STATISTICS IN SUMMARY

Randomized Comparative Experiment

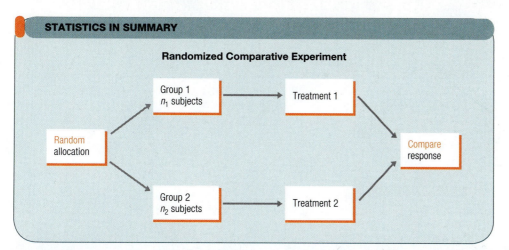

STATISTICS IN SUMMARY

The Idea of a Confidence Interval

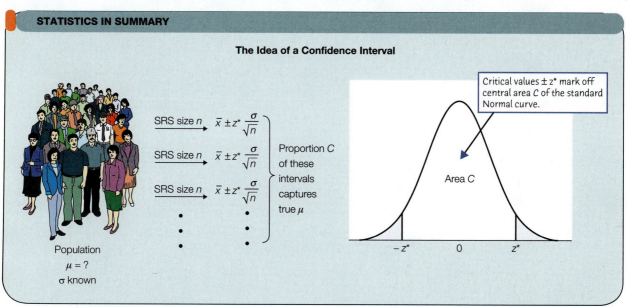

SRS size n → $\bar{x} \pm z^* \dfrac{\sigma}{\sqrt{n}}$

SRS size n → $\bar{x} \pm z^* \dfrac{\sigma}{\sqrt{n}}$

SRS size n → $\bar{x} \pm z^* \dfrac{\sigma}{\sqrt{n}}$

Proportion C of these intervals captures true μ

Population
$\mu = ?$
σ known

Critical values $\pm z^*$ mark off central area C of the standard Normal curve.

Area C

$-z^*$ 0 z^*

STATISTICS IN SUMMARY

The Idea of a Significance Test

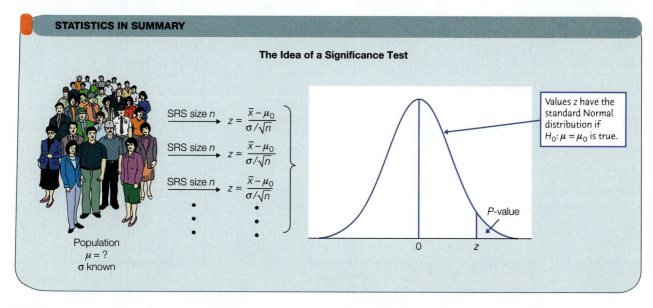

SRS size n → $z = \dfrac{\bar{x} - \mu_0}{\sigma/\sqrt{n}}$

SRS size n → $z = \dfrac{\bar{x} - \mu_0}{\sigma/\sqrt{n}}$

SRS size n → $z = \dfrac{\bar{x} - \mu_0}{\sigma/\sqrt{n}}$

Population
$\mu = ?$
σ known

Values z have the standard Normal distribution if $H_0: \mu = \mu_0$ is true.

P-value

0   z

Essential Statistics

Second Edition

DAVID S. MOORE
Purdue University

WILLIAM I. NOTZ
The Ohio State University

MICHAEL A. FLIGNER
The Ohio State University

W. H. Freeman and Company
New York

Senior Publisher: Ruth Baruth

Acquisitions Editor: Karen Carson

Executive Marketing Manager: Jennifer Somerville

Developmental Editor: Andrew Sylvester

Assistant Editor: Jackson Tucker

Senior Media Editor: Laura Capuano

Associate Media Editor: Catriona Kaplan

Associate Media Editor: Courtney M. Elezovic

Editorial Assistant: Barbara M. Scanlon

Marketing Assistant: Alyssa Nigro

Photo Editor: Cecilia Varas

Cover and Text Designer: Blake Logan

Senior Project Editor: Mary Louise Byrd

Illustrations and Composition: Aptara

Production Coordinator: Ellen Cash

Printing and Binding: Quad Graphics

Library of Congress Control Number: 2012936398

ISBN-13: 978-1-4292-5517-2
ISBN-10: 1-4292-5517-X

Printed in the United States of America

First printing

W. H. Freeman and Company
41 Madison Avenue
New York, NY 10010
Houndmills, Basingstoke RG21 6XS, England

www.whfreeman.com

Brief Contents

Starred material is not required for later parts of the text.

Detailed Table of Contents

*E*ssential Statistics is what its name suggests: a basic introduction to statistical ideas and methods that aims to equip students to carry out common statistical procedures and to follow statistical reasoning in their fields of study and in their future employment.

Despite its rather low mathematical level, *Essential Statistics* is designed to reflect the actual practice of statistics, where data analysis and design of data production join with probability-based inference to form a coherent science of data. There are good pedagogical reasons for beginning with data analysis (Chapters 1 to 7), then moving to data production (Chapters 8 and 9), and then to probability (Chapters 10 to 13) and inference (Chapters 14 to 26). In studying data analysis, students learn useful skills immediately and get over some of their fear of statistics. Data analysis is a necessary preliminary to inference in practice, because inference requires clean data. Designed data production is the surest foundation for inference, and the deliberate use of chance in random sampling and randomized comparative experiments motivates the study of probability in a course that emphasizes data-oriented statistics. *Essential Statistics* gives a full presentation of basic probability and inference (17 of the 26 chapters) but places it in the context of statistics as a whole.

GUIDING PRINCIPLES AND THE GAISE GUIDELINES

Essential Statistics is based on three principles: balanced content, experience with data, and the importance of ideas. These principles are widely accepted by statisticians concerned about teaching and are directly connected to and reflected by the themes of the College Report of the Guidelines in Assessment and Instruction for Statistics Education (GAISE) Project.

The GAISE Guidelines includes six recommendations for the introductory statistics course. The content, coverage, and features of *Essential Statistics* are closely aligned to these recommendations:

1. Emphasize statistical literacy and develop statistical thinking. The intent of *Essential Statistics* is to be modern *and* accessible. The exposition is straightforward and concentrates on major ideas and skills. One principle of writing for beginners is not to try to tell your students everything you know. Another principle is to offer frequent stopping points, marking off digestible bites of material. Statistical literacy is promoted throughout *Essential Statistics* in the many examples and exercises drawn from the popular press and from many fields of study. Statistical thinking is promoted in examples and exercises that give enough background to allow students to consider the meaning of their calculations. Exercises often ask for conclusions that are more than a number (or "reject H_0"). Some exercises require judgment in addition to right-or-wrong calculations and conclusions. Statistics, more than mathematics, depends on judgment for effective use. *Essential Statistics* begins to develop students' judgment about statistical studies.

2. Use real data. The study of statistics is supposed to help students work with data in their varied academic disciplines and in their unpredictable later employment. Students learn to work with data by working with data. *Essential Statistics* is full of data from many fields of study and from everyday life. Data are more than mere numbers—they are numbers with a context that should play a role in making sense of the numbers and in stating conclusions. Examples and exercises in *Essential Statistics*, though intended for beginners, use real data and give enough background to allow students to consider the meaning of their calculations.

3. Stress conceptual understanding rather than mere knowledge of procedures. A first course in statistics introduces many skills, from making a stemplot and calculating a correlation to choosing and carrying out a significance test. In practice (even if not always in the course), calculations and graphs are automated. Moreover, anyone who makes serious use of statistics will need some specific procedures not taught in her college stat course. *Essential Statistics* therefore tries to make clear the larger patterns and big ideas of statistics, not in the abstract, but in the context of learning specific skills and working with specific data. Many of the big ideas are summarized in graphical outlines. Three of the most useful appear inside the front cover. Formulas without guiding principles do students little good once the final exam is past, so it is worth the time to slow down a bit and explain the ideas.

4. Foster active learning in the classroom. Fostering active learning is the business of the teacher, though an emphasis on working with data helps. To this end, we have created interactive applets to our specifications and available online. These are designed primarily to help in learning statistics rather than in doing statistics. We suggest using selected applets for classroom demonstrations even if you do not ask students to work with them. The *Correlation and Regression*, *Confidence Interval*, and *P-value* applets, for example, convey core ideas more clearly than any amount of chalk and talk.

   We also provide Web exercises at the end of each chapter. Our intent is to take advantage of the fact that most undergraduates are "Web savvy." These exercises require students to search the Web for either data or statistical examples and then evaluate what they find. Teachers can use these as classroom activities or assign them as homework projects.

5. Use technology for developing conceptual understanding and analyzing data. Automating calculations increases students' ability to complete problems, reduces their frustration, and helps them concentrate on ideas and problem recognition rather than mechanics. At a minimum, students should have a "two-variable statistics" calculator with functions for correlation and the least-squares regression line as well as for the mean and standard deviation.

Many instructors will take advantage of more elaborate technology, as ASA/ MAA and GAISE recommend. And many students who don't use technology in their college statistics course will find themselves using (for example) Excel on the job. *Essential Statistics* does not assume or require use of software except in Part IV, where the work is otherwise too tedious. It does accommodate software use and tries to convince students that they are gaining knowledge that will enable them to read and use output from almost any source. There are regular Using Technology sections throughout the text. Each of these sections displays and comments on output from the same three technologies, representing graphing calculators (the Texas Instruments TI-83 or TI-84), spreadsheets (Microsoft Excel), and statistical software (Minitab and CrunchIt!). The output always concerns one of the main teaching examples, so that students can compare text and output.

6. Use assessments to improve and evaluate student learning.

Within chapters, a few Apply Your Knowledge exercises follow each new idea or skill for a quick check of basic mastery—and also to mark off digestible bites of material. Each of the first three parts of the book ends with a review chapter that includes a summary of the big ideas covered in the previous chapters, problems students can use to test themselves, and a set of supplementary exercises. The review chapters present supplementary exercises without the "I just studied that" context, thus asking for another level of learning. We think it is helpful to assign some supplementary exercises. Many instructors will find that the review chapters appear at the right points for pre-examination review. The Test Yourself questions can be used by students to review, self-assess, and prepare for such an examination.

In addition, assessment materials in the form of a test bank and quizzes are available online.

WHAT'S NEW?

The new edition of *Essential Statistics* brings many **new examples and exercises.** There are new data sets from a variety of sources, including marketing (methods for waitpersons to improve the size of tips), exercise physiology (improving swimming performance), psychology (the effect of colors on performance of cognitive tasks), and the environment (water quality in Ohio State Parks). Popular examples and exercises such as the Florida manatee regression example return, many with updated data. These are just a few of a large number of new data settings in this edition.

A new edition is also an opportunity to introduce new features and polish the exposition in ways intended to help students learn. Here are some of the changes

■ Chapter summaries consist of two sections. One, titled Chapter Specifics, summarizes the material presented in the chapter. The other, titled Link It, describes how the chapter links to material in previous and upcoming chapters. Together, Chapter Specifics and Link It help students understand how individual chapters relate to each other and to the overall practice of statistics.

■ Each chapter now contains a few exercises that have students investigate data or statistical issues that can be found on the Web. Problems include locating data on the Web and exploring the material to answer questions about it, or discussing statistical statements found online (much as we do in exercises asking students to evaluate statistical statements found in newspapers and magazines). These exercises appear in a section called Exploring the Web at the end of each chapter.

■ The Part Reviews have been revised to include a section titled Test Yourself. This section provides multiple-choice questions, short-answer questions, and calculations to help students review the basic ideas and skills presented in that part's chapters. These questions replace the Review Exercises in the first edition.

■ Data icons are located next to examples and exercises involving data sets. Data sets are now given descriptive names and are available in a variety of formats online.

■ We have added an introductory section, "Getting Started," that instructors may wish to assign to students on the first day of class. This section provides an overview of statistical thinking and real examples where the use of statistics can provide valuable insight. It expands on material that was previously in the "To the Student" preface, adding motivating examples.

■ We have added a new chapter (Chapter 6) that introduces two-way tables and discusses association for categorical data. Students are likely to encounter two-way tables in newspapers and magazines, on the Web, and in research articles, and this new chapter allows coverage of this important topic for courses that don't cover Chapter 23.

■ In response to reviewer requests, the essay on data ethics that appeared only on the Website in the first edition has been added to the text as a special section following Chapter 9.

■ Also in response to reviewer request, the introduction to inference has been split into three chapters, with separate chapters on confidence intervals (Chapter 14), tests of significance (Chapter 15), and inference in practice (Chapter 16). The two-chapter approach adopted in the first edition of *Essential Statistics* was intended to emphasize the relation between confidence intervals and tests of significance for means. Although confidence intervals and hypothesis tests have a natural connection, we realize it is simpler for students to first learn them as separate ideas and then explore the connection. We don't discuss one-sided intervals, so it may be prudent to avoid overemphasizing the connection and raising questions about how one-sided tests connect to confidence intervals.

FEATURES OF *ESSENTIAL STATISTICS,*
Second Edition

In this chapter we cover... Each chapter opener gives a brief look at where the chapter is heading, often with references to previous chapters, and includes a bulleted list of the major topics covered.

FOUR-STEP EXAMPLES

In Chapter 2, students learn how to use the four-step process for working through statistical problems: State, Plan, Solve, and Conclude. By observing this framework at work in selected examples throughout the text and practicing it in selected exercises, students develop the ability to solve and write reports on real statistical problems encountered outside the classroom setting.

© Kevin Schafer/Alamy

TROPICALFLOWER

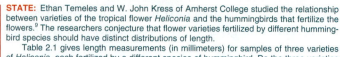

EXAMPLE 2.9 Comparing tropical flowers

STATE: Ethan Temeles and W. John Kress of Amherst College studied the relationship between varieties of the tropical flower *Heliconia* and the hummingbirds that fertilize the flowers.[9] The researchers conjecture that flower varieties fertilized by different hummingbird species should have distinct distributions of length.

Table 2.1 gives length measurements (in millimeters) for samples of three varieties of *Heliconia,* each fertilized by a different species of hummingbird. Do the three varieties display distinct distributions of length? How do the mean lengths compare?

PLAN: Use graphs and numerical descriptions to describe and compare these three distributions of flower length.

SOLVE: We might use boxplots to compare the distributions, but stemplots preserve more detail and work well for data sets of these sizes. Figure 2.4 displays stemplots with the stems lined up for easy comparison. The lengths have been rounded to the nearest tenth of a millimeter. The *bihai* and red varieties have somewhat skewed distributions, so we might choose to compare the five-number summaries. But because

TABLE 2.1 Flower lengths (millimeters) for three *Heliconia* varieties

H. BIHAI							
47.12	46.75	46.81	47.12	46.67	47.43	46.44	46.64
48.07	48.34	48.15	50.26	50.12	46.34	46.94	48.36
H. CARIBAEA RED							
41.90	42.01	41.93	43.09	41.47	41.69	39.78	40.57
39.63	42.18	40.66	37.87	39.16	37.40	38.20	38.07
38.10	37.97	38.79	38.23	38.87	37.78	38.01	
H. CARIBAEA YELLOW							
36.78	37.02	36.52	36.11	36.03	35.45	38.13	37.10
35.17	36.82	36.66	35.68	36.03	34.57	34.63	

the researchers plan to use $\bar{x}$ and s for further analysis, we instead calculate these measures:

Variety	Mean length	Standard deviation
bihai	47.60	1.213
red	39.71	1.799
yellow	36.18	0.975

CONCLUDE: The three varieties differ so much in flower length that there is little overlap among them. In particular, the flowers of *bihai* are longer than either red or yellow. The mean lengths are 47.6 mm for *H. bihai*, 39.7 mm for *H. caribaea* red, and 36.2 mm for *H. caribaea* yellow. ■

APPLY YOUR KNOWLEDGE

4.8 Coral reefs. Exercise 4.2 discusses a study in which scientists examined data on mean sea surface temperatures (in degrees Celsius) and mean coral growth (in millimeters per year) over a several-year period at locations in the Red Sea. Here are the data:[5] CORAL

Sea surface temperature	29.68	29.87	30.16	30.22	30.48	30.65	30.90
Growth	2.63	2.58	2.60	2.48	2.26	2.38	2.26

(a) Make a scatterplot. Which is the explanatory variable? The plot shows a negative linear pattern.

(b) Find the correlation r step-by-step. You may wish to round off to two decimal places in each step. First find the mean and standard deviation of each variable. Then find the seven standardized values for each variable. Finally, use the formula for r. Explain how your value for r matches your graph in (a).

(c) Enter these data into your calculator or software and use the correlation function to find r. Check that you get the same result as in (b), up to roundoff error.

Apply Your Knowledge

Major concepts are immediately reinforced with problems that are interspersed throughout the chapter (often following examples), allowing students to practice their skills as they work through the text.

Using Technology

Located throughout the text, these special sections display and comment on the output from graphing calculators, spreadsheets, and statistical software in the context of examples from the text.

USING TECHNOLOGY

Computer software or a graphing calculator will do calculations and make graphs as you command, freeing you to concentrate on choosing the right methods and interpreting your results. Figure 2.3 displays output describing the travel times to work of 20 people in New York State (Example 2.3). Can you find $\bar{x}$, s, and the five-number summary in each output? The big message of this section is: *once you know what to look for, you can read output from any technological tool.*

The displays in Figure 2.3 come from a Texas Instruments graphing calculator, the Minitab and CrunchIt! statistical programs, and the Microsoft Excel spreadsheet program. Minitab allows you to choose what descriptive measures you want, while the descriptive measures in the CrunchIt! output are provided by default. Excel and the calculator give some things we don't need. Just ignore the extras. Excel's "Descriptive Statistics" menu item doesn't give the quartiles. We used the spreadsheet's separate quartile function to get Q_1 and Q_3.

LINK IT

The methods of Chapters 1 to 6 can be used to describe data regardless of how the data were obtained. However, if we want to reason from data to give answers to specific questions or to draw conclusions about the larger population, then the method that was used to collect the data is important. Sampling is one way to collect data, but it does not guarantee that we can draw meaningful conclusions. Biased sampling methods, such as convenience sampling and voluntary response samples, produce data that can be misleading, resulting in incorrect conclusions. Simple random sampling avoids bias and produces data that can lead to valid conclusions regarding the population. Even with perfect sampling methods, there is still sample-to-sample variation; we will begin our study of the connection between sampling variation and drawing conclusions in Chapter 11.

Even when we take a simple random sample, our conclusions can be weakened by undercoverage, nonresponse, and poor wording of questions. Careful attention must be given to all aspects of the sampling process to ensure that the conclusions we make are valid. In many cases more complex sampling designs are required. But the use of impersonal chance to select the sample remains a key ingredient in the sampling process. And issues such as undercoverage and nonresponse still remain for these more complex designs.

Chapter Summary and Link It

At the conclusion of each chapter, students get a summary of the chapter specifics, including major terms and processes, followed by a brief discussion of how the chapter "links" to material in the previous and upcoming chapters.

Check Your Skills and Chapter Exercises Each chapter ends with a series of multiple-choice problems that test the students' understanding of basic concepts and their ability to apply those concepts to real-world statistical situations. These multiple-choice problems are followed by a set of more in-depth exercises that allow students to make judgments and draw conclusions based on real data and real scenarios.

CHAPTER 8 EXERCISES

In all exercises asking for an SRS, you may use either Table B or software.

8.20 Immigration reform priorities. A Gallup Poll asked, "If you had to choose, what should be the main focus of the U.S. government in dealing with the issue of illegal immigration—developing a plan for halting the flow of illegal immigrants into the U.S. (or) developing a plan to deal with immigrants who are currently in the U.S. illegally?" Gallup's report said, "Results are based on telephone interviews conducted June 11–13, 2010, with a random sample of 1,014 adults, aged 18 and older, living in the continental U.S."[11] What is the population for this sample survey? What is the sample?

8.21 Sampling stuffed envelopes. A large retailer prepares its customers' monthly credit card bills using an automatic machine that folds the bills, stuffs them into envelopes, and seals the envelopes for mailing. Are the envelopes completely sealed? Inspectors choose 40 envelopes from the 1000 stuffed each hour for visual inspection. What is the population for this sample survey? What is the sample?

8.22 Do you trust the Internet? You want to ask a sample of college students the question "How much do you trust information about health that you find on the Internet—a great deal, somewhat, not much, or not at all?" You try out this and other questions on a pilot group of 8 students chosen from your class. The class members are

Adams	Devore	Guo	Newberg	Shoepf
Aeffner	Ding	Heaton	Paulsen	Spagnola
Barnes	Drake	Huling	Payton	Terry
Bower	Eckstein	Kahler	Prince	Vore
Burke	Fassnacht	Kessis	Pulak	Wallace
Cao	Fullmer	Lu	Rabin	Wanner
Cisse	Gandhi	Mattos	Roberts	Zhang

Choose an SRS of 8 students. If you use Table B, start at line 131.

8.23 Sampling telephone area codes. The United States currently has approximately 287 Numbering Plan Areas (NPAs) in service, corresponding to geographic regions. Each NPA is identified by a three-digit code, commonly called an

EXPLORING THE WEB

3.47 Are the data Normal? Comparing quartiles. The Web site http://professionals.collegeboard.com/data-reports-research/sat presents data for high school seniors who participated in the SAT Program during the current year as well as previous years. Under SAT Data & Reports, click on the link *College-Bound Seniors* for the most recent year given. In the window that opens, click on the link *Total Group Report: College-Bound Seniors* for this year. The Total Group Profile will open and contains several tables, each giving different summary information. Go to the Overall Mean Scores table. How many students took the Critical Reading portion of the SAT? What were the mean and standard deviation of the scores? Assuming that the distribution of scores is Normal with the mean and standard deviation given in the Overall Mean Scores table, what are the first and third quartiles of the distribution? Now go to the Percentiles for the Total Group table, and compare the actual first and third quartiles from the data with the values obtained from the Normal curve. Does this give any evidence that the distribution of Critical Reading scores is not Normal?

Exploring the Web A final set of exercises asks students to investigate data or statistical issues by researching online. These exercises tend to be more involved and provide an opportunity for students to dig deep into contemporary issues and special applications of statistics.

ORIGINS

Instructors who have seen our other texts will recognize that *Essential Statistics* is based on the new sixth edition of the successful text *The Basic Practice of Statistics* (*BPS*). It is more than 20% shorter than *BPS* in word count, and the figures and tables have been reduced in size to lower the cost and reduce the physical size of the book. In addition to removing much of the optional material in *BPS*, we have carefully rewritten the text to shorten and simplify explanations. Although the reduction in length and detail is often subtle, there are considerable savings in places. The key Chapters 14, 15, and 16 that introduce inference, for example, are about 25% shorter than the corresponding chapters in *BPS*.

Some instructors will find the shorter-and-simpler book ideal for their students. Others will miss some of the fine points and added material that appear in *BPS*.

One feature of *BPS* that is loved by some instructors and ignored by others has been included on the Web site: the 28 exercises that guide use of a set of interactive applets to aid learning. We like and use this feature, but the applets naturally belong to electronic, rather than print, media.

WHY DID YOU DO THAT?

There is no single best way to organize the presentation of statistics to beginners. That said, our choices reflect thinking about both content and pedagogy. Here are comments on several "frequently asked questions" about the order and selection of material in *Essential Statistics*.

Why does the distinction between population and sample not appear in Part I? There is more to statistics than inference. In fact, statistical inference is appropriate only in rather special circumstances. The chapters in Part I present tools and tactics for describing data—any data. These tools and tactics do not depend on the idea of inference from sample to population. Many data sets in these chapters (for example, the several sets of data about the 50 states) do not lend themselves to inference because they represent an entire population. John Tukey of Bell Labs and Princeton, the philosopher of modern data analysis, insisted that the population-sample distinction be avoided when it is not relevant. He used the word "batch" for data sets in general. We see no need for a special word, but we think Tukey was right.

Why not begin with data production? It is certainly reasonable to do so—the natural flow of a planned study is from design to data analysis to inference. But in their future employment most students will use statistics mainly in settings other than planned research studies. We place the design of data production (Chapters 8 and 9) after data analysis to emphasize that data-analytic techniques apply to any data. One of the primary purposes of statistical designs for producing data is to make inference possible, so the discussion in Chapters 8 and 9 opens Part II and motivates the study of probability.

Why do Normal distributions appear in Part I? Density curves such as the Normal curves are just another tool to describe the distribution of a quantitative variable, along with stemplots, histograms, and boxplots. Professional statistical software offers to make density curves from data just as it offers histograms. We prefer not to suggest that this material is essentially tied to probability, as the traditional order does. And we find it helpful to break up the indigestible lump of probability that troubles students so much. Meeting Normal distributions early does this and strengthens the "probability distributions are like data distributions" way of approaching probability.

Why not delay discussing correlation and regression until late in the course, as was traditional? *Essential Statistics* begins by offering experience working with data and gives a conceptual structure for this nonmathematical but essential part of statistics.

Students profit from more experience with data and from seeing the conceptual structure worked out in relations among variables as well as in describing single-variable data. Correlation and least-squares regression are very important descriptive tools and are often used in settings where there is no population-sample distinction, such as studies of all of a firm's employees. Perhaps most important, the *Essential Statistics* approach asks students to think about what kind of relationship lies behind the data (confounding, lurking variables, association doesn't imply causation, and so on), without overwhelming them with the demands of formal inference methods. Inference in the correlation and regression setting is a bit complex, demands software, and often comes right at the end of the course. We find that delaying all mention of correlation and regression to that point means that students often don't master the basic uses and properties of these methods. We consider Chapters 4 and 5 (correlation and regression) essential and Chapter 24 (regression inference) optional.

Why use the *z* procedures for a population mean to introduce the reasoning of inference? This is a pedagogical issue, not a question of statistics in practice. Sometime in the golden future we will start with resampling methods. We think that permutation tests make the reasoning of tests clearer than any traditional approach. For now the main choices are z for a mean and z for a proportion.

We find z for means quite a bit more accessible to students. Positively, we can say up front that we are going to explore the reasoning of inference in the overly simple setting described in the box on page 286 titled Simple Conditions for Inference about a Mean. As this box suggests, exactly Normal population and true simple random sample are as unrealistic as known σ. All the issues of practice—robustness against lack of Normality and application when the data aren't an SRS as well as the need to estimate σ—are put off until, with the reasoning in hand, we discuss the practically useful t procedures. This separation of initial reasoning from messier practice works well.

Negatively, starting with inference for p introduces many side issues: no exact Normal sampling distribution but a Normal approximation to a discrete distribution; use of $\hat{p}$ in both the numerator and the denominator of the test statistic to estimate both the parameter p and $\hat{p}$'s own standard deviation; loss of the direct link between test and confidence interval; and the need to avoid small and moderate sample sizes because the Normal approximation for the test is quite unreliable.

Why didn't you cover Topic X? Introductory texts ought not to be encyclopedic. We chose topics on two grounds: they are the most commonly used in practice, and they are suitable vehicles for learning broader statistical ideas. Students who have completed the core of the book, Chapters 1 to 11 and 14 to 22, will have little difficulty moving on to more elaborate methods. Chapters 23 to 25 offer a choice of slightly more advanced topics, as does the chapter on nonparametric tests available online.

We have enjoyed the opportunity to once again rethink how to help beginning students achieve a practical grasp of basic statistics. What students actually learn is not identical to what we teachers think we have "covered," so the virtues of concentrating on the essentials are considerable. We hope that the new edition of *Essential Statistics* offers a mix of concrete skills and clearly explained concepts that will help many teachers guide their students toward useful knowledge.

ACKNOWLEDGMENTS

We are grateful to colleagues from two-year and four-year colleges and universities who commented on *Essential Statistics*:

Betty Anderson, *Howard Community College*
Murray Besler, *Langara College*
Prabha Betne, *LaGuardia Community College*
Daniel Birmajer, *Nazareth College*
Sherri Boyd, *Rollins College*
Patricia M. Buchanan, *The Pennsylvania State University*
Patti Collings, *Brigham Young University*
Lacey Echols, *Butler University*
Karen A. Estes, *St. Petersburg College*
Jim Hartman, *College of Wooster*
Susan Hollingsworth, *Edgewood College*
Patricia B. Humphrey, *Georgia Southern University*
Martin Jones, *College of Charleston*

Victor Kane, *Kennessaw State University*
Linda M. Myers, *Brookdale Community College*
Kane Nashimoto, *James Madison University*
Nabendu Pal, *University of Louisiana at Lafayette*
Mary R. Parker, *Austin Community College*
Ginger Rowell, *Middle Tennessee State University*
Barbara Savage, *Roxbury Community College*
Robb Sinn, *North Georgia College & State University*
Shawn Smith, *Nicholls State University*
Dave Tomkins, *Thompson Rivers University*
Mikhail Turegun, *Oklahoma City Community College*
Sasha Verkhovtseva, *Anoka Ramsey Community College*

Thanks also to Professor Jackie Miller of The Ohio State University for carefully reading all chapters, spotting many errors, and making numerous useful suggestions.

Special thanks are due to Brigitte Baldi (California State University, Long Beach) and Bradley Hartlaub (Kenyon College) for providing exercises, and to Ann Cannon (Cornell College) for carefully checking the manuscript. We are also grateful to Ruth Baruth, Karen Carson, Andrew Sylvester, Mary Louise Byrd, Blake Logan, Pamela Bruton, and the other editorial and design professionals who have contributed greatly to the attractiveness of this book.

Finally, we are indebted to the many statistics teachers with whom we have discussed the teaching of our subject over many years; to people from diverse fields with whom we have worked to understand data; and especially to students whose compliments and complaints have changed and improved our teaching. Working with teachers, colleagues in other disciplines, and students constantly reminds us of the importance of hands-on experience with data and of statistical thinking in an era when computer routines quickly handle statistical details.

David S. Moore, William I. Notz, and Michael A. Fligner

Media and Supplements

FOR STUDENTS

STATS P◮RTAL

www.yourstatsportal.com (access code or online purchase required) StatsPortal is the digital gateway to *Essential Statistics*, second edition (*ESS 2e*), designed to enrich the course and enhance students' study skills through a collection of Web-based tools. StatsPortal integrates a rich suite of diagnostic, assessment, tutorial, and enrichment features, enabling students to master statistics at their own pace. It is organized around three main teaching and learning components:

1. Interactive eBook offers a complete and customizable online version of the text, fully integrated with all the media resources available with *ESS 2e*. The eBook allows students to quickly search the text, highlight key areas, and add notes about what they're reading. Instructors can customize the eBook to add, hide, and reorder content, add their own material, and highlight key text for students.

2. Resources organizes all the resources for *ESS 2e* into one location for ease of use.

Student Resources
- **NEW! Statistical Video Series** consisting of StatClips, StatClips Examples, and Statistically Speaking "Snapshots." View animated lecture videos, whiteboard lessons, and documentary-style footage that illustrate key statistical concepts and help students visualize statistics in real-world scenarios.

- **StatTutor Tutorials** offer audio-multimedia tutorials tied directly to the textbook, containing videos, applets, and animations.

- **NEW! *LEARNINGCurve*** is a formative quizzing system that offers immediate feedback at the question level to help students master course material.

- **Statistical Applets** are a series of interactive applets to help students master key statistical concepts and work exercises from the text.

- **CrunchIt!® Statistical Software** allows users to analyze data from any Internet location. Designed with the novice user in mind, the software is not only easily accessible but also easy to use. CrunchIt!® offers all the basic statistical routines covered in introductory statistics courses and more.

- **Stats@Work Simulations** put students in the role of the statistical consultant, helping them better understand statistics interactively within the context of real-life scenarios.

- **EESEE Case Studies,** developed by The Ohio State University Statistics Department, teach students to apply their statistical skills by exploring actual case studies using real data.

■ **Data sets** are available in ASCII, Excel, TI, Minitab, SPSS (an IBM Company),[1] S-PLUS, and JMP formats.

■ **Student Solutions Manual** provides solutions to the odd-numbered exercises, with stepped-out solutions to select problems.

■ **Statistical Software Manuals** for TI-83/84, Minitab, Excel, JMP, and SPSS provide instruction, examples, and exercises using specific statistical software packages.

■ **Interactive Table Reader** allows students to use statistical tables interactively to seek the information they need.

■ **Tables**

Instructor Resources

■ **Instructor's Guide with Full Solutions** includes teaching suggestions, chapter comments, and detailed solutions to all exercises.

■ **Test Bank** offers hundreds of multiple-choice questions.

■ **Lecture PowerPoint slides** offer a detailed lecture presentation of statistical concepts covered in each chapter of *ESS 2e*.

■ NEW! **SolutionMaster** is a Web-based version of the solutions in the Instructor's Guide with Full Solutions. This easy-to-use tool allows instructors to generate a solution file for any set of homework exercises. Solutions can be downloaded in PDF format for convenient printing and posting. For more information or a demonstration, contact your local W. H. Freeman sales representative.

3. Assignments organizes assignments and guides instructors through an easy-to-create assignment process providing access to questions from the Test Bank and from the exercises in the text, including many algorithmic problems. The Assignment Center enables instructors to create their own assignments from a variety of question types for machine-gradable assignments. This powerful assignment manager allows instructors to select their preferred policies in regard to scheduling, maximum attempts, time limitations, feedback, and more!

Online Study Center

www.whfreeman.com/osc/ess2e

(access code or online purchase required)
The Online Study Center offers all the resources available in StatsPortal except the eBook and Assignment Center.

---

[1] SPSS was acquired by IBM in October 2009.

Companion Web Site

www.whfreeman.com/ess2e

This open-access Web site includes statistical applets, data sets, supplementary exercises, statistical profiles, and self-quizzes. The Web site also offers an optional companion chapter covering nonparametric tests.

Special Software Packages

Student versions of JMP, Minitab, S-PLUS, and SPSS are available on the student CD-ROM. This software is not sold separately and must be packaged with a text or a manual. Contact your W. H. Freeman representative for information or visit www.whfreeman.com.

NEW! Video Tool Kit

(Access code or online purchase required)

This new Statistical Video Series consists of three types of videos aimed to illustrate key statistical concepts and help students visualize statistics in real-world scenarios:

- **StatClips** lecture videos, created and presented by Alan Dabney, PhD, Texas A&M University, are innovative visual tutorials that illustrate key statistical concepts. In three to five minutes, each StatClips video combines dynamic animation, data sets, and interesting scenarios to help students understand the concepts presented in an introductory statistics course.

- In **StatClips Examples,** Alan Dabney walks students through step-by-step examples related to the StatClips lecture videos to reinforce the concepts through problem solving.

- **SnapShots** videos are abbreviated, student-friendly versions of the *Statistically Speaking* video series and bring the world of statistics into the classroom. Based on the successful PBS series *Against All Odds, Statistically Speaking* uses new and updated documentary footage and interviews that show real people using data analysis to make important decisions in their careers and in their daily lives. From business to medicine, from the environment to understanding the U.S. census, **SnapShots** focus on why statistics is important for students' careers and how statistics can be a powerful tool for understanding the world.

Student Solutions Manual

by R. Scott Linder, Ohio Wesleyan University

This printed manual provides stepped-out solutions for all odd-numbered exercises in the text. ISBN: 1-4292-5-6540

Software Manuals

Software manuals covering Minitab, Excel, SPSS, TI-83/84, and JMP are offered within StatsPortal and the Online Study Center. These manuals are also available in printed versions through custom publishing. They serve as basic introductions to popular statistical software options and guides to their use with *ESS 2e*.

FOR INSTRUCTORS

Instructor's Web Site

www.whfreeman.com/ess2e

This Web site requires user registration as an instructor and features all the student Web materials plus the following:

■ **Instructor version of EESEE** (Electronic Encyclopedia of Statistical Examples and Exercises), with solutions to the exercises in the student version.

■ **PowerPoint slides** containing all textbook figures and tables.

■ **Lecture PowerPoint slides** offering a detailed lecture presentation of statistical concepts covered in each chapter of *ESS 2e*.

■ **Full answers** to the **supplementary exercises** on the student Web site.

Instructor's Guide with Full Solutions

by Scott Linder, Ohio Wesleyan University

This printed guide includes full solutions to all exercises and provides additional examples and data sets for class use, Internet resources, and sample examinations. It also contains brief discussions of the *ESS* approach for each chapter. ISBN: 1-4292-5-6427

Test Bank

The Test Bank contains hundreds of multiple-choice questions to generate quizzes and tests for each chapter of the text. It is available in print as well as electronically on CD-ROM (for Windows and Mac), where questions can be downloaded, edited, and resequenced to suit each instructor's needs.
   Printed Version, ISBN: 1-4292-5-6583
   Computerized (CD) Version, ISBN: 1-4292-5-5846

Enhanced Instructor's Resource CD-ROM

This CD-ROM allows instructors to **search** and **export** (by key term or chapter) all the material from the student CD, plus

■ all text images and tables

■ Instructor's Guide with Full Solutions

- PowerPoint files and lecture slides
- Test Bank files
  ISBN: 1-4292-5-6508

Course Management Systems

W. H. Freeman and Company provides courses for Blackboard, WebCT (Campus Edition and Vista), Angel, Desire2Learn, Moodle, and Sakai course management systems. These are completely integrated solutions that you can easily customize and adapt to meet your teaching goals and course objectives. Visit www.bfwpub.com/lms for more information.

i-clicker

Developed by educators for educators, i-clicker is a two-way radio-frequency classroom response solution. University of Illinois physicists Tim Stelzer, Gary Gladding, Mats Selen, and Benny Brown created the i-clicker system after using competing classroom response solutions and discovering they were neither classroom-appropriate nor student-friendly. Each step of i-clicker's development has been informed by teaching and learning. From both a pedagogical and a technical standpoint, i-clicker is superior to other systems. To learn more about packaging i-clicker with this textbook, please contact your local sales representative or visit www.iclicker.com.

David S. Moore is Shanti S. Gupta Distinguished Professor of Statistics, Emeritus, at Purdue University and was 1998 president of the American Statistical Association. He received his AB from Princeton University and his PhD from Cornell University, both in mathematics. He has written many research papers in statistical theory and served on the editorial boards of several major journals. Professor Moore is an elected fellow of the American Statistical Association and of the Institute of Mathematical Statistics and an elected member of the International Statistical Institute. He has served as program director for statistics and probability at the National Science Foundation.

Professor Moore has long had an interest in the teaching of statistics. He was the content developer for the Annenberg/Corporation for Public Broadcasting college-level telecourse *Against All Odds: Inside Statistics* and for the series of video modules *Statistics: Decisions through Data*, intended to aid the teaching of statistics in schools. He is the author of influential articles on statistics education and of several leading texts. Professor Moore has served as president of the International Association for Statistical Education and has received the Mathematical Association of America's national award for distinguished college or university teaching of mathematics.

William I. Notz is Professor of Statistics at the Ohio State University. He received his BS in physics from the Johns Hopkins University and his PhD in mathematics from Cornell University. His first academic job was as Assistant Professor in the Department of Statistics at Purdue University. While there, he taught the introductory concepts course with Professor Moore, and as a result of this experience he developed an interest in statistical education. Professor Notz is a coauthor of EESEE (the Electronic Encyclopedia of Statistical Examples and Exercises) and coauthor of *Statistics: Concepts and Controversies*.

Professor Notz's research interests have focused on experimental design and computer experiments. He is the author of several research papers and of a book on the design and analysis of computer experiments. He is an elected fellow of the American Statistical Association. He has served as the editor of the journal *Technometrics* and as editor of the *Journal of Statistics Education*. At the Ohio State University he has served as the Director of the Statistical Consulting Service, as Acting Chair of the Department of Statistics for a year, and as an Associate Dean in the College of Mathematical and Physical Sciences. He is a winner of the Ohio State University's Alumni Distinguished Teaching Award.

Michael A. Fligner is Professor Emeritus at the Ohio State University. He received his BS in mathematics from the State University of New York at Stony Brook and his PhD from the University of Connecticut. He has spent his entire professional career at the Ohio State University, where he was Vice Chair of the Department for over

10 years and also served as Director of the Statistical Consulting Service. He has done consulting work with several large corporations in central Ohio.

Professor Fligner's research interests are in nonparametric statistical methods, and he received the Statistics in Chemistry award from the American Statistical Association for work on detecting biologically active compounds. He is coauthor of the book *Statistical Methods for Behavioral Ecology* and received a Fulbright scholarship under the American Republics Research program to work at the Charles Darwin Research Station in the Galapagos Islands. He has been an associate editor of the *Journal of Statistical Education*.

Data Are All Around

What's hot in popular music this week? SoundScan knows. SoundScan collects data electronically from the cash registers in more than 14,000 retail outlets and also collects data on download sales from Web sites. When you buy a CD or download a digital track, the checkout scanner or Web site is probably telling SoundScan what you bought. SoundScan provides this information to *Billboard magazine*, MTV, and VH1, as well as to record companies and artists' agents.

Should women take hormones such as estrogen after menopause, when natural production of these hormones ends? In 1992, several prominent medical organizations said "Yes." In particular, women who took hormones seemed to reduce their risk of a heart attack by 35% to 50%. The risks of taking hormones appeared small compared with the benefits. But in 2002, the National Institutes of Health declared these findings wrong. Use of hormones after menopause immediately plummeted. Both recommendations were based on extensive studies. What happened?

Is the climate warming? Is it becoming more extreme? An overwhelming majority of scientists now agree that the earth is undergoing major changes in climate. Enormous quantities of data are continuously being collected from weather stations, satellites, and other sources to monitor factors such as the surface temperature on land and sea, precipitation, solar activity, and the chemical composition of air and water. Climate models incorporate this

1

information to make projections of future climate change and can help us understand the effectiveness of proposed solutions.

SoundScan, medical studies, and climate research all produce data (numerical facts), and lots of them. Using data effectively is a large and growing part of most professions, and reacting to data is part of everyday life. In fact, we define statistics as **the science of learning from data.**

Although data are numbers, they are not "just numbers." *Data are numbers with a context.* The number 10.5, for example, carries no information by itself. But if we hear that a friend's new baby weighed 10.5 pounds at birth, we congratulate her on the healthy size of the child. The context engages our background knowledge and allows us to make judgments. We know that a baby weighing 10.5 pounds is quite large, and that a human baby is unlikely to weigh 10.5 ounces or 10.5 kilograms. The context makes the number informative.

To gain insight from data, we make graphs and do calculations. But graphs and calculations are guided by ways of thinking that amount to educated common sense. Let's begin our study of statistics with an informal look at three important principles of statistical thinking.[1]

WHERE THE DATA COME FROM MATTERS

Although data can be collected in a variety of ways, the type of conclusion that can be reached from the data depends on how the data were obtained. Let's take a closer look at the hormone replacement data to understand these issues.

EXAMPLE 1 Hormone replacement therapy

What's behind the flip-flop in the advice offered to women about hormone replacement? The evidence in favor of hormone replacement came from a number of studies that observed women who were taking hormones and compared them with others who were not. In such an *observational study* the women chose whether or not to take hormones. But women who choose to take hormones are very different from women who do not: they are richer and better educated and see doctors more often. These women do many things to maintain their health. It isn't surprising that they have fewer heart attacks.

Observational studies are usually easier to conduct than careful *experiments*. Experiments don't let women decide what to do. They assign women to either hormone replacement or to dummy pills that look and taste the same as the hormone pills. The assignment is done by a coin toss, so that all kinds of women are equally likely to get either treatment. Part of the difficulty of a good experiment is persuading women to accept the result—invisible to them—of the coin toss. By 2002, several experiments agreed that hormone replacement does *not* reduce the risk of heart attacks, at least for older women. Faced with this better evidence, medical authorities changed their recommendations.[2] ▪

Women who chose hormone replacement after menopause were on the average richer and better educated than those who didn't. No wonder they had fewer heart attacks. Children who play soccer tend to have prosperous and well-educated parents. No wonder they tend to do better in school than children who don't play soccer. We can't conclude that hormone replacement reduces heart attacks or that playing soccer increases school grades just because we see these relationships in data. In both examples, education and affluence are *lurking variables*, background factors that help explain the relationships between hormone replacement and good health and between soccer and good grades.

Almost all relationships between two variables are influenced by other variables lurking in the background. To understand the relationship between two variables, you must often look at other variables. Careful statistical studies try to think of and measure possible lurking variables in order to correct for their influence. As the hormone saga illustrates, this doesn't always work well. News reports often just ignore possible lurking variables that might ruin a good headline like "Playing soccer can improve your grades." The habit of asking, "What might lie behind this relationship?" is part of thinking statistically.

Of course, observational studies are still quite useful. We can learn from observational studies how chimpanzees behave in the wild or which popular songs sold best last week or what percent of workers were unemployed last month. SoundScan's data on popular music and the government's data on employment and unemployment come from *sample surveys*, an important kind of observational study that chooses a part (the sample) to represent a larger whole. Opinion polls interview perhaps 1000 of the 235 million adults in the United States to report the public's views on current issues. Can we trust the results? We'll see that this isn't a simple Yes or No question. Let's just say that the government's unemployment rate is much more trustworthy than opinion poll results, and not just because the Bureau of Labor Statistics interviews 60,000 people rather than 1000. We can, however, say right away that some samples can't be trusted. Consider the following write-in poll.

EXAMPLE 2 Would you have children again?

The advice columnist Ann Landers once asked her readers, "If you had it to do over again, would you have children?" A few weeks later, her column was headlined "70% OF PARENTS SAY KIDS NOT WORTH IT." Indeed, 70% of the nearly 10,000 parents who wrote in said they would not have children if they could make the choice again. Those 10,000 parents were upset enough with their children to write Ann Landers. Most parents are happy with their kids and don't bother to write. ■

Statistically designed samples, even opinion polls, don't let people choose themselves for the sample. They interview people selected by impersonal chance so that everyone has an equal opportunity to be in the sample. Such a poll showed that 91% of parents *would* have children again. Where data come from matters a lot. If you are careless about how you get your data, you may announce 70% "No" when the truth is close to 90% "Yes." Understanding the importance of where data come from and the relationship of the source of the data to the conclusions that can be reached is an important part of learning to think statistically.

ALWAYS LOOK AT THE DATA

Yogi Berra, former New York Yankee catcher and manager, said it: "You can observe a lot by just watching." That's a good motto for learning from data. *A few carefully chosen graphs are often more instructive than great piles of numbers.* Consider the outcome of the 2000 presidential election in Florida.

EXAMPLE 3 Palm Beach County

Elections don't come much closer: after much recounting, state officials declared that George Bush had carried Florida by 537 votes out of almost 6 million votes cast. Florida's vote decided the election and made George Bush, rather than Al Gore, president. Let's look at some data. Figure 1 displays a graph that plots votes for the third-party candidate Pat Buchanan against votes for the Democratic candidate Al Gore in Florida's 67 counties.

What happened in Palm Beach County? The question leaps out from the graph. In this large and heavily Democratic county, a conservative third-party candidate did far better relative to the Democratic candidate than in any other county. The points for the other 66 counties show votes for both candidates increasing together in a roughly straight-line pattern. Both counts go up as county population goes up. Based on this pattern, we would expect Buchanan to receive around 800 votes in Palm Beach County. He actually received more than 3400 votes. That difference determined the election result in Florida and in the nation. ■

Ruce Weaver/AFP/Getty Images

The graph demands an explanation. It turns out that Palm Beach County used a confusing "butterfly" ballot (pictured above), in which candidate names on both left and right pages led to a voting column in the center. It would be easy for a voter who intended to vote for Gore to in fact cast a vote for Buchanan. The graph is convincing evidence that this in

FIGURE 1

Votes in the 2000 presidential election for Al Gore and Patrick Buchanan in Florida's 67 counties, for Example 3. What happened in Palm Beach County?

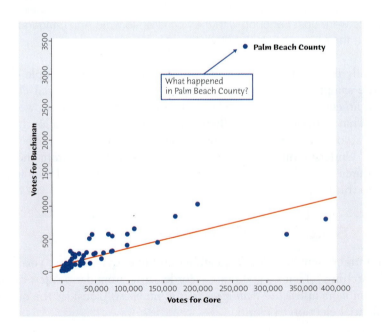

fact happened, more convincing than the complaints of voters who (later) were unsure where their votes ended up.

With a few simple commands, most statistical software will draw a variety of graphs. Examining your data with appropriate graphs and numerical summaries is the correct place to begin most data analyses. These can often reveal important patterns or trends that will help you understand what your data have to say.

VARIATION IS EVERYWHERE

The company's sales reps file into their monthly meeting. The sales manager rises. "Congratulations! Our sales were up 2% last month, so we're all drinking champagne this morning. You remember that when sales were down 1% last month, I fired half of our reps." This picture is only slightly exaggerated. Many managers overreact to small short-term variations in key figures. Here is Arthur Nielsen, former head of the country's largest market research firm, describing his experience:

> *Too many business people assign equal validity to all numbers printed on paper. They accept numbers as representing Truth and find it difficult to work with the concept of probability. They do not see a number as a kind of shorthand for a range that describes our actual knowledge of the underlying condition.*[3]

Business data such as sales and prices vary from month to month for reasons ranging from the weather to a customer's financial difficulties to the inevitable errors in gathering the data. The manager's challenge is to say when there is a real pattern behind the variation. We'll see that statistics provides tools for understanding variation and for seeking patterns behind the screen of variation. Let's look at some more data.

EXAMPLE 4 The price of gas

Figure 2 plots the average price of a gallon of regular unleaded gasoline each week from September 1990 to June 2011.[4] There certainly is variation! But a close look shows a yearly pattern: gas prices go up during the summer driving season, then down as demand drops in the fall. On top of this regular pattern we see the effects of international events. For example, prices rose when the 1990 Gulf War threatened oil supplies and dropped when the world economy turned down after the September 11, 2001, terrorist attacks in the United States. The years 2007 and 2008 brought the perfect storm: the ability to produce oil and refine gasoline was overwhelmed by high demand from China and the United States and continued turmoil in the oil-producing areas of the Middle East and Nigeria. Add in a rapid fall in the value of the dollar, and prices at the pump skyrocketed to more than $4 per gallon. In 2010 the Gulf oil spill also affected supply and hence prices. The data carry an important message: retail gas prices can vary wildly due to many extraneous factors. ■

Taylor Avelar/Bloomberg via Getty Images

Variation is everywhere. Individuals vary; repeated measurements on the same individual vary; almost everything varies over time. One reason we need to know some statistics is that it helps us to deal with variation and to describe the uncertainty in our conclusions. Let's look at another example to see how variation affects our conclusions.

FIGURE 2

Variation is everywhere: the average retail price of regular unleaded gasoline, 1990 to mid 2011, for Example 4.

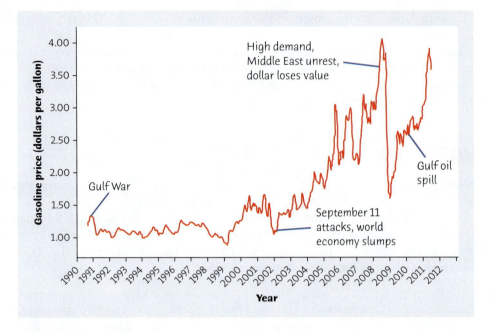

EXAMPLE 5 The HPV vaccine

Cervical cancer is second only to breast cancer as a cause of cancer deaths in women. Almost all cervical cancers are caused by human papillomavirus (HPV). The first vaccine to protect against the most common varieties of HPV became available in 2006. The Centers for Disease Control and Prevention (CDC) recommend that all girls be vaccinated at age 11 or 12. In 2011, the CDC made the same recommendation for boys, to protect against anal and throat cancers caused by HPV.

How well does the vaccine work? Doctors rely on experiments (called "clinical trials" in medicine) that give some women the new vaccine and others a dummy vaccine. (This is ethical when it is not yet known whether or not the vaccine is safe and effective.) The conclusion of the most important trial was that an estimated 98% of women up to age 26 who are vaccinated before they are infected with HPV will avoid cervical cancers over a 3-year period.[5]

On the average, women who get the vaccine are much less likely to get cervical cancer. But because variation is everywhere, the results are different for different women. Some vaccinated women will get cancer, and many who are not vaccinated will escape. Statistical conclusions are "on the average" statements only, and even these "on the average" statements have an element of uncertainty. Although we can't be 100% certain that the vaccine reduces risk on the average, statistics allows us to state how confident we are that this is the case. ■

Because variation is everywhere, conclusions are uncertain. Statistics gives us a language for talking about uncertainty that is used and understood by statistically literate people everywhere. We will soon learn to understand this language. Although we can't escape variation and uncertainty, learning statistics enables us to live more comfortably with these realities.

WHAT LIES AHEAD IN THIS BOOK

The purpose of *Essential Statistics* is to give you a working knowledge of the ideas and tools of practical statistics. We will divide practical statistics into three main areas.

■ **Data analysis** concerns methods and strategies for exploring, organizing, and describing data using graphs and numerical summaries. Your thoughtful exploration allows data to illuminate reality. Part I of this book (Chapters 1 to 7) discusses data analysis.

■ **Data production** provides methods for producing data that can give clear answers to specific questions. Where data come from is often the most important limitation on their usefulness. Basic concepts about how to select samples and design experiments are the most influential ideas in statistics. These concepts are the subject of Chapters 8 and 9.

■ **Statistical inference** moves beyond the data in hand to draw conclusions about some wider universe. Statistical conclusions aren't Yes or No answers—they must take into account variability among people, animals, or objects and uncertainty in data. To describe variation and uncertainty, inference uses the language of probability, introduced in Chapters 10 and 11. Because we are concerned with practice rather than theory, we need only a limited knowledge of probability. Chapters 12 and 13 offer more probability for those who want it. Chapters 14, 15, and 16 discuss the reasoning of statistical inference. These chapters are the key to the rest of the book. Chapters 18 to 22 present inference as used in practice in the most common settings. Chapters 23 to 25 concern more advanced or specialized kinds of inference.

Because data are numbers with a context, doing statistics means more than manipulating numbers. You must **state** a problem in its real-world context, **plan** your specific statistical work in detail, **solve** the problem by making the necessary graphs and calculations, and **conclude** by explaining what your findings say about the real-world setting. We'll make regular use of this four-step process to encourage good habits that go beyond graphs and calculations to ask, "What do the data tell me?"

Statistics does involve lots of calculating and graphing. The text presents the techniques you need, but you should use technology to automate calculations and graphs as much as possible. Because the big ideas of statistics don't depend on any particular level of access to technology, *Essential Statistics* does not require software or a graphing calculator until we reach the more advanced methods in Part IV of the text. Even if you make little use of technology, you should look at the Using Technology sections throughout the book. You will see at once that you can read and apply the output from almost any technology used for statistical calculations. The ideas really are more important than the details of how to do the calculations.

Unless you have constant access to software or a graphing calculator, *you will need a basic calculator with some built-in statistical functions*. Specifically, your calculator should find means and standard deviations and calculate correlations and regression lines. Look for a calculator that claims to do "two-variable statistics" or mentions "regression."

Although ability to carry out statistical procedures is very useful in academics and employment, the most important asset you can gain from the study of statistics is an understanding of the big ideas about working with data. *Essential Statistics* tries to explain the most important ideas of statistics, not just teach methods. Some examples of big ideas that you will meet (one from each of the three areas of statistics) are "always plot your data," "randomized comparative experiments," and "statistical significance."

You learn statistics by doing statistical problems. As you read, you will see several levels of exercises, arranged to help you learn. Short Apply Your Knowledge problem sets appear after each major idea. These are straightforward exercises that help you solidify the main points as you read. Be sure you can do these exercises before going on. The end-of-chapter exercises begin with multiple-choice Check Your Skills exercises (with all answers in the back of the book). Use them to check your grasp of the basics. The regular Chapter Exercises help you combine all the ideas of a chapter. Finally, the three Part Review chapters (Chapters 7, 17, and 22) look back over major blocks of learning, with many review exercises. At each step you are given less advance knowledge of exactly what statistical ideas and skills the problems will require, so each type of exercise requires more understanding.

The key to learning is persistence. The main ideas of statistics, like the main ideas of any important subject, took a long time to discover and take some time to master. The gain will be worth the pain.

Exploring Data

"What do the data say?" is the first question we ask in any statistical study. *Data analysis* answers this question by open-ended exploration of the data. The tools of data analysis are graphs such as histograms and scatterplots and numerical measures such as means and correlations. At least as important as the tools are principles that organize our thinking as we examine data. The six chapters in Part I present the principles and tools of statistical data analysis. They equip you with skills that are immediately useful whenever you deal with numbers.

These chapters reflect the strong emphasis on exploring data that characterizes modern statistics. Sometimes we hope to draw conclusions that apply to a setting that goes beyond the data in hand. This is *statistical inference,* the topic of much of the rest of the book. Data analysis is essential if we are to trust the results of inference, but data analysis isn't just preparation for inference. Roughly speaking, you can always do data analysis but inference requires rather special conditions.

One of the organizing principles of data analysis is to first look at one thing at a time and then at relationships. Our presentation follows this principle. In Chapters 1, 2, and 3 you will study *variables and their distributions.* Chapters 4, 5, and 6 concern *relationships among variables.* Chapter 7 reviews this part of the text.

Picturing Distributions with Graphs

S tatistics is the science of data. To work with data, we begin by organizing our thinking.

INDIVIDUALS AND VARIABLES

Any set of data contains information about some group of *individuals*. The information is organized in *variables*.

INDIVIDUALS AND VARIABLES

Individuals are the objects described by a set of data. Individuals may be people, but they may also be animals or things.

A **variable** is any characteristic of an individual. A variable can take different values for different individuals.

When you examine a set of data, ask *what individuals* the data describe and *what variables* the data contain. Some variables, like a person's sex or college major, simply place individuals into categories. Others, like height and grade point average, take numerical values for which we can do arithmetic. It makes sense to give an average income for a company's employees, but it does not make sense to give an "average" sex.

CATEGORICAL AND QUANTITATIVE VARIABLES

A **categorical variable** places an individual into one of several groups or categories.

A **quantitative variable** takes numerical values for which arithmetic operations such as adding and averaging make sense. The values of a quantitative variable are usually recorded in a **unit of measurement** such as seconds or kilograms.

EXAMPLE 1.1 The American Community Survey

The Census Bureau's American Community Survey collects data from 3,000,000 households each year, chosen at random from all the households in the country. You can view the detailed data online, though of course the identities of people and households are protected. If you choose the file of data on people, the *individuals* are the people living in the households contacted by the survey. Over 100 variables are recorded for each individual. Figure 1.1 displays a small part of the data. Most data tables follow this format—each row records data on one individual, and each column contains the values of one *variable* for all the individuals.

Translated from the Census Bureau's abbreviations, the variables are

SERIALNO	An identifying number for the household.
PWGTP	Weight in pounds.
AGEP	Age in years.
JWMNP	Travel time to work in minutes.
SCHL	Highest level of education. The numbers designate categories, *not* specific grades. For example, 9 = high school graduate, 10 = some college but no degree, and 13 = bachelor's degree.
SEX	Sex, designated by 1 = male and 2 = female.
WAGP	Wage and salary income last year, in dollars.

eg01-01.csv

	SERIALNO	PWGTP	AGEP	JWMNP	SCHL	SEX	WAGP
1	SERIALNO	PWGTP	AGEP	JWMNP	SCHL	SEX	WAGP
2	283	187	66		6	1	24000
3	283	158	66		9	2	0
4	323	176	54	10	12	2	11900
5	346	339	37	10	11	1	6000
6	346	91	27	10	10	2	30000
7	370	234	53	10	13	1	83000
8	370	181	46	15	10	2	74000
9	370	155	18		9	2	0
10	487	233	26		14	2	800
11	487	146	23		12	2	8000
12	511	236	53		9	2	0
13	511	131	53		11	1	0
14	515	213	38		11	2	12500
15	515	194	40		9	1	800
16	515	221	18	20	9	1	2500
17	515	193	11		3	1	

eg01-01

Each row in the spreadsheet contains data on one individual.

FIGURE 1.1

A spreadsheet displaying data from the American Community Survey, for Example 1.1.

Look at the highlighted row in Figure 1.1. This individual is a 53-year-old man who weighs 234 pounds, travels 10 minutes to work, has a bachelor's degree, and earned $83,000 last year.

In addition to the household serial number, there are six variables. Education and sex are categorical variables. The values for education and sex are stored as numbers, but these numbers are just labels for the categories and have no units of measurement. The other four variables are quantitative. Their values do have units. These variables are weight in pounds, age in years, travel time in minutes, and income in dollars. ■

When you examine data, pay attention to the *exact definition* of each variable. You might, for example, look into exactly what the Census Bureau means by "wage and salary income." Pay attention also to the *unit of measurement* of each quantitative variable. Weight in Example 1.1 is measured in pounds, but most countries would measure weight in kilograms.

APPLY YOUR KNOWLEDGE

1.1 Fuel economy. Here is a small part of a data set that describes the fuel economy (in miles per gallon) of model year 2010 motor vehicles:

Make and model	Vehicle type	Transmission type	Number of cylinders	City mpg	Highway mpg	Carbon footprint (tons)
⋮						
Aston Martin Vantage	Two-seater	Manual	8	12	19	13.1
Honda Civic	Subcompact	Automatic	4	25	36	6.3
Toyota Prius	Midsize	Automatic	4	51	48	3.7
Chevrolet Impala	Large	Automatic	6	18	29	8.3
⋮						

The *carbon footprint* measures a vehicle's impact on climate change in tons of carbon dioxide emitted annually.

(a) What are the individuals in this data set?

(b) For each individual, what variables are given? Which of these variables are categorical and which are quantitative?

1.2 Students and exercise. You are preparing to study the exercise habits of college students. Describe two categorical variables and two quantitative variables that you might measure for each student. Give the units of measurement for the quantitative variables.

CATEGORICAL VARIABLES: Pie charts and bar graphs

Statistical tools and ideas help us examine data in order to describe their main features. This examination is called **exploratory data analysis.** Like an explorer crossing unknown lands, we want first to simply describe what we see. Here are two principles that help us organize our exploration of a set of data.

exploratory data analysis

EXPLORING DATA

1. Begin by examining each variable by itself. Then move on to study the relationships among the variables.

2. Begin with a graph or graphs. Then add numerical summaries of specific aspects of the data.

We will follow these principles in organizing our learning. Chapters 1 to 3 present methods for describing a single variable. We study relationships among several variables in Chapters 4 and 5. In each case, we begin with graphical displays, then add numerical summaries for more complete description.

The proper choice of graph depends on the nature of the variable. To examine a single variable, we usually want to display its *distribution*.

DISTRIBUTION OF A VARIABLE

The **distribution** of a variable tells us what values it takes and how often it takes these values.

The values of a categorical variable are labels for the categories. The **distribution of a categorical variable** lists the categories and gives either the count or the percent of individuals that fall in each category.

 **MAJORS**

EXAMPLE 1.2 Which major?

About 1.8 million students enroll in colleges and universities each year. What do they plan to study? Here are data from 2008 on the percents of first-year students who plan to major in several discipline areas:[1]

Field of study	Percent of students
Arts and humanities	13.5
Biological sciences	9.3
Business	16.8
Education	8.2
Engineering	9.4
Physical sciences	3.2
Professional	13.8
Social science	11.5
Technical	1.0
Other majors and undeclared	13.2
Total	99.9

It's a good idea to check data for consistency. The percents should add to 100%. In fact, they add to 99.9%. What happened? Each percent is rounded to the nearest tenth. The exact percents would add to 100, but the rounded percents only come close. This is **roundoff error.** Roundoff errors don't point to mistakes in our work, just to the effect of rounding off results. ■

roundoff error

Columns of numbers take time to read. You can use a pie chart or a bar graph to display the distribution of a categorical variable more vividly. Figures 1.2 and 1.3 illustrate these displays for the distribution of intended college majors.

Pie charts show the distribution of a categorical variable as a "pie" whose slices are sized by the counts or percents for the categories. Pie charts are awkward to make by hand, but software will do the job for you. *A pie chart must include all the categories that make up a whole. Use a pie chart only when you want to emphasize each category's relation to the whole.* We need the "Other majors" category in Example 1.2 to complete the whole (all intended majors) and allow us to make the pie chart in Figure 1.2.

pie chart

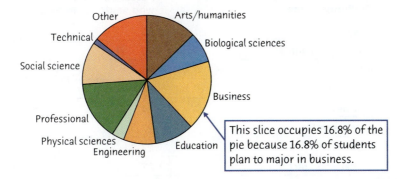

This slice occupies 16.8% of the pie because 16.8% of students plan to major in business.

FIGURE 1.2

You can use a pie chart to display the distribution of a categorical variable. Here is a pie chart of the distribution of intended majors of students entering college, for Example 1.2.

Bar graphs represent each category as a bar. The bar heights show the category counts or percents. Bar graphs are easier to make than pie charts and also easier to read. Figure 1.3 displays two bar graphs of the data on intended majors. The first orders the bars alphabetically by field of study (with "Other" at the end). It is often better to arrange the bars in order of height, as in Figure 1.3(b). This helps us immediately see which majors appear most often.

bar graph

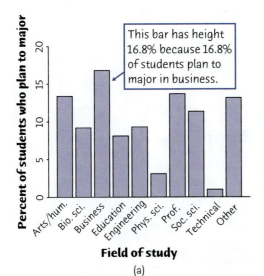

This bar has height 16.8% because 16.8% of students plan to major in business.

(a)

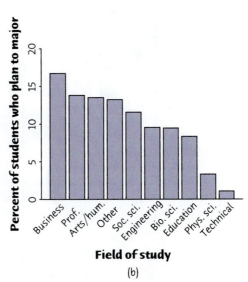

(b)

FIGURE 1.3

Bar graphs of the distribution of intended majors of students entering college, for Example 1.2. In (a), the bars follow the alphabetical order of fields of study. In (b), the same bars appear in order of height.

Bar graphs are more flexible than pie charts. Both pie charts and bar graphs can display the distribution of a categorical variable. But a bar graph can also compare any set of quantities that are measured in the same units, as in the following example.

CELLPHONES

EXAMPLE 1.3 Cell phones have biggest impact!

The rating service Arbitron asked Americans over 12 years old who used several high-tech platforms/devices to answer the question "How much of an impact on your life has (platform/device) had?" with 5 = Big impact and 1 = No impact at all. Here are the percents in decreasing order who said "Big impact." Only those platforms/devices for which 20% or more said "Big impact" are reported.[2]

Platform/Device	Percent of users who said "Big impact"
Cell phone	54
Broadband Internet	49
iPhone	45
BlackBerry	44
Television	34
Satellite radio	27
iPod	27
Digital video recorder	27
E-reader	24
Local AM/FM radio	22
Social-networking Web site	20

We can't make a pie chart to display these data. Each percent in the table refers to a different platform/device, not to parts of a single whole. Figure 1.4 is a bar graph comparing the eleven platforms/devices. We have again arranged the bars in order of height. ■

FIGURE 1.4

You can use a bar graph to compare quantities that are not part of a whole. This bar graph compares the percents of users who said "Big Impact" when asked how much of an impact a certain platform/device had on their lives, for Example 1.3.

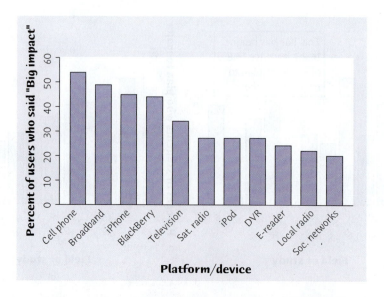

1.3 Do you listen to country radio? The rating service Arbitron places U.S. radio stations into more than 50 categories that describe the kind of programs they broadcast. Which formats attract the largest audiences? Here are Arbitron's measurements of the share of the listening audience for adults aged 18 to 24 years at a given time. The table includes only those formats with at least 3% of the listening audience:[3]

RADIOFORMAT

Format	Audience share
Pop Contempory Hit	16.1%
Country + New Country	14.0%
Rhythmic Contemporary Hit	8.7%
Adult Contemporary	6.8%
Urban Contemporary	6.6%
Hot Adult Contemporary	5.0%
Active Rock	4.6%
Classic Rock	4.5%
Mexican Regional	4.3%
Alternative	3.8%
Classic Hits	3.1%
Urban Adult Contemporary	3.1%

(a) What is the sum of the audience shares for these formats? What percent of the radio audience listens to stations with other formats?

(b) Make a bar graph to display these data. Be sure to include an "Other format" category.

(c) Would it be correct to display these data in a pie chart? Why?

1.4 How do students pay for college? The Higher Education Research Institute's Freshman Survey includes over 200,000 first-time full-time freshmen who entered college in 2010.[4] The survey reports the following data on the sources students use to pay for college expenses. COLLEGEPAY

Source for college expenses	Students
Family resources	78.4%
Student resources	64.3%
Aid—not to be repaid	73.4%
Aid—to be repaid	53.1%
Other	7.1%

(a) Explain why it is *not* correct to use a pie chart to display these data.

(b) Make a bar graph of the data. Notice that because the data contrast groups such as family and student resources it is better to keep these bars next to each other rather than to arrange the bars in order of height.

1.5 Never on Sunday? Births are not, as you might think, evenly distributed across the days of the week. Here are the average numbers of babies born on each day of the week in 2008:[5]  **BIRTHS**

Day	Births
Sunday	7,534
Monday	12,371
Tuesday	13,415
Wednesday	13,171
Thursday	13,147
Friday	12,919
Saturday	8,617

Present these data in a well-labeled bar graph. Would it also be correct to make a pie chart? Suggest some possible reasons why there are fewer births on weekends.

QUANTITATIVE VARIABLES: Histograms

Quantitative variables often take many values. The distribution tells us what values the variable takes and how often it takes these values. A graph of the distribution is clearer if nearby values are grouped together. The most common graph of the distribution of one quantitative variable is a **histogram.**

histogram

DATA FILE
FOREIGNBORN

EXAMPLE 1.4 Making a histogram

What percent of your home state's residents were born outside the United States? The country as a whole has 12.5% foreign-born residents, but the states vary from 1.2% in West Virginia to 27.2% in California. Table 1.1 presents the data for all 50 states and the District of Columbia.[6] The *individuals* in this data set are the states. The *variable* is the percent of a state's residents who are foreign-born. It's easier to see how your state compares with other states from a graph than from the table. To make a histogram of the distribution of this variable, proceed as follows:

Step 1. Choose the classes. Divide the range of the data into classes of equal width. The data in Table 1.1 range from 1.2 to 27.2, so we decide to use the following classes:

percent foreign-born between 0.1 and 5.0
percent foreign-born between 5.1 and 10.0
⋮
percent foreign-born between 25.1 and 30.0

Be sure to specify the classes precisely so that each individual falls into exactly one class. Pennsylvania, with 5.1% foreign-born, falls into the second class, but a state with 5.0% would fall into the first.

TABLE 1.1 Percent of state population born outside the United States

STATE	PERCENT	STATE	PERCENT	STATE	PERCENT
Alabama	2.8	Louisiana	2.9	Ohio	3.6
Alaska	7.0	Maine	3.2	Oklahoma	4.9
Arizona	15.1	Maryland	12.2	Oregon	9.7
Arkansas	3.8	Massachusetts	14.1	Pennsylvania	5.1
California	27.2	Michigan	5.9	Rhode Island	12.6
Colorado	10.3	Minnesota	6.6	South Carolina	4.1
Connecticut	12.9	Mississippi	1.8	South Dakota	2.2
Delaware	8.1	Missouri	3.3	Tennessee	3.9
Florida	18.9	Montana	1.9	Texas	15.9
Georgia	9.2	Nebraska	5.6	Utah	8.3
Hawaii	16.3	Nevada	19.1	Vermont	3.9
Idaho	5.6	New Hampshire	5.4	Virginia	10.1
Illinois	13.8	New Jersey	20.1	Washington	12.4
Indiana	4.2	New Mexico	10.1	West Virginia	1.2
Iowa	3.8	New York	21.6	Wisconsin	4.4
Kansas	6.3	North Carolina	6.9	Wyoming	2.7
Kentucky	2.7	North Dakota	2.1	Dist. of Columbia	12.7

Step 2. Count the individuals in each class. Here are the counts:

Class	Count
0.1 to 5.0	20
5.1 to 10.0	13
10.1 to 15.0	10
15.1 to 20.0	5
20.1 to 25.0	2
25.1 to 30.0	1

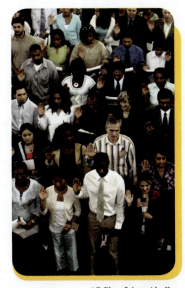

AP Photo/Mary Altaffer

Check that the counts add to 51, the number of individuals in the data (the 50 states and the District of Columbia).

Step 3. Draw the histogram. Mark the scale for the variable whose distribution you are displaying on the horizontal axis. That's the percent of a state's residents who are foreign-born. The scale runs from 0 to 30 because that is the span of the classes we chose. The vertical axis contains the scale of counts. Each bar represents a class. The base of the bar covers the class, and the bar height is the class count. Draw the bars with no horizontal space between them unless a class is empty, so that its bar has height zero. Figure 1.5 is our histogram. ■

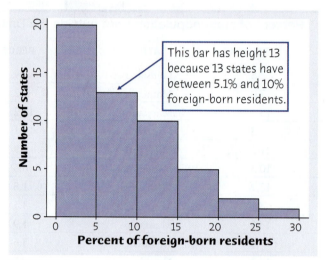

This bar has height 13 because 13 states have between 5.1% and 10% foreign-born residents.

FIGURE 1.5

Histogram of the distribution of the percent of foreign-born residents in the 50 states and the District of Columbia, for Example 1.4.

Although histograms resemble bar graphs, their details and uses are different. A histogram displays the distribution of a quantitative variable. The horizontal axis of a histogram is marked in the units of measurement for the variable. A bar graph compares the sizes of different quantities. The horizontal axis of a bar graph need not have any measurement scale but simply identifies the quantities being compared. Draw bar graphs with blank space between the bars to separate the quantities being compared. Draw histograms with no space, to indicate that all values of the variable are covered.

Our eyes respond to the *area* of the bars in a histogram.[7] Because the classes are all the same width, bar areas are proportional to heights, that is, to the class counts. So our eyes see an accurate picture of the distribution. There is no one right choice of the classes in a histogram. You must use your judgment in choosing classes to display the shape of a distribution. Statistics software will choose the classes for you. The software's choice is usually a good one, but you can change it if you want.

APPLY YOUR KNOWLEDGE

1.6 Older Americans. Where are older Americans more likely to live? Table 1.2 gives the percent of residents aged 65 years and over in each of the 50 states and the District of Columbia.[8] Make a histogram of the percents using classes of width 1% starting at 7%. That is, the first bar covers 7.0% to 7.9%, the second covers 8.0% to 8.9%, and so on. (Make this histogram by hand even if you have software, to be sure you understand the process. You may then want to compare your histogram with your software's choice.) 🔴 **OVER65**

TABLE 1.2 Percent of residents aged 65 and over

STATE	PERCENT	STATE	PERCENT	STATE	PERCENT
Alabama	13.8	Louisiana	12.3	Ohio	13.9
Alaska	7.6	Maine	15.6	Oklahoma	13.5
Arizona	13.1	Maryland	12.2	Oregon	13.5
Arkansas	14.3	Massachusetts	13.6	Pennsylvania	15.4
California	11.2	Michigan	13.4	Rhode Island	14.3
Colorado	10.6	Minnesota	12.7	South Carolina	13.7
Connecticut	13.9	Mississippi	12.8	South Dakota	14.5
Delaware	14.3	Missouri	13.7	Tennessee	13.4
Florida	17.2	Montana	14.6	Texas	10.3
Georgia	10.3	Nebraska	13.4	Utah	9.0
Hawaii	14.5	Nevada	11.6	Vermont	14.5
Idaho	12.1	New Hampshire	13.5	Virginia	12.2
Illinois	12.4	New Jersey	13.5	Washington	12.1
Indiana	12.9	New Mexico	13.0	West Virginia	15.8
Iowa	14.8	New York	13.4	Wisconsin	13.5
Kansas	13.0	North Carolina	12.7	Wyoming	12.3
Kentucky	13.2	North Dakota	14.7	Dist. of Columbia	11.7

INTERPRETING HISTOGRAMS

Making a statistical graph is not an end in itself. *The purpose of graphs is to help us understand the data.* After you make a graph, always ask, "What do I see?" Once you have displayed a distribution, you can see its important features as follows.

EXAMINING A HISTOGRAM

In any graph of data, look for the **overall pattern** and for striking **deviations** from that pattern.

You can describe the overall pattern of a histogram by its **shape, center,** and **spread.**

An important kind of deviation is an **outlier,** an individual value that falls outside the overall pattern.

One way to describe the center of a distribution is by its *midpoint*, the value with roughly half the observations taking smaller values and half taking larger values. For now, we will describe the spread of a distribution by giving the *smallest and largest values*. We will learn better ways to describe center and spread in Chapter 2.

EXAMPLE 1.5 Describing a distribution

Look again at the histogram in Figure 1.5. **Shape:** The distribution has a *single peak* at the left, which represents states in which between 0% and 5% of residents are foreign-born. The distribution is *skewed to the right*. A majority of states have no more than 10% foreign-born residents, but several states have much higher percents, so that the graph extends quite far to the right of its peak. **Center:** Arranging the observations from Table 1.1 in order of size shows that 6.3% (Kansas) is the midpoint of the distribution. There are 25 states with smaller percents foreign-born and 25 with larger. **Spread:** The spread is from 1.2% to 27.2%.

Outliers: Figure 1.5 shows no observations outside the overall single-peaked, right-skewed pattern of the distribution. Figure 1.6 is another histogram of the same distribution, with classes half as wide. Now California, at 27.2%, stands a bit apart to the right of the rest of the distribution. Is California an outlier or just the largest observation in a strongly skewed distribution? Unfortunately, there is no rule. Let's agree to call attention to only strong outliers that suggest something special about an observation—or an error such as typing 10.1 as 101. California is certainly not a strong outlier. ▪

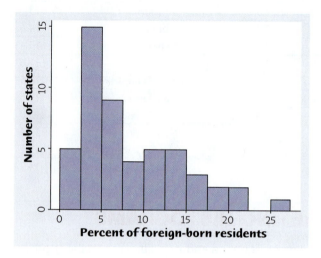

FIGURE 1.6

Another histogram of the distribution of the percent of foreign-born residents, with classes half as wide as in Figure 1.5, for Example 1.5. Histograms with more classes show more detail but may have a less clear pattern.

Figures 1.5 and 1.6 remind us that interpreting graphs calls for judgment. We also see that *the choice of classes in a histogram can influence the appearance of a distribution*. Because of this, and to avoid worrying about minor details, concentrate on the main features of a distribution. Look for major peaks, not for minor ups and downs, in the bars of the histogram. (For example, don't conclude that Figure 1.6 shows a second peak between 10% and 15%.) Look for clear outliers, not just for the smallest and largest observations. Look for rough *symmetry* or clear *skewness*.

SYMMETRIC AND SKEWED DISTRIBUTIONS

A distribution is **symmetric** if the right and left sides of the histogram are approximately mirror images of each other.

A distribution is **skewed to the right** if the right side of the histogram (containing the half of the observations with larger values) extends much farther out than the left side. It is **skewed to the left** if the left side of the histogram extends much farther out than the right side.

Here are more examples of describing the overall pattern of a histogram.

EXAMPLE 1.6 Iowa Test scores

Figure 1.7 displays the scores of all 947 seventh-grade students in the public schools of Gary, Indiana, on the vocabulary part of the Iowa Tests of Basic Skills.[9] Notice that the vertical scale is not the *count* of students but the *percent* of students in each histogram class. The distribution is *single-peaked* and *symmetric*. In mathematics, the two sides of symmetric patterns are exact mirror images. Real data are almost never exactly symmetric. We are content to describe Figure 1.7 as symmetric. The center (half above, half below) is close to 7. This is seventh-grade reading level. The scores range from 2.0 (second-grade level) to 12.1 (twelfth-grade level). ■

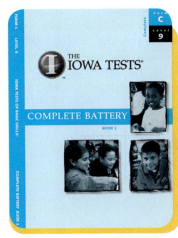

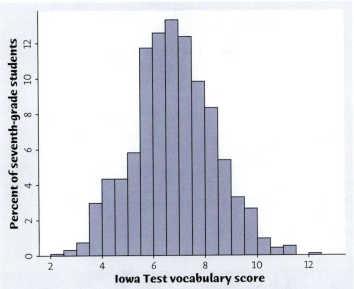

FIGURE 1.7

Histogram of the Iowa Test vocabulary scores of all seventh-grade students in Gary, Indiana, for Example 1.6. This distribution is single-peaked and symmetric.

EXAMPLE 1.7 Who takes the SAT?

Figure 1.8 is a histogram of the percent of high school graduates in each state who took the SAT Reasoning test.[10] The histogram shows two peaks, a high peak at the left and a lower but broader peak centered in the 60% to 80% class. The presence of two or more peaks suggests that a distribution mixes two or more kinds of individuals. That's the case here. There are two major tests of readiness for college, the ACT and the SAT. Most states have a strong preference for one or the other. In some states, many students take the ACT exam and few take the SAT—these states form the peak on the left. In other states, many students take the SAT and few choose the ACT—these states form the broader peak at the right.

> Giving the center and spread of this distribution is not very useful. The midpoint falls in the 20% to 40% class, between the two peaks. The story told by the histogram is in the two peaks corresponding to ACT states and SAT states. ■

FIGURE 1.8

Histogram of the percent of high school graduates in each state who took the SAT Reasoning test, for Example 1.7. The graph shows two groups of states: ACT states (where few students take the SAT) at the left and SAT states at the right.

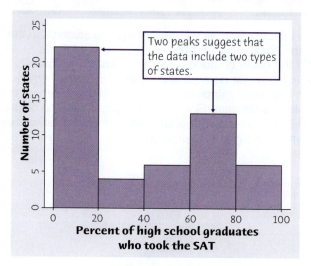

The overall shape of a distribution is important information about a variable. Many biological measurements on specimens from the same species and sex—lengths of bird bills, heights of young women—have symmetric distributions. On the other hand, data on people's incomes are usually strongly skewed to the right. There are many moderate incomes, some large incomes, and a few enormous incomes. Many distributions have irregular shapes that are neither symmetric nor skewed. Some data show other patterns, such as the two peaks in Figure 1.8. Use your eyes, describe the pattern you see, and then try to explain the pattern.

APPLY YOUR KNOWLEDGE

1.7 Older Americans. In Exercise 1.6, you made a histogram of the percent of residents aged 65 years and over in each of the 50 states and the District of Columbia, given in Table 1.2. Describe the shape of the distribution. Is it closer to symmetric or skewed? About where is the center (midpoint) of the data? What is the spread in terms of the smallest and largest values? Are there any states with unusually large or small percent of residents over 65?   OVER65

1.8 Unmarried women. Figure 1.9 shows the distribution of the state percents of women aged 15 and over who have never been married.   UNMARRIED

(a) The main body of the distribution is slightly skewed to the right. There is one clear outlier, the District of Columbia. Why is it not surprising that the percent of never-married women is higher in DC than in the 50 states?

(b) The midpoint of the distribution is the 26th state in order of percent of never-married women. In which class does the midpoint fall? About what is the spread (smallest to largest) of the distribution?

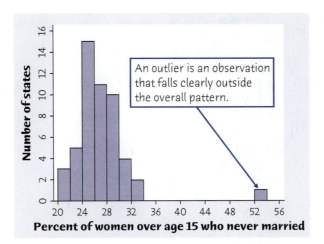

FIGURE 1.9
Histogram of the state percents of women aged 15 and over who have never been married, for Exercise 1.8.

QUANTITATIVE VARIABLES: Stemplots

Histograms are not the only graphical display of distributions. For small data sets, a *stemplot* is quicker to make and presents more detailed information.

STEMPLOT

To make a **stemplot:**

1. Separate each observation into a **stem,** consisting of all but the final (rightmost) digit, and a **leaf,** the final digit. Stems may have as many digits as needed, but each leaf contains only a single digit.

2. Write the stems in a vertical column with the smallest at the top, and draw a vertical line at the right of this column. Be sure to include all the stems needed to span the data, even when some will have no leaves.

3. Write each leaf in the row to the right of its stem, in increasing order out from the stem.

EXAMPLE 1.8 Making a stemplot

Table 1.1 presents the percents of state residents who were born outside the United States. To make a stemplot of these data, take the whole-number part of the percent as the stem and the final digit (tenths) as the leaf. Write stems from 1 for Mississippi, Montana, and West Virginia to 27 for California. Now add leaves. Arizona, 15.1%, has leaf 1 on the 15 stem. Texas, at 15.9%, places leaf 9 on the same stem. These are the only observations on this stem. Arrange the leaves in order, so that 15 | 19 is one row in the stemplot. Figure 1.10 is the complete stemplot for the data in Table 1.1. ■

FIGURE 1.10

Stemplot of the percents of foreign-born residents in the states, for Example 1.8. Each stem is a percent, and leaves are tenths of a percent.

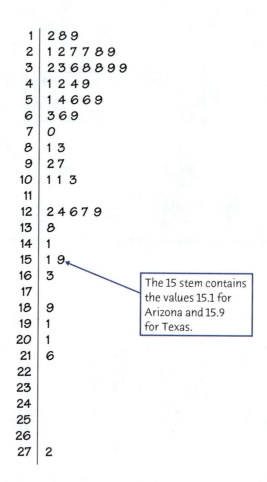

```
 1 | 2 8 9
 2 | 1 2 7 7 8 9
 3 | 2 3 6 8 8 9 9
 4 | 1 2 4 9
 5 | 1 4 6 6 9
 6 | 3 6 9
 7 | 0
 8 | 1 3
 9 | 2 7
10 | 1 1 3
11 |
12 | 2 4 6 7 9
13 | 8
14 | 1
15 | 1 9
16 | 3
17 |
18 | 9
19 | 1
20 | 1
21 | 6
22 |
23 |
24 |
25 |
26 |
27 | 2
```

The 15 stem contains the values 15.1 for Arizona and 15.9 for Texas.

A stemplot looks like a histogram turned on end. Compare the stemplot in Figure 1.10 with the histograms of the same data in Figures 1.5 and 1.6. All three graphs show a distribution that has one peak and is right-skewed. Figures 1.6 and 1.10 have enough classes to show that California (27.2%) stands slightly apart from the long right tail of the skewed distribution. You can choose the classes in a histogram. The classes (the stems) of a stemplot are given to you. But the stemplot, unlike the histogram, preserves the actual value of each observation. Stemplots do not work well for large data sets, where each stem must hold a large number of leaves. Don't try to make a stemplot of a large data set, such as the 947 Iowa Test scores in Figure 1.7.

EXAMPLE 1.9 Pulling wood apart

Although handbooks give the strength of a material as a single number, in fact the strength varies from piece to piece. Here are data from a typical student laboratory exercise: the load in pounds needed to pull apart pieces of Douglas fir.

33,190	31,860	32,590	26,520	33,280
32,320	33,020	32,030	30,460	32,700
23,040	30,930	32,720	33,650	32,340
24,050	30,170	31,300	28,730	31,920

A stemplot of these data would have very many stems and either no leaves or just one leaf on most stems. So we first **round** the data to the nearest hundred pounds and then drop the two 0s from the end of each rounded number. The rounded data are

332	319	326	265	333	323	330	320	305	327
230	309	327	337	323	241	302	313	287	319

rounding

 WOOD

Now we can make a stemplot with the first two digits (thousands of pounds) as stems and the third digit (hundreds of pounds) as leaves. Figure 1.11 is the stemplot. The distribution is *skewed to the left.* The *midpoint* is around 320 (32,000 pounds) and the *spread* is from 230 to 337. Because of the strong skew, we are reluctant to call the smallest observations outliers. They appear to be part of the long left tail of the distribution. Before using wood like this in construction, we should ask why some pieces are much weaker than the rest. ■

```
23 | 0
24 | 1
25 |
26 | 5
27 |
28 | 7
29 |
30 | 2 5 9
31 | 3 9 9
32 | 0 3 3 6 7 7
33 | 0 2 3 7
```

FIGURE 1.11

Stemplot of the breaking strength of pieces of wood, rounded to the nearest hundred pounds, for Example 1.9. Stems are thousands of pounds, and leaves are hundreds of pounds.

Comparing Figures 1.10 (right-skewed) and 1.11 (left-skewed) reminds us that *the direction of skewness is the direction of the long tail, not the direction where most observations are clustered.*

You can also **split stems** in a stemplot to double the number of stems when all the leaves would otherwise fall on just a few stems. Each stem then appears twice. Leaves 0 to 4 go on the upper stem, and leaves 5 to 9 go on the lower stem. If you split the stems in the stemplot of Figure 1.11, for example, the 32 and 33 stems become

splitting stems

```
32 | 033
32 | 677
33 | 023
33 | 7
```

Rounding and splitting stems are matters for judgment, like choosing the classes in a histogram. The wood strength data require rounding but don't require splitting stems.

APPLY YOUR KNOWLEDGE

1.9 Older Americans. Make a stemplot of percent of residents aged 65 years and over in each of the 50 states and the District of Columbia in Table 1.2. Use whole percents as your stems. Because the stemplot preserves the actual value of the observations, it is easy to find the midpoint (26th of the 51 observations in order) and the spread. What are they? **OVER65**

1.10 Health care spending. Table 1.3 shows the 2009 health care expenditure per capita in 35 countries with the highest gross domestic product in 2009.[11] Health expenditure per capita is the sum of public and private health expenditure (in international dollars, based on purchasing-power parity, or PPP) divided by population. Health expenditures include the provision of health services, family-planning activities, nutrition activities, and emergency aid designated for health but exclude the provision of water and sanitation. Make a stemplot of the data after rounding to the nearest $100 (so that stems are thousands of dollars, and leaves are hundreds of dollars). Split the stems, placing leaves 0 to 4 on the first stem and leaves 5 to 9 on the second stem of the same value. Describe the shape, center, and spread of the distribution. Which country is the high outlier? ● HEALTHCOST

TABLE 1.3 Annual health expenditure per capita (international dollars)

COUNTRY	DOLLARS	COUNTRY	DOLLARS	COUNTRY	DOLLARS
Argentina	1387	India	132	Saudi Arabia	1150
Australia	3382	Indonesia	99	South Africa	862
Austria	4243	Iran	685	Spain	3152
Belgium	4237	Italy	3027	Sweden	3690
Brazil	943	Japan	2713	Switzerland	5072
Canada	4196	Korea, South	1829	Thailand	345
China	308	Mexico	862	Turkey	965
Denmark	4118	Netherlands	4389	United Arab Emirates	1756
Finland	3357	Norway	5395	United Kingdom	3399
France	3934	Poland	1359	United States	7410
Germany	4129	Portugal	2703	Venezuela	737
Greece	3085	Russia	1038		

TIME PLOTS

Many variables are measured at intervals over time. We might, for example, measure the height of a growing child or the price of a stock at the end of each month. In these examples, our main interest is change over time. To display change over time, make a *time plot*.

TIME PLOT

A **time plot** of a variable plots each observation against the time at which it was measured. Always put time on the horizontal scale of your plot and the variable you are measuring on the vertical scale. Connecting the data points by lines helps emphasize any change over time.

WATERLEVEL

EXAMPLE 1.10 Water levels in the Everglades

Water levels in Everglades National Park are critical to the survival of this unique region. The photo shows a water-monitoring station in Shark River Slough, the main path for surface water moving through the "river of grass" that is the Everglades. Each day the mean gauge height, the height of the water surface above the gauge datum, is measured at the Shark River Slough monitoring station. (The gauge datum is a vertical control measure established in 1929 and is used as a reference for establishing varying elevations. It establishes a zero point from which to measure the gauge height.) Figure 1.12 is a time plot of mean daily gauge height at this station from October 1, 2000, to October 13, 2010.[12] ■

Courtesy U.S. Geological Survey

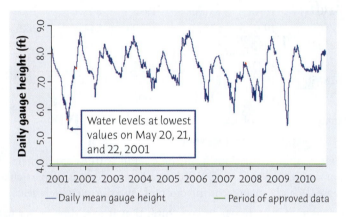

FIGURE 1.12

Time plot of water depth at a monitoring station in Everglades National Park over a period of ten years, for Example 1.10. The yearly cycles reflect Florida's wet and dry seasons.

When you examine a time plot, look once again for an overall pattern and for strong deviations from the pattern. Figure 1.12 shows strong **cycles,** regular up-and-down movements in water level. The cycles show the effects of Florida's wet season (roughly June to November) and dry season (roughly December to May). Water levels are highest in late fall. If you look closely, you can see the year-to-year variation. The dry season in 2003 ended early, with the first-ever April tropical storm. In consequence, the dry-season water level in 2003 did not dip as low as in other years. The drought in the southeastern portion of the country in 2008 and 2009 shows up in the steep drop in the mean gauge height in 2009, with water levels rising again after this period. The lower peaks in 2006 and 2007 reflect lower water levels during the wet seasons in these years.

cycles

Another common overall pattern in a time plot is a **trend,** a long-term upward or downward movement over time. Many economic variables show an upward trend. Incomes, house prices, and (alas) college tuitions tend to move generally upward over time.

trend

It is simplest to have statistics software draw the time plot for you. The software will often provide several options for drawing the time scale axis. Figure 1.17 (page 39) is an example of a time plot of monthly housing starts produced by Minitab.

APPLY YOUR KNOWLEDGE

1.11 The cost of college. Here are data on the average tuition and fees charged to in-state students by public four-year colleges and universities for the 1980 to 2010 academic years. Because almost any variable measured in dollars increases over time due to inflation (the falling buying power of a dollar), the values are given in "constant dollars," adjusted to have the same buying power that a dollar had in 2010.[13]

COLLEGECOST

Year	Tuition	Year	Tuition	Year	Tuition	Year	Tuition
1980	$2119	1988	$2903	1996	$4131	2004	$5900
1981	$2163	1989	$2972	1997	$4226	2005	$6128
1982	$2305	1990	$3190	1998	$4338	2006	$6218
1983	$2505	1991	$3373	1999	$4397	2007	$6480
1984	$2572	1992	$3622	2000	$4426	2008	$6532
1985	$2665	1993	$3827	2001	$4626	2009	$7137
1986	$2815	1994	$3974	2002	$4961	2010	$7605
1987	$2845	1995	$4019	2003	$5507		

(a) Make a time plot of average tuition and fees.

(b) What overall pattern does your plot show?

(c) Some possible deviations from the overall pattern are outliers, periods when charges went down (in 2010 dollars), and periods of particularly rapid increase. Which are present in your plot, and during which years?

(d) In looking for patterns, do you think that it would be better to study a time series of the tuition or the percent increase for each year? Why?

CHAPTER 1 SUMMARY

CHAPTER SPECIFICS

- A data set contains information on a number of **individuals.** Individuals may be people, animals, or things. For each individual, the data give values for one or more **variables.** A variable describes some characteristic of an individual, such as a person's height, sex, or salary.

- Some variables are **categorical** and others are **quantitative.** A categorical variable places each individual into a category, such as male or female. A quantitative variable has numerical values that measure some characteristic of each individual, such as height in centimeters or salary in dollars.

- **Exploratory data analysis** uses graphs and numerical summaries to describe the variables in a data set and the relations among them.

- After you understand the background of your data (individuals, variables, units of measurement), the first thing to do is almost always **plot your data.**

- The **distribution** of a variable describes what values the variable takes and how often it takes these values. **Pie charts** and **bar graphs** display the distribution of a categorical variable. Bar graphs can also compare any set of quantities measured in the same units. **Histograms** and **stemplots** graph the distribution of a quantitative variable.

- When examining any graph, look for an **overall pattern** and for notable **deviations** from the pattern.

- **Shape, center, and spread** describe the overall pattern of the distribution of a quantitative variable. Some distributions have simple shapes, such as **symmetric** or **skewed.** Not all distributions have a simple overall shape, especially when there are few observations.

- **Outliers** are observations that lie outside the overall pattern of a distribution. Always look for outliers and try to explain them.

- When observations on a variable are taken over time, make a **time plot** that graphs time horizontally and the values of the variable vertically. A time plot can reveal **trends, cycles,** or other changes over time.

LINK IT

Practical statistics uses data to draw conclusions about some wider universe. You should reread Example 1.1 of this chapter, as it will help you understand this basic idea. For the American Community Survey described in the example, the data are the responses from those households responding to the survey, although the wider universe of interest is the entire nation.

In our study of practical statistics, we will divide the subject into three main areas. In exploratory data analysis, graphs and numerical summaries are used for exploring, organizing, and describing data so that the patterns become apparent. Data production concerns where the data come from and helps us to understand whether what we learn from our data can be generalized to a wider universe. And statistical inference provides tools for generalizing what we learn to a wider universe.

In this chapter we have begun to learn about data analysis. A data set can consist of hundreds of observations on many variables. Even if we consider only one variable at a time, it is difficult to see what the data have to say by scanning a list containing many data values. Graphs provide a visual tool for organizing and identifying patterns in data and are a good starting point in the exploration of the distribution of a variable. Pie charts and bar graphs can summarize the information in a categorical variable by giving us the percent of the distribution in each category. Although a table containing the categories and percents gives the same information as a bar graph, a substantial advantage of the bar graph over a tabular presentation is that the bar graph allows us to visually compare percents among all categories simultaneously by means of the heights of the bars. Histograms and stemplots are graphical tools for summarizing the information provided by a quantitative variable. The overall pattern in a histogram or stemplot illustrates some of the important features of the distribution of a variable that will be of interest as we continue our study of practical statistics. The center of the histogram tells us about the value of a "typical" observation on this variable, while the spread gives us a sense of how close most of the observations are to this value. Other interesting features are the presence of outliers and the general shape of the plot. For data collected over time, time plots can show patterns such as seasonal variation and trends in the variable. In the next chapter we will see how the information about the distribution of a variable can also be described using numerical summaries.

CHECK YOUR SKILLS

The multiple-choice exercises in Check Your Skills ask straightfor-ward questions about basic facts from the chapter. Answers to all these exercises appear in the back of the book. You should expect almost all your answers to be correct.

1.12 A description of different houses on the market includes the variables square footage of the house and the average monthly gas bill. Which of the following is true?

  (a) Square footage and average monthly gas bill are both categorical variables.

  (b) Square footage and average monthly gas bill are both quantitative variables.

  (c) Square footage is a categorical variable, and aver-age monthly gas bill is a quantitative variable.

1.13 To display the distribution of grades (A, B, C, D, F) among students in a course, it would be correct to use

  (a) a pie chart but not a bar graph.

  (b) a bar graph but not a pie chart.

  (c) either a pie chart or a bar graph.

1.14 Figure 1.9 (page 25) is a histogram of the percent of women in each state aged 15 and over who have never been married. The leftmost bar in the histogram covers percents of never-married women ranging from about

  (a) 20% to 24%. (b) 20% to 22%. (c) 0% to 20%.

1.15 Here are the amounts of money (cents) in coins carried by 10 students in a statistics class:

    50 35 0 97 76 0 0 87 23 65

To make a stemplot of these data, you would use stems

  (a) 0, 1, 2, 3, 4, 5, 6, 7, 8, 9.

  (b) 0, 2, 3, 5, 6, 7, 8, 9.

  (c) 00, 10, 20, 30, 40, 50, 60, 70, 80, 90.

1.16 Here is a stemplot of the average travel times to work for workers in each state and the District of Columbia who are at least 16 years of age and don't work at home.[14] The stems are whole minutes, and the leaves are tenths of a minute.

```
15 | 59
16 |
17 | 6779
18 | 25
19 |
20 | 017889
21 | 28
22 | 01333499
23 | 445669
24 | 01266
25 | 0012569
26 | 689
27 | 39
28 |
29 | 12
30 | 69
```

The state with the longest average travel time is New York. On average, how long does it take New Yorkers to travel to work each day?

  (a) 30.69 minutes

  (b) 309 minutes

  (c) 30.9 minutes

1.17 The shape of the distribution in Exercise 1.16 is

  (a) clearly skewed to the right.

  (b) roughly symmetric.

  (c) clearly skewed to the left.

1.18 You look at real estate ads for houses in Naples, Florida. There are many houses ranging from $200,000 to $500,000 in price. The few houses on the water, however, have prices up to $15 million. The distribution of house prices will be

  (a) skewed to the left.

  (b) roughly symmetric.

  (c) skewed to the right.

CHAPTER 1 EXERCISES

1.19 Medical students. Students who have finished medi-cal school are assigned to residencies in hospitals to receive further training in a medical specialty. Here is part of a hypothetical database of students seeking residency posi-tions. USMLE is the student's score on Step 1 of the national medical-licensing examination.

Name	Medical school	Sex	Age	USMLE	Specialty sought
Abrams, Laurie	Florida	F	28	238	Family medicine
Brown, Gordon	Meharry	M	25	205	Radiology
Cabrera, Maria	Tufts	F	26	191	Pediatrics
Ismael, Miranda	Indiana	F	32	245	Internal medicine

(a) What individuals does this data set describe?

(b) In addition to the student's name, how many variables does the data set contain? Which of these variables are categorical and which are quantitative?

1.20 Buying a refrigerator. *Consumer Reports* is doing an article comparing refrigerators in their next issue. Some of the characteristics to be included in the report are the brand name and model; whether it has a top, bottom, or side-by-side freezer; the estimated energy consumption per year (kilowatts); whether or not it is Energy Star compliant; the width, depth, and height in inches; and both the freezer and refrigerator net capacity in cubic feet. Which of these variables are categorical and which are quantitative? Give the units for the quantitative variables and the categories for the categorical variables. What are the individuals in the report?

1.21 What color is your car? The most popular colors for cars and light trucks vary with region and over time. In North America white remains the top color choice, with black the top choice in Europe and silver the top choice in South America. Here is the distribution of the top colors for vehicles sold globally in 2010:[15] CARCOLOR

Color	Popularity
Silver	26%
Black	24%
White	16%
Gray	16%
Red	6%
Blue	5%
Beige, brown	3%
Other colors	

Fill in the percent of vehicles that are in other colors. Make a graph to display the distribution of color popularity.

1.22 Facebook and MySpace audience. Although most social-networking Web sites in the United States have fairly short histories, the growth of these sites has been exponential. Two of the most visited social-networking sites are Facebook.com and MySpace.com. Here is the age distribution for users over 18 years old for the two sites in November 2010:[16] FACEBOOK

Age group	Facebook users	MySpace users
18 to 22 years	16%	29%
23 to 35 years	33%	42%
36 to 49 years	25%	17%
50 to 65 years	19%	10%
Over 65 years	6%	3%

(a) Draw a bar graph for the age distribution of Facebook visitors. The leftmost bar should correspond to "18 to 22," the next bar to "23 to 35," and so on. Do the same for MySpace, using the same scale for the percent axis.

(b) Describe the most important difference in the age distribution of the audience for Facebook and MySpace. How does this difference show up in the bar graphs? Do you think it was important to order the bars by age to make the comparison easier?

(c) Explain why it *is* appropriate to use a pie chart to display either of these distributions. Draw a pie chart for each distribution. Do you think it is easier to compare the two distributions with bar graphs or pie charts? Explain your reasoning.

1.23 Deaths among young people. Among persons aged 15 to 24 years in the United States, the leading causes of death and number of deaths in 2009 were: accidents, 12,351; homicide, 4820; suicide, 4341; cancer, 1659; heart disease, 1010; congenital defects, 451.[17]

(a) Make a bar graph to display these data.

(b) To make a pie chart, you need one additional piece of information. What is it?

1.24 Canadian students rate their universities. The National Survey of Student Engagement asked students at many universities, "How would you evaluate your entire educational experience at this university?" Here are the percents of senior-year students at Canada's 10 largest primarily English-speaking universities who responded "Excellent":[18] CANADAUNIV

University	Excellent rating
Toronto	23%
York	18%
Alberta	22%
Ottawa	16%
Western Ontario	41%
British Columbia	18%
Calgary	15%
McGill	31%
Waterloo	35%
Concordia	21%

(a) The list is arranged in order of undergraduate enrollment. Make a bar graph with the bars in order of student rating.

(b) Explain carefully why it is not correct to make a pie chart of these data.

1.25 Do adolescent girls eat fruit? We all know that fruit is good for us. Figure 1.13 is a histogram of the number of servings of fruit per day claimed by 74 seventeen-year-old girls in a study in Pennsylvania.[19] Describe the shape, center, and spread of this distribution. What percent of these girls ate fewer than two servings per day?

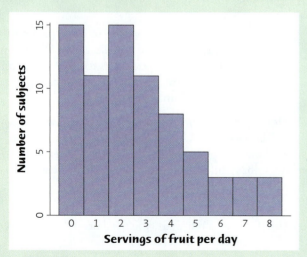

FIGURE 1.13

The distribution of fruit consumption in a sample of 74 seventeen-year-old girls, for Exercise 1.25.

1.26 IQ test scores. Figure 1.14 is a stemplot of the IQ test scores of 78 seventh-grade students in a rural midwestern school.[20] IQSCORES

(a) Four students had low scores that might be considered outliers. Ignoring these, describe the shape, center, and spread of the distribution. (Notice that it looks roughly bell-shaped.)

(b) We often read that IQ scores for large populations are centered at 100. What percent of these 78 students have scores above 100?

```
 7 | 2 4
 7 | 7 9
 8 |
 8 | 6 9
 9 | 0 1 3 3
 9 | 6 7 7 8
10 | 0 0 2 2 3 3 3 3 4 4
10 | 5 5 5 6 6 6 7 7 7 7 8 9
11 | 0 0 0 0 1 1 1 1 2 2 2 2 3 3 3 4 4 4 4
11 | 5 5 6 8 8 9 9 9
12 | 0 0 3 3 4 4
12 | 6 7 7 8 8 8
13 | 0 2
13 | 6
```

FIGURE 1.14

The distribution of IQ scores for 78 seventh-grade students, for Exercise 1.26.

1.27 Name that variable. A survey of a large college class asked the following questions:

1. Are you female or male? (In the data, male = 0, female = 1.)

2. Are you right-handed or left-handed? (In the data, right = 0, left = 1.)

3. What is your height in inches?

4. How many minutes do you study on a typical weeknight?

Figure 1.15 shows histograms of the student responses, in scrambled order and without scale markings. Which histogram goes with each variable? Explain your reasoning.

1.28 Food oils and health. Fatty acids are necessary for human health. Two types of essential fatty acids, called omega-3 and omega-6, are not produced by our bodies and so must be obtained from our food. Food oils, widely used in food processing and cooking, are major sources of these compounds. There is some evidence that a healthy diet should have more omega-3 than omega-6. Table 1.4 gives the ratio of omega-3 to

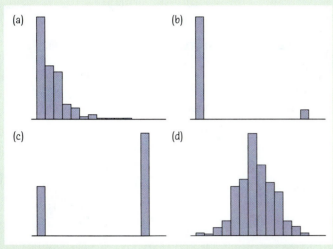

FIGURE 1.15

Histograms of four distributions, for Exercise 1.27.

omega-6 in some common food oils.[21] Values greater than 1 show that an oil has more omega-3 than omega-6. 🏺 **FOODOILS**

(a) Make a histogram of these data, using classes bounded by the whole numbers from 0 to 6.

(b) What is the shape of the distribution? How many of the 30 food oils have more omega-3 than omega-6? What does this distribution suggest about the possible health effects of modern food oils?

(c) Table 1.4 contains entries for several fish oils (cod, herring, menhaden, salmon, sardine). How do these values support the idea that eating fish is healthy?

1.29 Where are the nurses? Table 1.5 (page 36) gives the number of active nurses per 100,000 people in each state.[22]
🏺 **NURSES**

(a) Why is the number of nurses per 100,000 people a better measure of the availability of nurses than a simple count of the number of nurses in a state?

(b) Make a histogram that displays the distribution of nurses per 100,000 people. Write a brief description of the distribution. Are there any outliers? If so, can you explain them?

1.30 Carbon dioxide emissions. Burning fuels in power plants and motor vehicles emits carbon dioxide (CO_2), which contributes to global warming. Table 1.6 displays the 2007 CO_2 emissions per person from countries with populations of at least 30 million in that year.[23]
🏺 **CO2EMISSIONS**

(a) Why do you think we choose to measure emissions per person rather than total CO_2 emissions for each country?

(b) Make a stemplot to display the data of Table 1.6 (page 36). The data will first need to be rounded.

TABLE 1.4 Omega-3 fatty acids as a fraction of omega-6 fatty acids in food oils

OIL	RATIO	OIL	RATIO
Perilla	5.33	Flaxseed	3.56
Walnut	0.20	Canola	0.46
Wheat germ	0.13	Soybean	0.13
Mustard	0.38	Grape seed	0.00
Sardine	2.16	Menhaden	1.96
Salmon	2.50	Herring	2.67
Mayonnaise	0.06	Soybean, hydrogenated	0.07
Cod liver	2.00	Rice bran	0.05
Shortening (household)	0.11	Butter	0.64
Shortening (industrial)	0.06	Sunflower	0.03
Margarine	0.05	Corn	0.01
Olive	0.08	Sesame	0.01
Shea nut	0.06	Cottonseed	0.00
Sunflower (oleic)	0.05	Palm	0.02
Sunflower (linoleic)	0.00	Cocoa butter	0.04

TABLE 1.5 Nurses per 100,000 people, by state

STATE	NURSES	STATE	NURSES	STATE	NURSES
Alabama	889	Louisiana	890	Ohio	997
Alaska	777	Maine	1065	Oklahoma	734
Arizona	581	Maryland	897	Oregon	792
Arkansas	802	Massachusetts	1218	Pennsylvania	1027
California	657	Michigan	866	Rhode Island	1078
Colorado	799	Minnesota	1065	South Carolina	819
Connecticut	1010	Mississippi	930	South Dakota	1244
Delaware	1034	Missouri	1009	Tennessee	987
Florida	793	Montana	773	Texas	676
Georgia	669	Nebraska	1062	Utah	632
Hawaii	680	Nevada	610	Vermont	950
Idaho	710	New Hampshire	992	Virginia	770
Illinois	847	New Jersey	873	Washington	792
Indiana	884	New Mexico	599	West Virginia	932
Iowa	1008	New York	867	Wisconsin	919
Kansas	894	North Carolina	911	Wyoming	807
Kentucky	958	North Dakota	988	Dist. of Columbia	1566

TABLE 1.6 Annual carbon dioxide emissions in 2007 (metric tons per person)

COUNTRY	CO_2	COUNTRY	CO_2	COUNTRY	CO_2
Afghanistan	0.0272	India	1.3844	Poland	8.3231
Algeria	4.1384	Indonesia	1.7677	Russia	10.8309
Argentina	4.6525	Iran	6.8472	South Africa	8.8163
Bangladesh	0.2773	Italy	7.6923	Spain	8.1555
Brazil	1.9373	Japan	9.8476	Sudan	0.2850
Canada	16.9171	Kenya	0.2976	Tanzania	0.1464
China	4.9194	Korea, South	10.4941	Thailand	4.1432
Colombia	1.4301	Mexico	4.3862	Turkey	3.9543
Congo	0.0389	Morocco	1.4862	Uganda	0.1046
Egypt	2.3065	Myanmar	0.2685	Ukraine	6.8598
Ethiopia	0.0828	Nigeria	0.6449	United Kingdom	8.8608
France	6.0207	Pakistan	0.9031	United States	18.9144
Germany	9.5690	Philippines	0.7993	Vietnam	1.2935

What units are you going to use for the stems? The leaves? You should round the data to the units you are planning to use for the leaves before drawing the stemplot. Describe the shape, center, and spread of the distribution. Which countries are outliers?

1.31 Fur seals on St. George Island. Every year hundreds of thousands of northern fur seals return to their haul-outs in the Pribilof Islands in Alaska to breed, give birth, and teach their pups to swim, hunt, and survive in the Bering Sea. U.S. commercial fur sealing operations continued until 1983, but despite a reduction in harvest, the population of fur seals has continued to decline. Here are data on the number of fur seal pups born on St. George Island (in thousands) from 1975 to 2006:[24] **FURSEALS**

Year	Pups born (thousands)	Year	Pups born (thousands)
1975	53.70	1991	24.28
1976	56.16	1992	25.16
1977	43.41	1993	23.70
1978	47.25	1994	22.24
1979	47.47	1995	24.82
1980	39.34	1996	27.39
1981	38.15	1997	24.74
1982	39.29	1998	22.09
1983	31.44	1999	21.13
1984	33.44	2000	20.18
1985	28.87	2001	18.89
1986	32.36	2002	17.59
1987	33.12	2003	17.24
1988	24.82	2004	16.88
1989	33.11	2005	16.97
1990	23.40	2006	17.07

Make a stemplot to display the distribution of pups born per year. (Round to the nearest whole number and split the stems.) Describe the shape, center, and spread of the distribution. Are there any outliers?

1.32 Do women study more than men? We asked the students in a large first-year college class how many minutes they studied on a typical weeknight. Here are the responses of random samples of 30 women and 30 men from the class: **STUDYTIMES**

Women					Men				
270	150	180	360	180	120	120	30	45	200
120	180	120	240	170	90	90	30	120	75
150	120	180	180	150	150	90	60	240	300
200	150	180	120	240	240	60	150	60	30
120	60	120	180	180	30	230	120	95	150
90	240	180	115	120	0	200	120	120	180

(a) Examine the data. Why are you not surprised that most responses are multiples of 10 minutes? We eliminated one student who claimed to study 30,000 minutes per night. Are there any other responses you consider suspicious?

(b) Make a **back-to-back stemplot** to compare the two samples. That is, use one set of stems with two sets of leaves, one to the right and one to the left of the stems. (Draw a line on either side of the stems to separate stems and leaves.) Order both sets of leaves from smallest at the stem to largest away from the stem. Report the approximate midpoints of both groups. Does it appear that women study more than men (or at least claim that they do)?

back-to-back stemplot

1.33 Fur seals on St. George Island. Make a time plot of the number of fur seals born per year from Exercise 1.31. What does the time plot show that your stemplot in Exercise 1.31 did not show? When you have data collected over time, a time plot is often needed to understand what is happening. **FURSEALS**

1.34 Marijuana and traffic accidents. Researchers in New Zealand interviewed 907 drivers at age 21. They had data on traffic accidents and they asked the drivers about marijuana use. Here are data on the numbers of accidents caused by these drivers at age 19, broken down by marijuana use at the same age:[25]

	Marijuana Use per Year			
	Never	1–10 times	11–50 times	51+ times
Drivers	452	229	70	156
Accidents caused	59	36	15	50

(a) Explain carefully why a useful graph must compare *rates* (accidents per driver) rather than *counts* of accidents in the four marijuana use classes.

(b) Make a graph that displays the accident rate for each class. What do you conclude? (You can't conclude that marijuana use *causes* accidents, because risk takers are more likely both to drive aggressively and to use marijuana.)

1.35 Dates on coins. Sketch a histogram for a distribution that is skewed to the left. Suppose that you and your friends emptied your pockets of coins and recorded the year marked on each coin. The distribution of dates would be skewed to the left. Explain why.

1.36 El Niño and the monsoon. It appears that El Niño, the periodic warming of the Pacific Ocean west of South America, affects the monsoon rains that are essential for agriculture in India. Here are the monsoon rains (in millimeters) for the 23 strong El Niño years between 1871 and 2004:[26]

ELNINO

628	669	740	651	710	736	717	698
653	604	781	784	790	811	830	858
858	896	806	790	792	957	872	

(a) To make a stemplot of these rainfall amounts, round the data to the nearest 10, so that stems are hundreds of millimeters and leaves are tens of millimeters. Make two stemplots, with and without splitting the stems. Which plot do you prefer?

(b) Describe the shape, center, and spread of the distribution.

(c) The average monsoon rainfall for all years from 1871 to 2004 is about 850 millimeters. What effect does El Niño appear to have on monsoon rains?

1.37 Watch those scales! Figures 1.16(a) and 1.16(b) both show time plots of tuition charged to in-state students from 1980 through 2010.[27]

(a) Which graph appears to show the biggest increase in tuition between 2000 and 2010?

(b) Read the graphs and compute the actual increase in tuition between 2000 and 2010 in each graph. Do you think these graphs are for the same or different data sets? Why?

The impression that a time plot gives depends on the scales you use on the two axes. Changing the scales can make tuition appear to increase very rapidly or to have only a gentle increase. The moral of this exercise is: always pay close attention to the scales when you look at a time plot.

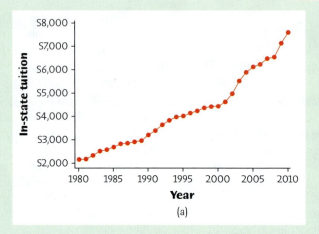

(a)

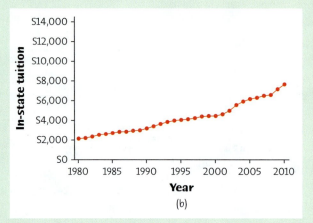

(b)

FIGURE 1.16

Time plots of in-state tuition between 1980 and 2010, for Exercise 1.37.

1.38 Housing starts. Figure 1.17 is a time plot of the number of single-family homes started by builders each month from January 1990 to August 2011.[28] The counts are in thousands of homes. HOUSESTARTS

(a) The most notable pattern in this time plot is yearly up-and-down cycles. At what season of the year are housing starts highest? Lowest? The cycles are explained by the weather in the northern part of the country.

(b) Is there a longer-term trend visible in addition to the cycles? If so, describe it.

(c) The big economic news of 2007 was a severe downturn in housing that began in mid-2006. This was followed by the financial crisis in 2008. How are these economic events reflected in the time plot?

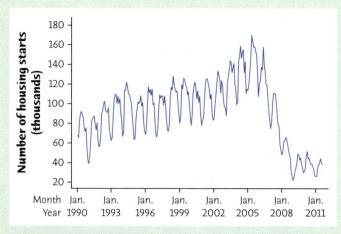

FIGURE 1.17

Time plot of the monthly count of new single-family houses started (in thousands) between January 1990 and August 2011, for Exercise 1.38.

Year	Area (millions of km²)	Year	Area millions (of km²)	Year	Area (millions of km²)
1979	0.1	1990	19.3	2001	25.0
1980	1.2	1991	19.0	2002	11.9
1981	0.6	1992	22.3	2003	25.8
1982	4.6	1993	24.2	2004	19.0
1983	7.7	1994	23.5	2005	23.9
1984	9.8	1995		2006	26.2
1985	14.1	1996	22.8	2007	21.6
1986	11.2	1997	22.1	2008	24.7
1987	19.3	1998	25.9	2009	21.6
1988	10.0	1999	23.3	2010	19.0
1989	18.8	2000	24.8		

1.39 Ozone hole. The ozone hole is a region in the stratosphere over the Antarctic with exceptionally depleted ozone. The size of the hole is not constant over the year but is largest at the beginning of the Southern Hemisphere spring (August–October). The increase in the size of the ozone hole led to the Montreal Protocol in 1987, an international treaty designed to protect the ozone layer by phasing out the production of substances, such as chlorofluorocarbons (CFCs), believed to be responsible for ozone depletion. The following table gives the average ozone hole size for the period September 7 to October 13 for each of the years from 1979 through 2010 (note that no data were acquired in 1995).[29] To get a better feel for the magnitude of the numbers, the area of North America is approximately 24.5 million square kilometers (km²). OZONEHOLE

The two parts of this exercise will have you draw two graphs of these data.

(a) First make a time plot of the data. The severity of the ozone hole will vary from year to year depending on the meteorology of the atmosphere above Antarctica. Does the time plot illustrate only year-to-year variation or are other patterns apparent? Specifically, is there a trend over any period of years? What about cyclical fluctuation? Explain in words the change in the average size of the ozone hole over this 30-year period.

(b) Now make a stemplot of the data. What is the midpoint of the distribution of ozone hole size? Do you think that the stemplot and the midpoint are a good description of this data set? Is there important information in the time plot that is not contained in the stemplot? When data are collected over time, you should always make a time plot.

EXPLORING THE WEB

1.40 Natural-gas prices. The Department of Energy Web site contains information about monthly wholesale and retail prices for natural gas in each state. Go to www.eia.gov/naturalgas/data.cfm and then click on the link *Monthly Wholesale and Retail Prices*. Under Area, choose a state of interest to you, make sure the Period is monthly, and then under Residential Price click on *View History*. A window will open with a time plot covering approximately a 20-year period, along with a table of the monthly residential prices for each year.

(a) If you have access to statistical software, you should use the *Download Data (XLS File)* link to save the data as an Excel (.xls) file on your computer. Then enter the data into your software package, and reproduce the time plot using the graphic capabilities of your software package. Be sure you use an appropriate title and axis labels. If you do not have access to appropriate software, provide a rough sketch of the time plot that is given on the Web site.

(b) Is there a regular pattern of seasonal variation that repeats each year? Describe it. Are the prices increasing over time?

1.41 Hank Aaron's home run record. The all-time home run leader prior to 2007 was Hank Aaron. You can find his career statistics by going to the Web site www.baseball-reference.com and then clicking on the *players* tab at the top of the page and going to *Hank Aaron*.

(a) Make a stemplot or a histogram of the number of home runs that Hank Aaron hit in each year during his career. Is the distribution roughly symmetric, clearly skewed, or neither? About how many home runs did Aaron hit in a typical year? Are there any outliers?

(b) Would a time plot be appropriate for these data? If so, what information would be included in the time plot that is not in the stemplot?

Logan Mock-Bunting/Getty Images

Describing Distributions with Numbers

H ere are the travel times in minutes for 15 workers in North Carolina, chosen at random by the Census Bureau:[1]

30 20 10 40 25 20 10 60 15 40 5 30 12 10 10

We aren't surprised that most people estimate their travel time in multiples of 5 minutes. Here is a stemplot of these data:

```
0 | 5
1 | 0 0 0 0 2 5
2 | 0 0 5
3 | 0 0
4 | 0 0
5 |
6 | 0
```

The distribution is single-peaked and right-skewed. The longest travel time (60 minutes) may be an outlier. Our goal in this chapter is to describe with numbers the center and spread of this and other distributions.

Chapter 2

IN THIS CHAPTER WE COVER...

- Measuring center: the mean
- Measuring center: the median
- Comparing the mean and the median
- Measuring spread: the quartiles
- The five-number summary and boxplots
- Spotting suspected outliers*
- Measuring spread: the standard deviation
- Choosing measures of center and spread
- Using technology
- Organizing a statistical problem

41

MEASURING CENTER: The mean

The most common measure of center is the ordinary arithmetic average, or *mean*.

> ### THE MEAN $\bar{x}$
>
> To find the **mean** of a set of observations, add their values and divide by the number of observations. If the n observations are $x_1, x_2, \ldots, x_n$, their mean is
>
> $$\bar{x} = \frac{x_1 + x_2 + \cdots + x_n}{n}$$
>
> or, in more compact notation,
>
> $$\bar{x} = \frac{1}{n}\sum x_i$$

The Σ (capital Greek sigma) in the formula for the mean is short for "add them all up." The subscripts on the observations x_i are just a way of keeping the n observations distinct. They do not necessarily indicate order or any other special facts about the data. The bar over the x indicates the mean of all the x-values. Pronounce the mean $\bar{x}$ as "x-bar." This notation is very common. When writers who are discussing data use $\bar{x}$ or $\bar{y}$, they are talking about a mean.

 **NCTRAVELTIME**

EXAMPLE 2.1 Travel times to work

The mean travel time of our 15 North Carolina workers is

$$\bar{x} = \frac{x_1 + x_2 + \cdots + x_n}{n}$$

$$= \frac{30 + 20 + \cdots + 10}{15}$$

$$= \frac{337}{15} = 22.5 \text{ minutes}$$

In practice, you can enter the data into your calculator and ask for the mean. You don't have to actually add and divide. But you should know that this is what the calculator is doing. ■

If we leave out the longest single travel time, 60 minutes, the mean for the remaining 14 people drops from 22.5 minutes to 19.8 minutes. One large observation raises the mean by 2.7 minutes. This is an important fact about the mean as a measure of center: it is sensitive to the influence of a few extreme observations. These may be outliers, but a skewed distribution that has no outliers will also pull the mean toward its long tail. Because the mean cannot resist the influence of extreme observations, we say that it is

resistant measure   not a **resistant measure** of center.

2.1 Pulling wood apart. Example 1.9 (page 26) gives the breaking strength in pounds of 20 pieces of Douglas fir. Find the mean breaking strength. How many of the pieces of wood have strengths less than the mean? What feature of the stemplot (Figure 1.11, page 27) explains the fact that the mean is smaller than most of the observations? **WOOD**

2.2 Health care spending. Table 1.3 (page 28) gives the 2009 health care expenditure per capita in 35 countries with the highest gross domestic product in 2009. The United States, at 7410 international dollars per person, is a high outlier. Find the mean health care spending in these nations with and without the United States. How much does the one outlier increase the mean? **HEALTHCOST**

MEASURING CENTER: The median

In Chapter 1, we used the midpoint of a distribution as an informal measure of center. The *median* is the formal version of the midpoint, with a specific rule for calculation.

THE MEDIAN *M*

The **median M** is the midpoint of a distribution, the number such that half the observations are smaller and the other half are larger. To find the median of a distribution:

1. Arrange all observations in order of size, from smallest to largest.

2. If the number of observations n is odd, the median M is the center observation in the ordered list. If the number of observations n is even, the median M is midway between the two center observations in the ordered list.

3. You can always locate the median in the ordered list of observations by counting up $(n + 1)/2$ observations from the start of the list.

EXAMPLE 2.2 Finding the median: odd *n*

What is the median travel time for our 15 North Carolina workers? Here are the data arranged in order:

5 10 10 10 10 12 15 **20** 20 25 30 30 40 40 60

The count of observations $n = 15$ is odd. The bold **20** is the center observation in the ordered list, with 7 observations to its left and 7 to its right. This is the median, $M = 20$ minutes.

Because $n = 15$, our rule for the location of the median gives

$$\text{location of } M = \frac{n + 1}{2} = \frac{16}{2} = 8$$

That is, the median is the 8th observation in the ordered list. Pay attention: the formula $(n + 1)/2$ does *not* give the median, just the location of the median in the ordered list. ■

NYTRAVELTIME

EXAMPLE 2.3 Finding the median: even *n*

Travel times to work in New York State are (on the average) longer than in North Carolina. Here are the travel times in minutes of 20 randomly chosen New York workers:

10   30   5   25   40   20   10   15   30   20   15   20   85   15   65   15   60   60   40   45

A stemplot not only displays the distribution but makes finding the median easy because it arranges the observations in order:

```
0 | 5
1 | 0 0 5 5 5 5
2 | 0 0 0 5
3 | 0 0
4 | 0 0 5
5 |
6 | 0 0 5
7 |
8 | 5
```

The distribution is single-peaked and right-skewed, with several travel times of an hour or more. There is no center observation, but there is a center pair. These are the bold **20** and **25** in the stemplot, which have 9 observations before them in the ordered list and 9 after them. The median is midway between these two observations:

$$M = \frac{20 + 25}{2} = 22.5 \text{ minutes}$$

With $n = 20$, the rule for locating the median in the list gives

$$\text{location of } M = \frac{n + 1}{2} = \frac{21}{2} = 10.5$$

The location 10.5 means "halfway between the 10th and 11th observations in the ordered list." That agrees with what we found by eye. ■

COMPARING THE MEAN AND THE MEDIAN

Examples 2.1 and 2.2 illustrate an important difference between the mean and the median. The median travel time (the midpoint of the distribution) in North Carolina is 20 minutes. The mean travel time is higher, 22.5 minutes. The mean is pulled toward the right tail of this right-skewed distribution. The median, unlike the mean, is *resistant*. If the longest travel time were 600 minutes rather than 60 minutes, the mean would increase to more than 58 minutes but the median would not change at all.

COMPARING THE MEAN AND THE MEDIAN

The mean and median of a roughly symmetric distribution are close together. If the distribution is exactly symmetric, the mean and median are exactly the same. In a skewed distribution, the mean is usually farther out in the long tail than is the median.[2]

Many economic variables have distributions that are skewed to the right. For example, the median endowment of colleges and universities in the United States and Canada in 2010 was about $74 million—but the mean endowment was almost $408 million. Most institutions have modest endowments, but a few are very wealthy. Harvard's endowment was over $27 billion.[3] The few wealthy institutions pull the mean up but do not affect the median. Reports about incomes and other strongly skewed distributions usually give the median ("midpoint") rather than the mean ("arithmetic average").

APPLY YOUR KNOWLEDGE

2.3 New York travel times. Find the mean of the travel times to work for the 20 New York workers in Example 2.3. Compare the mean and median for these data. What general fact does your comparison illustrate? ■ NYTRAVELTIME

2.4 House prices. The mean and median sales prices of new homes sold in the United States in August 2011 were $209,100 and $246,000.[4] Which of these numbers is the mean and which is the median? Explain how you know.

2.5 Carbon dioxide emissions. Table 1.6 (page 36) gives the 2007 carbon dioxide (CO_2) emissions per person for countries with populations of at least 30 million. Find the mean and the median for these data. Make a histogram of the data. What features of the distribution explain why the mean is larger than the median? ■ CO2EMISSIONS

Jose Antonio Sancho/Photolibrary

MEASURING SPREAD: The quartiles

The mean and median provide two different measures of the center of a distribution. A measure of center alone can be misleading. The Census Bureau reports that in 2009 the median income of American households was $49,777. Half of all households had incomes below $49,777, and half had higher incomes. The mean was much higher, $67,976, because the distribution of incomes is skewed to the right. But the median and mean don't tell the whole story. The bottom 10% of households had incomes less than $12,120, and households in the top 5% took in more than $180,001.[5] We are interested in the *spread* or *variability* of incomes as well as their center. *The simplest useful numerical description of a distribution requires both a measure of center and a measure of spread.*

The full spread of the data runs from the smallest to the largest observation. Because the smallest and largest observations may be outliers, we can improve our description of spread by also looking at the spread of the middle half of the data. The *quartiles* mark out the middle half. Count up the ordered list of observations, starting from the smallest. The *first quartile* lies one-quarter of the way up the list. The *third quartile* lies three-quarters of the way up the list. The second quartile is the median, which is halfway up the list. That's the idea of quartiles. We need a rule to make the idea exact. The rule for calculating the quartiles uses the rule for the median.

> **THE QUARTILES Q_1 AND Q_3**
>
> To calculate the **quartiles:**
>
> 1. Arrange the observations in increasing order and locate the median M in the ordered list of observations.
> 2. The **first quartile** Q_1 is the median of the observations whose position in the ordered list is to the left of the location of the overall median.
> 3. The **third quartile** Q_3 is the median of the observations whose position in the ordered list is to the right of the location of the overall median.

Here are examples that show how the rules for the quartiles work for both odd and even numbers of observations.

EXAMPLE 2.4 Finding the quartiles: odd *n*

Our North Carolina sample of 15 workers' travel times, arranged in increasing order, is

5   10   10   10   10   12   15   **20**   20   25   30   30   40   40   60

There is an odd number of observations, so the median is the middle one, the bold **20** in the list. The first quartile is the median of the 7 observations to the left of the median. This is the 4th of these 7 observations, so $Q_1 = 10$ minutes. If you want, you can use the rule for the location of the median with $n = 7$:

$$\text{location of } Q_1 = \frac{n + 1}{2} = \frac{7 + 1}{2} = 4$$

The third quartile is the median of the 7 observations to the right of the median, $Q_3 = 30$ minutes. *When there is an odd number of observations, leave out the overall median when you locate the quartiles in the ordered list.*

The quartiles are *resistant* because they are not affected by a few extreme observations. For example, Q_3 would still be 30 if the outlier were 600 rather than 60. ■

EXAMPLE 2.5 Finding the quartiles: even *n*

Here are the travel times to work of the 20 New Yorkers from Example 2.3, arranged in increasing order:

5   10   10   15   15   15   15   20   20   20 | 25   30   30   40   40   45   60   60   65   85

There is an even number of observations, so the median lies midway between the middle pair, the 10th and 11th in the list. Its value is $M = 22.5$ minutes. We have marked the location of the median by |. The first quartile is the median of the first 10 observations, because these are the observations to the left of the location of the median. Check that $Q_1 = 15$ minutes and $Q_3 = 42.5$ minutes. *When the number of observations is even, include all the observations when you locate the quartiles.* ■

Be careful when, as in these examples, several observations take the same numerical value. Write down all of the observations, arrange them in order, and apply the rules just as if they all had distinct values.

THE FIVE-NUMBER SUMMARY AND BOXPLOTS

The smallest and largest observations tell us little about the distribution as a whole, but they give information about the tails of the distribution that is missing if we know only the median and the quartiles. To get a quick summary of both center and spread, combine all five numbers.

THE FIVE-NUMBER SUMMARY

The **five-number summary** of a distribution consists of the smallest observation, the first quartile, the median, the third quartile, and the largest observation, written in order from smallest to largest. In symbols, the five-number summary is

$$\text{Minimum} \quad Q_1 \quad M \quad Q_3 \quad \text{Maximum}$$

These five numbers offer a reasonably complete description of center and spread. The five-number summaries of travel times to work from Examples 2.4 and 2.5 are

North Carolina:	5	10	20	30	60
New York:	5	15	22.5	42.5	85

The five-number summary of a distribution leads to a new graph, the *boxplot*. Figure 2.1 shows boxplots comparing travel times to work in North Carolina and New York.

BOXPLOT

A **boxplot** is a graph of the five-number summary.

■ A central box spans the quartiles Q_1 and Q_3.

■ A line in the box marks the median M.

■ Lines extend from the box out to the smallest and largest observations.

Boxplots show less detail than histograms or stemplots, so they are best used for side-by-side comparison of more than one distribution, as in Figure 2.1. When you look at a boxplot, first find the median, which marks the center of the distribution. Then look at the spread. The span of the central box shows the spread of the middle half of the data, and the smallest and largest observations show the spread of the entire data set. We see from Figure 2.1 that travel times to work are in general a bit longer in New York than in North Carolina. The median, both quartiles, and the maximum are all larger in New York. New York travel times are also more variable, as shown by the span of the box and the spread from smallest to largest time.

FIGURE 2.1

Boxplots comparing the travel times to work of samples of workers in North Carolina and New York.

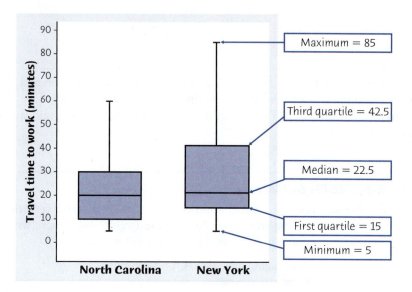

Finally, the New York data are more strongly right-skewed. In a symmetric distribution, the first and third quartiles are equally distant from the median. In most distributions that are skewed to the right, the third quartile will be farther above the median than the first quartile is below it. The smallest and largest observations behave the same way, but remember that they may be outliers.

APPLY YOUR KNOWLEDGE

AP Photo/Greg Trott

2.6 The Pittsburgh Steelers. The 2010 roster of the Pittsburgh Steelers professional football team included 7 defensive linemen and 9 offensive linemen. The weights in pounds of the defensive linemen were 🏈 STEELERS

$$305 \quad 325 \quad 305 \quad 300 \quad 285 \quad 280 \quad 298$$

and the weights of the offensive linemen were

$$338 \quad 324 \quad 325 \quad 304 \quad 344 \quad 315 \quad 304 \quad 319 \quad 318$$

(a) Make a stemplot of the weights of the defensive linemen and find the five-number summary.

(b) Make a stemplot of the weights of the offensive linemen and find the five-number summary.

(c) Does either group contain one or more clear outliers? Which group of players tends to be heavier?

2.7 Fuel economy for midsize cars. The Department of Energy provides fuel economy ratings for all cars and light trucks sold in the United States. Here are the estimated miles per gallon for city driving for the 129 cars classified as midsize in 2010, arranged in increasing order:[6] 🏈 MIDSIZECARS

9	10	10	11	11	11	12	13	14	14	15	15	15	15	15
15	15	16	16	16	16	16	16	16	16	16	16	16	16	16
16	16	16	16	17	17	17	17	17	17	17	17	17	17	17
17	17	17	17	18	18	18	18	18	18	18	18	18	18	18
18	18	18	18	18	18	18	18	18	18	18	18	19	19	19
19	19	19	19	19	19	19	19	20	20	20	21	21	21	21
21	22	22	22	22	22	22	22	22	22	22	22	22	22	22
22	22	22	23	23	23	23	24	24	24	25	26	26	26	26
26	26	26	28	33	35	41	41	51						

(a) Give the five-number summary of this distribution.

(b) Draw a boxplot of these data. What is the shape of the distribution shown by the boxplot? Which features of the boxplot led you to this conclusion? Are any observations unusually small or large?

SPOTTING SUSPECTED OUTLIERS*

Look again at the stemplot of travel times to work in New York in Example 2.3. The five-number summary for this distribution is

$$5 \quad 15 \quad 22.5 \quad 42.5 \quad 85$$

How shall we describe the spread of this distribution? The smallest and largest observations are extremes that don't describe the spread of the majority of the data. The distance between the quartiles (the range of the center half of the data) is a more resistant measure of spread. This distance is called the *interquartile range*.

> **THE INTERQUARTILE RANGE *IQR***
>
> The **interquartile range IQR** is the distance between the first and third quartiles,
>
> $$IQR = Q_3 - Q_1$$

For our data on New York travel times, $IQR = 42.5 - 15 = 27.5$ minutes. However, *no single numerical measure of spread, such as IQR, is very useful for describing skewed distributions*. The two sides of a skewed distribution have different spreads, so one number can't summarize them. That's why we give the full five-number summary. The interquartile range is mainly used as the basis for a rule of thumb for identifying suspected outliers. In some software, suspected outliers are identified in a boxplot with a special plotting symbol such as *.

*This short section is optional.

> **THE 1.5 × *IQR* RULE FOR OUTLIERS**
>
> Call an observation a suspected outlier if it falls more than 1.5 × IQR above the third quartile or below the first quartile.

EXAMPLE 2.6 Using the 1.5 × *IQR* rule

For the New York travel time data, *IQR* = 27.5 and

$$1.5 \times IQR = 1.5 \times 27.5 = 41.25$$

Any values not falling between

$$Q_1 - (1.5 \times IQR) = 15.0 - 41.25 = -26.25 \text{ and}$$
$$Q_3 + (1.5 \times IQR) = 42.5 + 41.25 = 83.75$$

are flagged as suspected outliers. Look again at the stemplot in Example 2.3: the only suspected outlier is the longest travel time, 85 minutes. The 1.5 × *IQR* rule suggests that the three next-longest travel times (60 and 65 minutes) are just part of the long right tail of this skewed distribution. ■

The 1.5 × *IQR* rule is not a replacement for looking at the data. It is most useful when large volumes of data are scanned automatically.

APPLY YOUR KNOWLEDGE

2.8 Travel time to work. We noted the influence of one long travel time of 60 minutes in our sample of 15 North Carolina workers, from Example 2.1. Does the 1.5 × *IQR* rule identify this travel time as a suspected outlier?

2.9 Fuel economy for midsize cars. Exercise 2.7 gives the estimated miles per gallon (mpg) for city driving for the 129 cars classified as midsize in 2010. In that exercise we noted that several of the mpg values were unusually large. Which of these are suspected outliers by the 1.5 × *IQR* rule? While outliers can be produced by errors or incorrectly recorded observations, they are often observations that differ from the others in some particular way. In this case, the cars producing the high outliers share a common feature. What do you think that is? ■ MIDSIZECARS

MEASURING SPREAD: The standard deviation

The five-number summary is not the most common numerical description of a distribution. That distinction belongs to the combination of the mean to measure center and the *standard deviation* to measure spread. The standard deviation and its close relative, the *variance*, measure spread by looking at how far the observations are from their mean.

THE STANDARD DEVIATION s

The **variance** s^2 of a set of observations is an average of the squares of the deviations of the observations from their mean. In symbols, the variance of n observations $x_1, x_2, \ldots, x_n$ is

$$s^2 = \frac{(x_1 - \bar{x})^2 + (x_2 - \bar{x})^2 + \cdots + (x_n - \bar{x})^2}{n - 1}$$

or, more compactly,

$$s^2 = \frac{1}{n - 1} \sum (x_i - \bar{x})^2$$

The **standard deviation** s is the square root of the variance s^2:

$$s = \sqrt{\frac{1}{n - 1} \sum (x_i - \bar{x})^2}$$

In practice, use software or your calculator to obtain the standard deviation from keyed-in data. Doing an example step-by-step will help you understand how the variance and standard deviation work, however.

EXAMPLE 2.7 Calculating the standard deviation

Georgia Southern University had 2417 students with regular admission in their freshman class of 2010. For each student, data are available on their SAT and ACT scores (if taken), high school GPA, and the college within the university to which they were admitted.[7] In Exercise 3.44, the full data set for the SAT Critical Reading scores will be examined. Here are the first five observations from that data set:

SATCR

650   490   580   450   570

We will compute $\bar{x}$ and s for these students. First find the mean:

$$\bar{x} = \frac{650 + 490 + 580 + 450 + 570}{5}$$

$$= \frac{2740}{5} = 548$$

Figure 2.2 displays the data as points above the number line, with their mean marked by an asterisk (*). The arrows mark two of the deviations from the mean. The deviations

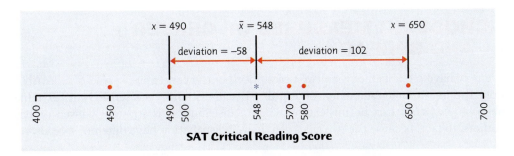

FIGURE 2.2

SAT Critical Reading scores for five students, with their mean (*) and the deviations of two observations from the mean shown, for Example 2.7.

show how spread out the data are about their mean. They are the starting point for calculating the variance and the standard deviation.

Observations x_i	Deviations $x_i - \bar{x}$	Squared deviations $(x_i - \bar{x})^2$
650	650–548 = 102	102^2 = 10,404
490	490–548 = −58	$(-58)^2$ = 3,364
580	580–548 = 32	32^2 = 1,024
450	450–548 = −98	$(-98)^2$ = 9,604
570	570–548 = 22	22^2 = 484
	sum = 0	sum = 24,880

The variance is the sum of the squared deviations divided by 1 less than the number of observations:

$$s^2 = \frac{1}{n-1} \sum (x_i - \bar{x})^2 = \frac{24{,}880}{4} = 6220$$

The standard deviation is the square root of the variance:

$$s = \sqrt{6220} = 78.87 \ \blacksquare$$

Notice that the "average" in the variance s^2 divides the sum by 1 fewer than the number of observations: $n - 1$ rather than n. The reason is that the n deviations $x_i - \bar{x}$ always sum to exactly 0, so that knowing $n - 1$ of them determines the last one. The number $n - 1$ is called the **degrees of freedom** of the variance or standard deviation.

degrees of freedom

Here are the most important properties of the standard deviation:

■ s measures *spread about the mean* and should be used only when the mean is chosen as the measure of center.

■ s is *always zero or greater than zero*. $s = 0$ only when there is no spread. This happens only when all observations have the same value. Otherwise, $s > 0$. As the observations become more spread out about their mean, s gets larger.

■ s has the *same units of measurement as the original observations*. For example, if you measure metabolic rates in calories, both the mean $\bar{x}$ and the standard deviation s are also in calories. This is one reason to prefer s to the variance s^2, which is in squared calories.

■ Like the mean $\bar{x}$, s is *not resistant*. A few outliers can make s very large.

CHOOSING MEASURES OF CENTER AND SPREAD

We now have a choice between two descriptions of the center and spread of a distribution: the five-number summary, or $\bar{x}$ and s. Because $\bar{x}$ and s are sensitive to extreme observations, they can be misleading when a distribution is strongly skewed or has outliers. In fact, because the two sides of a skewed distribution have different spreads, no single number such as *s* describes the spread well. The five-number summary, with its two quartiles and two extremes, does a better job.

CHOOSING A SUMMARY

The five-number summary is usually better than the mean and standard deviation for describing a skewed distribution or a distribution with strong outliers. Use $\bar{x}$ and *s* only for reasonably symmetric distributions that are free of outliers.

Outliers can greatly affect the values of the mean $\bar{x}$ and the standard deviation *s*, the most common measures of center and spread. Many more elaborate statistical procedures also can't be trusted when outliers are present. *Whenever you find outliers in your data, try to find an explanation for them.* Sometimes the explanation is as simple as a typing error, such as typing 10.1 as 101. In such cases you can simply correct or remove the outlier. When outliers are "real data," like the long travel times of some New York workers, you should choose statistical methods that are not greatly disturbed by the outliers. For example, use the five-number summary rather than $\bar{x}$ and *s* to describe a distribution with extreme outliers.

Remember that a graph gives the best overall picture of a distribution. Numerical measures of center and spread report specific facts about a distribution, but they do not describe its entire shape. Numerical summaries do not disclose the presence of multiple peaks or clusters, for example. Exercise 2.11 shows how misleading numerical summaries can be.

APPLY YOUR KNOWLEDGE

2.10 $\bar{x}$ **and s by hand.** Radon is a naturally occurring gas and is the second leading cause of lung cancer in the United States.[8] It comes from the natural breakdown of uranium in the soil and enters buildings through cracks and other holes in the foundations. Found throughout the United States, levels vary considerably from state to state. There are several methods to reduce the levels of radon in your home, and the Environmental Protection Agency recommends using one of these if the measured level in your home is above 4 picocuries per liter. Four readings from Franklin County, Ohio, where the county average is 9.32 picocuries per liter, were 5.2, 13.8, 8.6, and 16.8.

T. Jacobs/Custom Medical Stock Photo/ Newscom

(a) Find the mean step-by-step. That is, find the sum of the 4 observations and divide by 4.

(b) Find the standard deviation step-by-step. That is, find the deviation of each observation from the mean, square the deviations, then obtain the variance and the standard deviation. Example 2.7 shows the method.

(c) Now enter the data into your calculator and use the mean and standard deviation buttons to obtain $\bar{x}$ and *s*. Do the results agree with your hand calculations?

2.11 **x̄ and s are not enough.** Data sets with different shapes can have the same mean and standard deviation. To demonstrate this fact, use your calculator to find $\bar{x}$ and s for these two small data sets. Then make a stemplot of each and comment on the shape of each distribution. 🔴 **2DATASETS**

| Data A | 9.14 | 8.14 | 8.74 | 8.77 | 9.26 | 8.10 | 6.13 | 3.10 | 9.13 | 7.26 | 4.74 |
| Data B | 6.58 | 5.76 | 7.71 | 8.84 | 8.47 | 7.04 | 5.25 | 5.56 | 7.91 | 6.89 | 12.50 |

2.12 **Choose a summary.** The shape of a distribution is a rough guide to whether the mean and standard deviation are a helpful summary of center and spread. For which of the following distributions would $\bar{x}$ and s be useful? In each case, give a reason for your decision.

(a) Percents of high school graduates in the states taking the SAT, Figure 1.8 (page 24)

(b) Iowa Test scores, Figure 1.7 (page 23)

(c) New York travel times, Figure 2.1 (page 41)

USING TECHNOLOGY

Computer software or a graphing calculator will do calculations and make graphs as you command, freeing you to concentrate on choosing the right methods and interpreting your results. Figure 2.3 displays output describing the travel times to work of 20 people in New York State (Example 2.3). Can you find $\bar{x}$, s, and the five-number summary in each output? The big message of this section is: *once you know what to look for, you can read output from any technological tool.*

The displays in Figure 2.3 come from a Texas Instruments graphing calculator, the Minitab and CrunchIt! statistical programs, and the Microsoft Excel spreadsheet program. Minitab allows you to choose what descriptive measures you want, while the descriptive measures in the CrunchIt! output are provided by default. Excel and the calculator give some things we don't need. Just ignore the extras. Excel's "Descriptive Statistics" menu item doesn't give the quartiles. We used the spreadsheet's separate quartile function to get Q_1 and Q_3.

EXAMPLE 2.8 What is the third quartile?

In Example 2.5, we saw that the quartiles of the New York travel times are $Q_1 = 15$ and $Q_3 = 42.5$. Look at the output displays in Figure 2.3. The calculator and Excel agree with our work. Minitab and CrunchIt! say that $Q_3 = 43.75$. What happened? *There are several rules for finding the quartiles. Some calculators and software use rules that give results different from ours for some sets of data.* This is true of Minitab, CrunchIt!, and also Excel, though Excel agrees with our work in this example. Results from the various rules are always close to each other, so the differences are never important in practice. Our rule is the simplest for hand calculation. ■

Texas Instruments Graphing Calculator

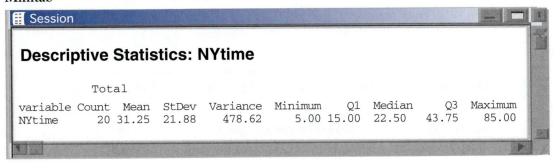

FIGURE 2.3

Output from a graphing calculator, two statistical software packages, and a spreadsheet program describing the data on travel times to work in New York State.

Minitab

Session

Descriptive Statistics: NYtime

		Total							
variable	Count	Mean	StDev	Variance	Minimum	Q1	Median	Q3	Maximum
NYtime	20	31.25	21.88	478.62	5.00	15.00	22.50	43.75	85.00

CrunchIt

Results - Descriptive Statistics   ▲ ☒

Export ▾

	n	Sample Mean	Median	Standard Deviation	Max	Min	Q1	Q3
NYtime	20	31.25	22.50	21.88	85	5	15	43.75

Microsoft Excel

Book1   _ ☐ ✕

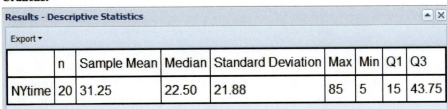

	A	B	C	D
1		*minutes*		
2				
3	Mean	31.25		
4	Standard Error	4.891924064		
5	Median	22.5	QUARTILE(A2:A21,1)	15
6	Mode	15	QUARTILE(A2:A21,3)	42.5
7	Standard Deviation	21.8773495		
8	Sample Variance	478.6184211		
9	Kurtosis	0.329884126		
10	Skewness	1.040110836		
11	Range	80		
12	Minimum	5		
13	Maximum	85		
14	Sum	625		
15	Count	20		
16				

Sheet4 / Sheet1 / Sheet2 / Sheet

ORGANIZING A STATISTICAL PROBLEM

Making graphs and calculations isn't all there is to doing statistics—we need to use data to draw conclusions about real-world settings. For example, water depth in the Everglades has a yearly cycle that reflects Florida's wet and dry seasons, and travel times to work are generally longer in New York than in North Carolina.

As you learn more statistical tools and principles, you will face more complex statistical problems. Although no framework accommodates all the varied issues that arise in applying statistics to real settings, the following four-step thought process gives useful guidance. In particular, the first and last steps emphasize that statistical problems are tied to specific real-world settings.

ORGANIZING A STATISTICAL PROBLEM: A FOUR-STEP PROCESS

STATE: What is the practical question, in the context of the real-world setting?

PLAN: What specific statistical operations does this problem call for?

SOLVE: Make the graphs and carry out the calculations needed for this problem.

CONCLUDE: Give your practical conclusion in the setting of the real-world problem.

To help you master the basics, many exercises will continue to tell you what to do—make a histogram, find the five-number summary, and so on. Real statistical problems don't come with detailed instructions. From now on, especially in the later chapters of the book, you will meet some exercises that are more realistic. Use the four-step process as a guide to solving and reporting these problems. They are marked with the four-step icon, as the following example illustrates.

EXAMPLE 2.9 Comparing tropical flowers

STATE: Ethan Temeles and W. John Kress of Amherst College studied the relationship between varieties of the tropical flower *Heliconia* and the hummingbirds that fertilize the flowers.[9] The researchers conjecture that flower varieties fertilized by different hummingbird species should have distinct distributions of length.

Table 2.1 gives length measurements (in millimeters) for samples of three varieties of *Heliconia,* each fertilized by a different species of hummingbird. Do the three varieties display distinct distributions of length? How do the mean lengths compare?

PLAN: Use graphs and numerical descriptions to describe and compare these three distributions of flower length.

SOLVE: We might use boxplots to compare the distributions, but stemplots preserve more detail and work well for data sets of these sizes. Figure 2.4 displays stemplots with the stems lined up for easy comparison. The lengths have been rounded to the nearest tenth of a millimeter. The *bihai* and red varieties have somewhat skewed distributions, so we might choose to compare the five-number summaries. But because

© Kevin Schafer/Alamy

TABLE 2.1 Flower lengths (millimeters) for three *Heliconia* varieties

H. BIHAI

47.12	46.75	46.81	47.12	46.67	47.43	46.44	46.64
48.07	48.34	48.15	50.26	50.12	46.34	46.94	48.36

H. CARIBAEA RED

41.90	42.01	41.93	43.09	41.47	41.69	39.78	40.57
39.63	42.18	40.66	37.87	39.16	37.40	38.20	38.07
38.10	37.97	38.79	38.23	38.87	37.78	38.01	

H. CARIBAEA YELLOW

36.78	37.02	36.52	36.11	36.03	35.45	38.13	37.10
35.17	36.82	36.66	35.68	36.03	34.57	34.63	

the researchers plan to use $\bar{x}$ and s for further analysis, we instead calculate these measures:

Variety	Mean length	Standard deviation
bihai	47.60	1.213
red	39.71	1.799
yellow	36.18	0.975

TROPICALFLOWER

CONCLUDE: The three varieties differ so much in flower length that there is little overlap among them. In particular, the flowers of *bihai* are longer than either red or yellow. The mean lengths are 47.6 mm for *H. bihai,* 39.7 mm for *H. caribaea* red, and 36.2 mm for *H. caribaea* yellow. ■

```
       bihai                    red                     yellow
    34 |                   34 |                     34 | 6 6
    35 |                   35 |                     35 | 2 5 7
    36 |                   36 |                     36 | 0 0 1 5 7 8 8
    37 |                   37 | 4 8 9               37 | 0 1
    38 |                   38 | 0 0 1 1 2 2 8 9     38 | 1
    39 |                   39 | 2 6 8               39 |
    40 |                   40 | 6 7                 40 |
    41 |                   41 | 5 7 9 9             41 |
    42 |                   42 | 0 2                 42 |
    43 |                   43 | 1                   43 |
    44 |                   44 |                     44 |
    45 |                   45 |                     45 |
    46 | 3 4 6 7 8 8 9     46 |                     46 |
    47 | 1 1 4             47 |                     47 |
    48 | 1 2 3 4           48 |                     48 |
    49 |                   49 |                     49 |
    50 | 1 3               50 |                     50 |
```

FIGURE 2.4

Stemplots comparing the distributions of flower lengths from Table 2.1, for Example 2.8. The stems are whole millimeters and the leaves are tenths of a millimeter.

APPLY YOUR KNOWLEDGE

2.13 Logging in the rain forest. "Conservationists have despaired over destruction of tropical rain forest by logging, clearing, and burning." These words begin a report on a statistical study of the effects of logging in Borneo.[10] Charles Cannon of Duke University and his coworkers compared forest plots that had never been logged (Group 1) with similar plots nearby that had been logged 1 year earlier (Group 2) and 8 years earlier (Group 3). All plots were 0.1 hectare in area. Here are the counts of trees for plots in each group: ◉ **LOGGING**

Group 1:	27	22	29	21	19	33	16	20	24	27	28	19
Group 2:	12	12	15	9	20	18	17	14	14	2	17	19
Group 3:	18	4	22	15	18	19	22	12	12			

To what extent has logging affected the count of trees? Follow the four-step process in reporting your work.

2.14 Diplomatic scofflaws. Until Congress allowed some enforcement in 2002, foreign diplomats in New York City could freely violate parking laws. Two economists looked at the number of unpaid parking tickets per diplomat over a five-year period ending when enforcement reduced the problem.[11] They concluded that large numbers of unpaid tickets lined up well with measures of the degree of corruption in various countries. The data file on the text Web site and CD contains data for 145 countries. The first 32 countries in the list (Australia to Trinidad and Tobago) are classified by the World Bank as "developed" based on their national income. The remaining countries (Albania to Zimbabwe) are "developing." ◉ **SCOFFLAWS**

Give a full description of the distribution of unpaid tickets for both groups of countries and identify any high outliers. Compare the two groups. Does national income alone do a good job of distinguishing countries whose diplomats do and do not obey parking laws?

CHAPTER 2 SUMMARY

CHAPTER SPECIFICS

■ A numerical summary of a distribution should report at least its **center** and its **spread** or **variability.**

■ The **mean $\bar{x}$** and the **median M** describe the center of a distribution in different ways. The mean is the arithmetic average of the observations, and the median is the midpoint of the values.

■ When you use the median to indicate the center of the distribution, describe its spread by giving the **quartiles.** The **first quartile Q_1** has one-fourth of the observations below it, and the **third quartile Q_3** has three-fourths of the observations below it.

■ The **five-number summary** consists of the median, the quartiles, and the smallest and largest individual observations. The median describes the center, and the quartiles and extremes show the spread.

■ **Boxplots** based on the five-number summary are useful for comparing several distributions. The box spans the quartiles and shows the spread of the central half of the distribution. The median is marked within the box. Lines extend from the box to the smallest and largest observations to show the full spread of the data.

- The **variance s^2** and especially its square root, the **standard deviation s,** measure spread about the mean as center. The standard deviation s is zero when there is no spread and gets larger as the spread increases.

- A **resistant measure** of any aspect of a distribution is relatively unaffected by changes in the numerical value of a small proportion of the total number of observations, no matter how large these changes are. The median and quartiles are resistant, but the mean and the standard deviation are not.

- The mean and standard deviation are good descriptions for symmetric distributions without outliers. The five-number summary is a better description for skewed distributions.

- Numerical summaries do not fully describe the shape of a distribution. Always plot your data.

- A statistical problem has a real-world setting. You can organize many problems using the four steps **state, plan, solve,** and **conclude.**

LINK IT

In this chapter we have continued our study of exploratory data analysis. Graphs are an important visual tool for organizing and identifying patterns in data. They give a fairly complete description of a distribution, although for many problems the important information in your data can be described by a few numbers. These numerical summaries can be useful for describing a single distribution as well as for comparing the distributions from several groups of observations.

Two important features of a distribution are the center and the spread. For distributions that are approximately symmetric without outliers, the mean and standard deviation are important numeric summaries for describing and comparing distributions. But if the distribution is not symmetric and/or has outliers, the five-number summary often provides a better description.

The boxplot gives a picture of the five-number summary that is useful for a simple comparison of several distributions. Remember that the boxplot is based only on the five-number summary and does not have any information beyond these five numbers. Certain features of a distribution that are revealed in histograms and stemplots will not be evident from a boxplot alone. These include gaps in the data and the presence of several peaks. You must be careful when reducing a distribution to a few numbers to make sure that important information has not been lost in the process.

CHECK YOUR SKILLS

2.15 The respiratory system can be a limiting factor in maximal exercise performance. Researchers from the United Kingdom studied the effect of two breathing frequencies on both performance times and several physiological parameters in swimming.[12] Subjects were 10 male collegiate swimmers. Here are their times in seconds to swim 200 meters at 90% of race pace when breathing every second stroke in front crawl swimming: 🔴 SWIMTIMES

| 151.6 | 165.1 | 159.2 | 163.5 | 174.8 | 173.2 | 177.6 |
| | | 174.3 | 164.1 | 171.4 | | |

The mean of these data is

(a) 165.10. (b) 167.48. (c) 168.25.

2.16 The median of the data in Exercise 2.15 is

(a) 167.48. (b) 168.25. (c) 174.00.

2.17 The five-number summary of the data in Exercise 2.15 is

(a) 151.6, 159.2, 167.48, 174.8, 177.6.

(b) 151.6, 163.5, 168.25, 174.3, 177.6.

(c) 151.6, 159.2, 168.25, 174.8, 177.6.

2.18 If a distribution is skewed to the right,

    (a) the mean is less than the median.

    (b) the mean and median are equal.

    (c) the mean is greater than the median.

2.19 What percent of the observations in a distribution lie between the first quartile and the third quartile?

    (a) 25% (b) 50% (c) 75%

2.20 The correct units for the standard deviation of the swim times in Exercise 2.15 are

    (a) no units—it's just a number.

    (b) seconds.

    (c) seconds squared.

2.21 Which of the following is least affected if an extreme high outlier is added to your data?

    (a) The median

    (b) The mean

    (c) The standard deviation

CHAPTER 2 EXERCISES

2.22 Incomes of college grads. According to the Census Bureau's 2010 Current Population Survey, the mean and median 2009 income of people at least 25 years old who had a bachelor's degree but no higher degree were $46,931 and $58,762. Which of these numbers is the mean and which is the median? Explain your reasoning.

2.23 Saving for retirement. Retirement seems a long way off and we need money now, so saving for retirement is hard. Once every three years, the Board of Governors of the Federal Reserve System collects data on household assets and liabilities through the Survey of Consumer Finances (SCF). The most recent such survey was conducted in 2007, and the survey results were released to the public in February 2009. The survey presents data on household ownership of, and balances in, retirement savings accounts. Only 53.6% of households own retirement accounts. The mean value per household is $148,579, but the median value is just $45,000. For households in which the head of household is under 35, 42.6% own retirement accounts, the mean is $25,279, and the median is $9600.[13] What explains the differences between the two measures of center, both for all households and for the under-35 age group?

2.24 University endowments. The National Association of College and University Business Officers collects data on college endowments. In 2010, 865 colleges and universities reported the value of their endowments. When the endowment values are arranged in order, what are the locations of the median and the quartiles in this ordered list?

2.25 Pulling wood apart. Example 1.9 (page 26) gives the breaking strengths of 20 pieces of Douglas fir. WOOD

    (a) Give the five-number summary of the distribution of breaking strengths. (The stemplot, Figure 1.11, helps because it arranges the data in order, but you should use the unrounded values in numerical work.)

    (b) The stemplot shows that the distribution is skewed to the left. Does the five-number summary show the skew? Remember that only a graph gives a clear picture of the shape of a distribution.

2.26 Comparing tropical flowers. An alternative presentation of the flower length data in Table 2.1 reports the five-number summary and uses boxplots to display the distributions. Do this. Do the boxplots fail to reveal any important information visible in the stemplots in Figure 2.4? TROPICALFLOWER

2.27 How much fruit do adolescent girls eat? Figure 1.13 (page 34) is a histogram of the number of servings of fruit per day claimed by 74 seventeen-year-old girls.

    (a) With a little care, you can find the median and the quartiles from the histogram. What are these numbers? How did you find them?

    (b) With a little care, you can also find the mean number of servings of fruit claimed per day. First use the information in the histogram to compute the sum of the 74 observations, and then use this to compute the mean. What is the relationship between the mean and median? Is this what you expected?

2.28 Guinea pig survival times. Here are the survival times in days of 72 guinea pigs after they were injected with infectious bacteria in a medical experiment.[14] Survival times, whether of machines under stress or cancer patients after treatment, usually have distributions that are skewed to the right. GUINEAPIGS

43	45	53	56	56	57	58	66	67	73	74	79
80	80	81	81	81	82	83	83	84	88	89	91
91	92	92	97	99	99	100	100	101	102	102	102
103	104	107	108	109	113	114	118	121	123	126	128
137	138	139	144	145	147	156	162	174	178	179	184
191	198	211	214	243	249	329	380	403	511	522	598

(a) Graph the distribution and describe its main features. Does it show the expected right-skew?

(b) Which numerical summary would you choose for these data? Calculate your chosen summary. How does it reflect the skewness of the distribution?

2.29 Weight of newborns. Here is the distribution of the weight at birth for all babies born in the United States in 2008:[15]

Weight (grams)	Count	Weight (grams)	Count
Less than 500	6,581	3,000 to 3,499	1,663,512
500 to 999	23,292	3,500 to 3,999	1,120,642
1,000 to 1,499	31,900	4,000 to 4,499	280,270
1,500 to 1,999	67,140	4,500 to 4,999	39,109
2,000 to 2,499	218,296	5,000 to 5,499	4,443
2,500 to 2,999	788,148		

(a) For comparison with other years and with other countries, we prefer a histogram of the *percents* in each weight class rather than the counts. Explain why.

(b) How many babies were there?

(c) Make a histogram of the distribution, using percents on the vertical scale.

(d) What are the locations of the median and quartiles in the ordered list of all birth weights? In which weight classes do the median and quartiles fall?

2.30 More on study times. In Exercise 1.32 (page 37) you examined the nightly study time claimed by first-year college men and women. The most common methods for formal comparison of two groups use $\bar{x}$ and s to summarize the data.

STUDYTIMES

(a) What kinds of distributions are best summarized by $\bar{x}$ and s? Do you think these summary measures are appropriate in this case?

(b) One student in each group claimed to study at least 300 minutes (five hours) per night. How much does removing these observations change $\bar{x}$ and s for each group? You will need to compute $\bar{x}$ and s for each group, both with and without the high outlier.

2.31 Never on Sunday: also in Canada? Exercise 1.5 (page 18) gives the number of births in the United States on each day of the week during an entire year. The boxplots in Figure 2.5 are based on more detailed data from Toronto, Canada: the number of births on each of the 365 days in a year, grouped by day of the week.[16] Based on these plots, compare

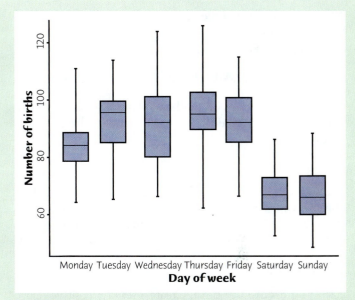

FIGURE 2.5

Boxplots of the distributions of numbers of births in Toronto, Canada, on each day of the week during a year, for Exercise 2.31.

the day-of-the-week distributions using shape, center, and spread. Summarize your findings.

2.32 Thinking about means. Table 1.1 (page 19) gives the percent of foreign-born residents in each of the states. For the nation as a whole, 12.5% of residents are foreign-born. Find the mean of the 51 entries in Table 1.1. It is *not* 12.5%. Explain carefully why this happens. (*Hint:* The states with the largest populations are California, Texas, New York, and Florida. Look at their entries in Table 1.1.)

2.33 Thinking about medians. A report says that "the median credit card debt of American households is zero." We know that many households have large amounts of credit card debt. In fact, the mean household credit card debt is close to $8000. Explain how the median debt can nonetheless be zero.

2.34 A standard deviation contest. This is a standard deviation contest. You must choose four numbers from the whole numbers 0 to 10, with repeats allowed.

(a) Choose four numbers that have the smallest possible standard deviation.

(b) Choose four numbers that have the largest possible standard deviation.

(c) Is more than one choice possible in either (a) or (b)? Explain.

2.35 Test your technology. This exercise requires a calculator with a standard deviation button or statistical software on a computer. The observations

$$10,001 \quad 10,002 \quad 10,003$$

have mean $\bar{x} = 10,002$ and standard deviation $s = 1$. Adding a 0 in the center of each number, the next set becomes

$$100,001 \quad 100,002 \quad 100,003$$

The standard deviation remains $s = 1$ as more 0s are added. Use your calculator or software to find the standard deviation of these numbers, adding extra 0s until you get an incorrect answer. How soon did you go wrong? This demonstrates that calculators and software cannot handle an arbitrary number of digits correctly.

2.36 You create the data. Create a set of 5 positive numbers (repeats allowed) that have median 7 and mean 10. What thought process did you use to create your numbers?

2.37 You create the data. Give an example of a small set of data for which the mean is smaller than the first quartile.

2.38 Adolescent obesity. Adolescent obesity is a serious health risk affecting more than 5 million young people in the United States alone. Laparoscopic adjustable gastric banding has the potential to provide a safe and effective treatment. Fifty adolescents between 14 and 18 years old with a body mass index (BMI) higher than 35 were recruited from the Melbourne, Australia, community for the study.[17] Twenty-five were randomly selected to undergo gastric banding, and the remaining twenty-five were assigned to a supervised lifestyle intervention program involving diet, exercise, and behavior modification. All subjects were followed for two years. Here are the weight losses in kilograms for the subjects who completed the study: 🔵 GASTRICBANDS

Gastric banding

35.6	81.4	57.6	32.8	31.0	37.6
36.5	−5.4	27.9	49.0	64.8	39.0
43.0	33.9	29.7	20.2	15.2	41.7
53.4	13.4	24.8	19.4	32.3	22.0

Lifestyle intervention

6.0	2.0	−3.0	20.6	11.6	15.5
−17.0	1.4	4.0	−4.6	15.8	34.6
6.0	−3.1	−4.3	−16.7	−1.8	−12.8

(a) In the context of this study, what do the negative values in the data set mean?

(b) Give a graphical comparison of the weight loss distribution for both groups using side-by-side boxplots. Provide appropriate numerical summaries for the two distributions and identify any high outliers in either group. What can you say about the effects of gastric banding versus lifestyle intervention on weight loss for the subjects in this study?

(c) The measured variable was weight loss in kilograms. Would two subjects with the same weight loss always have similar benefits from a weight reduction program? Does it depend on their initial weights? Other variables considered in this study were the percent of excess weight lost and the reduction in BMI. Do you see any advantages to using either of these variables when comparing weight loss for the two groups?

(d) One subject from the gastric-banding group dropped out of the study, and seven subjects from the lifestyle group dropped out. Of the seven dropouts in the lifestyle group, six had gained weight at the time they dropped out. If all subjects had completed the study, how do you think it would have affected the comparison between the two groups?

Exercises 2.39 to 2.44 ask you to analyze data without having the details outlined for you. The exercise statements give you the **State** *step of the four-step process. In your work, follow the* **Plan, Solve,** *and* **Conclude** *steps as illustrated in Example 2.9.*

2.39 Athletes' salaries. The Montreal Canadiens were founded in 1909 and are the longest continuously operating professional ice hockey team. They have won 24 Stanley Cups, making them one of the most successful professional sports teams of the traditional four major sports of Canada and the United States. Table 2.2 (page 63) gives the salaries of the 2010–2011 roster.[18] Provide the team owner with a full description of the distribution of salaries and a brief summary of its most important features. 🔵 HOCKEYSALARIES

2.40 Returns on stocks. How well have stocks done over the past generation? The Wilshire 5000 index describes the average performance of all U.S. stocks. The average is weighted by the total market value of each company's stock, so think of the index as measuring the performance of the average investor. Here are the percent returns on the Wilshire 5000 index for the years from 1971 to 2010:

Year	Return	Year	Return	Year	Return
1971	16.19	1985	31.46	1999	24.23
1972	17.34	1986	15.61	2000	−10.89
1973	−18.78	1987	1.75	2001	−10.97
1974	−27.87	1988	17.59	2002	−20.86
1975	37.38	1989	28.53	2003	31.64
1976	26.77	1990	−6.03	2004	12.48
1977	−2.97	1991	33.58	2005	6.38
1978	8.54	1992	9.02	2006	15.77
1979	24.40	1993	10.67	2007	5.62
1980	33.21	1994	0.06	2008	−37.23
1981	−3.98	1995	36.41	2009	28.30
1982	20.43	1996	21.56	2010	17.16
1983	22.71	1997	31.48		
1984	3.27	1998	24.31		

What can you say about the distribution of yearly returns on stocks? ⬤ WILSHIRE5000

2.41 Do good smells bring good business? Businesses know that customers often respond to background music. Do they also respond to odors? Nicolas Guéguéen and his colleagues studied this question in a small pizza restaurant in France on Saturday evenings in May. On one evening, a relaxing lavender odor was spread through the restaurant; on another evening, a stimulating lemon odor; a third evening served as a control, with no odor. Table 2.3 (page 64) shows the amounts (in euros) that customers spent on each of these evenings.[19] Compare the three distributions. Were both odors associated with increased customer spending? ⬤ ODORS

2.42 Daily activity and obesity. People gain weight when they take in more energy from food than they expend. Table 2.4 (page 64) compares volunteer subjects who were lean with others who were mildly obese. None of the subjects followed an exercise program. The subjects wore sensors that recorded every move for 10 days. The table shows the average minutes per day spent in activity (standing and walking) and in lying down.[20] Compare the distributions of time spent actively for lean and obese subjects and also the distributions of time spent lying down. How does the behavior of lean and mildly obese people differ? ⬤ OBESITY

2.43 Good weather and tipping. Favorable weather has been shown to be associated with increased tipping. Will just the belief that future weather will be favorable lead to higher tips? The researchers gave 60 index cards to a waitress at an Italian restaurant in New Jersey. Before delivering the bill to each customer, the waitress randomly selected a card and wrote on the bill the same message that was printed on the index card. Twenty of the cards had the message "The weather is supposed to be really good tomorrow. I hope you enjoy the day!" Another 20 cards contained the message "The weather is supposed to be not so good tomorrow. I hope you enjoy the day anyway!" The remaining 20 cards were blank, indicating that the waitress was not supposed to write any message. Choosing a card at random ensured that there was a random assignment of the customers to the three experimental conditions. Here are the tip percents for the three messages:[21] ⬤ TIPPING

Good weather report:	20.8 18.7 19.9 20.6 22.0 23.4 22.8 24.9 22.2 20.3
	24.9 22.3 27.0 20.4 22.2 24.0 21.2 22.1 22.0 22.7
Bad weather report:	18.0 19.0 19.2 18.8 18.4 19.0 18.5 16.1 16.8 14.0
	17.0 13.6 17.5 19.9 20.2 18.8 18.0 23.2 18.2 19.4
No weather report:	19.9 16.0 15.0 20.1 19.3 19.2 18.0 19.2 21.2 18.8
	18.5 19.3 19.3 19.4 10.8 19.1 19.7 19.8 21.3 20.6

Compare the three distributions. How did the tip percents vary with the weather report information?

TABLE 2.2 Salaries (U.S. dollars) for the 2010–2011 Montreal Canadiens

PLAYER	SALARY	PLAYER	SALARY	PLAYER	SALARY
Scott Gomez	$8,000,000	Andrei Markov	$5,750,000	Roman Hamrlik	$5,500,000
Mike Cammalleri	$5,000,000	Brian Gionta	$5,000,000	Tomas Plekanec	$5,000,000
Jaroslav Spacek	$3,833,000	Andrei Kostitsyn	$3,250,000	James Wisniewski	$3,250,000
Carey Price	$2,500,000	Hal Gill	$2,250,000	Travis Moen	$1,500,000
Benoit Pouliot	$1,350,000	Josh Gorges	$1,300,000	Alex Auld	$1,000,000
Max Pacioretty	$875,000	Lars Eller	$875,000	P. K. Subban	$875,000
Yannick Weber	$637,500	Jeff Halpern	$600,000	Alexandre Picard	$600,000
David Desharnais	$550,000	Mathieu Darche	$500,000	Tom Pyatt	$500,000

TABLE 2.3 Amount spent (euros) by customers in a restaurant when exposed to odors

NO ODOR									
15.9	18.5	15.9	18.5	18.5	21.9	15.9	15.9	15.9	15.9
15.9	18.5	18.5	18.5	20.5	18.5	18.5	15.9	15.9	15.9
18.5	18.5	15.9	18.5	15.9	18.5	15.9	25.5	12.9	15.9

LEMON ODOR									
18.5	15.9	18.5	18.5	18.5	15.9	18.5	15.9	18.5	18.5
15.9	18.5	21.5	15.9	21.9	15.9	18.5	18.5	18.5	18.5
25.9	15.9	15.9	15.9	18.5	18.5	18.5	18.5		

LAVENDER ODOR									
21.9	18.5	22.3	21.9	18.5	24.9	18.5	22.5	21.5	21.9
21.5	18.5	25.5	18.5	18.5	21.9	18.5	18.5	24.9	21.9
25.9	21.9	18.5	18.5	22.8	18.5	21.9	20.7	21.9	22.5

TABLE 2.4 Time (minutes per day) active and lying down by lean and obese subjects

LEAN SUBJECTS			OBESE SUBJECTS		
SUBJECT	STAND/WALK	LIE	SUBJECT	STAND/WALK	LIE
1	511.100	555.500	11	260.244	521.044
2	607.925	450.650	12	464.756	514.931
3	319.212	537.362	13	367.138	563.300
4	584.644	489.269	14	413.667	532.208
5	578.869	514.081	15	347.375	504.931
6	543.388	506.500	16	416.531	448.856
7	677.188	467.700	17	358.650	460.550
8	555.656	567.006	18	267.344	509.981
9	374.831	531.431	19	410.631	448.706
10	504.700	396.962	20	426.356	412.919

2.44 Canadians' earnings in 1901. Table 2.5 presents the "earnings from occupation or trade" in the year 1901 of a random sample of those Canadians who did have earnings in that year. The amounts are in Canadian dollars. If they seem low, remember that a loaf of bread cost 4 cents and a pound of beef 14 cents.[22] Of course, Canadians today have much higher incomes, even after adjusting for inflation. Give a complete graphical and numerical description of these data, and briefly describe your findings.

Exercises 2.45 to 2.48 make use of the optional material on the $1.5 \times IQR$ rule for suspected outliers.

2.45 Older Americans. In Exercise 1.9 you were asked to use a stemplot to display the distribution of the percents of

TABLE 2.5 Earnings (dollars) of a sample of 200 Canadians in 1901

400	360	400	200	150	175	60	96	600	100
125	525	500	200	175	360	50	300	175	480
300	500	160	960	300	96	500	170	380	600
300	10	250	200	124	350	150	225	600	100
250	250	220	100	200	250	100	256	399	125
100	360	250	600	400	450	150	550	250	240
100	970	240	300	100	400	450	125	250	225
480	350	300	100	144	500	200	150	225	240
250	300	250	150	100	225	96	200	500	20
250	500	100	165	350	200	200	500	300	57
1000	200	800	415	450	190	360	180	1200	100
320	240	100	208	8	142	420	300	700	600
205	150	75	205	300	300	350	150	450	350
450	462	350	1500	120	200	300	225	475	2000
150	325	300	150	720	140	350	150	85	400
184	125	300	500	340	150	160	480	300	376
220	1000	300	2200	350	290	700	120	700	600
375	150	450	360	500	575	500	400	350	180
600	300	1000	600	300	80	1000	300	390	499
210	500	550	450	520	200	300	200	540	1200

residents aged 65 and older in the states. Stemplots help you find the five-number summary because they arrange the observations in increasing order. OVER65

(a) Give the five-number summary of this distribution.

(b) Use the five-number summary to draw a boxplot of the data. What is the shape of the distribution?

(c) Which observations does the $1.5 \times IQR$ rule flag as suspected outliers? (The rule flags several observations that are not that extreme. The reason is that the center half of the observations are close together, so that the IQR is small. This example reminds us to use our eyes, not a rule, to spot outliers.)

2.46 Carbon dioxide emissions. Table 1.6 (page 36) gives the 2007 carbon dioxide (CO_2) emissions per person for countries with populations of at least 30 million in that year. A stemplot or histogram shows that the distribution is strongly skewed to the right. The United States and several other countries appear to be high outliers. CO2EMISSIONS

(a) Give the five-number summary. Explain why this summary suggests that the distribution is right-skewed.

(b) Which countries are outliers according to the $1.5 \times IQR$ rule? Make a stemplot of the data or look at your stemplot from Exercise 1.30. Do you agree with the rule's suggestions about which countries are and are not outliers?

2.47 Athletes' salaries. Which members of the Montreal Canadiens (Table 2.2) have salaries that are suspected outliers by the $1.5 \times IQR$ rule? HOCKEYSALARIES

2.48 Canadians' earnings in 1901. The Canadians' earnings in Exercise 2.44 are right-skewed, with a few large incomes. Which incomes are suspected outliers by the $1.5 \times IQR$ rule?

EXPLORING THE WEB

2.49 Home run leaders. The three top players on the career home run list are Barry Bonds, Hank Aaron, and Babe Ruth. You can find their home run statistics by going to the Web site www.baseball-reference.com and then clicking on the *players* tab at the top of the page. Construct three side-by-side boxplots comparing the yearly home run production of Barry Bonds, Hank Aaron, and Babe Ruth. Describe any differences that you observe. It is worth noting that in his first four seasons, Babe Ruth was primarily a pitcher. If these four seasons are ignored, how does Babe Ruth compare with Barry Bonds and Hank Aaron?

2.50 Crime rates and outliers. The *Statistical Abstract of the United States* is a comprehensive summary of statistics on the social, political, and economic organization of the United States. It can be found at the Web site www.census.gov/compendia/statab/. Go to the section Law Enforcement, Courts, and Prisons, and then to the subsection Crimes and Crime Rates. Several tables of data will be available.

(a) Open the table *Crime Rates by State, 2008 and 2009, and by Type, 2009*, or for the latest year given. Why do you think they use rates per 100,000 population rather than the number of crimes committed? The District of Columbia is a high outlier in almost every crime category.

(b) Open the table *Crime Rates by Type—Selected Large Cities*. This table includes the District of Columbia, which is listed as Washington, DC. Without doing any formal calculations, does the District of Columbia look like a high outlier in the table for large cities? Whether or not the District of Columbia is an outlier depends on more than its crime rate. It also depends on the other observations included in the data set. Which data set do you feel is more appropriate for the District of Columbia?

(c) Using the *Crime Rates by State, 2008 and 2009, and by Type, 2009*, or for the latest year given, choose a crime category, and give a full description of its distribution over the 50 states, omitting the District of Columbia. Your description of the distribution should include appropriate graphical and numerical summaries and a brief report describing the main features of the distribution. You can open the data as an Excel file and import it into your statistical software.

ImageSource/Photolibrary

The Normal Distributions

W e now have a kit of graphical and numerical tools for describing distributions. What is more, we have a clear strategy for exploring data on a single quantitative variable.

EXPLORING A DISTRIBUTION

1. Plot your data: make a graph, usually a histogram or a stemplot.
2. Look for the overall pattern (shape, center, spread) and for striking deviations such as outliers.
3. Calculate a numerical summary to briefly describe center and spread.

In this chapter, we add one more step to this strategy:

4. Sometimes the overall pattern of a large number of observations is so regular that we can describe it by a smooth curve.

67

DENSITY CURVES

Figure 3.1 is a histogram of the scores of all 947 seventh-grade students in Gary, Indiana, on the vocabulary part of the Iowa Tests of Basic Skills.[1] Scores of many students on this national test have a quite regular distribution. The histogram is symmetric, and both tails fall off smoothly from a single center peak. There are no large gaps or obvious outliers.

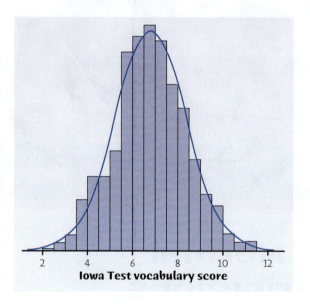

Iowa Test vocabulary score

FIGURE 3.1

Histogram of the Iowa Test vocabulary scores of all seventh-grade students in Gary, Indiana. The smooth curve shows the overall shape of the distribution.

EXAMPLE 3.1 From histogram to density curve

Our eyes respond to the *areas* of the bars in a histogram. The bar areas represent proportions of the observations. Figure 3.2(a) is a copy of Figure 3.1 with the leftmost bars shaded. The area of the shaded bars in Figure 3.2(a) represents the students with vocabulary scores 6.0 or lower. There are 287 such students, who make up the proportion 287/947 = 0.303 of all Gary seventh-graders.

Now look at the curve drawn through the bars. In Figure 3.2(b), the area under the curve to the left of 6.0 is shaded. We can draw histogram bars taller or shorter by adjusting the vertical scale. In moving from histogram bars to a smooth curve, we make a specific choice: adjust the scale of the graph so that *the total area under the curve is exactly 1*. The total area represents the proportion 1, that is, all the observations. We can then interpret areas under the curve as proportions of the observations. The curve is now a *density curve*. The shaded area under the density curve in Figure 3.2(b) represents the proportion of students with score 6.0 or lower. This area is 0.293, only 0.010 away from the actual proportion 0.303. Areas under the density curve give quite good approximations to the actual distribution of the 947 test scores. ■

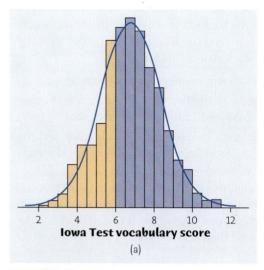

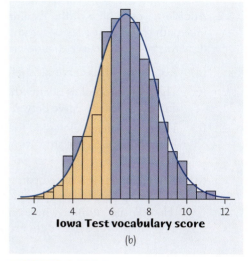

FIGURE 3.2(a)

The proportion of scores less than or equal to 6.0 in the actual data is 0.303.

FIGURE 3.2(b)

The proportion of scores less than or equal to 6.0 from the density curve is 0.293. The density curve is a good approximation to the distribution of the data.

DENSITY CURVE

A **density curve** is a curve that

■ is always on or above the horizontal axis, and

■ has area exactly 1 underneath it.

A density curve describes the overall pattern of a distribution. The area under the curve and above any range of values is the proportion of all observations that fall in that range.

Density curves, like distributions, come in many shapes. A density curve is often a good description of the overall pattern of a distribution. Outliers, which are deviations from the overall pattern, are not described by the curve. *No set of real data is exactly described by a density curve. The curve is an idealized description that is easy to use and accurate enough for practical use.*

APPLY YOUR KNOWLEDGE

3.1 Sketch density curves. Sketch density curves that describe distributions with the following shapes:

(a) Symmetric, but with two peaks (that is, two strong clusters of observations)

(b) Single peak and skewed to the left

3.2 Accidents on a bike path. Examining the location of accidents on a level, 5-mile bike path shows that they occur uniformly along the length of the path. Figure 3.3 displays the density curve that describes the distribution of accidents.

(a) Explain why this curve satisfies the two requirements for a density curve.

(b) The proportion of accidents that occur in the first mile of the path is the area under the density curve between 0 miles and 1 mile. What is this area?

(c) There is a stream alongside the bike path between the 0.8-mile mark and the 1.3-mile mark. What proportion of accidents happen on the bike path alongside the stream?

(d) The bike path is a paved path through the woods, and there is a road at each end. What proportion of accidents happen more than 1 mile from either road? (*Hint:* First determine where on the bike path the accident needs to occur to be more than 1 mile from either road, and then find the area.)

FIGURE 3.3

The density curve for the location of accidents along a 5-mile bike path, for Exercise 3.2.

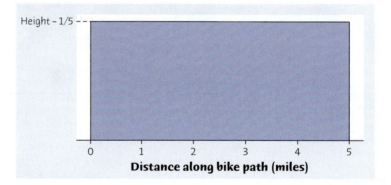

DESCRIBING DENSITY CURVES

Our measures of center and spread apply to density curves as well as to actual sets of observations. Areas under a density curve represent proportions of the total number of observations. The **median** and **quartiles** of a density curve divide the area under the curve into four equal parts. One-fourth of the area under the curve is to the left of the first quartile, one-half is to the left of the median, and three-fourths of the area is to the left of the third quartile. You can therefore roughly locate the median and quartiles of a density curve by eye. In particular, the median of a symmetric density curve is at its center. Figure 3.4 shows a symmetric density curve and a skewed curve with their medians marked.

The **mean** of a set of observations is their arithmetic average. If we think of the observations as weights strung out along a thin rod, the mean is the point at which the rod would balance. This fact is also true of density curves. The mean is the point at which the curve would balance if made of solid material. A symmetric curve balances at its center because the two sides are identical. *The mean and median of a symmetric density curve are equal*, as in Figure 3.4(a). We know that the mean of a skewed distribution is pulled toward the long tail. Figure 3.4(b) shows how the mean of a skewed density curve is pulled toward the long tail more than is the median. It's hard to locate the balance point by eye on a skewed curve.

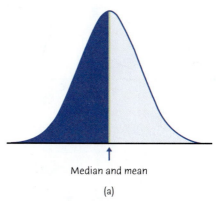

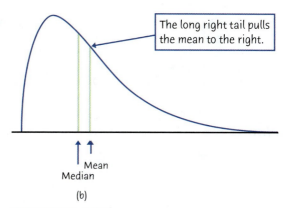

The long right tail pulls the mean to the right.

Median and mean

(a)

Mean
Median

(b)

FIGURE 3.4(a)

The median and mean of a symmetric density curve both lie at the center of symmetry.

FIGURE 3.4(b)

The median and mean of a right-skewed density curve. The mean is pulled away from the median toward the long tail.

MEDIAN AND MEAN OF A DENSITY CURVE

The **median** of a density curve is the equal-areas point, the point that divides the area under the curve in half.

The **mean** of a density curve is the balance point, at which the curve would balance if made of solid material.

The median and mean are the same for a symmetric density curve. They both lie at the center of the curve. The mean of a skewed curve is pulled away from the median in the direction of the long tail.

Because a density curve is an idealized description of a distribution of data, we need to distinguish between the mean and standard deviation of the density curve and the mean $\bar{x}$ and standard deviation s computed from the actual observations. We write the **mean of a density curve** as μ (the Greek letter mu). We write the **standard deviation of a density curve** as σ (the Greek letter sigma). You can roughly locate the mean μ of any density curve by eye, as the balance point. There is no easy way to locate the standard deviation σ by eye for density curves in general.

mean μ

standard deviation σ

APPLY YOUR KNOWLEDGE

3.3 Mean and median. What is the mean μ of the density curve pictured in Figure 3.3? (That is, where would the curve balance?) What is the median? (That is, where is the point with area 0.5 on either side?)

3.4 Mean and median. Figure 3.5 (on page 72) displays three density curves, each with three points marked on them. At which of these points on each curve do the mean and the median fall?

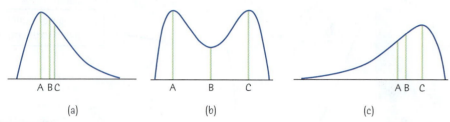

FIGURE 3.5

Three density curves, for Exercise 3.4.

NORMAL DISTRIBUTIONS

Normal curve

Normal distribution

One particularly important class of density curves has already appeared in Figures 3.1 and 3.2. They are called **Normal curves.** The distributions they describe are called **Normal distributions.** Normal distributions play a large role in statistics, but they are rather special and not at all "normal" in the sense of being usual or average. We capitalize Normal to remind you that these curves are special. Look at the two Normal curves in Figure 3.6. They illustrate several important facts:

◼ All Normal curves have the same overall shape: symmetric, single-peaked, bell-shaped.

◼ Any specific Normal curve is completely described by giving its mean μ and its standard deviation σ.

◼ The mean is located at the center of the symmetric curve and is the same as the median. Changing μ without changing σ moves the Normal curve along the horizontal axis without changing its spread.

◼ The standard deviation σ controls the spread of a Normal curve. Curves with larger standard deviations are more spread out.

The standard deviation σ is the natural measure of spread for Normal distributions. Not only do μ and σ completely determine the shape of a Normal curve, but we can locate σ by eye on a Normal curve. Here's how. Imagine that you are skiing down a

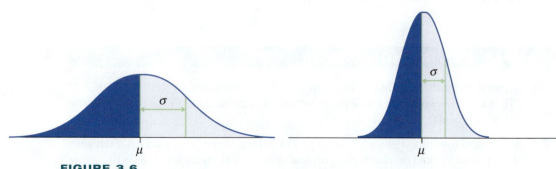

FIGURE 3.6

Two Normal curves, showing the mean μ and standard deviation σ.

mountain that has the shape of a Normal curve. At first, you descend at an ever-steeper angle as you go out from the peak:

Fortunately, before you find yourself going straight down, the slope begins to grow flatter rather than steeper as you go out and down:

The points at which this change of curvature takes place are located at distance σ on either side of the mean μ. You can feel the change as you run a pencil along a Normal curve, and so find the standard deviation. Remember that *μ and σ alone do not specify the shape of most distributions*, and that the shape of density curves in general does not reveal σ. These are special properties of Normal distributions.

> **NORMAL DISTRIBUTIONS**
>
> A **Normal distribution** is described by a Normal density curve. Any particular Normal distribution is completely specified by two numbers, its mean μ and standard deviation σ.
>
> The mean of a Normal distribution is at the center of the symmetric Normal curve. The standard deviation is the distance from the center to the change-of-curvature points on either side.

Normal distributions are good descriptions for some distributions of real data. Distributions that are often close to Normal include scores on tests taken by many people (such as Iowa Tests and SAT exams), repeated careful measurements of the same quantity, and characteristics of biological populations (such as lengths of crickets and yields of corn). However, many sets of data do not follow a Normal distribution. Most income distributions, for example, are skewed to the right and so are not Normal.

THE 68—95—99.7 RULE

Although there are many Normal curves, they all have common properties. In particular, all Normal distributions obey the following rule.

> **THE 68—95—99.7 RULE**
>
> In the Normal distribution with mean μ and standard deviation σ:
>
> - Approximately **68%** of the observations fall within σ of the mean μ.
> - Approximately **95%** of the observations fall within 2σ of μ.
> - Approximately **99.7%** of the observations fall within 3σ of μ.

FIGURE 3.7

The 68–95–99.7 rule for Normal distributions.

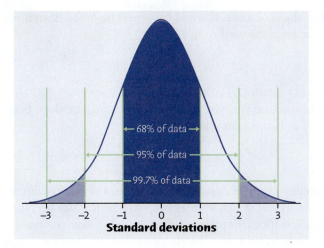

Figure 3.7 illustrates the 68–95–99.7 rule. By remembering these three numbers, you can think about Normal distributions without constantly making detailed calculations.

EXAMPLE 3.2 Iowa Test scores

Figures 3.1 and 3.2 show that the distribution of Iowa Test vocabulary scores for seventh-grade students in Gary, Indiana, is close to Normal. Suppose that the distribution is exactly Normal with mean $\mu = 6.84$ and standard deviation $\sigma = 1.55$. (These are the mean and standard deviation of the 947 actual scores.)

Figure 3.8 applies the 68–95–99.7 rule to the Iowa Test scores. The 95 part of the rule says that 95% of all scores are between

$$\mu - 2\sigma = 6.84 - (2)(1.55) = 6.84 - 3.10 = 3.74$$

and

$$\mu + 2\sigma = 6.84 + (2)(1.55) = 6.84 + 3.10 = 9.94$$

The other 5% of scores are outside this range. Because Normal distributions are symmetric, half of these scores are lower than 3.74 and half are higher than 9.94. That is, 2.5% of the scores are below 3.74 and 2.5% are above 9.94. ■

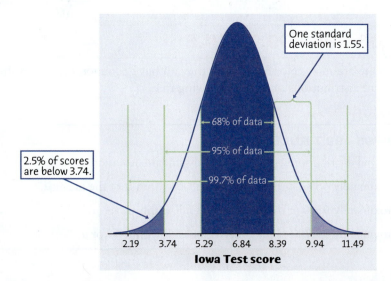

FIGURE 3.8

The 68–95–99.7 rule applied to the distribution of Iowa Test scores for seventh-grade students in Gary, Indiana, for Example 3.2. The mean and standard deviation are $\mu = 6.84$ and $\sigma = 1.55$.

EXAMPLE 3.3   Iowa Test scores

Look again at Figure 3.8. A score of 5.29 is one standard deviation below the mean. What percent of scores are higher than 5.29? Find the answer by adding areas in the figure. Here is the calculation in pictures:

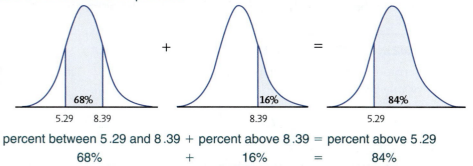

percent between 5.29 and 8.39 + percent above 8.39 = percent above 5.29

68%   +   16%   =   84%

Be sure you see where the 16% came from. We know that 68% of scores are between 5.29 and 8.39, so 32% of scores are outside that range. Because the curve is symmetric, these are equally split between the two tails, 16% below 5.29 and 16% above 8.39. ■

Because we will mention Normal distributions often, a short notation is helpful. We abbreviate the Normal distribution with mean μ and standard deviation σ as $N(\mu, \sigma)$. For example, the distribution of Gary Iowa Test scores is approximately $N(6.84, 1.55)$.

APPLY YOUR KNOWLEDGE

3.5 Fruit flies. The common fruit fly *Drosophila melanogaster* is the most studied organism in genetic research because it is small, easy to grow, and reproduces rapidly. The length of the thorax (where the wings and legs attach) in a population of male fruit flies is approximately Normal with mean 0.800 millimeters (mm) and standard deviation 0.078 mm. Draw a Normal curve on which this mean and standard deviation are correctly located. (*Hint:* Draw an unlabeled Normal curve, locate the points where the curvature changes, then add number labels on the horizontal axis.)

3.6 Fruit flies. The length of the thorax in a population of male fruit flies is approximately Normal with mean 0.800 millimeters (mm) and standard deviation 0.078 mm. Use the 68–95–99.7 rule to answer the following questions. (Start by making a sketch like Figure 3.8.)

(a) What range of lengths covers almost all (99.7%) of this distribution?

(b) What percent of male fruit flies have a thorax length exceeding 0.878 mm?

3.7 Monsoon rains. The summer monsoon brings 80% of India's rainfall and is essential for the country's agriculture. Records going back more than a century show that the amount of monsoon rainfall varies from year to year according to a distribution that is approximately Normal with mean 852 millimeters (mm) and standard deviation 82 mm.[2] Use the 68–95–99.7 rule to answer the following questions.

(a) Between what values do the monsoon rains fall in 95% of all years?

(b) How small are the monsoon rains in the dryest 2.5% of all years?

Plastiquel/Dreamtime.com

THE STANDARD NORMAL DISTRIBUTION

As the 68–95–99.7 rule suggests, all Normal distributions share many properties. In fact, all Normal distributions are the same if we measure in units of size σ about the mean μ as center. Changing to these units is called *standardizing*. To standardize a value, subtract the mean of the distribution and then divide by the standard deviation.

STANDARDIZING AND z-SCORES

If x is an observation from a distribution that has mean μ and standard deviation σ, the **standardized value** of x is

$$z = \frac{x - \mu}{\sigma}$$

A standardized value is often called a **z-score.**

A z-score tells us how many standard deviations the original observation falls away from the mean, and in which direction. Observations larger than the mean are positive when standardized, and observations smaller than the mean are negative.

EXAMPLE 3.4 Standardizing women's heights

The heights of women aged 20 to 29 are approximately Normal with μ = 64.3 inches and σ = 2.7 inches.[3] The standardized height is

$$z = \frac{\text{height} - 64.3}{2.7}$$

A woman's standardized height is the number of standard deviations by which her height differs from the mean height of all young women. A woman 70 inches tall, for example, has standardized height

$$z = \frac{70 - 64.3}{2.7} = 2.11$$

or 2.11 standard deviations above the mean. Similarly, a woman 5 feet (60 inches) tall has standardized height

$$z = \frac{60 - 64.3}{2.7} = -1.59$$

or 1.59 standard deviations less than the mean height. ■

We often standardize observations from symmetric distributions to express them in a common scale. We might, for example, compare the heights of two children of different ages by calculating their z-scores. The standardized heights tell us where each child stands in the distribution for his or her age group.

If the variable we standardize has a Normal distribution, standardizing does more than give a common scale. It makes all Normal distributions into a single distribution, and this distribution is still Normal. Standardizing a variable that has any Normal distribution produces a new variable that has the *standard Normal distribution*.

STANDARD NORMAL DISTRIBUTION

The **standard Normal distribution** is the Normal distribution $N(0, 1)$ with mean 0 and standard deviation 1.

If a variable x has any Normal distribution $N(\mu, \sigma)$ with mean μ and standard deviation σ, then the standardized variable

$$z = \frac{x - \mu}{\sigma}$$

has the standard Normal distribution.

APPLY YOUR KNOWLEDGE

3.8 SAT versus ACT. In 2010, when she was a high school senior, Alysha scored 670 on the Mathematics part of the SAT.[4] The distribution of SAT Math scores in 2010 was Normal with mean 516 and standard deviation 116. John took the ACT and scored 26 on the Mathematics portion. ACT Math scores for 2010 were Normally distributed with mean 21.0 and standard deviation 5.3. Find the standardized scores for both students. Assuming that both tests measure the same kind of ability, who had the higher score?

3.9 Men's and women's heights. The heights of women aged 20 to 29 are approximately Normal with mean 64.3 inches and standard deviation 2.7 inches. Men the same age have mean height 69.9 inches with standard deviation 3.1 inches.[5] What are the z-scores for a woman 6 feet tall and a man 6 feet tall? Say in simple language what information the z-scores give that the original nonstandardized heights do not.

FINDING NORMAL PROPORTIONS

Areas under a Normal curve represent proportions of observations from that Normal distribution. There is no formula for areas under a Normal curve. Calculations use either software that calculates areas or a table of areas. Most tables and software calculate one kind of area, *cumulative proportions*. The idea of "cumulative" is "everything that came before." Here is the exact statement.

CUMULATIVE PROPORTIONS

The **cumulative proportion** for a value x in a distribution is the proportion of observations in the distribution that are less than or equal to x.

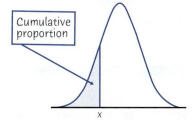

The key to calculating Normal proportions is to match the area you want with areas that represent cumulative proportions. If you make a sketch of the area you want, you will almost never go wrong. Find areas for cumulative proportions either from software or (with an extra step) from a table. The following example shows the method in a picture.

EXAMPLE 3.5 Who qualifies for college sports?

The National Collegiate Athletic Association (NCAA) uses a sliding scale for eligibility for Division I athletes.[6] Those students with a 2.5 high school GPA must have a combined score of at least 820 on the Mathematics and Reading parts of the SAT to compete in their first college year. The scores of the 1.5 million high school seniors taking the SAT this year are approximately Normal with mean 1026 and standard deviation 209. What percent of high school seniors meet this NCAA requirement of a combined SAT score of 820 or better?

Here is the calculation in a picture: the proportion of scores above 820 is the area under the curve to the right of 820. That's the total area under the curve (which is always 1) minus the cumulative proportion up to 820.

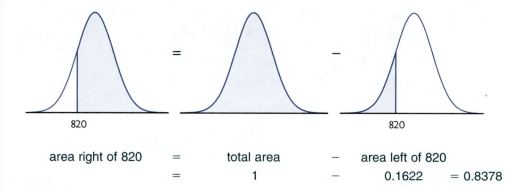

area right of 820	=	total area	−	area left of 820
	=	1	−	0.1622 = 0.8378

About 84% of all high school seniors meet this requirement of a combined Math and Reading score of 820 or higher.

To find the numerical value 0.1622 of the cumulative proportion using software, plug in mean 1026 and standard deviation 209 and ask for the cumulative proportion for 820. Here, for example, is Minitab's output:

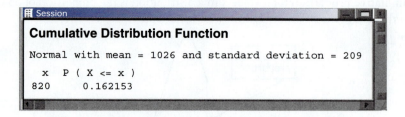

```
Session

Cumulative Distribution Function

Normal with mean = 1026 and standard deviation = 209

    x   P ( X <= x )
  820     0.162153
```

If you are not using software, you can find cumulative proportions for Normal curves from a table. This requires an extra step. ■

The actual data may contain a student who scored exactly 820 on the SAT, so that the proportion of scores ≥ 820 is slightly larger than the proportion of scores > 820. These two proportions are equal for a Normal distribution, because there is no area under a smooth curve exactly over the point 820. This is a consequence of the idealized smoothing of Normal distributions.

USING THE STANDARD NORMAL TABLE

The extra step in finding cumulative proportions from a table is that we must first standardize to express the problem in the standard scale of z-scores. This allows us to get by with just one table, a table of *standard Normal cumulative proportions*. Table A in the back of the book gives cumulative proportions for the standard Normal distribution. The pictures at the top of the table remind us that the entries are cumulative proportions, areas under the curve to the left of a value z.

EXAMPLE 3.6 The standard Normal table

What proportion of observations on a standard Normal variable z take values less than 1.47?

Solution: To find the area to the left of 1.47, locate 1.4 in the left-hand column of Table A, then locate the remaining digit 7 as .07 in the top row. The entry opposite 1.4 and under .07 is 0.9292. This is the cumulative proportion we seek. Figure 3.9 illustrates this area. ■

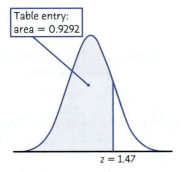

Table entry:
area = 0.9292

$z = 1.47$

FIGURE 3.9

The area under a standard Normal curve to the left of the point $z = 1.47$ is 0.9292. Table A gives cumulative proportions for the standard Normal curve.

Now that you see how Table A works, let's redo Example 3.5 using the table. We can break Normal calculations using the table into three steps.

EXAMPLE 3.7 Who qualifies for college sports?

Scores of high school seniors on the SAT follow the Normal distribution with mean $\mu = 1026$ and standard deviation $\sigma = 209$. What proportion of seniors score at least 820?

Step 1. Draw a picture. The picture is exactly as in Example 3.5. It shows that

area to the right of 820 = 1 − area to the left of 820

Step 2. Standardize. Call the SAT score x. Subtract the mean and then divide by the standard deviation to transform the problem about x into a problem about a standard Normal z:

$$x \geq 820$$

$$\frac{x - 1026}{209} \geq \frac{820 - 1026}{209}$$

$$z \geq -0.99$$

Step 3. Use the table. The picture shows that we need the cumulative proportion for $x = 820$. Step 2 says that this is the same as the cumulative proportion for $z = -0.99$. The Table A entry for $z = -0.99$ says that this cumulative proportion is 0.1611. The area to the right of -0.99 is therefore $1 - 0.1611 = 0.8389$. ■

The area from the table in Example 3.7 (0.8389) is slightly less accurate than the area from software in Example 3.5 (0.8378) because we must round z to two decimal places when we use Table A. The difference is rarely important in practice. Here's the method in outline form.

> **USING TABLE A TO FIND NORMAL PROPORTIONS**
>
> **Step 1. State the problem** in terms of the observed variable x. **Draw a picture** that shows the proportion you want in terms of cumulative proportions.
>
> **Step 2. Standardize** x to restate the problem in terms of a standard Normal variable z.
>
> **Step 3. Use Table A** and the fact that the total area under the curve is 1 to find the required area under the standard Normal curve.

EXAMPLE 3.8 Who qualifies for college sports?

Recall that the NCAA uses a sliding scale for eligibility for Division I athletics. Students with a 2.5 GPA must have a combined SAT score of 820 or higher to be eligible. Students with lower GPAs will require higher SAT scores for eligibility, while students with higher GPAs can have a lower SAT score and still be eligible. For example, students with a 2.75 GPA are only required to have a combined SAT score that is at least 720. What proportion of all students who take the SAT would meet an SAT requirement of at least 720, but not 820?

Step 1. State the problem and draw a picture. Call the SAT score x. The variable x has the $N(1026, 209)$ distribution. What proportion of SAT scores fall between 720 and 820? Here is the picture:

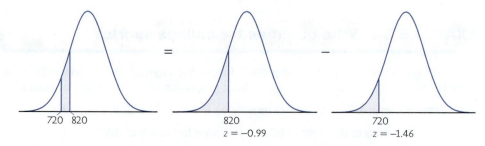

720 820   820   720
              z = −0.99   z = −1.46

Step 2. Standardize. Subtract the mean and then divide by the standard deviation to turn x into a standard Normal z:

$$720 \leq x < 820$$
$$\frac{720 - 1026}{209} \leq \frac{x - 1026}{209} < \frac{820 - 1026}{209}$$
$$-1.46 \leq z < -0.99$$

Step 3. Use the table. Follow the picture (we added the z-scores to the picture to help you):

area between -1.46 and -0.99 = (area left of -0.99) − (area left of -1.46)

$$= 0.1611 - 0.0721 = 0.0890$$

About 9% of high school seniors have SAT scores between 720 and 820. ■

Sometimes we encounter a value of z more extreme than those appearing in Table A. For example, the area to the left of $z = -4$ is not given directly in the table. The z-values in Table A leave only area 0.0002 in each tail unaccounted for. For practical purposes, we can act as if there is zero area outside the range of Table A.

APPLY YOUR KNOWLEDGE

3.10 Use the Normal table. Use Table A to find the proportion of observations from a standard Normal distribution that satisfies each of the following statements. In each case, sketch a standard Normal curve and shade the area under the curve that is the answer to the question.

(a) $z < -1.42$ (b) $z > -1.42$ (c) $z < 2.35$ (d) $-1.42 < z < 2.35$

3.11 Monsoon rains. The summer monsoon rains in India follow approximately a Normal distribution with mean 852 millimeters (mm) of rainfall and standard deviation 82 mm.

(a) In the drought year 1987, 697 mm of rain fell. In what percent of all years will India have 697 mm or less of monsoon rain?

(b) "Normal rainfall" means within 20% of the long-term average, or between 683 and 1022 mm. In what percent of all years is the rainfall normal?

3.12 The Medical College Admission Test. Almost all medical schools in the United States require students to take the Medical College Admission Test (MCAT).[7] The exam is composed of three multiple-choice sections (Physical Sciences, Verbal Reasoning, and Biological Sciences). The score on each section is converted to a 15-point scale so that the total score has a maximum value of 45. The total scores follow a Normal distribution, and in 2010 the mean was 25.0 with a standard deviation of 6.4. There is little change in the distribution of scores from year to year.

(a) What proportion of students taking the MCAT had a score over 30?

(b) What proportion had scores between 20 and 25?

FINDING A VALUE WHEN GIVEN A PROPORTION

Examples 3.5 to 3.8 illustrate the use of software or Table A to find what proportion of the observations satisfies some condition, such as "SAT score above 820." We may instead want to find the observed value with a given proportion of the observations above or below it. Statistical software will do this directly.

EXAMPLE 3.9 Find the top 10% using software

Scores on the SAT Reading test in recent years follow approximately the $N(504, 111)$ distribution. How high must a student score to place in the top 10% of all students taking the SAT?

We want to find the SAT score x with area 0.1 to its *right* under the Normal curve with mean $\mu = 504$ and standard deviation $\sigma = 111$. That's the same as finding the SAT score x with area 0.9 to its *left*. Figure 3.10 poses the question in graphical form. Most software will tell you x when you plug in mean 504, standard deviation 111, and cumulative proportion 0.9. Here is Minitab's output:

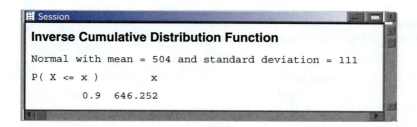

```
Session

Inverse Cumulative Distribution Function

Normal with mean = 504 and standard deviation = 111

P( X <= x )        x
      0.9  646.252
```

Minitab gives $x = 646.252$. So scores 647 or above are in the top 10%. (Round up because SAT scores can only be whole numbers.) ■

Without software, use Table A backward. Find the given proportion in the body of the table and then read the corresponding z from the left column and top row. There are again three steps.

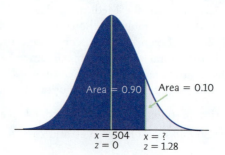

FIGURE 3.10

Locating the point on a Normal curve with area 0.10 to its right, for Examples 3.9 and 3.10.

EXAMPLE 3.10 Find the top 10% using Table A

Scores on the SAT Reading test in recent years follow approximately the $N(504, 111)$ distribution. How high must a student score to place in the top 10% of all students taking the SAT?

Step 1. State the problem and draw a picture. This step is exactly as in Example 3.9. The picture is Figure 3.10.

Step 2. Use the table. Look in the body of Table A for the entry closest to 0.9. It is 0.8997. This is the entry corresponding to $z = 1.28$. So $z = 1.28$ is the standardized value with area 0.9 to its left.

Step 3. Unstandardize to transform z back to the original x scale. We know that the standardized value of the unknown x is $z = 1.28$. This means that x itself lies 1.28 standard deviations above the mean on this particular Normal curve. That is,

$$x = \text{mean} + (1.28)(\text{standard deviation})$$
$$= 504 + (1.28)(111) = 646.1$$

A student must score at least 647 to place in the highest 10%. ■

EXAMPLE 3.11 Find the first quartile

High levels of cholesterol in the blood increase the risk of heart disease. For 14-year-old boys, the distribution of blood cholesterol is approximately Normal with mean $\mu = 170$ milligrams of cholesterol per deciliter of blood (mg/dl) and standard deviation $\sigma = 30$ mg/dl.[8] What is the first quartile of the distribution of blood cholesterol?

Step 1. State the problem and draw a picture. Call the cholesterol level x. The variable x has the $N(170, 30)$ distribution. The first quartile is the value with 25% of the distribution to its left. Figure 3.11 is the picture.

Step 2. Use the table. Look in the body of Table A for the entry closest to 0.25. It is 0.2514. This is the entry corresponding to $z = -0.67$. So $z = -0.67$ is the standardized value with area 0.25 to its left.

Step 3. Unstandardize. The cholesterol level corresponding to $z = -0.67$ lies 0.67 standard deviations below the mean, so

$$x = \text{mean} - (0.67)(\text{standard deviation})$$
$$= 170 - (0.67)(30) = 149.9$$

The first quartile of blood cholesterol levels in 14-year-old boys is about 150 mg/dl. ■

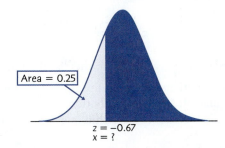

FIGURE 3.11

Locating the first quartile of a Normal curve, for Example 3.11.

APPLY YOUR KNOWLEDGE

3.13 **Table A.** Use Table A to find the value z of a standard Normal variable that satisfies each of the following conditions. (Use the value of z from Table A that comes closest to satisfying the condition.) In each case, sketch a standard Normal curve with your value of z marked on the axis.

(a) The point z with 15% of the observations falling below it

(b) The point z with 70% of the observations falling above it

3.14 **The Medical College Admission Test.** The total scores on the Medical College Admission Test (MCAT) follow a Normal distribution with mean 25.0 and standard deviation 6.4. What are the median and the first and third quartiles of the MCAT scores?

▌ CHAPTER 3 SUMMARY

CHAPTER SPECIFICS

■ We can sometimes describe the overall pattern of a distribution by a **density curve.** A density curve has total area 1 underneath it. An area under a density curve gives the proportion of observations that fall in a range of values.

■ A density curve is an idealized description of the overall pattern of a distribution that smooths out the irregularities in the actual data. We write the **mean of a density curve** as μ and the **standard deviation of a density curve** as σ to distinguish them from the mean $\bar{x}$ and standard deviation s of the actual data.

■ The mean, the median, and the quartiles of a density curve can be located by eye. The **mean** μ is the balance point of the curve. The **median** divides the area under the curve in half. The **quartiles** and the median divide the area under the curve into quarters. The **standard deviation** σ cannot be located by eye on most density curves.

■ The mean and median are equal for symmetric density curves. The mean of a skewed curve is located farther toward the long tail than is the median.

■ The **Normal distributions** are described by a special family of bell-shaped, symmetric density curves, called **Normal curves.** The mean μ and standard deviation σ completely specify a Normal distribution $N(\mu, \sigma)$. The mean is the center of the curve, and σ is the distance from μ to the change-of-curvature points on either side.

■ To **standardize** any observation x, subtract the mean of the distribution and then divide by the standard deviation. The resulting z-**score**

$$z = \frac{x - \mu}{\sigma}$$

says how many standard deviations x lies from the distribution mean.

■ All Normal distributions are the same when measurements are transformed to the standardized scale. In particular, all Normal distributions satisfy the **68–95–99.7 rule,** which describes what percent of observations lie within one, two, and three standard deviations of the mean.

■ If x has the $N(\mu, \sigma)$ distribution, then the **standardized variable** $z = (x - \mu)/\sigma$ has the **standard Normal distribution** $N(0, 1)$ with mean 0 and standard deviation 1. Table A gives the **cumulative proportions** of standard Normal observations that are less than z for many values of z. By standardizing, we can use Table A for any Normal distribution.

LINK IT

When exploring data, some data sets can be shown to closely follow the Normal distribution. When this is true, the description of the data can be greatly simplified without much loss of information. We can calculate the percent of the distribution in an interval for *any* Normal distribution if we know its mean and standard deviation. This also shows why the mean and standard deviation can be important numerical summaries. For distributions that are approximately Normal, these two numerical summaries give a complete description of the distribution of our data. It is important to remember that not all distributions can be well approximated by a Normal curve. In these cases, calculations based on the Normal distribution can be misleading.

Normal distributions are also good approximations to many kinds of chance outcomes such as the proportion of heads in many tosses of a coin (this setting will be described in more detail in Chapter 20). And when we discuss statistical inference in Part III of the text, we will find that many procedures based on Normal distributions work well for other roughly symmetric distributions.

CHECK YOUR SKILLS

3.15 Which of these variables is most likely to have a Normal distribution?

    (a) Income per person for 150 different countries

    (b) Sale prices of 200 homes in a suburb of Chicago

    (c) Heights of 100 white pine trees in a forest

3.16 Figure 3.12 shows a Normal curve. The mean of this distribution is

    (a) 0.   (b) 2.   (c) 3.

3.17 The standard deviation of the Normal distribution in Figure 3.12 is

    (a) 2.   (b) 3.   (c) 5.

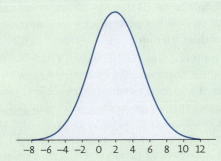

FIGURE 3.12
A Normal curve, for Exercises 3.16 and 3.17.

3.18 The length of human pregnancies from conception to birth varies according to a distribution that is approximately Normal with mean 266 days and standard deviation 16 days. 95% of all pregnancies last between

    (a) 250 and 282 days.   (c) 218 and 314 days.

    (b) 234 and 298 days.

3.19 The scores of adults on an IQ test are approximately Normal with mean 100 and standard deviation 15. The organization MENSA, which calls itself "the high IQ society," requires an IQ score of 130 or higher for membership. What percent of adults would qualify for membership?

    (a) 95%   (b) 5%   (c) 2.5%

3.20 The scores of adults on an IQ test are approximately Normal with mean 100 and standard deviation 15. Clara scores 127 on such a test. Her z-score is about

    (a) 1.27.   (b) 1.80.   (c) 8.47.

3.21 The scores of adults on an IQ test are approximately Normal with mean 100 and standard deviation 15. Clara scores 127 on such a test. She scores higher than what percent of all adults?

    (a) About 10%   (b) About 90%   (c) About 96%

CHAPTER 3 EXERCISES

3.22 Daily activity. It appears that people who are mildly obese are less active than leaner people. One study looked at the average number of minutes per day that people spend standing or walking.[9] Among mildly obese people, minutes of activity varied according to the $N(373, 67)$ distribution. Minutes of activity for lean people had the $N(526, 107)$ distribution. Within what limits do the active minutes for 95% of the people in each group fall? Use the 68–95–99.7 rule.

3.23 Low IQ test scores. Scores on the Wechsler Adult Intelligence Scale (WAIS) are approximately Normal with mean 100 and standard deviation 15. People with WAIS scores below 70 are considered mentally retarded when, for example, applying for Social Security disability benefits. According to the 68–95–99.7 rule, about what percent of adults are retarded by this criterion?

3.24 Standard Normal drill. Use Table A to find the proportion of observations from a standard Normal distribution that fall in each of the following regions. In each case, sketch a standard Normal curve and shade the area representing the region.

 (a) $z \leq -1.25$ (b) $z \geq -1.25$ (c) $z > 2.17$
 (d) $-1.25 < z < 2.17$

3.25 Standard Normal drill.

 (a) Find the number z such that the proportion of observations that are less than z in a standard Normal distribution is 0.6.

 (b) Find the number z such that 15% of all observations from a standard Normal distribution are greater than z.

3.26 Fruit flies. The thorax lengths in a population of male fruit flies follow a Normal distribution with mean 0.800 millimeters (mm) and standard deviation 0.078 mm.

 (a) What proportion of flies have thorax lengths less than 0.7 mm?

 (b) What proportion have thorax lengths greater than 1 mm?

 (c) What proportion have thorax lengths between 0.7 and 1 mm?

3.27 Acid rain? Emissions of sulfur dioxide by industry set off chemical changes in the atmosphere that result in "acid rain." The acidity of liquids is measured by pH on a scale of 0 to 14. Distilled water has pH 7.0, and lower pH values indicate acidity. Normal rain is somewhat acidic, so acid rain is sometimes defined as rainfall with a pH below 5.0. The pH of rain at one location varies among rainy days according to a Normal distribution with mean 5.43 and standard deviation 0.54. What proportion of rainy days have rainfall with pH below 5.0?

3.28 Runners. In a study of exercise, a large group of male runners walk on a treadmill for 6 minutes. Their heart rates in beats per minute at the end vary from runner to runner according to the $N(104, 12.5)$ distribution. The heart rates for male nonrunners after the same exercise have the $N(130, 17)$ distribution.

 (a) What percent of the runners have heart rates above 130?

 (b) What percent of the nonrunners have heart rates above 130?

3.29 A milling machine. Automated manufacturing operations are quite precise but still vary, often with distributions that are close to Normal. The width in inches of slots cut by a milling machine follows approximately the $N(0.8750, 0.0012)$ distribution. The specifications allow slot widths between 0.8720 and 0.8780 inch. What proportion of slots meet these specifications?

3.30 Body mass index. Your body mass index (BMI) is your weight in kilograms divided by the square of your height in meters. Many online BMI calculators allow you to enter weight in pounds and height in inches. High BMI is a common but controversial indicator of overweight or obesity. A study by the National Center for Health Statistics found that the BMI of American young women (ages 20 to 29) is approximately Normal with mean 26.5 and standard deviation 6.4.[10]

 (a) People with BMI less than 18.5 are often classified as "underweight." What percent of young women are underweight by this criterion?

 (b) People with BMI over 30 are often classified as "obese." What percent of young women are obese by this criterion?

Miles per gallon. *In its* Fuel Economy Guide *for model year 2010 vehicles, the Environmental Protection Agency gives data on 1101 vehicles. There are a number of high outliers, mainly hybrid gas-electric vehicles. If we ignore the vehicles identified as outliers, however, the combined city and highway gas mileage of the other 1082 vehicles is approximately Normal with mean 20.3 miles per gallon (mpg) and standard deviation 4.3 mpg. Exercises 3.31 to 3.34 concern this distribution.*

3.31 In my Chevrolet. The 2010 Chevrolet Camaro with an eight-cylinder engine and automatic transmission has a combined gas mileage of 19 mpg. What percent of all vehicles have better gas mileage than the Camaro?

3.32 The bottom 10%. How low must a 2010 vehicle's gas mileage be in order to fall in the bottom 10% of all vehicles?

3.33 The middle half. The quartiles of any distribution are the values with cumulative proportions 0.25 and 0.75. They span the middle half of the distribution. What are the quartiles of the distribution of gas mileage?

3.34 Quintiles. The quintiles of any distribution are the values with cumulative proportions 0.20, 0.40, 0.60, and 0.80. What are the quintiles of the distribution of gas mileage?

3.35 What's your percentile? Reports on a student's ACT, SAT, or MCAT usually give the percentile as well as the actual score. The percentile is just the cumulative proportion stated as a percent: the percent of all scores that were lower than this one. In 2010, the total MCAT scores were close to Normal with mean 25.0 and standard deviation 6.4. William scored 32. What was his percentile?

3.36 Perfect SAT scores. It is possible to score higher than 1600 on the combined Mathematics and Reading portions of the SAT, but scores of 1600 and above are reported as 1600. The distribution of SAT scores (combining Mathematics and Reading) was close to Normal with mean 1021 and standard deviation 211. What proportion of SAT scores for these two parts were reported as 1600?

3.37 Heights of women. The heights of women aged 20 to 29 follow approximately the $N(64.3, 2.7)$ distribution. Men the same age have heights distributed as $N(69.9, 3.1)$. What percent of young women are taller than the mean height of young men?

3.38 Weights aren't Normal. The heights of people of the same sex and similar ages follow a Normal distribution reasonably closely. Weights, on the other hand, are not Normally distributed. The weights of women aged 20 to 29 have mean 155.9 pounds and median 144.0 pounds. The first and third quartiles are 124.1 pounds and 173.7 pounds. What can you say about the shape of the weight distribution? Why?

3.39 Grading managers. Some companies "grade on a bell curve" to compare the performance of their managers and professional workers. This forces the use of some low performance ratings so that not all workers are listed as "above average." Ford Motor Company's "performance management process" for a time assigned 10% A grades, 80% B grades, and 10% C grades to the company's managers. Suppose that Ford's performance scores really are Normally distributed. This year, managers with scores less than 25 received C's and those with scores above 475 received A's. What are the mean and standard deviation of the scores?

3.40 Osteoporosis. Osteoporosis is a condition in which the bones become brittle due to loss of minerals. To diagnose osteoporosis, measure bone mineral density (BMD). BMD is usually reported in standardized form. The standardization is based on a population of healthy young adults. The World Health Organization (WHO) criterion for osteoporosis is a BMD 2.5 standard deviations below the mean for young adults. BMD measurements in a population of people similar in age and sex roughly follow a Normal distribution.

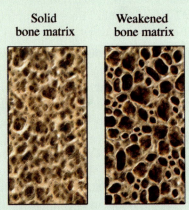

Solid bone matrix   Weakened bone matrix

(a) What percent of healthy young adults have osteoporosis by the WHO criterion?

(b) Women aged 70 to 79 are of course not young adults. The mean BMD in this age is about -2 on the standard scale for young adults. Suppose that the standard deviation is the same as for young adults. What percent of this older population have osteoporosis?

In later chapters we will meet many statistical procedures that work well when the data are "close enough to Normal." Exercises 3.41 to 3.46 concern data that are mostly close enough to Normal for statistical work. These exercises ask you to do data analysis and Normal calculations to investigate how close to Normal real data are.

3.41 Normal is only approximate: IQ test scores. Here are the IQ test scores of 31 seventh-grade girls in a Midwest school district:[11] 🔴 **MIDWESTIQ**

114	100	104	89	102	91	114	114	103	105	108
130	120	132	111	128	118	119	86	72	111	103
74	112	107	103	98	96	112	112	93		

(a) We expect IQ scores to be approximately Normal. Make a stemplot to check that there are no major departures from Normality.

(b) Nonetheless, proportions calculated from a Normal distribution are not always very accurate for small numbers of observations. Find the mean $\bar{x}$ and standard deviation s for these IQ scores. What proportion of the scores are within one standard deviation of the mean? Within two standard deviations of the mean? What would these proportions be in an exactly Normal distribution?

3.42 Normal is only approximate: ACT scores. Scores on the ACT test for the 2010 high school graduating class had mean 21.0 and standard deviation 5.2. In all, 1,568,835 students in this class took the test. Of these, 145,000 had scores higher than 28 and another 50,860 had scores exactly 28. ACT scores are always whole numbers. The exactly Normal $N(21.0, 5.2)$ distribution can include any value, not just whole numbers. What is more, there is *no* area exactly above 28 under the smooth Normal curve. So ACT scores can be only approximately Normal. To illustrate this fact, find

(a) the percent of 2010 ACT scores greater than 28.

(b) the percent of 2010 ACT scores greater than or equal to 28.

(c) the percent of observations from the $N(21.0, 5.2)$ distribution that are greater than 28. (The percent greater than or equal to 28 is the same, because there is no area exactly above 28.)

3.43 Are the data Normal? Acidity of rainfall. Exercise 3.27 concerns the acidity (measured by pH) of rainfall. A sample of 105 rainwater specimens had mean pH 5.43, standard deviation 0.54, and five-number summary 4.33, 5.05, 5.44, 5.79, 6.81.[12]

(a) Compare the mean and median and also the distances of the two quartiles from the median. Does it appear that the distribution is quite symmetric? Why?

(b) If the distribution is really $N(5.43, 0.54)$, what proportion of observations would be less than 5.05? Less than 5.79? Do these proportions suggest that the distribution is close to Normal? Why?

3.44 Are the data Normal? SAT Critical Reading scores. Georgia Southern University (GSU) had 2417 students with regular admission in their freshman class of 2010. For each student, data are available on their SAT and ACT scores, if taken, high school GPA, and the college within the university to which they were admitted.[13] Here are the first 20 SAT Critical Reading scores from that data set: 🔴 **SATCR**

650	490	580	450	570	540	510	530	510	560
560	590	470	690	530	570	460	590	530	490

The complete data set is on the text Web site and CD, which contains both the original scores and the ordered scores.

(a) Make a histogram of the distribution (if your software allows it, superimpose a Normal curve over the histogram as in Figure 3.1). Although the resulting histogram depends a bit on your choice of classes, the distribution appears roughly symmetric with no outliers.

(b) Find the mean, median, standard deviation, and quartiles for these data. Comparing the mean and the median and comparing the distances of the two quartiles from the median suggest that the distribution is quite symmetric. Why?

(c) In 2010, the mean score on the Critical Reading portion of the SAT for all college-bound seniors was 501. If the distribution were exactly Normal with the mean and standard deviation you found in part (b), what proportion of regularly admitted GSU freshmen scored above the mean for all college-bound seniors?

(d) Compute the exact proportion of regularly admitted GSU freshmen who scored above the mean for all college-bound seniors. It will be simplest to use the ordered scores in the data file to calculate this. How does this percent compare with the percent calculated in part (c)? Despite the discrepancy, this distribution is "close enough to Normal" for statistical work in later chapters.

3.45 Are the data Normal? Monsoon rains. Here are the amounts of summer monsoon rainfall (millimeters) for India in the 100 years from 1901 to 2000:[14] 🔴 **MONSOONS**

722.4	792.2	861.3	750.6	716.8	885.5	777.9	897.5	889.6	935.4
736.8	806.4	784.8	898.5	781.0	951.1	1004.7	651.2	885.0	719.4
866.2	869.4	823.5	863.0	804.0	903.1	853.5	768.2	821.5	804.9
877.6	803.8	976.2	913.8	843.9	908.7	842.4	908.6	789.9	853.6
728.7	958.1	868.6	920.8	911.3	904.0	945.9	874.3	904.2	877.3
739.2	793.3	923.4	885.8	930.5	983.6	789.0	889.6	944.3	839.9
1020.5	810.0	858.1	922.8	709.6	740.2	860.3	754.8	831.3	940.0
887.0	653.1	913.6	748.3	963.0	857.0	883.4	909.5	708.0	882.9
852.4	735.6	955.9	836.9	760.0	743.2	697.4	961.7	866.9	908.8
784.7	785.0	896.6	938.4	826.4	857.3	870.5	873.8	827.0	770.2

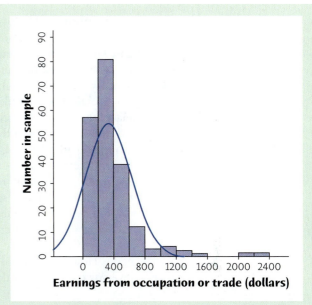

(a) Make a histogram of these rainfall amounts. Find the mean and the median.

(b) Although the distribution is reasonably Normal, your work shows some departure from Normality. In what way are the data not Normal?

3.46 Are the data Normal? Canadians' earnings in 1901. Table 2.5 (page 65) gives data on the earnings of a sample of 200 Canadians in 1901. The mean of the earnings is $350.30, and the standard deviation is $292.20. Figure 3.13 gives a histogram of the data along with a smooth curve representing an $N(350.30, 292.20)$ distribution. From the figure, the Normal curve does not appear to follow the pattern in the histogram that closely. Because of this, the use of areas under the Normal curve may not provide a good approximation to incomes in various intervals. CANADIANEARNS

FIGURE 3.13

Histogram of the earnings of 200 Canadians in 1901, with a Normal curve superimposed, for Exercise 3.46.

(a) Referring to Table 2.5, what proportion of earnings are above $375? What percent of the $N(350.30, 292.20)$ distribution is above $375?

(b) There are no negative incomes. What percent of the $N(350.30, 292.20)$ distribution is below zero?

(c) Based on your answers in (a) and (b), do you think it is a good idea to summarize the distribution of incomes by an $N(350.30, 292.20)$ distribution?

EXPLORING THE WEB

3.47 Are the data Normal? Comparing quartiles. The Web site http://professionals. collegeboard.com/data-reports-research/sat presents data for high school seniors who participated in the SAT Program during the current year as well as previous years. Under SAT Data & Reports, click on the link *College-Bound Seniors* for the most recent year given. In the window that opens, click on the link *Total Group Report: College-Bound Seniors* for this year. The Total Group Profile will open and contains several tables, each giving different summary information. Go to the Overall Mean Scores table. How many students took the Critical Reading portion of the SAT? What were the mean and standard deviation of the scores? Assuming that the distribution of scores is Normal with the mean and standard deviation given in the Overall Mean Scores table, what are the first and third quartiles of the distribution? Now go to the Percentiles for the Total Group table, and compare the actual first and third quartiles from the data with the values obtained from the Normal curve. Does this give any evidence that the distribution of Critical Reading scores is not Normal?

3.48 Are the data Normal? Comparing proportions. The Web site http://professionals. collegeboard.com/data-reports-research/sat presents data for high school seniors who participated in the SAT Program during the current year as well as previous years. Under SAT Data & Reports, click on the link *College-Bound Seniors* for the most recent year given. In the window that opens, click on the link *Total Group Report: College-Bound Seniors* for this year. The Total Group Profile will open and contains several tables, each giving different summary information. Go to the Overall Mean Scores table. How many students took the Critical Reading portion of the SAT? What were the mean and standard deviation of the scores? Now go to the Score Distribution table. The scores are broken into intervals: 200–290, 300–390, etc. Using the "Total" column, find the actual percent of students who scored in each of the six intervals reported for the Critical Reading portion of the SAT. Now, assuming that the distribution of scores is Normal with the mean and standard deviation given in the Overall Mean Scores table, find the area under the Normal curve for each interval. Because the actual scores are discrete numbers, take the interval 200–290 as the interval 200–300, the interval 300–390 as the interval 300–400, etc., when finding the areas under the Normal curve. How do the actual percents compare with the areas under the Normal curve? Does this give any evidence that the distribution of Critical Reading scores is not Normal?

Georgie Holland/Photolibrary

Scatterplots and Correlation

A medical study finds that short women are more likely to have heart attacks than women of average height, while tall women have the fewest heart attacks. An insurance group reports that heavier cars have fewer deaths per 10,000 vehicles registered than do lighter cars. These and many other statistical studies look at the *relationship between two variables*. To understand a statistical relationship between two variables, we measure both variables on the same individuals. Then we apply our basic principles: plot the data, look for the overall pattern and striking deviations, then add numerical summaries.

EXPLANATORY AND RESPONSE VARIABLES

We think that car weight helps explain accident deaths and that smoking influences life expectancy. In each of these relationships, the two variables play different roles: one explains or influences the other.

91

> ### RESPONSE VARIABLE, EXPLANATORY VARIABLE
>
> A **response variable** measures an outcome of a study. An **explanatory variable** may explain or influence changes in a response variable.

EXAMPLE 4.1 Explanatory and response variables

How does drinking beer affect the level of alcohol in our blood? Student volunteers at Ohio State University drank different numbers of cans of beer. Thirty minutes later, a police officer measured their blood alcohol content. Number of beers consumed is the explanatory variable, and percent of alcohol in the blood is the response variable.

Record the SAT scores of high school students and then their first-year grades in college. We think that SAT score (explanatory variable) helps to predict college grades (response variable).

More beers *cause* higher blood alcohol. But high SAT scores don't *cause* high college grades. A cause-and-effect relationship is not necessary for the distinction between explanatory and response variables. ▪

APPLY YOUR KNOWLEDGE

4.1 Explanatory and response variables? You have data on a large group of college students. Here are four pairs of variables measured on these students. For each pair, is it more reasonable to simply explore the relationship between the two variables or to view one of the variables as an explanatory variable and the other as a response variable? In the latter case, which is the explanatory variable and which is the response variable?

(a) Amount of time spent studying for a statistics exam and grade on the exam.

(b) Weight in kilograms and height in centimeters.

(c) Hours per week spent online using Facebook and grade point average.

(d) Score on the SAT Mathematics exam and score on the SAT Critical Reading exam.

4.2 Coral reefs. How sensitive to changes in water temperature are coral reefs? To find out, scientists examined data on sea surface temperatures and coral growth per year at locations in the Red Sea.[1] What are the explanatory and response variables? Are they categorical or quantitative?

Georgette Douwma/Getty

DISPLAYING RELATIONSHIPS: Scatterplots

The most useful graph for displaying the relationship between two quantitative variables is a *scatterplot*.

EXAMPLE 4.2 State SAT Mathematics scores

In some states most high school graduates take the SAT test of readiness for college, and in other states most take the ACT. Who takes a test may influence the average score. Let's follow our four-step process (page 56) to examine this influence.[2]

STATE: The percent of high school students who take the SAT varies from state to state. Does this fact help explain differences among the states in average SAT Mathematics score?

PLAN: Examine the relationship between percent taking the SAT and state mean score on the Mathematics part of the SAT. Choose the explanatory and response variables (if any). Make a *scatterplot* to display the relationship between the variables. Interpret the plot to understand the relationship.

SOLVE (make the plot): We suspect that "percent taking" will help explain "mean score." So "percent taking" is the explanatory variable and "mean score" is the response variable. We want to see how mean score changes when percent taking changes, so we put percent taking (the explanatory variable) on the horizontal axis. Figure 4.1 is the scatterplot. Each point represents a single state. In Colorado, for example, 24% took the SAT, and their mean SAT Math score was 565. Find 24 on the *x* (horizontal) axis and 565 on the *y* (vertical) axis. Colorado appears as the point above 24 and to the right of 565. ■

  **MATHSAT**

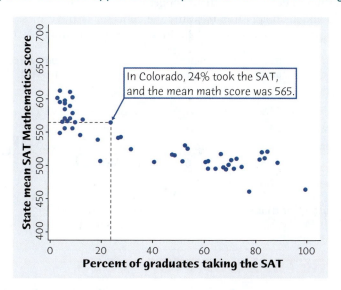

FIGURE 4.1

Scatterplot of the mean SAT Mathematics score in each state against the percent of that state's high school graduates who take the SAT, for Example 4.2. The dashed lines intersect at the point (24, 565), the data for Colorado.

SCATTERPLOT

A **scatterplot** shows the relationship between two quantitative variables measured on the same individuals. The values of one variable appear on the horizontal axis, and the values of the other variable appear on the vertical axis. Each individual in the data appears as the point in the plot fixed by the values of both variables for that individual.

Always plot the explanatory variable, if there is one, on the horizontal axis (the *x* axis) of a scatterplot. As a reminder, we usually call the explanatory variable *x* and the response variable *y*. If there is no explanatory-response distinction, either variable can go on the horizontal axis.

APPLY YOUR KNOWLEDGE

4.3 Do heavier people burn more energy? Metabolic rate, the rate at which the body consumes energy, is important in studies of weight gain, dieting, and exercise. We have data on the lean body mass and resting metabolic rate for 12 women who are subjects in a study of dieting. Lean body mass, given in kilograms, is a person's weight leaving out all fat. Metabolic rate is measured in calories burned per 24 hours. 🔴 **METABOLIC**

Mass	36.1	54.6	48.5	42.0	50.6	42.0
	40.3	33.1	42.4	34.5	51.1	41.2
Rate	995	1425	1396	1418	1502	1256
	1189	913	1124	1052	1347	1204

The researchers believe that lean body mass is an important influence on metabolic rate. Make a scatterplot to examine this belief.

4.4 Outsourcing by airlines. Airlines have increasingly outsourced the maintenance of their planes to other companies. A concern voiced by critics is that the maintenance may be less carefully done, so that outsourcing creates a safety hazard. In addition, flight delays are often due to maintenance problems, so one might look at government data on percent of major maintenance outsourced and percent of flight delays blamed on the airline to determine if these concerns are justified. This was done, and data from 2005 and 2006 appeared to justify the concerns of the critics. Do more recent data still support the concerns of the critics? Here are data from 2010:[3] 🔴 **AIRLINES**

Airline	Outsource percent	Delay percent	Airline	Outsource percent	Delay percent
AirTran	74.5	17.2	Hawaiian	74.7	7.5
Alaska	55.9	12.4	JetBlue	54.5	24.3
American	24.3	20.4	Southwest	60.1	20.5
Continental	42.2	18.6	United	40.0	14.8
Delta	39.3	22.6	US Airways	57.6	17.0
Frontier	7.8	18.6			

Make a scatterplot that shows how delays depend on outsourcing.

INTERPRETING SCATTERPLOTS

To interpret a scatterplot, adapt the strategies of data analysis learned in Chapters 1 and 2 to the new two-variable setting.

EXAMINING A SCATTERPLOT

In any graph of data, look for the **overall pattern** and for striking **deviations** from that pattern.

You can describe the overall pattern of a scatterplot by the **direction, form,** and **strength** of the relationship.

An important kind of deviation is an **outlier,** an individual value that falls outside the overall pattern of the relationship.

EXAMPLE 4.3 Understanding state SAT scores

SOLVE (interpret the plot): Figure 4.1 shows a clear *direction:* the overall pattern moves from upper left to lower right. That is, states in which higher percents of high school graduates take the SAT tend to have lower mean SAT Mathematics scores. We call this a *negative association* between the two variables.

The *form* of the relationship is roughly a straight line with a slight curve to the right as it moves down. What is more, most states fall into two distinct **clusters.** The ACT states cluster at the left and the SAT states at the right. In 22 states, fewer than 20% of seniors took the SAT; in another 22 states, more than 50% took the SAT.

clusters

The *strength* of a relationship in a scatterplot is determined by how closely the points follow a clear form. The overall relationship in Figure 4.1 is moderately strong: states with similar percents taking the SAT tend to have roughly similar mean SAT Math scores.

CONCLUDE: Percent taking explains much of the variation among states in average SAT Mathematics score. States in which a higher percent of students take the SAT tend to have lower mean scores because the mean includes a broader group of students. SAT states as a group have lower mean SAT scores than ACT states. ■

POSITIVE ASSOCIATION, NEGATIVE ASSOCIATION

Two variables are **positively associated** when above-average values of one tend to accompany above-average values of the other, and below-average values also tend to occur together.

Two variables are **negatively associated** when above-average values of one tend to accompany below-average values of the other, and vice versa.

Not all relationships have a clear direction that we can describe as positive association or negative association. Exercise 4.11 (page 101) gives an example that does not have a single direction. Here is an example of a strong positive association with a simple and important form.

EXAMPLE 4.4 The endangered manatee

STATE: Manatees are large, gentle, slow-moving creatures found along the coast of Florida. Many manatees are injured or killed by boats. Table 4.1 contains data on the number of boats registered in Florida (in thousands) and the number of manatees killed by boats for the years 1977 to 2009.[4] Examine the relationship. Is it plausible that restricting the number of boats would help protect manatees?

PLAN: Make a scatterplot with "boats registered" as the explanatory variable and "manatees killed" as the response variable. Describe the direction, form, and strength of the relationship.

SOLVE: Figure 4.2 is the scatterplot. There is a positive association—the more boats, the more manatees are killed. The form of the relationship is **linear.** That is, the overall pattern follows a straight line from lower left to upper right. The relationship is strong because the points don't deviate greatly from a line.

linear relationship

CONCLUDE: As more boats are registered, the number of manatees killed by boats goes up linearly. The Florida Wildlife Commission says that in recent years boats accounted for 24% of manatee deaths and 31% of all wildlife deaths whose causes could be determined. Although many manatees die from other causes, it appears that fewer boats would mean fewer manatee deaths. ■

TABLE 4.1 Florida boat registrations (thousands) and manatees killed by boats

YEAR	BOATS	MANATEES	YEAR	BOATS	MANATEES	YEAR	BOATS	MANATEES
1977	447	13	1989	711	50	2001	944	81
1978	460	21	1990	719	47	2002	962	95
1979	481	24	1991	681	53	2003	978	73
1980	498	16	1992	679	38	2004	983	69
1981	513	24	1993	678	35	2005	1010	79
1982	512	20	1994	696	49	2006	1024	92
1983	526	15	1995	713	42	2007	1027	73
1984	559	34	1996	732	60	2008	1010	90
1985	585	33	1997	755	54	2009	982	97
1986	614	33	1998	809	66			
1987	645	39	1999	830	82			
1988	675	43	2000	880	78			

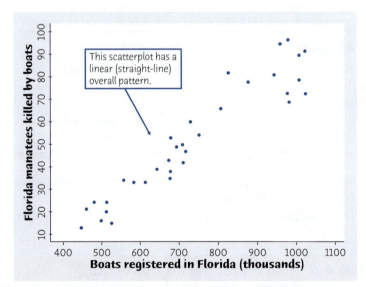

FIGURE 4.2

Scatterplot of the number of Florida manatees killed by boats in the years 1977 to 2009 against the number of boats registered in Florida that year, for Example 4.4. There is a strong linear (straight-line) pattern.

APPLY YOUR KNOWLEDGE

4.5 Do heavier people burn more energy? Describe the direction, form, and strength of the relationship between lean body mass and metabolic rate, as displayed in your plot for Exercise 4.3. METABOLIC

4.6 Outsourcing by airlines. Does your plot for Exercise 4.4 show a positive association between maintenance outsourcing and delays caused by the airline? One airline is a low outlier in delay percent. Which airline is this? Aside from the outlier, does the plot show a roughly linear form? Is the relationship very strong? AIRLINES

4.7 Do heavier people burn more energy? The study of dieting described in Exercise 4.3 collected data on the lean body mass (in kilograms) and metabolic rate (in calories) for both female and male subjects: METABOLIC2

Sex	F	F	F	F	F	F	F	F	F	F
Mass	36.1	54.6	48.5	42.0	50.6	42.0	40.3	33.1	42.4	34.5
Rate	995	1425	1396	1418	1502	1256	1189	913	1124	1052
Sex	F	F	M	M	M	M	M	M	M	
Mass	51.1	41.2	51.9	46.9	62.0	62.9	47.4	48.7	51.9	
Rate	1347	1204	1867	1439	1792	1666	1322	1614	1460	

(a) Make a scatterplot of metabolic rate versus lean body mass for all 19 subjects. Use separate symbols to distinguish women and men. (*This is a common method to compare two groups of individuals in a scatterplot.*)

(b) Does the same overall pattern hold for both women and men? What is the most important difference between women and men?

MEASURING LINEAR ASSOCIATION: Correlation

A scatterplot displays the direction, form, and strength of the relationship between two quantitative variables. Linear (straight-line) relations are particularly important because a straight line is a simple pattern that is quite common. A linear relation is strong if the points lie close to a straight line, and weak if they are widely scattered about a line. *Correlation* is a numerical measure of the strength and direction of a linear relationship.

CORRELATION

The **correlation** measures the direction and strength of the linear relationship between two quantitative variables. Correlation is usually written as r.

Suppose that we have data on variables x and y for n individuals. The values for the first individual are x_1 and y_1, the values for the second individual are x_2 and y_2, and so on. The means and standard deviations of the two variables are $\bar{x}$ and s_x for the x-values, and $\bar{y}$ and s_y for the y-values. The correlation r between x and y is

$$r = \frac{1}{n-1}\left[\left(\frac{x_1 - \bar{x}}{s_x}\right)\left(\frac{y_1 - \bar{y}}{s_y}\right) + \left(\frac{x_2 - \bar{x}}{s_x}\right)\left(\frac{y_2 - \bar{y}}{s_y}\right)\right.$$
$$\left. + \cdots + \left(\frac{x_n - \bar{x}}{s_x}\right)\left(\frac{y_n - \bar{y}}{s_y}\right)\right]$$

or, more compactly,

$$r = \frac{1}{n-1}\sum\left(\frac{x_i - \bar{x}}{s_x}\right)\left(\frac{y_i - \bar{y}}{s_y}\right)$$

Correlation uses *standardized observations*. Suppose that x is height in centimeters and y is weight in kilograms. Then $\bar{x}$ and s_x are the mean and standard deviation in centimeters of all the heights in our data. The value

$$\frac{x_i - \bar{x}}{s_x}$$

that appears in the formula for r is the standardized height of the ith person. Standardized height has no units—it just says how many standard deviations above or below the mean this person's height lies. The correlation r is an average of the products of the standardized height and the standardized weight for all the individuals. Just as in the case of the standard deviation s, the "average" here divides by one fewer than the number of individuals. The formula helps us see what correlation is, but in practice you should use software or a calculator that finds r from keyed-in values of two variables x and y.

APPLY YOUR KNOWLEDGE

4.8 Coral reefs. Exercise 4.2 discusses a study in which scientists examined data on mean sea surface temperatures (in degrees Celsius) and mean coral growth (in millimeters per year) over a several-year period at locations in the Red Sea. Here are the data:[5] CORAL

Sea surface temperature	29.68	29.87	30.16	30.22	30.48	30.65	30.90
Growth	2.63	2.58	2.60	2.48	2.26	2.38	2.26

(a) Make a scatterplot. Which is the explanatory variable? The plot shows a negative linear pattern.

(b) Find the correlation r step-by-step. You may wish to round off to two decimal places in each step. First find the mean and standard deviation of each variable. Then find the seven standardized values for each variable. Finally, use the formula for r. Explain how your value for r matches your graph in (a).

(c) Enter these data into your calculator or software and use the correlation function to find r. Check that you get the same result as in (b), up to roundoff error.

FACTS ABOUT CORRELATION

How correlation behaves is more important than the details of the formula. Here is what you need to know in order to interpret correlation:

1. *Correlation makes no distinction between explanatory and response variables.* It makes no difference which variable you call x and which you call y in calculating the correlation.

2. Because r uses the standardized values of the observations, *r does not change when we change the units of measurement of x, y, or both.* Measuring height in inches rather than centimeters and weight in pounds rather than kilograms does not change the correlation between height and weight. The correlation r itself has no unit of measurement; it is just a number.

3. *Positive r indicates positive association between the variables, and negative r indicates negative association.*

4. *The correlation r is always a number between* −1 *and* 1. Values of r near 0 indicate a very weak linear relationship. The strength of the linear relationship increases as r moves away from 0 toward either −1 or 1. Values of r close to −1 or 1 indicate that the points in a scatterplot lie close to a straight line. The extreme values $r = -1$ and $r = 1$ occur only in the case of a perfect linear relationship, when the points lie exactly along a straight line.

EXAMPLE 4.5 From scatterplot to correlation

The scatterplots in Figure 4.3 illustrate how values of r closer to 1 or −1 correspond to stronger linear relationships. To make the meaning of r clearer, the standard deviations of both variables in these plots are equal, and the horizontal and vertical scales are the same.

The scatterplots in Figure 4.4 show four sets of real data. The patterns are less regular than those in Figure 4.3, but they also illustrate how correlation measures the strength of linear relationships.[6]

(a) This repeats the manatee plot in Figure 4.2. There is a strong positive linear relationship, $r = 0.951$.

(b) Here are the number of named tropical storms each year between 1984 and 2010 plotted against the number predicted before the start of hurricane season by William Gray of Colorado State University. There is a moderate linear relationship, $r = 0.613$.

(c) These data come from an experiment that studied how quickly cuts in the limbs of newts heal. Each point represents the healing rate in micrometers (millionths of a meter) per hour for the two front limbs of the same newt. This relationship is weaker than those in (a) and (b), with $r = 0.358$.

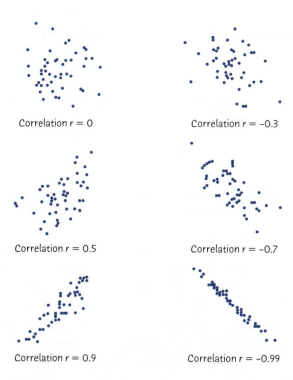

Correlation $r = 0$ Correlation $r = -0.3$

Correlation $r = 0.5$ Correlation $r = -0.7$

Correlation $r = 0.9$ Correlation $r = -0.99$

FIGURE 4.3

How correlation measures the strength of a linear relationship, for Example 4.5. Patterns closer to a straight line have correlations closer to 1 or −1.

FIGURE 4.4

How correlation measures the strength of a linear relationship, for Example 4.5. Four sets of real data with (a) $r = 0.951$, (b) $r = 0.613$, (c) $r = 0.358$, and (d) $r = -0.081$.

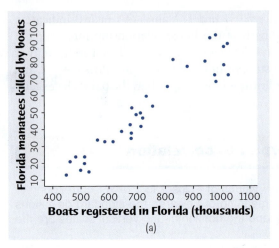

(a)

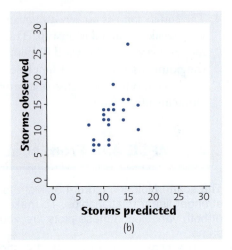

(b)

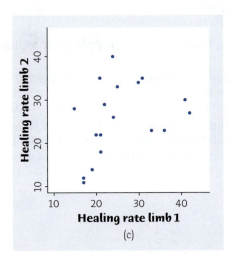

(c)

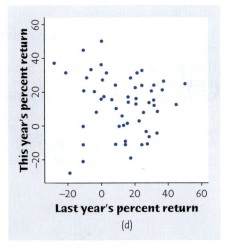

(d)

(d) Does last year's stock market performance help predict how stocks will do this year? No. The correlation between last year's percent return and this year's percent return over 56 years is only $r = -0.081$. The scatterplot shows a cloud of points with no visible linear pattern. ▪

    Describing the relationship between two variables is a more complex task than describing the distribution of one variable. Here are some cautions to keep in mind when you use correlation:

1. *Correlation requires that both variables be quantitative, so that it makes sense to do the arithmetic indicated by the formula for r.* We cannot calculate a correlation between the incomes of a group of people and what city they live in, because city is a categorical variable.

2. Correlation measures the strength of only the linear relationship between two variables. *Correlation does not describe curved relationships between variables, no matter how strong they are.* Exercise 4.11 illustrates this important fact.

3. *Like the mean and standard deviation, the correlation is not resistant: r is strongly affected by a few outlying observations.* Use r with caution when outliers appear in the scatterplot. Figure 4.4(b) contains an outlier, the disastrous 2005 season, whose named storms included Hurricane Katrina. Adding this 1 point to the other 26 decreases the correlation from 0.621 to 0.613. Because the outlier does not follow the linear pattern of the other points, it decreases the correlation.

4. *Correlation is not a complete summary of two-variable data*, even when the relationship between the variables is linear. You should give the means and standard deviations of both x and y along with the correlation.

Because the formula for correlation uses the means and standard deviations, these measures are the proper choice to accompany a correlation. Of course, even giving means, standard deviations, and the correlation for state SAT scores and percent taking will not point out the clusters in Figure 4.1. Numerical summaries complement plots of data, but they don't replace them.

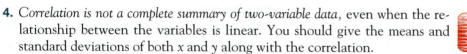

APPLY YOUR KNOWLEDGE

4.9 Changing the units. The healing rates plotted in Figure 4.4(c) are measured in micrometers (millionths of a meter) per hour. The correlation between healing rates for the two front limbs of newts is $r = 0.358$. If the measurements were made in inches per day, would the correlation change? Explain your answer.

4.10 Changing the correlation. Use your calculator or software to demonstrate how outliers can affect correlation.

(a) What is the correlation between lean body mass and metabolic rate for the 12 women in Exercise 4.3? **METABOLIC**

(b) Make a scatterplot of the data with two new points added. Point A: mass 65 kilograms, metabolic rate 1761 calories. Point B: mass 35 kilograms, metabolic rate 1400 calories. Find two new correlations: one for the original data plus Point A, and another for the original data plus Point B.

(c) By looking at your plot, explain why adding Point A makes the correlation stronger (closer to 1) and adding Point B makes the correlation weaker (closer to 0). **METABOLIC3**

4.11 Strong association but no correlation. The gas mileage of an automobile first increases and then decreases as the speed increases. Suppose that this relationship is very regular, as shown by the following data on speed (miles per hour) and mileage (miles per gallon):

Speed	30	40	50	60	70
Mileage	24	28	30	28	24

Make a scatterplot of mileage versus speed. Show that the correlation between speed and mileage is $r = 0$. Explain why the correlation is 0 even though there is a strong relationship between speed and mileage. **MPG**

CHAPTER 4 SUMMARY

CHAPTER SPECIFICS

■ To study relationships between variables, we measure the variables on the same group of individuals.

■ If we think that a variable x may explain or even cause changes in another variable y, we call x an **explanatory variable** and y a **response variable.**

■ A **scatterplot** displays the relationship between two quantitative variables measured on the same individuals. Mark values of one variable on the horizontal axis (x axis) and values of the other variable on the vertical axis (y axis). Plot each individual's data as a point on the graph. Always plot the explanatory variable, if there is one, on the x axis of a scatterplot.

■ In examining a scatterplot, look for an overall pattern showing the **direction, form,** and **strength** of the relationship and then for **outliers** or other deviations from this pattern.

■ **Direction:** If the relationship has a clear direction, we speak of either **positive association** (high values of the two variables tend to occur together) or **negative association** (high values of one variable tend to occur with low values of the other variable).

■ **Form: Linear relationships,** where the points show a straight-line pattern, are an important form of relationship between two variables. Curved relationships and **clusters** are other forms to watch for.

■ **Strength:** The **strength** of a relationship is determined by how close the points in the scatterplot lie to a simple form such as a line.

■ The **correlation r** measures the direction and strength of the linear association between two quantitative variables x and y. Although you can calculate a correlation for any scatterplot, r measures only straight-line relationships.

■ Correlation indicates the direction of a linear relationship by its sign: $r > 0$ for a positive association and $r < 0$ for a negative association. Correlation always takes values between -1 and 1 and indicates the strength of a relationship by how close it is to -1 or 1. Perfect correlation, $r = 1$ or $r = -1$, occurs only when the points on a scatterplot lie exactly on a straight line.

■ Correlation ignores the distinction between explanatory and response variables. The value of r is not affected by changes in the unit of measurement of either variable. Correlation is not resistant, so outliers can greatly change the value of r.

LINK IT

In this chapter we continue our study of exploratory data analysis but for the purpose of examining relationships *between* variables. Scatterplots are a type of graph that can be used to visualize patterns in the relationship between two variables. We look for an overall pattern showing the direction, form, and strength of the relationship and then for outliers or other deviations from this pattern. The direction of the pattern is often summarized as either a positive association (high values of the two variables tend to occur together) or a negative association (high values of one variable tend to occur with low values of the other variable). Forms to watch for are straight-line patterns, curved patterns, and clusters. The strength of a relationship is determined by how close the points in the scatterplot lie to a simple form such as a straight line or curve.

One of the simplest forms is a linear relationship, where the points suggest a straight-line pattern. Correlation is a number that summarizes the strength and direction of a linear relation. Positive values of the correlation correspond to a positive association. Negative values correspond to a negative association. The closer the absolute value of the correlation is to 1, the stronger the linear relationship (the more closely the points in the scatterplot come to lying on a straight line).

It is tempting to assume that the patterns we observe in our data hold for values of our variables that we have not observed—in other words, that additional data would continue to conform to these patterns. The process of identifying underlying patterns would seem to assume that this is the case. But is this assumption justified? We will return to this issue in Part IV of the book.

CHECK YOUR SKILLS

4.12 In a scatterplot of the average price of a barrel of oil and the average retail price of a gallon of gasoline, you expect to see

  (a) a positive association.

  (b) very little association.

  (c) a negative association.

4.13 Figure 4.5 is a scatterplot of school GPA against IQ test scores for 15 seventh-grade students. There is one low outlier in the plot. The IQ and GPA scores for this student are

  (a) IQ = 0.5, GPA = 103.

  (b) IQ = 103, GPA = 0.5.

  (c) IQ = 103, GPA = 7.6.

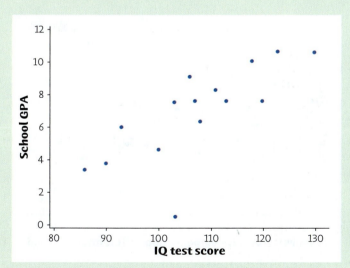

FIGURE 4.5
Scatterplot of school GPA against IQ test score for seventh-grade students, for Exercises 4.13 and 4.14.

4.14 If we leave out the low outlier, the correlation for the remaining 14 points in Figure 4.5 is closest to

  (a) 0.9   (b) −0.9.   (c) 0.1.

4.15 If the correlation between two variables is close to 0, you can conclude that a scatterplot would show

  (a) a strong straight-line pattern.

  (b) a cloud of points with no visible pattern.

  (c) no straight-line pattern, but there might be a strong pattern of another form.

4.16 The points on a scatterplot lie very close to the line whose equation is $y = 4 - 3x$. The correlation between x and y is close to

  (a) −3.   (b) −1.   (c) 1.

4.17 For a biology project, you measure the weight in grams and the tail length in millimeters of a group of mice. The correlation is $r = 0.7$. If you had measured tail length in centimeters instead of millimeters, what would be the correlation? (There are 10 millimeters in a centimeter.)

  (a) 0.7/10 = 0.07   (b) 0.7   (c) (0.7)(10) = 7

4.18 Because elderly people may have difficulty standing to have their heights measured, a study looked at predicting overall height from height to the knee. Here are data (in centimeters) for six elderly men: 🌐 KNEEHT

Knee height x	57.7	47.4	43.5	44.8	55.2	54.6
Height y	192.1	153.3	146.4	162.7	169.1	177.8

Use your calculator or software: the correlation between knee height and overall height is about

  (a) $r = 0.08$.   (b) $r = 0.89$.   (c) $r = 0.74$.

CHAPTER 4 EXERCISES

4.19 Scores at the Masters. The Masters is one of the four major golf tournaments. Figure 4.6 is a scatterplot of the scores for the first two rounds of the 2010 Masters for all the golfers entered. Only the 60 golfers with the lowest two-round total advance to the final two rounds. The plot has a grid pattern because golf scores must be whole numbers.[7] 🔴 MASTERS10

(a) What was the lowest score in the first round of play? How many golfers had this low score? What were their scores in the second round?

(b) Sandy Lyle had the highest score in the second round. What was this score? What was Lyle's score in the first round?

(c) Is the correlation between first-round scores and second-round scores closest to $r = 0.1$, $r = 0.5$, or $r = 0.9$? Explain your choice. Does the graph suggest that knowing a professional golfer's score for one round is much help in predicting his score for another round on the same course?

4.20 Happy states. Human happiness or well-being can be assessed either subjectively or objectively. Subjective assessment can be accomplished by listening to what people say. Objective assessment can be made from data related to well-being such as income, climate, availability of entertainment, housing prices, lack of traffic congestion, etc. Do subjective and objective assessments agree? To study this, investigators made both subjective and objective assessments of happiness

for each of the 50 states. The subjective measurement was the mean score on a life-satisfaction question found on the Behavioral Risk Factor Surveillance System (BRFSS), which is a state-based system of health surveys. Lower scores indicate a greater degree of happiness. To objectively assess happiness, the investigators computed a mean well-being score (called the compensating-differentials score) for each state, based on objective measures that have been found to be related to happiness or well-being. The states were then ranked according to this score (Rank 1 being the happiest). Figure 4.7 is a scatterplot of mean BRFSS scores (response) against the rank based on the compensating-differentials scores (explanatory).[8] 🔴 HAPPY

(a) Is there an overall positive association or an overall negative association between mean BRFSS score and rank based on the compensating-differentials method?

(b) Are there any outliers? If so, what are the BRFSS scores corresponding to these outliers?

4.21 Wine and cancer in women. Some studies have suggested that a nightly glass of wine may not only take the edge off a day but also improve health. Is wine good for your health? A study of nearly 1.3 million middle-aged British women examined wine consumption and the risk of breast cancer. The researchers were interested in how risk changed as wine consumption increased. Risk is based on breast cancer rates in

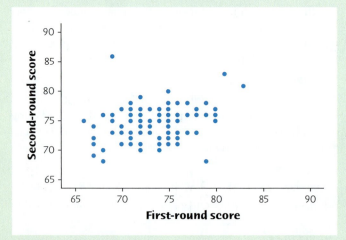

FIGURE 4.6

Scatterplot of the scores in the first two rounds of the 2010 Masters Tournament, for Exercise 4.19.

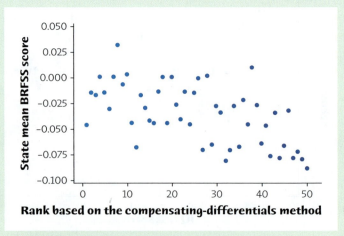

FIGURE 4.7

Scatterplot of mean BRFSS score in each state against each state's well-being rank, for Exercise 4.20.

drinkers relative to breast cancer rates in nondrinkers in the study, with higher values indicating greater risk. In particular, a value greater than 1 indicates a greater breast cancer rate than that of nondrinkers. Wine intake is the mean wine intake, in grams per day, of all women in the study who drank approximately the same amount of wine per week. Here are the data (for drinkers only):[9] ☕ **CANCER**

Wine intake x (grams per day)	2.5	8.5	15.5	26.5
Relative risk y	1.00	1.08	1.15	1.22

(a) Make a scatterplot of these data. Based on the scatterplot, do you expect the correlation to be positive or negative? Near ± 1 or not?

(b) Find the correlation r between wine intake and relative risk. Do the data show that women who consume more wine tend to have higher relative risks of breast cancer?

4.22 Ebola and gorillas. The deadly Ebola virus is a threat to both people and gorillas in Central Africa. An outbreak in 2002 and 2003 killed 91 of the 95 gorillas in 7 home ranges in the Congo. To study the spread of the virus, measure "distance" by the number of home ranges separating a group of gorillas from the first group infected. Here are data on distance and time in number of days until deaths began in each later group:[10] ☕ **EBOLA**

Distance	1	3	4	4	4	5
Time	4	21	33	41	43	46

(a) Make a scatterplot. Which is the explanatory variable? What kind of pattern does your plot show?

(b) Find the correlation r between distance and time.

(c) If time in days were replaced by time in number of weeks until death began in each later group (fractions allowed so that 4 days becomes 4/7 weeks), would the correlation between distance and time change? Explain your answer.

4.23 Sparrowhawk colonies. One of nature's patterns connects the percent of adult birds in a colony that return from the previous year and the number of new adults that join the colony. Here are data for 13 colonies of sparrowhawks:[11]

☕ **SPARROWHAWKS**

Percent return	74	66	81	52	73	62	52	45	62	46	60	46	38
New adults	5	6	8	11	12	15	16	17	18	18	19	20	20

(a) Plot the count of new adults (response) against the percent of returning birds (explanatory). Describe the direction and form of the relationship. Is the correlation r an appropriate measure of the strength of this relationship? If so, find r.

(b) For short-lived birds, the association between these variables is positive: changes in weather and food supply drive the populations of new and returning birds up or down together. For long-lived territorial birds, on the other hand, the association is negative because returning birds claim their territories in the colony and don't leave room for new recruits. Which type of species is the sparrowhawk?

4.24 Our brains don't like losses. Most people dislike losses more than they like gains. In money terms, people are about as sensitive to a loss of $10 as to a gain of $20. To discover what parts of the brain are active in decisions about gain and loss, psychologists presented subjects with a series of gambles with different odds and different amounts of winnings and losses. From a subject's choices, they constructed a measure of "behavioral loss aversion." Higher scores show greater sensitivity to losses. Observing brain activity while subjects made their decisions pointed to specific brain regions. Here are data for 16 subjects on behavioral loss aversion and "neural loss aversion," a measure of activity in one region of the brain:[12] ☕ **BRAINS**

Neural	−50.0	−39.1	−25.9	−26.7	−28.6	−19.8
Behavioral	0.08	0.81	0.01	0.12	0.68	0.11
Neural	−17.6	5.5	2.6	20.7	12.1	15.5
Behavioral	0.36	0.34	0.53	0.68	0.99	1.04
Neural	28.8	41.7	55.3	155.2		
Behavioral	0.66	0.86	1.29	1.94		

(a) Make a scatterplot that shows how behavior responds to brain activity.

(b) Describe the overall pattern of the data. There is one clear outlier.

(c) Find the correlation r between neural and behavioral loss aversion both with and without the outlier. Does the outlier have a strong influence on the value of r? By looking at your plot, explain why adding the outlier to the other data points causes r to increase.

4.25 Sulfur, the ocean, and the sun. Sulfur in the atmosphere affects climate by influencing formation of clouds. The main natural source of sulfur is dimethyl sulfide (DMS) produced by small organisms in the upper layers of the oceans. DMS production is in turn influenced by the amount of energy the upper ocean receives from sunlight. Here are monthly data on solar radiation dose (SRD, in watts per square meter) and surface DMS concentration (in nanomolars) for a region in the Mediterranean:[13]
🔥 SULFUR

SRD	12.55	12.91	14.34	19.72	21.52
DMS	0.796	0.692	1.744	1.062	0.682
SRD	22.41	37.65	48.41	74.41	94.14
DMS	1.517	0.736	0.720	1.820	1.099
SRD	109.38	157.79	262.67	268.96	289.23
DMS	2.692	5.134	8.038	7.280	8.872

(a) Make a scatterplot that shows how DMS responds to SRD.

(b) Describe the overall pattern of the data. Find the correlation r between DMS and SRD. Because SRD changes with the seasons of the year, the close relationship between SRD and DMS helps explain other seasonal patterns.

4.26 Alcohol and cancer in women. Exercise 4.21 discusses a study of the relationship between wine consumption and the risk of breast cancer in women. The researchers were also interested in how risk changed as consumption of alcoholic beverages other than wine increased. Intake of alcoholic beverages other than wine is the mean intake, in grams per day, of all women in the study who drank approximately the same amount of alcohol other than wine per week. Here are the data for both women who drank wine and women who drank alcoholic beverages other than wine: 🔥 CANCER

Wine intake (grams per day)	2.5	8.5	15.5	26.5
Relative risk	1.00	1.08	1.15	1.22
Alcohol intake (grams per day)	2.0	7.0	13.0	24.0
Relative risk	0.96	1.06	1.11	1.20

(a) Make a scatterplot of the relative risk versus intake, using separate symbols for the two types of drinks.

(b) What does your plot show about the pattern of risk? What does it show about the effect of type of drink on risk?

4.27 Feed the birds. Canaries provide more food to their babies when the babies beg more intensely. Researchers wondered if begging was the main factor determining how much food baby canaries receive, or if parents also take into account whether the babies are theirs or not. To investigate, researchers conducted an experiment allowing canary parents to raise two broods: one of their own and one fostered from a different pair of parents. If begging determines how much food babies receive, then differences in the "begging intensities" of the broods should be strongly associated with differences in the amount of food the broods receive. The researchers decided to use the relative growth rates (the growth rate of the foster babies relative to that of the natural babies, with values greater than 1 indicating that the foster babies grew more rapidly than the natural babies) as a measure of the difference in the amount of food received. They recorded the difference in begging intensities (the begging intensity of the foster babies minus that of the natural babies) and relative growth rates. Here are data from the experiment:[14] 🔥 CANARIES

Difference in begging intensity	−14.0	−12.5	−12.0	−8.0	−8.0	−6.5
Relative growth rate	0.85	1.00	1.33	0.85	0.90	1.15
Difference in begging intensity	−5.5	−3.5	−3.0	−2.0	−1.5	−1.5
Relative growth rate	1.00	1.30	1.33	1.03	0.95	1.15
Difference in begging intensity	0.0	0.0	2.00	2.00	3.00	4.50
Relative growth rate	1.13	1.00	1.07	1.14	1.00	0.83
Difference in begging intensity	7.00	8.00	8.50			
Relative growth rate	1.15	0.93	0.70			

(a) Make a scatterplot that shows how relative growth rate responds to the difference in begging intensity.

(b) Describe the overall pattern of the relationship. Is it linear? Is there a positive or negative association, or neither? Find the correlation r. Is r a helpful description of this relationship?

(c) If begging intensity is the main factor determining food received, with higher intensity leading to more food, one would expect the relative growth rate to increase as the difference in begging intensity increases. However, if both begging intensity and a preference for their own babies determine the amount of food received (and hence the relative growth rate), we might expect growth rate to increase initially as begging intensity increases but then to level off (or even decrease) as the parents begin to ignore increases in begging by the foster babies. Which of these theories do the data appear to support? Explain your answer.

4.28 Good weather and tipping. Favorable weather has been shown to be associated with increased tipping. Will just the belief that future weather will be favorable lead to higher tips? Researchers gave 60 index cards to a waitress at an Italian restaurant in New Jersey. Before delivering the bill to each customer, the waitress randomly selected a card and wrote on the bill the same message that was printed on the index card. Twenty of the cards had the message "The weather is supposed to be really good tomorrow. I hope you enjoy the day!" Another 20 cards contained the message "The weather is supposed to be not so good tomorrow. I hope you enjoy the day anyway!" The remaining 20 cards were blank, indicating that the waitress was not supposed to write any message. Choosing a card at random ensured that there was a random assignment of the diners to the three experimental conditions. Here are the tip percents for the three messages:[15] **TIPPING**

Weather report	Tip percents				
Good	20.8	18.7	19.9	20.6	22.0
	23.4	22.8	24.9	22.2	20.3
	24.9	22.3	27.0	20.4	22.2
	24.0	21.2	22.1	22.0	22.7
Bad	18.0	19.0	19.2	18.8	18.4
	19.0	18.5	16.1	16.8	14.0
	17.0	13.6	17.5	19.9	20.2
	18.8	18.0	23.2	18.2	19.4
None	19.9	16.0	15.0	20.1	19.3
	19.2	18.0	19.2	21.2	18.8
	18.5	19.3	19.3	19.4	10.8
	19.1	19.7	19.8	21.3	20.6

(a) Make a plot of tip percent against the weather report on the bill (space the three weather reports equally on the horizontal axis). Which weather report appears to lead to the best tip?

(b) Does it make sense to speak of a positive or negative association between weather report and tip percent? Why? Is correlation r a helpful description of the relationship? Why?

4.29 Thinking about correlation. Exercise 4.21 presents data on wine intake and the relative risk of breast cancer in women.

(a) If wine intake is measured in ounces per day rather than grams per day, how would the correlation change? (There are 0.035 ounces in a gram.)

(b) How would r change if all the relative risks were 0.25 less than the values given in the table? Does the correlation tell us that among women who drink, those who drink more wine tend to have a greater relative risk of cancer than women who don't drink at all?

(c) If drinking an additional gram of wine each day raised the relative risk of breast cancer by exactly 0.01, what would be the correlation between wine intake and relative risk of breast cancer? (*Hint:* Draw a scatterplot for several values of wine intake.)

4.30 The effect of changing units. Changing the units of measurement can dramatically alter the appearance of a scatterplot. Return to the data on knee height and overall height in Exercise 4.18: **KNEEHT**

Knee height x	57.7	47.4	43.5	44.8	55.2	54.6
Height y	192.1	153.3	146.4	162.7	169.1	177.8

Both heights are measured in centimeters. A mad scientist decides to measure knee height in millimeters and height in meters. The same data in these units are

Knee height x	577	474	435	448	552	546
Height y	1.921	1.533	1.464	1.627	1.691	1.778

(a) Make a plot with the x axis extending from 0 to 600 and the y axis from 0 to 250. Plot the original data on these axes. Then plot the new data using a different color or symbol. The two plots look very different.

(b) Nonetheless, the correlation is exactly the same for the two sets of measurements. Why do you know that this is true without doing any calculations? Find the two correlations to verify that they are the same.

4.31 Statistics for investing. A mutual funds company's newsletter says, "A well-diversified portfolio includes assets with low correlations." The newsletter includes a table of correlations between the returns on various classes of investments. For example, the correlation between municipal bonds and large-cap stocks is 0.50, and the correlation between municipal bonds and small-cap stocks is 0.21.

(a) Rachel invests heavily in municipal bonds. She wants to diversify by adding an investment whose returns do not closely follow the returns on her bonds. Should she choose large-cap stocks or small-cap stocks for this purpose? Explain your answer.

(b) If Rachel wants an investment that tends to increase when the return on her bonds drops, what kind of correlation should she look for?

4.32 Teaching and research. A college newspaper interviews a psychologist about student ratings of the teaching of faculty members. The psychologist says, "The evidence indicates that the correlation between the research productivity and teaching rating of faculty members is close to zero." The paper reports this as "Professor McDaniel said that good researchers tend to be poor teachers, and vice versa." Explain why the paper's report is wrong. Write a statement in plain language (don't use the word "correlation") to explain the psychologist's meaning.

4.33 Sloppy writing about correlation. Each of the following statements contains a blunder. Explain in each case what is wrong.

(a) "There is a high correlation between the gender of American workers and their income."

(b) "We found a high correlation ($r = 1.09$) between students' ratings of faculty teaching and ratings made by other faculty members."

(c) "The correlation between height and weight of the subjects was $r = 0.63$ centimeter."

*The following exercises ask you to answer questions from data without having the details outlined for you. The exercise statements give you the **State** step of the four-step process. In your work, follow the **Plan, Solve,** and **Conclude** steps of the process, described on page 56.*

4.34 Brighter sunlight? The brightness of sunlight at the earth's surface changes over time depending on whether the earth's atmosphere is more or less clear.

Sunlight dimmed between 1960 and 1990. After 1990, air pollution dropped in industrial countries. Did sunlight brighten? Here are annual averages computed by researchers from data from Ny Alesund, Spitsbergen, Norway, averaging over only clear days each year. (Other locations show similar trends.) The response variable is solar radiation in watts per square meter.[16] **SUNLIGHT**

Year	1993	1994	1995	1996	1997	1998	1999	2000
Sun	116.0	120.0	123.0	123.5	125.5	125.0	129.0	128.0

4.35 Will women outrun men? Does the physiology of women make them better suited than men to long distance running? Will women eventually outperform men in long-distance races? Researchers examined data on world record times (in seconds) for men and women in the marathon. Here are data for women:[17] **MARATHON**

Year	1926	1964	1967	1970	1971
Time	13,222.0	11,973.0	11,246.0	10,973.0	9990.0
Year	1974	1975	1977	1980	1981
Time	9834.5	9499.0	9287.5	9027.0	8806.0
Year	1982	1983	1985		
Time	8771.0	8563.0	8466.0		

Here are data for men:

Year	1908	1909	1913	1920	1925	1935
Time	10,518.4	9751.0	9366.6	9155.8	8941.8	8802.0
Year	1947	1952	1953	1954	1958	1960
Time	8739.0	8442.2	8314.8	8259.4	8117.0	8116.2
Year	1963	1964	1965	1967	1969	1981
Time	8068.0	7931.2	7920.0	7776.4	7713.6	7698.0
Year	1984	1985	1988			
Time	7685.0	7632.0	7610.0			

(a) What do the data show about women's and men's times in the marathon? (Start by plotting both sets of data on the same plot, using two different plotting symbols.)

(b) Based on these data, researchers (in 1992) predicted that women would outrun men in the marathon in 1998. How do you think they arrived at this date? Was their prediction accurate? (You may want to look on the Web; try doing a Google search on "women's world record marathon times.")

4.36 Toucan beaks. The toco toucan, the largest member of the toucan family, possesses the largest beak relative to body size of all birds. This exaggerated feature has received various interpretations, such as being a refined adaptation for feeding. However, the large surface area may also be an important mechanism for radiating heat (and hence cooling the bird) as outdoor temperature increases. Here are data for beak heat loss, as a percent of total body heat loss, at various temperatures in degrees Celsius:[18] 🔶 TOUCAN

Temperature (°C)	15	16	17	18	19	20	21	22
Percent heat loss from beak	32	34	35	33	37	46	55	51
Temperature (°C)	23	24	25	26	27	28	29	30
Percent heat loss from beak	43	52	45	53	58	60	62	62

Investigate the relationship between outdoor temperature and beak heat loss as a percent of total body heat loss.

4.37 Does social rejection hurt? We often describe our emotional reaction to social rejection as "pain." Does social rejection cause activity in areas of the brain that are known to be activated by physical pain? If it does, we really do experience social and physical pain in similar ways. Psychologists first included and then deliberately excluded individuals from a social activity while they measured changes in brain activity. After each activity, the subjects filled out questionnaires that assessed how excluded they felt. Here are data for 13 subjects:[19] 🔶 REJECTION

Subject	Social distress	Brain activity
1	1.26	−0.055
2	1.85	−0.040
3	1.10	−0.026
4	2.50	−0.017
5	2.17	−0.017
6	2.67	0.017
7	2.01	0.021
8	2.18	0.025
9	2.58	0.027
10	2.75	0.033
11	2.75	0.064
12	3.33	0.077
13	3.65	0.124

The explanatory variable is "social distress" measured by each subject's questionnaire score after exclusion relative to the score after inclusion. (So values greater than 1 show the degree of distress caused by exclusion.) The response variable is change in activity in a region of the brain that is activated by physical pain. Discuss what the data show.

EXPLORING THE WEB

4.38 Drive for show, putt for dough. A popular saying in golf is "You drive for show but you putt for dough." The point is that hitting the golf ball a long way with a driver looks impressive, but putting well is more important for the final score and hence the amount of money you win. You can find this season's Professional Golfers Association (PGA) Tour statistics at the PGA Tour Web site: www.pgatour.com/r/stats (click on View All under any category displayed to see the statistics for all golfers). You can also find these statistics at the ESPN Web site: espn.go.com/golf/statistics/_/year. Look at the most recent putting, driving, and money earnings data for the current season on the PGA Tour.

(a) Make a scatterplot of earnings and putting average. Use earnings as the response variable. Describe the direction, form, and strength of the relationship in the plot. Are there any outliers?

(b) Make a scatterplot of earnings and driving distance. Use earnings as the response variable. Describe the direction, form, and strength of the relationship in the plot. Are there any outliers?

(c) Do your plots support the maxim "You drive for show but you putt for dough"?

4.39 Olympic medals. Go to the *Chance News* Web site at www.causeweb.org/wiki/chance/index.php/Chance_News_61#Predicting_medal_counts and read the article "Predicting Medal Counts." Next, search the Web and locate the Winter Olympics medal counts for 2002 and 2006 (we found Winter Olympics medal counts on Wikipedia). Make a scatterplot that is similar to the one in the *Chance News* article but that uses the 2002 medal counts to predict the 2010 medal counts. How does your plot compare with the plot in the *Chance News* article?

Regression

Linear (straight-line) relationships between two quantitative variables are easy to understand and quite common. In Chapter 4, we found linear relationships in settings as varied as Florida manatee deaths, the risk of cancer, and predicting tropical storms. Correlation measures the direction and strength of these relationships. When a scatterplot shows a linear relationship, we would like to summarize the overall pattern by drawing a line on the scatterplot.

REGRESSION LINES

A *regression line* summarizes the relationship between two variables, but only in a specific setting: one of the variables helps explain or predict the other. That is, regression describes a relationship between an explanatory variable and a response variable.

REGRESSION LINE

A **regression line** is a straight line that describes how a response variable y changes as an explanatory variable x changes. We often use a regression line to predict the value of y for a given value of x.

FATGAIN

EXAMPLE 5.1 Does fidgeting keep you slim?

Here, following our four-step process (page 56), is an account of a study that sheds some light on gaining weight.

STATE: Some people don't gain weight even when they overeat. Perhaps fidgeting and other "nonexercise activity" (NEA) explains why. These people may spontaneously increase nonexercise activity when fed more. Researchers deliberately overfed 16 healthy young adults for 8 weeks. They measured fat gain (in kilograms) and, as an explanatory variable, change in energy use (in calories) from activity other than deliberate exercise—fidgeting, daily living, and the like. Here are the data:[1]

NEA change (cal)	−94	−57	−29	135	143	151	245	355
Fat gain (kg)	4.2	3.0	3.7	2.7	3.2	3.6	2.4	1.3
NEA change (cal)	392	473	486	535	571	580	620	690
Fat gain (kg)	3.8	1.7	1.6	2.2	1.0	0.4	2.3	1.1

Negative values for NEA change correspond to a decrease in spontaneous NEA. Do people with larger increases in NEA tend to have smaller gains in fat?

PLAN: Make a scatterplot of the data and examine the pattern. If it is linear, use correlation to measure its strength and draw a regression line on the scatterplot to predict fat gain from change in NEA.

SOLVE: Figure 5.1 is a scatterplot of these data. The plot shows a moderately strong negative linear association with no outliers. The correlation is $r = -0.7786$. The line on the plot is a regression line for predicting fat gain from change in NEA.

CONCLUDE: People with larger increases in NEA do indeed gain less fat. To add to this conclusion, we must study regression lines in more detail. ■

FIGURE 5.1

Weight gain after 8 weeks of overeating, plotted against increase in nonexercise activity over the same period, for Example 5.1.

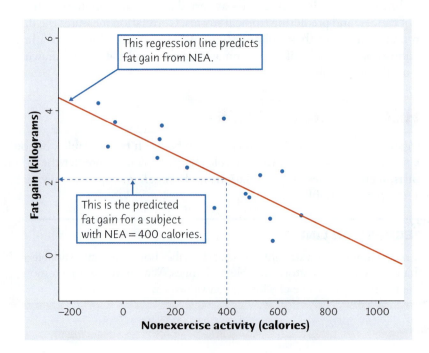

Many calculators and software programs will give you the equation of a regression line from keyed-in data. Understanding and using the line are more important than the details of where the equation comes from.

REVIEW OF STRAIGHT LINES

Suppose that y is a response variable (plotted on the vertical axis) and x is an explanatory variable (plotted on the horizontal axis). A straight line relating y to x has an equation of the form

$$y = a + bx$$

In this equation, b is the **slope,** the amount by which y changes when x increases by one unit. The number a is the **intercept,** the value of y when $x = 0$.

EXAMPLE 5.2 Using a regression line

Any straight line describing the NEA data has the form

$$\text{fat gain} = a + (b \times \text{NEA change})$$

The line in Figure 5.1 is the regression line with the equation

$$\text{fat gain} = 3.505 - 0.00344 \times \text{NEA change}$$

Be sure you understand the role of the two numbers in this equation:

■ The slope $b = -0.00344$ tells us that fat gained goes down by 0.00344 kilogram for each added calorie of NEA. The slope of a regression line is the *rate of change* in the response as the explanatory variable changes.

■ The intercept, $a = 3.505$ kilograms, is the estimated fat gain if NEA does not change when a person overeats.

The equation of the regression line makes it easy to predict fat gain. If a person's NEA increases by 400 calories when she overeats, substitute $x = 400$ in the equation. The predicted fat gain is

$$\text{fat gain} = 3.505 - (0.00344 \times 400) = 2.13 \text{ Kilograms}$$

Figure 5.1 shows the prediction graphically: go "up and over" from $x = 400$.
  To **plot the line** on the scatterplot, use the equation to find the predicted y for two values of x, one near each end of the range of x in the data. Plot each y above its x-value and draw the line through the two points. ■

plotting a line

The slope $b = -0.00344$ in Example 5.2 looks small. This does *not* mean that change in NEA has little effect on fat gain. The size of the slope depends on the units in which we measure the two variables. In this example, the slope is the change in fat gain in kilograms when NEA increases by one calorie. There are 1000 grams in a kilogram. If we measured fat gain in grams, the slope would be 1000 times larger, $b = -3.44$. *You can't say how important a relationship is by looking at the size of the slope of the regression line.*

APPLY YOUR KNOWLEDGE

5.1 City mileage, highway mileage. We expect a car's highway gas mileage (mpg) to be related to its city gas mileage. Data for all 1040 vehicles in the government's *2010 Fuel Economy Guide* give the regression line

$$\text{highway mpg} = 6.554 + (1.016 \times \text{city mpg})$$

for predicting highway mileage from city mileage.

(a)   What is the slope of this line? Say in words what the numerical value of the slope tells you.

(b)   What is the intercept? Explain why the value of the intercept is not statistically meaningful.

(c)   Find the predicted highway mileage for a car that gets 16 miles per gallon in the city. Do the same for a car with a city mileage of 28 mpg.

5.2 What's the line? You use the same bar of soap to shower each morning. The bar weighs 80 grams when it is new. Its weight goes down by 5 grams per day on the average. What is the equation of the regression line for predicting weight from days of use?

THE LEAST-SQUARES REGRESSION LINE

How should we draw a regression line on a scatterplot? Because we use the line to predict y from x, the prediction errors we make are errors in y, the vertical direction in the scatterplot. A *good regression line makes the vertical distances of the points from the line as small as possible*. The most common way to make the collection of vertical distances "as small as possible" is the *least-squares* method.

LEAST-SQUARES REGRESSION LINE

The **least-squares regression line** of y on x is the line that makes the sum of the squares of the vertical distances of the data points from the line as small as possible.

We can give the equation for the least-squares line in terms of the means and standard deviations of the two variables and the correlation between them.

> ### EQUATION OF THE LEAST-SQUARES REGRESSION LINE
>
> We have data on an explanatory variable x and a response variable y for n individuals. From the data, calculate the means $\bar{x}$ and $\bar{y}$ and the standard deviations s_x and s_y of the two variables, and their correlation r. The least-squares regression line is the line
>
> $$\hat{y} = a + bx$$
>
> with **slope**
>
> $$b = r\frac{s_y}{s_x}$$
>
> and **intercept**
>
> $$a = \bar{y} - b\bar{x}$$

We write $\hat{y}$ (read "y hat") in the equation of the regression line to emphasize that the line gives a *predicted* response $\hat{y}$ for any x. Because of the scatter of points about the line, the predicted response will usually not be exactly the same as the actually *observed* response y. In practice, you don't need to calculate the means, standard deviations, and correlation first. Software or your calculator will give the slope b and intercept a of the least-squares line from the values of the variables x and y. You can then concentrate on understanding and using the regression line.

USING TECHNOLOGY

Least-squares regression is one of the most common statistical procedures. Any technology for statistical calculations will give you the least-squares line and related information. Figure 5.2 displays the regression output for the data of Examples 5.1 and 5.2 from a graphing calculator, two statistical programs, and a spreadsheet program. Each output records the slope and intercept of the least-squares line. The software also provides information that we do not yet need, although we will use much of it later. (In fact, we left out part of the Minitab and Excel outputs.) Be sure that you can locate the slope and intercept on all three outputs. *Once you understand the statistical ideas, you can read and work with almost any software output.*

APPLY YOUR KNOWLEDGE

5.3 Coral reefs. Exercises 4.2 and 4.8 discuss a study in which scientists examined data on mean sea surface temperatures (in degrees Celsius) and mean coral growth (in millimeters per year) over a several-year period at locations in the Red Sea. Here are the data:[2] CORAL

Sea surface temperature	29.68	29.87	30.16	30.22	30.48	30.65	30.90
Growth	2.63	2.58	2.60	2.48	2.26	2.38	2.26

FIGURE 5.2

Least-squares regression for the nonexercise activity data: output from a graphing calculator, two statistical programs, and a spreadsheet program.

Texas Instruments Graphing Calculator

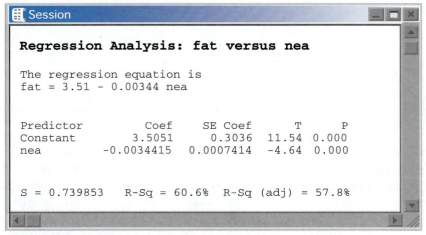

```
LinReg
 y=a+bx
 a=3.505122916
 b=-.003441487
 r²=.6061492049
 r=-.7785558457
```

Minitab

```
Session                                            _ □ ✕

  Regression Analysis: fat versus nea

  The regression equation is
  fat = 3.51 - 0.00344 nea


  Predictor          Coef     SE Coef        T      P
  Constant         3.5051      0.3036    11.54  0.000
  nea           -0.0034415   0.0007414   -4.64  0.000


  S = 0.739853   R-Sq = 60.6%   R-Sq (adj) = 57.8%
```

CrunchIt!

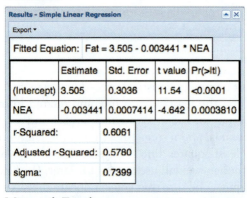

Results – Simple Linear Regression   ▲ ✕

Export ▾

Fitted Equation: Fat = 3.505 - 0.003441 * NEA

	Estimate	Std. Error	t value	Pr(>|t|)
(Intercept)	3.505	0.3036	11.54	<0.0001
NEA	-0.003441	0.0007414	-4.642	0.0003810

r-Squared:	0.6061
Adjusted r-Squared:	0.5780
sigma:	0.7399

Microsoft Excel

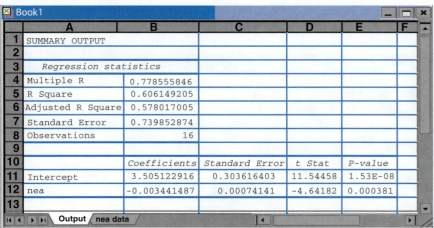

	A	B	C	D	E	F
1	SUMMARY OUTPUT					
2						
3	*Regression statistics*					
4	Multiple R	0.778555846				
5	R Square	0.606149205				
6	Adjusted R Square	0.578017005				
7	Standard Error	0.739852874				
8	Observations	16				
9						
10		*Coefficients*	*Standard Error*	*t Stat*	*P-value*	
11	Intercept	3.505122916	0.303616403	11.54458	1.53E-08	
12	nea	-0.003441487	0.00074141	-4.64182	0.000381	
13						

Output / nea data

116

(a) Use your calculator to find the mean and standard deviation of both sea surface temperature x and growth y and the correlation r between x and y. Use these basic measures to find the equation of the least-squares line for predicting y from x.

(b) Enter the data into your software or calculator and use the regression function to find the least-squares line. The result should agree with your work in (a) up to roundoff error.

5.4 Do heavier people burn more energy? We have data on the lean body mass and resting metabolic rate for 12 women who are subjects in a study of dieting. Lean body mass, given in kilograms, is a person's weight leaving out all fat. Metabolic rate, in calories burned per 24 hours, is the rate at which the body consumes energy. 🔴 METABOLIC

Mass	36.1	54.6	48.5	42.0	50.6	42.0	40.3	33.1	42.4	34.5	51.1	41.2
Rate	995	1425	1396	1418	1502	1256	1189	913	1124	1052	1347	1204

(a) Make a scatterplot that shows how metabolic rate depends on body mass. There is a quite strong linear relationship, with correlation $r = 0.876$.

(b) Find the least-squares regression line for predicting metabolic rate from body mass. Add this line to your scatterplot.

(c) Explain in words what the slope of the regression line tells us.

(d) Another woman has a lean body mass of 45 kilograms. What is her predicted metabolic rate?

FACTS ABOUT LEAST-SQUARES REGRESSION

One reason for the popularity of least-squares regression lines is that they have many convenient properties. Here are some facts about least-squares regression lines.

Fact 1. The distinction between explanatory and response variables is essential in regression. Least-squares regression makes the distances of the data points from the line small only in the y direction. If we reverse the roles of the two variables, we get a different least-squares regression line.

Fact 2. The least-squares regression line always passes through the point $(\bar{x}, \bar{y})$ on the graph of y against x.

Fact 3. The correlation r describes the strength of a straight-line relationship. In the regression setting, this description takes a specific form: **the square of the correlation, r^2, is the fraction of the variation in the values of y that is explained by the least-squares regression of y on x.**

The idea is that when there is a linear relationship, some of the variation in y is accounted for by the fact that as x changes it pulls y along with it. More exactly, the predicted response $\hat{y}$ moves along the regression line as we move x from one end of its scale to the other. This is the variation in y that is explained by regression. Unless all the data points lie exactly on a line, there is additional variation in the actual response y that appears as the scatter of points above and below the line. Although we will skip the algebra, it's possible to write

$$r^2 = \frac{\text{variation in } \hat{y} \text{ as } x \text{ pulls it along the line}}{\text{total variation in observed values of } y}$$

EXAMPLE 5.3 Using r^2

For the NEA data, $r = -0.7786$ and $r^2 = (-0.7786)^2 = 0.6062$. About 61% of the variation in fat gained is accounted for by the linear relationship with change in NEA. The other 39% is individual variation among subjects that is not explained by the linear relationship.

Figure 4.2 (page 96) shows a stronger linear relationship between boat registrations in Florida and manatees killed by boats. The correlation is $r = 0.951$ and $r^2 = (0.951)^2 = 0.904$. Slightly more than 90% of the year-to-year variation in number of manatees killed by boats is explained by regression on number of boats registered. Only about 10% is variation among years with similar numbers of boats registered. ■

You can find a regression line for any relationship between two quantitative variables, but the usefulness of the line for prediction depends on the strength of the linear relationship. So r^2 is almost as important as the equation of the line in reporting a regression. All the outputs in Figure 5.2 include r^2, either in decimal form or as a percent.

Facts 2 and 3 are special properties of least-squares regression. They are not true for other methods of fitting a line to data.

APPLY YOUR KNOWLEDGE

5.5 How useful is regression? Figure 4.6 (page 104) displays the relationship between golfers' scores on the first and second rounds of the 2010 Masters Tournament. The correlation is $r = 0.347$. Exercise 4.25 (page 106) gives data on solar radiation (SRD) and concentration of dimethyl sulfide (DMS) over a region of the Mediterranean. The correlation is $r = 0.969$. Explain in simple language why knowing only these correlations enables you to say that prediction of DMS from SRD by a regression line will be much more accurate than prediction of a golfer's second-round score from his first-round score.

5.6 Feed the birds. Exercise 4.27 (page 106) gives data from a study in which canary parents cared both for their own babies and for those of other parents. Investigators looked at how the growth rate of the foster babies relative to the growth rate of the natural babies changed as the begging intensity for food by the foster babies increased over the begging intensity of the natural babies. If begging intensity is the main factor determining food received, with higher intensity leading to more food, one would expect the relative growth rate to increase as the difference in begging intensity increases. However, if both begging intensity and a preference for their own babies determine the amount of food received (and hence the relative growth rate), we might expect growth rate to increase initially as begging intensity increases but then to level off (or even decrease) as the parents begin to ignore further increases in begging by the foster babies. CANARIES

(a) Make a scatterplot of the data. Find the least-squares regression line for predicting relative growth rate of the foster brood from the difference in begging intensity between the foster brood and the actual babies of the parents and add this line to your plot. Should we *not* use the regression line for prediction in this setting?

(b) What is r^2? What does this value say about the success of the regression line in predicting relative growth rate?

RESIDUALS

One of the principles of data analysis is to look for an overall pattern and also for striking deviations from the pattern. A regression line describes the overall pattern of a linear relationship between an explanatory variable and a response variable. Deviations from this pattern appear in the scatter of the data points above and below the regression line. Because the vertical distances from the points to the line represent "left-over" variation in the response after fitting the regression line, we call these distances *residuals*.

RESIDUALS

A **residual** is the difference between an observed value of the response variable and the value predicted by the regression line. That is, a residual is the prediction error that remains after we have chosen the regression line:

$$\text{residual} = \text{observed } y - \text{predicted } y$$
$$= y - \hat{y}$$

EXAMPLE 5.4 I feel your pain

"Empathy" means being able to understand what others feel. To see how the brain expresses empathy, researchers recruited 16 couples in their midtwenties who were married or had been dating for at least two years. They zapped the man's hand with an electrode while the woman watched, and measured the activity in several parts of the woman's brain that would respond to her own pain. Brain activity was recorded as a fraction of the activity observed when the woman herself was zapped with the electrode. The women also completed a psychological test that measures empathy. Will women who score higher in empathy respond more strongly when their partner has a painful experience? Here are data for one brain region:[3]

Subject	1	2	3	4	5	6	7	8
Empathy score	38	53	41	55	56	61	62	48
Brain activity	−0.120	0.392	0.005	0.369	0.016	0.415	0.107	0.506
Subject	9	10	11	12	13	14	15	16
Empathy score	43	47	56	65	19	61	32	105
Brain activity	0.153	0.745	0.255	0.574	0.210	0.722	0.358	0.779

Figure 5.3 is a scatterplot, with empathy score as the explanatory variable x and brain activity as the response variable y. The plot shows a positive association. That is, women who score higher in empathy do indeed react more strongly to their partner's pain. The overall pattern is moderately linear, with correlation $r = 0.515$.

The line on the plot is the least-squares regression line of brain activity on empathy score. Its equation is

$$\hat{y} = -0.0578 + 0.00761x$$

For Subject 1, with empathy score 38, we predict

$$\hat{y} = -0.0578 + (0.00761)(38) = 0.231$$

This subject's actual brain activity level was −0.120. The residual is

$$\text{residual} = \text{observed } y - \text{predicted } y$$
$$= -0.120 - 0.231 = -0.351$$

The residual is negative because the data point lies below the regression line. The dashed line segment in Figure 5.3 shows the size of the residual. ■

FIGURE 5.3

Scatterplot of activity in a region of the brain that responds to pain versus score on a test of empathy, for Example 5.4. Brain activity is measured as the subject watches her partner experience pain. The line is the least-squares regression line.

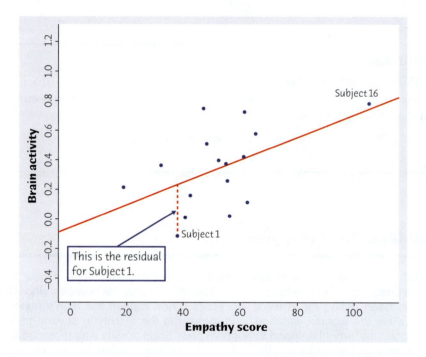

There is a residual for each data point. Finding the residuals is a bit unpleasant because you must first find the predicted response for every x. Software or a graphing calculator gives you the residuals all at once. Here are the 16 residuals for the empathy study data, from software:

```
residuals:
-0.3515  -0.2494  -0.3526  -0.3072  -0.1166  -0.1136  0.1231  0.1721
 0.0463   0.0080   0.0084   0.1983   0.4449   0.1369  0.3154  0.0374
```

Because the residuals show how far the data fall from our regression line, examining the residuals helps us assess how well the line describes the data. Although residuals can be calculated from any curve or line fitted to the data, the residuals from the least-squares line have a special property: **the mean of the least-squares residuals is always zero.**

Compare the scatterplot in Figure 5.3 with the *residual plot* for the same data in Figure 5.4. The horizontal line at zero in Figure 5.4 helps orient us. This "residual = 0" line corresponds to the regression line in Figure 5.3. A residual plot in effect turns the regression line horizontal and magnifies the deviations of the points from the line. This makes it easier to see unusual observations and patterns.

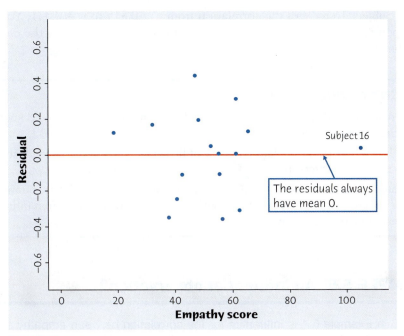

FIGURE 5.4

Residual plot for the data shown in Figure 5.3. The horizontal line at zero residual corresponds to the regression line in Figure 5.3.

RESIDUAL PLOTS

A **residual plot** is a scatterplot of the regression residuals against the explanatory variable. Residual plots help us assess how well a regression line fits the data.

APPLY YOUR KNOWLEDGE

5.7 Residuals by hand. In Exercise 5.3 (page 115) you found the equation of the least-squares line for predicting coral growth y from mean sea surface temperature x.

(a) Use the equation to obtain the 7 residuals step-by-step. That is, find the prediction $\hat{y}$ for each observation and then find the residual $y - \hat{y}$.

(b) Check that (up to roundoff error) the residuals add to 0.

(c) The residuals are the part of the response y left over after the straight-line tie between y and x is removed. Show that the correlation between the residuals and x is 0 (up to roundoff error). That this correlation is always 0 is another special property of least-squares regression.

INFLUENTIAL OBSERVATIONS

Figures 5.3 and 5.4 show one unusual observation. Subject 16 is an outlier in the x direction, with empathy score 40 points higher than any other subject. Because of its extreme position on the empathy scale, this point has a strong influence on the correlation.

Dropping Subject 16 reduces the correlation from $r = 0.515$ to $r = 0.331$. You can see that this point extends the linear pattern in Figure 5.3 and so increases the correlation. We say that Subject 16 is *influential* for calculating the correlation.

INFLUENTIAL OBSERVATIONS

An observation is **influential** for a statistical calculation if removing it would markedly change the result of the calculation.

The result of a statistical calculation may be of little practical use if it depends strongly on a few influential observations.

Points that are outliers in either the x or the y direction of a scatterplot are often influential for the correlation. Points that are outliers in the x direction are often influential for the least-squares regression line.

EXAMPLE 5.5 An influential observation?

Subject 16 in Example 5.4 is influential for the correlation between empathy score and brain activity because removing it reduces r from 0.515 to 0.331. Is this observation also influential for the least-squares line? Figure 5.5 shows that it is not. The regression line calculated without Subject 16 (dashed) differs little from the line that uses all the observations (solid). The reason that the outlier has little influence on the regression line is that it lies close to the dashed regression line calculated from the other observations. ▪

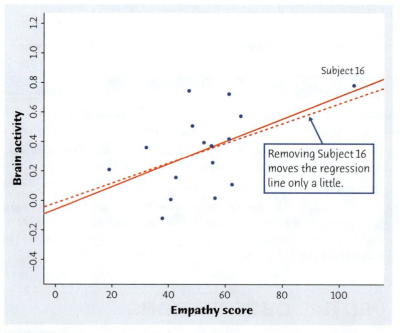

FIGURE 5.5

Subject 16 is an outlier in the x direction. The outlier is not influential for least-squares regression, because removing it moves the regression line only a little.

To see why points that are outliers in the *x* direction are often influential for regression, let's try an experiment. Suppose that Subject 16's point in the scatterplot moves straight down. What happens to the regression line? Figure 5.6 gives the answer. The dashed line is the regression line with the outlier in its new, lower position. Because there are no other points with similar *x*-values, the line chases the outlier. *An outlier in x pulls the least-squares line toward itself. If the outlier does not lie close to the line calculated from the other observations, it will be influential.*

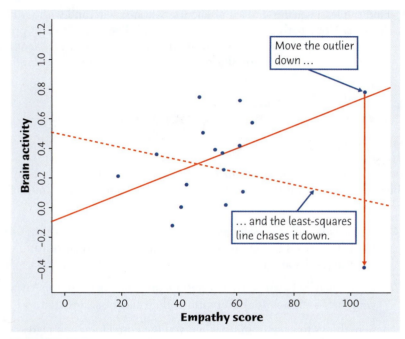

FIGURE 5.6

An outlier in the *x* direction pulls the least-squares line to itself because there are no other observations with similar values of *x* to hold the line in place. When the outlier moves down, the regression line chases it down. The original regression line is solid, and the final position of the regression line is dashed.

APPLY YOUR KNOWLEDGE

5.8 Do heavier people burn more energy? Return to the data of Exercise 5.4 (page 117) on lean body mass and metabolic rate. We will use these data to illustrate influence.

METABOLIC2

(a) Make a scatterplot of the data that is suitable for predicting metabolic rate from body mass, with two new points added. Point A: mass 42 kilograms, metabolic rate 1500 calories. Point B: mass 70 kilograms, metabolic rate 1400 calories. In which direction is each of these points an outlier?

(b) Add three least-squares regression lines to your plot: for the original 12 women, for the original women plus Point A, and for the original women plus Point B. Which new point is more influential for the regression line? Explain in simple language why each new point moves the line in the way your graph shows.

5.9 Outsourcing by airlines. Exercise 4.4 (page 94) gives data for 11 airlines on the percent of major maintenance outsourced and the percent of flight delays blamed on the airline. **AIRLINES**

(a) Make a scatterplot with outsourcing percent as x and delay percent as y. Would you consider Hawaiian Airlines to be influential?

(b) Find the correlation r with and without Hawaiian Airlines. How influential is the outlier for correlation?

(c) Find the least-squares line for predicting y from x with and without Hawaiian Airlines. Draw both lines on your scatterplot. Use both lines to predict the percent of delays blamed on an airline that has outsourced 74.7% of its major maintenance. How influential is the outlier for the least-squares line?

CAUTIONS ABOUT CORRELATION AND REGRESSION

Correlation and regression are powerful tools for describing the relationship between two variables. When you use these tools, you must be aware of their limitations. You already know that

- *Correlation and regression lines describe only linear relationships.* You can do the calculations for any relationship between two quantitative variables, but the results are useful only if the scatterplot shows a linear pattern.

- *Correlation and least-squares regression lines are not resistant.* Always plot your data and look for observations that may be influential.

Here are two more things to keep in mind when you use correlation and regression.

Beware extrapolation Suppose that you have data on a child's growth between 3 and 8 years of age. You find a strong linear relationship between age x and height y. If you fit a regression line to these data and use it to predict height at age 25 years, you will predict that the child will be 8 feet tall. Growth slows down and then stops at maturity, so extending the straight line to adult ages is foolish. *Few relationships are linear for all values of x. Don't make predictions far outside the range of x that actually appears in your data.*

EXTRAPOLATION

Extrapolation is the use of a regression line for prediction far outside the range of values of the explanatory variable x that you used to obtain the line. Such predictions are often not accurate.

 Beware the lurking variable Another caution is even more important: *the relationship between two variables can often be understood only by taking other variables into account. Lurking variables* can make a correlation or regression misleading.

LURKING VARIABLE

A **lurking variable** is a variable that is not among the explanatory or response variables in a study and yet may influence the interpretation of relationships among those variables.

You should always think about possible lurking variables before you draw conclusions based on correlation or regression.

EXAMPLE 5.6 Magic Mozart?

The Kalamazoo (Michigan) Symphony once advertised a "Mozart for Minors" program with this statement: "Question: Which students scored 51 points higher in verbal skills and 39 points higher in math? Answer: Students who had experience in music."[4]

We could as well answer "Students who played soccer." Why? Children with prosperous and well-educated parents are more likely than poorer children to have experience with music and also to play soccer. They are also likely to attend good schools, get good health care, and be encouraged to study hard. These advantages lead to high test scores. Family background is a lurking variable that explains why test scores are related to experience with music. ■

APPLY YOUR KNOWLEDGE

5.10 The endangered manatee. Table 4.1 gives 33 years of data on boats registered in Florida and manatees killed by boats. Figure 4.2 (page 96) shows a strong positive linear relationship. The correlation is $r = 0.951$. **MANATEES**

Photodisc

(a) Find the equation of the least-squares line for predicting manatees killed from thousands of boats registered. Because the linear pattern is so strong, we expect predictions from this line to be quite accurate—but only if conditions in Florida remain similar to those of the past 33 years.

(b) In 2009, experts predicted that the number of boats registered in Florida would be 975,000 in 2010. How many manatees do you predict would be killed by boats if there are 975,000 boats registered? Explain why we can trust this prediction.

(c) Predict manatee deaths if there were *no* boats registered in Florida. Explain why the predicted count of deaths is impossible. (We use $x = 0$ to find the intercept of the regression line, but unless the explanatory variable x actually takes values near 0, prediction for $x = 0$ is an example of extrapolation.)

5.11 Is math the key to success in college? A College Board study of 15,941 high school graduates found a strong correlation between how much math minority students took in high school and their later success in college. News articles quoted the head of the College Board as saying that "math is the gatekeeper for success in college."[5] Maybe so, but we should also think about lurking variables. What might lead minority students to take more or fewer high school math courses? Would these same factors influence success in college?

ASSOCIATION DOES NOT IMPLY CAUSATION

Thinking about lurking variables leads to the most important caution about correlation and regression. When we study the relationship between two variables, we often hope to show that changes in the explanatory variable *cause* changes in the response variable. *A strong association between two variables is not enough to draw conclusions about cause and effect.* Sometimes an observed association really does reflect cause and effect. A household that heats with natural gas uses more gas in colder months because cold weather requires burning more gas to stay warm. In other cases, an association is explained by lurking variables, and the conclusion that x causes y is either wrong or not proved.

EXAMPLE 5.7   Does having more cars make you live longer?

A serious study once found that people with two cars live longer than people who own only one car.[6] Owning three cars is even better, and so on. There is a substantial positive correlation between number of cars x and length of life y.

   The basic meaning of causation is that by changing x we can bring about a change in y. Could we lengthen our lives by buying more cars? No. The study used number of cars as a quick indicator of affluence. Well-off people tend to have more cars. They also tend to live longer, probably because they are better educated, take better care of themselves, and get better medical care. The cars have nothing to do with it. There is no cause-and-effect tie between number of cars and length of life. ■

Correlations such as that in Example 5.7 are sometimes called "nonsense correlations." The correlation is real. What is nonsense is the conclusion that changing one of the variables causes changes in the other. A lurking variable—such as personal affluence in Example 5.7—that influences both x and y can create a high correlation even though there is no direct connection between x and y.

ASSOCIATION DOES NOT IMPLY CAUSATION

An association between an explanatory variable x and a response variable y, even if it is very strong, is not by itself good evidence that changes in x actually cause changes in y.

EXAMPLE 5.8   Overweight mothers, overweight daughters

Overweight parents tend to have overweight children. The results of a study of Mexican American girls aged 9 to 12 years are typical. The investigators measured body mass index (BMI), a measure of weight relative to height, for both the girls and their mothers. People with high BMI are overweight. The correlation between the BMI of daughters and the BMI of their mothers was $r = 0.506$.[7]

Body type is in part determined by heredity. Daughters inherit half their genes from their mothers. There is therefore a direct cause-and-effect link between the BMI of mothers and daughters. But perhaps mothers who are overweight also set an example of little exercise, poor eating habits, and lots of television. Their daughters may pick up these habits, so the influence of heredity is mixed up with influences from the girls' environment. Both contribute to the mother-daughter correlation. ■

The lesson of Example 5.8 is that *even when direct causation is present, it may not be the whole explanation for a correlation*. You must still worry about lurking variables. The best way to get good evidence that x causes y is to do an **experiment** in which we change x and keep lurking variables under control. We will discuss experiments in Chapter 9.

experiment

EXAMPLE 5.9 Does smoking cause lung cancer?

Despite the difficulties, it is sometimes possible to build a strong case for causation in the absence of experiments. The evidence that smoking causes lung cancer is about as strong as nonexperimental evidence can be.

Doctors had long observed that most lung cancer patients were smokers. Comparison of smokers and "similar" nonsmokers showed a very strong association between smoking and death from lung cancer. Could the association be explained by lurking variables? Might there be, for example, a genetic factor that predisposes people both to nicotine addiction and to lung cancer? Smoking and lung cancer would then be positively associated even if smoking had no direct effect on the lungs. How were these objections overcome? ■

James Leynse/CORBIS

Let's answer this question in general terms: what are the criteria for establishing causation when we cannot do an experiment?

■ *The association is strong.* The association between smoking and lung cancer is very strong.

■ *The association is consistent.* Many studies of different kinds of people in many countries link smoking to lung cancer. That reduces the chance that a lurking variable specific to one group or one study explains the association.

■ *Higher doses are associated with stronger responses.* People who smoke more cigarettes per day or who smoke over a longer period get lung cancer more often. People who stop smoking reduce their risk.

■ *The alleged cause precedes the effect in time.* Lung cancer develops after years of smoking. The number of men dying of lung cancer rose as smoking became more common, with a lag of about 30 years. Lung cancer kills more men than any other form of cancer. Lung cancer was rare among women until women began to smoke. Lung cancer in women rose along with smoking, again with a lag of about 30 years, and has now passed breast cancer as the leading cause of cancer death among women.

■ *The alleged cause is plausible.* Experiments with animals show that tars from cigarette smoke do cause cancer.

Medical authorities do not hesitate to say that smoking causes lung cancer. The U.S. Surgeon General has long stated that cigarette smoking is "the largest avoidable cause of death and disability in the United States."[8] The evidence for causation is overwhelming—but it is not as strong as the evidence provided by well-designed experiments.

APPLY YOUR KNOWLEDGE

5.12 Another reason not to smoke? A stop-smoking booklet says, "Children of mothers who smoked during pregnancy scored nine points lower on intelligence tests at ages three and four than children of nonsmokers." Suggest some lurking variables that may help explain the association between smoking during pregnancy and children's later test scores. The association by itself is not good evidence that mothers' smoking *causes* lower scores.

5.13 Education and income. There is a strong positive association between workers' education and their income. For example, the U.S. Census Bureau reported in 2008 that the median income of young adults (ages 25 to 34) who worked full-time increased from $20,260 for those with less than a ninth-grade education, to $30,543 for high school graduates, to $46,932 for holders of a bachelor's degree, and on up for yet more education. In part, this association reflects causation—education helps people qualify for better jobs. Suggest several lurking variables that also contribute. (Ask yourself what kinds of people tend to get more education.)

5.14 To earn more, get married? Data show that men who are married, and also divorced or widowed men, earn quite a bit more than men the same age who have never been married. This does not mean that a man can raise his income by getting married, because men who have never been married are different from married men in many ways other than marital status. Suggest several lurking variables that might help explain the association between marital status and income.

CHAPTER 5 SUMMARY

CHAPTER SPECIFICS

■ A **regression line** is a straight line that describes how a response variable y changes as an explanatory variable x changes. You can use a regression line to **predict** the value of y for any value of x by substituting this x into the equation of the line.

■ The **slope** b of a regression line $\hat{y} = a + bx$ is the rate at which the predicted response $\hat{y}$ changes along the line as the explanatory variable x changes. Specifically, b is the change in $\hat{y}$ when x increases by 1 unit.

■ The **intercept** a of a regression line $\hat{y} = a + bx$ is the predicted response $\hat{y}$ when the explanatory variable $x = 0$. This prediction is of no practical interest unless x can actually take values near 0.

- The most common method of fitting a line to a scatterplot is least squares. The **least-squares regression line** is the straight line $\hat{y} = a + bx$ that minimizes the sum of the squares of the vertical distances of the observed points from the line.

- The least-squares regression line of y on x is the line with slope $b = rs_y/s_x$ and intercept $a = \bar{y} - b\bar{x}$. This line always passes through the point $(\bar{x}, \bar{y})$.

- **Correlation and regression** are closely connected. The correlation r and the regression slope b always have the same sign. The **square of the correlation r^2** is the fraction of the variation in one variable that is explained by least-squares regression on the other variable.

- Correlation and regression must be **interpreted with caution. Plot the data** to be sure the relationship is roughly linear and to detect outliers and influential observations. A plot of the **residuals** makes these effects easier to see.

- Look for **influential observations,** individual points that substantially change the correlation or the regression line. Outliers in either x or y can influence correlation. Outliers in the x direction are often influential for the regression line.

- Avoid **extrapolation,** the use of a regression line for prediction for values of the explanatory variable far outside the range of the data from which the line was calculated.

- **Lurking variables** may explain the relationship between the explanatory and response variables. Correlation and regression can be misleading if you ignore important lurking variables.

- Most of all, be careful not to conclude that there is a cause-and-effect relationship between two variables just because they are strongly associated. **High correlation does not imply causation.** The best evidence that an association is due to causation comes from an **experiment** in which the explanatory variable is directly changed and other influences on the response are controlled.

LINK IT

In this chapter we use the least-squares regression line to describe the straight-line relationship between two variables when such a pattern is seen in a scatterplot. The equation of the least-squares regression line is a numerical summary that makes precise the notion of "straight-line relationship."

To help us assess whether the least-squares regression line is a sensible description of the relationship between two variables, we examine residual plots. Outliers and, in particular, influential observations may indicate that the least-squares regression line is not a good description of this relationship.

Even if the least-squares regression line is a good description of the relationship between the observed values of two variables, we must exercise caution in how we interpret this relationship. Such interpretations rest on the assumption that the relationship is valid in some broader sense. We will explore this more carefully later in this book, but in this chapter we have issued some cautions. Association, as indicated by a large correlation, does not imply that there is an underlying cause-and-effect relation between the response and explanatory variables. There may, in fact, be a lurking variable that influences the interpretation of any relation between the response and explanatory variables. Finally, be careful not to use the least-squares regression line to make predictions outside the range of values of the explanatory variable that you used to obtain the line.

CHECK YOUR SKILLS

5.15 Figure 5.7 is a scatterplot of school GPA against IQ test scores for 15 seventh-grade students. The line is the least-squares regression line for predicting school GPA from IQ score. If another child in this class has an IQ score of 110, you predict the school GPA to be close to

(a) 2. (b) 7.5. (c) 11.

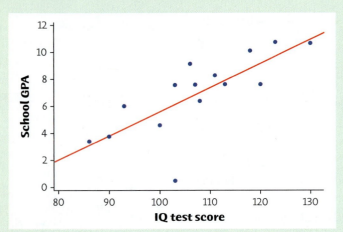

FIGURE 5.7

Scatterplot of IQ test scores and school GPA for 15 seventh-grade students, for Exercises 5.15 and 5.16.

5.16 The slope of the line in Figure 5.7 is closest to

(a) −11. (b) 0.2. (c) 2.0.

5.17 Smokers don't live as long (on the average) as non-smokers, and heavy smokers don't live as long as light smokers. You regress the age at death of a group of male smokers on the number of packs per day they smoked. The slope of your regression line

(a) will be greater than 0.

(b) will be less than 0.

(c) Can't tell without seeing the data.

5.18 An owner of a home in the Midwest installed solar panels to reduce heating costs. After installing the solar panels, he measured the amount of natural gas used y (in cubic feet) to heat the home and outside temperature x (in degree-days, where a day's degree-days are the number of degrees its average temperature falls below 65° F) over a 23-month period. He then computed the least-squares regression line for predicting y from x and found it to be[9]

$$\hat{y} = 85 + 16x$$

How much, on average, does gas used increase for each additional degree-day?

(a) 23 cubic feet

(b) 85 cubic feet

(c) 16 cubic feet

5.19 According to the regression line in Exercise 5.18, the predicted amount of gas used when the outside temperature is 20 degree-days is about

(a) 405 cubic feet.

(b) 320 cubic feet.

(c) 105 cubic feet.

5.20 By looking at the equation of the least-squares regression line in Exercise 5.18, you can see that the correlation between amount of gas used and degree-days is

(a) greater than zero.

(b) less than zero.

(c) Can't tell without seeing the data.

5.21 The software used to compute the least-squares regression line in Exercise 5.18 says that $r^2 = 0.98$. This suggests that

(a) although degree-days and gas used are correlated, degree-days does not predict gas used very accurately.

(b) gas used increases by $\sqrt{0.98} = 0.99$ cubic feet for each additional degree-day.

(c) prediction of gas used from degree-days will be quite accurate.

5.22 Because elderly people may have difficulty standing to have their heights measured, a study looked at predicting overall height from height to the knee. Here are data (in centimeters) for six elderly men: KNEEHT

Knee height x	57.7	47.4	43.5	44.8	55.2	54.6
Height y	192.1	153.3	146.4	162.7	169.1	177.8

Use your calculator or software: what is the equation of the least-squares regression line for predicting overall height from knee height?

(a) $\hat{y} = 42.9 + 2.5x$

(b) $\hat{y} = -3.4 + 0.3x$

(c) $\hat{y} = 2.5 + 42.9x$

CHAPTER 5 EXERCISES

5.23 Penguins diving. A study of king penguins looked for a relationship between how deep the penguins dive to seek food and how long they stay underwater.[10] There is a linear relationship that is different for different penguins. The study report gives a scatterplot for one penguin titled "The relation of dive duration (DD) to depth (D)." Duration DD is measured in minutes and depth D is in meters. The report then says, "The regression equation for this bird is: DD = 2.69 + 0.0138D."

(a) What is the slope of the regression line? Explain in specific language what this slope says about this penguin's dives.

(b) According to the regression line, how long does a typical dive to a depth of 200 meters last?

(c) The dives varied from 40 meters to 300 meters in depth. Plot the regression line from D = 40 to D = 300.

5.24 The price of diamond rings. A newspaper advertisement in the *Straits Times* of Singapore contained pictures of diamond rings and listed their prices, diamond weight (in carats), and gold purity. Based on data for only the 20-carat gold ladies' rings in the advertisement, the least-squares regression line for predicting price (in Singapore dollars) from the weight of the diamond (in carats) is[11]

$$price = 259.63 + 3721.02 \text{ carats}$$

(a) What does the slope of this line say about the relationship between price and number of carats?

(b) What is the predicted price when number of carats = 0? How would you interpret this price?

5.25 Does social rejection hurt? Exercise 4.37 (page 109) gives data from a study that shows that social exclusion causes "real pain." That is, activity in an area of the brain that responds to physical pain goes up as distress from social exclusion goes up. A scatterplot shows a moderately strong linear relationship. Figure 5.8 shows Minitab regression output for these data. ⬛ REJECTION

(a) What is the equation of the least-squares regression line for predicting brain activity from social distress score? Use the equation to predict brain activity for a social distress score of 2.0.

(b) What percent of the variation in brain activity among these subjects is explained by the straight-line relationship with social distress score?

(c) Use the information in Figure 5.8 to find the correlation *r* between social distress score and brain activity. How do you know whether the sign of *r* is + or −?

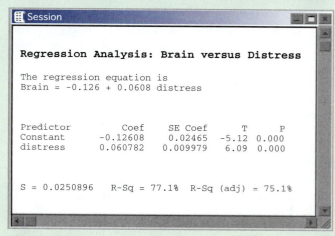

FIGURE 5.8

Minitab regression output for a study of the effects of social rejection on brain activity, for Exercise 5.25.

5.26 Toucan beaks. Exercise 4.36 (page 109) gives data on beak heat loss, as a percent of total body heat loss from all sources, at various temperatures. The data show that beak heat loss is higher at higher temperatures and that the relationship is roughly linear. Figure 5.9 shows Minitab regression output for these data. ⬛ TOUCAN

(a) What is the equation of the least-squares regression line for predicting beak heat loss, as a percent of total body heat loss from all sources, from temperature? Use the equation to predict beak heat loss, as a percent of total body heat loss from all sources, at a temperature of 25 degrees Celsius.

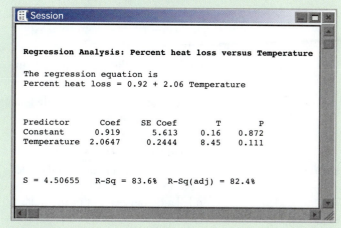

FIGURE 5.9

Minitab regression output for a study of how temperature affects beak heat loss in toucans, for Exercise 5.26.

(b) What percent of the variation in beak heat loss is explained by the straight-line relationship with temperature?

(c) Use the information in Figure 5.9 to find the correlation r between beak heat loss and temperature. How do you know whether the sign of r is + or −?

5.27 Husbands and wives. The mean height of American women in their twenties is about 64.3 inches, and the standard deviation is about 2.7 inches. The mean height of men the same age is about 69.9 inches, with standard deviation about 3.1 inches. Suppose that the correlation between the heights of husbands and wives is about $r = 0.5$.

(a) What are the slope and intercept of the regression line of the husband's height on the wife's height in young couples?

(b) Draw a graph of this regression line for heights of wives between 56 and 72 inches. Predict the height of the husband of a woman who is 67 inches tall, and plot the wife's height and predicted husband's height on your graph.

(c) You don't expect this prediction for a single couple to be very accurate. Why not?

5.28 What's my grade? In Professor Krugman's economics course the correlation between the students' total scores prior to the final examination and their final-examination scores is $r = 0.5$. The pre-exam totals for all students in the course have mean 280 and standard deviation 40. The final-exam scores have mean 75 and standard deviation 8. Professor Krugman has lost Julie's final exam but knows that her total before the exam was 300. He decides to predict her final-exam score from her pre-exam total.

(a) What is the slope of the least-squares regression line of final-exam scores on pre-exam total scores in this course? What is the intercept?

(b) Use the regression line to predict Julie's final-exam score.

(c) Julie doesn't think this method accurately predicts how well she did on the final exam. Use r^2 to argue that her actual score could have been much higher (or much lower) than the predicted value.

5.29 Going to class. A study of class attendance and grades among first-year students at a state university showed that in general students who attended a higher percent of their classes earned higher grades. Class attendance explained 16% of the variation in grade index among the students. What is the numerical value of the correlation between percent of classes attended and grade index?

5.30 Sisters and brothers. How strongly do physical characteristics of sisters and brothers correlate? Here are data on the heights (in inches) of 12 adult pairs:[12] BROSIS

Brother	71	68	66	67	70	71	70	73	72	65	66	70
Sister	69	64	65	63	65	62	65	64	66	59	62	64

(a) Use your calculator or software to find the correlation and the equation of the least-squares line for predicting sister's height from brother's height. Make a scatterplot of the data and add the regression line to your plot.

(b) Damien is 70 inches tall. Predict the height of his sister Tonya. Based on the scatterplot and the correlation r, do you expect your prediction to be very accurate? Why?

5.31 Sparrowhawk colonies. One of nature's patterns connects the percent of adult birds in a colony that return from the previous year and the number of new adults that join the colony. Here are data for 13 colonies of sparrowhawks:[13]

 SPARROWHAWKS

Percent return x	74	66	81	52	73	62	52
New adults y	5	6	8	11	12	15	16
Percent return x	45	62	46	60	46	38	
New adults y	17	18	18	19	20	20	

You saw in Exercise 4.23 that there is a moderately strong linear relationship, with correlation $r = -0.748$.

(a) Find the least-squares regression line for predicting y from x. Make a scatterplot and draw your line on the plot.

(b) Explain in words what the slope of the regression line tells us.

(c) An ecologist uses the line, based on 13 colonies, to predict how many new birds will join another colony, to which 60% of the adults from the previous year return. What is the prediction?

5.32 Our brains don't like losses. Exercise 4.24 (page 105) describes an experiment that showed a linear relationship between how sensitive people are to monetary losses ("behavioral loss aversion") and activity in one part of their brains ("neural loss aversion"). LOSSES

(a) Make a scatterplot with neural loss aversion as x and behavioral loss aversion as y. One point is a high outlier in both the x and y directions.

(b) Find the least-squares line for predicting y from x, *leaving out the outlier*, and add the line to your plot.

(c) The outlier lies very close to your regression line. Looking at the plot, you now expect that adding the outlier will increase the correlation but will have little effect on the least-squares line. Explain why.

(d) Find the correlation and the equation of the least-squares line with and without the outlier. Your results verify the expectations from (c).

5.33 Keeping water clean. Keeping water supplies clean requires regular measurement of levels of pollutants. The measurements are indirect—a typical analysis involves forming a dye by a chemical reaction with the dissolved pollutant, then passing light through the solution and measuring its "absorbence." To calibrate such measurements, the laboratory measures known standard solutions and uses regression to relate absorbence and pollutant concentration. This is usually done every day. Here is one series of data on the absorbence for different levels of nitrates. Nitrates are measured in milligrams per liter of water.[14] **NITRATES**

Nitrates	50	50	100	200	400
Absorbence	7.0	7.5	12.8	24.0	47.0
Nitrates	800	1200	1600	2000	2000
Absorbence	93.0	138.0	183.0	230.0	226.0

(a) Chemical theory says that these data should lie on a straight line. If the correlation is not at least 0.997, something went wrong and the calibration procedure is repeated. Plot the data and find the correlation. Must the calibration be done again?

(b) The calibration process sets nitrate level and measures absorbence. The linear relationship that results is used to estimate the nitrate level in water from a measurement of absorbence. What is the equation of the line used to estimate nitrate level? What is the estimated nitrate level in a water specimen with absorbence 40?

(c) Do you expect estimates of nitrate level from absorbence to be quite accurate? Why?

5.34 Always plot your data! Table 5.1 presents four sets of data prepared by the statistician Frank Anscombe to illustrate the dangers of calculating without first plotting the data.[15] **ANSCOMBECA**

(a) Without making scatterplots, find the correlation and the least-squares regression line for each of the four data sets. What do you notice? Use the regression line to predict y for $x = 10$. **ANSCOMBECB**

(b) Make a scatterplot for each of the data sets and add the regression line to each plot. **ANSCOMBECC**

(c) In which of the four cases would you be willing to use the regression line to describe the dependence of y on x? Explain your answer in each case. **ANSCOMBECD**

5.35 Managing diabetes. People with diabetes measure their fasting plasma glucose (FPG) after fasting for at least 8 hours. Another measurement, made at regular medical checkups, is called HbA. This is roughly the percent of red blood cells that have a glucose molecule attached. It measures average exposure to glucose over a period of several months. Table 5.2 gives data on both HbA and FPG for 18 diabetics five months after they had completed a diabetes education class.[16]

TABLE 5.1 Four data sets for exploring correlation and regression

					DATA SET A						
x	10	8	13	9	11	14	6	4	12	7	5
y	8.04	6.95	7.58	8.81	8.33	9.96	7.24	4.26	10.84	4.82	5.68

					DATA SET B						
x	10	8	13	9	11	14	6	4	12	7	5
y	9.14	8.14	8.74	8.77	9.26	8.10	6.13	3.10	9.13	7.26	4.74

					DATA SET C						
x	10	8	13	9	11	14	6	4	12	7	5
y	7.46	6.77	12.74	7.11	7.81	8.84	6.08	5.39	8.15	6.42	5.73

					DATA SET D						
x	8	8	8	8	8	8	8	8	8	8	19
y	6.58	5.76	7.71	8.84	8.47	7.04	5.25	5.56	7.91	6.89	12.50

TABLE 5.2 Two measures of glucose level in diabetics

SUBJECT	HbA (%)	FPG (mg/ml)	SUBJECT	HbA (%)	FPG (mg/ml)	SUBJECT	HbA (%)	FPG (mg/ml)
1	6.1	141	7	7.5	96	13	10.6	103
2	6.3	158	8	7.7	78	14	10.7	172
3	6.4	112	9	7.9	148	15	10.7	359
4	6.8	153	10	8.7	172	16	11.2	145
5	7.0	134	11	9.4	200	17	13.7	147
6	7.1	95	12	10.4	271	18	19.3	255

(a) Make a scatterplot with HbA as the explanatory variable. There is a positive linear relationship, but it is surprisingly weak.

(b) Subject 15 is an outlier in the y direction. Subject 18 is an outlier in the x direction. Find the correlation for all 18 subjects, for all except Subject 15, and for all except Subject 18. Are either or both of these subjects influential for the correlation? Explain in simple language why r changes in opposite directions when we remove each of these points.

5.36 The effect of changing units. The equation of a regression line, unlike the correlation, depends on the units we use to measure the explanatory and response variables. Here are data on knee height and overall height (in centimeters) for six elderly men: **KNEEHT2**

Knee height x	57.7	47.4	43.5	44.8	55.2	54.6
Height y	192.1	153.3	146.4	162.7	169.1	177.8

(a) Find the equation of the regression line for predicting overall height in centimeters from knee height in centimeters.

(b) A mad scientist decides to measure knee height in millimeters and height in meters. The same data in these units are

Knee height x	577	474	435	448	552	546
Height y	1.921	1.533	1.464	1.627	1.691	1.778

Find the equation of the regression line for predicting overall height in meters from knee height in millimeters.

(c) Use both lines to predict the overall height of a man whose knee height is 50 centimeters, which is the same as 500 millimeters. Use the fact that there are 100 centimeters in a meter to show that the two predictions are the same (up to roundoff error).

5.37 Managing diabetes, continued. Add three regression lines for predicting FPG from HbA to your scatterplot from Exercise 5.35: for all 18 subjects, for all except Subject 15, and for all except Subject 18. Is either Subject 15 or Subject 18 strongly influential for the least-squares line? Explain in simple language what features of the scatterplot explain the degree of influence. **DIABETES**

5.38 Do artificial sweeteners cause weight gain? People who use artificial sweeteners in place of sugar tend to be heavier than people who use sugar. Does this mean that artificial sweeteners cause weight gain? Give a more plausible explanation for this association.

5.39 Learning online. Many colleges offer online versions of courses that are also taught in the classroom. It often happens that the students who enroll in the online version do better than the classroom students on the course exams. This does not show that online instruction is more effective than classroom teaching, because the people who sign up for online courses are often quite different from the classroom students. Suggest some differences between online and classroom students that might explain why online students do better.

5.40 Some regression math. Use the equation of the least-squares regression line (box on page 115) to show that the regression line for predicting y from x always passes through the point $(\bar{x}, \bar{y})$. That is, when $x = \bar{x}$, the equation gives $\hat{y} = \bar{y}$.

5.41 Regression to the mean. Figure 4.6 (page 104) displays the relationship between golfers' scores on the first and second rounds of the 2010 Masters Tournament. The least-squares line for predicting second-round scores from first-round scores has equation $\hat{y} = 52.74 + 0.297x$. Find the predicted second-round scores for a player who shot 80 in the first round and for a player who shot 70. The mean second-round score for all players was 74.48. So a player who does well in the first round is predicted to do less well, but still better than average, in the second round. And a player who does poorly in the first is predicted to do better, but still worse than average, in the second.

(*Comment:* This is **regression to the mean.** If you select individuals with extreme scores on some measure, they tend to have less extreme scores when measured again. That's because their extreme position is partly merit and partly luck. The luck will be different next time. Regression to the mean contributes to lots of "effects." The rookie of the year often doesn't do as well the next year; a student who feels she needs coaching after taking the SAT often does better on the next try without coaching.)

*The following exercises ask you to answer questions from data without having the details outlined for you. The exercise statements give you the **State** step of the four-step process. In your work, follow the **Plan, Solve,** and **Conclude** steps of the process, described on page 56.*

5.42 Beavers and beetles. Do beavers benefit beetles? Researchers laid out 23 circular plots, each 4 meters in diameter, in an area where beavers were cutting down cottonwood trees. In each plot, they counted the number of stumps from trees cut by beavers and the number of clusters of beetle larvae. Ecologists think that the new sprouts from stumps are more tender than other cottonwood growth, so that beetles prefer them. If so, more stumps should produce more beetle larvae. Here are the data:[17]

BEAVERS

Stumps	2	2	1	3	3	4	3	1	2	5	1	3
Beetle larvae	10	30	12	24	36	40	43	11	27	56	18	40
Stumps	2	1	2	2	1	1	4	1	2	1	4	
Beetle larvae	25	8	21	14	16	6	54	9	13	14	50	

Analyze these data to see if they support the "beavers benefit beetles" idea.

5.43 A computer game. A multimedia statistics learning system includes a test of skill in using the computer's mouse. The software displays a circle at a random location on the computer screen. The subject clicks in the circle with the mouse as quickly as possible. A new circle appears as soon as the subject clicks the old one. Table 5.3

TABLE 5.3 Reaction times (in milliseconds) in a computer game

TIME	DISTANCE	HAND	TIME	DISTANCE	HAND
115	190.70	right	240	190.70	left
96	138.52	right	190	138.52	left
110	165.08	right	170	165.08	left
100	126.19	right	125	126.19	left
111	163.19	right	315	163.19	left
101	305.66	right	240	305.66	left
111	176.15	right	141	176.15	left
106	162.78	right	210	162.78	left
96	147.87	right	200	147.87	left
96	271.46	right	401	271.46	left
95	40.25	right	320	40.25	left
96	24.76	right	113	24.76	left
96	104.80	right	176	104.80	left
106	136.80	right	211	136.80	left
100	308.60	right	238	308.60	left
113	279.80	right	316	279.80	left
123	125.51	right	176	125.51	left
111	329.80	right	173	329.80	left
95	51.66	right	210	51.66	left
108	201.95	right	170	201.95	left

gives data for one subject's trials, 20 with each hand. Distance is the distance from the cursor location to the center of the new circle, in units whose actual size depends on the size of the screen. Time is the time required to click in the new circle, in milliseconds.[18] We suspect that time depends on distance. We also suspect that performance will not be the same with the right and left hands. Analyze the data with a view to predicting performance separately for the two hands. COMPUTER GAME

5.44 Predicting tropical storms. William Gray heads the Tropical Meteorology Project at Colorado State University (well away from the hurricane belt). His forecasts before each year's hurricane season attract lots of attention. Here are data on the number of named Atlantic tropical storms predicted by Dr. Gray and the actual number of storms for the years 1984 to 2010:[19] STORM2

Year	Forecast	Actual	Year	Forecast	Actual
1984	10	12	1998	10	14
1985	11	11	1999	14	12
1986	8	6	2000	12	14
1987	8	7	2001	12	15
1988	11	12	2002	11	12
1989	7	11	2003	14	16
1990	11	14	2004	14	14
1991	8	8	2005	15	27
1992	8	6	2006	17	10
1993	11	8	2007	17	14
1994	9	7	2008	15	16
1995	12	19	2009	11	9
1996	10	13	2010	18	19
1997	11	7			

Analyze these data. How accurate are Dr. Gray's forecasts? How many tropical storms would you expect in a year when his preseason forecast calls for 16 storms? What is the effect of the disastrous 2005 season on your answers?

5.45 Great Arctic rivers. One effect of global warming is to increase the flow of water into the Arctic Ocean from rivers. Such an increase may have major effects on the world's climate. Six rivers (Yenisey, Lena, Ob, Pechora, Kolyma, and Severnaya Dvina) drain two-thirds of the Arctic in Europe and Asia. Several of these are among the largest rivers on earth. Table 5.4 presents the total discharge from

TABLE 5.4 Arctic river discharge (cubic kilometers), 1936 to 2008

YEAR	DISCHARGE	YEAR	DISCHARGE	YEAR	DISCHARGE	YEAR	DISCHARGE
1936	1721	1955	1656	1974	2000	1993	1845
1937	1713	1956	1721	1975	1928	1994	1902
1938	1860	1957	1762	1976	1653	1995	1842
1939	1739	1958	1936	1977	1698	1996	1849
1940	1615	1959	1906	1978	2008	1997	2007
1941	1838	1960	1736	1979	1970	1998	1903
1942	1762	1961	1970	1980	1758	1999	1970
1943	1709	1962	1849	1981	1774	2000	1905
1944	1921	1963	1774	1982	1728	2001	1890
1945	1581	1964	1606	1983	1920	2002	2085
1946	1834	1965	1735	1984	1823	2003	1780
1947	1890	1966	1883	1985	1822	2004	1900
1948	1898	1967	1642	1986	1860	2005	1930
1949	1958	1968	1713	1987	1732	2006	1910
1950	1830	1969	1742	1988	1906	2007	2270
1951	1864	1970	1751	1989	1932	2008	2078
1952	1829	1971	1879	1990	1861		
1953	1652	1972	1736	1991	1801		
1954	1589	1973	1861	1992	1793		

these rivers each year from 1936 to 2008. Discharge is measured in cubic kilometers of water. Analyze these data to uncover the nature and strength of the trend in total discharge over time. ARCTIC

5.46 Will women outrun men? Does the physiology of women make them better suited than men to long-distance

running? Will women eventually outperform men in long-distance races? Researchers examined data on world record times (in seconds) for men and women in the marathon. Based on these data, researchers (in 1992) attempted to predict when women would outrun men in the marathon. Here are data for women:[21]

Year	1926	1964	1967	1970	1971	1974	1975
Time	13,222.0	11,973.0	11,246.0	10,973.0	9990.0	9834.5	9499.0
Year	1977	1980	1981	1982	1983	1985	
Time	9287.5	9027.0	8806.0	8771.0	8563.0	8466.0	

Here are data for men:

Year	1908	1909	1913	1920	1925	1935	1947
Time	10,518.4	9751.0	9366.6	9155.8	8941.8	8802.0	8739.0
Year	1952	1953	1954	1958	1960	1963	1964
Time	8442.2	8314.8	8259.4	8117.0	8116.2	8068.0	7931.2
Year	1965	1967	1969	1981	1984	1985	1988
Time	7920.0	7776.4	7713.6	7698.0	7685.0	7632.0	7610.0

Analyze these data using least-squares regression to estimate when men and women's record times will be equal. How reliable is your estimate?

 EXPLORING THE WEB

5.47 Association and causation. Find an example of a study in which the issue of association and causation is present. This can be either an example in which association is confused with causation or an example in which the association is not confused with causation. Summarize the study and its conclusions in your own words. Be sure to include either a copy of the actual article or at least the Web source, title, and where the article was published. The *Chance News* Web site at www.causeweb.org/wiki/chance/index.php/Main_Page is a good place to look for examples.

5.48 Predicting batting averages. Go to www.mlb.com and find the batting averages for a diverse set of 30 players for both the 2010 and 2011 seasons. You can click on the Stats tab to find the results for the current season as well as historical data. You should select only players who played in at least 50 games both seasons. Make a scatterplot of the batting averages using the 2010 season average as the explanatory variable and the 2011 season average as the response. Is it reasonable to fit a straight line to these data? If so, find the least-squares regression line for predicting batting average in 2011 from that in 2010 based on your sample of

30 players. In 2010, the major league leader in batting was Joe Mauer, who had a batting average of .365. What does your least-squares regression line predict for the 2011 batting average of someone who hit .365 in 2010? Is the 2011 predicted batting average higher or lower than .365?

5.49 Predicting the federal budget. Go to the Congressional Budget Office Web site, www.cbo.gov/topics/budget/budget-projections/reports. Click on the Updated Budget Projections report. Next, find the Budget Projections Excel file in the left hand column. What is the current prediction for the federal budget in five years' time? Is a surplus or a deficit predicted? Do you think this prediction is accurate? Why or why not?

Luc Beziat/Getty Images

Two-Way Tables

We have concentrated on relationships in which at least the response variable is quantitative. Now we will describe relationships between two categorical variables. Some variables—such as sex, race, and occupation—are categorical by nature. Other categorical variables are created by grouping values of a quantitative variable into classes. Published data often appear in grouped form to save space. To analyze categorical data, we use the *counts* or *percents* of individuals that fall into various categories.

EXAMPLE 6.1 I think I'll be rich by age 30

A sample survey of young adults (aged 19 to 25) asked, "What do you think are the chances you will have much more than a middle-class income at age 30?" Table 6.1 shows the responses, omitting a few people who refused to respond or who said they were already rich.[1] This is a **two-way table** because it describes two categorical variables: sex and opinion about becoming rich. Opinion is the **row variable** because each row in the table describes young adults who held one of the five opinions about their chances. Because the opinions have a natural order from "Almost no chance" to "Almost certain," the rows are also in this order. Sex is the **column variable** because each column describes one sex. The entries in the table are the counts of individuals in each opinion-by-sex class. ■

two-way table

row and column variables

139

TABLE 6.1 Young adults by sex and chance of getting rich

| | SEX | | |
OPINION	FEMALE	MALE	TOTAL
Almost no chance	96	98	194
Some chance but probably not	426	286	712
A 50-50 chance	696	720	1416
A good chance	663	758	1421
Almost certain	486	597	1083
Total	2367	2459	4826

MARGINAL DISTRIBUTIONS

How can we best grasp the information contained in Table 6.1? First, *look at the distribution of each variable separately*. The distribution of a categorical variable says how often each outcome occurred. The "Total" column at the right of the table contains the totals for each of the rows. These row totals give the distribution of opinions about becoming rich in the entire group of 4826 young adults: 194 felt that they had almost no chance, 712 thought they had just some chance, and so on.

marginal distribution

If the row and column totals are missing, the first thing to do in studying a two-way table is to calculate them. The distributions of opinion alone and sex alone are called **marginal distributions** because they appear at the right and bottom margins of the two-way table.

Percents are often more informative than counts. We can display the marginal distribution of opinions in percents by dividing each row total by the table total and converting to a percent.

EXAMPLE 6.2 Calculating a marginal distribution

The percent of these young adults who think they are almost certain to be rich by age 30 is

$$\frac{\text{almost certain total}}{\text{table total}} = \frac{1083}{4826} = 0.224 = 22.4\%$$

Do four more such calculations to obtain the marginal distribution of opinion in percents. Here is the complete distribution:

Response	Percent
Almost no chance	$\frac{194}{4826} = 4.0\%$
Some chance	$\frac{712}{4826} = 14.8\%$
A 50-50 chance	$\frac{1416}{4826} = 29.3\%$
A good chance	$\frac{1421}{4826} = 29.4\%$
Almost certain	$\frac{1083}{4826} = 22.4\%$

It seems that many young adults are optimistic about their future income. The total should be 100% because everyone holds one of the five opinions. In fact, the percents add to 99.9% because we rounded each one to the nearest tenth. This is **roundoff error.** ■

Each marginal distribution from a two-way table is a distribution for a single categorical variable. As we saw in Chapter 1, we can use a bar graph or a pie chart to display such a distribution. Figure 6.1 is a bar graph of the distribution of opinion among young adults.

In working with two-way tables, you must calculate lots of percents. Here's a tip to help you decide what fraction gives the percent you want. Ask, "What group represents the total of which I want a percent?" The count for that group is the denominator of the fraction that leads to the percent. In Example 6.2, we want a percent "of young adults," so the count of young adults (the table total) is the denominator.

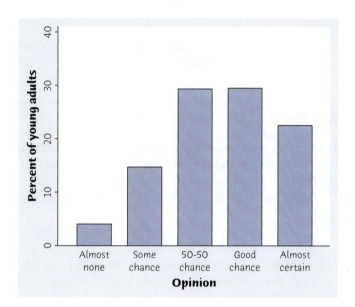

FIGURE 6.1

Bar graph of the distribution of opinions of young adults about becoming rich by age 30. This is one of the marginal distributions for Table 6.1.

APPLY YOUR KNOWLEDGE

6.1 Video-gaming and grades. The popularity of computer, video, online, and virtual reality games has raised concerns about their ability to negatively impact youth. The data in this exercise are based on a recent survey of 14- to 18-year-olds in Connecticut high schools. Here are the grade distributions of boys who have and have not played video games:[2] 🎮 GAMING

Keith Bedford/The New York Times/Redux

	Grade Average		
	A's and B's	C's	D's and F's
Played games	736	450	193
Never played games	205	144	80

(a) How many people does this table describe? How many of these have played video games?

(b) Give the marginal distribution of the grades. What percent of the boys represented in the table received a grade of C or lower?

6.2 Undergraduates' ages. Here is a two-way table of U.S. Census Bureau data describing the age and sex of all American undergraduate college students. The table entries are counts in thousands of students.[3] UNDERGRADAGES

Age group	Female	Male
15 to 19 years	2124	1876
20 to 24 years	2814	2648
25 to 34 years	703	536
35 years or older	518	159

(a) How many college undergraduates are there?

(b) Find the marginal distribution of age group. What percent of undergraduates are in the 20 to 24 college age group?

CONDITIONAL DISTRIBUTIONS

Table 6.1 contains much more information than the two marginal distributions of opinion alone and sex alone. *Marginal distributions tell us nothing about the relationship between two variables.* To describe a relationship between two categorical variables, we must calculate some well-chosen percents from the counts given in the body of the table.

Let's say that we want to compare the opinions of women and men. To do this, compare percents for women alone with percents for men alone. To study the opinions of women, we look only at the "Female" column in Table 6.1. To find the percent of *young women* who think they are almost certain to be rich by age 30, divide the count of such women by the total number of women (the column total):

$$\frac{\text{women who are almost certain}}{\text{column total}} = \frac{486}{2367} = 0.205 = 20.5\%$$

Doing this for all five entries in the "Female" column gives the *conditional distribution* of opinion among women. We use the term "conditional" because this distribution describes only young adults who satisfy the condition that they are female.

MARGINAL AND CONDITIONAL DISTRIBUTIONS

The **marginal distribution** of one of the categorical variables in a two-way table of counts is the distribution of values of that variable among all individuals described by the table.

A **conditional distribution** of a variable is the distribution of values of that variable among only individuals who have a given value of the other variable. There is a separate conditional distribution for each value of the other variable.

EXAMPLE 6.3 Comparing women and men

STATE: How do young men and young women differ in their responses to the question "What do you think are the chances you will have much more than a middle-class income at age 30?"

PLAN: Make a two-way table of response by sex. Find the two conditional distributions of response for men alone and for women alone. Compare these two distributions.

SOLVE: Table 6.1 is the two-way table we need. Look first at just the "Female" column to find the conditional distribution for women, then at just the "Male" column to find the conditional distribution for men. Here are the calculations and the two conditional distributions:

Response	Female	Male
Almost no chance	$\frac{96}{2367} = 4.1\%$	$\frac{98}{2459} = 4.0\%$
Some chance	$\frac{426}{2367} = 18.0\%$	$\frac{286}{2459} = 11.6\%$
A 50-50 chance	$\frac{696}{2367} = 29.4\%$	$\frac{720}{2459} = 29.3\%$
A good chance	$\frac{663}{2367} = 28.0\%$	$\frac{758}{2459} = 30.8\%$
Almost certain	$\frac{486}{2367} = 20.5\%$	$\frac{597}{2459} = 24.3\%$

Each set of percents adds to 100% because everyone holds one of the five opinions.

CONCLUDE: Men are somewhat more optimistic about their future income than are women. Men are less likely to say that they have "some chance but probably not" and more likely to say that they have "a good chance" or are "almost certain" to have much more than a middle-class income by age 30. ■

Software will do these calculations for you. Most programs allow you to choose which conditional distributions you want to compare. The output in Figure 6.2 presents the two conditional distributions of opinion, for women and for men, and also the marginal distribution of opinion for all the young adults. The distributions agree (up to roundoff) with the results in Examples 6.2 and 6.3.

Remember that there are two sets of conditional distributions for any two-way table. Example 6.3 looked at the conditional distributions of opinion for the two sexes. We could also examine the five conditional distributions of sex, one for each of the five opinions, by looking separately at the five rows in Table 6.1. Figure 6.3 makes this comparison in a bar graph. Each bar is divided (segmented) into two parts, represented by two colors. The lower portion of each bar represents the percent of women among young adults who hold each opinion. The upper portion represents the percent of men. Each bar has a height of 100%, because each bar represents all the young adults in each different group of people. Bar graphs like that in Figure 6.3 in which each bar is divided into parts, each part representing a different category, are sometimes called **segmented bar graphs.**

segmented bar graphs

No single graph (such as a scatterplot) portrays the form of the relationship between categorical variables. No single numerical measure (such as the correlation) summarizes the strength of the association. Bar graphs are flexible enough to be helpful, but you must think about what comparisons you want to display. For numerical measures, we rely on well-chosen percents. You must decide which percents you need. Here is a hint: *if there is an explanatory-response relationship, compare the conditional*

FIGURE 6.2

Minitab and CrunchIt! output for the two-way table of young adults by sex and chance of getting rich. Each entry in the Minitab output includes the percent of its column total. The "Female" and "Male" columns give the conditional distributions of responses for women and men, and the "All" column shows the marginal distribution of responses for all these young adults. Each entry in the CrunchIt! output includes the percent of its row total, the percent of its column total, and the percent of the entire table total. The second entry in each cell gives the conditional distribution of responses for the different opinions. The third entry in each cell for the "Female" and "Male" columns gives the conditional distributions of responses for women and men. The "All" row and column show the corresponding marginal distribution of responses for all these young adults.

Minitab

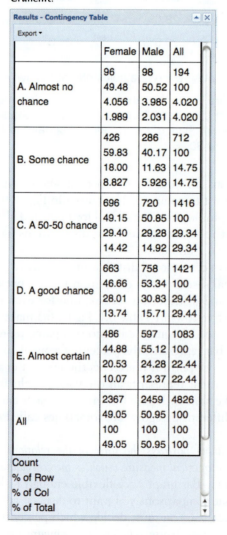

CrunchIt!

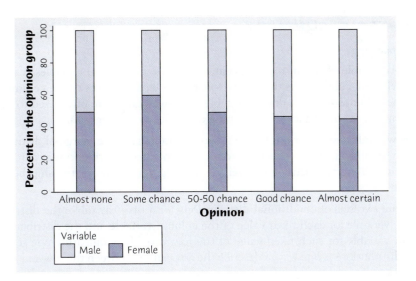

FIGURE 6.3
Bar graph comparing the percents of females and the percents of males among those who hold each opinion about their chances of getting rich by age 30.

distributions of the response variable for the separate values of the explanatory variable. If you think that sex influences young adults' opinions about their chances of getting rich by age 30, compare the conditional distributions of opinion for women and for men, as in Example 6.3.

APPLY YOUR KNOWLEDGE

6.3 Video-gaming and grades. Exercise 6.1 (page 141) gives data on the grade distribution of boys who have and have not played video games. The popularity of computer, video, online, and virtual reality games has raised concerns about their ability to negatively impact youth. Do those who play such games tend to do worse in school than those who do not play? To see the relationship between grades and game-playing experience, find the conditional distributions of grades (the response variable) for players and nonplayers. What do you conclude? 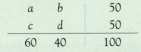 GAMING

6.4 Undergraduates' ages. Exercise 6.2 (page 142) gives U.S. Census Bureau data describing the age and sex of all American college undergraduates. We suspect that the percent of women is higher among students in the 25- to 34-year-old age group than in the 20- to 24-year-old age group. Do the data support this suspicion? Follow the four-step process as illustrated in Example 6.3. UNDERGRADAGES

6.5 Marginal distributions aren't the whole story. Here are the row and column totals for a two-way table with two rows and two columns:

a	*b*	50
c	*d*	50
60	40	100

Make up *two different* sets of counts *a*, *b*, *c*, and *d* for the body of the table that give these same totals. This shows that the relationship between two variables cannot be obtained from the two individual distributions of the variables.

CHAPTER 6 SUMMARY

CHAPTER SPECIFICS

- A **two-way table** of counts organizes data about two categorical variables. Values of the **row variable** label the rows that run across the table, and values of the **column variable** label the columns that run down the table. Two-way tables are often used to summarize large amounts of information by grouping outcomes into categories.

- The **row totals** and **column totals** in a two-way table give the **marginal distributions** of the two individual variables. It is clearer to present these distributions as percents of the table total. Marginal distributions tell us nothing about the relationship between the variables.

- There are two sets of **conditional distributions** for a two-way table: the distributions of the row variable for each fixed value of the column variable and the distributions of the column variable for each fixed value of the row variable. Comparing one set of conditional distributions is one way to describe the association between the row and the column variables.

- To find the **conditional distribution** of the row variable for one specific value of the column variable, look only at that one column in the table. Find each entry in the column as a percent of the column total.

- **Bar graphs** are a flexible means of presenting categorical data. There is no single best way to describe an association between two categorical variables.

LINK IT

In Chapters 4 and 5 we considered relationships between two quantitative variables. In this chapter we use two-way tables to describe relationships between two *categorical* variables. To explore relationships between two categorical variables, we examine their conditional distributions. The conditional distribution of one of the categorical variables is the distribution of that variable among only individuals who have a given value of the other variable. There is a separate conditional distribution for each value of this other variable. Changes in the pattern of the conditional distribution of one variable as the value of the other varies provide information about the relationship between the variables. No change in this pattern suggests that there is no relationship.

Although it provides no information about the relationship between two categorical variables, we can examine each variable separately by looking at its marginal distributions. The marginal distribution of one of the categorical variables is the distribution of values of that variable among all individuals described in the table. The marginal distributions allow us to see how frequently the values of each variable occur, ignoring the other variable.

CHECK YOUR SKILLS

The Pew Internet and American Life Project interviewed several hundred teens (ages 12 to 17). One question asked was "How often do you take your cell phone to school?" Here is a two-way table of the responses by how permissive the school is with regard to cell phone use:[4]

Frequency	Forbid	Allow in school but not in class	Allow in class
Never	25	19	4
Less often	14	31	6
At least several times per week	14	23	8
Every day	97	314	57

Exercises 6.6 to 6.14 are based on this table. CELLPHONE

6.6 How many individuals are described by this table?

    (a) 468   (b) 612   (c) Need more information

6.7 How many teens from schools that forbid cell phones were among the respondents?

    (a) 48   (b) 150   (c) Need more information

6.8 The percent of teens from schools that forbid cell phones among the respondents was

    (a) about 8%.   (b) about 25%.   (c) about 48%.

6.9 Your percent from the previous exercise is part of

    (a) the marginal distribution of school permissiveness.

    (b) the marginal distribution of the frequency that a teen brought a cell phone to school.

    (c) the conditional distribution of the frequency that a teen brought a cell phone to school among schools with a given level of permissiveness.

6.10 What percent of teens from schools that forbid cell phones brought their cell phone to school every day?

    (a) about 16%   (b) about 21%   (c) about 65%

6.11 Your percent from the previous exercise is part of

    (a) the marginal distribution of the frequency that a teen brought a cell phone to school.

    (b) the conditional distribution of school permissiveness among those who brought a cell phone to school every day.

    (c) the conditional distribution of the frequency that a teen brought a cell phone to school among schools that forbid cell phones.

6.12 What percent of those who brought their cell phone to school every day were from schools that forbid cell phones?

    (a) about 16%

    (b) about 21%

    (c) about 65%

6.13 Your percent from the previous exercise is part of

    (a) the marginal distribution of the frequency that a teen brought a cell phone to school.

    (b) the conditional distribution of school permissiveness among those who brought a cell phone to school every day.

    (c) the conditional distribution of the frequency that a teen brought a cell phone to school among schools with a given level of permissiveness.

6.14 A bar graph showing the conditional distribution of the frequency that a teen brought a cell phone to school among schools with a given level of permissiveness would have

    (a) 3 bars.   (b) 4 bars.   (c) 12 bars.

CHAPTER 6 EXERCISES

6.15 Is astrology scientific? The University of Chicago's General Social Survey (GSS) is the nation's most important social science sample survey. The GSS asked a random sample of adults their opinion about whether astrology is very scientific, sort of scientific, or not at all scientific. Here is a two-way table of counts for people in the sample who had three levels of higher education degrees:[5] ASTROLOGY

Opinion	Degree Held		
	Junior college	Bachelor	Graduate
Not at all scientific	87	198	111
Very or sort of scientific	43	57	28

Find the two conditional distributions of degree held, one for those who hold the opinion that astrology is not at all scientific and one for those who say astrology is very or sort of scientific. Based on your calculations, describe with a graph and in words the differences between those who say astrology is not at all scientific and those who say it is very or sort of scientific.

6.16 Weight-lifting injuries. Resistance training is a popular form of conditioning aimed at enhancing sports performance and is widely used among high school, college, and professional athletes, although its use for younger athletes is controversial. A random sample of 4111 patients between the ages of 8 and 30 admitted to U.S. emergency rooms with the injury code "weightlifting" was obtained. These injuries were classified as "accidental" if caused by dropped weight or improper equipment use. The patients were also classified into the four age categories 8 to 13 years, 14 to 18, 19 to 22, and 23 to 30. Here is a two-way table of the results:[6]

WEIGHTLIFTING

Age	Accidental	Not accidental
8–13	295	102
14–18	655	916
19–22	239	533
23–30	363	1008

Compare the distributions of ages for accidental and nonaccidental injuries. Use percents and draw a bar graph. What do you conclude?

Marital status and job level. *We sometimes hear that getting married is good for your career. Table 6.2 presents data from one of the studies behind this generalization. To avoid gender effects, the investigators looked only at men. The data describe the marital status and the job level of all 8235 male managers and professionals employed by a large manufacturing firm.[7] The firm assigns each position a grade that reflects the value of that particular job to the company. The authors of the study grouped the many job grades into quarters. Grade 1 contains jobs in the lowest quarter of the job grades, and Grade 4 contains those in the highest quarter. Exercises 6.17 to 6.21 are based on these data.* MARITALSTAT

TABLE 6.2   Marital status and job grade

JOB GRADE	MARITAL STATUS				TOTAL
	SINGLE	MARRIED	DIVORCED	WIDOWED	
1	58	874	15	8	955
2	222	3927	70	20	4239
3	50	2396	34	10	2490
4	7	533	7	4	551
Total	337	7730	126	42	8235

6.17 Marginal distributions. Give (in percents) the two marginal distributions, for marital status and for job grade. Do each of your two sets of percents add to exactly 100%? If not, why not?

6.18 Percents. What percent of single men hold Grade 1 jobs? What percent of Grade 1 jobs are held by single men?

6.19 Conditional distribution. Give (in percents) the conditional distribution of job grade among single men. Should your percents add to 100% (up to roundoff error)?

6.20 Marital status and job grade. One way to see the relationship is to look at who holds Grade 1 jobs.

(a) There are 874 married men with Grade 1 jobs, and only 58 single men with such jobs. Explain why these counts by themselves don't describe the relationship between marital status and job grade.

(b) Find the percent of men in each marital status group who have Grade 1 jobs. Then find the percent in each marital group who have Grade 4 jobs. What do these percents say about the relationship?

6.21 Association is not causation. The data in Table 6.2 show that single men are more likely to hold lower-grade jobs than are married men. We should not conclude that single men can help their career by getting married. What lurking variables might help explain the association between marital status and job grade?

*The following exercises ask you to answer questions from data without having the details outlined for you. The exercise statements give you the **State** step of the four-step process. In your work, follow the **Plan, Solve,** and **Conclude** steps of the process as illustrated in Example 6.3 (page 143).*

6.22 Smoking cessation. A large randomized trial was conducted to assess the efficacy of Chantix for smoking cessation compared with bupropion (more commonly known as Wellbutrin or Zyban) and a placebo. Chantix is different from most other quit-smoking products in that it targets nicotine receptors in the brain, attaches to them, and blocks nicotine from reaching them, while bupropion is an antidepressant often used to help people stop smoking. Generally healthy smokers who smoked at least 10 cigarettes per day were assigned at random to take Chantix ($n = 352$), bupropion ($n = 329$), or a placebo ($n = 344$). The response measure is continuous cessation from smoking for Weeks 9 through 12 of the study. Here is a two-way table of the results:[8] SMOKECESS

	Treatment		
	Chantix	Bupropion	Placebo
No smoking in Weeks 9–12	155	97	61
Smoked in Weeks 9–12	197	232	283

How does whether a subject smoked in Weeks 9 to 12 depend on the treatment received?

6.23 Animal testing. "It is right to use animals for medical testing if it might save human lives." The General Social Survey asked 1152 adults to react to this statement. Here is the two-way table of their responses: 🔴 ANTESTING

Response	Male	Female
Strongly agree	76	59
Agree	270	247
Neither agree nor disagree	87	139
Disagree	61	123
Strongly disagree	22	68

How do the distributions of opinion differ between men and women?

6.24 College degrees. "Colleges and universities across the country are grappling with the case of the mysteriously vanishing male." So said an article in the *Washington Post*. Here are data on the numbers of degrees earned in 2012–2013, as projected by the National Center for Education Statistics. The table entries are counts of degrees in thousands.[9] 🔴 DEGREES

Degree	Female	Male
Associate's	519	304
Bachelor's	989	731
Master's	418	266
Professional	49	50
Doctor's	40	35

Briefly contrast the counts and distributions of men and women in earning degrees. Are men "vanishing" from colleges and universities across the country?

6.25 Complications of bariatric surgery. Bariatric surgery, or weight-loss surgery, includes a variety of procedures performed on people who are obese. Weight loss is achieved by reducing the size of the stomach with an implanted medical device (gastric banding), by removing a portion of the stomach (sleeve gastrectomy), or by resecting and rerouting the small intestines to a small stomach pouch (gastric bypass surgery). Because there can be complications using any of these methods, the National Institutes of Health recommends bariatric surgery for obese people with a body mass index (BMI) of at least 40 and for people with a BMI of at least 35 and serious coexisting medical conditions such as diabetes. Serious complications include potentially life-threatening, permanently disabling, and fatal outcomes. Here is a two-way table for data collected in Michigan over several years giving counts of non-life-threatening complications, serious complications, and no complications for these three types of surgeries:[10] 🔴 BARIATRIC

Surgery	Type of Complication			Total
	Non-life-threatening	Serious	None	
Gastric banding	81	46	5253	5380
Sleeve gastrectomy	31	19	804	854
Gastric bypass	606	325	8110	9041

What do the data say about differences in complications for the three types of surgeries?

6.26 Smokers rate their health. The University of Michigan Health and Retirement Study (HRS) surveys more than 22,000 Americans over the age of 50 every two years. A subsample of the HRS participated in a 2009 Internet-based survey that collected information on a number of topical areas, including health (physical and mental health behaviors), psychosocial items, economics (income, assets, expectations, and consumption), and retirement.[11] Two of the questions asked were "Would you say your health is excellent, very good, good, fair, or poor?" and "Do you smoke cigarettes now?" The two-way table summarizes the answers on these two questions. 🔴 SMOKERATING

Health	Current Smoker	
	Yes	No
Excellent	25	484
Very good	115	1557
Good	145	1309
Fair	90	545
Poor	29	11

What do the data say about differences in self-evaluation of health for current smokers and nonsmokers?

6.27 Python eggs. How is the hatching of water python eggs influenced by the temperature of the snake's nest? Researchers placed 104 newly laid eggs in a hot environment, 56 in a neutral environment, and 27 in a cold environment. Hot duplicates the warmth provided by the mother python. Neutral and cold are cooler, as when the mother is absent. The results: 75 of the hot eggs hatched, along with 38 of the neutral eggs and 16 of the cold eggs.[12]

(a) Make a two-way table of "environment temperature" against "hatched or not."

(b) The researchers anticipated that eggs would hatch less well at cooler temperatures. Do the data support that anticipation?

EXPLORING THE WEB

6.28 Promoting women. In academics, faculty typically start as assistant professors, are promoted to associate professor (and gain tenure), and finally reach the rank of full professor. Some have argued that women have a harder time gaining promotion to associate and full professor than do men. Do data support this argument? Search the Web to find the number of faculty by rank and gender at some university. Organize the data in a two-way table with columns labeled assistant, associate, and full professor, and rows labeled female and male. Calculate the conditional distributions of rank for females and males. Do you see a pattern that suggests that the proportion of women decreases as rank increases? We found several sources of data by doing a Google search on "faculty head count by rank and gender." In addition to discussing the pattern you find, provide the data, the name of the school, and the source of the data.

6.29 Accidental deaths and age. Accidental deaths are shocking and tragic. Do the ways in which people die by accident change with age? Look at the most recent *Statistical Abstract of the United States* (http://www.census.gov/compendia/statab/). From the list under Browse Subjects on the left side of the page, select "Births, Deaths, Marriages, and Divorces" then "Death". Next, select the report for "Deaths by Age and Selected Causes" and make a two-way table that provides the counts of deaths due to accidents from various causes for three different age groups. What do you conclude?

Ben Cranke/Getty Images

Chapter 7

IN THIS CHAPTER
WE COVER...

■ Part I Summary

■ Test Yourself

■ Supplementary Exercises

Exploring Data: Part I Review

PART 1 SUMMARY

Data analysis is the art of describing data using graphs and numerical summaries. The purpose of data analysis is to help us see and understand the most important features of a set of data. Chapter 1 commented on graphs to display distributions: pie charts and bar graphs for categorical variables, histograms and stemplots for quantitative variables. In addition, time plots show how a quantitative variable changes over time. Chapter 2 presented numerical tools for describing the center and spread of the distribution of one variable. Chapter 3 discussed density curves for describing the overall pattern of a distribution, with emphasis on the Normal distributions.

The first STATISTICS IN SUMMARY figure on the next page organizes the big ideas for exploring a quantitative variable. Plot your data, then describe their center and spread using either the mean and standard deviation or the five-number summary. The last step, which makes sense only for some data, is to summarize the data in compact form by using a Normal curve as a

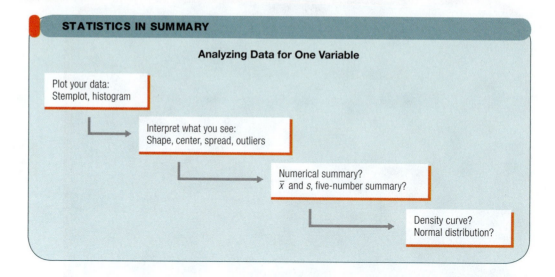

description of the overall pattern. The question marks at the last two stages remind us that the usefulness of numerical summaries and Normal distributions depends on what we find when we examine graphs of our data. No short summary does justice to irregular shapes or to data with several distinct clusters.

Chapters 4 and 5 applied the same ideas to relationships between two quantitative variables. The second STATISTICS IN SUMMARY figure retraces the big ideas, with details that fit the new setting. Always begin by making graphs of your data. In the case of a scatterplot, we have learned a numerical summary only for data that show a roughly linear pattern on the scatterplot. The summary is then the means and standard deviations of the two variables and their correlation. A regression line drawn on the plot gives a compact description of the overall pattern that we can use for prediction. Once again there are question marks at the last two stages to remind us that correlation and regression describe only straight-line relationships. Chapter 6 shows how to understand relationships between two categorical variables; comparing well-chosen percents is the key.

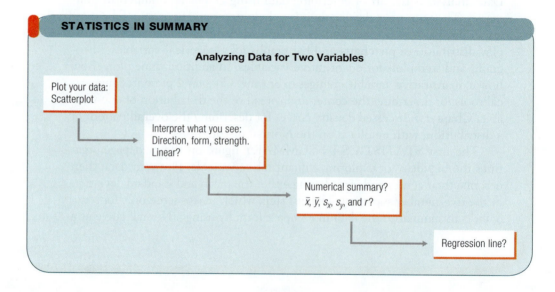

You can organize your work in any open-ended data analysis setting by following the four-step STATE, PLAN, SOLVE, and CONCLUDE process first introduced in Chapter 2. After we have mastered the extra background needed for statistical inference, this process will also guide practical work on inference later in the book.

TEST YOURSELF

The questions below include multiple-choice, calculations, and short-answer questions. They will help you review the basic ideas and skills presented in Chapters 1 to 6.

7.1 As part of a database on new births at a hospital some variables recorded are the age of the mother, marital status of the mother (single, married, divorced, other), weight of the baby, and sex of the baby. Of these variables

(a) age, marital status, and weight are quantitative variables.

(b) age and weight are categorical variables.

(c) sex and marital status are categorical variables.

(d) sex, marital status, and age are categorical variables.

7.2 You are interested in obtaining information about the performance of students in your statistics class and seeing how this performance is affected by several factors such as sex. To do this you are going to give a questionnaire to all students in the class. Give two questions for which the response is categorical and two questions for which the response is quantitative. For the categorical variables, give the possible values.

Pocket change. *In a statistics class with 136 students, the professor records how much money each student has in his or her possession during the first class of the semester. Figure 7.1 gives the histogram of the data collected. Use this histogram to help answer Questions 7.3 to 7.5.*

7.3 The *number* of students with under $10 in their possession is closest to

(a) 40.   (b) 50.   (c) 60.   (d) 70.

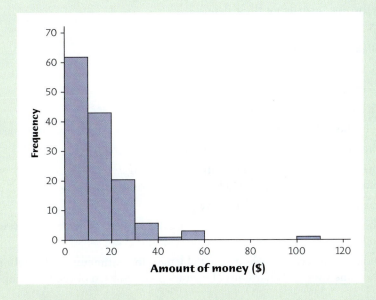

FIGURE 7.1

Histogram of the distribution of the amount of money carried by each student on the first day of class, for Questions 7.3 to 7.5.

7.4 The histogram

(a) is skewed right. (c) is asymmetric.

(b) has an outlier. (d) is all of the above.

7.5 The *percent* of students with $20 or more in their possession is

(a) about 10%. (c) about 30%.

(b) about 20%. (d) over 40%.

7.6 A reporter wishes to portray baseball players as overpaid. Which measure of center should he report as the average salary of major league players?

(a) The mean

(b) The median

(c) Either the mean or the median. It doesn't matter since they will be equal.

(d) Neither the mean nor the median. Both will be much lower than the actual average salary.

Genetic engineering for cancer treatment. *Here's a new idea for treating advanced melanoma, the most serious kind of skin cancer. Genetically engineer white blood cells to better recognize and destroy cancer cells, then infuse these cells into patients. The subjects in a small initial study were 11 patients whose melanoma had not responded to existing treatments. One question was how rapidly the new cells would multiply after infusion, as measured by the doubling time in days.[1] Use the following doubling times in days to answer Questions 7.7 to 7.10.*

1.4   1.0   1.3   1.0   1.3   2.0   0.6   0.8   0.7   0.9   1.9

7.7 What is the mean number of days for the 11 doubling times?

(a) 1.17 days (c) 0.9 days

(b) 1.0 day (d) 0.46 days

7.8 What is the median number of days for the 11 doubling times?

(a) 2.0 days (c) 1.0 day

(b) 1.17 days (d) 0.9 days

7.9 What is the first quartile for these data?

(a) 1.3 days (c) 0.85 days

(b) 1.0 day (d) 0.8 days

7.10 (Optional) What is the interquartile range for these data?

(a) 1.3 days (c) 0.6 days

(b) 0.8 days (d) 0.4 days

7.11 Which of the following is likely to have a mean that is smaller than the median?

(a) The salaries of all National Football League players

(b) The scores of students (out of 100 points) on a very easy exam in which most students score perfectly, but a few do very poorly

(c) The prices of homes in a large city

(d) The scores of students (out of 100 points) on a very difficult exam in which most students score poorly, but a few do very well

7.12 For a biology project, you measure the tail length in centimeters and weight in grams of 12 mice of the same variety. What units of measurement do each of the following have?

(a) The mean length of the tails

(b) The first quartile of the tail lengths

(c) The standard deviation of the tail lengths

(d) The variance of the weights

Employment times. *A sample of 40 employees from the local Honda plant was obtained, and the length of time (in months) worked was recorded for each employee. A stemplot of these data follows. Use the stemplot to answer Questions 7.13 and 7.14. In the stemplot 5|2 represents 52 months.*

```
5 | 2 2 3 3 4 5 7 8 9 9
6 | 0 0 0 2 3 4 4 4 5 6 7 7 8 8 8 9
7 | 3 4 5 5 6 6 7 7 7 8 8 9 9
8 |
9 | 8
```

7.13 What would be a better way to represent this data set?

(a) Display the data in a time plot

(b) Split the stems

(c) Use a pie chart

(d) Use a histogram with class width equal to 10

7.14 The *percent* of employees in the sample who have worked at the plant for less than 5 years is

(a) approximately zero. (c) 15%.

(b) 10%. (d) 25%.

What color is your car? *The bar graph in Figure 7.2 gives the distribution of the most popular colors for vehicles sold in North America in 2010.[2] Use the bar graph to help answer Questions 7.15 and 7.16.*

7.15 Approximately what percent of vehicles sold in North America in 2010 were beige or brown?

(a) 5% (b) 10% (c) 15% (d) 20%

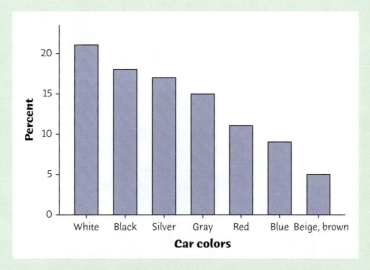

FIGURE 7.2

Bar graph of the distribution of the most popular colors for vehicles sold in North America in 2010, for Questions 7.15 and 7.16.

7.16 The total of the percents of the bars in the graph add to 96%. Which of the following are true?

(a) The percent of green cars sold must be less than 2%.

(b) A pie chart could be drawn for the colors given in the bar graph.

(c) The percent of vehicles sold that are either silver or white is just over 40%.

(d) None of the above.

7.17 Mechanical measurements on supposedly identical objects usually vary. The variation often follows a Normal distribution. The stress required to break a type of bolt varies Normally with mean 75 kilopounds per square inch (ksi) and standard deviation 8.3 ksi.

(a) What percent of these bolts will withstand a stress of 90 ksi without breaking?

(b) What range covers the middle 50% of breaking strengths for these bolts?

7.18 A professor knows from past experience that the time for students to complete a quiz has an $N(19, 3)$ distribution.

(a) If he allows 20 minutes for the quiz, what percent of the students will not complete the quiz?

(b) Suppose that he wants to allow sufficient time so that 95% of the students will complete the quiz in the allotted time. How much time should he allow for the quiz?

7.19 The Aleppo pine and the Torrey pine are widely planted as ornamental trees in Southern California. Here are the lengths (centimeters) of 15 Aleppo pine needles:[3]

10.2   7.2   7.6   9.3   12.1   10.9   9.4   11.3   8.5   8.5   12.8   8.7   9.0   9.0   9.4

(a) Find the five-number summary for the distribution of Aleppo pine needles.

Figure 7.3 gives a boxplot for the distribution of the lengths (centimeters) of 18 Torrey pine needles. Use this information to help answer the remainder of this question.

(b) The median of the distribution of Torrey pine needles is closest to which of the following values?

24   25   27   30

(c) Twenty-five percent of the Torrey pine needles exceed what value?

(d) Given only the length of a needle, do you think you could say which pine species it comes from? Explain briefly.

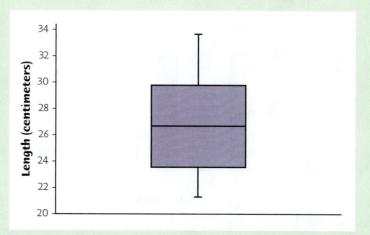

FIGURE 7.3

Boxplot for the distribution of the lengths (centimeters) of 18 Torrey pine needles, for Question 7.19.

Soap in the shower. *From Rex Boggs in Australia comes an unusual data set. Before showering in the morning, he weighed the bar of soap in his shower stall. The weight goes down as the soap is used. The data appear below (weights in grams). Notice that Mr. Boggs forgot to weigh the soap on some days. Questions 7.20 to 7.23 are based on the soap data set.* SOAP

Day	Weight	Day	Weight	Day	Weight
1	124	8	84	16	27
2	121	9	78	18	16
5	103	10	71	19	12
6	96	12	58	20	8
7	90	13	50	21	6

7.20 Figure 7.4 is a scatterplot of the weight of the bar of soap against day. How would you describe the overall pattern?

    (a) Sharply curved.

    (b) There are two distinct clusters that are widely separated.

    (c) A very weak positive association.

    (d) A strong negative association.

7.21 The equation of the least-squares regression line for predicting soap weight from day is

$$\text{weight} = 133.2 - 6.3 \times \text{day}$$

What does this tell us about the rate at which the soap lost weight?

    (a) The soap lost about −6.3 grams per day.

    (b) The soap lost about 6.3 grams per day.

    (c) The soap lost about −133.2 grams per day.

    (d) The soap lost about 133.2 grams per day.

7.22 The equation of the least-squares regression line for predicting soap weight from day is

$$\text{weight} = 133.2 - 6.3 \times \text{day}$$

Mr. Boggs did not measure the weight of the soap on Day 4. Use the regression equation to predict that weight.

    (a) 108 grams   (b) 126.9 grams   (c) 157.3 grams   (d) 526.5 grams

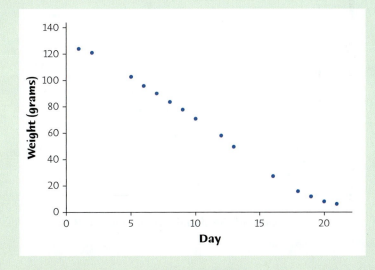

FIGURE 7.4

Scatterplot of the weight of a bar of soap against day, for Question 7.20.

7.23 The equation of the least-squares regression line for predicting soap weight from day is

$$\text{weight} = 133.2 - 6.3 \times \text{day}$$

I use the regression equation to predict the weight of the soap on Day 30. I conclude that

(a) the soap will last at least a month.

(b) the prediction is not sensible, because the prediction is far outside the range of values of the response variable.

(c) the prediction is not sensible, because 30 days is far outside the range of values of the explanatory variable.

(d) the prediction is not sensible, because of the outlier present in the data.

Squirrels and their food supply. *The fact that animal species produce more offspring when their supply of food goes up isn't surprising. The fact that some animals appear able to anticipate unusual food abundance is surprising. Red squirrels eat seeds from pine cones, a food source that occasionally has very large crops (called seed masting). Below are data on an index of the abundance of pine cones (larger values indicate greater abundance) and average number of offspring per female over 16 years.[4] What makes these data interesting is that the offspring are conceived in the spring, before the cones mature in the fall to feed the new young squirrels through the winter. Questions 7.24 to 7.26 are based on these data.* 🔴 **SQUIRRELS**

Cone index x	0.00	2.02	0.25	3.22	4.68	0.31	3.37	3.09
Offspring y	1.49	1.10	1.29	2.71	4.07	1.29	3.36	2.41
Cone index x	2.44	4.81	1.88	0.31	1.61	1.88	0.91	1.04
Offspring y	1.97	3.41	1.49	2.02	3.34	2.41	2.15	2.12

7.24 Figure 7.5 is a scatterplot of average number of offspring per female against cone index. Which of the following is a plausible value of the correlation, r, between average number of offspring per female and cone index?

(a) 0   (b) 1   (c) 0.75   (d) −0.75

7.25 The equation of the least-squares regression line for predicting average number of offspring per female from cone index is

$$\text{offspring} = 1.41 + 0.44 \times \text{cone index}$$

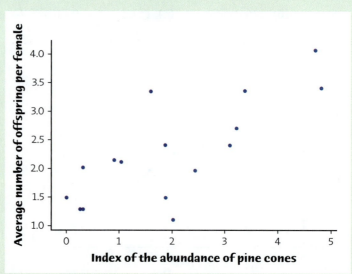

FIGURE 7.5

Scatterplot of the average number of offspring per female against cone index, for Question 7.24.

What does the intercept of 1.41 tell us?

(a) The average number of offspring per female is 1.41.

(b) The predicted number of offspring per female is 1.41.

(c) The predicted number of offspring per female when the cone index is 0 is 1.41.

(d) All of the above.

7.26 The equation of the least-squares regression line for predicting average number of offspring per female from cone index is

$$\text{offspring} = 1.41 + 0.44 \times \text{cone index}$$

Use this to predict the average number of offspring per female for a year with a cone index of 0.25.

(a) 1.52   (b) 1.29   (c) 0.44   (d) 0.11

7.27 How well do people remember their past diet? Data are available for 91 people who were asked about their diet when they were 18 years old. Researchers asked them at about age 55 to describe their eating habits at age 18. For each subject, the researchers calculated the correlation between actual intakes of many foods at age 18 and the intakes the subjects now remember. The median of the 91 correlations was $r = 0.217$.[5] Which of the following conclusions is consistent with this correlation?

(a) We conclude that subjects remember approximately 21.7% of their food intakes at age 18.

(b) We conclude that subjects remember approximately $r^2 = (0.217)^2 = 0.047$ of their food intakes at age 18.

(c) We conclude that food intake at age 55 is about 21.7% that of food intake at age 18.

(d) We conclude that memory of food intake in the distant past is fair to poor.

7.28 Joe's retirement plan invests in stocks through an "index fund" that follows the behavior of the stock market as a whole, as measured by the Standard & Poor's (S&P) 500 stock index. Joe wants to buy a mutual fund that does not track the index closely. He reads that monthly returns from Fidelity Technology Fund have correlation $r = 0.77$ with the S&P 500 index and that Fidelity Real Estate Fund has correlation $r = 0.37$ with the index. Which of the following is correct?

(a) The Fidelity Technology Fund has a closer relationship to returns from the stock market as a whole and also has higher returns than the Fidelity Real Estate Fund.

(b) The Fidelity Technology Fund has a closer relationship to returns from the stock market as a whole, but we cannot say that it has higher returns than the Fidelity Real Estate Fund.

(c) The Fidelity Real Estate Fund has a closer relationship to returns from the stock market as a whole and also has higher returns than the Fidelity Technology Fund.

(d) The Fidelity Real Estate Fund has a closer relationship to returns from the stock market as a whole, but we cannot say that it has higher returns than the Fidelity Technology Fund.

Monkey calls. *The usual way to study the brain's response to sounds is to have subjects listen to "pure tones." The response to recognizable sounds may differ. To compare responses, researchers anesthetized macaque monkeys. They fed pure tones and also monkey calls directly to their brains by inserting electrodes. Response to the stimulus was measured by the firing rate (electrical spikes per second) of neurons in various areas of the brain. Table 7.1 contains the responses for 37 neurons.[6] Figure 7.6 is a scatterplot of monkey call response against pure-tone response (explanatory variable). Questions 7.29 and 7.30 refer to these data and the scatterplot.* 🐵 **MONKEYCALLS**

TABLE 7.1 Neuron response (electrical firing rate per second) to pure tones and monkey calls

NEURON	TONE	CALL	NEURON	TONE	CALL	NEURON	TONE	CALL
1	474	500	14	145	42	26	71	134
2	256	138	15	141	241	27	68	65
3	241	485	16	129	194	28	59	182
4	226	338	17	113	123	29	59	97
5	185	194	18	112	182	30	57	318
6	174	159	19	102	141	31	56	201
7	176	341	20	100	118	32	47	279
8	168	85	21	74	62	33	46	62
9	161	303	22	72	112	34	41	84
10	150	208	23	20	193	35	26	203
11	19	66	24	21	129	36	28	192
12	20	54	25	26	135	37	31	70
13	35	103						

7.29 We might expect some neurons to have strong responses to any stimulus and others to have consistently weak responses. There would then be a strong relationship between tone response and call response. From the scatterplot of monkey call response against pure-tone response in Figure 7.6 what would you estimate the correlation r to be?

    (a) −0.6   (c) 0.1

    (b) −0.1   (d) 0.6

7.30 Which of the following statements about the scatterplot in Figure 7.6 is correct?

    (a) There is moderate evidence that pure-tone response causes monkey call response.

    (b) There is moderate evidence that monkey call response causes pure-tone response.

    (c) There are one or two outliers and at least one of these may also be influential.

    (d) None of the above.

FIGURE 7.6

Scatterplot of monkey tone response against pure-tone response, for Questions 7.29 and 7.30.

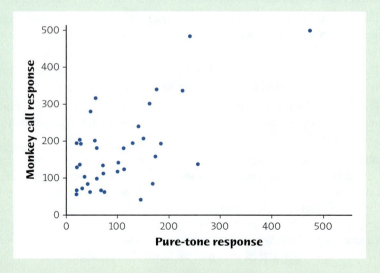

Catalog shopping. *What is the most important reason that students buy from catalogs? The answer may differ for different groups of students. Here are counts for samples of American and East Asian students at a large midwestern university.*[7] *Use these counts to answer Questions 7.31 to 7.33.* ⬤ SHOPPING

Reason	American	Asian
Save time	29	10
Easy	28	11
Low price	17	34
Live far from stores	11	4
No pressure to buy	10	3
Other	20	7
Total	115	69

7.31 What percent of all students say that the most important reason to buy from a catalog is to save time?

(a) 74%   (b) 25%   (c) 21%   (d) 14%

7.32 What percent of East Asian students say that the most important reason to buy from a catalog is low price?

(a) 67%   (b) 49%   (c) 28%   (d) 18%

7.33 What are the most important differences between the two groups of students?

(a) The most important reasons for American students to buy from a catalog are to save time and because it is easy, while for East Asian students it is low price.

(b) American students appear to be almost three times more likely to live far from stores than East Asian students.

(c) East Asian students are twice as likely to purchase from a catalog because of low price than American students.

(d) All of the above.

Investment strategies. *One reason to invest abroad is that markets in different countries don't move in step. When American stocks go down, foreign stocks may go up. So an investor who holds both bears less risk. That's the theory. But then we read in a magazine article that the correlation between changes in American and European stock prices rose from 0.4 in the mid-1990s to 0.8 in 2000.*[8] *Questions 7.34 and 7.35 refer to this article.*

7.34 Explain to an investor who knows no statistics why the fact stated in this article reduces the protection provided by buying European stocks.

7.35 The same article that claims that the correlation between changes in stock prices in Europe and the United States is 0.8 goes on to say: "Crudely, that means that movements on Wall Street can explain 80% of price movements in Europe."

(a) Is this true?

(b) What is the percent explained if $r = 0.8$?

7.36 People who get angry easily tend to have more heart disease. That's the conclusion of a study that followed a random sample of 12,986 people from three locations for about four years. All subjects were free of heart disease at the beginning of the study. The subjects took the Spielberger Trait Anger Scale test, which measures how prone a person is to sudden anger. Here are data for the 8474 people in the sample who had normal blood pressure. CHD stands for "coronary heart disease." This includes people who had heart attacks and those who needed medical treatment for heart disease.[9] ⬤ ANGER

	Low anger	Moderate anger	High anger	Total
CHD	53	110	27	190
No CHD	3057	4621	606	8284
Total	3110	4731	633	8474

(a) What percent of all 8474 people with normal blood pressure had CHD?

(b) What percent of all 8474 people were classified as having high anger?

(c) What percent of those classified as having high anger had CHD?

(d) What percent of those with no CHD were classified as having moderate anger?

(e) Do these data provide any evidence that as anger score increases, the percent who suffer CHD increases? Explain.

■ SUPPLEMENTARY EXERCISES

*Supplementary exercises apply the skills you have learned in ways that require more thought or more elaborate use of technology. Some of these exercises ask you to follow the **Plan, Solve,** and **Conclude** steps of the four-step process introduced on page 56.*

7.37 The Mississippi River. Table 7.2 gives the volume of water discharged by the Mississippi River into the Gulf of Mexico for each year from 1954 to 2001.[10] The units are cubic kilometers of water. 🌀 MISSISSIPPI

(a) Make a graph of the distribution of water volume. Describe the overall shape of the distribution and any outliers.

(b) Based on the shape of the distribution, do you expect the mean to be close to the median, clearly less than the median, or clearly greater than the median? Why? Find the mean and the median to check your answer.

(c) Based on the shape of the distribution, does it seem reasonable to use $\bar{x}$ and s to describe the center and spread of this distribution? Why? Find $\bar{x}$ and s if you think they are a good choice. Otherwise, find the five-number summary.

7.38 More on the Mississippi River. The data in Table 7.2 are a time series. Make a time plot that shows how the volume of water in the Mississippi changed between 1954 and 2001. What does the time plot reveal that the histogram from the previous exercise does not? It is a good idea to always make a time plot of time series data because a histogram cannot show changes over time. 🌀 MISSISSIPPI

TABLE 7.2 Yearly discharge (cubic kilometers of water) of the Mississippi River

YEAR	DISCHARGE	YEAR	DISCHARGE	YEAR	DISCHARGE	YEAR	DISCHARGE
1954	290	1966	410	1978	560	1990	680
1955	420	1967	460	1979	800	1991	700
1956	390	1968	510	1980	500	1992	510
1957	610	1969	560	1981	420	1993	900
1958	550	1970	540	1982	640	1994	640
1959	440	1971	480	1983	770	1995	590
1960	470	1972	600	1984	710	1996	670
1961	600	1973	880	1985	680	1997	680
1962	550	1974	710	1986	600	1998	690
1963	360	1975	670	1987	450	1999	580
1964	390	1976	420	1988	420	2000	390
1965	500	1977	430	1989	630	2001	580

Falling through the ice. *The Nenana Ice Classic is an annual contest to guess the exact time in the spring when a tripod erected on the frozen Tanana River near Nenana, Alaska, will fall through the ice. The 2010 jackpot prize was $279,030. The contest has been run since 1917. Table 7.3 gives simplified data that record only the date on which the tripod fell each year. The earliest date so far is April 20. To make the data easier to use, the table gives the date each year in days starting with April 20. That is, April 20 is 1, April 21 is 2, and so on. Exercises 7.39 to 7.41 concern these data.*[11] **TANANA**

7.39 When does the ice break up? We have 94 years of data on the date of ice breakup on the Tanana River. Describe the distribution of the breakup date with both a graph or graphs and appropriate numerical summaries. What is the median date (month and day) for ice breakup?

7.40 Global warming? Because of the high stakes, the falling of the tripod has been carefully observed for many years. If the date the tripod falls has been getting earlier, that may be evidence for the effects of global warming.

(a) Make a time plot of the date the tripod falls against year.

(b) There is a great deal of year-to-year variation. Fitting a regression line to the data may help us see the trend. Fit the least-squares line and add it to your time plot. What do you conclude?

(c) There is much variation about the line. Give a numerical description of how much of the year-to-year variation in ice breakup time is accounted for by the time trend represented by the regression line. (This simple example is typical of more complex evidence for the effects of global warming: large year-to-year variation requires many years of data to see a trend.)

7.41 More on global warming. Side-by-side boxplots offer a different look at the data. Group the data into periods of roughly equal length: 1917 to 1939, 1940 to 1962, 1963 to 1985, and 1986 to 2010. Make boxplots to compare ice breakup dates in these four time periods. Write a brief description of what the plots show.

7.42 Big government? The data file **GDP** on the text CD and Web site contains the percent of gross domestic product (GDP, the total value of all goods and services a country produces) taken by the government in 82 countries. For example, the government share of GDP is 12.28% in Canada and 10.54% in the United States.[12] **GDP**

(a) Make a stemplot or a histogram to display the distribution of government share of GDP.

(b) There are several high outliers. What countries are these? (In the most extreme case, the government took more than the total annual GDP!) What is the overall shape of the distribution if you ignore the outliers?

TABLE 7.3 Days from April 20 for the Tanana River tripod to fall

YEAR	DAY	YEAR	DAY	YEAR	DAY	YEAR	DAY	YEAR	DAY	YEAR	DAY
1917	11	1933	19	1949	25	1965	18	1981	11	1997	11
1918	22	1934	11	1950	17	1966	19	1982	21	1998	1
1919	14	1935	26	1951	11	1967	15	1983	10	1999	10
1920	22	1936	11	1952	23	1968	19	1984	20	2000	12
1921	22	1937	23	1953	10	1969	9	1985	23	2001	19
1922	23	1938	17	1954	17	1970	15	1986	19	2002	18
1923	20	1939	10	1955	20	1971	19	1987	16	2003	10
1924	22	1940	1	1956	12	1972	21	1988	8	2004	5
1925	16	1941	14	1957	16	1973	15	1989	12	2005	9
1926	7	1942	11	1958	10	1974	17	1990	5	2006	13
1927	23	1943	9	1959	19	1975	21	1991	12	2007	8
1928	17	1944	15	1960	13	1976	13	1992	25	2008	16
1929	16	1945	27	1961	16	1977	17	1993	4	2009	12
1930	19	1946	16	1962	23	1978	11	1994	10	2010	10
1931	21	1947	14	1963	16	1979	11	1995	7		
1932	12	1948	24	1964	31	1980	10	1996	16		

(c) Based on your work in (b), give a numerical summary of the center and spread of the distribution, omitting the outliers.

(d) Some Americans complain about big government and heavy taxes. Where does the United States (10.54%) stand in this international comparison?

7.43 Cicadas as fertilizer? Periodically, swarms of cicadas emerge from the ground in the eastern United States, live for about six weeks, then die. There are so many cicadas that their dead bodies can serve as fertilizer and increase plant growth. In an experiment, a researcher added 10 cicadas under some plants in a natural plot of bellflowers in a forest, leaving other plants undisturbed. One of the response variables was the size of seeds produced by the plants. Here are data (seed mass in milligrams) for 39 cicada plants and 33 undisturbed (control) plants:[13] CICADA

Cicada plants				Control plants			
0.237	0.277	0.241	0.142	0.212	0.188	0.263	0.253
0.109	0.209	0.238	0.277	0.261	0.265	0.135	0.170
0.261	0.227	0.171	0.235	0.203	0.241	0.257	0.155
0.276	0.234	0.255	0.296	0.215	0.285	0.198	0.266
0.239	0.266	0.296	0.217	0.178	0.244	0.190	0.212
0.238	0.210	0.295	0.193	0.290	0.253	0.249	0.253
0.218	0.263	0.305	0.257	0.268	0.190	0.196	0.220
0.351	0.245	0.226	0.276	0.246	0.145	0.247	0.140
0.317	0.310	0.223	0.229	0.241			
0.192	0.201	0.211					

Describe and compare the two distributions. Do the data support the idea that dead cicadas can serve as fertilizer?

7.44 A big-toe problem. Hallux abducto valgus (call it HAV) is a deformation of the big toe that is not common in youth and often requires surgery. Doctors used X-rays to measure the angle (in degrees) of deformity in 38 consecutive patients under the age of 21 who came to a medical center for surgery to correct HAV.[14] The angle is a measure of the seriousness of the deformity. The data appear in Table 7.4 as "HAV angle." Describe the distribution of the angle of deformity among young patients needing surgery for this condition. DEFORMITY

7.45 Prey attract predators. Here is one way in which nature regulates the size of animal populations: high population density attracts predators, who remove a higher proportion of the population than when the density of the prey is low. One study looked at kelp perch and their common predator, the kelp bass. The researcher set up four large circular pens on sandy ocean bottom in Southern California. He chose young perch at random from a large group and placed 10, 20, 40, and 60 perch in the four pens. Then he dropped the nets protecting the pens, allowing bass to swarm in, and counted the perch left after 2 hours. Here are data on the proportions of perch eaten in four repetitions of this setup:[15]

Perch	Proportion killed			
10	0.0	0.1	0.3	0.3
20	0.2	0.3	0.3	0.6
40	0.075	0.3	0.6	0.725
60	0.517	0.55	0.7	0.817

Do the data support the principle that "more prey attract more predators, who drive down the number of prey"?

TABLE 7.4 Angle of deformity (degrees) for two types of foot deformity

HAV ANGLE	MA ANGLE	HAV ANGLE	MA ANGLE	HAV ANGLE	MA ANGLE
28	18	21	15	16	10
32	16	17	16	30	12
25	22	16	10	30	10
34	17	21	7	20	10
38	33	23	11	50	12
26	10	14	15	25	25
25	18	32	12	26	30
18	13	25	16	28	22
30	19	21	16	31	24
26	10	22	18	38	20
28	17	20	10	32	37
13	14	18	15	21	23
20	20	26	16		

7.46 Predicting foot problems. Metatarsus adductus (call it MA) is a turning in of the front part of the foot that is common in adolescents and usually corrects itself. Table 7.4 gives the severity of MA ("MA angle"). Doctors speculate that the severity of MA can help predict the severity of HAV. Describe the relationship between MA and HAV. Do you think the data confirm the doctors' speculation? Why or why not? **DEFORMITY**

7.47 Change in the Serengeti. Long-term records from the Serengeti National Park in Tanzania show interesting ecological relationships. When wildebeest are more abundant, they graze the grass more heavily, so there are fewer fires and more trees grow. Lions feed more successfully when there are more trees, so the lion population increases. Here are data on one part of this cycle, wildebeest abundance (in thousands of animals) and the percent of the grass area that burned in the same year:[16] **SERENGETI**

Wildebeest (1000s)	Percent burned	Wildebeest (1000s)	Percent burned	Wildebeest (1000s)	Percent burned
396	56	360	88	1147	32
476	50	444	88	1173	31
698	25	524	75	1178	24
1049	16	622	60	1253	24
1178	7	600	56	1249	53
1200	5	902	45		
1302	7	1440	21		

To what extent do these data support the claim that more wildebeest reduce the percent of grasslands that burn? How rapidly does burned area decrease as the number of wildebeest increases? Include a graph and suitable calculations.

7.48 Casting aluminum. In casting metal parts, molten metal flows through a "gate" into a die that shapes the part. The gate velocity (the speed at which metal is forced through the gate) plays a critical role in die casting. A firm that casts cylindrical aluminum pistons examined 12 types formed from the same alloy. How does the piston wall thickness (inches) influence the gate velocity (feet per second) chosen by the skilled workers who do the casting? If there is a clear pattern, it can be used to direct new workers or to automate the process. Analyze these data and report your findings.[17] **ALUMINUM**

Thickness	Velocity	Thickness	Velocity	Thickness	Velocity
0.248	123.8	0.524	228.6	0.697	145.2
0.359	223.9	0.552	223.8	0.752	263.1
0.366	180.9	0.628	326.2	0.806	302.4
0.400	104.8	0.697	302.4	0.821	302.4

7.49 How are schools doing? The nonprofit group Public Agenda conducted telephone interviews with parents of high school children. Interviewers chose equal numbers of black, Hispanic, and non-Hispanic white parents at random. One question asked was "Are the high schools in your state doing an excellent, good, fair or poor job, or don't you know enough to say?" Here are the survey results:[18] **SCHOOLS**

Opinion	Black parents	Hispanic parents	White parents
Excellent	12	34	22
Good	69	55	81
Fair	75	61	60
Poor	24	24	24
Don't know	22	28	14
Total	202	202	201

Write a brief analysis of these results that focuses on the relationship between parent group and opinions about schools.

7.50 Influence: hot sector funds? Investment advertisements always warn that "past performance does not guarantee future results." Here is an example that shows why you should pay attention to this warning. Stocks fell sharply in 2002, then rose sharply in 2003. The table below gives the percent returns from 23 Fidelity Investments "sector funds" in these two years. Sector funds invest in narrow segments of the stock market. They often rise and fall faster than the market as a whole. **SECTORFUNDS**

2002 return	2003 return	2002 return	2003 return	2002 return	2003 return
−17.1	23.9	−0.7	36.9	−37.8	59.4
−6.7	14.1	−5.6	27.5	−11.5	22.9
−21.1	41.8	−26.9	26.1	−0.7	36.9
−12.8	43.9	−42.0	62.7	64.3	32.1
−18.9	31.1	−47.8	68.1	−9.6	28.7
−7.7	32.3	−50.5	71.9	−11.7	29.5
−17.2	36.5	−49.5	57.0	−2.3	19.1
−11.4	30.6	−23.4	35.0		

(a) Make a scatterplot of 2003 return (response) against 2002 return (explanatory). The funds with the best performance in 2002 tend to have the worst performance in 2003. Fidelity Gold Fund, the only fund with a positive return in both years, is an extreme outlier.

(b) To demonstrate that correlation is not resistant, find r for all 23 funds and then find r for the 22 funds other than Gold. Explain from Gold's position in your plot why omitting this point makes r more negative.

(c) Find the equations of two least-squares lines for predicting 2003 return from 2002 return, one for all 23 funds and one omitting Fidelity Gold Fund. Add both lines to your scatterplot. Starting with the least-squares idea, explain why adding Fidelity Gold Fund to the other 22 funds moves the line in the direction that your graph shows.

7.51 Influence: monkey calls. Table 7.1 contains data on the response of 37 monkey neurons to pure tones and to monkey calls. Figure 7.6 is a scatterplot of these data.

MONKEYCALLS

(a) Find the least-squares line for predicting a neuron's call response from its pure-tone response. Add the line to your scatterplot. Mark on your plot the point (call it A) with the largest residual (either positive or negative) and also the point (call it B) that is an outlier in the x direction.

(b) How influential are each of these points for the correlation r?

(c) How influential are each of these points for the regression line?

7.52 Canadian students gambling. Here are the percents of students at four universities in Ontario who engage in several types of gambling:[19]

Type of gambling	Percent of males	Percent of females
Instant game tickets	38.8	52.6
LOTTO 6/49 or similar	27.8	19.1
Pro-Line	27.8	2.2
Bingo	7.0	14.7
Casino slots	30.7	41.1
Casino blackjack	16.4	6.4
Card games for money	23.5	7.3
Raffles or fundraising tickets	34.2	46.5
Sports pools	29.1	4.1
Horse races	8.9	7.1

(LOTTO 6/49 is a nationwide Canadian lottery. Pro-Line is a sports betting game offered by the Ontario provincial government.) Make a graph that compares the gambling behaviors of male and female students, and briefly discuss what the data show.

From Exploration to Inference

The purpose of statistics is to gain understanding from data. We can seek understanding in different ways, depending on the circumstances. We have studied one approach to data, *exploratory data analysis*, in some detail. Now we move from data analysis toward *statistical inference*. Both types of reasoning are essential to effective work with data. Here is a brief sketch of the differences between them.

EXPLORATORY DATA ANALYSIS	STATISTICAL INFERENCE
Purpose is unrestricted exploration of the data, searching for interesting patterns.	Purpose is to answer specific questions, posed before the data were produced.
Conclusions apply only to the individuals and circumstances for which we have data in hand.	Conclusions apply to a larger group of individuals or a broader class of circumstances.
Conclusions are informal, based on what we see in the data.	Conclusions are formal, backed by a statement of our confidence in them.

Our journey toward inference begins in Chapters 8 and 9, which describe statistical designs for *producing data* by samples and experiments. The conclusions of inference use the language of *probability*, the mathematics of chance. Chapters 10 and 11 present the ideas we need, and the optional Chapters 12 and 13 add more detail. Armed with designs for producing trustworthy data, data analysis to examine the data, and the language of probability, we are prepared to understand the big ideas of inference in Chapters 14, 15, and 16. These chapters are the foundation for the discussion of inference in practice that occupies the rest of the book.

Associated Press

Producing Data: Sampling

Exploratory data analysis helps us understand data that describe some group of individuals. But sometimes we have specific questions and no data to answer them. To get answers, we must *produce data*.

Suppose our question is "What percent of college students think that people should not obey laws that violate their personal values?" To answer the question, we interview undergraduate college students. We can't afford to ask all students, so we put the question to a *sample* chosen to represent the entire student *population*. How shall we choose a sample that truly represents the opinions of the entire population? Statistical designs for choosing samples are the topic of this chapter. We will see that

- a sound statistical design is necessary if we are to trust data from a sample;

- in sampling from large human populations, however, "practical problems" can overwhelm even sound designs.

POPULATION VERSUS SAMPLE

A political scientist wants to know what percent of college-age adults consider themselves conservatives. An automaker hires a market research firm to learn what percent of adults aged 18 to 35 recall seeing television advertisements for a new gas-electric hybrid car. Government economists inquire about average household income. In all these cases, we want information about a large group of individuals. In practice, we can afford to contact only part of the group in order to draw conclusions about the whole.

POPULATION, SAMPLE, SAMPLING DESIGN

The **population** in a statistical study is the entire group of individuals about which we want information.

A **sample** is a part of the population from which we actually collect information. We use a sample to draw conclusions about the entire population.

A **sampling design** describes exactly how to choose a sample from the population.

sample survey

Pay careful attention to the details of the definitions of "population" and "sample." Look at Exercise 8.1 right now to check your understanding. The first step in planning a **sample survey** is to say exactly *what population* we want to describe. The second step is to say exactly *what we want to measure*, that is, to give exact definitions of our variables.

EXAMPLE 8.1 The Current Population Survey

The government's Current Population Survey (CPS) contacts about 60,000 households each month. It produces the monthly unemployment rate and much other economic and social information. (See Figure 8.1.) To measure unemployment, we must first specify the *population* we want to describe. The CPS defines its population as all U.S. residents (including illegal immigrants) 16 years of age and over who are civilians and are not in an

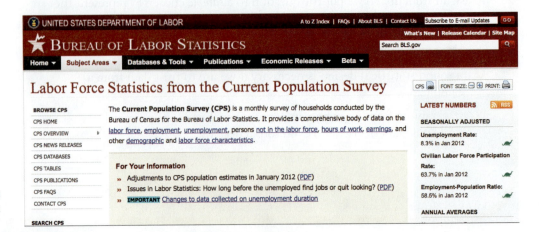

FIGURE 8.1

The home page of the Current Population Survey at the Bureau of Labor Statistics.

institution such as a prison. The unemployment rate announced in the news refers to this specific population.

To define the unemployment rate carefully, the CPS must say what it means to be "unemployed." Someone who is not looking for work—for example, a full-time student—should not be called unemployed just because she is not working for pay. If you are chosen for the CPS sample, the interviewer first asks whether you are available to work and whether you actually looked for work in the past four weeks. If not, you are neither employed nor unemployed—you are not in the labor force.

If you are in the labor force, the interviewer goes on to ask about employment. If you did any work for pay or in your own business during the week of the survey, you are employed. If you worked at least 15 hours in a family business without pay, you are employed. You are also employed if you have a job but didn't work because of vacation, being on strike, or other good reason. An unemployment rate of 8.7% means that 8.7% of the sample was unemployed, using the exact CPS definitions of both "labor force" and "unemployed." ■

APPLY YOUR KNOWLEDGE

8.1 Sampling students. A political scientist wants to know how college students feel about the Social Security system. She obtains a list of the 3456 undergraduates at her college and mails a questionnaire to 250 students selected at random. Only 104 questionnaires are returned.

(a) What is the population in this study? Be careful: what group does she *want information about?*

(b) What is the sample? Be careful: from what group does she *actually obtain information?*

8.2 Student archaeologists. An archaeological dig turns up large numbers of pottery shards, broken stone implements, and other artifacts. Students working on the project classify each artifact and assign it a number. The counts in different categories are important for understanding the site, so the project director chooses 2% of the artifacts at random and checks the students' work. What are the population and the sample here?

8.3 Customer satisfaction. A department store mails a customer satisfaction survey to people who make credit card purchases at the store. This month, 45,000 people made credit card purchases. Surveys are mailed to 1000 of these people, chosen at random, and 137 people return the survey form.

(a) What is the population of interest for this survey?

(b) What is the sample? From what group is information actually obtained?

HOW TO SAMPLE BADLY

The final step in planning a sample survey is the sampling design. A sampling design is a specific method for choosing a sample from the population. The easiest—but not the best—design just chooses individuals close at hand. A sample selected by taking the members of the population that are easiest to reach is called a **convenience sample.** Convenience samples often produce unrepresentative data.

convenience sample

EXAMPLE 8.2 Sampling at the mall

A sample of mall shoppers is fast and cheap. But people at shopping malls tend to be more prosperous than typical Americans. They are also more likely to be teenagers or retired. Moreover, unless interviewers are carefully trained, they tend to question well-dressed, respectable-looking people and avoid poorly dressed or tough-looking individuals. In short, mall interviews will not contact a sample that is representative of the entire population. ■

Interviews at shopping malls will almost always overrepresent middle-class and retired people and underrepresent the poor. This is *bias*: the outcomes of mall surveys will repeatedly miss the truth about the population in the same ways. Bias isn't bad luck on one sample but rather a systematic error caused by a bad sampling design.

BIAS

The design of a statistical study is **biased** if it systematically favors certain outcomes.

EXAMPLE 8.3 Online polls

Former CNN evening commentator Lou Dobbs doesn't like illegal immigration. One of his broadcasts in 2007 was largely devoted to attacking a proposal by the governor of New York State to offer driver's licenses to illegal immigrants as a public safety measure. During the show, Mr. Dobbs invited his viewers to go to loudobbs.com to vote on the question "Would you be more or less likely to vote for a presidential candidate who supports giving driver's licenses to illegal aliens?" We aren't surprised that 97% of the 7350 people who voted by the end of the broadcast said, "Less likely." ■

The loudobbs.com poll was biased because people chose whether or not to participate. Most who voted were viewers of Lou Dobbs's program who had just heard him denounce the governor's idea. *People who take the trouble to respond to an open invitation are usually not representative of any clearly defined population.* That's true of the people who bother to respond to write-in, call-in, or online polls in general. Polls like these are examples of *voluntary response sampling*.

VOLUNTARY RESPONSE SAMPLE

A **voluntary response sample** consists of people who choose themselves by responding to a broad appeal. Voluntary response samples are biased because people with strong opinions are most likely to respond.

APPLY YOUR KNOWLEDGE

8.4 Sampling on campus. You see a woman student standing in front of the student center, now and then stopping other students to ask them questions. She says that she is collecting student opinions for a class assignment. Explain why this sampling method is almost certainly biased.

8.5 More sampling on campus. You would like to start a club for psychology majors on campus, and you are interested in finding out what proportion of psychology majors would join. The dues would be $35 and used to pay for speakers to come to campus. You ask 5 psychology majors from your senior psychology honors seminar whether they would be interested in joining this club and find that 4 of the 5 students questioned are interested. Is this sampling method biased, and, if so, what is the likely direction of bias?

SIMPLE RANDOM SAMPLES

In a voluntary response sample, people choose whether to respond. In a convenience sample, the interviewer makes the choice. In both cases, personal choice produces bias. *Choosing a sample by chance* attacks bias by giving all individuals an equal chance to be chosen. Rich and poor, young and old, black and white, all have the same chance to be in the sample. The simplest way to use chance to select a sample is to place names in a hat (the population) and draw out a handful (the sample). This is the idea of *simple random sampling*.

SIMPLE RANDOM SAMPLE

A **simple random sample (SRS)** of size n consists of n individuals from the population chosen in such a way that every set of n individuals has an equal chance to be the sample actually selected.

An SRS not only gives each individual an equal chance to be chosen but also gives every possible sample an equal chance to be chosen. There are other random sampling designs that give each individual, but not each sample, an equal chance. Exercise 8.36 describes one such design.

When you think of an SRS, picture drawing names from a hat to remind yourself that an SRS doesn't favor any part of the population. That's why an SRS is a better method of choosing samples than convenience or voluntary response sampling. But writing names on slips of paper and drawing them from a hat is slow and inconvenient. In practice, samplers use software. If you don't use software, you can randomize by using a *table of random digits*. In fact, software for choosing samples starts by generating random digits, so using a table just does by hand what the software does more quickly.

RANDOM DIGITS

A **table of random digits** is a long string of the digits 0, 1, 2, 3, 4, 5, 6, 7, 8, 9 with these two properties:

1. Each entry in the table is equally likely to be any of the 10 digits 0 through 9.

2. The entries are independent of each other. That is, knowledge of one part of the table gives no information about any other part.

Table B at the back of the book is a table of random digits. Table B begins with the digits 19223950340575628713. To make the table easier to read, the digits appear in groups of five and in numbered rows. The groups and rows have no meaning—the table is just a long list of randomly chosen digits. There are two steps in using the table to choose a simple random sample.

USING TABLE B TO CHOOSE AN SRS

Label: Give each member of the population a numerical label of the *same length*.

Table: To choose an SRS, read from Table B successive groups of digits of the length you used as labels. Your sample contains the individuals whose labels you find in the table.

You can label up to 100 items with two digits: 01, 02, . . . , 99, 00. Up to 1000 items can be labeled with three digits, and so on. Always use the shortest labels that will cover your population. We recommend that you begin with label 1 (or 01 or 001, as needed). Reading groups of digits from the table gives all individuals the same chance to be chosen because all labels of the same length have the same chance to be found in the table. For example, any pair of digits in the table is equally likely to be any of the 100 possible labels 01, 02, . . . , 99, 00. Ignore any group of digits that was not used as a label or that duplicates a label already in the sample.

EXAMPLE 8.4 Sampling spring break resorts

Robert Daly/Getty Images

A campus newspaper plans a major article on spring break destinations. The authors intend to call 4 randomly chosen resorts at each destination to ask about their attitudes toward groups of students as guests. Here are the resorts listed in one city:

01	Aloha Kai	08	Captiva	15	Palm Tree	22	Sea Shell
02	Anchor Down	09	Casa del Mar	16	Radisson	23	Silver Beach
03	Banana Bay	10	Coconuts	17	Ramada	24	Sunset Beach
04	Banyan Tree	11	Diplomat	18	Sandpiper	25	Tradewinds
05	Beach Castle	12	Holiday Inn	19	Sea Castle	26	Tropical Breeze
06	Best Western	13	Lime Tree	20	Sea Club	27	Tropical Shores
07	Cabana	14	Outrigger	21	Sea Grape	28	Veranda

Label: Because two digits are needed to label the 28 resorts, all labels will have two digits. We have added labels 01 to 28 to the list of resorts. Always say how you labeled the members of the population. To sample from the 1240 resorts in a major vacation area, you would label the resorts 0001, 0002, . . . , 1239, 1240.

Table: Read two-digit groups from Table B until you have chosen four resorts. Starting at line 130 (any line will do), we find

69051	64817	87174	09517	84534	06489	87201	97245

Because the labels are two digits long, read successive two-digit groups from the table. Ignore groups not used as labels, like the initial 69. Also ignore any repeated labels, like the second and third 17s in this row, because you can't choose the same resort twice. Your sample contains the resorts labeled 05, 16, 17, and 20. These are Beach Castle, Radisson, Ramada, and Sea Club. ■

Random sampling, the use of impersonal chance to avoid bias, is the basic idea of sampling design. Online polls and mall interviews also produce samples, but these samples are chosen in ways that invite bias. *The first question to ask about any sample is whether it was chosen at random.*

random sampling

EXAMPLE 8.5 Texting while driving

"Do you think sending a text message while driving, either on a cell phone or other electronic device, should be legal or illegal?" When the *New York Times* and CBS News asked this question of 829 adults in October 2009, 97% said "illegal" and just 1% said "legal." Can we trust the opinions of this sample to fairly represent the opinions of all adults? Here's part of the statement by the *Times* on how the poll was conducted:

> The latest *New York Times/CBS News* poll is based on telephone interviews conducted October 5 through October 8 with 829 adults throughout the United States.
>
> The sample of land line telephone exchanges called was randomly selected by a computer from a complete list of more than 69,000 active residential exchanges across the country. The exchanges were chosen so as to ensure that each region of the country was represented in proportion to its population.
>
> Within each exchange, random digits were added to form a complete telephone number, thus permitting access to listed and unlisted numbers alike. Within each household, one adult was designated by a random procedure to be the respondent for the survey.[1]

iStockphoto

This is a good description of a common method for choosing national samples, called **random digit dialing.** We'll come back to random digit dialing and its problems later (see Example 8.6 and Exercise 8.29), but this statement is a good start toward gaining our confidence. We know the size of the sample and when the poll was taken, and the comforting word "random" appears three times. ■

random digit dialing

Large-scale sample surveys often use random sampling designs more complicated than an SRS. For example, the opinion poll described in Example 8.5 uses a three-stage design: choose a random sample of telephone exchanges, then a random sample of household telephone numbers within each exchange, then a random adult in each household. Analysis of data from sampling designs more complex than an SRS takes us beyond basic statistics. But the SRS is the building block of more elaborate designs, and analysis of other designs differs more in complexity of detail than in fundamental concepts.

APPLY YOUR KNOWLEDGE

8.6 Apartment living. You are planning a report on apartment living in a college town. You decide to select three apartment complexes at random for in-depth interviews with residents. Use software or Table B to select a simple random sample of 4 of the following apartment complexes. If you use Table B, start at line 122.

Ashley Oaks	Country View	Mayfair Village
Bay Pointe	Country Villa	Nobb Hill
Beau Jardin	Crestview	Pemberly Courts
Bluffs	Del-Lynn	Peppermill

Brandon Place	Fairington	Pheasant Run
Briarwood	Fairway Knolls	River Walk
Brownstone	Fowler	Sagamore Ridge
Burberry Place	Franklin Park	Salem Courthouse
Cambridge	Georgetown	Village Square
Chauncey Village	Greenacres	Waterford Court

8.7 Minority managers. A firm wants to understand the attitudes of its minority managers toward its system for assessing management performance. Below is a list of all the firm's managers who are members of minority groups. Use software or Table B at line 134 to choose 5 to be interviewed in detail about the performance appraisal system.

Adelaja	Draguljic	Huo	Modur
Ahmadiani	Fernandez	Ippolito	Rettiganti
Barnes	Fox	Jiang	Rodriguez
Bonds	Gao	Jung	Sanchez
Burke	Gemayel	Mani	Sgambellone
Deis	Gupta	Mazzeo	Yajima
Ding	Hernandez		

8.8 Sampling gravestones. The local genealogical society in Coles County, Illinois, has compiled records on all 55,914 gravestones in cemeteries in the county for the years 1825 to 1985. Historians plan to use these records to learn about African Americans in Coles County's history. They first choose an SRS of 395 records to check their accuracy by visiting the actual gravestones.[2]

(a) How would you label the 55,914 records?

(b) Use Table B, beginning at line 120, to choose the first 5 records for the SRS.

©*The Photo Works*

INFERENCE ABOUT THE POPULATION

inference

The purpose of a sample is to give us information about a larger population. The process of drawing conclusions about a population on the basis of sample data is called **inference** because we *infer* information about the population from what we *know* about the sample.

Inference from convenience samples or voluntary response samples would be misleading because these methods of choosing a sample are biased. We are almost certain that the sample does *not* fairly represent the population. *The first reason to rely on random sampling is to eliminate bias in selecting samples from the list of available individuals.*

Nonetheless, it is unlikely that results from a random sample are exactly the same as for the entire population. Sample results, like the unemployment rate obtained from the monthly Current Population Survey, are only estimates of the truth about the population. If we select two samples at random from the same population, we will almost certainly draw different individuals. So the sample results will differ somewhat, just by chance.

Why can we trust random samples? The big idea is that the results of random sampling don't change haphazardly from sample to sample. Because we deliberately use chance, the results obey the laws of probability that govern chance behavior. These laws allow us to say how likely it is that sample results are close to the truth about the population. *The second reason to use random sampling is that the laws of probability allow trustworthy inference about the population.* Results from random samples come with a margin of error that sets bounds on the size of the likely error. We will begin to learn the details in Chapter 14.

One point is worth making now: *larger random samples give more accurate results than smaller samples.* By taking a very large sample, you can be confident that the sample result is very close to the truth about the population. The Current Population Survey contacts about 60,000 households, so it estimates the national unemployment rate quite accurately. Opinion polls that contact 1000 or 1500 people give less accurate results. Of course, only samples chosen by chance carry this guarantee. Lou Dobbs's online sample tells us little about overall American public opinion even though 7350 people clicked a response.

APPLY YOUR KNOWLEDGE

8.9 Ask more people. Just before a presidential election, a national opinion-polling firm increases the size of its weekly sample from the usual 1500 people to 4000 people. Why do you think the firm does this?

8.10 Sampling Pentecostals. Pentecostals are among the fastest-growing Christian groups in many countries. The Pew Forum on Religion and Public Life surveyed Pentecostal Christians in 10 countries and compared their opinions with those of the general population. In South Korea, random samples by Gallup Korea had margins of error (we will give more detail in later chapters) of ±4% for the general public and ±9% for Pentecostals.[3] What do you think explains the fact that estimates for Pentecostals were less accurate?

CAUTIONS ABOUT SAMPLE SURVEYS

Random selection eliminates bias in the choice of a sample from a list of the population. When the population consists of human beings, however, accurate information from a sample requires more than a good sampling design.

To begin, we need an accurate and complete list of the population. Because such a list is rarely available, most samples suffer from some degree of *undercoverage*. A sample survey of households, for example, will miss not only homeless people but prison inmates and students in dormitories. An opinion poll conducted by calling landline telephone numbers will miss households that have only cell phones as well as households without a phone. The results of national sample surveys therefore have some bias if the people not covered differ from the rest of the population.

A more serious source of bias in most sample surveys is *nonresponse*, which occurs when a selected individual cannot be contacted or refuses to cooperate. Nonresponse to sample surveys often exceeds 50%, even with careful planning and several callbacks. Because nonresponse is higher in urban areas, many sample surveys substitute other people in the same area to avoid favoring rural areas in the final sample. If the people contacted differ from those who are rarely at home or who refuse to answer questions, some bias remains.

UNDERCOVERAGE AND NONRESPONSE

Undercoverage occurs when some groups in the population are left out of the process of choosing the sample.

Nonresponse occurs when an individual chosen for the sample can't be contacted or refuses to participate.

EXAMPLE 8.6 Cell phones and undercoverage

A few national sample surveys, especially government surveys, interview some or all of their subjects in person. Most national surveys contact subjects by telephone using the random digit dialing (RDD) method described in Example 8.5. Technology, especially the spread of cell phones, is making traditional RDD methods outdated.

The number of *cell-phone-only households* is increasing rapidly. By mid-2007, 14% of American households had a cell phone but no landline phone, and by the end of 2009 that number had increased to almost 25%. Even if the United States and Canada don't approach the 61% of households in Finland that have no landline phone, it's clear that RDD reaching only landline numbers suffers from undercoverage. Can surveys just add cell phone numbers? Not easily. Federal regulations require hand dialing of cell phone numbers, ruling out computerized RDD sampling and adding expense. A cell phone can be anywhere, and many people keep their cell number despite moving, so breaking down a sample by location becomes difficult. And a cell phone user may be driving or otherwise unable to talk safely.

People who screen calls and people who have only a cell phone tend to be younger than the general population. By the end of 2009 almost half of adults aged 25 to 29 years (48.6%) lived in households with no landline phone. So RDD surveys using only landline phones may be biased (see Exercise 8.29). Many polling organizations include a minimum quota of cell phone users in their samples to help adjust for bias (see Exercise 8.41).[4] ■

EXAMPLE 8.7 How bad is nonresponse?

The Census Bureau's American Community Survey (ACS) has the lowest nonresponse rate of any poll we know: only about 1% of the households in the sample refuse to respond; the overall nonresponse rate, including "never at home" and other causes, is just 2.5%.[5] This monthly survey of about 250,000 households replaces the "long form" that in the past was sent to some households in the every-ten-years national census. Participation in the ACS is mandatory, and the Census Bureau follows up by telephone and then in person if a household fails to return the mail questionnaire.

The University of Chicago's General Social Survey (GSS) is the nation's most important social science survey. (See Figure 8.2.) The GSS contacts its sample in person, and it is run by a university. Despite these advantages, a recent survey had a 30% rate of nonresponse.

What about opinion polls by news media and opinion-polling firms? Polls don't tell us how bad their nonresponse is. The Pew Research Center for the People and the Press imitated a careful random digit dialing survey and published the results: over 5 days, the survey reached 76% of the households in its chosen sample, but "because of busy schedules, skepticism and outright refusals, interviews were completed in just 38% of households that were reached." Combining households that could not be contacted with those who did not complete the interview gave a nonresponse rate of 73%.[6] ■

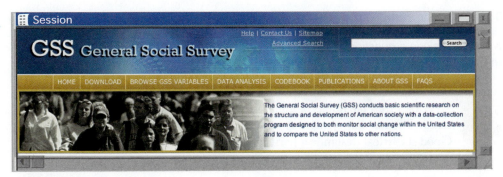

FIGURE 8.2

The home page of the General Social Survey at the University of Chicago's National Opinion Research Center. The GSS has tracked opinions about a wide variety of issues since 1972.

In addition, the behavior of the respondent or the interviewer can cause **response bias** in sample results. People know that they should take the trouble to vote, for example, so many who didn't vote in the last election will tell an interviewer that they did. Answers to questions that ask respondents to recall past events are often inaccurate because of faulty memory. For example, many people "telescope" events in the past, bringing them forward in memory to more recent time periods. "Have you visited a dentist in the last 6 months?" will often draw a "Yes" from someone who last visited a dentist 8 months ago.[7] Careful training of interviewers and careful supervision to avoid variation among interviewers can reduce response bias. Good interviewing technique is another aspect of a well-done sample survey.

response bias

The **wording of questions** is the most important influence on the answers given to a sample survey. Confusing or leading questions can introduce strong bias, and changes in wording can greatly change a survey's outcome. Even the order in which questions are asked matters. Here are some examples.[8]

wording effects

EXAMPLE 8.8 What was that question?

How do Americans feel about illegal immigrants? "Should illegal immigrants be prosecuted and deported for being in the U.S. illegally, or shouldn't they?" Asked this question in an opinion poll, 69% favored deportation. But when the very same sample was asked whether illegal immigrants who have worked in the United States for two years "should be given a chance to keep their jobs and eventually apply for legal status," 62% said that they should. Different questions give quite different impressions of attitudes toward illegal immigrants.

What about government help for the poor? Only 13% think we are spending too much on "assistance to the poor," but 44% think we are spending too much on "welfare." ■

EXAMPLE 8.9 Are you happy?

Ask a sample of college students these two questions:

"How happy are you with your life in general?" (Answers on a scale of 1 to 5)

"How many dates did you have last month?"

The correlation between answers is $r = -0.012$ when asked in this order. It appears that dating has little to do with happiness. Reverse the order of the questions, however, and $r = 0.66$. Asking a question that brings dating to mind makes dating success a big factor in happiness. ■

 Don't trust the results of a sample survey until you have read the exact questions asked. The amount of nonresponse and the date of the survey are also important. Good statistical design is a part, but only a part, of a trustworthy survey.

APPLY YOUR KNOWLEDGE

8.11   Ring-no-answer. A common form of nonresponse in telephone surveys is "ring-no-answer." That is, a call is made to an active number but no one answers. The Italian National Statistical Institute looked at nonresponse to a government survey of households in Italy during the periods January 1 to Easter and July 1 to August 31. All calls were made between 7 and 10 P.M., but 21.4% gave "ring-no-answer" in one period versus 41.5% "ring-no-answer" in the other period.[9] Which period do you think had the higher rate of no answers? Why? Explain why a high rate of nonresponse makes sample results less reliable.

8.12   Gays in the military. In 2010, a Quinnipiac University Poll and a CNN Poll each asked a nationwide sample about their views on openly gay men and women serving in the military.[10] Here are the two questions:

> Question A: *Federal law currently prohibits openly gay men and women from serving in the military. Do you think this law should be repealed or not?*

> Question B: *Do you think people who are openly gay or homosexual should or should not be allowed to serve in the U.S. military?*

One of these questions had 78% responding "should," and the other question had only 57% responding "should." Which wording is slanted toward a more negative response on gays in the military? Why?

CHAPTER 8   SUMMARY

CHAPTER SPECIFICS

■ A **sample survey** selects a **sample** from the **population** of all individuals about which we desire information. We base conclusions about the population on data from the sample. It is important to specify exactly what population you are interested in and what variables you will measure.

■ The **design** of a sample describes the method used to select the sample from the population. **Random sampling** designs use chance to select a sample.

■ The basic random sampling design is a **simple random sample (SRS).** An SRS gives every possible sample of a given size the same chance to be chosen.

■ Choose an SRS by labeling the members of the population and using **random digits** to select the sample. Software can automate this process.

- Failure to use random sampling often results in **bias,** or systematic errors in the way the sample represents the population. **Voluntary response samples,** in which the respondents choose themselves, are particularly prone to large bias.

- In human populations, even random samples can suffer from bias due to **undercoverage** or **nonresponse,** from **response bias,** or from misleading results due to **poorly worded questions.** Sample surveys must deal expertly with these potential problems in addition to using a random sampling design.

- Most national sample surveys are carried out by telephone, using **random digit dialing** to choose residential telephone numbers at random. Call screening is increasing nonresponse to such surveys, and the rise of cell-phone-only households is increasing undercoverage.

LINK IT

The methods of Chapters 1 to 6 can be used to describe data regardless of how the data were obtained. However, if we want to reason from data to give answers to specific questions or to draw conclusions about the larger population, then the method that was used to collect the data is important. Sampling is one way to collect data, but it does not guarantee that we can draw meaningful conclusions. Biased sampling methods, such as convenience sampling and voluntary response samples, produce data that can be misleading, resulting in incorrect conclusions. Simple random sampling avoids bias and produces data that can lead to valid conclusions regarding the population. Even with perfect sampling methods, there is still sample-to-sample variation; we will begin our study of the connection between sampling variation and drawing conclusions in Chapter 11.

Even when we take a simple random sample, our conclusions can be weakened by undercoverage, nonresponse, and poor wording of questions. Careful attention must be given to all aspects of the sampling process to ensure that the conclusions we make are valid. In many cases more complex sampling designs are required. But the use of impersonal chance to select the sample remains a key ingredient in the sampling process. And issues such as undercoverage and nonresponse still remain for these more complex designs.

CHECK YOUR SKILLS

8.13 An online store contacts 1000 customers from its list of customers who have purchased something from them in the last year. In all, 696 of the 1000 say that they are very satisfied with the store's Web site. The population in this setting is

(a) all customers who have purchased something in the last year.

(b) the 1000 customers contacted.

(c) the 696 customers who were very satisfied with the store's Web site.

8.14 A state representative wants to know how voters in his district feel about enacting a statewide smoking ban in all enclosed public places, including bars and restaurants, as well as several other current statewide issues. He mails a questionnaire addressing these issues to an SRS of 800 voters in his district. Of the 800 questionnaires mailed, 152 were returned. The sample is

(a) the 800 voters receiving the questionnaire.

(b) the 152 voters returning the questionnaire.

(c) all voters in his district.

8.15 The Web site www.twiigs.com allows you to vote on polls that interest you or to post one of your own. Once you have found a poll of interest, you just click on "Vote" and your response becomes part of the sample. One of the questions in July 2010 was "How many times have you been pulled over by the police?" Of the 780 people responding, 70% said "1–5 times." You can conclude that

    (a) about 70% of Americans have been pulled over by the police "1–5 times."

    (b) the poll uses voluntary response, so the results tell us little about the population of all adults.

    (c) more people still need to vote on the question, as a larger sample is required to reduce bias.

8.16 You must choose an SRS of 10 of the 440 retail outlets in New York that sell your company's products. How would you label this population in order to use Table B?

    (a) 001, 002, 003, . . . , 439, 440

    (b) 000, 001, 002, . . . , 439, 440

    (c) 1, 2, . . . , 439, 440

8.17 You are using the table of random digits to choose a simple random sample of 6 students from a class of 30 students. You label the students 01 to 30 in alphabetical order. You are going to select the sample using Table B. Which of the following is a possible sample that could be obtained?

    (a) 45, 74, 04, 18, 07, 65

    (b) 04, 18, 07, 13, 02, 07

    (c) 04, 18, 07, 13, 02, 05

8.18 A sample of households in a community is selected at random from the telephone directory. In this community, 4% of households have no telephone, 10% have only cell phones, and another 25% have unlisted telephone numbers. The sample will certainly suffer from

    (a) nonresponse.

    (b) undercoverage.

    (c) false responses.

8.19 The Pew Research Center survey asked a random sample of 1500 adults, "Do you think the use of marijuana should be made legal, or not?" In the entire sample, 41% said, "Yes, legal." But only 24% of the Republicans in the sample said, "Yes, legal." Which of these two sample percents will be more accurate as an estimate of the truth about the population?

    (a) The result for Republicans is more accurate because it is easier to estimate a proportion for a smaller group.

    (b) The result for the entire sample is more accurate because it comes from a larger sample.

    (c) Both are equally accurate because both come from the same sample.

CHAPTER 8 EXERCISES

In all exercises asking for an SRS, you may use either Table B or software.

8.20 Immigration reform priorities. A Gallup Poll asked, "If you had to choose, what should be the main focus of the U.S. government in dealing with the issue of illegal immigration—developing a plan for halting the flow of illegal immigrants into the U.S. (or) developing a plan to deal with immigrants who are currently in the U.S. illegally?" Gallup's report said, "Results are based on telephone interviews conducted June 11–13, 2010, with a random sample of 1,014 adults, aged 18 and older, living in the continental U.S."[11] What is the population for this sample survey? What is the sample?

8.21 Sampling stuffed envelopes. A large retailer prepares its customers' monthly credit card bills using an automatic machine that folds the bills, stuffs them into envelopes, and seals the envelopes for mailing. Are the envelopes completely sealed? Inspectors choose 40 envelopes from the 1000 stuffed each hour for visual inspection. What is the population for this sample survey? What is the sample?

8.22 Do you trust the Internet? You want to ask a sample of college students the question "How much do you trust information about health that you find on the Internet—a great deal, somewhat, not much, or not at all?" You try out this and other questions on a pilot group of 8 students chosen from your class. The class members are

Adams	Devore	Guo	Newberg	Shoepf
Aeffner	Ding	Heaton	Paulsen	Spagnola
Barnes	Drake	Huling	Payton	Terry
Bower	Eckstein	Kahler	Prince	Vore
Burke	Fassnacht	Kessis	Pulak	Wallace
Cao	Fullmer	Lu	Rabin	Wanner
Cisse	Gandhi	Mattos	Roberts	Zhang

Choose an SRS of 8 students. If you use Table B, start at line 131.

8.23 Sampling telephone area codes. The United States currently has approximately 287 Numbering Plan Areas (NPAs) in service, corresponding to geographic regions. Each NPA is identified by a three-digit code, commonly called an area code. (More are created regularly.)[12] Choose an SRS of 20 of these area codes for a study of available telephone numbers. (If you use Table B, start at line 135 and choose only the first 5 area codes in the sample.)

8.24 Sampling the forest. To gather data on a 1200-acre pine forest in Louisiana, the U.S. Forest Service laid a grid of 1410 equally spaced circular plots over a map of the forest. A ground survey visited a sample of 10% of these plots.[13]

(a) How would you label the plots?

(b) Choose the first 5 plots in an SRS of 141 plots. (If you use Table B, start at line 105.)

8.25 Sampling students. The freshman class at the Ohio State University contains 6168 students. The Office of International Affairs is considering increasing its programming staff for its study abroad program and is going to sample the entering freshman class to see how many students are considering taking advantage of the opportunity to travel abroad while attending Ohio State.

(a) How would you label the names in order to select an SRS?

(b) Use software or Table B, starting at line 135, to select an SRS of 8 Ohio State freshmen.

8.26 Random digits. In using Table B repeatedly to choose random samples, you should not always begin at the same place, such as line 101. Why not?

8.27 Random digits. Which of the following statements are true of a table of random digits, and which are false? Briefly explain your answers.

(a) There are exactly four 0s in each row of 40 digits.

(b) Each pair of digits has chance 1/100 of being 00.

(c) The digits 0000 can never appear as a group, because this pattern is not random.

8.28 Movie viewing. An opinion poll calls 2000 randomly chosen residential telephone numbers and asks to speak with an adult member of the household. The interviewer asks, "How many movies have you watched in a movie theater in the past 12 months?"

(a) What population do you think the poll has in mind?

(b) In all, 831 people respond. What is the rate (percent) of nonresponse?

(c) What source of response error is likely for the question asked?

8.29 More on random digit dialing. By the end of 2009 about 25% of adults lived in households with a cell phone and no landline phone, and among adults aged 25 to 29 this number was almost 50%.

(a) Write a survey question for which the opinions of adults with landline phones only are likely to differ from the opinions of adults with cell phones only. Give the direction of the difference of opinion.

(b) For the survey question in (a), suppose a survey was conducted using random digit dialing of landline phones only. Would the results be biased? What would be the direction of bias?

8.30 Nonresponse. Academic sample surveys, unlike commercial polls, often discuss nonresponse. In a survey of drivers, researchers called a random sample of all listed residential telephone numbers in the United States. Of 45,956 calls, 5029 were completed.[14] What was the rate of nonresponse for this sample? (Only one call was made to each number. Nonresponse would be lower if more calls were made.)

8.31 Running red lights. The sample described in the previous exercise produced a list of 5024 licensed drivers. The investigators then chose an SRS of 880 of these drivers to answer questions about their driving habits.

(a) How would you assign labels to the 5024 drivers? Use Table B, starting at line 104, to choose the first 5 drivers in the sample.

(b) One question asked was "Recalling the last ten traffic lights you drove through, how many of them were red when you entered the intersections?" Of the 880 respondents, 171 admitted that at least one light had been red. A practical problem with this survey is that people may not give truthful answers. What is the likely direction of the bias: do you think more or fewer than 171 of the 880 respondents really ran a red light? Why?

8.32 The Canadian census. The Canadian government's decision to eliminate the mandatory long-form version of the census and to move these questions to an optional survey has many concerned. Economists and many members of the business community stressed the importance of the census data for crafting public policy. The minister of industry was given the task of defending the government's decision. In response to an argument that making the long form of the census voluntary would skew the data by eliminating the statistical randomness of the survey, the minister replied, "Wrong. Statisticians can ensure validity with a larger sample size."[15] Is the minister correct? If not, explain in simple terms the error in his statement.

8.33 Sampling at a party. At a party there are 40 men and 30 women. You want to ask opinions about how to improve the next party. You choose at random 4 of the men and separately choose at random 3 of the women to interview.

(a) What is the probability that any of the 40 men is in your random sample of 4 men to be interviewed? What is the probability that any of the 30 women is in your random sample of 3 women to be interviewed?

(b) If you have done the calculations correctly in part (a), the probability of any person at the party being interviewed is the same. Why is your sample of 7 men and women not an SRS of people from the party?

8.34 Stratified random samples. Cook County, Illinois, has the second-largest population of any county in the United States (after Los Angeles County, California). Cook County has 30 suburban townships and an additional 8 townships that make up the city of Chicago. The suburban townships are

Barrington	Hanover	Norwood Park	Riverside
Berwyn	Lemont	Oak Park	Schaumburg
Bloom	Leyden	Orland	Stickney
Bremen	Lyons	Palatine	Thornton
Calumet	Maine	Palos	Wheeling
Cicero	New Trier	Proviso	Worth
Elk Grove	Niles	Rich	
Evanston	Northfield	River Forest	

The Chicago townships are

Hyde Park	Lake View	South Chicago
Jefferson	North Chicago	West Chicago
Lake	Rogers Park	

Because city and suburban areas may differ, the first stage of a multistage sample chooses an SRS of 6 suburban townships and a separate SRS of 4 of the more heavily populated Chicago townships. This is called a **stratified random sample:** divide the population into groups using information available in advance, then take separate SRSs in each group. Use Table B or software to choose this sample. (If you use Table B, assign labels in alphabetical order and start at line 105 for the suburbs and at line 115 for Chicago.)

8.35 Sampling pharmacists. All pharmacists in the Canadian province of Ontario are required to be members of the Ontario College of Pharmacists. In 2009, there were 11,361 members of the college divided into 17 electoral districts, with each district having an elected member on the Council. The number of members in each district follow:[16]

District	1	2	3	4	5	6	7	8	9
Membership	997	803	694	771	536	1126	1104	864	286

District	10	11	12	13	14	15	16	17
Membership	414	458	572	537	303	263	743	890

Suppose that the Council is interested in obtaining members' views on the Minor Ailments Program, which proposes making pharmacists the primary source of care for patients with some 30 minor ailments. To be sure that the opinions of all districts are represented, you decide to choose a *stratified random sample* (see the previous exercise) of 5 pharmacists from each district. Explain how you will assign labels within each district, and then give the labels of the pharmacists from Districts 1 and 2 in your sample. If you use Table B, start at line 122 for District 1 and at line 131 for District 2. Why should you not start at the same line in Table B to obtain your samples for Districts 1 and 2?

8.36 Systematic random samples. *Systematic random samples* go through a list of the population and choose individuals at fixed intervals from a randomly chosen starting point. For example, a study of dating among college students chose a systematic sample of 200 single male students at a university as follows.[17] Start with a list of all 9000 single male students. Because 9000/200 = 45, choose one of the first 45 names on the list at random and then every 45th name after that. For example, if the first name chosen is at position 23, the systematic sample consists of the names at positions 23, 68, 113, 158, and so on up to 8978.

(a) Use Table B to choose a systematic random sample of 5 names from a list of 200. Enter the table at line 120.

(b) Like an SRS, a systematic sample gives all individuals the same chance to be chosen. Explain why this is true, then explain carefully why a systematic sample is nonetheless *not* an SRS.

8.37 Sampling frame. The list of individuals from which a sample is actually selected is called the *sampling frame*. Ideally, the frame should list every individual in the population, but in practice this is often difficult. A frame that leaves out part of the population is a common source of undercoverage.

(a) Suppose that a sample of households in a community is selected at random from the telephone directory. What households are omitted from this frame? What types of people do you think are likely to live in these households? These people will probably be underrepresented in the sample.

(b) It is usual in telephone surveys to use random digit dialing equipment that selects the last four digits of a telephone number at random after being given the exchange (the first three digits), as described in Example 8.5 (page 175). Which of the households you mentioned in your answer to (a) will be included in the sampling frame by random digit dialing?

8.38 Canadian health care survey. The Tenth Annual Health Care in Canada Survey is a survey of the opinions of the Canadian public and health care providers on a variety of health care issues, including quality of health care, access to health care, health and the environment, and so forth. A description of the survey follows:

> The 10th edition of the Health Care in Canada Survey was conducted by POLLARA Research between October 3rd and November 8th, 2007. Results for the survey are based on telephone interviews with nationally representative samples of 1,223 members of the Canadian public, 202 doctors, 201 nurses, 202 pharmacists and 201 health managers. Public results are considered to be accurate within ±2.8%, while the margin of error for results for doctors, nurses, pharmacists and managers is ±6.9%.[18]

(a) Why is the accuracy greater for the public than for health care providers and managers?

(b) Why do you think they sampled the public as well as health care providers and managers?

8.39 Wording survey questions. Comment on each of the following as a potential sample survey question. Is the question clear? Is it slanted toward a desired response?

(a) "Some cell phone users have developed brain cancer. Should all cell phones come with a warning label explaining the danger of using cell phones?"

(b) "Do you agree that a national system of health insurance should be favored because it would provide health insurance for everyone and would reduce administrative costs?"

(c) "In view of the negative externalities in parent labor force participation and pediatric evidence associating increased group size with morbidity of children in day care, do you support government subsidies for day care programs?"

8.40 Your own bad questions. Write your own examples of bad sample survey questions.

(a) Write a biased question designed to get one answer rather than another.

(b) Write a question to which many people may not give truthful answers.

8.41 Gulf oil spill. Two months after the Gulf oil spill began in April 2010, nearly half of Americans (49%) believed that at least some of the affected beaches would never recover, according to a Gallup Poll conducted June 11–13, 2010. Results are based on telephone interviews of a random sample of 1014 adults, aged 18 and older, selected using random digit dialing sampling. In the survey methods section, Gallup reports: "Interviews are conducted with respondents on landline telephones (for respondents with a landline telephone) and cellular phones (for respondents who are cell phone–only). Each sample includes a minimum quota of 150 cell phone–only respondents and 850 landline respondents, with additional minimum quotas among landline respondents for gender within region."[19]

(a) What is automated random digit dialing? Why is it a practical method for obtaining (almost) an SRS of households with landline phones?

(b) The survey wants the opinion of an individual adult. Several adults may live in a household. In that case, the survey interviewed the adult with the most recent birthday. Why is this preferable to simply interviewing the person who answers the phone?

(c) The survey included both landline telephones and cellular phones. Why do you think this may be important?

8.42 Seat belt use. A study in El Paso, Texas, looked at seat belt use by drivers. Drivers were observed at randomly chosen convenience stores. After they left their cars, they were invited to answer questions that included questions about seat belt use. In all, 75% said they always used seat belts, yet only 61.5% were wearing seat belts when they pulled into the store parking lots.[20] Explain the reason for the bias observed in responses to the survey. Do you expect bias in the same direction in most surveys about seat belt use?

8.43 Online polls. Example 8.3 reports an online poll in which 97% of the respondents opposed issuing driver's licenses to illegal immigrants. National random samples taken at the same time showed about 70% of the respondents opposed to such licenses. Explain briefly to someone who knows no statistics why the random samples report public opinion more reliably than the online poll.

EXPLORING THE WEB

8.44 Poor survey designs. The Web site for the American Association for Public Opinion Research discusses several issues about polls. This information can be found at www.aapor. org/Poll_andamp_Survey_FAQs.htm. Click on the link *Questions to Ask When Writing about*

Polls for suggestions about how to determine if a poll is good or bad. Click on the link *What Is a Random Sample?* and then the link *Bad Samples* for some examples of flawed samples.

(a) You are going to design a survey at your university. Give a question of interest and two examples of bad ways to collect your sample, along with the likely direction of bias that would result. Explain your answers.

(b) How would you modify your examples in (a) to produce a better sample? What are some difficulties you might encounter when collecting your sample?

8.45 Find a survey. The Web site for the Pew Research Center for the People and the Press is www.people-press.org. Go to the Web site and read one of the featured surveys. Which questions listed under Questions to Ask When Writing about Polls from the previous exercise can be answered from the information in the featured survey you have read? You may find the concluding section entitled About the Survey and some of the links at the end of the featured survey helpful for finding answers to these questions.

David Caudery/Digital Camera Magazine via Getty Images

Producing Data: Experiments

IN THIS CHAPTER WE COVER...

- Observation versus experiment
- Subjects, factors, treatments
- How to experiment badly
- Randomized comparative experiments
- The logic of randomized comparative experiments
- Cautions about experimentation
- Matched pairs designs

A **sample survey aims to gather information about a population without disturbing the population in the process.** Sample surveys are one kind of *observational study*. Other observational studies observe the behavior of animals in the wild or the interactions between teacher and students in the classroom. This chapter is about statistical designs for *experiments*, a quite different way to produce data.

OBSERVATION VERSUS EXPERIMENT

Experiments don't just observe individuals or ask them questions. They actively impose some treatment in order to observe the response. Experiments can answer questions such as "Does aspirin reduce the chance of a heart attack?" and "Do a majority of college students prefer Pepsi to Coke when they taste both without knowing which they are drinking?"

> ### OBSERVATION VERSUS EXPERIMENT
>
> An **observational study** observes individuals and measures variables of interest but does not attempt to influence the responses. The purpose of an observational study is to describe some group or situation.
>
> An **experiment,** on the other hand, deliberately imposes some treatment on individuals in order to observe their responses. The purpose of an experiment is to study whether the treatment causes a change in the response.

An observational study, even one based on a statistical sample, is a poor way to gauge the effect of a treatment. To see the response to a change, we must actually impose the change. *When our goal is to understand cause and effect, experiments are the only source of fully convincing data.* For this reason, the distinction between observation and experiment is one of the most important in statistics.

EXAMPLE 9.1 Drink a little, but not a lot

Many observational studies show that people who drink a moderate amount of alcohol have less heart disease than people who drink no alcohol or who drink heavily.[1] ("Moderate" means one or two drinks a day for men and one drink a day for women.) Is this *association* good reason to think that moderate drinking actually *causes* less heart disease? People who choose to drink in moderation are, as a group, different from both heavy drinkers and abstainers. They are more likely to maintain a healthy weight, get enough sleep, and exercise regularly. Moderate drinkers may be healthier because of these healthy habits rather than because of the effect of alcohol on health.

It is easy to imagine an experiment that would settle the issue of whether moderate drinking really *causes* reduced heart disease. Choose half of a large group of adults at random to be the "treatment" group. The remaining half becomes the "control" group. Require the treatment group to have one alcoholic drink every day. Require the control group to abstain from alcohol. Follow both groups for a decade. This experiment isolates the effect of alcohol. Of course, it isn't practical to carry out such an experiment. ■

The point of Example 9.1 is the contrast between observing people who choose for themselves what to drink and an experiment that requires some people to drink and others to abstain. When we simply observe people's drinking choices, the effect of moderate drinking is *confounded* with (mixed up with) the characteristics of people who choose to drink in moderation. These characteristics are lurking variables (see page 125) that make it hard to see the true relationship between the explanatory and response variables. Figure 9.1 shows the confounding in picture form.

> ### CONFOUNDING
>
> Two variables (explanatory variables or lurking variables) are **confounded** when their effects on a response variable cannot be distinguished from each other.

 Observational studies of the effect of one variable on another often fail because the explanatory variable is confounded with lurking variables. Well-designed experiments take steps to prevent confounding.

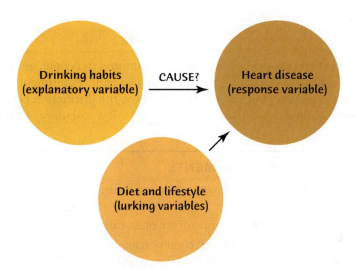

FIGURE 9.1
Confounding: We can't distinguish the effects of drinking habits from the effects of overall diet and lifestyle.

APPLY YOUR KNOWLEDGE

9.1 **Cell phones and brain cancer.** A study of cell phones and the risk of brain cancer looked at a group of 469 people who have brain cancer. The investigators matched each cancer patient with a person of the same sex, age, and race who did not have brain cancer, then asked about use of cell phones. Result: "Our data suggest that use of handheld cellular telephones is not associated with risk of brain cancer."[2] Is this an observational study or an experiment? Why? What are the explanatory and response variables?

9.2 **The font matters!** In general, when trying to change your behavior, if the effort required is perceived as high this will be an impediment to change, whether it is modifying your diet or your study habits. Divide 40 students into two groups of 20. The first group reads instructions for an exercise program printed in an easy-to-read font (Arial, 12 point), and the second group reads identical instructions in a difficult-to-read font (Brush, 12 point). Each subject estimates how many minutes the program would take and also uses a 7-point rating scale to report whether they are likely to include the exercise program as part of their daily routine (7 = very likely). The researchers hypothesized that those reading about the exercise program in the more difficult-to-read font would estimate that the program would take longer and would be less likely to make the exercise program part of their regular routine.[3] Is this an experiment? Why or why not? What are the explanatory and response variables?

9.3 **Quitting smoking and risk for type 2 diabetes.** Researchers studied a group of 10,892 middle-aged adults over a period of nine years. They found that smokers who quit had a higher risk for diabetes within three years of quitting than either non-smokers or continuing smokers.[4] Does this show that stopping smoking causes the short-term risk for diabetes to increase? (Weight gain has been shown to be a major risk factor for developing type 2 diabetes and is often a side effect of quitting smoking.) Based on this research, should you tell a middle-aged adult who smokes that stopping smoking can *cause* diabetes and advise him or her to continue smoking? Carefully explain your answers to both questions.

Paula Solloway/Alamy

SUBJECTS, FACTORS, TREATMENTS

A study is an experiment when we actually do something to people, animals, or objects in order to observe the response. Because the purpose of an experiment is to reveal the response of one variable to changes in other variables, the distinction between explanatory and response variables is essential. Here is the basic vocabulary of experiments.

SUBJECTS, FACTORS, TREATMENTS

The **individuals** studied in an experiment are often called **subjects,** particularly when they are people.

The explanatory variables in an experiment are often called **factors.**

A **treatment** is any specific experimental condition applied to the subjects. If an experiment has more than one factor, a treatment is a combination of specific values of each factor.

EXAMPLE 9.2 Foster care versus orphanages

Do abandoned children placed in foster homes do better than similar children placed in an institution? The Bucharest Early Intervention Project found that the answer is a clear "Yes." The *subjects* were 136 young children abandoned at birth and living in orphanages in Bucharest, Romania. Half of the children, chosen at random, were placed in foster homes (paid for by the study). The other half remained in the orphanages. The experiment compared these two *treatments.* There is a single *factor,* type of care (foster versus institutional care). The *response variables* included measures of mental and physical development.[5] ■

EXAMPLE 9.3 Effects of TV advertising

What are the effects of watching an ad on TV? The answer may depend both on the length of the ad and on how often it is repeated. An experiment investigated this question using undergraduate students as *subjects.* All subjects viewed a 40-minute television program that included ads for a digital camera. Some subjects saw a 30-second commercial; others, a 90-second version. The same commercial was shown either 1, 3, or 5 times during the program.

This experiment has 2 *factors:* length of the commercial, with 2 values, and repetitions, with 3 values. The 6 combinations of 1 value of each factor form 6 *treatments.* Figure 9.2 shows the layout of the treatments. After viewing, all the subjects answered questions about their recall of the ad, their attitude toward the camera, and their intention to purchase it. These are the *response variables.* ■

Examples 9.2 and 9.3 illustrate the advantages of experiments over observational studies. In an experiment, we can study the effects of the specific treatments we are interested in. By assigning subjects to treatments, we can avoid confounding. For example,

Factor B
Repetitions

	1 time	3 times	5 times
30 seconds	1	2	3
90 seconds	4	5	6

Factor A Length

Subjects assigned to Treatment 3 see a 30-second ad five times during the program.

FIGURE 9.2
The treatments in the experimental design of Example 9.3. Combinations of values of the two factors form six treatments.

observational studies of the effects of foster homes versus institutions on the development of children have often been biased because healthier or more alert children tend to be placed in homes. The random assignment in Example 9.2 eliminates bias in placing the children. Moreover, in experiments we can control the environment of the subjects to hold constant factors that are of no interest to us, such as the specific product advertised in Example 9.3.

APPLY YOUR KNOWLEDGE

For each of the following experiments, identify the subjects, the factors, the treatments, and the response variables.

9.4 Ginkgo extract and the post-lunch dip. The post-lunch dip is the drop in mental alertness after a midday meal. Does an extract of the leaves of the ginkgo tree reduce the post-lunch dip? Assign healthy people aged 18 to 40 to take either ginkgo extract or a placebo pill. After lunch, ask them to read seven pages of random letters and place an X over every *e*. Count the number of misses.

9.5 Growing in the shade. Ability to grow in shade may help pines in the dry forests of Arizona resist drought. How well do these pines grow in shade? Plant pine seedlings in a greenhouse in either full light, light reduced to 25% of normal by shade cloth, or light reduced to 5% of normal. At the end of the study, dry the young trees and weigh them.

9.6 Reactions to simulated news reports. A sample of University of Colorado students each viewed one of two simulated news reports about a terrorist bombing against the United States by a fictitious country. One report showed the bombing attack on a military target; and the other, on a cultural/educational site. Additionally, before viewing the news report, each student read one of two "primes." The first was a prime for *forgiveness* based on the biblical saying "Love thy enemy," while the second was a *retaliatory* prime based on the biblical saying "An eye for an eye, and a tooth for a tooth." After viewing the news report, the students were asked to rate on a scale of 1 to 12 what the U.S. reaction should be, with the lowest score (1) corresponding to the United States sending a special ambassador to the country and the highest score (12) corresponding to an all-out nuclear attack against the country.[6] (Use a diagram like Figure 9.2 to display the factors and treatments.)

Howard Bjornson/Getty Images

HOW TO EXPERIMENT BADLY

Statistical designs are often essential for effective experiments. To see why, let's look at an example in which an experiment suffers from confounding.

EXAMPLE 9.4 An uncontrolled experiment

A college offers a review course to prepare candidates for the Graduate Management Admission Test (GMAT). This year, it offers only an online version of the course. The average GMAT score of students in the online course is 10% higher than the longtime average for those who took the classroom review course. Is the online course more effective?

This experiment has a very simple design. A group of subjects (the students) were exposed to a treatment (the online course), and the outcome (GMAT scores) was observed. Here is the design:

$$\text{Subjects} \longrightarrow \text{Online course} \longrightarrow \text{GMAT scores}$$

The students in the online review course were different from the students who in past years took the classroom course—they were older and more likely to be employed. We can't compare the performance of these mature students with that of the undergraduates who previously dominated the course. The online course might even be less effective than the classroom version. The effect of online versus in-class instruction is confounded with the effect of lurking variables. ■

Most laboratory experiments use a design like that in Example 9.4:

$$\text{Subjects} \longrightarrow \text{Treatment} \longrightarrow \text{Measure response}$$

In the controlled environment of the laboratory, simple designs often work well. Field experiments and experiments with living subjects are exposed to more variable conditions and deal with more variable subjects. *Outside the laboratory, uncontrolled experiments often yield worthless results because of confounding with lurking variables.*

APPLY YOUR KNOWLEDGE

9.7 Reducing unemployment. Will cash bonuses speed the return to work of unemployed people? A state department of labor notes that last year 41% of people who filed claims for unemployment insurance found a new job within 15 weeks. As an experiment, the state offers $500 to people filing unemployment claims if they find a job within 15 weeks. The percent who do so increases to 53%. Suggest some conditions that might make it easier or harder to find a job this year as opposed to last year. Confounding with these lurking variables makes it impossible to say whether the bonus really caused the increase.

RANDOMIZED COMPARATIVE EXPERIMENTS

control group

The remedy for the confounding in Example 9.4 is to do a *comparative experiment* in which some students are taught in the classroom and other, similar students take the course online. The classroom group is called a **control group.** Most well-designed experiments compare two or more treatments.

Comparison alone isn't enough to produce results we can trust. If the treatments are given to groups that differ markedly when the experiment begins, bias will result. For example, if we allow students to elect online or classroom instruction, students who are older and employed are likely to sign up for the online course. Personal choice will bias our results in the same way that volunteers bias the results of online opinion polls. The solution to the problem of bias in sampling is random selection, and the same is true in experiments. The subjects assigned to any treatment should be chosen at random from the available subjects.

RANDOMIZED COMPARATIVE EXPERIMENT

An experiment that uses both comparison of two or more treatments and random assignment of subjects to treatments is a **randomized comparative experiment.**

EXAMPLE 9.5 Classroom versus online

The college decides to compare the progress of 25 students taught in the classroom with that of 25 students taught the same material online. Select the students who will be taught online by taking a simple random sample of size 25 from the 50 available subjects. The remaining 25 students form the control group. They will receive classroom instruction. The result is a randomized comparative experiment with two groups. Figure 9.3 outlines the design in graphical form.

The selection procedure is exactly the same as it is for sampling. **Label:** Label the 50 students 01 to 50. **Table:** Go to the table of random digits and read successive two-digit groups. The first 25 labels encountered select the online group. As usual, ignore repeated labels and groups of digits not used as labels. For example, if you begin at line 125 in Table B, the first 5 students chosen are those labeled 21, 49, 37, 18, and 44. You can also use software to choose treatment groups at random. ■

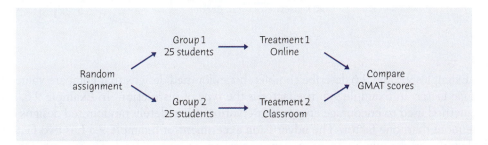

FIGURE 9.3

Outline of a randomized comparative experiment to compare online and classroom instruction, for Example 9.5.

The design in Example 9.5 is *comparative* because it compares two treatments (the two instructional settings). It is *randomized* because the subjects are assigned to the treatments by chance. This "flowchart" outline in Figure 9.3 presents all the essentials: randomization, the sizes of the groups and which treatment they receive, and the response variable. We call designs like that in Figure 9.3 *completely randomized.*

COMPLETELY RANDOMIZED DESIGN

In a **completely randomized** experimental design, all the subjects are allocated at random among all the treatments.

Completely randomized designs can compare any number of treatments. Here is an example that compares three treatments.

EXAMPLE 9.6 Conserving energy

How can an electric company encourage energy conservation among its customers? One approach places small digital displays in households that show what the cost would be if current electricity use continued for a month. Will the displays reduce electricity use? Would cheaper methods work almost as well? The company decides to conduct an experiment.

One cheaper approach is to give customers a chart and information about monitoring their electricity use from their outside meter. The experiment compares these two approaches (display, chart) and also a control. The control group of customers receives information about energy conservation but no help in monitoring electricity use. The response variable is total electricity used in a year. The company finds 60 single-family residences in the same city willing to participate, so it assigns 20 residences at random to each of the three treatments. Figure 9.4 outlines the design.

To use Table B, label the 60 households 01 to 60. Enter the table to select an SRS of 20 to receive the displays. Continue in Table B, selecting 20 more to receive charts. The remaining 20 form the control group. ■

FIGURE 9.4

Outline of a completely randomized design comparing three energy-saving programs, for Example 9.6.

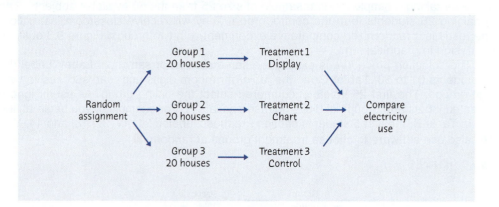

Examples 9.5 and 9.6 describe completely randomized designs that compare values of a single factor. In Example 9.5, the factor is the type of instruction. In Example 9.6, it is the method used to encourage energy conservation. Completely randomized designs can have more than one factor. The advertising experiment of Example 9.3 has two factors: the length and the number of repetitions of a television commercial. Their combinations form the six treatments outlined in Figure 9.2. A completely randomized design assigns subjects at random to these six treatments. Once the layout of treatments is set, the randomization needed for a completely randomized design is tedious but straightforward.

APPLY YOUR KNOWLEDGE

9.8 Adolescent obesity. Adolescent obesity is a serious health risk affecting more than 5 million young people in the United States alone. Laparoscopic adjustable gastric banding has the potential to provide a safe and effective treatment. Fifty adolescents between 14 and 18 years old with a body mass index higher than 35 were recruited from the Melbourne, Australia, community for the study. Twenty-five were randomly selected to undergo gastric banding, and the remaining 25 were assigned to a supervised lifestyle intervention program involving diet, exercise, and behavior modification. All subjects were followed for two years and their weight loss was recorded.[7]

(a) Outline the design of this experiment, following the model of Figure 9.3. What is the response variable?

(b) Carry out the random assignment of 25 adolescents to the gastric-banding group using software or Table B, starting at line 130.

9.9   More rain for California? The changing climate will probably bring more rain to California, but we don't know whether the additional rain will come during the winter wet season or extend into the long dry season in spring and summer. Kenwyn Suttle of the University of California at Berkeley and his coworkers carried out a randomized controlled experiment to study the effects of more rain in either season. They randomly assigned plots of open grassland to 3 treatments: added water equal to 20% of annual rainfall either during January to March (winter) or during April to June (spring), and no added water (control). Thirty-six circular plots of area 70 square meters were available, of which 18 were used for this study. One response variable was total plant biomass, in grams per square meter, produced in a plot over a year.[8]

(a) Outline the design of the experiment, following the model of Figure 9.4.

(b) Number all 36 plots and choose 6 at random for each of the 3 treatments. Be sure to explain how you did the random selection.

9.10   Effects of TV advertising. Figure 9.2 (page 191) displays the 6 treatments for the two-factor experiment on TV advertising described in Example 9.3. The 24 students named below will serve as subjects. Outline the design and randomly assign the subjects to the 6 treatments, an equal number of subjects to each treatment. If you use Table B, start at line 132.

Abramson	Biery	Cohen	Greenberg	Linder	Stanley
Anthony	Blake	Cote	Kessis	Minor	Tory
Austen	Brower	Delp	Koster	Schwartz	Truitt
Baker	Carroll	Disbro	Kruger	Shi	Walsh

THE LOGIC OF RANDOMIZED COMPARATIVE EXPERIMENTS

Randomized comparative experiments are designed to give good evidence that differences in the treatments actually *cause* the differences we see in the response. The logic is as follows:

■ Random assignment of subjects forms groups that should be similar in all respects before the treatments are applied.

■ Comparative design ensures that influences other than the experimental treatments operate equally on all groups.

■ Therefore, differences in average response must be due either to the treatments or to the play of chance in the random assignment of subjects to the treatments.

Be careful about that "either-or." In Example 9.5, we cannot say that *any* difference between the average GMAT scores of students enrolled online and in the classroom must be caused by a difference in the effectiveness of the two types of instruction. There would be some difference even if both groups received the same instruction, because of variation among students in background and study habits. Chance assigns students to one group or the other, and this creates a chance difference between the groups. If we assign many subjects to each group, the effects of chance will average out, and there will be little difference in the average responses in the two groups unless the treatments themselves cause a difference. "Use enough subjects to reduce chance variation" is the third big idea of statistical design of experiments.

PRINCIPLES OF EXPERIMENTAL DESIGN

The basic principles of statistical design of experiments are

1. **Control** the effects of lurking variables on the response, most simply by comparing two or more treatments.

2. **Randomize**—use chance to assign subjects to treatments.

3. **Use enough subjects** in each group to reduce chance variation in the results.

We hope to see a difference in the responses so large that it is unlikely to happen just because of chance variation. We can use the laws of probability, which describe chance behavior, to learn if the treatment effects are larger than we would expect to see if only chance were operating. If they are, we call them *statistically significant*.

STATISTICAL SIGNIFICANCE

An observed effect so large that it would rarely occur by chance is called **statistically significant**.

If we observe statistically significant differences among the groups in a randomized comparative experiment, we have good evidence that the treatments actually caused these differences. You will often see the phrase "statistically significant" in reports of investigations in many fields of study.

APPLY YOUR KNOWLEDGE

9.11 Prayer and meditation. You read in a magazine that "nonphysical treatments such as meditation and prayer have been shown to be effective in controlled scientific studies for such ailments as high blood pressure, insomnia, ulcers, and asthma." Explain in simple language what the article means by "controlled scientific studies." Why can such studies in principle provide good evidence that, for example, meditation is an effective treatment for high blood pressure?

9.12 **Conserving energy.** Example 9.6 describes an experiment to learn whether providing households with digital displays or charts will reduce their electricity consumption. An executive of the electric company objects to including a control group. He says: "It would be simpler to just compare electricity use last year (before the display or chart was provided) with consumption in the same period this year. If households use less electricity this year, the display or chart must be working." Explain clearly why this design is inferior to that in Example 9.6.

9.13 **Healthy diet and cataracts.** The relationship between healthy diet and prevalence of cataracts was assessed using a sample of 1808 participants from the Women's Health Initiative Observational Study. Having a high Healthy Eating Index score was the strongest predictor of a reduced risk of cataracts, among modifiable behaviors considered. The Healthy Eating Index score was created by the U.S. Department of Agriculture and measures how well a person's diet conforms to recommended healthy eating patterns. The report concludes: "These data add to the body of evidence suggesting that eating foods rich in a variety of vitamins and minerals may contribute to postponing the occurrence of the most common type of cataract in the United States."[9]

(a) Explain why this is an observational study rather than an experiment.

(b) Although the result was statistically significant, the authors did not use strong language in stating their conclusions, using words such as "suggesting" and "may." Do you think that their language is appropriate given the nature of the study? Why?

CAUTIONS ABOUT EXPERIMENTATION

The logic of a randomized comparative experiment depends on our ability to treat all the subjects identically in every way except for the actual treatments being compared. Good experiments therefore require careful attention to details to ensure that all subjects really are treated identically.

EXAMPLE 9.7 Vitamin E and heart disease

Will daily doses of vitamin E reduce the risk of heart disease? Divide the subjects at random into two groups. All the subjects receive the same medical attention during the several years of the experiment. All of them take a pill every day: vitamin E in the treatment group and a dummy pill (called a *placebo*) in the control group. Many patients respond favorably to any treatment, even a placebo, perhaps because they trust the doctor. The response to a dummy treatment is called the *placebo effect*. If the control group did not take any pills, the effect of vitamin E in the treatment group would be confounded with the placebo effect, the effect of simply taking pills.

In addition, the experiment is *double-blind*. The subjects don't know whether they are taking vitamin E or a placebo. Neither do the medical personnel who work with them. The double-blind method avoids unconscious bias by, for example, a doctor who is convinced that a vitamin must be better than a placebo. ■

> ## THE PLACEBO AND DOUBLE-BLIND METHODS
>
> A **placebo** is a dummy treatment. Experiments in medicine and psychology often give a placebo to a control group because just being in an experiment can affect responses.
>
> In a **double-blind** experiment, neither the subjects nor the people who interact with them know which treatment each subject is receiving.

lack of realism   Even well-designed experiments often face another problem: **lack of realism.** Practical constraints may mean that the subjects or treatments or setting of an experiment don't realistically duplicate the conditions we really want to study. Here are two examples.

EXAMPLE 9.8 Response to advertising

The study of television advertising in Example 9.3 showed a 40-minute video to students who knew an experiment was going on. We can't be sure that the results apply to everyday television viewers. Many behavioral science experiments use as subjects students or other volunteers who know they are subjects in an experiment. That's not a realistic setting. ■

EXAMPLE 9.9 Center brake lights

© Aurimas0508/Dreamstime.com

Do those high center brake lights, required on all cars sold in the United States since 1986, really reduce rear-end collisions? Randomized comparative experiments with fleets of rental and business cars, done before the lights were required, showed that the third brake light reduced rear-end collisions by as much as 50%. Alas, requiring the third light in all cars led to only a 5% drop.

What happened? Most cars did not have the extra brake light when the experiments were carried out, so it caught the eye of following drivers. Now that almost all cars have the third light, they no longer capture attention. ■

Lack of realism can limit our ability to apply the conclusions of an experiment to the settings of greatest interest. Most experimenters want to generalize their conclusions to some setting wider than that of the actual experiment. *Statistical analysis of an experiment cannot tell us how far the results will generalize*. Nonetheless, the randomized comparative experiment, because of its ability to give convincing evidence for causation, is one of the most important ideas in statistics.

APPLY YOUR KNOWLEDGE

9.14 Testosterone for older men. As men age, their testosterone levels gradually decrease. This may cause a reduction in lean body mass, an increase in fat, and other undesirable changes. Do testosterone supplements reverse some of these effects? A study in the Netherlands assigned 237 men aged 60 to 80 with low or low-normal testosterone levels to either a testosterone supplement or a placebo. The report in the *Journal of the American Medical Association* described the study as a "double-blind, randomized, placebo-controlled trial."[10] Explain each of these terms to someone who knows no statistics.

9.15 Does meditation reduce anxiety? An experiment that claimed to show that meditation reduces anxiety proceeded as follows. The experimenter interviewed the subjects and rated their level of anxiety. Then the subjects were randomly assigned to two groups. The experimenter taught one group how to meditate and they meditated daily for a month. The other group was simply told to relax more. At the end of the month, the experimenter interviewed all the subjects again and rated their anxiety level. The meditation group now had less anxiety. Psychologists said that the results were suspect because the ratings were not blind. Explain what this means and how lack of blindness could bias the reported results.

MATCHED PAIRS DESIGNS

Completely randomized designs are the simplest statistical designs for experiments. They illustrate clearly the principles of control, randomization, and adequate number of subjects. However, more elaborate designs are common. In particular, matching the subjects in various ways can produce more precise results than simple randomization. One common design that combines matching with randomization is the *matched pairs design*.

MATCHED PAIRS DESIGN

A **matched pairs design** compares two treatments. Choose pairs of subjects that are as closely matched as possible. Use chance to decide which subject in a pair gets the first treatment. The other subject in that pair gets the other treatment.

Sometimes each "pair" in a matched pairs design consists of just one subject, who gets both treatments one after the other. Use chance to decide the order in which subjects receive the treatments.

EXAMPLE 9.10 Cell phones and driving

Does talking on a hands-free cell phone distract drivers? Undergraduate students "drove" in a high-fidelity driving simulator equipped with a hands-free cell phone. The car ahead brakes: how quickly does the subject react? Let's compare two designs for this experiment. There are 40 student subjects available.

In a *completely randomized design,* all 40 subjects are assigned at random, 20 to simply drive and the other 20 to talk on the cell phone while driving. In the *matched pairs design* that was actually used, all subjects drive both with and without using the cell phone. The two drives are on separate days to reduce carryover effects. The *order* of the two treatments is assigned at random: 20 subjects are chosen to drive first with the phone, and the remaining 20 drive first without the phone.[11]

Royalty Free/CORBIS

Some subjects naturally react faster than others. The completely randomized design relies on chance to distribute the faster subjects roughly evenly between the two groups. The matched pairs design compares each subject's reaction time with and without the cell phone. This makes it easier to see the effects of using the phone. ■

Matched pairs designs use the principles of comparison of treatments and randomization. However, the randomization is not complete—we do not randomly assign all the subjects at once to the two treatments. Instead, we randomize only within each matched pair. This allows matching to reduce the effect of variation among the subjects.

Like the design of samples, the design of complex experiments is a job for experts. Now that we have seen a bit of what is involved, we will concentrate for the most part on completely randomized experiments.

APPLY YOUR KNOWLEDGE

9.16　Comparing breathing frequencies in swimming. Researchers from the United Kingdom studied the effect of two breathing frequencies on performance times and on several physiological parameters in front crawl swimming.[12] The breathing frequencies were one breath every second stroke (B2) and one breath every fourth stroke (B4). Subjects were 10 male collegiate swimmers. Each subject swam 200 meters, once with breathing frequency B2 and once on a different day with breathing frequency B4.

(a) Describe the design of this matched pairs experiment, including the randomization required by this design.

(b) Could this experiment be conducted using a completely randomized design? How would the design differ from the matched pairs experiment?

(c) Are there any problems with having swimmers choose their own breathing frequency and then swim 200 meters using their selected frequency?

9.17　How long did I work? A psychologist wants to know if the difficulty of a task influences our estimate of how long we spend working at it. She designs two sets of mazes that subjects can work through on a computer. One set has easy mazes and the other has hard mazes. Subjects work until told to stop. They are then asked to estimate how long they worked. The psychologist has 30 students available to serve as subjects.

(a) Describe the design of a completely randomized experiment to learn the effect of difficulty on estimated time.

(b) Describe the design of a matched pairs experiment using the same 30 subjects.

CHAPTER 9 SUMMARY

CHAPTER SPECIFICS

■ We can produce data intended to answer specific questions by **observational studies** or **experiments.** Sample surveys that select a part of a population to represent the whole are one type of observational study. **Experiments,** unlike observational studies, actively impose some treatment on the subjects of the experiment.

- Variables are **confounded** when their effects on a response can't be distinguished from each other. Observational studies and uncontrolled experiments often fail to show that changes in an explanatory variable actually cause changes in a response variable because the explanatory variable is confounded with lurking variables.

- In an experiment, we impose one or more **treatments** on individuals, often called **subjects.** Each treatment is a combination of values of the explanatory variables, which we call **factors.**

- The **design** of an experiment describes the choice of treatments and the manner in which the subjects are assigned to the treatments. The basic principles of statistical design of experiments are **control** and **randomization** to combat bias and **using enough subjects** to reduce chance variation.

- The simplest form of control is **comparison.** Experiments should compare two or more treatments in order to avoid confounding of the effect of a treatment with other influences, such as lurking variables.

- **Randomization** uses chance to assign subjects to the treatments. Randomization creates treatment groups that are similar (except for chance variation) before the treatments are applied. Randomization and comparison together prevent **bias,** or systematic favoritism, in experiments.

- You can carry out randomization by using software or by giving numerical labels to the subjects and using a **table of random digits** to choose treatment groups.

- Applying each treatment to many subjects reduces the role of chance variation and makes the experiment more sensitive to differences among the treatments.

- Good experiments require attention to detail as well as good statistical design. Many behavioral and medical experiments are **double-blind.** Some give a **placebo** to a control group. **Lack of realism** in an experiment can prevent us from generalizing its results.

- **A matched pairs design** compares just two treatments. In some matched pairs designs, each subject receives both treatments in a random order. In others, the subjects are matched in pairs as closely as possible, and each subject in a pair receives one of the treatments.

LINK IT

Observational studies and experiments are two methods for producing data. Observational studies are useful when the conclusion involves describing a group or situation without disturbing the scene we observe. Sample surveys, discussed in Chapter 8, are an important type of observational study in which we draw conclusions about a population by observing only a part of the population (the sample). In contrast, experiments are used when the situation calls for a conclusion about whether a treatment *causes* a change in a response. The distinction between observational studies and experiments will be important when stating your conclusions in later chapters.

In a simple comparative experiment, two treatments are imposed on two groups of individuals. Reaching the conclusion that the difference between the groups is caused by the treatments, rather than lurking variables, requires that the two groups of individuals be similar at the outset. A randomized comparative experiment is used to create groups that are similar. If there is a sufficiently large difference between the groups after imposing the treatments, we can say that the results are statistically significant and conclude that the differences in the response were *caused* by the treatments. In later chapters, the specific statistical procedures for reaching these conclusions will be described.

As with sampling, when conducting an experiment, attention to detail is important because our conclusions can be weakened by several circumstances. A lack of blinding can result in the expectations of the researcher influencing the results, while the placebo effect can confound the comparison between a treatment and a control group. In many instances, a more complex design is required to overcome difficulties and can produce more precise results.

CHECK YOUR SKILLS

9.18 The Nurses' Health Study has interviewed a sample of more than 100,000 female registered nurses every two years since 1976. The study finds that "light-to-moderate drinkers had a significantly lower risk of death" than either nondrinkers or heavy drinkers. The Nurses' Health Study is

(a) an observational study.

(b) an experiment.

(c) Can't tell without more information.

9.19 Do violence and sex in television programs help sell products in advertisements? Subjects were randomly assigned to watch one of four types of TV shows: (1) neither sex nor violence in the content code; (2) violence but no sex in the content code; (3) sex but no violence in the content code; and (4) both sex and violence in the content code. For each TV show, the original advertisements were replaced with the same set of twelve advertisements. Subjects were not told the purpose of the study but were instead told that the researchers were studying attitudes toward TV shows. After viewing the show, subjects received a surprise memory test to check their recall of the products advertised.[13] This experiment has

(a) four factors, the four TV shows being compared.

(b) twelve factors, the advertisements being shown.

(c) two factors, with/without violent content and with/without sexual content.

9.20 In the experiment of the previous exercise, the 336 subjects are labeled 001 to 336. Labels are selected at random by software, with the first 84 selected assigned to view TV show 1, the next 84 to view TV show 2, and the next 84 to view TV show 3. The 84 remaining subjects view TV show 4. This is a

(a) matched pairs design because subjects are matched to the TV shows.

(b) completely randomized design.

(c) stratified random sample.

9.21 A medical experiment compares an antidepression medicine with a placebo for relief of chronic headaches. There are 36 headache patients available to serve as subjects. To choose 18 patients to receive the medicine, you would

(a) assign labels 01 to 36 and use Table B to choose 18.

(b) assign labels 01 to 18, because only 18 need to be chosen.

(c) assign the first 18 who signed up to get the medicine.

9.22 The Community Intervention Trial for Smoking Cessation asked whether a community-wide advertising campaign would reduce smoking. The researchers located 11 pairs of communities, each pair similar in location, size, economic status, and so on. One community in each pair participated in the advertising campaign and the other did not. This is

(a) an observational study.

(b) a matched pairs experiment.

(c) a completely randomized experiment.

9.23 To decide which community in each pair in the previous exercise should get the advertising campaign, it is best to

(a) toss a coin.

(b) choose the community that will help pay for the campaign.

(c) choose the community with a mayor who will participate.

9.24 A marketing class designs two videos advertising a Mercedes sports car. They test the videos by asking fellow students to view both (in random order) and say which makes them more likely to buy the car. Mercedes should be reluctant to agree that the video favored in this study will sell more cars because

(a) the study used a matched pairs design instead of a completely randomized design.

(b) results from students may not generalize to the older and richer customers who might buy a Mercedes.

(c) this is an observational study, not an experiment.

CHAPTER 9 EXERCISES

In all exercises that require randomization, you may use either Table B or software.

9.25 Alcohol and heart attacks. Many studies have found that people who drink alcohol in moderation have lower risk of heart attacks than either nondrinkers or heavy drinkers. Does alcohol consumption also improve survival after a heart attack? One study followed 1913 people who were hospitalized after severe heart attacks. In the year before their heart attacks, 47% of these people did not drink, 36% drank moderately, and 17% drank heavily. After four years, fewer of the moderate drinkers had died.[14]

(a) Is this an observational study or an experiment? Why? What are the explanatory and response variables?

(b) Suggest some lurking variables that may be confounded with the drinking habits of the subjects. The possible confounding makes it difficult to conclude that drinking habits explain death rates.

9.26 Reducing nonresponse. How can we reduce the rate of refusals in telephone surveys? Most people who answer at all listen to the interviewer's introductory remarks and then decide whether to continue. One study made telephone calls to randomly selected households to ask opinions about the next election. In some calls, the interviewer gave her name, in others she identified the university she was representing, and in still others she identified both herself and the university. The study recorded what percent of each group of interviews was completed. Is this an observational study or an experiment? Why? What are the explanatory and response variables?

9.27 Samples versus experiments. Give an example of a question about college students, their behavior, or their opinions that would best be answered by

(a) a sample survey.

(b) an experiment.

9.28 Observation versus experiment. Observational studies had suggested that vitamin E reduces the risk of heart disease. Careful experiments, however, showed that vitamin E has no effect. According to a commentary in the *Journal of the American Medical Association*:

> Thus, vitamin E enters the category of therapies that were promising in epidemiologic and observational studies but failed to deliver in adequately powered randomized controlled trials. As in other studies, the "healthy user" bias must be considered, ie, the healthy lifestyle behaviors that characterize individuals who

care enough about their health to take various supplements are actually responsible for the better health, but this is minimized with the rigorous trial design.[15]

A friend who knows no statistics asks you to explain this.

(a) What is the difference between observational studies and experiments?

(b) What is a "randomized controlled trial"?

(c) How does "healthy user bias" explain how people who take vitamin E supplements have better health in observational studies but not in controlled experiments?

9.29 Attitudes toward homeless people. Are attitudes toward poor people more negative when a person is homeless? To find out, read to subjects a description of a poor person. There are two versions. One begins

> Jim is a 30-year-old single man. He is currently living in a small single-room apartment.

The other description begins

> Jim is a 30-year-old single man. He is currently homeless and lives in a shelter for homeless people.

After reading the description, ask subjects what they believe about Jim and what they think should be done to help him. The subjects are 544 adults interviewed by telephone.[16] Outline the design of this experiment.

9.30 Getting teachers to come to school. Elementary schools in rural India are usually small, with a single teacher. The teachers often fail to show up for work. Here is an idea for improving attendance: give the teacher a digital camera with a tamper-proof time and date stamp and ask a student to take a photo of the teacher and class at the beginning and end of the day. Offer the teacher better pay for good attendance verified by the photos. Will this work? A randomized comparative experiment started with 120 rural schools in Rajasthan and assigned 60 to this treatment and 60 to a control group. Random checks for teacher attendance showed that 21% of teachers in the treatment group were absent, as opposed to 42% in the control group.[17]

(a) Outline the design of this experiment.

(b) Label the schools and choose the first 10 schools for the treatment group. If you use Table B, start at line 108.

9.31 Marijuana and work. How does smoking marijuana affect willingness to work? Canadian researchers persuaded young adult men who used marijuana to live for 98 days in a "planned environment." One group smoked two potent marijuana cigarettes every evening. The other group smoked two weak marijuana cigarettes. All subjects could buy more cigarettes but were given strong or weak cigarettes depending on their group. Did the weak and strong groups differ in work output?[18]

(a) Outline the design of this experiment.

(b) Here are the names of the 30 subjects. Use software or Table B at line 120 to carry out the randomization your design requires.

Abel	DeVore	Kennedy	Reichert	Stout
Aeffner	Fleming	Lamone	Riddle	Williams
Birkel	Fritz	Mani	Sawant	Wilson
Bower	Giriunas	Mattos	Scannell	Worbis
Burke	Glosup	Molnar	Sheldon	Zaccai
Deis	Heaton	Newlen	Simmons	Zelaski

(c) Do you think this can be run as a double-blind experiment? Explain.

9.32 The benefits of red wine. Some people think that red wine protects moderate drinkers from heart disease better than other alcoholic beverages. This calls for a randomized comparative experiment. The subjects were healthy men aged 35 to 65. They were randomly assigned to drink red wine (9 subjects), drink white wine (9 subjects), drink white wine and also take polyphenols from red wine (6 subjects), take polyphenols alone (9 subjects), or drink vodka and lemonade (6 subjects).[19] Outline the design of the experiment and randomly assign the 39 subjects to the 5 groups. If you use Table B, start at line 107.

9.33 Can low-fat food labels lead to obesity? What are the effects of low-fat food labels on food consumption? Do people eat more of a snack food when the food is labeled as low-fat? The answer may depend both on whether the snack food is labeled low-fat and whether the label includes serving-size information. An experiment investigated this question using university staff, graduate students, and undergraduate students at a large university as subjects. Subjects were asked to evaluate a pilot episode for an upcoming TV show in a theater on campus and were given a cold 24-ounce bottle of water and a bag of granola from a respected campus restaurant called The Spice Box. They were told to enjoy as much or as little of the granola as they wanted. Depending on the treatment randomly assigned to the subjects, the granola was labeled as either "Regular Rocky Mountain Granola" or "Low-Fat Rocky Mountain Granola." Below this, the label indicated "Contains 1 Serving" or "Contains 2 Servings," or it provided no serving-size information.[20] Twenty subjects are assigned to each treatment, and their granola bags were weighed at the end of the session to determine how much granola was eaten.

(a) What are the factors and the treatments? How many subjects does the experiment require?

(b) Outline a completely randomized design for this experiment. (You need not actually do the randomization.)

9.34 Relieving headaches. Can antidepressant medications or stress management training reduce the number and severity of chronic headaches? Are both together more effective than either alone?

(a) Use a diagram like Figure 9.2 to display the treatments in a design with two factors: "medication, yes or no" and "stress management, yes or no." Then outline the design of a completely randomized experiment to compare these treatments.

(b) The headache sufferers named below have agreed to participate in the study. Randomly assign the subjects to the treatments. If you use software, assign all the subjects. If you use Table B, start at line 125 and assign subjects to only the first treatment group.

Abbott	Decker	Herrera	Lucero	Richter
Abdalla	Devlin	Hersch	Masters	Riley
Alawi	Engel	Hurwitz	Morgan	Samuels
Broden	Fuentes	Irwin	Nelson	Smith
Chai	Garrett	Jiang	Nho	Suarez
Chuang	Gill	Kelley	Ortiz	Upasani
Cordoba	Glover	Kim	Ramdas	Wilson
Custer	Hammond	Landers	Reed	Xiang

Treating sinus infections. *Sinus infections are common, and doctors often treat them with antibiotics. Another treatment is to spray a steroid solution into the nose. A well-designed clinical trial found that these treatments, alone or in combination, do not reduce the severity or the length of sinus infections.*[21] *Exercises 9.35 to 9.37 concern this trial.*

9.35 Experimental design. The clinical trial was a completely randomized experiment that assigned 240 patients at random among 4 treatments as follows:

	Antibiotic pill	Placebo pill
Steroid spray	53	64
Placebo spray	60	63

(a) Outline the design of the experiment.

(b) How will you label the 240 subjects?

(c) Explain briefly how you would do the random assignment of patients to treatments. Assign the first 5 patients who will receive the first treatment.

9.36 Describing the design. The report of this study in the *Journal of the American Medical Association* describes it as a "double-blind, randomized, placebo-controlled factorial trial." "Factorial" means that the treatments are formed from more than one factor. What are the factors? What do "double-blind" and "placebo-controlled" mean?

9.37 Checking the randomization. If the random assignment of patients to treatments did a good job of eliminating bias, possible lurking variables such as smoking history, asthma, and hay fever should be similar in all 4 groups. After recording and comparing many such variables, the investigators said that "all showed no significant difference between groups." Explain to someone who knows no statistics what "no significant difference" means. Does it mean that the presence of all these variables was exactly the same in all four treatment groups?

9.38 Frappuccino light? Here's the opening of a Starbucks press release: "Starbucks Corp. on Monday said it would roll out a line of blended coffee drinks intended to tap into the growing popularity of reduced-calorie and reduced-fat menu choices for Americans." You wonder if Starbucks customers like the new "Mocha Frappuccino Light" as well as the regular Mocha Frappuccino coffee.

(a) Describe a matched pairs design to answer this question. Be sure to include proper blinding of your subjects.

(b) You have 20 regular Starbucks customers on hand. Use software or Table B at line 141 to do the randomization that your design requires.

9.39 Growing trees faster. Carbon dioxide (CO_2) in the atmosphere is increasing due to our use of fossil fuels. Because green plants use CO_2 to fuel photosynthesis, more CO_2 may cause trees to grow faster. An elaborate apparatus allows researchers to pipe extra CO_2 to a 30-meter circle of forest. We want to compare the growth in base area of trees in treated and untreated areas to see if extra CO_2 does in fact increase growth. We can afford to treat three circular areas.[22]

(a) Describe the design of a completely randomized experiment using six well-separated 30-meter circular areas in a pine forest. Sketch the circles and carry out the randomization your design calls for.

(b) Areas within the forest may differ in soil fertility. Describe a matched pairs design using three pairs of circles that will reduce the extra variation due to different fertility. Sketch the circles and carry out the randomization your design calls for.

9.40 Athletes taking oxygen. We often see players on the sidelines of a football game inhaling oxygen. Their coaches think this will speed their recovery. We might measure recovery from intense exertion as follows: Have a football player run 100 yards three times in quick succession. Then allow three minutes to rest before running 100 yards again. Time the final run. Because players vary greatly in speed, you plan a matched pairs experiment using 25 football players as subjects. Discuss the design of such an experiment to investigate the effect of inhaling oxygen during the rest period.

9.41 Do antioxidants prevent cancer? People who eat lots of fruits and vegetables have lower rates of colon cancer than those who eat little of these foods. Fruits and vegetables are rich in "antioxidants" such as vitamins A, C, and E. Will taking antioxidants help prevent colon cancer? A medical experiment studied this question with 864 people who were at risk of colon cancer. The subjects were divided into four groups: daily beta-carotene, daily vitamins C and E, all three vitamins every day, or daily placebo. After four years, the researchers were surprised to find no significant difference in colon cancer among the groups.[23]

(a) What are the explanatory and response variables in this experiment?

(b) Outline the design of the experiment. Use your judgment in choosing the group sizes.

(c) The study was double-blind. What does this mean?

(d) What does "no significant difference" mean in describing the outcome of the study?

(e) Suggest some lurking variables that could explain why people who eat lots of fruits and vegetables have lower rates of colon cancer. The experiment suggests that these variables, rather than the antioxidants, may be responsible for the observed benefits of fruits and vegetables.

9.42 An herb for depression? Does the herb Saint-John's-wort relieve major depression? Here are some excerpts from the report of a study of this issue.[24] The study concluded that the herb is no more effective than a placebo.

(a) "Design: Randomized, double-blind, placebo-controlled clinical trial. . . ." A clinical trial is a medical experiment using actual patients as subjects. Explain the meaning of each of the other terms in this description.

(b) "Participants . . . were randomly assigned to receive either Saint-John's-wort extract ($n = 98$) or placebo ($n = 102$). . . . The primary outcome measure was the rate of change in the Hamilton Rating Scale for Depression over the treatment period." Based on this information, use a diagram to outline the design of this clinical trial.

EXPLORING THE WEB

9.43 Smoking cessation. Go to the *New England Journal of Medicine* Web site, www.nejm. org, and find the article "A Randomized, Controlled Trial of Financial Incentives for Smoking Cessation" by Volpp et al. in the February 12, 2009, issue. Under the *ISSUES* link, you need to go to the *Browse full index* link and then to the February 12, 2009, issue. You can then download the pdf of the article for free. Was this a comparative study? Was randomization used? How many subjects took part? There were 22 subjects in the control group and 64 in the incentive group who were still not smoking six months after they stopped. What were the percents in each group? This difference is statistically significant. Explain in simple language what this means.

9.44 Find an experiment. You can find the latest medical research in the *Journal of the American Medical Association* at www.jama.ama-assn.org and the *New England Journal of Medicine* at www.nejm.org. Many of the articles describe randomized comparative experiments and use the language of statistical significance when giving conclusions. Look through the abstracts and find an experiment of interest to you. If your institution has a subscription to these journals, you should be able to view the entire article. Otherwise, use the information in the abstract to answer as many of these questions as you can. What was the purpose of the experiment? How many factors were in the experiment, and what were the values of the factors? What response(s) were measured? How many subjects were assigned to each of the treatments, and was randomization used? Was it a double-blind experiment? What were the conclusions, and were the results statistically significant?

Commentary: Data Ethics*

T he production and use of data, like all human endeavors, raise ethical questions. We won't discuss the telemarketer who begins a telephone sales pitch with "I'm conducting a survey." Such deception is clearly unethical. It enrages legitimate survey organizations, which find the public less willing to talk with them. Neither will we discuss those few researchers who, in the pursuit of professional advancement, publish fake data. There is no ethical question here—faking data to advance your career is just wrong. It will end your career when uncovered. But just how honest must researchers be about real, unfaked data? Here is an example that suggests the answer is "More honest than they often are."

EXAMPLE 1 The whole truth?

Papers reporting scientific research are supposed to be short, with no extra baggage. Brevity, however, can allow researchers to avoid complete honesty about their data. Did they choose their subjects in a biased way? Did they report data on only some of their subjects? Did they try several statistical analyses and report only the ones that looked best? The statistician John Bailar

*This short essay concerns a very important topic, but the material is not needed to read the rest of the book.

207

screened more than 4000 medical papers in more than a decade as consultant to the *New England Journal of Medicine*. He says, "When it came to the statistical review, it was often clear that critical information was lacking, and the gaps nearly always had the practical effect of making the authors' conclusions look stronger than they should have."[1] The situation is no doubt worse in fields that screen published work less carefully. ■

The most complex issues of data ethics arise when we collect data from people. The ethical difficulties are more severe for experiments that impose some treatment on people than for sample surveys that simply gather information. Trials of new medical treatments, for example, can do harm as well as good to their subjects. Here are some basic standards of data ethics that must be obeyed by all studies that gather data from human subjects, both observational studies and experiments.

BASIC DATA ETHICS

All planned studies must be reviewed in advance by an **institutional review board** charged with protecting the safety and well-being of the subjects.

All individuals who are subjects in a study must give their **informed consent** before data are collected.

All individual data must be kept **confidential.** Only statistical summaries for groups of subjects may be made public.

The law requires that studies carried out or funded by the federal government obey these principles.[2] But neither the law nor the consensus of experts is completely clear about the details of their application.

INSTITUTIONAL REVIEW BOARDS

The purpose of an institutional review board is not to decide whether a proposed study will produce valuable information or whether it is statistically sound. The board's purpose is, in the words of one university's board, "to protect the rights and welfare of human subjects (including patients) recruited to participate in research activities." The board reviews the plan of the study and can require changes. It reviews the consent form to ensure that subjects are informed about the nature of the study and about any potential risks. Once research begins, the board monitors the study's progress at least once a year.

The most pressing issue concerning institutional review boards is whether their workload has become so large that their effectiveness in protecting subjects drops. When the government temporarily stopped human subject research at Duke University Medical Center in 1999 due to inadequate protection of subjects, more than 2000 studies were going on. That's a lot of review work. There are shorter review procedures for projects that involve only minimal risks to subjects, such as most sample surveys. When a board is overloaded, there is a temptation to put more proposals in the minimal-risk category to speed the work.

Institutional Review Board (IRB)

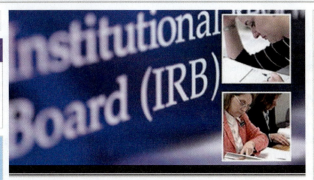

Home

More Pages

Education and Training
Federalwide Assurance
Glossary of Terms
Policy Manual

Support Mayo Now

Director, Mayo Clinic Office
of Human Research
Protection

William J Tremaine, M.D.

Overview

The Mayo Clinic Institutional Review Board (IRB) reviews all human subject research conducted at Mayo Clinic Florida (MCF), Mayo Clinic Rochester (MCR), or Mayo Clinic Arizona (MCA) and research conducted at other facilities under the direction of MCF, MCR, or MCA staff. A guarantee that all human subject research at Mayo will be reviewed by the IRB has been given to the U.S. Department of Health and Human Services (HHS) in a Federalwide Assurance (FWA00005001).

⇨ **Read More**

Mission

The primary mission of Mayo Clinic's IRB is to ensure the protection of rights, privacy and welfare of all human participants in research programs conducted by Mayo Clinic and associated faculty, professional staff, and students. Coexistent with participant protection is the goal of providing quality service to enhance the conduct of research. To achieve this goal, the IRB has the authority to review, approve, modify or disapprove research protocols submitted by faculty, staff and student investigators. The IRB review process is guided by federal rules and regulations, and is based on the Protection of Human Subject Code of Federal Regulations, the Belmont Report and provisions of 45CFR46 – Protection of Human Subjects requiring institutions receiving federal funds to have all research involving human participants be approved by an IRB.

Related Resources

Food and Drug Administration (FDA)

Guidance for Institutional Review Boards and Clinical Investigators (FDA)

Office for Human Research Protections (OHRP)

National Institutes of Health (NIH)

The Web page of the Mayo Clinic's institutional review board. It begins by describing the job of such boards.

INFORMED CONSENT

Both words in the phrase "informed consent" are important, and both can be controversial. Subjects must be *informed* in advance about the nature of a study and any risk of harm it may bring. In the case of a sample survey, physical harm is not possible. The subjects should be told what kinds of questions the survey will ask and about how much of their time it will take. Experimenters must tell subjects the nature and purpose of the study and outline possible risks. Subjects must then *consent* in writing.

EXAMPLE 2 Who can consent?

Are there some subjects who can't give informed consent? It was once common, for example, to test new vaccines on prison inmates who gave their consent in return for good-behavior credit. Now we worry that prisoners are not really free to refuse, and the law forbids almost all medical research in prisons.

Children can't give fully informed consent, so the usual procedure is to ask their parents. A study of new ways to teach reading is about to start at a local elementary school, so the study team sends consent forms home to parents. Many parents don't return the forms. Can their children take part in the study because the parents did not say "No," or should we allow only children whose parents returned the form and said "Yes"?

What about research into new medical treatments for people with mental disorders? What about studies of new ways to help emergency room patients who may be unconscious? In most cases, there is not time to get the consent of the family. Does the principle of informed consent bar realistic trials of new treatments for unconscious patients?

These are questions without clear answers. Reasonable people differ strongly on all of them. There is nothing simple about informed consent.[3] ■

The difficulties of informed consent do not vanish even for capable subjects. Some researchers, especially in medical trials, regard consent as a barrier to getting patients to participate in research. They may not explain all possible risks; they may not point out that there are other therapies that might be better than those being studied; they may be too optimistic in talking with patients even when the consent form has all the right details. On the other hand, mentioning every possible risk leads to very long consent forms that really are barriers. "They are like rental car contracts," one lawyer said. Some subjects don't read forms that run five or six printed pages. Others are frightened by the large number of possible (but unlikely) disasters that might happen and so refuse to participate. Of course, unlikely disasters sometimes happen. When they do, lawsuits follow and the consent forms become yet longer and more detailed.

CONFIDENTIALITY

Ethical problems do not disappear once a study has been cleared by the review board, has obtained consent from its subjects, and has actually collected data about the subjects. It is important to protect the subjects' privacy by keeping all data about individuals confidential. The report of an opinion poll may say what percent of the 1200 respondents felt that legal immigration should be reduced. It may not report what *you* said about this or any other issue.

anonymity   Confidentiality is not the same as **anonymity.** Anonymity means that subjects are anonymous—their names are not known even to the director of the study. Anonymity is rare in statistical studies. Even where it is possible (mainly in surveys conducted by mail), anonymity prevents any follow-up to improve nonresponse or inform subjects of results.

Any breach of confidentiality is a serious violation of data ethics. The best practice is to separate the identity of the subjects from the rest of the data at once. Sample surveys, for example, use the identification only to check on who did or did not respond. In an era of advanced technology, however, it is no longer enough to be sure that each individual set of data protects people's privacy. The United States government, for example, maintains a vast amount of information about citizens in many separate databases—census responses, tax returns, Social Security information, data from surveys such as the Current Population Survey, and so on. Many of these databases can be searched by computers for statistical studies. A clever computer search of several databases might be able, by combining information, to identify you and learn a great deal about you even if your name and other identification have been removed from the data available for search. A colleague from Germany once remarked that "female full professor of statistics with a PhD from the United States" was enough to identify her among all the 83 million residents of Germany. Privacy and confidentiality of data are hot issues among statisticians in the computer age.

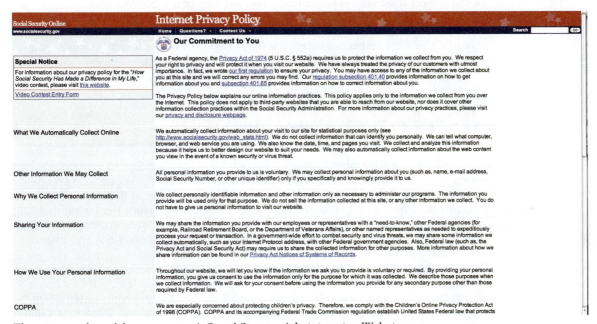

The privacy policy of the government's Social Security Administration Web site.

EXAMPLE 3 Uncle Sam knows

Citizens of the United States are required to give information to the government. Think of tax returns and Social Security contributions. The government needs these data for administrative purposes—to see if you paid the right amount of tax and how large a Social Security benefit you are owed when you retire. Some people feel that individuals should be able to forbid any other use of their data, even with all identification removed. This would prevent using government records to study, say, the ages, incomes, and household sizes of Social Security recipients. Such a study could well be vital to debates on reforming Social Security. ■

CLINICAL TRIALS

Clinical trials are experiments that study the effectiveness of medical treatments on actual patients. Medical treatments can harm as well as heal, so clinical trials spotlight the ethical problems of experiments with human subjects. Here are the starting points for a discussion:

■ Randomized comparative experiments are the only way to see the true effects of new treatments. Without them, risky treatments that are no more effective than placebos will become common.

■ Clinical trials produce great benefits, but most of these benefits go to future patients. The trials also pose risks, and these risks are borne by the subjects of the trial. So we must balance future benefits against present risks.

■ Both medical ethics and international human rights standards say that "the interests of the subject must always prevail over the interests of science and society."

The quoted words are from the 1964 Helsinki Declaration of the World Medical Association, the most respected international standard. The most outrageous examples of unethical experiments are those that ignore the interests of the subjects.

EXAMPLE 4 The Tuskegee study

In the 1930s, syphilis was common among black men in the rural South, a group that had almost no access to medical care. The Public Health Service Tuskegee study recruited 399 poor black sharecroppers with syphilis and 201 others without the disease in order to observe how syphilis progressed when no treatment was given. Beginning in 1943, penicillin became available to treat syphilis. The study subjects were not treated. In fact, the Public Health Service prevented any treatment until word leaked out and forced an end to the study in the 1970s.

The Tuskegee study is an extreme example of investigators following their own interests and ignoring the well-being of their subjects. A 1996 review said, "It has come to symbolize racism in medicine, ethical misconduct in human research, paternalism by physicians, and government abuse of vulnerable people." In 1997, President Clinton formally apologized to the surviving participants in a White House ceremony.[4] ■

Because "the interests of the subject must always prevail," medical treatments can be tested in clinical trials only when there is reason to hope that they will help the patients who are subjects in the trials. Future benefits aren't enough to justify experiments with human subjects. Of course, if there is already strong evidence that a treatment works and is safe, it is unethical *not* to give it. Here are the words of Dr. Charles Hennekens of the Harvard Medical School, who directed the large clinical trial that showed that aspirin reduces the risk of heart attacks:

There's a delicate balance between when to do or not do a randomized trial. On the one hand, there must be sufficient belief in the agent's potential to justify exposing half the subjects to it. On the other hand, there must be sufficient doubt about its efficacy to justify withholding it from the other half of subjects who might be assigned to placebos.[5]

Why is it ethical to give a control group of patients a placebo? Well, we know that placebos often work. Moreover, placebos have no harmful side effects. So in the state of balanced doubt described by Dr. Hennekens, the placebo group may be getting a better treatment than the drug group. If we knew which treatment was better, we would give it to everyone. When we don't know, it is ethical to try both and compare them.

BEHAVIORAL AND SOCIAL SCIENCE EXPERIMENTS

When we move from medicine to the behavioral and social sciences, the direct risks to experimental subjects are less acute, but so are the possible benefits to the subjects. Consider, for example, the experiments conducted by psychologists in their study of human behavior.

EXAMPLE 5 Psychologists in the men's room

Psychologists observe that people have a "personal space" and are uneasy if others come too close to them. We don't like strangers to sit at our table in a coffee shop if other tables are available, and we see people move apart in elevators if there is room to do so. Americans tend to require more personal space than people in most other cultures. Can violations of personal space have physical, as well as emotional, effects?

Investigators set up shop in a men's public restroom. They blocked off urinals to force men walking in to use either a urinal next to an experimenter (treatment group) or a urinal separated from the experimenter (control group). Another experimenter, using a periscope from a toilet stall, measured how long the subject took to start urinating and how long he continued.[6] ■

David Pollack/CORBIS

This personal space experiment illustrates the difficulties facing those who plan and review behavioral studies.

■ There is no risk of harm to the subjects, although they would certainly object to being watched through a periscope. What should we protect subjects from when physical harm is unlikely? Possible emotional harm? Undignified situations? Invasion of privacy?

■ What about informed consent? The subjects did not even know they were participating in an experiment. Many behavioral experiments rely on hiding the true purpose of the study. The subjects would change their behavior if told in advance what the investigators were looking for. Subjects are asked to consent on the basis of vague information. They receive full information only after the experiment.

The "Ethical Principles" of the American Psychological Association require consent unless a study merely observes behavior in a public place. They allow deception only when it is necessary to the study, does not hide information that might influence a subject's willingness to participate, and is explained to subjects as soon as possible. The personal space study (from the 1970s) does not meet current ethical standards.

We see that the basic requirement for informed consent is understood differently in medicine and psychology. Here is an example of another setting with yet another interpretation of what is ethical. The subjects get no information and give no consent. They don't even know that an experiment may be sending them to jail for the night.

EXAMPLE 6 Reducing domestic violence

How should police respond to domestic violence calls? In the past, the usual practice was to remove the offender and order him to stay out of the household overnight. Police were reluctant to make arrests because the victims rarely pressed charges. Women's groups argued that arresting offenders would help prevent future violence even if no charges were filed. Is there evidence that arrest will reduce future offenses? That's a question that experiments have tried to answer.

A typical domestic violence experiment compares two treatments: arrest the suspect and hold him overnight, or warn the suspect and release him. When police officers reach the scene of a domestic violence call, they calm the participants and investigate. Weapons or death threats require an arrest. If the facts permit an arrest but do not require it, an officer radios headquarters for instructions. The person on duty opens the next envelope in a file prepared in advance by a statistician. The envelopes contain the treatments in random order. The police either arrest the suspect or warn and release him, depending on the contents of the envelope. The researchers then watch police records and visit the victim to see if the domestic violence reoccurs.

Such experiments show that arresting domestic violence suspects does reduce their future violent behavior.[7] As a result of this evidence, arrest has become the common police response to domestic violence. ■

The domestic violence experiments shed light on an important issue of public policy. Because there is no informed consent, the ethical rules that govern clinical trials and most social science studies would forbid these experiments. They were cleared by review boards because, in the words of one domestic violence researcher, "These people became subjects by committing acts that allow the police to arrest them. You don't need consent to arrest someone."

In summary, data ethics begin with some principles that go beyond just being honest. These include screening by an institutional review board, informed consent, and confidentiality. These principles are a good start, but many ethical debates remain, especially in the area of experiments with human subjects. Many of the debates concern the right balance between the welfare of the subjects and the future benefits of the experiment. Remember that randomized comparative experiments can answer questions that can't be answered without them. But also remember that "the interests of the subject must always prevail over the interests of science and society."

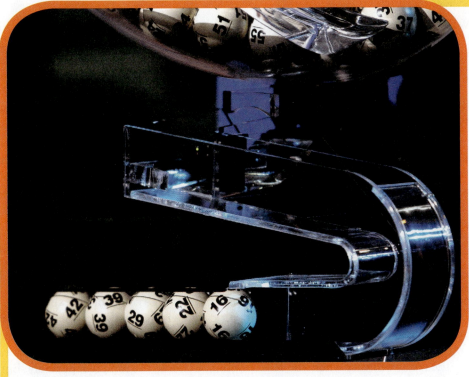

AP Photo/Shiho Fukada

Introducing Probability

Why is probability, the mathematics of chance behavior, needed to understand statistics, the science of data? Let's look at a typical sample survey.

EXAMPLE 10.1 Do you lotto?

What proportion of all adults bought a lottery ticket in the past 12 months? We don't know, but we do have results from the Gallup Poll. Gallup took a random sample of 1027 adults. The poll found that 472 of the people in the sample bought tickets. The proportion who bought tickets was

$$\text{sample proportion} = \frac{472}{1027} = 0.46 \text{ (that is, 46\%)}$$

If the sample was a simple random sample of all adults,[1] then all adults had the same chance to be among the chosen 1027. It would be reasonable to use this 46% as an estimate of the unknown proportion in the population. It's a *fact* that 46% of the sample bought lottery tickets—we know because Gallup asked them. We don't know what percent of *all* adults bought tickets, but we *estimate* that about 46% did. This is a basic move in statistics: use a result from a sample to estimate something about a population. ■

215

What if Gallup took a second random sample of 1027 adults? The new sample would have different people in it. It is almost certain that there would not be exactly 472 positive responses. That is, Gallup's estimate of the proportion of adults who bought a

lottery ticket will vary from sample to sample. *Random samples eliminate bias from the act of choosing a sample, but they can still be wrong because of the variability that results when we choose at random.*

This is why we need facts about probability to make progress in statistics. Because Gallup uses chance to choose its samples, the laws of probability govern the behavior of the samples. Gallup says that the probability is 0.95 that an estimate from one of their samples comes within ±3 percentage points of the truth about the population of all adults. The first step toward understanding this statement is to understand what "probability 0.95" means. Our purpose in this chapter is to understand the language of probability, but without going into the mathematics of probability theory.

THE IDEA OF PROBABILITY

To understand why we can trust random samples and randomized comparative experiments, we must look closely at chance behavior. The big fact that emerges is this: **chance behavior is unpredictable in the short run but has a regular and predictable pattern in the long run.**

Toss a coin, or choose a random sample. The result can't be predicted in advance, because the result will vary when you toss the coin or choose the sample repeatedly. But there is still a regular pattern in the results, a pattern that emerges clearly only after many repetitions. This remarkable fact is the basis for the idea of probability.

EXAMPLE 10.2 Coin tossing

When you toss a coin, there are only two possible outcomes, heads or tails. Figure 10.1 shows the results of tossing a coin 5000 times twice. For each number of tosses from 1 to 5000, we have plotted the proportion of those tosses that gave a head. Trial A (solid

FIGURE 10.1

The proportion of tosses of a coin that give a head changes as we make more tosses. Eventually, however, the proportion approaches 0.5, the probability of a head. This figure shows the results of two trials of 5000 tosses each.

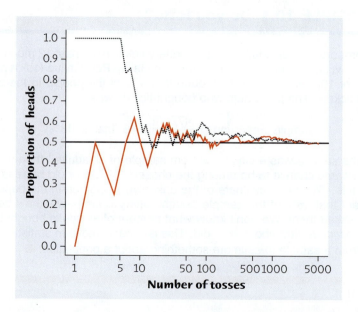

red line) begins tail, head, tail, tail. You can see that the proportion of heads for Trial A starts at 0 on the first toss, rises to 0.5 when the second toss gives a head, then falls to 0.33 and 0.25 as we get two more tails. Trial B, on the other hand, starts with five straight heads, so the proportion of heads is 1 until the sixth toss.

The proportion of tosses that produce heads is quite variable at first. Trial A starts low and Trial B starts high. As we make more and more tosses, however, the proportion of heads for both trials gets close to 0.5 and stays there. If we made yet a third trial at tossing the coin a great many times, the proportion of heads would again settle down to 0.5 in the long run. This is the intuitive idea of probability. Probability 0.5 means "occurs half the time in a very large number of trials." The probability 0.5 appears as a horizontal line on the graph. ■

> ### RANDOMNESS AND PROBABILITY
>
> We call a phenomenon **random** if individual outcomes are uncertain but there is none-theless a regular distribution of outcomes in a large number of repetitions.
>
> The **probability** of any outcome of a random phenomenon is the proportion of times the outcome would occur in a very long series of repetitions.

We might suspect that a coin has probability 0.5 of coming up heads just because the coin has two sides. But we can't be sure. In fact, spinning a penny on a flat surface, rather than tossing the coin, gives heads probability about 0.45 rather than 0.5.[2] The best way to understand randomness is to observe random behavior, as in Figure 10.1. We are willing to say that most coins have probability 0.5 of giving a head when tossed because some people have actually made thousands of tosses. Experience shows that the proportion of heads gradually settles down close to 0.5. Equally important, experience shows that *the proportion in a small or moderate number of tosses can be far from the probability. Probability describes only what happens in the long run.* Of course, we can never observe a probability exactly. We could always continue tossing the coin, for example. Mathematical probability is an idealization based on imagining what would happen in an indefinitely long series of trials.

APPLY YOUR KNOWLEDGE

10.1 Texas hold 'em. In the popular Texas hold 'em variety of poker, players make their best five-card poker hand by combining the two cards they are dealt with three of five cards available to all players. You read in a book on poker that if you hold a pair (two cards of the same rank) in your hand, the probability of getting four of a kind (four cards of the same rank) is 2/245. Explain carefully what this means. In particular, explain why it does *not* mean that if you play 245 such hands, exactly 2 hands will contain four of a kind.

10.2 Probability says . . . Probability is a measure of how likely an event is to occur. Match one of the probabilities that follow with each statement of likelihood given. (The probability is usually a more exact measure of likelihood than is the verbal statement.)

$$0 \qquad 0.01 \qquad 0.45 \qquad 0.50 \qquad 0.55 \qquad 0.99 \qquad 1$$

(a) This event is impossible. It can never occur.

(b) This event is certain. It will occur on every trial.

Cut and Deal Ltd./Alamy

(c) This event is very likely, but once in a while it will not occur in a long sequence of trials.

(d) This event will occur slightly less often than not.

10.3 Random digits. The table of random digits (Table B) was produced by a random mechanism that gives each digit probability 0.1 of being a 0. So random digits can illustrate the idea of probability.

(a) Count the number of 0s in each of the first 5 rows of Table B. Each row has 40 digits. What are the proportions of 0s in each of the first 5 rows? You see that proportions in just 40 trials need not be very close to the probability 0.1.

(b) Combine your counts: how many 0s are there among the 200 digits in the first 5 rows of the table? Of course, 200 trials is not the long run, but already the proportion is closer to the probability 0.1.

PROBABILITY MODELS

The idea of probability rests on the observed fact that the average result of many thousands of chance outcomes can be known with near certainty. How can we give a mathematical description of this long-run regularity?

Think first about a very simple random phenomenon, tossing a coin once. When we toss a coin, we cannot know the outcome in advance. What *do* we know? We are willing to say that the outcome will be either heads or tails. We believe that each of these outcomes has probability 1/2. This description of coin tossing has two parts:

■ a list of possible outcomes

■ a probability for each outcome

Such a description is the basis for all *probability models*. Here is the basic vocabulary we use.

PROBABILITY MODELS

The **sample space** *S* of a random phenomenon is the set of all possible outcomes.

An **event** is an outcome or a set of outcomes of a random phenomenon. That is, an event is a subset of the sample space.

A **probability model** is a mathematical description of a random phenomenon consisting of two parts: a sample space *S* and a way of assigning probabilities to events.

A sample space *S* can be very simple or very complex. When we toss a coin once, there are only two outcomes, heads and tails. The sample space is $S = \{H, T\}$. When Gallup draws a random sample of 1027 adults, the sample space contains all possible choices of 1027 of the 235 million adults in the country. This *S* is extremely large. Each member of *S* is a possible sample, which explains the term *sample space*.

EXAMPLE 10.3 Rolling dice

Rolling two dice is a common way to lose money in casinos. There are 36 possible outcomes when we roll two dice and record the up-faces in order (first die, second die). Figure 10.2 displays these outcomes. They make up the sample space S. "Roll a 5" is an event, call it A, that contains 4 of these 36 outcomes:

$$A = \{\boxed{\cdot}\ \boxed{::}\quad \boxed{\cdot\cdot}\ \boxed{\therefore}\quad \boxed{\therefore}\ \boxed{\cdot\cdot}\quad \boxed{::}\ \boxed{\cdot}\}$$

What probabilities should we assign to this sample space? Different dice may be unbalanced in different ways, and so may have different probabilities. Let's assume that we have ideal, perfectly balanced dice. Carefully made casino dice are close to this ideal.

If the dice are perfectly balanced, all 36 outcomes in Figure 10.2 will be *equally likely*. That is, each of the 36 outcomes will come up on one thirty-sixth of all rolls in the long run. So each outcome has probability 1/36. There are 4 outcomes in the event A ("roll a 5"), so this event has probability 4/36. In this way we can assign a probability to any event. So we have a complete probability model. ■

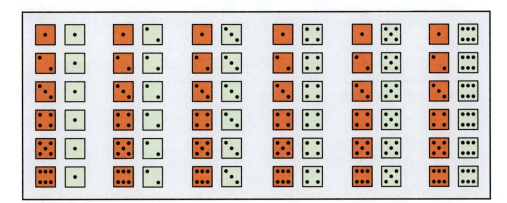

FIGURE 10.2

The 36 possible outcomes in rolling two dice, for Example 10.3. If the dice are carefully made, all these outcomes have the same probability.

EXAMPLE 10.4 Rolling dice and counting the spots

Gamblers care only about the total number of spots on the up-faces of the dice. The sample space for rolling two dice and counting the spots is

$$S = \{2, 3, 4, 5, 6, 7, 8, 9, 10, 11, 12\}$$

Comparing this S with Figure 10.2 reminds us that *we can change S by changing the detailed description of the random phenomenon we are describing.*

What are the probabilities for this new sample space? The 11 possible outcomes are *not* equally likely, because there are six ways to roll a 7 and only one way to roll a 2 or a 12. That's the key: each outcome in Figure 10.2 has probability 1/36. So "roll a 7" has probability 6/36 because this event contains 6 of the 36 outcomes. Similarly, "roll a 2" has probability 1/36, and "roll a 5" (4 outcomes from Figure 10.2) has probability 4/36. Here is the complete probability model:

Spots	2	3	4	5	6	7	8	9	10	11	12
Probability	1/36	2/36	3/36	4/36	5/36	6/36	5/36	4/36	3/36	2/36	1/36

10.4 **Sample space.** Choose a student at random from a large statistics class. Describe a sample space *S* for each of the following. (In some cases you may have some freedom in specifying *S*.)

(a) Does the student live on campus or off campus?

(b) What is the student's age in years?

(c) Ask how much money in coins (not bills) the student is carrying.

(d) Record the student's letter grade at the end of the course.

10.5 **Role-playing games.** Computer games in which the players take the roles of characters go back to earlier tabletop games such as Dungeons & Dragons. These games use many different types of dice. A four-sided die has faces indicating an outcome of 1, 2, 3, or 4.

(a) What is the sample space for rolling a four-sided die twice (outcomes on the first and second rolls)? Follow the example of Figure 10.2.

(b) What is the assignment of probabilities to outcomes in this sample space? Assume that the die is perfectly balanced, and follow the method of Example 10.3.

10.6 **Role-playing games.** The intelligence of a character in a game is determined by rolling the four-sided die twice and adding 1 to the sum of the spots. Start with your work in the previous exercise to give a probability model (sample space and probabilities of outcomes) for the character's intelligence. Follow the method of Example 10.4.

Slpix/Dreamstime.com

PROBABILITY RULES

In Examples 10.3 and 10.4 we found probabilities for tossing perfectly balanced dice. As random phenomena go, dice are pretty simple. In most situations, it isn't easy to give a "correct" probability model. We can make progress by listing some facts that must be true for *any* assignment of probabilities. These facts follow from the idea of probability as "the long-run proportion of repetitions on which an event occurs."

1. **Any probability is a number between 0 and 1.** Any proportion is a number between 0 and 1, so any probability is also a number between 0 and 1. An event with probability 0 never occurs, and an event with probability 1 occurs on every trial. An event with probability 0.5 occurs in half the trials in the long run.

2. **All possible outcomes together must have probability 1.** Because some outcome must occur on every trial, the sum of the probabilities for all possible outcomes must be exactly 1.

3. **If two events have no outcomes in common, the probability that one or the other occurs is the sum of their individual probabilities.** If one event occurs in 40% of all trials, a different event occurs in 25% of all trials, and the two can never occur together, then one or the other occurs on 65% of all trials because 40% + 25% = 65%.

4. **The probability that an event does not occur is 1 minus the probability that the event does occur.** If an event occurs in 70% of all trials, it fails to occur in the other 30%. The probability that an event occurs and the probability that it does not occur always add to 100%, or 1.

We can use mathematical notation to state Facts 1 to 4 more concisely. Capital letters near the beginning of the alphabet denote events. If A is any event, we write its probability as $P(A)$. Here are our probability facts in formal language. As you apply these rules, remember that they are just another form of intuitively true facts about long-run proportions.

PROBABILITY RULES

Rule 1. The probability $P(A)$ of any event A satisfies $0 \leq P(A) \leq 1$.

Rule 2. If S is the sample space in a probability model, then $P(S) = 1$.

Rule 3. Two events A and B are **disjoint** if they have no outcomes in common and so can never occur together. If A and B are disjoint,

$$P(A \text{ or } B) = P(A) + P(B)$$

This is the **addition rule for disjoint events.**

Rule 4. For any event A,

$$P(A \text{ does not occur}) = 1 - P(A)$$

The addition rule extends to more than two events that are disjoint in the sense that no two have any outcomes in common. If events A, B, and C are disjoint, the probability that one of these events occurs is $P(A) + P(B) + P(C)$.

EXAMPLE 10.5 Using the probability rules

We already used the addition rule, without calling it by that name, to find the probabilities in Example 10.4. The event "roll a 5" contains the four disjoint outcomes displayed in Example 10.3, so the addition rule (Rule 3) says that its probability is

$$P(\text{roll a 5}) = P(\boxed{\cdot}\ \boxed{\vdots}) + P(\boxed{\cdot}\ \boxed{\because}) + P(\boxed{\because}\ \boxed{\cdot}) + P(\boxed{\vdots}\ \boxed{\cdot})$$

$$= \frac{1}{36} + \frac{1}{36} + \frac{1}{36} + \frac{1}{36}$$

$$= \frac{4}{36} = 0.111$$

What is the probability of rolling anything other than a 5? By Rule 4,

$$P(\text{roll does not give a 5}) = 1 - P(\text{roll a 5})$$

$$= 1 - 0.111 = 0.889$$

Our model assigns probabilities to individual outcomes. To find the probability of an event, just add the probabilities of the outcomes that make up the event. For example:

$$P(\text{outcome is odd}) = P(3) + P(5) + P(7) + P(9) + P(11)$$

$$= \frac{2}{36} + \frac{4}{36} + \frac{6}{36} + \frac{4}{36} + \frac{2}{36}$$

$$= \frac{18}{36} = \frac{1}{2} \ ■$$

10.7 Who takes the GMAT? In many settings, the "rules of probability" are just basic facts about percents. The Graduate Management Admission Test (GMAT) Web site provides the following information about the undergraduate majors of those who took the test in 2009–2010: 53% majored in business or commerce; 17% majored in engineering; 16% majored in the social sciences; 6% majored in the sciences; 5% majored in the humanities; and 3% listed some major other than the preceding.[3]

(a) What percent of those who took the test in 2009–2010 majored in either engineering or science? Which rule of probability did you use to find the answer?

(b) What percent of those who took the test in 2009–2010 majored in something other than business or commerce? Which rule of probability did you use to find the answer?

10.8 Overweight? Although the rules of probability are just basic facts about percents or proportions, we need to be able to use the language of events and their probabilities. Choose an American adult at random. Define two events:

A = the person chosen is obese

B = the person chosen is overweight, but not obese

According to the National Center for Health Statistics, $P(A) = 0.34$ and $P(B) = 0.33$.

(a) Explain why events A and B are disjoint.

(b) Say in plain language what the event "A or B" is. What is $P(A$ or $B)$?

(c) If C is the event that the person chosen has normal weight or less, what is $P(C)$?

10.9 Languages in Canada. Canada has two official languages, English and French. Choose a Canadian at random and ask, "What is your mother tongue?" Here is the distribution of responses, combining many separate languages, from the province of Quebec:[4]

Language	English	French	Italian	Other
Probability	0.08	0.80	0.02	?

(a) What probability should replace "?" in the distribution?

(b) What is the probability that a Canadian's mother tongue is not English?

(c) What is the probability that a Canadian's mother tongue is a language other than English or French?

FINITE AND DISCRETE PROBABILITY MODELS

Examples 10.3, 10.4, and 10.5 illustrate one way to assign probabilities to events: assign a probability to every individual outcome, then add these probabilities to find the probability of any event. This idea works well when there are only a finite (fixed and limited) number of outcomes.

> **FINITE PROBABILITY MODEL**
>
> A probability model with a finite sample space is called **finite.**
>
> To assign probabilities in a finite model, list the probabilities of all the individual outcomes. These probabilities must be numbers between 0 and 1 that add to exactly 1. The probability of any event is the sum of the probabilities of the outcomes making up the event.

Finite probability models are sometimes called **discrete** probability models. However, discrete probability models include not only finite sample spaces but sample spaces that are infinite and equivalent to the set of all positive integers. An example of a discrete but not finite sample space would be the sample space for the number of free-throw attempts until a basketball player makes her first free throw. This could occur on her first attempt, her second attempt, her third attempt, etc. Assigning probabilities to individual outcomes in an infinite discrete sample space is more complicated than for a finite sample space. In this book we will often refer to finite probability models as discrete, and in practice statisticians often refer to finite probability models as discrete.

EXAMPLE 10.6 Benford's law

Dishonest people try to fake numbers in tax returns, invoices, or expense account claims. It's hard to make up numbers that are fully realistic. One reason is that the first digits of numbers in legitimate records often follow a model known as Benford's law.[5] Call the first digit of a randomly chosen record X for short. Benford's law gives this probability model for X (note that a first digit can't be 0):

First digit X	1	2	3	4	5	6	7	8	9
Probability	0.301	0.176	0.125	0.097	0.079	0.067	0.058	0.051	0.046

Check that the probabilities of the outcomes sum to exactly 1. This is therefore a legitimate finite (or discrete) probability model. Investigators can detect fraud by comparing the first digits in records such as invoices paid by a business with these probabilities.

The probability that a first digit is equal to or greater than 6 is

$$P(X \geq 6) = P(X = 6) + P(X = 7) + P(X = 8) + P(X = 9)$$
$$= 0.067 + 0.058 + 0.051 + 0.046 = 0.222$$

This is less than the probability that a record has first digit 1,

$$P(X = 1) = 0.301$$

Fraudulent records tend to have too few 1s and too many higher first digits.

Note that the probability that a first digit is greater than or equal to 6 is not the same as the probability that a first digit is strictly greater than 6. The latter probability is

$$P(X > 6) = 0.058 + 0.051 + 0.046 = 0.155$$

The outcome $X = 6$ is included in "greater than or equal to" and is not included in "strictly greater than." ■

APPLY YOUR KNOWLEDGE

10.10 Rolling a die. Figure 10.3 displays several finite probability models for rolling a die. We can learn which model is actually *accurate* for a particular die only by rolling the die many times. However, some of the models are not *legitimate*. That is, they do not obey the rules. Which are legitimate and which are not? In the case of the illegitimate models, explain what is wrong.

FIGURE 10.3

Four assignments of probabilities to the six faces of a die, for Exercise 10.10.

	Probability			
Outcome	Model 1	Model 2	Model 3	Model 4
⚀	1/7	1/3	1/3	1
⚁	1/7	1/6	1/6	1
⚂	1/7	1/6	1/6	2
⚃	1/7	0	1/6	1
⚄	1/7	1/6	1/6	1
⚅	1/7	1/6	1/6	2

10.11 Benford's law. The first digit of a randomly chosen expense account claim follows Benford's law (Example 10.6). Consider the events

$$A = \{\text{first digit is 4 or greater}\}$$
$$B = \{\text{first digit is even}\}$$

(a) What outcomes make up the event A? What is $P(A)$?

(b) What outcomes make up the event B? What is $P(B)$?

(c) What outcomes make up the event "A or B"? What is $P(A \text{ or } B)$? Why is this probability not equal to $P(A) + P(B)$?

10.12 Weighty behavior. Choose an adult in the United States at random and ask, "How many days per week do you lift weights?" Call the response X for short. Based on a large sample survey, here is a probability model for the answer you will get:[6]

Days	0	1	2	3	4	5	6	7
Probability	0.73	0.06	0.06	0.06	0.04	0.02	0.01	0.02

(a) Verify that this is a legitimate finite probability model.

(b) Describe the event $X < 4$ in words. What is $P(X < 4)$?

(c) Express the event "lifted weights at least once" in terms of X. What is the probability of this event?

CONTINUOUS PROBABILITY MODELS

When we use the table of random digits to select a digit between 0 and 9, the finite probability model assigns probability 1/10 to each of the 10 possible outcomes. Suppose that we want to choose a number at random between 0 and 1, allowing *any* number between 0 and 1 as the outcome. Software random number generators will do this. The sample space is now an entire interval of numbers:

$$S = \{\text{all numbers between 0 and 1}\}$$

Call the outcome of the random number generator Y for short. How can we assign probabilities to such events as $\{0.3 \le Y \le 0.7\}$? As in the case of selecting a random digit, we would like all possible outcomes to be equally likely. But we cannot assign probabilities to each individual value of Y and then add them, because there are infinitely many possible values.

We use a new way of assigning probabilities directly to events—as *areas under a density curve*. Any density curve has area exactly 1 underneath it, corresponding to total probability 1. We met density curves as models for data in Chapter 3 (page 68).

CONTINUOUS PROBABILITY MODEL

A **continuous probability model** assigns probabilities as areas under a density curve. The area under the curve and above any range of values is the probability of an outcome in that range.

EXAMPLE 10.7 Random numbers

The random number generator will spread its output uniformly across the entire interval from 0 to 1 as we allow it to generate a long sequence of numbers. Figure 10.4 is a histogram of 10,000 random numbers. They are quite uniform, but not exactly so. The bar heights would all be exactly equal (1000 numbers for each bar) if the 10,000 numbers were exactly uniform. In fact, the counts vary from a low of 960 to a high of 1022.

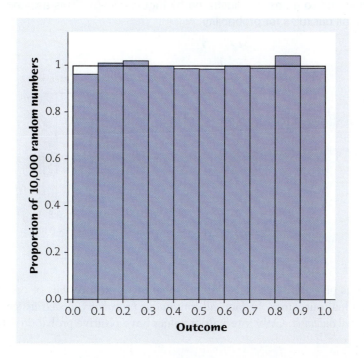

FIGURE 10.4

The probability model for the outcomes of a software random number generator, for Example 10.7. Compare the histogram of 10,000 actual outcomes with the uniform density curve that spreads probability evenly between 0 and 1.

uniform distribution

As in Chapter 3, we have adjusted the histogram scale so that the total area of the bars is exactly 1. Now we can add the density curve that describes the distribution of perfectly random numbers. This density curve also appears in Figure 10.4. It has height 1 over the interval from 0 to 1. This is the density curve of a **uniform distribution.** It is the continuous probability model for the results of generating very many random numbers. Like the probability model for perfectly balanced dice, the density curve is an idealized description of the outcomes of a perfectly uniform random number generator. It is a good approximation for software outcomes, but even 10,000 tries isn't enough for actual outcomes to look exactly like the idealized model. ■

EXAMPLE 10.8 Probabilities for random numbers

The uniform density curve has height 1 over the interval from 0 to 1. The area under the curve is 1, and the probability of any event is the area under the curve and above the event in question. Figure 10.5 illustrates finding probabilities as areas under the density curve. The probability that the random number generator produces a number between 0.3 and 0.7 is

$$P(0.3 \le Y \le 0.7) = 0.4$$

because the area under the density curve and above the interval from 0.3 to 0.7 is 0.4, as Figure 10.5(a) shows. The height of the curve is 1 and the area of a rectangle is the product of height and length, so the probability of any interval of outcomes is just the length of the interval. Similarly,

$$P(Y \le 0.5) = 0.5$$
$$P(Y > 0.8) = 0.2$$
$$P(Y \le 0.5 \text{ or } Y > 0.8) = 0.7$$

The last event consists of two nonoverlapping intervals, so the total area above the event is found by adding two areas, as illustrated by Figure 10.5(b). This assignment of probabilities obeys all our rules for probability. ■

FIGURE 10.5

Probability as area under a density curve, for Example 10.8. The uniform density curve spreads probability evenly between 0 and 1.

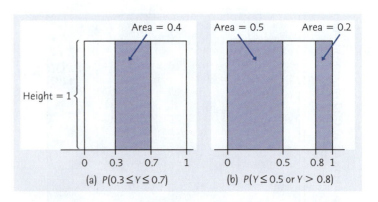

(a) $P(0.3 \le Y \le 0.7)$ (b) $P(Y \le 0.5 \text{ or } Y > 0.8)$

Continuous probability models assign probabilities to intervals of outcomes rather than to individual outcomes. In fact, *all continuous probability models assign probability 0 to every individual outcome.* Only intervals of values have positive probability. For example, the probability $P(Y = 0.8)$ in Example 10.8 is 0 because there is 0 area under the density curve and exactly above 0.8. Put another way, $P(Y > 0.8)$ and $P(Y \geq 0.8)$ are both 0.2 because that is the area in Figure 10.5(b) between 0.8 and 1.

We can use any density curve to assign probabilities. The density curves that are most familiar to us are the Normal curves. **Normal distributions are continuous probability models** as well as descriptions of data. There is a close connection between a Normal distribution as an idealized description for data and a Normal probability model. If we look at the heights of all young women, we find that they closely follow the Normal distribution with mean $\mu = 64.3$ inches and standard deviation $\sigma = 2.7$ inches. This is a distribution for a large set of data. Now choose one young woman at random. Call her height X. If we repeat the random choice very many times, the distribution of values of X is the same Normal distribution that describes the heights of all young women.

EXAMPLE 10.9 The heights of young women

What is the probability that a randomly chosen young woman has height between 68 and 70 inches? The height X of the woman we choose has the $N(64.3, 2.7)$ distribution. We want $P(68 \leq X \leq 70)$. This is the area under the Normal curve in Figure 10.6. Software gives us the answer at once: $P(68 \leq X \leq 70) = 0.0679$.

We can also find the probability by standardizing and using Table A, the table of standard Normal probabilities. We will reserve capital Z for a standard Normal variable.

$$P(68 \leq X \leq 70) = P\left(\frac{68 - 64.3}{2.7} \leq \frac{X - 64.3}{2.7} \leq \frac{70 - 64.3}{2.7}\right)$$
$$= P(1.37 \leq Z \leq 2.11)$$
$$= 0.9826 - 0.9147 = 0.0679$$

The calculation is the same as those we did in Chapter 3. Only the language of probability is new. ■

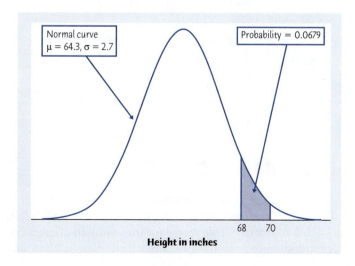

Normal curve
$\mu = 64.3, \sigma = 2.7$

Probability = 0.0679

68   70

Height in inches

FIGURE 10.6

The probability in Example 10.9 as an area under a Normal curve.

APPLY YOUR KNOWLEDGE

10.13 Random numbers. Let Y be a random number between 0 and 1 produced by the idealized random number generator described in Example 10.7 and Figure 10.4. Find the following probabilities:

(a) $P(Y \leq 0.6)$

(b) $P(Y < 0.6)$

(c) $P(0.4 \leq Y \leq 0.8)$

10.14 Adding random numbers. Generate two random numbers between 0 and 1 and take X to be their sum. The sum X can take any value between 0 and 2. The density curve of X is the triangle shown in Figure 10.7.

(a) Verify by geometry that the area under this curve is 1.

(b) What is the probability that X is less than 1? (Sketch the density curve, shade the area that represents the probability, then find that area. Do this for (c) also.)

(c) What is the probability that X is less than 0.5?

FIGURE 10.7

The density curve for the sum of two random numbers, for Exercise 10.14. This density curve spreads probability between 0 and 2.

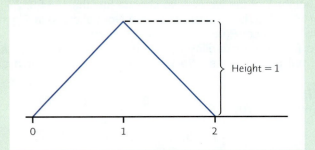

10.15 The Medical College Admission Test. The Normal distribution with mean $\mu = 25.0$ and standard deviation $\sigma = 6.4$ is a good description of the total score on the Medical College Admission Test (MCAT). This is a continuous probability model for the score of a randomly chosen student. Call the score of a randomly chosen student X for short.

(a) Write the event "the student chosen has a score of 35 or higher" in terms of X.

(b) Find the probability of this event.

RANDOM VARIABLES

Examples 10.6 to 10.9 use a convenient shorthand notation. In Example 10.9, we let X stand for the result of choosing a woman at random and measuring her height. We know that X would take a different value if we made another random choice. Because its value changes from one random choice to another, we call the height X a *random variable*.

RANDOM VARIABLE

A **random variable** is a variable whose value is a numerical outcome of a random phenomenon.

The **probability distribution** of a random variable X tells us what values X can take and how to assign probabilities to those values.

We usually denote random variables by capital letters near the end of the alphabet, such as X or Y. Of course, the random variables of greatest interest to us are outcomes such as the mean $\bar{x}$ of a random sample, for which we will keep the familiar notation. There are two main types of random variables, corresponding to two types of probability models: *discrete (or finite)* and *continuous*.

EXAMPLE 10.10 Discrete and continuous random variables

The first digit X in Example 10.6 is a random variable whose possible values are the whole numbers {1, 2, 3, 4, 5, 6, 7, 8, 9}. The distribution of X assigns a probability to each of these outcomes. Random variables that have a finite list of possible outcomes are called **discrete**.

discrete random variable

Compare the output Y of the random number generator in Example 10.7. The values of Y fill the entire interval of numbers between 0 and 1. The probability distribution of Y is given by its density curve, shown in Figure 10.4. Random variables that can take on any value in an interval, with probabilities given as areas under a density curve, are called **continuous**.

continuous random variable

APPLY YOUR KNOWLEDGE

10.16 Grades in an economics course. Indiana University posts the grade distributions for its courses online.[7] Students in Economics 201 in the fall 2009 semester received 9% A's, 8% A−'s, 10% B+'s, 14% B's, 13% B−'s, 10% C+'s, 12% C's, 4% C−'s, 4% D+'s, 8% D's, and 8% F's. Choose an Economics 201 student at random. To "choose at random" means to give every student the same chance to be chosen. The student's grade on a four-point scale (with A = 4, A− = 3.7, B+ = 3.3, B = 3.0, B− = 2.7, C+ = 2.3, C = 2.0, C− = 1.7, D+ = 1.3, D = 1.0, and F = 0.0) is a discrete random variable X with this probability distribution:

Value of X	0.0	1.0	1.3	1.7	2.0	2.3	2.7	3.0	3.3	3.7	4.0
Probability	0.08	0.08	0.04	0.04	0.12	0.10	0.13	0.14	0.10	0.08	0.09

(a) Say in words what the meaning of $P(X \geq 3.0)$ is. What is this probability?

(b) Write the event "the student got a grade poorer than B−" in terms of values of the random variable X. What is the probability of this event?

10.17 Running a mile. A study of 12,000 able-bodied male students at the University of Illinois found that their times for the mile run were approximately Normal with mean 7.11 minutes and standard deviation 0.74 minute.[8] Choose a student at random from this group and call his time for the mile Y.

(a) Say in words what the meaning of $P(Y \geq 8)$ is. What is this probability?

(b) Write the event "the student could run a mile in less than 6 minutes" in terms of values of the random variable Y. What is the probability of this event?

CHAPTER 10 SUMMARY

CHAPTER SPECIFICS

■ A **random phenomenon** has outcomes that we cannot predict but that nonetheless have a regular distribution in very many repetitions.

■ The **probability** of an event is the proportion of times the event occurs in many repeated trials of a random phenomenon.

■ A **probability model** for a random phenomenon consists of a sample space S and an assignment of probabilities P.

■ The **sample space S** is the set of all possible outcomes of the random phenomenon. Sets of outcomes are called **events.** P assigns a number $P(A)$ to an event A as its probability.

■ Any assignment of probability must obey the rules that state the basic properties of probability:

1. $0 \leq P(A) \leq 1$ for any event A.
2. $P(S) = 1$.
3. **Addition rule:** Events A and B are **disjoint** if they have no outcomes in common. If A and B are disjoint, then $P(A \text{ or } B) = P(A) + P(B)$.
4. For any event A, $P(A \text{ does not occur}) = 1 - P(A)$.

■ When a sample space S contains finitely many possible values, a finite probability model assigns each of these values a probability between 0 and 1 such that the sum of all the probabilities is exactly 1. The probability of any event is the sum of the probabilities of all the values that make up the event.

■ A sample space can contain all values in some interval of numbers. A **continuous probability model** assigns probabilities as areas under a **density curve.** The probability of any event is the area under the curve and above the values that make up the event.

■ A **random variable** is a variable taking numerical values determined by the outcome of a random phenomenon. The **probability distribution** of a random variable X tells us what the possible values of X are and how probabilities are assigned to those values.

■ A random variable X and its distribution can be **discrete** or **continuous.** A **discrete random variable** has finitely many possible values. Its distribution gives the probability of each value. A **continuous random variable** takes all values in some interval of numbers. A density curve describes the probability distribution of a continuous random variable.

LINK IT

This chapter begins our study of probability. The important fact is that random phenomena are unpredictable in the short run but have a regular and predictable behavior in the long run. Probability rules and probability models provide the tools for describing and predicting the long-run behavior of random phenomena.

Probability helps us understand why we can trust random samples and randomized comparative experiments, the subjects of Chapters 8 and 9. It is the key to generalizing what we learn from data produced by random samples and randomized comparative experiments to some wider universe or population. How we use probability to do this will be the topic of the remainder of this book.

CHECK YOUR SKILLS

10.18 You read in a book on poker that the probability of being dealt two pairs in a five-card poker hand is 1/20. This means that

   (a) if you deal thousands of poker hands, the fraction of them that contain two pairs will be very close to 1/20.

   (b) if you deal 20 poker hands, exactly 1 of them will contain two pairs.

   (c) if you deal 10,000 poker hands, exactly 500 of them will contain two pairs.

10.19 A basketball player shoots 5 free throws during a game. The sample space for counting the number she makes is

   (a) S = any number between 0 and 1.

   (b) S = whole numbers 0 to 5.

   (c) S = all sequences of 5 hits or misses, like HMMHH.

Here is the probability model for the political affiliation of a randomly chosen adult in the United States.[9] Exercises 10.20 and 10.21 use this information.

Political affiliation	Republican	Independent	Democrat	Other
Probability	0.28	0.42	0.28	?

10.20 This probability model is

   (a) continuous.   (b) finite.   (c) equally likely.

10.21 The probability that a randomly chosen American adult's political affiliation is "Other" must be

   (a) any number between 0 and 1.

   (b) 0.02.   (c) 0.2.

10.22 In a table of random digits such as Table B, each digit is equally likely to be any of 0, 1, 2, 3, 4, 5, 6, 7, 8, or 9. What is the probability that a digit in the table is 7 or greater?

   (a) 7/10   (b) 4/10   (c) 3/10

10.23 Choose an American household at random and let the random variable X be the number of cars (including SUVs and light trucks) they own. Here is the probability model if we ignore the few households that own more than 6 cars:

Number of cars X	0	1	2	3	4	5	6
Probability	0.09	0.29	0.38	0.16	0.05	0.02	0.01

A housing company builds houses with two-car garages. What percent of households have more cars than the garage can hold?

   (a) 16%   (b) 24%   (c) 62%

10.24 Choose a common fruit fly *Drosophila melanogaster* at random. Call the length of the thorax (where the wings and legs attach) Y. The random variable Y has the Normal distribution with mean $\mu = 0.800$ millimeter (mm) and standard deviation $\sigma = 0.078$ mm. The probability $P(Y > 1)$ that the fly you choose has a thorax more than 1 mm long is about

   (a) 0.995.   (b) 0.5.   (c) 0.005.

CHAPTER 10 EXERCISES

10.25 Sample space. In each of the following situations, describe a sample space S for the random phenomenon.

   (a) A basketball player shoots four free throws. You record the sequence of hits and misses.

   (b) A basketball player shoots four free throws. You record the number of baskets she makes.

10.26 Probability models? In each of the following situations, state whether or not the given assignment of probabilities to individual outcomes is legitimate, that is, satisfies the rules of probability. If not, give specific reasons for your answer.

   (a) Roll a die and record the count of spots on the up-face:

$$P(1) = 0 \qquad P(2) = 1/6 \quad P(3) = 1/3$$
$$P(4) = 1/3 \quad P(5) = 1/6 \quad P(6) = 0$$

(b) Deal a card from a shuffled deck:

P (clubs) = 12/52 P (diamonds) = 12/52

P (hearts) = 12/52 P (spades) = 16/52

(c) Choose a college student at random and record sex and enrollment status:

P (female full-time) = 0.56 P (male full-time) = 0.44

P (female part-time) = 0.24 P (male part-time) = 0.17

10.27 Education among young adults. Choose a young adult (aged 25 to 29) at random. The probability is 0.13 that the person chosen did not complete high school, 0.31 that the person has a high school diploma but no further education, and 0.29 that the person has at least a bachelor's degree.

(a) What must be the probability that a randomly chosen young adult has some education beyond high school but does not have a bachelor's degree?

(b) What is the probability that a randomly chosen young adult has at least a high school education?

10.28 Land in Canada. Canada's national statistics agency, Statistics Canada, says that the land area of Canada is 9,094,000 square kilometers. Of this land, 4,176,000 square kilometers are forested. Choose a square kilometer of land in Canada at random.

(a) What is the probability that the area you choose is forested?

(b) What is the probability that it is not forested?

10.29 Foreign-language study. Choose a student in a U.S. public high school at random and ask if he or she is studying a language other than English. Here is the distribution of results:

Language	Spanish	French	German	All others	None
Probability	0.30	0.08	0.02	0.03	0.57

(a) Explain why this is a legitimate probability model.

(b) What is the probability that a randomly chosen student is studying a language other than English?

(c) What is the probability that a randomly chosen student is studying French, German, or Spanish?

10.30 Car colors. Choose a new car or light truck at random and note its color. Here are the probabilities of the most popular colors for vehicles sold globally in 2010:[10]

Color	Silver	Black	White	Gray	Red	Blue	Beige, brown
Probability	0.26	0.24	0.16	0.16	0.06	0.05	0.03

(a) What is the probability that the vehicle you choose has any color other than those listed?

(b) What is the probability that a randomly chosen vehicle is neither silver nor white?

10.31 Drawing cards. You are about to draw a card at random (that is, all choices have the same probability) from a set of 7 cards. Although you can't see the cards, here they are:

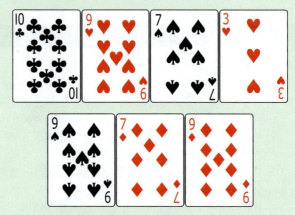

(a) What is the probability that you draw a 9?

(b) What is the probability that you draw a red 9?

(c) What is the probability that you do not draw a 7?

10.32 Loaded dice. There are many ways to produce crooked dice. To *load* a die so that 6 comes up too often and 1 (which is opposite 6) comes up too seldom, add a bit of lead to the filling of the spot on the 1 face. If a die is loaded so that 6 comes up with probability 0.2 and the probabilities of the 2, 3, 4, and 5 faces are not affected, what is the assignment of probabilities to the six faces?

10.33 A door prize. A party host gives a door prize to one guest chosen at random. There are 48 men and 42 women at the party. What is the probability that the prize goes to a woman? Explain how you arrived at your answer.

10.34 Race and ethnicity. The U.S. Census Bureau allows each person to choose from a long list of races. That is, in the eyes of the U.S. Census Bureau, you belong to whatever race you say you belong to. "Hispanic/Latino" is a separate category; Hispanics may be of any race. If we choose a resident of the United States at random, the U.S. Census Bureau gives these probabilities:[11]

	Hispanic	Not Hispanic
Asian	0.001	0.044
Black	0.006	0.124
White	0.144	0.667
Other	0.005	0.009

(a) Verify that this is a legitimate assignment of probabilities.

(b) What is the probability that a randomly chosen American is Hispanic?

(c) Non-Hispanic whites are the historical majority in the United States. What is the probability that a randomly chosen American is not a member of this group?

Who do you live with? *Choose at random a person aged 15 to 44 years. Ask their age and who they live with (alone, with spouse, with other persons). Here is the probability model for 12 possible answers:*[12]

	Age in Years			
	15–19	20–24	25–34	35–44
Alone	0.001	0.011	0.031	0.030
With spouse	0.001	0.023	0.155	0.216
With others	0.169	0.132	0.142	0.089

Exercises 10.35 to 10.37 use this probability model.

10.35 Living arrangements.

(a) Why is this a legitimate finite probability model?

(b) What is the probability that the person chosen is a 15- to 19-year-old who lives alone?

(c) What is the probability that the person is 15 to 19 years old?

(d) What is the probability that the person chosen lives alone?

10.36 Living arrangements, continued.

(a) List the outcomes that make up the event

A = {The person chosen is *either* 15 to 19 years old *or* lives alone, or both}

(b) What is P(A)? Explain carefully why P(A) is not the sum of the probabilities you found in parts (b) and (c) of the previous exercise.

10.37 Living arrangements, continued.

(a) What is the probability that the person chosen is 20 years old or older?

(b) What is the probability that the person chosen does not live alone?

10.38 Spelling errors. Spell-checking software catches "nonword errors" that result in a string of letters that is not a word, as when "the" is typed as "teh." When undergraduates are asked to type a 250-word essay (without spell-checking), the number X of nonword errors has the following distribution:

Value of X	0	1	2	3	4
Probability	0.1	0.2	0.3	0.3	0.1

(a) Is the random variable X discrete or continuous? Why?

(b) Write the event "at least one nonword error" in terms of X. What is the probability of this event?

(c) Describe the event X ≤ 2 in words. What is its probability? What is the probability that X < 2?

10.39 First digits again. A crook who never heard of Benford's law (page 223) might fake invoices so that the first digits of the amounts are equally likely to be any of 1, 2, 3, 4, 5, 6, 7, 8, or 9. Call the first digit of a randomly chosen fake invoice W for short.

(a) Write the probability distribution for the random variable W.

(b) Find P(W ≥ 6) and compare your result with the Benford's law probability from Example 10.6.

10.40 Who gets interviewed? Abby, Deborah, Mei-Ling, Sam, and Roberto are students in a small seminar course. Their professor decides to choose two of them to interview about the course. To avoid unfairness, the choice will be made by drawing two names from a hat. (This is an SRS of size 2.)

(a) Write down all possible choices of two of the five names. This is the sample space.

(b) The random drawing makes all choices equally likely. What is the probability of each choice?

(c) What is the probability that Mei-Ling is chosen?

(d) Abby, Deborah, and Mei-Ling liked the course. Sam and Roberto did not like the course. What is the probability that both people selected liked the course?

10.41 Birth order. A couple plans to have three children. There are 8 possible arrangements of girls and boys. For example, GGB means the first two children are girls and the third child is a boy. All 8 arrangements are (approximately) equally likely.

(a) Write down all 8 arrangements of the sexes of three children. What is the probability of any one of these arrangements?

(b) Let X be the number of girls the couple has. What is the probability that X = 2?

(c) Starting from your work in (a), find the distribution of X. That is, what values can X take, and what are the probabilities for each value?

10.42 Random numbers. Many random number generators allow users to specify the range of the random numbers to be produced. Suppose that you specify that the random number Y can take any value between 0 and 2. Then the density curve of the outcomes has constant height between 0 and 2, and height 0 elsewhere.

(a) Is the random variable Y discrete or continuous? Why?

(b) What is the height of the density curve between 0 and 2? Draw a graph of the density curve.

(c) Use your graph from (b) and the fact that probability is area under the curve to find $P(Y \le 1)$.

10.43 More random numbers. Find these probabilities as areas under the density curve you sketched in Exercise 10.42.

(a) $P(0.5 < Y < 1.3)$

(b) $P(Y \ge 0.8)$

10.44 Survey accuracy. A sample survey contacted an SRS of 3050 registered voters shortly before the 2008 presidential election and asked respondents whom they planned to vote for. Election results show that 53% of registered voters voted for Barack Obama. We will see later that in this situation the proportion of the sample who planned to vote for Barack Obama (call this proportion V) has approximately the Normal distribution with mean $\mu = 0.53$ and standard deviation $\sigma = 0.009$.

(a) If the respondents answer truthfully, what is $P(0.51 \le V \le 0.55)$? This is the probability that the sample proportion V estimates the population proportion 0.53 within plus or minus 0.02.

(b) In fact, 55% of the respondents said they planned to vote for Barack Obama ($V = 0.55$). If respondents answer truthfully, what is $P(V \ge 0.55)$?

10.45 Friends. How many close friends do you have? Suppose that the number of close friends adults claim to have varies from person to person with mean $\mu = 9$ and standard deviation $\sigma = 2.5$. An opinion poll asks this question of an SRS of 1100 adults. We will see later that in this situation the sample mean response $\bar{x}$ has approximately the Normal distribution with mean 9 and standard deviation 0.075. What is $P(8.9 \le \bar{x} \le 9.1)$, the probability that the sample result $\bar{x}$ estimates the population truth $\mu = 9$ to within ± 0.1?

10.46 Unusual dice. Nonstandard dice can produce interesting distributions of outcomes. You have two balanced, six-sided dice. One is a standard die, with faces having 1, 2, 3, 4, 5, and 6 spots. The other die has three faces with 0 spots and three faces with 6 spots. Find the probability distribution for the total number of spots Y on the up-faces when you roll these two dice. (*Hint:* Start with a picture like Figure 10.2 (page 219) for the possible up-faces. Label the three 0 faces on the second die 0a, 0b, 0c in your picture, and similarly distinguish the three 6 faces.)

10.47 Playing Pick 4. The Pick 4 games in many state lotteries announce a four-digit winning number each day. Each of the 10,000 possible numbers 0000 to 9999 has the same chance of winning. You win if your choice matches the winning digits. Suppose your chosen number is 5974.

(a) What is the probability that the winning number matches your number exactly?

(b) What is the probability that the winning number has the same digits as your number *in any order*?

 EXPLORING THE WEB

10.48 Super Bowl odds. Oddsmakers often list the odds for certain sporting events on the Web. For example, one can find the current odds of winning the next Super Bowl for each NFL team. We found a list of such odds at www.vegas.com/gaming/futures/superbowl.html. When an oddsmaker says the odds are A to B of winning, he or she means that the probability of winning is $B/(A + B)$. For example, when we checked the Web site listed above, in early 2012 the odds that the New York Giants would win Super Bowl XLVII were 10 to 1. This corresponds to a probability of winning of $1/(10 + 1) = 1/11$.

On the Web, find the current odds, at the time you read this according to an oddsmaker, of winning the Super Bowl for each NFL team. Convert these odds to probabilities. Do these probabilities satisfy Rules 1 and 2 given in this chapter? If they don't, can you think of a reason why?

Age Fotostock/SuperStock

Sampling Distributions

What is the average income of American households? Each March, the government's Current Population Survey asks detailed questions about income. The 97,263 households contacted in March 2010 had a mean "total money income" of $67,976 in 2009.[1] (The median income was of course lower, $49,777.) That $67,976 describes the sample, but we use it to estimate the mean income of all households. This is an example of statistical inference: we use information from a sample to infer something about a wider population.

Because the results of random samples and randomized comparative experiments include an element of chance, we can't guarantee that our inferences are correct. What we can guarantee is that our methods usually give correct answers. The reasoning of statistical inference rests on asking, "How often would this method give a correct answer if I used it very many times?" If our data come from random sampling or randomized comparative experiments, the laws of probability answer the question "What would happen if we did this many times?" This chapter presents some facts about probability that help answer this question.

PARAMETERS AND STATISTICS

As we begin to use sample data to draw conclusions about a wider population, we must take care to keep straight whether a number describes a sample or a population. Here is the vocabulary we use.

PARAMETER, STATISTIC

A **parameter** is a number that describes the population. In statistical practice, the value of a parameter is not known because we cannot examine the entire population.

A **statistic** is a number that can be computed from the sample data without making use of any unknown parameters. In practice, we often use a statistic to estimate an unknown parameter.

EXAMPLE 11.1 Household earnings

The mean income of the sample of 97,263 households contacted by the Current Population Survey was $\bar{x}$ = $67,976. The number $67,976 is a *statistic* because it describes this one Current Population Survey sample. The population that the poll wants to draw conclusions about is all 117 million U.S. households. The *parameter* of interest is the mean income of all these households. We don't know the value of this parameter. ■

population mean μ
sample mean x̄

Remember **s** and **p**: statistics come from **s**amples, and **p**arameters come from **p**opulations. As long as we were just doing data analysis, the distinction between population and sample was not important. Now, however, it is essential. The notation we use reflects this distinction. We write μ (the Greek letter mu) for the **mean of a population.** This parameter has a fixed value, but we don't know what it is. The **mean of the sample** is the familiar $\bar{x}$, the average of the observations in the sample. This statistic would almost certainly take a different value if we chose another sample from the same population. The sample mean $\bar{x}$ from a sample or an experiment is an estimate of the mean μ of the underlying population.

APPLY YOUR KNOWLEDGE

11.1 Genetic engineering. Here's a new idea for treating advanced melanoma, the most serious kind of skin cancer. Genetically engineer white blood cells to better recognize and destroy cancer cells, then infuse these cells into patients. The subjects in a small initial study of this approach were 11 patients whose melanoma had not responded to existing treatments. One outcome of this experiment was measured by a test for the presence of cells that trigger an immune response in the body and so may help fight cancer. The mean counts of active cells per 100,000 cells for the 11 subjects were **3.8** before infusion and **160.2** after infusion. Is each of the boldface numbers a parameter or a statistic?

11.2 Florida voters. Florida played a key role in the 2000 and 2004 presidential elections. Voter registration records show that **41%** of Florida voters are registered as Democrats and **37%** as Republicans. (Most of the others did not choose a party.) To test a random digit dialing device, you use it to call 250 randomly chosen residential telephones in Florida. Of the registered voters contacted, **33%** are registered Democrats. Is each of the boldface numbers a parameter or a statistic?

STATISTICAL ESTIMATION AND THE LAW OF LARGE NUMBERS

Statistical inference uses sample data to draw conclusions about the entire population. Because good samples are chosen randomly, statistics such as $\bar{x}$ are random variables. We can describe the behavior of a sample statistic by a probability model that answers the question "What would happen if we did this many times?" Here is an example that will lead us toward the probability ideas most important for statistical inference.

 WINE

EXAMPLE 11.2 Does this wine smell bad?

Sulfur compounds such as dimethyl sulfide (DMS) cause "off-odors" in wine, so winemakers want to know the odor threshold, the lowest concentration of DMS that the human nose can detect. Different people have different thresholds, so we start by asking about the mean threshold μ in the population of all adults. The number μ is a parameter that describes this population.

To estimate μ, we present subjects with both natural wine and the same wine spiked with DMS at different concentrations to find the lowest concentration at which they identify the spiked wine. Here are the odor thresholds (measured in micrograms of DMS per liter of wine) for 10 randomly chosen subjects:

28   40   28   33   20   31   29   27   17   21

The mean threshold for these subjects is $\bar{x} = 27.4$. It seems reasonable to use the sample result $\bar{x} = 27.4$ to estimate the unknown μ. An SRS should fairly represent the population, so the mean $\bar{x}$ of the sample should be somewhere near the mean μ of the population. Of course, we don't expect $\bar{x}$ to be exactly equal to μ. We realize that if we choose another SRS, the luck of the draw will probably produce a different $\bar{x}$. ■

Foodpix/Getty Images

If $\bar{x}$ is rarely exactly right and varies from sample to sample, why is it nonetheless a reasonable estimate of the population mean μ? Here is one answer: *if we keep on taking larger and larger samples, the statistic $\bar{x}$ is guaranteed to get closer and closer to the parameter μ.* If we can afford to keep on measuring more subjects, eventually we will estimate the mean odor threshold of all adults very accurately. This remarkable fact is called the *law of large numbers*. It is remarkable because it holds for *any* population, not just for some special class such as Normal distributions.

LAW OF LARGE NUMBERS

Draw observations at random from any population with finite mean μ. As the number of observations drawn increases, the mean $\bar{x}$ of the observed values gets closer and closer to the mean μ of the population.

The behavior of $\bar{x}$ is similar to the idea of probability. In the long run, the *proportion* of outcomes taking any value gets close to the probability of that value, and the *average* outcome gets close to the population mean. Figure 10.1 (page 216) shows how proportions approach probability in one example. Here is an example of how sample means approach the population mean.

EXAMPLE 11.3 The law of large numbers in action

In fact, the distribution of odor thresholds among all adults has mean 25. The mean $\mu = 25$ is the true value of the parameter we seek to estimate. Figure 11.1 shows how the sample mean $\bar{x}$ of an SRS drawn from this population changes as we add more subjects to our sample.

The first subject in Example 11.2 had threshold 28, so the line in Figure 11.1 starts there. The mean for the first two subjects is

$$\bar{x} = \frac{28 + 40}{2} = 34$$

This is the second point on the graph. At first, the graph shows that the mean of the sample changes as we take more observations. Eventually, however, the mean of the observations gets close to the population mean $\mu = 25$ and settles down at that value.

If we started over, again choosing people at random from the population, we would get a different path from left to right in Figure 11.1. The law of large numbers says that whatever path we get will always settle down at 25 as we draw more and more people. ▪

FIGURE 11.1

The law of large numbers in action: as we take more observations, the sample mean $\bar{x}$ always approaches the mean μ of the population.

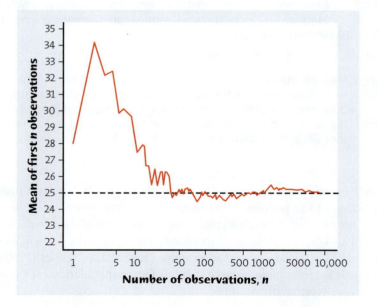

The law of large numbers is the foundation of such business enterprises as gambling casinos and insurance companies. The winnings (or losses) of a gambler on a few plays are uncertain—that's why some people find gambling exciting. In Figure 11.1, the mean has not settled down close to μ even after 100 observations. It is only *in the long run* that the mean outcome is predictable. The house plays tens of thousands of times. So the house, unlike individual gamblers, can count on the long-run regularity described by the law of large numbers. The average winnings of the house on tens of thousands of plays will be very close to the mean of the distribution of winnings. Needless to say, this mean guarantees the house a profit. That's why gambling can be a business.

APPLY YOUR KNOWLEDGE

11.3 Insurance. The idea of insurance is that we all face risks that are unlikely but carry high cost. Think of a fire or flood destroying your apartment. Insurance spreads the risk: we all pay a small amount, and the insurance policy pays a large amount to those few of us whose apartments are damaged. An insurance company looks at the records for millions of apartment owners and sees that the mean loss from apartment damage in a year is $\mu = \$75$ per person. (Most of us have no loss, but a few lose most of their possessions. The $75 is the average loss.) The company plans to sell fire insurance for $75 plus enough to cover its costs and profit. Explain clearly why it would be unwise to sell only 12 policies. Then explain why selling thousands of such policies is a safe business.

SAMPLING DISTRIBUTIONS

The law of large numbers assures us that if we measure enough subjects, the statistic $\bar{x}$ will eventually get very close to the unknown parameter μ. But the odor threshold study in Example 11.2 had just 10 subjects. What can we say about estimating μ by $\bar{x}$ from a sample of 10 subjects? Put this one sample in the context of all such samples by asking, "What would happen if we took many samples of 10 subjects from this population?" Here's how to answer this question:

- Take a large number of samples of size 10 from the population.

- Calculate the sample mean $\bar{x}$ for each sample.

- Make a histogram of the values of $\bar{x}$.

- Examine the shape, center, and spread of the distribution displayed in the histogram.

It is too expensive to take many samples from a large population such as all adult U.S. residents. But we can imitate many samples by using software. Using software to imitate chance behavior is called **simulation.**

simulation

EXAMPLE 11.4 What would happen in many samples?

Extensive studies have found that the DMS odor threshold of adults follows roughly a Normal distribution with mean $\mu = 25$ micrograms per liter and standard deviation $\sigma = 7$ micrograms per liter. We call this the *population distribution* of odor threshold.

Figure 11.2 illustrates the process of choosing many samples and finding the sample mean threshold $\bar{x}$ for each one. Follow the flow of the figure from the population at the left, to choosing an SRS and finding the $\bar{x}$ for this sample, to collecting together the $\bar{x}$'s from many samples. The first sample has $\bar{x} = 26.42$. The second sample contains a different 10 people, with $\bar{x} = 24.28$, and so on. The histogram at the right of the figure shows the distribution of the values of $\bar{x}$ from 1000 separate SRSs of size 10. This histogram displays the *sampling distribution* of the statistic $\bar{x}$. ▪

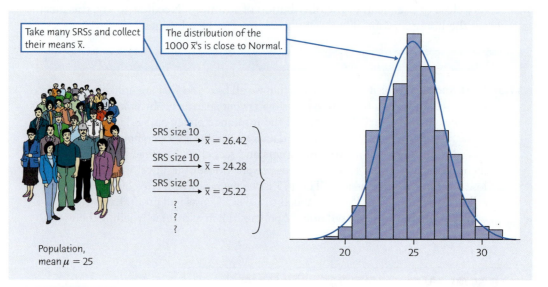

FIGURE 11.2

The idea of a sampling distribution: take many samples from the same population, collect the $\bar{x}$'s from all the samples, and display the distribution of the $\bar{x}$'s. The histogram shows the results of 1000 samples.

> ### POPULATION DISTRIBUTION, SAMPLING DISTRIBUTION
>
> The **population distribution** of a variable is the distribution of values of the variable among all the individuals in the population.
>
> The **sampling distribution** of a statistic is the distribution of values taken by the statistic in all possible samples of the same size from the same population.

Be careful: The population distribution describes the *individuals* that make up the population. A sampling distribution describes how a *statistic* varies in many samples from the population. Strictly speaking, the sampling distribution is the ideal pattern that would emerge if we looked at all possible samples of size 10 from our population. A distribution obtained from a fixed number of trials, like the 1000 trials in Figure 11.2, is only an approximation to the sampling distribution.

We can use the tools of data analysis to describe any distribution. Let's apply those tools to Figure 11.2. What can we say about the shape, center, and spread of this distribution?

▪ **Shape:** It looks Normal! Detailed examination confirms that the distribution of $\bar{x}$ from many samples is very close to Normal.

■ **Center:** The mean of the 1000 $\bar{x}$'s is 24.95. That is, the distribution is centered very close to the population mean $\mu = 25$.

■ **Spread:** The standard deviation of the 1000 $\bar{x}$'s is 2.217, notably smaller than the standard deviation $\sigma = 7$ of the population of individual subjects.

Although these results describe just one simulation of a sampling distribution, they reflect facts that are true whenever we use random sampling.

APPLY YOUR KNOWLEDGE

11.4 Sampling distribution versus population distribution. During World War II, 12,000 able-bodied male undergraduates at the University of Illinois participated in required physical training. Each student ran a timed mile. Their times followed the Normal distribution with mean 7.11 minutes and standard deviation 0.74 minute. An SRS of 100 of these students has mean time $\bar{x} = 7.15$ minutes. A second SRS of size 100 has mean $\bar{x} = 6.97$ minutes. After many SRSs, the many values of the sample mean $\bar{x}$ follow the Normal distribution with mean 7.11 minutes and standard deviation 0.074 minute.

(a) What is the population? What values does the population distribution describe? What is this distribution?

(b) What values does the sampling distribution of $\bar{x}$ describe? What is the sampling distribution?

11.5 Generating a sampling distribution. Let's illustrate the idea of a sampling distribution in the case of a very small sample from a very small population. The population is the scores of 10 students on an exam:

Student	0	1	2	3	4	5	6	7	8	9
Score	86	63	81	55	72	72	65	66	75	59

The parameter of interest is the mean score μ in this population. The sample is an SRS of size $n = 4$ drawn from the population. Because the students are labeled 0 to 9, a single random digit from Table B chooses one student for the sample.

(a) Find the mean of the 10 scores in the population. This is the population mean μ.

(b) Use the first digits in row 116 of Table B to draw an SRS of size 4 from this population. What are the four scores in your sample? What is their mean $\bar{x}$? This statistic is an estimate of μ.

(c) Repeat this process 9 more times, using the first digits in rows 117 to 125 of Table B. Make a histogram of the 10 values of $\bar{x}$. You are constructing the sampling distribution of $\bar{x}$. Is the center of your histogram close to μ?

THE MEAN AND STANDARD DEVIATION OF $\bar{x}$

Figure 11.2 suggests that when we choose many SRSs from a population, the sampling distribution of the sample means is centered at the mean of the original population and is less spread out than the distribution of individual observations. Here are the facts.

> **MEAN AND STANDARD DEVIATION OF A SAMPLE MEAN[2]**
>
> Suppose that $\bar{x}$ is the mean of an SRS of size n drawn from a large population with mean μ and standard deviation σ. Then the sampling distribution of $\bar{x}$ has **mean μ** and **standard deviation $\sigma/\sqrt{n}$.**

These facts about the mean and the standard deviation of the sampling distribution of $\bar{x}$ are true for *any* population, not just for some special class such as Normal distributions. They have important implications for statistical inference:

unbiased estimator

■ The mean of the statistic $\bar{x}$ is always equal to the mean μ of the population. That is, the sampling distribution of $\bar{x}$ is centered at μ. In repeated sampling, $\bar{x}$ will sometimes fall above the true value of the parameter μ and sometimes below, but there is no systematic tendency to overestimate or underestimate the parameter. This makes the idea of lack of bias in the sense of "no favoritism" more precise. Because the mean of $\bar{x}$ is equal to μ, we say that the statistic $\bar{x}$ is an **unbiased estimator** of the parameter μ.

■ An unbiased estimator is "correct on the average" in many samples. How close the estimator falls to the parameter in most samples is determined by the spread of the sampling distribution. If individual observations have standard deviation σ, then sample means $\bar{x}$ from samples of size n have standard deviation $\sigma/\sqrt{n}$. That is, **averages are less variable than individual observations.**

■ Not only is the standard deviation of the distribution of $\bar{x}$ smaller than the standard deviation of individual observations, but it gets smaller as we take larger samples. **The results of large samples are less variable than the results of small samples.**

The upshot of all this is that we can trust the sample mean from a large random sample to estimate the population mean accurately. If the sample size n is large, the standard deviation of $\bar{x}$ is small, and almost all samples will give values of $\bar{x}$ that lie very close to the true parameter μ. *However, the standard deviation of the sampling distribution gets smaller only at the rate $\sqrt{n}$. To cut the standard deviation of $\bar{x}$ in half, we must take four times as many observations, not just twice as many.* So very accurate estimates may be expensive.

APPLY YOUR KNOWLEDGE

11.6 Measurements in the lab. Juan makes a measurement in a chemistry laboratory and records the result in his lab report. The standard deviation of students' lab measurements is $\sigma = 10$ milligrams. Juan repeats the measurement 4 times and records the mean $\bar{x}$ of his 4 measurements.

(a) What is the standard deviation of Juan's mean result? (That is, if Juan kept on making 4 measurements and averaging them, what would be the standard deviation of all his $\bar{x}$'s?)

(b) How many times must Juan repeat the measurement to reduce the standard deviation of $\bar{x}$ to 2? Explain to someone who knows no statistics the advantage of reporting the average of several measurements rather than the result of a single measurement.

THE CENTRAL LIMIT THEOREM

The facts about the mean and standard deviation of $\bar{x}$ are true no matter what the shape of the population distribution may be. But what is the shape of the sampling distribution? *It is a remarkable fact that as the sample size increases, the distribution of $\bar{x}$ changes shape: it looks less like that of the population and more like a Normal distribution.* When the sample is large enough, the distribution of $\bar{x}$ is very close to Normal. This is true no matter what shape the population distribution has, as long as the population has a finite standard deviation σ. This famous fact of probability theory is called the *central limit theorem*.

CENTRAL LIMIT THEOREM

Draw an SRS of size n from any population with mean μ and finite standard deviation σ. The **central limit theorem** says that when n is large the sampling distribution of the sample mean $\bar{x}$ is approximately Normal:

$$\bar{x} \text{ is approximately } N\left(\mu, \frac{\sigma}{\sqrt{n}}\right)$$

The central limit theorem allows us to use Normal probability calculations to answer questions about sample means from many observations.

How large a sample size n is needed for $\bar{x}$ to be close to Normal depends on the population distribution. In fact, *if the population distribution itself is exactly Normal, then the sampling distribution of $\bar{x}$ is exactly Normal.* No real population has an exactly Normal distribution, so this fact is much less important than the central limit theorem. If the shape of the population distribution is far from Normal, more observations are required in order for $\bar{x}$ to be close to Normal. Here is an example in which the population is very far from Normal.

EXAMPLE 11.5 The central limit theorem in action

Figure 11.3(a) shows a strongly right-skewed population distribution that has its most probable outcomes near 0. The mean μ of this distribution is 1, and its standard deviation σ is also 1. This particular distribution is called an *exponential distribution*. Exponential distributions are used as models for the lifetime in service of electronic components and for the time required to serve a customer or repair a machine.

Figures 11.3(b), (c), and (d) are the density curves of the sample means of 2, 10, and 25 observations from this population. As n increases, the shape becomes more Normal. The mean remains at $\mu = 1$, and the standard deviation decreases, taking the value $1/\sqrt{n}$. The density curve for 10 observations is still somewhat skewed to the right but already resembles a Normal curve having $\mu = 1$ and $\sigma = 1/\sqrt{10} = 0.32$. The density curve for $n = 25$ is yet more Normal. The contrast between the shapes of the population distribution and of the distribution of the means of 10 or 25 observations is striking. ■

FIGURE 11.3

The central limit theorem in action, for Example 11.5. The distribution of sample means $\bar{x}$ from a strongly non-Normal population becomes more Normal as the sample size increases. (a) The distribution of 1 observation. (b) The distribution of $\bar{x}$ for 2 observations. (c) The distribution of $\bar{x}$ for 10 observations. (d) The distribution of $\bar{x}$ for 25 observations.

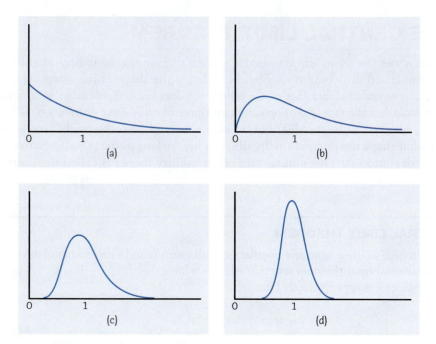

Comparing Figure 11.3(a) with Figures 11.3(b), (c), and (d) illustrates the two most important ideas of this chapter.

THINKING ABOUT SAMPLE MEANS

Means of random samples are **less variable** than individual observations.

Means of random samples are **more Normal** than individual observations.

Let's use Normal calculations based on the central limit theorem to answer a question about the very non-Normal distribution in Figure 11.3(a).

EXAMPLE 11.6 Maintaining air conditioners

STATE: The time (in hours) that a technician requires to perform preventive maintenance on an air-conditioning unit is governed by the exponential distribution whose density curve appears in Figure 11.3(a). The mean time is $\mu = 1$ hour and the standard deviation is $\sigma = 1$ hour. Your company has a contract to maintain 70 of these units in an apartment building. You must schedule technicians' time for a visit to this building. Is it safe to budget an average of 1.1 hours for each unit? Or should you budget an average of 1.25 hours?

PLAN: We can treat these 70 air conditioners as an SRS from all units of this type. What is the probability that the average maintenance time for 70 units exceeds 1.1 hours? That the average time exceeds 1.25 hours?

SOLVE: The central limit theorem says that the sample mean time $\bar{x}$ spent working on 70 units has approximately the Normal distribution with mean equal to the population mean $\mu = 1$ hour and standard deviation

$$\frac{\sigma}{\sqrt{70}} = \frac{1}{\sqrt{70}} = 0.12 \text{ hour}$$

The distribution of $\bar{x}$ is therefore approximately $N(1, 0.12)$. This Normal curve is the solid curve in Figure 11.4.

Using this Normal distribution, the probabilities we want are

$$P(\bar{x} > 1.10 \text{ hours}) = 0.2014$$

$$P(\bar{x} > 1.25 \text{ hours}) = 0.0182$$

Software gives these probabilities immediately, or you can standardize and use Table A. For example,

$$P(\bar{x} > 1.10) = P\left(\frac{\bar{x} - 1}{0.12}\right) > P\left(\frac{1.10 - 1}{0.12}\right)$$

$$= P(Z > 0.83) = 1 - 0.7967 = 0.2033$$

with the usual roundoff error. Don't forget to use standard deviation 0.12 in your software or when you standardize $\bar{x}$.

CONCLUDE: If you budget 1.1 hours per unit, there is a 20% chance that the technicians will not complete the work in the building within the budgeted time. This chance drops to 2% if you budget 1.25 hours. You therefore budget 1.25 hours per unit. ■

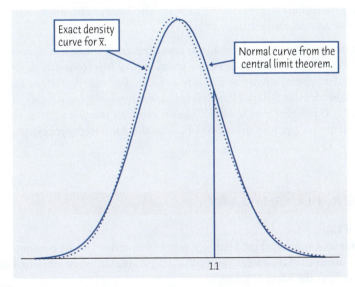

FIGURE 11.4
The exact distribution (dotted) and the Normal approximation from the central limit theorem (solid) for the average time needed to maintain an air conditioner, for Example 11.6. The probability we want is the area to the right of 1.1.

Using more mathematics, we can start with the exponential distribution and find the actual density curve of $\bar{x}$ for 70 observations. This is the dotted curve in Figure 11.4. You can see that the solid Normal curve is a good approximation. The exactly correct probability for 1.1 hours is the area to the right of 1.1 under the dotted density curve. It is 0.1977. The central limit theorem Normal approximation 0.2014 is off by only about 0.004.

APPLY YOUR KNOWLEDGE

11.7 **Population versus sample.** The blood cholesterol level of all men aged 20 to 34 follows the Normal distribution with mean $\mu = 188$ milligrams per deciliter (mg/dl) and standard deviation $\sigma = 41$ mg/dl. A sample survey measures the blood cholesterol level of an SRS of 10 such men.

    (a) What are the mean and standard deviation of the sampling distribution of the sample mean $\bar{x}$?

    (b) Draw two Normal curves on the same graph, one for the population distribution of individual measurements and another for the sampling distribution of the mean of 10 measurements. Comparing the two curves illustrates the fact that averages are less variable than individuals.

11.8 **Larger sample, more accurate estimate.** The blood cholesterol level of all men aged 20 to 34 follows a population distribution with mean $\mu = 188$ milligrams per deciliter (mg/dl) and standard deviation $\sigma = 41$ mg/dl.

    (a) Choose an SRS of 100 men from this population. According to the central limit theorem, what is the approximate sampling distribution of $\bar{x}$? What is the probability that $\bar{x}$ takes a value between 185 and 191 mg/dl? This is the probability that $\bar{x}$ estimates μ within ± 3 mg/dl.

    (b) Choose an SRS of 1000 men from this population. Now what is the probability that $\bar{x}$ falls within ± 3 mg/dl of μ? The larger sample is much more likely to give an accurate estimate of μ.

11.9 **More on insurance.** An insurance company knows that in the entire population of millions of apartment owners, the mean annual loss from damage is $\mu = \$75$ and the standard deviation of the loss is $\sigma = \$300$. The distribution of losses is strongly right-skewed: most policies have $0 loss, but a few have large losses. If the company sells 10,000 policies, can it safely base its rates on the assumption that its average loss will be no greater than $85? Follow the four-step process as illustrated in Example 11.6.

▌ CHAPTER 11 SUMMARY

CHAPTER SPECIFICS

- A **parameter** in a statistical problem is a number that describes a population, such as the **population mean** μ. To estimate an unknown parameter, use a **statistic** calculated from a sample, such as the **sample mean** $\bar{x}$.

- The **law of large numbers** states that the actually observed mean outcome $\bar{x}$ must approach the mean μ of the population as the number of observations increases.

- The **population distribution** of a variable describes the values of the variable for all individuals in a population.

- The **sampling distribution** of a statistic describes the values of the statistic in all possible samples of the same size from the same population.

- When the sample is an SRS from the population, the **mean** of the sampling distribution of the sample mean $\bar{x}$ is the same as the population mean μ. That is, $\bar{x}$ is an **unbiased estimator** of μ.

- The **standard deviation** of the sampling distribution of $\bar{x}$ is $\sigma/\sqrt{n}$ for an SRS of size n if the population has standard deviation σ. That is, averages are less variable than individual observations.

- Choose an SRS of size n from any population with mean μ and finite standard deviation σ. The **central limit theorem** states that when n is large the sampling distribution of $\bar{x}$ is approximately Normal. That is, averages are more Normal than individual observations. We can use the $N(\mu, \sigma/\sqrt{n})$ distribution to calculate approximate probabilities for events involving $\bar{x}$.

LINK IT

As we mentioned in Chapter 10, probability is the tool we will use to generalize from data produced by random samples and randomized comparative experiments to some wider population. In this chapter we begin to formalize this process. We use a statistic to estimate an unknown parameter. We use the sampling distribution to summarize the behavior of a statistic in all possible random samples of the same size from a population.

More specifically, in this chapter we begin to think about how a sample mean, $\bar{x}$, can provide information about a population mean, μ. When the sample mean is computed from an SRS drawn from a large population, its sampling distribution has properties that help us understand how the sample mean can be used to draw conclusions about a population mean. The law of large numbers tells us that a sample mean computed from a *random* sample from some population gets closer and closer to the population mean as the sample size increases. The central limit theorem describes the sampling distribution of the sample mean for "large" SRSs and allows us to make probability statements about possible values of the sample mean. Beginning with Chapter 14, we will develop specific methods for drawing conclusions about a population mean based on a sample mean computed from an SRS. These methods will use the tools developed in this chapter.

CHECK YOUR SKILLS

11.10 The Bureau of Labor Statistics announces that last month it interviewed all members of the labor force in a sample of 60,000 households; **9.5%** of the people interviewed were unemployed. The boldface number is a

  (a) sampling distribution.   (c) parameter.

  (b) statistic.

11.11 A study of voting chose 663 registered voters at random shortly after an election. Of these, 72% said they had voted in the election. Election records show that only **56%** of registered voters voted in the election. The boldface number is a

  (a) sampling distribution.   (c) statistic.

  (b) parameter.

11.12 Annual returns on the more than 5000 common stocks available to investors vary a lot. In a recent year, the mean return was 8.3% and the standard deviation of returns was 28.5%. The law of large numbers says that

  (a) you can get an average return higher than the mean 8.3% by investing in a large number of stocks.

  (b) as you invest in more and more stocks chosen at random, your average return on these stocks gets ever closer to 8.3%.

  (c) if you invest in a large number of stocks chosen at random, your average return will have approximately a Normal distribution.

11.13 Scores on the Critical Reading part of the SAT exam in a recent year were roughly Normal with mean 501 and standard deviation 112. You choose an SRS of 100 students and average their SAT Critical Reading scores. If you do this many times, the mean of the average scores you get will be close to

  (a) 501.   (c) $501/\sqrt{100} = 50.1$.

  (b) $501/100 = 5.01$.

11.14 Scores on the Critical Reading part of the SAT exam in a recent year were roughly Normal with mean 501 and standard deviation 112. You choose an SRS of 100 students and average their SAT Critical Reading scores. If you do this many times, the standard deviation of the average scores you get will be close to

(a) 112.

(b) 112/100 = 1.12.

(c) $112/\sqrt{100} = 11.2$.

11.15 The number of hours a battery lasts before failing varies from battery to battery. The distribution of failure times is strongly skewed to the right. The central limit theorem says that

(a) as we look at more and more batteries, their average failure time gets ever closer to the mean μ for all batteries of this type.

(b) the average failure time of a large number of batteries has a distribution of the same shape (strongly skewed) as the distribution for individual batteries.

(c) the average failure time of a large number of batteries has a distribution that is close to Normal.

11.16 The length of human pregnancies from conception to birth varies according to a distribution that is approximately Normal with mean 266 days and standard deviation 16 days. The probability that the average pregnancy length for 6 randomly chosen women exceeds 270 days is about

(a) 0.40. (b) 0.27. (c) 0.07.

CHAPTER 11 EXERCISES

11.17 Testing glass. How well materials conduct heat matters when designing houses. As a test of a new measurement process, 10 measurements are made on pieces of glass known to have conductivity **1**. The average of the 10 measurements is **1.07**. For each of the boldface numbers, indicate whether it is a parameter or a statistic. Explain your answer.

11.18 Statistics anxiety. What can teachers do to alleviate statistics anxiety in their students? To explore this question, statistics anxiety for students in two classes was compared. In one class, the instructor lectured in a formal manner, including dressing formally. In the other, the instructor was less formal, dressed informally, was more personal, used humor, and called on students by their first names. Anxiety was measured using a questionnaire. Higher scores indicate a greater level of anxiety. The mean anxiety score for students in the formal lecture class was **25.40**; in the informal class the mean was **20.41**. For each of the boldface numbers, indicate whether it is a parameter or a statistic. Explain your answer.

11.19 Roulette. A roulette wheel has 38 slots, of which 18 are black, 18 are red, and 2 are green. When the wheel is spun, the ball is equally likely to come to rest in any of the slots. One of the simplest wagers chooses red or black. A bet of $1 on red returns $2 if the ball lands in a red slot. Otherwise, the player loses his dollar. When gamblers bet on red or black, the two green slots belong to the house. Because the probability of winning $2 is 18/38, the mean payoff from a $1 bet is twice 18/38, or 94.7 cents. Explain what the law of large numbers tells us about what will happen if a gambler makes very many bets on red.

11.20 Monsoon rains. The summer monsoon rains in India follow approximately a Normal distribution with mean 852 millimeters (mm) of rainfall and standard deviation 82 mm. Rainfall is to be recorded each year for a decade and the mean rainfall $\bar{x}$ computed. What are the mean and standard deviation of $\bar{x}$, the mean rainfall per year?

11.21 The Medical College Admission Test. Almost all medical schools in the United States require students to take the Medical College Admission Test (MCAT). To estimate the mean score μ of those who took the MCAT on your campus, you will obtain the scores of an SRS of students. The scores follow a Normal distribution, and from published information you know that the standard deviation is 6.4. Suppose that (unknown to you) the mean score of those taking the MCAT on your campus is 25.0.

(a) If you choose one student at random, what is the probability that the student's score is between 20 and 30?

(b) You sample 25 students. What is the sampling distribution of their average score $\bar{x}$?

(c) What is the probability that the mean score of your sample is between 20 and 30?

11.22 Glucose testing. Shelia's doctor is concerned that she may suffer from gestational diabetes (high blood glucose levels during pregnancy). There is variation both in the actual glucose level and in the blood test that measures the level. A patient is classified as having gestational diabetes if the glucose level is above 140 milligrams per deciliter (mg/dl) one hour after having a sugary drink. Shelia's measured glucose level one hour after the sugary drink varies according to the Normal distribution with $\mu = 122$ mg/dl and $\sigma = 12$ mg/dl.

(a) If a single glucose measurement is made, what is the probability that Shelia is diagnosed as having gestational diabetes?

(b) If measurements are made on 4 separate days and the mean result is compared with the criterion 140 mg/dl, what is the probability that Shelia is diagnosed as having gestational diabetes?

11.23 Daily activity. It appears that people who are mildly obese are less active than leaner people. One study looked at the average number of minutes per day that people spend standing or walking.[3] Among mildly obese people, the mean number of minutes of daily activity (standing or walking) is approximately Normally distributed with mean 373 minutes and standard deviation 67 minutes. The mean number of minutes of daily activity for lean people is approximately Normally distributed with mean 526 minutes and standard deviation 107 minutes. A researcher records the minutes of activity for an SRS of 5 mildly obese people and an SRS of 5 lean people.

(a) What is the probability that the mean number of minutes of daily activity of the 5 mildly obese people exceeds 420 minutes?

(b) What is the probability that the mean number of minutes of daily activity of the 5 lean people exceeds 420 minutes?

11.24 Pollutants in auto exhausts. Light vehicles sold in the United States must emit an average of no more than 0.07 grams per mile (g/mi) of nitrogen oxides (NOX). NOX emissions for one car model vary Normally with mean 0.05 g/mi and standard deviation 0.01 g/mi.

(a) What is the probability that a single car of this model emits more than 0.07 g/mi of NOX?

(b) A company has 25 cars of this model in its fleet. What is the probability that the average NOX level $\bar{x}$ of these cars is above 0.07 g/mi?

11.25 Runners. In a study of exercise, a large group of male runners walk on a treadmill for 6 minutes. After this exercise, their heart rates vary with mean 8.8 beats per five seconds and standard deviation 1.0 beats per five seconds. This distribution takes only whole-number values, so it is certainly not Normal.

(a) Let $\bar{x}$ be the mean number of beats per five seconds after measuring heart rate for 12 five-second intervals (a minute). What is the approximate distribution of $\bar{x}$ according to the central limit theorem?

(b) What is the approximate probability that $\bar{x}$ is less than 8?

(c) What is the approximate probability that the heart rate of a runner is less than 100 beats per minute? (*Hint:* Restate this event in terms of $\bar{x}$.)

11.26 Returns on stocks. Andrew plans to retire in 40 years. He plans to invest part of his retirement funds in stocks, so he seeks out information on past returns. He learns that from 1960 to 2009, the annual returns on U.S. common stocks had mean 10.8% and standard deviation 17.1%.[4] The distribution of annual returns on common stocks is roughly symmetric, so the mean return over even a moderate number of years is close to Normal. What is the probability (assuming that the past pattern of variation continues) that the mean annual return on common stocks over the next 40 years will exceed 10%? What is the probability that the mean return will be less than 5%? Follow the four-step process as illustrated in Example 11.6.

11.27 Airline passengers get heavier. In response to the increasing weight of airline passengers, the Federal Aviation Administration (FAA) in 2003 told airlines to assume that passengers average 190 pounds in the summer, including clothing and carry-on baggage. But passengers vary, and the FAA did not specify a standard deviation. A reasonable standard deviation is 35 pounds. Weights are not Normally distributed, especially when the population includes both men and women, but they are not very non-Normal. A commuter plane carries 22 passengers. What is the approximate probability that the total weight of the passengers exceeds 4500 pounds? Use the four-step process to guide your work. (*Hint:* To apply the central limit theorem, restate the problem in terms of the mean weight.)

11.28 Sampling students. To estimate the mean score μ of those who took the Medical College Admission Test on your campus, you will obtain the scores of an SRS of students. From published information you know that the scores are approximately Normal with standard deviation about 6.4. How large an SRS must you take to reduce the standard deviation of the sample mean score to 1?

11.29 Sampling students, continued. To estimate the mean score μ of those who took the Medical College Admission Test on your campus, you will obtain the scores of an SRS of students. From published information you know that the scores are approximately Normal with standard deviation about 6.4. You want your sample mean $\bar{x}$ to estimate μ with an error of no more than 1 point in either direction.

(a) What standard deviation must $\bar{x}$ have so that 99.7% of all samples give an $\bar{x}$ within 1 point of μ? (Use the 68–95–99.7 rule.)

(b) How large an SRS do you need in order to reduce the standard deviation of $\bar{x}$ to the value you found in part (a)?

11.30 The numbers racket is a well-entrenched illegal gambling operation in most large cities. One version works as follows: you choose one of the 1000 three-digit numbers 000 to 999 and pay your local numbers runner a dollar to enter your bet. Each day, one three-digit number is chosen at random and pays off $600. The mean payoff for the population of thousands of bets is $\mu = 60$ cents. Joe makes one bet every day for many years. Explain what the law of large numbers says about Joe's results as he keeps on betting.

11.31 Playing the numbers: a gambler gets chance outcomes. The law of large numbers tells us what happens in the long run. Like many games of chance, the numbers racket has outcomes so variable—one three-digit number wins $600 and all others win nothing—that gamblers never reach "the long run." Even after many bets, their average winnings may not be close to the mean. For the numbers racket, the mean payout for single bets is $0.60 (60 cents) and the standard deviation of payouts is about $18.96. If Joe plays 350 days a year for 40 years, he makes 14,000 bets.

(a) What are the mean and standard deviation of the average payout $\bar{x}$ that Joe receives from his 14,000 bets?

(b) The central limit theorem says that his average payout is approximately Normal with the mean and standard deviation you found in part (a). What is the approximate probability that Joe's average payout per bet is between $0.50 and $0.70? You see that Joe's average may not be very close to the mean $0.60 even after 14,000 bets.

11.32 Playing the numbers: the house has a business. Unlike Joe (see the previous exercise) the operators of the numbers racket can rely on the law of large numbers. It is said that the New York City mobster Casper Holstein took as many as 25,000 bets per day in the Prohibition era. That's 150,000 bets in a week if he takes Sunday off. Casper's mean winnings per bet are $0.40 (he pays out 60 cents of each dollar bet to people like Joe and keeps the other 40 cents.) His standard deviation for single bets is about $18.96, the same as Joe's.

(a) What are the mean and standard deviation of Casper's average winnings $\bar{x}$ on his 150,000 bets?

(b) According to the central limit theorem, what is the approximate probability that Casper's average winnings per bet are between $0.30 and $0.50? After only a week, Casper can be pretty confident that his winnings will be quite close to $0.40 per bet.

 EXPLORING THE WEB

11.33 Online videos. There are several online videos of the law of large numbers and central limit theorem. Locate one such video, watch it, and write a brief summary of the video. We did a Google search of "videos for law of large numbers" and "videos for the central limit theorem" and found several links.

11.34 Work the law of large numbers. Read the online article at ezinearticles.com/?Work-The-Law-of-Large-Numbers-But-Remember-It-Only-Takes-One-to-Succeed!&id=932026. Does this article accurately describe the law of large numbers? Explain your answer.

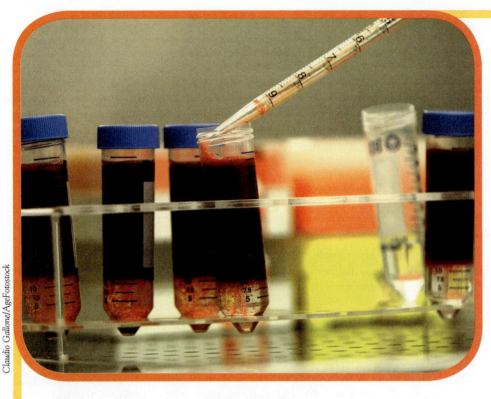

Claudio Gallone/AgeFotostock

General Rules
of Probability*

Although we are interested in probability mainly because it is the foundation for statistical inference, the mathematics of chance is important in many fields of study. Our introduction to probability in Chapter 10 concentrated on basic ideas and facts. Now we look at some further details. To start, recall the four rules of probability that we met in Chapter 10.

PROBABILITY RULES

Rule 1. For any event A, $0 \leq P(A) \leq 1$.

Rule 2. If S is the sample space, $P(S) = 1$.

Rule 3. Addition rule: If A and B are **disjoint** events,

$$P(A \text{ or } B) = P(A) + P(B)$$

Rule 4. For any event A,

$$P(A \text{ does not occur}) = 1 - P(A)$$

*This more advanced chapter introduces some of the mathematics of probability. The material is not needed to read the rest of the book.

INDEPENDENCE AND THE MULTIPLICATION RULE

Rule 3, the addition rule for disjoint events, describes the probability that *one or the other* of two events A and B occurs in the special situation when A and B cannot occur together. Now we will describe the probability that *both* events A and B occur, again only in a special situation. To display relations among several events, it is often helpful to draw a picture.

VENN DIAGRAM

A picture that shows the sample space S as a rectangular area and events as areas within S is called a **Venn diagram.**

Figures 12.1 and 12.2 are Venn diagrams. Events A and B in Figure 12.1 are disjoint because they do not overlap. Figure 12.2 illustrates two events that are not disjoint. The event $\{A \text{ and } B\}$ appears as the overlapping area that is common to both A and B. Can we find the probability $P(A \text{ and } B)$ that both events occur if we know the individual probabilities $P(A)$ and $P(B)$?

FIGURE 12.1

Venn diagram showing disjoint events A and B.

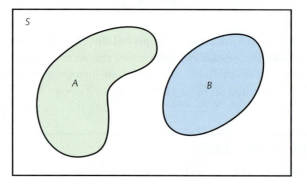

FIGURE 12.2

Venn diagram showing events A and B that are not disjoint. The event $\{A \text{ and } B\}$ consists of outcomes common to A and B.

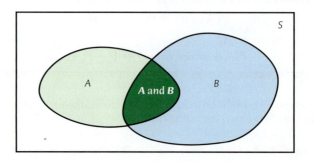

EXAMPLE 12.1 Can you taste PTC?

That molecule in the diagram to the left is PTC, a substance with an unusual property: 70% of people find that it has a bitter taste and the other 30% can't taste it at all. The difference is genetic, depending on a single gene. Ask two people chosen at random to taste PTC. We are interested in the events

$$A = \{\text{first person can taste PTC}\}$$
$$B = \{\text{second person can taste PTC}\}$$

We know that $P(A) = 0.7$ and $P(B) = 0.7$. What is the probability $P(A \text{ and } B)$ that both can taste PTC?

We can think our way to the answer. The first person chosen can taste PTC in 70% of all samples and then the second person can taste it in 70% of those samples. We will get two tasters in 70% of 70% of all samples. That's $P(A \text{ and } B) = 0.7 \times 0.7 = 0.49$. ■

The argument in Example 12.1 works because knowing that the first person can taste PTC tells us nothing about the second person. The probability is still 0.7 that the second person can taste PTC whether or not the first person can. We say that the events "first person can taste PTC" and "second person can taste PTC" are **independent.** Now we have another rule of probability.

independent events

MULTIPLICATION RULE FOR INDEPENDENT EVENTS

Two events A and B are **independent** if knowing that one occurs does not change the probability that the other occurs. If A and B are independent,

$$P(A \text{ and } B) = P(A)P(B)$$

EXAMPLE 12.2 Independent or not?

To use this multiplication rule, we must decide whether events are independent. In Example 12.1, we think that the ability of one randomly chosen person to taste PTC tells us nothing about whether or not a second person, also randomly chosen, can taste PTC. That's independence. But if the two people are members of the same family, the fact that ability to taste PTC is inherited warns us that they are not independent.

Independence is clearest in artificial settings such as games of chance. Because a coin has no memory, it is safe to assume that successive coin tosses are independent. On the other hand, the colors of successive cards dealt from the same deck are not independent. A standard 52-card deck contains 26 red and 26 black cards. For the first card dealt from a shuffled deck, the probability of a red card is $26/52 = 0.50$. Once we see that the first card is red, we know that there are only 25 reds among the remaining 51 cards. The probability that the second card is red is therefore only $25/51 = 0.49$. Knowing the outcome of the first deal changes the probabilities for the second. ■

If two events A and B are independent, the event that A does not occur is also independent of B, and so on. Moreover, the multiplication rule extends to collections of more than two events, provided that all are independent. Independence of several events means that no information about any collection of the events can change the probabilities of the remaining events.

EXAMPLE 12.3 Can you taste PTC?

Carmen buys a package of PTC taste strips online and offers them to friends at a party to see who can taste PTC. Take A_i to be the event that the ith person Carmen meets can taste PTC. The probability that the first 3 people can all taste PTC is

$$P(A_1 \text{ and } A_2 \text{ and } A_3) = P(A_1)P(A_2)P(A_3)$$
$$= (0.7)(0.7)(0.7) = 0.343$$

The probability that the 5th person is the first who can't taste PTC is

$$P(A_1)P(A_2)P(A_3)P(A_4)(1 - P(A_5)) = (0.7)(0.7)(0.7)(0.7)(0.3)$$
$$= (0.7)^4(0.3) = 0.072$$

You see how independence allows you to find the probability of any string of outcomes. ▪

EXAMPLE 12.4 Rapid HIV testing

STATE: Many people who come to clinics to be tested for HIV, the virus that causes AIDS, don't come back to learn the test results. Clinics now use "rapid HIV tests" that give a result while the client waits. The trade-off for fast results is that rapid tests are less accurate than slower laboratory tests. Applied to people who have no HIV antibodies, one rapid test has probability about 0.004 of producing a false-positive (that is, of falsely indicating that antibodies are present).[1] If a clinic tests 200 people who are free of HIV antibodies, what is the chance that at least one false-positive will occur?

PLAN: It is reasonable to assume that the test results for different individuals are independent. We have 200 independent events, each with probability 0.004. What is the probability that at least one of these events occurs?

SOLVE: "At least one positive" combines many outcomes. It is easier to find the probability of "no positives" and use the fact that

$$P(\text{at least one positive}) = 1 - P(\text{no positives})$$

The probability of a negative result for any one person is $1 - 0.004 = 0.996$. To find the probability that all 200 people tested have negative results, use the multiplication rule:

$$P(\text{no positives}) = P(\text{all 200 negative})$$
$$= (0.996)(0.996) \ldots (0.996)$$
$$= (0.996)^{200} = 0.4486$$

The probability we want is therefore

$$P(\text{at least one positive} = 1 - 0.4486 = 0.5514$$

CONCLUDE: The probability is greater than 1/2 that at least one of the 200 people will test positive for HIV even though no one has the virus. ▪

> The multiplication rule $P(A \text{ and } B) = P(A)P(B)$ holds if A and B are independent but not otherwise. The addition rule $P(A \text{ or } B) = P(A) + P(B)$ holds if A and B are disjoint but not otherwise. Resist the temptation to use these simple rules when the circumstances that justify them are not present. Be careful not to confuse disjointness and independence. If A and B are disjoint, then the fact that A occurs tells us that B cannot occur—look again at Figure 12.1. So disjoint events are not independent. Unlike disjointness, we cannot picture independence in a Venn diagram, because it involves the probabilities of the events rather than just the outcomes that make up the events.

APPLY YOUR KNOWLEDGE

12.1 Older college students. Government data show that 8% of adults are full-time college students and that 30% of adults are age 55 or older. Nonetheless, we can't conclude that, because $(0.08)(0.30) = 0.024$, about 2.4% of adults are college students 55 or older. Why not?

12.2 Common names. The Census Bureau says that the 10 most common names in the United States are (in order) Smith, Johnson, Williams, Brown, Jones, Miller, Davis, Garcia, Rodriguez, and Wilson. These names account for 9.6% of all U.S. residents. Out of curiosity, you look at the authors of the textbooks for your current courses. There are 9 authors in all. Would you be surprised if none of the names of these authors were among the 10 most common? (Assume that authors' names are independent and follow the same probability distribution as the names of all residents.)

12.3 Lost Internet sites. Internet sites often vanish or move, so that references to them can't be followed. In fact, 13% of Internet sites referenced in major scientific journals are lost within two years after publication.[2] If a paper contains seven Internet references, what is the probability that all seven are still good two years later? What specific assumptions did you make in order to calculate this probability?

THE GENERAL ADDITION RULE

We know that if A and B are disjoint events, then $P(A \text{ or } B) = P(A) + P(B)$. If events A and B are *not* disjoint, they can occur together. The probability that one or the other occurs is then *less* than the sum of their probabilities. As Figure 12.3 illustrates, outcomes common to both are counted twice when we add probabilities, so we must subtract this probability once. Here is the addition rule for any two events, disjoint or not.

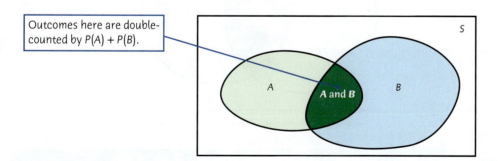

Outcomes here are double-counted by $P(A) + P(B)$.

FIGURE 12.3

The general addition rule: for any events A and B, $P(A \text{ or } B) = P(A) + P(B) - P(A \text{ and } B)$.

ADDITION RULE FOR ANY TWO EVENTS

For any two events A and B,

$$P(A \text{ or } B) = P(A) + P(B) - P(A \text{ and } B)$$

If A and B are disjoint, the event $\{A \text{ and } B\}$ that both occur contains no outcomes and therefore has probability 0. So the general addition rule includes Rule 3, the addition rule for disjoint events.

Justin Sullivan/Getty Images

> ### EXAMPLE 12.5 Motor vehicle sales
>
> Motor vehicles sold in the United States (ignoring heavy trucks) are classified as either cars or light trucks and as either domestic or imported. "Light trucks" include SUVs and minivans. "Domestic" means made in Canada, Mexico, or the United States, so that a Toyota made in Canada counts as domestic.
>
> In 2010, 76% of the new vehicles sold to individuals were domestic, 50% were light trucks, and 43% were domestic light trucks.[3] Choose a vehicle sale at random. Then
>
> $$P(\text{domestic or light truck}) = P(\text{domestic}) + P(\text{light truck}) - P(\text{domestic light truck})$$
>
> $$= 0.76 + 0.50 - 0.43 = 0.83$$
>
> That is, 83% of vehicles sold were domestic or light trucks. ▪

Venn diagrams clarify events and their probabilities because you can just think of adding and subtracting areas. Figure 12.4 shows all the events formed from "domestic" and "truck" in Example 12.5. The four probabilities that appear in the figure add to 1 because they refer to four disjoint events that make up the entire sample space. All these probabilities come from the information in Example 12.5. For example, the probability that a randomly chosen vehicle sale is a domestic car (" D and not T" in the figure) is

$$P(\text{domestic car}) = P(\text{domestic}) - P(\text{domestic light truck})$$

$$= 0.76 - 0.43 = 0.33$$

FIGURE 12.4

Venn diagram and probabilities for motor vehicle sales, for Example 12.5.

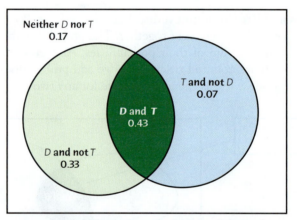

D = vehicle is domestic T = vehicle is a light truck

APPLY YOUR KNOWLEDGE

12.4 College degrees. Of all college degrees awarded in the United States, 50% are bachelor's degrees, 59% are earned by women, and 29% are bachelor's degrees earned by women. Make a Venn diagram and use it to answer these questions.

(a) What percent of all degrees are earned by men?

(b) What percent of all degrees are bachelor's degrees earned by men?

(c) Are the events earning a bachelor's degree and being a man independent? Why?

12.5 Distance-learning. A study of the students taking distance-learning courses at a university finds that they are mostly older students not living in the university town. Choose a distance-learning student at random. Let A be the event that the student is 25 years old or older and B the event that the student is local. The study finds that $P(A) = 0.7$, $P(B) = 0.25$, and $P(A \text{ and } B) = 0.05$.

(a) Make a Venn diagram similar to Figure 12.4 showing the events {A and B}, {A and not B}, {B and not A}, and {neither A nor B}.

(b) Describe each of these events in words.

(c) Find the probabilities of all four events and add the probabilities to your Venn diagram.

CONDITIONAL PROBABILITY

The probability we assign to an event can change if we know that some other event has occurred. This idea is the key to many applications of probability.

EXAMPLE 12.6 Trucks among imported motor vehicles

Figure 12.4, based on the information in Example 12.5, gives the following probabilities for a randomly chosen light motor vehicle sold at retail in the United States:

	Domestic	Imported	Total
Light truck	0.43	0.07	0.50
Car	0.33	0.17	0.50
Total	0.76	0.24	1

The four probabilities in the body of the table add to 1 because they describe all vehicles sold. We obtain the "Total" row and column from these probabilities by the addition rule.

Now we are told that the vehicle chosen is imported. That is, it is one of the 24% in the "Imported" column of the table. The probability that a vehicle is a light truck *given the information that it is imported* is the proportion of trucks in the "Imported" column,

$$P(\text{truck} \mid \text{imported}) = \frac{0.07}{0.24} = 0.29$$

This is a **conditional probability.** You can read the bar | as "given the information that." ■   *conditional probability*

Although 50% of all vehicles sold are trucks, only 29% of imported vehicles are trucks. It's common sense that knowing that one event (the vehicle is imported) occurs often changes the probability of another event (the vehicle is a truck). The example also shows how we should define conditional probability. The conditional probability $P(B \mid A)$ of one event B given that another event A occurs is the proportion *of all occurrences of A for which B also occurs.*

CONDITIONAL PROBABILITY

When $P(A) > 0$, the **conditional probability** of B given A is

$$P(B \mid A) = \frac{P(A \text{ and } B)}{P(A)}$$

Be sure to keep in mind the distinct roles of the events A and B in P(B | A). Event A represents the information we are given, and B is the event whose probability we are calculating. Here is an example that emphasizes this distinction.

EXAMPLE 12.7 Imports among trucks, trucks among imports

What is the conditional probability that a randomly chosen vehicle is imported *given the information that it is a truck?* Using the definition of conditional probability,

$$P(\text{imported} \mid \text{truck}) = \frac{P(\text{imported and truck})}{P(\text{truck})}$$

$$= \frac{0.07}{0.50} = 0.14$$

Only 14% of trucks sold are imports. We have now found two conditional probabilities:

$$P(\text{truck} \mid \text{imported}) = 0.29$$
$$P(\text{imported} \mid \text{truck}) = 0.14$$

The first answers the question "What proportion of imports are trucks?" The second answers "What proportion of trucks are imports?" ▪

The conditional probability $P(B \mid A)$ is generally not the same as the unconditional probability $P(B)$. If these two probabilities *are* the same, knowing that A occurs gives no additional information about B. That's what we mean when we say that A and B are independent. So the precise definition of independence is expressed in terms of conditional probability.

INDEPENDENT EVENTS

Two events A and B that both have positive probability are **independent** if
$$P(B \mid A) = P(B)$$

APPLY YOUR KNOWLEDGE

12.6 College degrees. In the setting of Exercise 12.4, what is the conditional probability that a degree is earned by a woman given that it is a bachelor's degree?

12.7 Distance learning. In the setting of Exercise 12.5, what is the conditional probability that a student is local given that he or she is less than 25 years old?

12.8 Independent? The Clemson University Fact Book for 2007 shows that 123 of the university's 338 assistant professors were women, along with 76 of the 263 associate professors and 73 of the 375 full professors.

(a) What is the probability that a randomly chosen Clemson professor is a woman?

(b) What is the conditional probability that a randomly chosen professor is a woman, given that the person chosen is a full professor?

(c) Are the rank and gender of Clemson professors independent? How do you know?

THE GENERAL MULTIPLICATION RULE

The definition of conditional probability reminds us that in principle all probabilities, including conditional probabilities, can be found from the assignment of probabilities to events that describe a random phenomenon. More often, however, conditional probabilities are part of the information given to us in a probability model. The definition of conditional probability then turns into a rule for finding the probability that both of two events occur.

MULTIPLICATION RULE FOR ANY TWO EVENTS

The probability that both of two events A and B happen together can be found by
$$P(A \text{ and } B) = P(A)P(B|A)$$

In words, this rule says that for both of two events to occur, first one must occur and then, given that the first event has occurred, the second must occur. If the A and B are independent, then the conditional probability $P(B|A)$ is the same as the unconditional probability $P(B)$. So the general multiplication rule includes the multiplication rule for independent events.

EXAMPLE 12.8 Teens with online profiles

The Pew Internet and American Life Project finds that 93% of teenagers (ages 12 to 17) use the Internet, and that 55% of online teens have posted a profile on a social-networking site.[4] What percent of teens are online *and* have posted a profile?
   Use the multiplication rule:

$$P(\text{online}) = 0.93$$
$$P(\text{profile} | \text{online}) = 0.55$$
$$P(\text{online and have profile}) = P(\text{online}) \times P(\text{profile} | \text{online})$$
$$= (0.93)(0.55) = 0.5115$$

That is, about 51% of all teens use the Internet and have a profile on a social-networking site.
   You can think your way through this: if 93% of teens are online and 55% *of these* have posted a profile, then 55% of 93% are both online and have a profile. ■

The multiplication rule extends to find the probability that all of several events occur. Just condition each event on the occurrence of *all* the preceding events. For any three events A, B, and C,

$$P(A \text{ and } B \text{ and } C) = P(A)P(B|A)P(C|\text{both } A \text{ and } B)$$

Here is an example of the extended multiplication rule.

EXAMPLE 12.9 Fundraising by telephone

STATE: A charity raises funds by calling a list of prospective donors to ask for pledges. It is able to talk with 40% of the names on its list. Of those the charity reaches, 30% make a pledge. But only half of those who pledge actually make a contribution. What percent of the donor list contributes?

PLAN: Express the information we are given in terms of events and their probabilities:

If A = {the charity reaches a prospect}   then $P(A) = 0.4$
If B = {the prospect makes a pledge}   then $P(B\,|\,A) = 0.3$
If C = {the prospect makes a contribution}   then $P(C\,|\,\text{both }A\text{ and }B) = 0.5$

We want to find $P(A \text{ and } B \text{ and } C)$.

SOLVE: Use the multiplication rule:

$$P(A \text{ and } B \text{ and } C) = P(A)P(B\,|\,A)P(C\,|\,\text{both }A\text{ and }B)$$
$$= 0.4 \times 0.3 \times 0.5 = 0.06$$

CONCLUDE: Only 6% of the prospective donors make a contribution. ■

APPLY YOUR KNOWLEDGE

12.9 At the gym. Suppose that 10% of adults belong to health clubs, and 40% of these health club members go to the club at least twice a week. What percent of all adults go to a health club at least twice a week? Write the information given in terms of probabilities and use the general multiplication rule.

12.10 Teens online. We saw in Example 12.8 that 93% of teenagers are online and that 55% of online teens have posted a profile on a social-networking site. Of online teens with a profile, 76% have placed comments on a friend's blog. What percent of all teens are online, have a profile, and comment on a friend's blog? Define events and probabilities and follow the pattern of Example 12.9.

12.11 The probability of a flush. A poker player holds a flush when all 5 cards in the hand belong to the same suit (clubs, diamonds, hearts, or spades). We will find the probability of a flush when 5 cards are dealt. Remember that a deck contains 52 cards, 13 of each suit, and that when the deck is well shuffled, each card dealt is equally likely to be any of those that remain in the deck.

(a) Concentrate on spades. What is the probability that the first card dealt is a spade? What is the conditional probability that the second card is a spade given that the first is a spade? (*Hint:* How many cards remain? How many of these are spades?)

(b) Continue to count the remaining cards to find the conditional probabilities of a spade on the third, the fourth, and the fifth card given in each case that all previous cards are spades.

(c) The probability of being dealt 5 spades is the product of the 5 probabilities you have found. What is this probability?

(d) The probability of being dealt 5 hearts or 5 diamonds or 5 clubs is the same as the probability of being dealt 5 spades. What is the probability of being dealt a flush?

Amana Productions Inc./Getty Images

TREE DIAGRAMS

Probability models often have several stages, with probabilities at each stage conditional on the outcomes of earlier states. These models require us to combine several of the basic rules into a more elaborate calculation. Here is an example.

EXAMPLE 12.10 Who visits YouTube?

STATE: Video-sharing sites, led by YouTube, are popular destinations on the Internet. Let's look only at adult Internet users, age 18 and over. About 27% of adult Internet users are 18 to 29 years old, another 45% are 30 to 49 years old, and the remaining 28% are 50 and over. The Pew Internet and American Life Project finds that 70% of Internet users aged 18 to 29 have visited a video-sharing site, along with 51% of those aged 30 to 49 and 26% of those 50 or older. What percent of all adult Internet users visit video-sharing sites?

PLAN: To use the tools of probability, restate all these percents as probabilities. If we choose an online adult at random,

$$P(\text{age 18 to 29}) = 0.27$$
$$P(\text{age 30 to 49}) = 0.45$$
$$P(\text{age 50 and older}) = 0.28$$

These three probabilities add to 1 because all adult Internet users are in one of the three age groups. The percents of each group who visit video-sharing sites are *conditional* probabilities:

$$P(\text{video yes} \mid \text{age 18 to 29}) = 0.70$$
$$P(\text{video yes} \mid \text{age 30 to 49}) = 0.51$$
$$P(\text{video yes} \mid \text{age 50 and older}) = 0.26$$

We want to find the unconditional probability $P(\text{video yes})$.

SOLVE: The **tree diagram** in Figure 12.5 organizes this information. Each segment in the tree is one stage of the problem. Each complete branch shows a path through the two stages. The probability written on each segment is the conditional probability of an Internet user following that segment given that he or she has reached the node from which it branches.

tree diagram

  Starting at the left, an Internet user falls into one of the three age groups. The probabilities of these groups mark the leftmost segments in the tree. Look at age 18 to 29, the top branch. The two segments going out from the "18 to 29" branch point carry the conditional probabilities

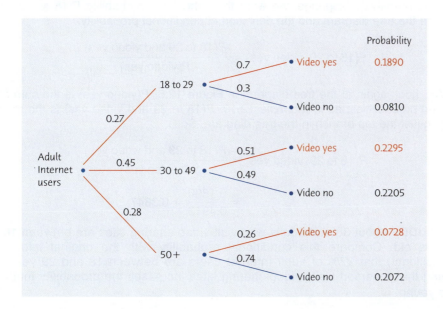

FIGURE 12.5

Tree diagram for use of the Internet and video-sharing sites such as YouTube, for Example 12.10. The three disjoint paths to the outcome that an adult Internet user visits video-sharing sites are colored red.

$$P(\text{video yes} \mid \text{age 18 to 29}) = 0.70$$
$$P(\text{video no} \mid \text{age 18 to 29}) = 0.30$$

The full tree shows the probabilities for all three age groups.

Now use the multiplication rule. The probability that a randomly chosen Internet user is an 18- to 29-year-old who visits video-sharing sites is

$$P(\text{18 to 29 and video yes}) = P(\text{18 to 29})P(\text{video yes} \mid \text{18 to 29})$$
$$= (0.27)(0.70) = 0.1890$$

This probability appears at the end of the topmost branch. The multiplication rule says that the probability of any complete branch in the tree is the product of the probabilities of the segments in that branch.

There are three disjoint paths to "video yes," one for each of the three age groups. These paths are colored red in Figure 11.5. Because the three paths are disjoint, the probability that an adult Internet user visits video-sharing sites is the sum of their probabilities:

$$P(\text{video yes}) = (0.27)(0.70) + (0.45)(0.51) + (0.28)(0.26)$$
$$= 0.1890 + 0.2295 + 0.0728 = 0.4913$$

CONCLUDE: About 49% of all adult Internet users have visited a video-sharing site. ■

It takes longer to explain a tree diagram than it does to use it. Once you have understood a problem well enough to draw the tree, the rest is easy. Here is another question about video-sharing sites that the tree diagram helps us answer.

EXAMPLE 12.11 Young adults at video-sharing sites

STATE: What percent of adult Internet users who visit video-sharing sites are age 18 to 29?

PLAN: In probability language, we want the conditional probability $P(\text{18 to 29} \mid \text{video yes})$. Use the tree diagram and the definition of conditional probability:

$$P(\text{18 to 29} \mid \text{video yes}) = \frac{P(\text{18 to 29 and video yes})}{P(\text{video yes})}$$

SOLVE: Look again at the tree diagram in Figure 12.5. $P(\text{video yes})$ is the sum of the three red probabilities, as in Example 12.10. $P(\text{18 to 29 and video yes})$ is the result of following just the top branch in the tree diagram. So

$$P(\text{18 to 29} \mid \text{video yes}) = \frac{P(\text{18 to 29 and video yes})}{P(\text{video yes})}$$
$$= \frac{0.1890}{0.4913} = 0.3847$$

CONCLUDE: About 38% of adults who visit video-sharing sites are between 18 and 29 years old. Compare this conditional probability with the original information (unconditional) that 27% of adult Internet users are between 18 and 29 years old. Knowing that a person visits video-sharing sites increases the probability that he or she is young. ■

Examples 12.10 and 12.11 illustrate a common setting for tree diagrams. Some outcome (such as visiting video-sharing sites) has several sources (such as the three age groups). Starting from

■ the probability of each source, and

■ the conditional probability of the outcome given each source

the tree diagram leads to the overall probability of the outcome. Example 12.10 does this. You can then use the probability of the outcome and the definition of conditional probability to find the conditional probability of one of the sources given that the outcome occurred. Example 12.11 shows how.

APPLY YOUR KNOWLEDGE

12.12 Peanut and tree nut allergies. About 1% of the American population is allergic to peanuts or tree nuts.[5] Choose 3 individuals at random and let the random variable X be the number in this sample who are allergic to peanuts or tree nuts. The possible values that X can take are 0, 1, 2, and 3. Make a three-stage tree diagram of the outcomes (allergic or not allergic) for the 3 individuals, and use it to find the probability distribution of X.

12.13 Testing for HIV. Enzyme immunoassay tests are used to screen blood specimens for the presence of antibodies to HIV, the virus that causes AIDS. Antibodies indicate the presence of the virus. The test is quite accurate but is not always correct. Here are approximate probabilities of positive and negative test results when the blood tested does and does not actually contain antibodies to HIV:[6]

	Test Result	
	Positive	**Negative**
Antibodies present	0.9985	0.0015
Antibodies absent	0.0060	0.9940

Suppose that 1% of a large population carry antibodies to HIV in their blood.

(a) Draw a tree diagram for selecting a person from this population (outcomes: antibodies present or absent) and testing his or her blood (outcomes: test positive or negative).

(b) What is the probability that the test is positive for a randomly chosen person from this population?

12.14 Peanut and tree nut allergies. Continue your work from Exercise 12.12. What is the conditional probability that exactly 2 of the people will be allergic to peanuts or tree nuts given that at least 1 of the 3 people suffers from one of these allergies?

12.15 False HIV positives. Continue your work from Exercise 12.13. What is the probability that a person has the antibody given that the test is positive? (Your result illustrates a fact that is important when considering proposals for widespread testing for HIV, illegal drugs, or agents of biological warfare: if the condition being tested is uncommon in the population, most positives will be false-positives.)

CHAPTER 12 SUMMARY

CHAPTER SPECIFICS

- Events A and B are **disjoint** if they have no outcomes in common. In that case, $P(A \text{ or } B) = P(A) + P(B)$.

- The **conditional probability** $P(B \mid A)$ of an event B given an event A is defined by

$$P(B \mid A) = \frac{P(A \text{ and } B)}{P(A)}$$

  when $P(A) > 0$. In practice, we most often find conditional probabilities from directly available information rather than from the definition.

- Events A and B are **independent** if knowing that one event occurs does not change the probability we would assign to the other event; that is, $P(B \mid A) = P(B)$. In that case, $P(A \text{ and } B) = P(A)P(B)$.

- Any assignment of probability obeys these rules:

  Addition rule for disjoint events: If events A, B, C, ... are all disjoint in pairs, then

$$P(\text{at least one of these events occurs}) = P(A) + P(B) + P(C) + \cdots$$

  Multiplication rule for independent events: If events A, B, C, ... are independent, then

$$P(\text{all of these events occur}) = P(A)P(B)P(C) \cdots$$

  General addition rule: For any two events A and B,

$$P(A \text{ or } B) = P(A) + P(B) - P(A \text{ and } B)$$

  General multiplication rule: For any two events A and B,

$$P(A \text{ and } B) = P(A)P(B \mid A)$$

- **Tree diagrams** organize probability models that have several stages.

LINK IT

Probability models provide the important connection between the observed data and the process that generated the data. Probability is also the foundation of statistical inference and provides the language by which we answer questions and draw conclusions from our data. For these reasons, it is important that we have at least a basic understanding of what we mean by probability and of some of the rules and properties of probabilities.

Chapter 10 introduced basic ideas and facts about probability, and in this chapter we have considered some further details. The conditional distributions discussed in Chapter 6 are an example of the computation of conditional probabilities. Conditional probabilities play a central role when studying the relationship between two categorical variables, and we will return to them in Chapter 23. In terms of later chapters, the most important idea of this chapter is independence. This is an assumption that many statistical procedures make about the observations in a data set, and therefore, it is an important assumption to fully understand.

CHECK YOUR SKILLS

12.16 An instant lottery game gives you probability 0.02 of winning on any one play. Plays are independent of each other. If you play 3 times, the probability that you win on none of your plays is about

(a) 0.98.   (b) 0.94.   (c) 0.000008.

12.17 Choose an American adult at random. The probability that you choose a woman is 0.52. The probability that the person you choose has never married is 0.25. The probability that you choose a woman who has never married is 0.11. The probability that the person you choose is either a woman or never married (or both) is therefore about

(a) 0.77.   (b) 0.66.   (c) 0.13.

What is the distribution of conferred doctorates by field and sex? Here are the counts from the most popular fields in 2009.[7] The physical sciences include mathematics and computer and information sciences; the life sciences include agricultural sciences/natural resources, biological/biomedical sciences, and health sciences; and the social sciences include psychology.

	Male	Female
Engineering	6,006	1,623
Physical sciences	5,868	2,450
Life sciences	5,180	6,212
Social sciences	3,259	4,575
Education	2,160	4,370
Other	3,865	3,960
Total	26,338	23,190

Exercises 12.18 to 12.21 are based on this table.

12.18 Choose a doctoral recipient at random from this group. The probability that the recipient is female is about

(a) 0.42.   (b) 0.47.   (c) 0.58.

12.19 The conditional probability that the recipient is female given that the degree is in engineering is about

(a) 0.03.   (b) 0.07.   (c) 0.21.

12.20 The conditional probability that the degree is in engineering given that the recipient is female is about

(a) 0.03.   (b) 0.07.   (c) 0.21.

12.21 Let A be the event that the degree is in engineering and B the event that the recipient is female. The proportion of engineering doctorates conferred on females is expressed in probability notation as

(a) $P(A \text{ and } B)$.   (b) $P(A|B)$.   (c) $P(B|A)$.

12.22 Of people who died in the United States in recent years, 86% were white, 12% were black, and 2% were Asian. (This ignores a small number of deaths among other races.) Diabetes caused 2.8% of deaths among whites, 4.4% among blacks, and 3.5% among Asians. The probability that a randomly chosen death is a white who died of diabetes is about

(a) 0.107.   (b) 0.030.   (c) 0.024.

CHAPTER 12 EXERCISES

12.23 Playing the lottery. New York State's Quick Draw lottery moves right along. Players choose between 1 and 10 numbers from the range 1 to 80; 20 winning numbers are displayed on a screen every four minutes. If you choose just 1 number, your probability of winning is 20/80, or 0.25. Lester plays 1 number 8 times as he sits in a bar. What is the probability that all 8 bets lose?

12.24 Universal blood donors. People with type O-negative blood are universal donors. That is, any patient can receive a transfusion of O-negative blood. Only 7.2% of the American population have O-negative blood. If 10 people appear at random to give blood, what is the probability that at least 1 of them is a universal donor?

12.25 Playing the slots. Before electronics took over, slot machines were like this: you pull the lever to spin three wheels; each wheel has 20 symbols, all equally likely to show when the wheel stops spinning; the three wheels are independent of each other. Suppose that the middle wheel has 9 cherries among its 20 symbols, and the left and right wheels have 1 cherry each.

(a) You win the jackpot if all three wheels show cherries. What is the probability of winning the jackpot?

(b) There are three ways that the three wheels can show 2 cherries and 1 symbol other than a cherry. Find the probability of each of these ways.

(c) What is the probability that the wheels stop with exactly 2 cherries showing among them?

12.26 A whale of a time. Hacksaw's Boats of St. Lucia takes tourists on a daily dolphin/whale watch cruise. Their brochure claims an 80% chance of sighting a dolphin or a whale, and you can assume that sightings from day to day are independent.

(a) If you take the dolphin/whale watch cruise on two consecutive days, what is the probability that you see a dolphin or a whale on both days?

(b) If you take the dolphin/whale watch cruise on two consecutive days, what is the probability that you see a dolphin or a whale on at least one day? (*Hint:* First compute the probability that you don't see a dolphin or a whale on either day.)

(c) If you want to have a 99% probability of seeing a dolphin or a whale at least once, what is the minimum number of days that you will need to take the cruise?

12.27 Tendon surgery. You have torn a tendon and are facing surgery to repair it. The surgeon explains the risks to you: infection occurs in 3% of such operations, the repair fails in 14%, and both infection and failure occur together in 1%. What percent of these operations succeed and are free from infection? Follow the four-step process in your answer.

12.28 A whale of a time, continued. Hacksaw's Boats of St. Lucia takes tourists on a daily dolphin/whale watch cruise. Their brochure claims an 80% chance of sighting a dolphin or a whale. Suppose that there is a 75% chance of seeing a dolphin and a 15% chance of seeing both a dolphin and a whale. Make a Venn diagram. Then answer these questions.

(a) What is the probability of seeing a whale on the cruise?

(b) What is the probability of seeing a whale but not a dolphin?

(c) Are seeing a whale and seeing a dolphin independent events?

12.29 Screening job applicants. A company retains a psychologist to assess whether job applicants are suited for assembly-line work. The psychologist classifies applicants as one of A (well suited), B (marginal), or C (not suited). The company is concerned about the event D that an employee leaves the company within a year of being hired. Data on all people hired in the past five years give these probabilities:

$P(A) = 0.4$ $P(B) = 0.3$ $P(C) = 0.3$
$P(A \text{ and } D) = 0.1$ $P(B \text{ and } D) = 0.1$ $P(C \text{ and } D) = 0.2$

Sketch a Venn diagram of the events A, B, C, and D and mark on your diagram the probabilities of all combinations of psychological assessment and leaving (or not) within a year. What is $P(D)$, the probability that an employee leaves within a year?

12.30 Type of high school attended. Choose a college freshman at random and ask what type of high school he or she attended. Here is the distribution of results:[8]

Type	Regular public	Public charter	Public magnet	Private religious	Private independent	Home school
Probability	0.781	0.018	0.031	0.105	0.059	0.006

What is the conditional probability that a college freshman was homeschooled given that he or she did not attend a regular public high school?

12.31 Income tax returns. Here is the distribution of the adjusted gross income (in thousands of dollars) reported on individual federal income tax returns in 2008:[9]

Income	<15	15–29	30–74	75–199	≥200
Probability	0.265	0.209	0.315	0.180	0.031

(a) What is the probability that a randomly chosen return shows an adjusted gross income of $30,000 or more?

(b) Given that a return shows an income of at least $30,000, what is the conditional probability that the income is at least $75,000?

12.32 Computer games. Here is the distribution of computer games sold by type of game:[10]

Game type	Probability
Strategy	0.354
Role playing	0.139
Family entertainment	0.127
Shooters	0.109
Children's	0.057
Other	0.214

What is the conditional probability that a computer game is a role-playing game given that it is not a strategy game?

12.33 A probability teaser. Suppose (as is roughly correct) that each child born is equally likely to be a boy or a girl and that the sexes of successive children are independent. If we let BG mean that the older child is a boy and the younger child is a girl, then each of the combinations BB, BG, GB, GG has probability 0.25. Ashley and Brianna each have two children.

(a) You know that at least one of Ashley's children is a boy. What is the conditional probability that she has two boys?

(b) You know that Brianna's older child is a boy. What is the conditional probability that she has two boys?

12.34 College degrees. A striking trend in higher education is that more women than men reach each level of attainment. The National Center for Education Statistics provides projections for the number of degrees earned, classified by level and by the sex of the degree recipient. Here are the projected number of earned degrees (in thousands) in the United States for the 2015–2016 academic year:[11]

	Associate's	Bachelor's	Master's	Professional	Doctorate	Total
Female	556	1034	450	54	45	2139
Male	311	737	282	53	38	1421
Total	867	1771	732	107	83	3560

(a) If you choose a degree recipient at random, what is the probability that the person you choose is a man?

(b) What is the conditional probability that you choose a man given that the person chosen received a master's?

(c) Are the events "choose a man" and "choose a master's degree recipient" independent? How do you know?

12.35 College degrees. Exercise 12.34 gives the projected counts (in thousands) of earned degrees in the United States in the 2015–2016 academic year. Use these data to answer the following questions.

(a) What is the probability that a randomly chosen degree recipient is a woman?

(b) What is the conditional probability that the person chosen received an associate's degree given that she is a woman?

(c) Use the multiplication rule to find the probability of choosing a female associate's degree recipient. Check your result by finding this probability directly from the table of counts.

12.36 Deer and pine seedlings. As suburban gardeners know, deer will eat almost anything green. In a study of pine seedlings at an environmental center in Ohio, researchers noted how deer damage varied with how much of the seedling was covered by thorny undergrowth:[12]

	Deer Damage	
Thorny cover	Yes	No
None	60	151
<1/3	76	158
1/3 to 2/3	44	177
>2/3	29	176

(a) What is the probability that a randomly selected seedling was damaged by deer?

(b) What are the conditional probabilities that a randomly selected seedling was damaged given each level of cover?

(c) Does knowing about the amount of thorny cover on a seedling change the probability of deer damage? If so, cover and damage are not independent.

12.37 Deer and pine seedlings. In the setting of Exercise 12.36, what percent of the trees that were *not* damaged by deer were more than two-thirds covered by thorny plants?

12.38 Deer and pine seedlings. In the setting of Exercise 12.36, what percent of the trees that were damaged by deer were less than one-third covered by thorny plants?

Julie graduates from college. *Julie has studied biology, chemistry, and computing and hopes to use her science background in crime investigation. Late one night she thinks about some jobs for which she has applied. Let A, B, and C be the events that Julie is offered a job by*

A = the Connecticut Office of the Chief Medical Examiner

B = the New Jersey Division of Criminal Justice

C = the federal Disaster Mortuary Operations Response Team

Julie writes down her probabilities for being offered these jobs:

$P(A) = 0.5$ $P(B) = 0.4$ $P(C) = 0.2$

$P(A \text{ and } B) = 0.1$ $P(A \text{ and } C) = 0.05$ $P(B \text{ and } C) = 0.05$

$P(A \text{ and } B \text{ and } C) = 0$

Make a Venn diagram of the events A, B, and C. As in Figure 12.4, mark the probabilities of every intersection involving these events. Use this diagram for Exercises 12.39 to 12.41.

12.39 Will Julie get a job offer? What is the probability that Julie is not offered any of the three jobs?

12.40 Will Julie get just these offers? What is the probability that Julie is offered the Connecticut job but not the New Jersey or federal job?

12.41 Julie's conditional probabilities. If Julie is offered the federal job, what is the conditional probability that she is also offered the New Jersey job? If Julie is offered the New Jersey job, what is the conditional probability that she is also offered the federal job?

12.42 The geometric distributions. You are tossing a pair of balanced dice in a board game. Tosses are independent. You land in a danger zone that requires you to roll doubles (both faces show the same number of spots) before you are allowed to play again. How long will you wait to play again?

(a) What is the probability of rolling doubles on a single toss of the dice? (If you need review, the possible outcomes appear in Figure 10.2 [page 252]. All 36 outcomes are equally likely.)

(b) What is the probability that you do not roll doubles on the first toss, but you do on the second toss?

(c) What is the probability that the first two tosses are not doubles and the third toss is doubles? This is the probability that the first doubles occurs on the third toss.

(d) Now you see the pattern. What is the probability that the first doubles occurs on the fourth toss? On the fifth toss? Give the general result: what is the probability that the first doubles occurs on the kth toss?

(*Comment:* The distribution of the number of trials to the first success is called a *geometric distribution*. In this problem you have found geometric distribution probabilities when the probability of a success on each trial is 1/6. The same idea works for any probability of success.)

12.43 Winning at tennis. A player serving in tennis has two chances to get a serve into play. If the first serve is out, the player serves again. If the second serve is also out, the player loses the point. Here are probabilities based on four years of the Wimbledon Championship:[13]

$$P(\text{1st serve in}) = 0.59$$
$$P(\text{win point} \mid \text{1st serve in}) = 0.73$$
$$P(\text{2nd serve in} \mid \text{1st serve out}) = 0.86$$
$$P(\text{win point} \mid \text{1st serve out and 2nd serve in}) = 0.59$$

Make a tree diagram for the results of the two serves and the outcome (win or lose) of the point. (The branches in your tree have different numbers of stages depending on the outcome of the first serve.) What is the probability that the serving player wins the point?

12.44 Urban voters. The voters in a large city are 40% white, 40% black, and 20% Hispanic. (Hispanics may be of any race in official statistics, but here we are speaking of political blocks.) A black mayoral candidate

anticipates attracting 30% of the white vote, 90% of the black vote, and 50% of the Hispanic vote. Draw a tree diagram with probabilities for the race (white, black, or Hispanic) and vote (for or against the candidate) of a randomly chosen voter. What percent of the overall vote does the candidate expect to get? Use the four-step process to guide your work.

12.45 Winning at tennis, continued. Based on your work in Exercise 12.43, in what percent of points won by the server was the first serve in? (Write this as a conditional probability and use the definition of conditional probability.)

12.46 Where do the votes come from? In the election described in Exercise 12.44, what percent of the candidate's votes come from black voters? (Write this as a conditional probability and use the definition of conditional probability.)

12.47 Teens and texting. The Pew Internet and American Life Project finds that 75% of teenagers (ages 12 to 17) now own cell phones, and of the teens who own cell phones, 87% use text messaging.[14]

(a) What percent of teens own cell phones *and* are "texters"?

(b) Among teens who own cell phones and are texters, 15% send more than 200 texts a day, or more than 6000 texts a month. What percent of all teens own a cell phone, are texters, and send more than 6000 texts a month?

12.48 Lactose intolerance. Lactose intolerance causes difficulty digesting dairy products that contain lactose (milk sugar). It is particularly common among people of African and Asian ancestry. In the United States (ignoring other groups and people who consider themselves to belong to more than one race), 82% of the population is white, 14% is black, and 4% is Asian. Moreover, 15% of whites, 70% of blacks, and 90% of Asians are lactose intolerant.[15]

(a) What percent of the entire population is lactose intolerant?

(b) What percent of people who are lactose intolerant are Asian?

12.49 Fundraising by telephone. Tree diagrams can organize problems having more than two stages. Figure 12.6 shows probabilities for a charity calling potential donors by telephone.[16] Each person called is either a recent donor, a past donor, or a new prospect. At the next stage, the person called either does or does not pledge to contribute, with conditional probabilities that depend on the donor class the person belongs to. Finally, those who make a pledge either do or don't actually make a contribution.

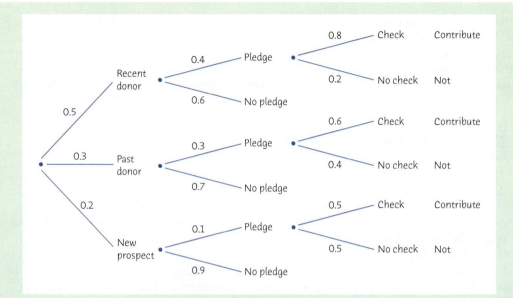

FIGURE 12.6
Tree diagram for fundraising by telephone, for Exercise 12.49. The three stages are the type of prospect called, whether or not the person makes a pledge, and whether or not a person who pledges actually makes a contribution.

(a) What percent of calls result in a contribution?

(b) What percent of those who contribute are recent donors?

DNA forensics. *When a suspect's DNA is compared with a sample of DNA collected at a crime scene, the comparison is made between certain sections of the DNA called loci. Each locus has two alleles (gene forms), one inherited from the mother and the other from the father. Suppose that there are two alleles, called A and B, for a particular locus. These alleles can be present at the locus in three combinations. A person's alleles at the locus could both be A, one allele could be A and the other B, or both alleles could be B, giving the three combinations (A and A), (A and B), and (B and B). Here's how the math works. If the proportion of the population with allele A as one of their alleles at the locus is a, and the proportion of the population with allele B as one of their alleles at the locus is b, then the proportions of the population with the three combinations of these allele types at the locus are*

Alleles at the locus	Population proportion with allele combination
A and A	a^2
A and B	$2ab$
B and B	b^2

Use this information in Exercises 12.50 and 12.51. The numbers used in the exercises are from the FBI database.[17]

12.50 Alleles at D21S11. Suppose that the locus D21S11 has two alleles called 29 and 31. The proportion of the Caucasian population with allele 29 is 0.181 and with allele 31 is 0.071. What proportion of the Caucasian population has the combination (29, 31) at the locus D21S11? What proportion has the combination (29, 29)?

12.51 Alleles at D3S1358. Suppose that the locus D3S1358 has two alleles called 16 and 17. The proportion of the Caucasian population with allele 16 is 0.232 and with allele 17 is 0.212. What proportion of the Caucasian population has the combination (16, 17) at the locus D3S1358.

12.52 Alleles at multiple loci. One important fact regarding the loci evaluated in such forensic tests is that the allele combinations at each locus have been shown to be independent. What proportion of the Caucasian population has the combination (29, 31) at locus D21S11 and combination (16, 17) at locus D3S1358? As we specify the alleles present at more loci, what will happen to the proportion of the Caucasian population that matches the allele combinations at all the loci?

12.53 How many match? A defendant in Ohio was indicted on December 17, 2009, on charges of aggravated burglary and assault. A hair found at the crime scene was tested at six loci and demonstrated a specific combination of alleles found in about 1 in 1.6 million individuals in the population. Comparison of the DNA profile found on the hair with a database of convicted felons revealed a match between the allelic profile found on the hair and an individual in the database (the defendant). Defense attorneys in the case requested that the

State perform additional DNA testing since several previously untested loci were available to test. The results of this testing revealed that the defendant did not match at some of these newly tested loci, indicating that the DNA from the hair was not the defendant's. The charges were dropped.

If the DNA profile (or combination of alleles) found on the hair is possessed by 1 in 1.6 million individuals, and the database of convicted felons contains 4.5 million individuals, approximately how many individuals in the database would demonstrate a match between their DNA and that found on the hair?

 EXPLORING THE WEB

12.54 SAT Mathematics scores. The Web site http://professionals.collegeboard.com/ data-reports-research/sat presents data for high school seniors who participated in the SAT Program during the current year as well as previous years. Under *SAT Data & Reports*, click on the link for *College-Bound Seniors* for the most recent year given. In the window that opens, click on the link for *Total Group Report: College-Bound Seniors* for this year. The Total Group Profile Report presents data for high school graduates who participated in the SAT Program that year. Students are counted only once, no matter how often they are tested, and only their latest scores are summarized. Suppose a high school graduate is selected at random. Use the information in the tables to answer the following questions.

(a) What is the probability that the selected student is female?

(b) What is the probability that the selected student scores 600 or over on the Mathematics section of the SAT?

(c) What is the conditional probability that the selected student scores 600 or over on the Mathematics section given that the student is male?

(d) What is the conditional probability that the selected student scores 600 or over on the Mathematics section given that the student is female?

(e) Are scoring over 600 on the Mathematics section and sex independent? If not, explain in a simple sentence the nature of the dependence.

12.55 Let's make a deal. The Monty Hall Problem is an example of a simple probability problem with an answer that is counterintuitive. The problem was made popular when Marilyn vos Savant published the problem in her *Parade Magazine* column in 1990. Here is the question:

Suppose you're on a game show, and you're given a choice of three doors: Behind one door is a car; behind the others, goats. You pick a door, say number 1, and the host, who knows what's behind the doors, opens another door, say number 3, which has a goat. He says to you, "Do you want to pick door number 2?" Is it to your advantage to switch your choice of doors?

Go to the Web site www.letsmakeadeal.com/problem.htm. Then use the *Three Doors Simulation* link further down on the Web page to play the game 30 times.

(a) What proportion of the time would you have won if you had switched doors? If you had not switched? Based on your simulation, does it seem better to switch or to stay with your initial choice?

(b) The Web site provides an explanation of why it is better to switch doors. The explanation uses conditional probabilities, and in the notation of the Web site, $P(A \wedge B)$ is another way of writing $P(A$ and $B)$. Following the guidelines on the Web site and using the notation in our text, show why the probability of getting the car is 1/3 if you do not switch doors and 2/3 if you do switch doors. How well do these probabilities agree with the proportions you found in your simulation?

Randy Duchaine/Alamy

Binomial Distributions*

A basketball player shoots 5 free throws. How many does she make? A sample survey dials 1200 residential phone numbers at random. How many live people answer the phone? You plant 10 dogwood trees. How many live through the winter? In all these situations, we want a probability model for a *count* of successful outcomes.

THE BINOMIAL SETTING AND BINOMIAL DISTRIBUTIONS

The distribution of a count depends on how the data are produced. Here is a common situation.

*This more advanced chapter concerns a special topic in probability. The material is not needed to read the rest of the book.

THE BINOMIAL SETTING

1. There are a fixed number n of observations.

2. The n observations are all **independent.** That is, knowing the result of one observation does not change the probabilities we assign to other observations.

3. Each observation falls into one of just two categories, which for convenience we call "success" and "failure."

4. The probability of a success, call it p, is the same for each observation.

Think of tossing a coin n times as an example of the binomial setting. Each toss gives either heads or tails. Knowing the outcome of one toss doesn't change the probability of a head on any other toss, so the tosses are independent. If we call heads a success, then p is the probability of a head and remains the same as long as we toss the same coin. For tossing a coin, p is close to 0.5. If we spin the coin on a flat surface rather than toss it, p is not equal to 0.5. The number of heads we count is a discrete random variable X. The distribution of X is called a **binomial distribution.**

BINOMIAL DISTRIBUTION

The count X of successes in the binomial setting has the **binomial distribution** with parameters n and p. The parameter n is the number of observations, and p is the probability of a success on any one observation. The possible values of X are the whole numbers from 0 to n.

The binomial distributions are an important class of finite probability models. *Pay attention to the binomial setting, because not all counts have binomial distributions.*

EXAMPLE 13.1   Counting boys

Choose two births at random from the last year's births at a large hospital and count the number of boys (0, 1, or 2). The sexes of children born to different mothers are surely independent. The probability that a randomly chosen birth in Canada and the United States is a boy is about 0.52. So the count of boys has a binomial distribution with $n = 2$ and $p = 0.52$.

Next, observe successive births at a large hospital and let X be the number of births until the first boy is born. Births are independent and each has probability 0.52 of being a boy. Yet X is *not* binomial, because there is no fixed number of observations. "Count observations until the first success" is a different setting than "count the number of successes in a fixed number of observations." ■

BINOMIAL DISTRIBUTIONS IN STATISTICAL SAMPLING

The binomial distributions are important in statistics when we wish to make inferences about the proportion p of "successes" in a population. Here is a typical example.

EXAMPLE 13.2 Choosing an SRS of DVDs

A distributor inspects an SRS of 10 DVDs from a shipment of 10,000 DVDs of a popular film. Suppose that (unknown to the distributor) 10% of the DVDs in the shipment have defective copy-protection schemes that will harm personal computers. Count the number X of bad DVDs in the sample.

This is not quite a binomial setting. Removing 1 DVD changes the proportion of bad DVDs remaining in the shipment. So the probability that the second DVD chosen is bad changes when we know whether the first is good or bad. But removing 1 DVD from a shipment of 10,000 changes the makeup of the remaining 9999 DVDs very little. In practice, the distribution of X is very close to the binomial distribution with $n = 10$ and $p = 0.1$. ■

© *Jeff Morgan 13/Alamy*

Example 13.2 shows how we can use the binomial distributions in the statistical setting of selecting an SRS. When the population is much larger than the sample, a count of successes in an SRS of size n has approximately the binomial distribution with n equal to the sample size and p equal to the proportion of successes in the population.

SAMPLING DISTRIBUTION OF A COUNT

Choose an SRS of size n from a population with proportion p of successes. When the population is much larger than the sample, the count X of successes in the sample has approximately the binomial distribution with parameters n and p.

APPLY YOUR KNOWLEDGE

In each of Exercises 13.1 to 13.3, X is a count. Does X have a binomial distribution? Give your reasons in each case.

13.1 Random digit dialing. When an opinion poll calls residential telephone numbers at random, only 20% of the calls reach a live person. You watch the random dialing machine make 15 calls. X is the number that reach a live person.

13.2 Random digit dialing. When an opinion poll calls residential telephone numbers at random, only 20% of the calls reach a live person. You watch the random dialing machine make calls. X is the number of calls until the first live person answers.

13.3 Boxes of tiles. Boxes of six-inch slate flooring tile contain 40 tiles per box. The count X is the number of cracked tiles in a box. You have noticed that most boxes contain no cracked tiles, but if there are cracked tiles in a box, then there are usually several.

13.4 Canadian Internet use. A survey finds that in 2009, 80% of Canadians aged 16 and older used the Internet for personal reasons.[1] In the survey, an "Internet user" is defined as someone who used the Internet for personal reasons from any location in the 12 months preceding the survey. If you take an SRS of 1500 Canadians aged 16 and over, what is the approximate distribution of the number in your sample who have used the Internet for personal reasons?

BINOMIAL PROBABILITIES

We can find a formula for the probability that a binomial random variable takes any value by starting from the multiplication rule for independent events (page 252).

BINOMIAL PROBABILITY

If X has the binomial distribution with n observations and probability p of success on each observation, the possible values of X are $0, 1, 2, \ldots, n$. If k is any one of these values, the **binomial probability** of k successes is

$$P(X = k) = \frac{n!}{k! \, (n - k)!} \, p^k(1 - p)^{n-k}$$

This expression uses the **factorial** notation:

$$n! = n \times (n - 1) \times (n - 2) \times \cdots \times 3 \times 2 \times 1$$

In addition, we define $0! = 1$.

EXAMPLE 13.3 Inheriting blood type

The blood types of successive children born to the same parents are independent and have fixed probabilities that depend on the genetic makeup of the parents. Each child born to a certain set of parents has probability 0.25 of having blood type O. If these parents have 5 children, what is the probability that exactly 2 of them have type O blood?

The number X of children with type O blood has the binomial distribution with $n = 5$ and $p = 0.25$. The probability we want is

$$P(X = 2) = \frac{5!}{2! \, 3!} (0.25)^2(0.75)^3$$

Calculating a binomial probability is made easier by the fact that the larger of the two factorials in the denominator will cancel much of the $n!$ in the numerator:

$$P(X = 2) = \frac{(5)(4)(3)(2)(1)}{(2)(1) \times (3)(2)(1)} (0.25)^2(0.75)^3$$

$$= \frac{(5)(4)}{(2)(1)} (0.25)^2(0.75)^3$$

$$= 10(0.25)^2(0.75)^3 = 0.2637 \ \blacksquare$$

The binomial probability formula is awkward to use unless the number of observations n is quite small. Graphing calculators and software will give you binomial probabilities $P(X = k)$ and cumulative probabilities $P(X \le k)$. Here, for example, is Minitab's output for the binomial probability in Example 13.3:

```
BINOMIAL with n = 5 and p = 0.25

x P( X = x )
2    0.263672
```

Optional: Where does the formula come from? We can arrive at the binomial probability formula used in Example 13.3 as follows. The multiplication rule says that the probability that (say) the first and third children have type O blood is

$$(0.25)(0.75)(0.25)(0.75)(0.75) = (0.25)^2(0.75)^3$$

You see that *any* arrangement of 2 successes and 3 failures among the 5 children has this same probability. So the overall probability of exactly 2 successes is $(0.25)^2(0.75)^3$ times the number of ways of arranging 2 successes and 3 failures. You can write these out as

SSFFF, SFSFF, and so on to see that there are 10 such arrangements. In general, the number of ways of arranging k successes and $n - k$ failures among n trials is the $n!/k!(n - k)!$ in the binomial probability formula. This expression is called a **binomial coefficient.**

binomial coefficient

APPLY YOUR KNOWLEDGE

13.5 Proofreading. Typing errors in a text are either nonword errors (as when "the" is typed as "teh") or word errors that result in a real but incorrect word. Spell-checking software will catch nonword errors but not word errors. Human proof-readers catch 70% of word errors. You ask a fellow student to proofread an essay in which you have deliberately made 10 word errors.

(a) If the student matches the usual 70% rate, what is the distribution of the number of errors caught? What is the distribution of the number of errors missed?

(b) Missing 3 or more out of 10 errors seems a poor performance. What is the probability that a proofreader who catches 70% of word errors misses exactly 3 out of 10? If you use software, also find the probability of missing 3 or more out of 10.

13.6 Random digit dialing. When an opinion poll calls residential telephone numbers at random, only 20% of the calls reach a live person. You watch the random digit dialing machine make 15 calls.

(a) What is the probability that exactly 3 calls reach a person?

(b) What is the probability that at most 3 calls reach a person?

(c) What is the probability that at least 3 calls reach a person?

(d) What is the probability that fewer than 3 calls reach a person?

(e) What is the probability that more than 3 calls reach a person?

BINOMIAL MEAN AND STANDARD DEVIATION

If a count X has the binomial distribution based on n observations with probability p of success, what is its mean μ? That is, in very many repetitions of the binomial setting, what will be the average count of successes? We can guess the answer. If a basketball player makes 80% of her free throws, the mean number made in 10 tries should be 80% of 10, or 8. In general, the mean of a binomial distribution should be $\mu = np$. Here are the facts.

> **BINOMIAL MEAN AND STANDARD DEVIATION**
>
> If a count X has the binomial distribution with number of observations n and probability of success p, the **mean** and **standard deviation** of X are
>
> $$\mu = np$$
> $$\sigma = \sqrt{np(1 - p)}$$

EXAMPLE 13.4 Inheriting blood type

Continuing Example 13.3, the count X of children with type O blood is binomial with $n = 5$ and $p = 0.25$. The histogram in Figure 13.1 displays this probability distribution. (Because probabilities are long-run proportions, using probabilities as the heights of the bars shows what the distribution of X would be in very many repetitions.) The distribution is skewed to the right.

The mean and standard deviation of the binomial distribution in Figure 13.1 are

$$\mu = np$$
$$= (5)(0.25) = 1.25$$
$$\sigma = \sqrt{np(1 - p)}$$
$$= \sqrt{(5)(0.25)(0.75)} = \sqrt{0.9375} = 0.9682$$

The mean is marked on the probability histogram in Figure 13.1. Notice that the mean need not be a whole number even though all the possible outcomes are whole numbers. If we look at very many couples with these genetic makeups who have 5 children, the average number of their children who have type O blood is 1.25. ■

FIGURE 13.1

Probability histogram for the binomial distribution with $n = 5$ and $p = 0.25$, for Example 13.4.

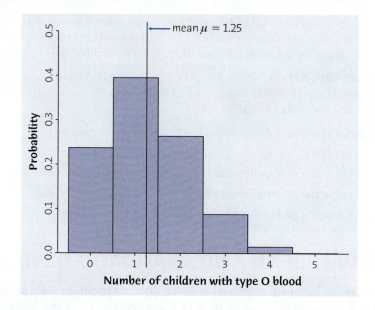

APPLY YOUR KNOWLEDGE

13.7 Proofreading. Return to the proofreading setting of Exercise 13.5.

(a) If X is the number of word errors missed, what is the distribution of X? If Y is the number of word errors caught, what is the distribution of Y?

(b) What is the mean number of errors caught? What is the mean number of errors missed? The mean counts of successes and of failures always add to n, the number of observations.

(c) What is the standard deviation of the number of errors caught? What is the standard deviation of the number of errors missed? The standard deviations of the count of successes and the count of failures are always the same.

13.8 Random digit dialing. When an opinion poll calls residential telephone numbers at random, only 20% of the calls reach a live person. You watch the random digit dialing machine make 15 calls.

(a) What is the mean number of calls that reach a person?

(b) What is the standard deviation σ of the count of calls that reach a person?

(c) If calls are made to New York City rather than nationally, the probability that a call reaches a person is only $p = 0.08$. How does this new p affect the standard deviation? What would be the standard deviation if $p = 0.01$? What does your work show about the behavior of the standard deviation of a binomial distribution as the probability of a success gets closer to 0?

THE NORMAL APPROXIMATION TO BINOMIAL DISTRIBUTIONS

It isn't practical to use the formula for binomial probabilities when the number of observations n is large. Software or a graphing calculator will handle many problems that are beyond the reach of hand calculation. If technology does not rescue you, there is another alternative: *as the number of observations n gets larger, the binomial distribution gets close to a Normal distribution*. When n is large, we can use Normal probability calculations to approximate binomial probabilities. Here are the facts.

NORMAL APPROXIMATION FOR BINOMIAL DISTRIBUTIONS

Suppose that a count X has the binomial distribution with n observations and success probability p. When n is large, the distribution of X is approximately Normal, $N(np, \sqrt{np(1 - p)})$.

As a rule of thumb, we will use the Normal approximation when n is so large that $np \geq 10$ and $n(1 - p) \geq 10$.

The Normal approximation is easy to remember because it says to act as if X is Normal with exactly the same mean and standard deviation as the binomial distribution. The accuracy of the Normal approximation improves as the sample size n increases. It is most accurate for any fixed n when p is close to $1/2$ and least accurate when p is near 0 or 1. This is why the rule of thumb in the box depends on p as well as n.

EXAMPLE 13.5 Attitudes toward shopping

How many people enjoy shopping? A survey asked a nationwide random sample of 2500 adults if they agreed or disagreed that "I like buying new clothes, but shopping is often frustrating and time-consuming."[2] The population that the poll wants to draw conclusions about is all U.S. residents aged 18 and over. Suppose that in fact 60% of all adult U.S. residents would say "Agree" if asked the same question. What is the probability that 1520 or more of the sample agree? ■

Because there are about 235 million adults in the United States, the responses of 2500 randomly chosen adults are very close to independent. So the number in our sample who agree that shopping is frustrating is a random variable X having the binomial distribution with $n = 2500$ and $p = 0.6$. Figure 13.2 is a probability histogram

Erica Shires/zefa/Corbis

FIGURE 13.2

Probability histogram for the binomial distribution with $n = 2500$, $p = 0.6$. The bars at and above 1520 are shaded to highlight the probability of getting at least 1520 successes. The shape of this binomial probability distribution closely resembles a Normal curve.

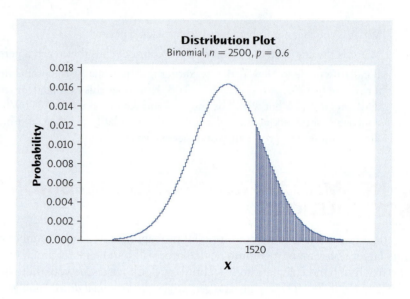

of this distribution, from Minitab. As the Normal approximation suggests, the shape of the distribution looks Normal.

To find the probability $P(X \geq 1520)$ that at least 1520 of the people in the sample find shopping frustrating, we must add the binomial probabilities of all outcomes from $X = 1520$ to $X = 2500$. This is the sum of the heights of the shaded bars in Figure 13.2. Statistical software can find the exact probability. In most cases, software finds cumulative probabilities $P(X \leq x)$. So start by writing

$$P(X \geq 1520) = 1 - P(X \leq 1519)$$

Here is Minitab's answer for $P(X \leq 1519)$:

```
    Binomial with n = 2500 and p = 0.6

      x      P(X <= x)
   1519    0.786861
```

The probability we want is $1 - 0.786861 = 0.213139$, correct to 6 decimal places. We can avoid the need for software by using the Normal approximation.

EXAMPLE 13.6 Normal calculation of a binomial probability

Act as though the count X has the Normal distribution with the same mean and standard deviation as the binomial distribution:

$$\mu = np = (2500)(0.6) = 1500$$
$$\sigma = \sqrt{np(1-p)} = \sqrt{(2500)(0.6)(0.4)} = 24.49$$

Standardizing X gives a standard Normal variable Z. The probability we want is

$$P(X \geq 1520) = P\left(\frac{X - 1500}{24.49} \geq \frac{1520 - 1500}{24.49}\right)$$
$$= P(Z \geq 0.82)$$
$$= 1 - 0.7939 = 0.2061$$

The Normal approximation 0.2061 misses the true probability by about 0.007. ■

Whether or not the Normal approximation is satisfactory depends on how accurate your calculations need to be. For most statistical purposes, great accuracy is not required. Our rule of thumb for use of the Normal approximation reflects this judgment.

APPLY YOUR KNOWLEDGE

13.9 Using Benford's law. According to Benford's law (Example 10.6, page 227) the probability that the first digit of the amount of a randomly chosen invoice is a 1 or a 2 is 0.477. You examine 90 invoices from a vendor and find that 29 have first digits 1 or 2. If Benford's law holds, the count of 1s and 2s will have the binomial distribution with $n = 90$ and $p = 0.477$. Too few 1s and 2s suggests fraud. What is the approximate probability of 29 or fewer if the invoices follow Benford's law? Do you suspect that the invoice amounts are not genuine?

13.10 College admissions. A small liberal arts college would like to have an entering class of 475 students next year. Past experience shows that about 31% of the students admitted will decide to attend. The college therefore plans to admit 1520 students. Suppose that students make their decisions independently and that the probability is 0.31 that a randomly chosen student will accept the offer of admission.

    (a) What are the mean and standard deviation of the number of students who accept the admissions offer from this college?

    (b) Use the Normal approximation: what is the approximate probability that the college gets more students than it wants?

    (c) Use software to compute the exact probability that the college gets more students than it wants. How good is the approximation in part (b)?

13.11 Checking for survey errors. One way of checking the effect of undercoverage, nonresponse, and other sources of error in a sample survey is to compare the sample with known facts about the population. About 24% of the Canadian population over 15 years of age are first generation; that is, they were born outside Canada. The number X of first-generation Canadians in random samples of 1000 persons over 15 should therefore vary with the binomial ($n = 1000$, $p = 0.24$) distribution.

    (a) What are the mean and standard deviation of X?

    (b) Use the Normal approximation to find the probability that the sample will contain between 210 and 270 first-generation Canadians. Be sure to check that you can safely use the approximation.

CHAPTER 13 SUMMARY

CHAPTER SPECIFICS

■ A count X of successes has a **binomial distribution** in the **binomial setting:** there are n observations; the observations are independent of each other; each observation results in a success or a failure; each observation has the same probability p of a success.

■ The binomial distribution with n observations and probability p of success gives a good approximation to the sampling distribution of the count of successes in an SRS of size n from a large population containing proportion p of successes.

■ If X has the binomial distribution with parameters n and p, the possible values of X are the whole numbers $0, 1, 2, \ldots, n$. The **binomial probability** that X takes any of these values is

$$P(X = k) = \frac{n!}{k! \, (n - k)!} \, p^k (1 - p)^{n-k}$$

In practice, binomial probabilities are best found using software. Here the **factorial n!** is

$$n! = n \times (n - 1) \times (n - 2) \times \cdots \times 3 \times 2 \times 1$$

for positive whole numbers n, and $0! = 1$.

■ The **mean** and **standard deviation** of a binomial count X are

$$\mu = np$$
$$\sigma = \sqrt{np(1 - p)}$$

■ The **Normal approximation** to the binomial distribution says that if X is a count having the binomial distribution with parameters n and p, then when n is large, X is approximately $N(np, \sqrt{np(1 - p)})$. Use this approximation only when $np \geq 10$ and $n(1 - p) \geq 10$.

LINK IT

The binomial distribution is used to compute probabilities for the count of successes among n observations that are produced under the binomial setting. An important situation for which the binomial setting can be used is when we choose an SRS from a population with a proportion p of successes. When the success probability p is known, probabilities associated with the number of successes among n observations can be computed using either the binomial formula or the Normal approximation when n and p are such that both the mean number of successes and the mean number of failures are large enough.

An important application of the binomial distribution is in making inferences about the *proportion* of some outcome in a population. This is described in Chapter 20, where our data are collected under the binomial setting, but the proportion with the given outcome in the population is not known. For example, we may be interested in learning about the proportion of young adults (ages 19 to 25) who still live at home with their parents based on a sample from the population of young adults. When we want to make inferences about an unknown proportion in a population, we generally work with the *proportion of successes in the sample* rather than the count of successes in the sample. When using the proportion of successes in the sample to answer questions and draw conclusions about this unknown proportion in the population, the statistical methods are still related to the binomial distribution and the Normal approximation to the binomial.

CHECK YOUR SKILLS

13.12 Stanley reads that 1 out of 4 eggs contains salmonella bacteria. So he never uses more than 3 eggs in cooking. If eggs do or don't contain salmonella independently of each other, the number of contaminated eggs when Stanley uses 3 chosen at random has the distribution

   (a) binomial with $n = 4$ and $p = 1/4$.

   (b) binomial with $n = 3$ and $p = 1/4$.

   (c) binomial with $n = 3$ and $p = 1/3$.

13.13 In a group of 10 college students, 4 are business majors. You choose 3 of the 10 students at random and ask their major. The distribution of the number of business majors you choose is

   (a) binomial with $n = 10$ and $p = 0.4$.

   (b) binomial with $n = 3$ and $p = 0.4$.

   (c) not binomial.

13.14 Virginia makes 40% of her free throws. She takes 5 free throws in a game. If the shots are independent of each other, the probability that she misses the first and last shot but makes the other 3 is about

(a) 0.230.   (b) 0.115.   (c) 0.023.

13.15 Virginia makes 40% of her free throws. She takes 5 free throws in a game. If the shots are independent of each other, the probability that she makes 3 out of the 5 shots is about

(a) 0.230.   (b) 0.115.   (c) 0.023.

Each entry in a table of random digits like Table B has probability 0.1 of being any of the ten digits 0 to 9, and digits are independent of each other. Exercises 13.16 to 13.18 use this setting.

13.16 The probability of an entry being either an 8 or a 9 is

(a) 0.1.   (b) 0.2.   (c) 0.4.

13.17 Each line in Table B has 40 digits. The number of times an 8 or a 9 occurs in *two lines* of the table has a

(a) binomial distribution with $n = 80$ and $p = 0.2$.

(b) binomial distribution with $n = 80$ and $p = 0.1$.

(c) binomial distribution with $n = 40$ and $p = 0.2$.

13.18 The mean number of times an 8 or a 9 occurs in *two lines* of the table is

(a) 16.   (b) 12.8.   (c) 8.

CHAPTER 13 EXERCISES

13.19 Binomial setting? In each situation below, is it reasonable to use a binomial distribution for the random variable X? Give reasons for your answer in each case.

(a) An auto manufacturer chooses one car from each hour's production for a detailed quality inspection. One variable recorded is the count X of finish defects (dimples, ripples, etc.) in the car's paint.

(b) The pool of potential jurors for a murder case contains 100 persons chosen at random from the adult residents of a large city. Each person in the pool is asked whether he or she opposes the death penalty; X is the number who say "Yes."

(c) Joe buys a ticket in his state's Pick 3 lottery game every week; X is the number of times in a year that he wins a prize.

13.20 Binomial setting? A binomial distribution will be approximately correct as a model for one of these two sports settings and not for the other. Explain why by briefly discussing both settings.

(a) A National Football League kicker has made 80% of his field goal attempts in the past. This season he attempts 20 field goals. The attempts differ widely in distance, angle, wind, and so on.

(b) A National Basketball Association player has made 80% of his free-throw attempts in the past. This season he takes 150 free throws. Basketball free throws are always attempted from 15 feet away with no interference from other players.

13.21 Testing ESP. In a test for ESP (extrasensory perception), a subject is told that cards the experimenter but not the subject can see contain either a star, a circle, a wave, or a square. As the experimenter looks at each of 20 cards in turn, the subject names the shape on the card. A subject who is just guessing has probability 0.25 of guessing correctly on each card.

(a) The count of correct guesses in 20 cards has a binomial distribution. What are n and p?

(b) What is the mean number of correct guesses in many repetitions of the experiment?

(c) What is the probability of exactly 5 correct guesses?

13.22 Random stock prices. A believer in the random walk theory of stock markets thinks that an index of stock prices has probability 0.65 of increasing in any year. Moreover, the change in the index in any given year is not influenced by whether it rose or fell in earlier years. Let X be the number of years among the next 5 years in which the index rises.

(a) X has a binomial distribution. What are n and p?

(b) What are the possible values that X can take?

(c) Find the probability of each value of X. Draw a probability histogram for the distribution of X. (See Figure 13.1 for an example of a probability histogram.)

(d) What are the mean and standard deviation of this distribution? Mark the location of the mean on your histogram.

13.23 Betting on red. A roulette wheel has 38 slots, numbered 0, 00, and 1 to 36. The slots 0 and 00 are colored green, 18 of the others are red, and 18 are black. The dealer spins the wheel and at the same time rolls a small ball along the wheel in the opposite direction. The wheel is carefully balanced so that the ball is equally likely to land in any slot when the wheel slows. Gamblers can bet on various combinations of numbers and colors.

(a) If you bet on "red," you win if the ball lands in a red slot. What is the probability of winning with a bet on red in a single play of roulette?

(b) You decide to play roulette 4 times, each time betting on red. What is the distribution of X, the number of times you win?

(c) If you bet the same amount on each play and win on exactly 2 of the 4 plays, you will "break even." What is the probability that you will break even?

(d) If you win on *fewer than* 2 of the 4 plays, you will lose money. What is the probability that you will lose money?

13.24 The birth control shot. The birth control shot is one of the most effective methods of birth control available, and it works best when you get the shot regularly, every 12 weeks. Under ideal conditions, only 1% of women getting the shot become pregnant within one year. In typical use, however, 3% become pregnant.[3] Choose at random 20 women using the shot as their method of birth control. We count the number who become pregnant in the next year.

(a) Explain why this is a binomial setting.

(b) What is the probability that at least 1 of the women becomes pregnant under ideal conditions? What is the probability in typical use?

13.25 Betting on red, continued. You decide to play roulette 200 times, each time betting the same amount on red. You will lose money if you win on fewer than 100 of the plays. Based on the information in Exercise 13.23, what is the probability that you will lose money? (Check that the Normal approximation is permissible, and use it to find this probability. If your software allows, find the exact binomial probability and compare the two results.) In general, if you bet the same amount on red every time, you will lose money if you win on fewer than half of the plays. What do you think happens to the probability of making money the longer you continue to play?

13.26 The birth control shot, continued. A study of the effectiveness of the birth control shot interviews a random sample of 600 women who are using the shot as their method of birth control.

(a) Based on the information about typical use in Exercise 13.24, what is the probability that at least 20 of these women become pregnant in the next year? (Check that the Normal approximation is permissible, and use it to find this probability. If your software allows, find the exact binomial probability and compare the two results.)

(b) We can't use the Normal approximation to the binomial distribution to find this probability under ideal conditions as described in Exercise 13.24. Why not?

13.27 Hitting the fairway. One statistic used to assess professional golfers is driving accuracy, the percent of drives that land in the fairway. In 2009, driving accuracy for PGA Tour professionals ranged from about 50% to about 75%. Phil Mickelson, the third-highest money winner on the PGA Tour in 2009, hits the fairway only about 52% of the time.[4] Phil is also one of the longest drivers on the tour, and increased distance is generally associated with decreased accuracy.

(a) Phil hits 14 drives in a round. What assumptions must you make in order to use a binomial distribution for the count X of fairways he hits? Which of these assumptions is least realistic?

(b) Assuming that a binomial distribution can be used, what is the expected number of fairways that Phil hits in a round in which he hits 14 drives?

13.28 Genetics. According to genetic theory, the blossom color in the second generation of a certain cross of sweet peas should be red or white in a 3:1 ratio. That is, each plant has probability 3/4 of having red blossoms, and the blossom colors of separate plants are independent.

(a) What is the probability that exactly 6 out of 8 of these plants have red blossoms?

(b) What is the mean number of red-blossomed plants when 80 plants of this type are grown from seeds?

(c) What is the probability of obtaining at least 60 red-blossomed plants when 80 plants are grown from seeds? Use the Normal approximation. If your software allows, find the exact binomial probability and compare the two results.

13.29 False-positives in testing for HIV. A rapid test for the presence in the blood of antibodies to HIV, the virus that causes AIDS, gives a positive result with probability about 0.004 when a person who is free of HIV antibodies is tested. A clinic tests 1000 people who are all free of HIV antibodies.

(a) What is the distribution of the number of positive tests?

(b) What is the mean number of positive tests?

(c) You cannot safely use the Normal approximation for this distribution. Explain why.

13.30 Chevrolet sales in 2010. Chevrolet sold 4.26 million vehicles globally in 2010, making it the only one among the top five global automakers to increase its market share. The five best-selling Chevrolet vehicles in 2010 were Silverado pickups, with approximately 435,000 sold; Cruze compact cars, with 335,000; Aveo compacts, with 322,000; Malibus, with 222,000; and Impalas, with 184,000.[5] Chevrolet wants to undertake a survey of buyers of these five vehicle types to ask them about satisfaction with their purchases.

(a) What proportion of the five best-selling vehicle types were Impalas?

(b) If they plan to survey a total of 1000 customers, what is the expected number and standard deviation of the number of Impala buyers in the sample?

(c) What is the probability that they will get more than 100 Impala buyers in their sample?

13.31 Retention rates in a weight-loss program. Americans spend over $30 billion on a variety of weight-loss products and services. In a study of retention rates of those using the Platinum Program at Jenny Craig from May 2001 to May 2002, it was found that about 25% of those who began the program dropped out in the first four weeks.[6] Assume that we have a random sample of 300 people who are beginning the program.

(a) What is the mean number of people who will drop out of the Platinum Program in the first four weeks in a sample of this size? What is the standard deviation?

(b) What is the approximate probability that at least 210 people in the sample will still be in the Platinum Program after the first four weeks?

13.32 Multiple-choice tests. Here is a simple probability model for multiple-choice tests. Suppose that each student has probability p of correctly answering a question chosen at random from a universe of possible questions. (A strong student has a higher p than a weak student.) Answers to different questions are independent.

(a) Jodi is a good student for whom $p = 0.75$. Use the Normal approximation to find the probability that Jodi scores between 70% and 80% on a 100-question test.

(b) If the test contains 250 questions, what is the probability that Jodi will score between 70% and 80%? You see that Jodi's score on the longer test is more likely to be close to her "true score."

13.33 Is this coin balanced? While he was a prisoner of war during World War II, John Kerrich tossed a coin 10,000 times. He got 5067 heads. If the coin is perfectly balanced, the probability of a head is 0.5. Is there reason to think that Kerrich's coin was not balanced? To answer this question, find the probability that tossing a balanced coin 10,000 times would give a count of heads at least this far from 5000 (that is, at least 5067 heads or no more than 4933 heads).

Whooping cough. *Whooping cough (pertussis) is a highly contagious bacterial infection that was a major cause of childhood deaths before the development of vaccines. About 80% of unvaccinated children who are exposed to whooping cough will develop* the infection, *as opposed to only about 5% of vaccinated children. Exercises 13.34 to 13.37 are based on this information.*

13.34 Vaccination at work. A group of 20 children at a nursery school are exposed to whooping cough by playing with an infected child.

(a) If all 20 have been vaccinated, what is the mean number of new infections? What is the probability that no more than 2 of the 20 children develop infections?

(b) If none of the 20 have been vaccinated, what is the mean number of new infections? What is the probability that 18 or more of the 20 children develop infections?

13.35 A whooping cough outbreak. In 2007, Bob Jones University ended its fall semester a week early because of a whooping cough outbreak; 158 students were isolated and another 1200 given antibiotics as a precaution.[7] Because the effect of childhood vaccination often wears off by late adolescence, treat the Bob Jones students as if they were unvaccinated. It appears that about 1400 students were exposed. What is the probability that at least 75% of these students develop infections if not treated? (Fortunately, whooping cough is much less serious after infancy.)

13.36 A mixed group: means. A group of 20 children at a nursery school are exposed to whooping cough by playing with an infected child. Of these children 17 have been vaccinated and 3 have not.

(a) What is the distribution of the number of new infections among the 17 vaccinated children? What is the mean number of new infections?

(b) What is the distribution of the number of new infections among the 3 unvaccinated children? What is the mean number of new infections?

(c) Add your means from parts (a) and (b). This is the mean number of new infections among all 20 exposed children.

13.37 A mixed group: probabilities. We would like to find the probability that exactly 2 of the 20 exposed children in the previous exercise develop whooping cough.

(a) One way to get 2 infections is to get 1 among the 17 vaccinated children and 1 among the 3 unvaccinated children. Find the probability of exactly 1 infection among the 17 vaccinated children. Find the probability of exactly 1 infection among the 3 unvaccinated children. These events are independent: what is the probability of exactly 1 infection in each group?

(b) Write down all the ways in which 2 infections can be divided between the two groups of children. Follow the pattern of part (a) to find the probability of each of these possibilities. Add all of your results, including the result of part (a), to obtain the probability of exactly 2 infections among the 20 children.

13.38 The continuity correction. One reason why the Normal approximation may fail to give accurate estimates of binomial probabilities is that the binomial distributions are discrete and the Normal distributions are continuous. That is, counts take only whole-number values but Normal variables can take any value. We can improve the Normal approximation by treating each whole-number count as if it occupied the interval from 0.5 below the number to 0.5 above the number. For example, approximate a binomial probability $P(X \geq 10)$ by finding the Normal probability $P(X \geq 9.5)$. Be careful: binomial $P(X > 10)$ is approximated by Normal $P(X \geq 10.5)$.

We saw in Exercise 13.27 that Phil Mickelson hits the fairway in 52% of his drives. We will assume that his drives are independent and that each has probability 0.52 of hitting the fairway. Suppose Phil drives 24 times. The exact binomial probability that he hits 17 or more fairways is 0.0487.

(a) Show that this setting satisfies the rule of thumb for use of the Normal approximation (just barely).

(b) What is the Normal approximation to $P(X \geq 17)$?

(c) What is the Normal approximation using the continuity correction? That's a lot closer to the true binomial probability.

 EXPLORING THE WEB

13.39 MCAT writing sample. Go to the Web site aamc.org/students/applying/mcat/admissionsadvisors/mcat_stats/, which reports the distribution of the total scaled MCAT composite score as well as the scores on the individual areas of assessment for recent years. The areas of assessment include four multiple-choice portions that are combined to give the overall composite score, plus a writing sample consisting of two essays. The essays are scored individually, with the results converted to an alphabetic score ranging from J (lowest) to T (highest). Most competitive medical schools look for a writing MCAT score of at least P or Q.

(a) Open the pdf with the percentage and scaled score tables for the most recent year provided. Can the distribution of writing-sample scores be assumed to be approximately Normal? Explain.

(b) A survey organization is planning on contacting an SRS of 1000 of the examinees from the most recent year to see how they prepared for the writing sample. What is the distribution of the number of examinees in the sample who had a score of at least P on the writing sample?

(c) Use the Normal distribution to approximate the probability that at least half of the examinees in the sample scored a P or higher.

(d) Use software or a calculator to compute the exact probability that at least half of the examinees in the sample scored a P or higher. How do the exact probability and the Normal approximation to this probability compare? Which of the two answers would you report to the survey organization? Why?

13.40 Binomial calculators. A number of Web sites will do exact binomial probability calculations for you.

(a) Find a Web site with a binomial calculator and give its URL.

(b) In Example 13.5, the number in the sample who agree that shopping is frustrating is a binomial random variable X with $n = 2500$ and $p = 0.6$. Use the binomial calculator to compute the probability that 1530 or more of the sample agree.

Chris Ryan/Getty Images

Confidence Intervals: The Basics

A fter we have selected a sample, we know the responses of the individuals in the sample. The usual reason for taking a sample is not to learn about the individuals in the sample but to *infer* from the sample data some conclusion about the wider population that the sample represents.

STATISTICAL INFERENCE

Statistical inference provides methods for drawing conclusions about a population from sample data.

Because a different sample might lead to different conclusions, we can't be certain that our conclusions are correct. Statistical inference uses the language of probability to say how trustworthy our conclusions are. This chapter introduces one of the two most common types of inference, *confidence intervals* for estimating the value of a population parameter. The next chapter discusses the other common type of inference, *tests of significance* for assessing the evidence for a claim about a population. Both types of inference are based on the sampling distributions of statistics. That is, both use probability to say what would happen if we applied the inference method many times.

This chapter presents the basic reasoning of statistical inference. To make the reasoning as clear as possible, we start with a setting that is too simple to be realistic. Here is the setting for our work in this chapter.

SIMPLE CONDITIONS FOR INFERENCE ABOUT A MEAN

1. We have an SRS from the population of interest. There is no nonresponse or other practical difficulty.
2. The variable we measure has an exactly Normal distribution $N(\mu, \sigma)$ in the population.
3. We don't know the population mean μ. But we do know the population standard deviation σ.

The conditions that we have a perfect SRS, that the population is exactly Normal, and that we know the population σ are all unrealistic. Chapter 16 begins to move from the "simple conditions" toward the reality of statistical practice. Later chapters deal with inference in fully realistic settings.

If these "simple conditions" are unrealistic, why study them? One reason is that under these simple conditions we can apply what we have learned in previous chapters about the Normal distribution and the sampling distribution of a sample mean to develop, step-by-step, methods for inference about a mean. The reasoning used under simple conditions applies to more realistic settings where the mathematics is more complicated.

Another reason for studying inference under these simple conditions is that we can carry out calculations using what we have already learned about the Normal distribution in previous chapters. This includes the sample size calculations used to plan statistical studies, which we discuss in Chapter 16. Unfortunately, under more realistic conditions, such calculations are more complicated, and the connection to previous material about the Normal distribution is less clear.

Finally, we take an important step by using a *mathematical model* to describe an unknown population. This is a fundamental idea in science. Use a mathematical model (mathematical equations) to describe a physical situation. This mathematical model is understood to be an approximation to the real physical situation, but it provides a compact description of it and allows us to make predictions about what will happen in this real physical situation. Our simple conditions provide us with a compact mathematical description of our unknown population and allow us to predict what will happen when we sample from it. For example, it allows us to describe the sampling distribution of the mean and so provides a basis for inference about the unknown mean of the population.

Although we never know whether a population is exactly Normal and we never know the population σ, the methods we discuss in this and the next two chapters are approximately correct for sufficiently large sample sizes, provided we treat the sample standard deviation as though it were the population σ. Thus, there are situations (admittedly rare) where these methods can be used in practice.

THE REASONING OF STATISTICAL ESTIMATION

Body mass index (BMI) is used to screen for possible weight problems. It is calculated as weight divided by the square of height, measuring weight in kilograms and height in meters. Many online BMI calculators allow you to enter weight in pounds and height in inches. Adults with BMI less than 18.5 are considered underweight, and those with BMI greater than 25 may be overweight. For data about BMI, we turn to the National Health and Nutrition Examination Survey (NHANES), a continuing government sample survey that monitors the health of the American population.

EXAMPLE 14.1 Body mass index of young women

An NHANES report gives data for 654 women aged 20 to 29 years.[1] The mean BMI of these 654 women was $\bar{x} = 26.8$. On the basis of this sample, we want to estimate the mean BMI μ in the population of all 20.6 million women in this age group.

To match the "simple conditions," we will treat the NHANES sample as an SRS from a Normal population with standard deviation $\sigma = 7.5$. ■

©SebastianKnight/Dreamstime.com

Here is the reasoning of statistical estimation in a nutshell:

1. To estimate the unknown population mean BMI μ, use the mean $\bar{x} = 26.8$ of the random sample. We don't expect $\bar{x}$ to be exactly equal to μ, so we want to say how accurate this estimate is.

2. We know the sampling distribution of $\bar{x}$. In repeated samples, $\bar{x}$ has the Normal distribution with mean μ and standard deviation $\sigma/\sqrt{n}$. So the average BMI $\bar{x}$ of an SRS of 654 young women has standard deviation

$$\frac{\sigma}{\sqrt{n}} = \frac{7.5}{\sqrt{654}} = 0.3 \ \text{(rounded off)}$$

3. The 95 part of the 68–95–99.7 rule for Normal distributions says that $\bar{x}$ is within 0.6 (that's two standard deviations) of the mean μ in 95% of all samples. That is, for 95% of all samples of size 654, the distance between the sample mean $\bar{x}$ and the population mean μ is less than 0.6. So if we estimate that μ lies somewhere in the interval from $\bar{x} - 0.6$ to $\bar{x} + 0.6$, we'll be right for 95% of all possible samples. For this particular sample, this interval is

$$\bar{x} - 0.6 = 26.8 - 0.6 = 26.2$$

to

$$\bar{x} + 0.6 = 26.8 + 0.6 = 27.4$$

4. Because we got the interval 26.2 to 27.4 from a method that captures the population mean for 95% of all possible samples, we say that we are 95% *confident* that the mean BMI μ of all young women is some value in that interval, no lower than 26.2 and no higher than 27.4.

The sampling distribution of $\bar{x}$ tells us how close to μ the sample mean $\bar{x}$ is likely to be. Statistical estimation just turns that information around to say how close to $\bar{x}$ the unknown population mean μ is likely to be. We call the interval of numbers between the values $\bar{x} \pm 0.6$ a 95% *confidence interval* for μ. For this sample, $\bar{x} = 26.8$, so our confidence interval is 26.8 ± 0.6. Most confidence intervals have this form:

$$\text{estimate} \pm \text{margin of error}$$

margin of error

The estimate ($\bar{x} = 26.8$ in our example) is our guess for the value of the unknown parameter. The **margin of error** ± 0.6 shows how accurate we believe our guess is, based on the variability of the estimate. We have a 95% confidence interval because the interval $\bar{x} \pm 0.6$ catches the unknown parameter in 95% of all possible samples.

CONFIDENCE INTERVAL

A **level C confidence interval** for a parameter has two parts:

■ An **interval** calculated from the data, usually of the form

$$\text{estimate} \pm \text{margin of error}$$

■ A **confidence level** C, which gives the probability that the interval will capture the true parameter value in repeated samples. That is, the confidence level is the success rate for the method.

We choose the confidence level we want: usually 90% or higher because we usually want to be quite sure of our conclusions. The most common confidence level is 95%.

EXAMPLE 14.2 Statistical estimation in pictures

Figure 14.1 shows how 95% confidence intervals behave. Draw many SRSs from the same population and calculate a 95% confidence interval from each sample. The center of each interval is at $\bar{x}$ and therefore varies from sample to sample. The sampling distribution

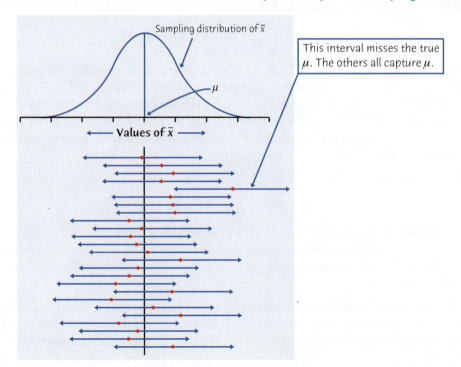

FIGURE 14.1

Twenty-five samples from the same population gave these 95% confidence intervals. In the long run, 95% of all samples give an interval that contains the population mean μ.

of $\bar{x}$ appears at the top of the figure to show the long-term pattern of this variation. The population mean μ is at the center of the sampling distribution. The 95% confidence intervals from 25 SRSs appear underneath. The center $\bar{x}$ of each interval is marked by a dot. The arrows on either side of the dot span the confidence interval. All except 1 of these 25 intervals capture the true value of μ. If we take a very large number of samples, 95% of the confidence intervals will contain μ. ■

INTERPRETING A CONFIDENCE LEVEL

The confidence level is the success rate of the method that produces the interval. We don't know whether the 95% confidence interval from a particular sample is one of the 95% that capture μ or one of the unlucky 5% that miss.

To say that we are **95% confident** that the unknown μ lies between 26.2 and 27.4 is shorthand for **"We got these numbers using a method that gives correct results 95% of the time."**

APPLY YOUR KNOWLEDGE

14.1 Number skills of high school seniors. The National Assessment of Educational Progress (NAEP) includes a mathematics test for high school seniors.[2] Scores on the test range from 0 to 300. Demonstrating the ability to use the Pythagorean theorem to determine the length of a hypotenuse is an example of the skills and knowledge associated with performance at the Basic level. An example of the knowledge and skills associated with the Proficient level is using trigonometric ratios to determine length.

In 2009, 51,000 12th-graders were in the NAEP sample for the mathematics test. The mean mathematics score was $\bar{x} = 153$. We want to estimate the mean score μ in the population of all 12th-graders. Consider the NAEP sample as an SRS from a Normal population with standard deviation $\sigma = 34$.

(a) If we take many samples, the sample mean $\bar{x}$ varies from sample to sample according to a Normal distribution with mean equal to the unknown mean score μ in the population. What is the standard deviation of this sampling distribution?

(b) According to the 95 part of the 68–95–99.7 rule, 95% of all values of $\bar{x}$ fall within _____ on either side of the unknown mean μ. What is the missing number?

(c) What is the 95% confidence interval for the population mean score μ based on this one sample?

14.2 Explaining confidence. A student reads that a 95% confidence interval for the mean body mass index (BMI) of young American women is 26.8 ± 0.6. Asked to explain the meaning of this interval, the student says, "95% of all young women have BMI between 26.2 and 27.4." Explain in simple language what a 95% confidence interval is and why the student's explanation is incorrect.

CONFIDENCE INTERVALS FOR A POPULATION MEAN

To find a 95% confidence interval for the mean BMI of young women, we first caught the central 95% of the Normal sampling distribution by going out two standard deviations in both directions from the mean. To find a level C confidence interval, we first catch the central area C under the Normal sampling distribution. Because all Normal distributions are the same in the standard scale, we can obtain everything we need from the standard Normal curve.

Figure 14.2 shows how the central area C under a standard Normal curve is marked off by two points z^* and $-z^*$. Numbers like z^* that mark off specified areas are called *critical value* **critical values** of the standard Normal distribution. Values of z^* for many choices of C appear at the bottom of Table C in the back of the book, in the row labeled z^*. Here are the entries for the most common confidence levels:

Confidence level C	90%	95%	99%
Critical value z^*	1.645	1.960	2.576

You see that for C = 95% the table gives $z^* = 1.960$. This is a bit more precise than the approximate value $z^* = 2$ based on the 68–95–99.7 rule. Software will give you critical values z^* for any confidence level, as well as the entire confidence interval.

FIGURE 14.2

The critical value z^* is the number that catches central probability C under a standard Normal curve between $-z^*$ and z^*.

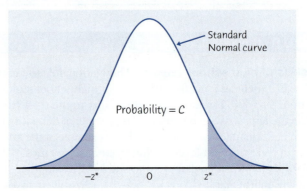

Standard
Normal curve

Probability = C

$-z^*$ 0 z^*

Because there is area C under the standard Normal curve between $-z^*$ and z^*, *any* Normal curve has area C within z^* standard deviations on either side of its mean. In particular, the Normal sampling distribution of $\bar{x}$ has area C within $z^*\sigma/\sqrt{n}$ on either side of the population mean μ because it has mean μ and standard deviation $\sigma/\sqrt{n}$. If we start at $\bar{x}$ and go out $z^*\sigma/\sqrt{n}$ in both directions, we get an interval that contains the population mean μ in a proportion C of all samples. This interval is

$$\text{from} \quad \bar{x} - z^*\frac{\sigma}{\sqrt{n}} \quad \text{to} \quad \bar{x} + z^*\frac{\sigma}{\sqrt{n}}$$

or

$$\bar{x} \pm z^*\frac{\sigma}{\sqrt{n}}$$

It is a level C confidence interval for μ.

CONFIDENCE INTERVAL FOR THE MEAN OF A NORMAL POPULATION

Draw an SRS of size n from a Normal population having unknown mean μ and known standard deviation σ. A level C **confidence interval for μ** is

$$\bar{x} \pm z^*\frac{\sigma}{\sqrt{n}}$$

The critical value z^* is illustrated in Figure 14.2 and found at the bottom of Table C.

The steps in finding a confidence interval mirror the overall four-step process for organizing statistical problems.

CONFIDENCE INTERVALS: THE FOUR-STEP PROCESS

STATE: What is the practical question that requires estimating a parameter?

PLAN: Identify the parameter, choose a level of confidence, and select the type of confidence interval that fits your situation.

SOLVE: Carry out the work in two phases:

1. **Check the conditions** for the interval you plan to use.

2. Calculate the **confidence interval.**

CONCLUDE: Return to the practical question to describe your results in this setting.

EXAMPLE 14.3 Good weather, good tips?

DATA FILE
TIPPING2

STATE: Does the expectation of good weather lead to more generous behavior? Psychologists studied the size of the tip in a restaurant when a message indicating that the next day's weather would be good was written on the bill. Here are tips from 20 patrons, measured in percent of the total bill:[3]

20.8	18.7	19.9	20.6	21.9	23.4	22.8	24.9	22.2	20.3
24.9	22.3	27.0	20.4	22.2	24.0	21.1	22.1	22.0	22.7

This is one of three sets of measurements made, the others being tips received when the message on the bill said that the next day's weather would not be good and tips received when there was no message on the bill. We want to estimate the mean tip for comparison with tips under the other conditions.

PLAN: We will give a 95% confidence interval to estimate the mean tip percent μ for all patrons of this restaurant when they receive a message on their bill indicating that the next day's weather will be good. The confidence interval just introduced fits this situation.

SOLVE: We should start by checking the conditions for inference. For this example, we will first find the interval and then discuss how statistical practice deals with conditions that are never perfectly satisfied.

The mean tip percent of the sample is $\bar{x} = 22.21$. As part of the "simple conditions," suppose that from past experience with patrons of this restaurant we know that the standard deviation of tip percents is $\sigma = 2$. For 95% confidence, the critical value is $z^* = 1.960$. A 95% confidence interval for μ is therefore

$$\bar{x} \pm z^* \frac{\sigma}{\sqrt{n}} = 22.21 \pm 1.960 \frac{2}{\sqrt{20}}$$

$$= 22.21 \pm 0.88$$

$$= 21.33 \text{ to } 23.09$$

CONCLUDE: We are 95% confident that the mean tip percent for all patrons of this restaurant when their bill contains a message that the next day's weather will be good is between 21.33 and 23.09. ■

Ariel Skelley/AgeFotostock

```
27 | 0
26 |
25 |
24 | 099
23 | 4
22 | 0122378
21 | 19
20 | 3468
19 | 9
18 | 7
```

FIGURE 14.3

Stemplot of the tip percents in Example 14.3.

In practice, the first part of the "Solve" step is to check the conditions for inference. The "simple conditions" are as follows:

1. **SRS:** We don't have an actual SRS from the population of all patrons of this restaurant. Scientists often act as if subjects are SRSs if there is nothing special about how the subjects were obtained. But it is always better to have an actual SRS because otherwise we can never be sure that hidden biases aren't present. This study was actually a randomized comparative experiment in which these 20 patrons were assigned at random from a larger group of patrons to get one of the treatments being compared.

2. **Normal distribution:** The psychologists expect from past experience that measurements like this on patrons of the same restaurant under the same conditions will follow approximately a Normal distribution. We can't look at the population, but we can examine the sample. Figure 14.3 is a stemplot. The shape is roughly bell-shaped, with perhaps a modest outlier but no strong skewness. Shapes like this often occur in small samples from Normal populations, so we have no reason to doubt that the population distribution is Normal.

3. **Known σ:** It really is unrealistic to suppose that we know that $\sigma = 2$. We will see in Chapter 18 that it is easy to do away with the need to know σ.

As this discussion suggests, inference methods are often used when conditions like SRS and Normal population are not exactly satisfied. In this introductory chapter, we act as though the "simple conditions" are satisfied. In reality, wise use of inference requires judgment. Chapter 16 and the later chapters on each inference method will give you a better basis for judgment.

APPLY YOUR KNOWLEDGE

14.3 Find a critical value. The critical value z^* for confidence level 85% is not in Table C. Use software or Table A of standard Normal probabilities to find z^*. Include in your answer a sketch like Figure 14.2 with $C = 0.85$ and your critical value z^* marked on the axis.

14.4 Measuring conductivity. The National Institute of Standards and Technology (NIST) supplies "standard materials" whose physical properties are supposed to be known. For example, you can buy from NIST an iron rod whose electrical conductivity is supposed to be 10.1 at 293 kelvins. (The units for conductivity are microsiemens per centimeter. Distilled water has conductivity 0.5.) Of course, no measurement is exactly correct. NIST knows the variability of its measurements very well, so it is quite realistic to assume that the population of all measurements of the same rod has the Normal distribution with mean μ equal to the true conductivity and standard deviation $\sigma = 0.1$. Here are 6 measurements on the same standard iron rod, which is supposed to have conductivity 10.1:

$$10.08 \quad 9.89 \quad 10.05 \quad 10.16 \quad 10.21 \quad 10.11$$

NIST wants to give the buyer of this iron rod a 90% confidence interval for its true conductivity. What is this interval? Follow the four-step process as illustrated in Example 14.3. 🔴 CONDUCTIVITY

14.5 IQ test scores. Here are the IQ test scores of 31 seventh-grade girls in a Midwest school district:[4] **MIDWESTIQ**

114	100	104	89	102	91	114	114	103	105
108	130	120	132	111	128	118	119	86	72
111	103	74	112	107	103	98	96	112	112	93

(a) These 31 girls are an SRS of all seventh-grade girls in the school district. Suppose that the standard deviation of IQ scores in this population is known to be $\sigma = 15$. We expect the distribution of IQ scores to be close to Normal. Make a stemplot of the distribution of these 31 scores (split the stems) to verify that there are no major departures from Normality. You have now checked the "simple conditions" to the extent possible.

(b) Estimate the mean IQ score for all seventh-grade girls in the school district, using a 99% confidence interval. Follow the four-step process as illustrated in Example 14.3.

HOW CONFIDENCE INTERVALS BEHAVE

The z confidence interval $\bar{x} \pm z^*\sigma/\sqrt{n}$ for the mean of a Normal population illustrates several important properties that are shared by all confidence intervals in common use. The user chooses the confidence level, and the margin of error follows from this choice. We would like high confidence and also a small margin of error. High confidence says that our method almost always gives correct answers. A small margin of error says that we have pinned down the parameter quite precisely. The factors that influence the margin of error of the z confidence interval are typical of most confidence intervals.

How do we get a small margin of error? The margin of error for the z confidence interval is

$$\text{margin of error} = z^*\frac{\sigma}{\sqrt{n}}$$

This expression has z^* and σ in the numerator and $\sqrt{n}$ in the denominator. Therefore, the margin of error gets smaller when

- z^* gets smaller. Smaller z^* is the same as lower confidence level C.

- σ is smaller. The standard deviation σ measures the variation in the population. You can think of the variation among individuals in the population as noise that obscures the average value μ. It is easier to pin down μ when σ is small.

- n gets larger. Increasing the sample size n reduces the margin of error for any confidence level. That is, larger samples thus allow more precise estimates.

You can't change the population standard deviation σ. But you can decide what confidence level you want and how many observations you will take. These decisions change the margin of error.

EXAMPLE 14.4 Changing the margin of error

In Example 14.3, psychologists recorded the size of the tip of 20 patrons in a restaurant when a message indicating that the next day's weather would be good was written on their bill. The data gave the mean size of the tip, as a percent of the total bill, as $\bar{x} = 22.21$, and we know that $\sigma = 2$. Here are the intervals for several levels of confidence:

$$99\% \text{ confidence} \qquad 22.21 \pm 2.576\frac{2}{\sqrt{20}} = 22.21 \pm 1.15$$

$$95\% \text{ confidence} \qquad 22.21 \pm 1.960\frac{2}{\sqrt{20}} = 22.21 \pm 0.88$$

$$90\% \text{ confidence} \qquad 22.21 \pm 1.645\frac{2}{\sqrt{20}} = 22.21 \pm 0.74$$

 There is a trade-off between the confidence level and the margin of error. To obtain a smaller margin of error from the same data, you must be willing to accept lower confidence.

Here are the 95% confidence intervals for 10, 20, and 40 patrons (the actual sample size 20, plus samples half as large and twice as large):

$$\text{sample size 10} \qquad 22.21 \pm 1.960\frac{2}{\sqrt{10}} = 22.21 \pm 1.24$$

$$\text{sample size 20} \qquad 22.21 \pm 1.960\frac{2}{\sqrt{20}} = 22.21 \pm 0.88$$

$$\text{sample size 40} \qquad 22.21 \pm 1.960\frac{2}{\sqrt{40}} = 22.21 \pm 0.62$$

 As the sample size increases, the margin of error gets smaller. The intervals are displayed in Figure 14.4. *Because the sample size n appears under a square root sign, you need four times as many observations to cut the margin of error in half.* ■

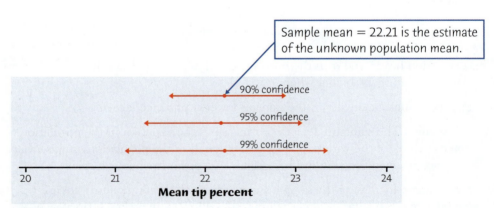

Sample mean = 22.21 is the estimate of the unknown population mean.

90% confidence

95% confidence

99% confidence

Mean tip percent

FIGURE 14.4

The lengths of three confidence intervals for Example 14.4. All three are centered at the estimate $\bar{x} = 22.21$. When the data and the sample size remain the same, higher confidence results in a larger margin of error.

APPLY YOUR KNOWLEDGE

14.6 Confidence level and margin of error. Example 14.1 described NHANES survey data on the body mass index (BMI) of 654 young women. The mean BMI in the sample was $\bar{x} = 26.8$. We treated these data as an SRS from a Normally distributed population with standard deviation $\sigma = 7.5$.

(a) Give three confidence intervals for the mean BMI μ in this population, using 90%, 95%, and 99% confidence.

(b) What are the margins of error for 90%, 95%, and 99% confidence? How does increasing the confidence level change the margin of error of a confidence interval when the sample size and population standard deviation remain the same?

14.7 Sample size and margin of error. Example 14.1 described NHANES survey data on the body mass index (BMI) of 654 young women. The mean BMI in the sample was $\bar{x} = 26.8$. We treated these data as an SRS from a Normally distributed population with standard deviation $\sigma = 7.5$.

(a) Suppose that we had an SRS of just 100 young women. What would be the margin of error for 95% confidence?

(b) Find the margins of error for 95% confidence based on SRSs of 400 young women and 1600 young women.

(c) Compare the three margins of error. How does increasing the sample size change the margin of error of a confidence interval when the confidence level and population standard deviation remain the same?

CHAPTER 14 SUMMARY

CHAPTER SPECIFICS

■ A **confidence interval** uses sample data to estimate an unknown population parameter with an indication of how accurate the estimate is and of how confident we are that the result is correct.

■ Any confidence interval has two parts: an interval calculated from the data and a confidence level C. The **confidence interval** often has the form

$$\text{estimate} \pm \text{margin of error}$$

■ The **confidence level** is the success rate of the method that produces the interval. That is, C is the probability that the method will give a correct answer. If you use 95% confidence intervals often, in the long run 95% of your intervals will contain the true parameter value. You do not know whether or not a 95% confidence interval calculated from a particular set of data contains the true parameter value.

■ A level C **confidence interval for the mean** μ of a Normal population with known standard deviation σ, based on an SRS of size n, is given by

$$\bar{x} \pm z^* \frac{\sigma}{\sqrt{n}}$$

■ The **critical value** z^* is chosen so that the standard Normal curve has area C between $-z^*$ and z^*.

- Other things being equal, the margin of error of a confidence interval gets smaller as
  - the confidence level C decreases,
  - the population standard deviation σ decreases,
  - the sample size n increases.

LINK IT

The reason we collect data is not to learn about the individuals that we observed but to infer from the data to some wider population that the individuals represent. Chapters 8 and 9 tell us that the way we produce the data (sampling, experimental design) affects whether we have a good basis for generalizing to some wider population. Chapters 10, 11, 12, and 13 discuss probability, the formal mathematical tool that determines the nature of the inferences we make. In particular, Chapter 11 discusses sampling distributions, which tell us how repeated SRSs behave and hence what a statistic (in particular, a sample mean) computed from our sample is likely to tell us about the corresponding parameter of the population (in particular, a population mean) from which the sample was selected.

In this chapter we discuss the basic reasoning of statistical estimation, with emphasis on estimating a population mean. To an estimate of the population mean we attach a margin of error and a confidence level. The result is a confidence interval. The sampling distribution of the sample mean, discussed in Chapter 11, provides the mathematical basis for constructing confidence intervals and understanding their properties. Although we apply the reasoning of statistical estimation in a simple and artificial setting (we assume that we know the population standard deviation), we will use the same logic in future chapters to construct confidence intervals for population parameters in more realistic settings.

CHECK YOUR SKILLS

14.8 To give a 99.9% confidence interval for a population mean μ, you would use the critical value

(a) $z^* = 1.960$.   (b) $z^* = 2.576$.   (c) $z^* = 3.291$

Use the following information for Exercises 14.9 through 14.11. A laboratory scale is known to have a standard deviation of $\sigma = 0.001$ gram in repeated weighings. Scale readings in repeated weighings are Normally distributed, with mean equal to the true weight of the specimen. Three weighings of a specimen on this scale give 3.412, 3.416, and 3.414 grams.

14.9 A 95% confidence interval for the true weight of this specimen is WEIGHTS

(a) 3.414 ± 0.00113.

(b) 3.414 ± 0.00065.

(c) 3.414 ± 0.00196.

14.10 You want a 99% confidence interval for the true weight of this specimen. The margin of error for this interval will be

(a) smaller than the margin of error for 95% confidence.

(b) greater than the margin of error for 95% confidence.

(c) about the same as the margin of error for 95% confidence.

14.11 Another specimen is weighed 8 times on this scale. The average weight is 4.1602 grams. A 99% confidence interval for the true weight of this specimen is

(a) 4.1602 ± 0.00032.

(b) 4.1602 ± 0.00069.

(c) 4.1602 ± 0.00091.

Use the following information for Exercises 14.12 through 14.15. The National Assessment of Educational Progress (NAEP) includes a mathematics test for high school seniors. Scores on the test range from 0 to 300. Suppose that you give the NAEP test to an SRS of 900 12th-graders from a large population in which the scores have mean $\mu = 150$ and standard deviation $\sigma = 35$. The mean $\bar{x}$ will vary if you take repeated samples.

14.12 The sampling distribution of $\bar{x}$ is approximately Normal. It has mean $\mu = 150$. What is its standard deviation?

(a) 35.   (b) 1.167.   (c) 0.039.

14.13 Suppose that an SRS of 900 12th-graders has $\bar{x} = 148$. Based on this sample, a 95% confidence interval for μ is

(a) 2.29.   (b) 148 ± 2.29.   (c) 150 ± 2.29.

14.14 In the previous exercise, suppose that we computed a 99% confidence interval for μ.

(a) This 99% confidence interval would have a smaller margin of error than the 95% confidence interval.

(b) This 99% confidence interval would have a larger margin of error than the 95% confidence interval.

(c) This 99% confidence interval could have either a smaller or a larger margin of error than the 95% confidence interval. This varies from sample to sample.

14.15 Suppose that we took an SRS of 1600 12th-graders and found $\bar{x} = 148$. Compared with an SRS of 900 12th-graders, the margin of error for a 95% confidence interval for μ is

(a) smaller.

(b) larger.

(c) either smaller or larger but we can't say which.

CHAPTER 14 EXERCISES

14.16 Student study times. A class survey in a large class for first-year college students asked, "About how many minutes do you study on a typical weeknight?" The mean response of the 463 students was $\bar{x} = 118$ minutes. Suppose that we know that the study time follows a Normal distribution with standard deviation $\sigma = 65$ minutes in the population of all first-year students at this university.

(a) Use the survey result to give a 99% confidence interval for the mean study time of all first-year students.

(b) What condition not yet mentioned must be met for your confidence interval to be valid?

14.17 I want more muscle. Young men in North America and Europe (but not in Asia) tend to think they need more muscle to be attractive. One study presented 200 young American men with 100 images of men with various levels of muscle.[5] Researchers measure level of muscle in kilograms per square meter (kg/m^2) of fat-free body mass. Typical young men have about 20 kg/m^2. Each subject chose two images, one that represented his own level of body muscle and one that he thought represented "what women prefer." The mean gap between self-image and "what women prefer" was 2.35 kg/m^2.

Suppose that the "muscle gap" in the population of all young men has a Normal distribution with standard deviation 2.5 kg/m^2. Give a 90% confidence interval for the mean amount of muscle young men think they should add to be attractive to women. (They are wrong: women actually prefer a level close to that of typical men.)

14.18 An outlier strikes. There were actually 464 responses to the class survey in Exercise 14.16. One student claimed to study 60,000 minutes per night. We know he's joking, so

we left out this value. If we did a calculation without looking at the data, we would get $\bar{x} = 247$ minutes for all 464 students. Now what is the 99% confidence interval for the population mean? (Continue to use $\sigma = 65$.) Compare the new interval with that in Exercise 14.16. The message is clear: always look at your data, because outliers can greatly change your result.

14.19 Explaining confidence. Here is an explanation from the Associated Press concerning one of its opinion polls. Explain briefly but clearly in what way this explanation is incorrect.

> *For a poll of 1,600 adults, the variation due to sampling error is no more than three percentage points either way. The error margin is said to be valid at the 95 percent confidence level. This means that, if the same questions were repeated in 20 polls, the results of at least 19 surveys would be within three percentage points of the results of this survey.*

*Exercises 14.20 to 14.22 ask you to answer questions from data. Assume that the "simple conditions" hold in each case. The exercise statements give you the **State** step of the four-step process. In your work, follow the **Plan, Solve,** and **Conclude** steps, illustrated in Example 14.3 for a confidence interval.*

14.20 Pulling wood apart. How heavy a load (pounds) is needed to pull apart pieces of Douglas fir 4 inches long and 1.5 inches square? Here are data from students doing a laboratory exercise:

33,190	31,860	32,590	26,520	33,280
32,320	33,020	32,030	30,460	32,700
23,040	30,930	32,720	33,650	32,340
24,050	30,170	31,300	28,730	31,920

(a) We are willing to regard the wood pieces prepared for the lab session as an SRS of all similar pieces of Douglas fir. Engineers also commonly assume that characteristics of materials vary Normally. Make a graph to show the shape of the distribution for these data. Does it appear safe to assume that the Normality condition is satisfied? Suppose that the strength of pieces of wood like these follows a Normal distribution with standard deviation 3000 pounds.

(b) Give a 95% confidence interval for the mean load required to pull the wood apart. 🔲 WOOD

14.21 Bone loss by nursing mothers. Breast-feeding mothers secrete calcium into their milk. Some of the calcium may come from their bones, so mothers may lose bone mineral. Researchers measured the percent change in mineral content of the spines of 47 mothers during three months of breast-feeding.[6] Here are the data:

−4.7	−2.5	−4.9	−2.7	−0.8	−5.3	−8.3	−2.1	−6.8	−4.3
2.2	−7.8	−3.1	−1.0	−6.5	−1.8	−5.2	−5.7	−7.0	−2.2
−6.5	−1.0	−3.0	−3.6	−5.2	−2.0	−2.1	−5.6	−4.4	−3.3
−4.0	−4.9	−4.7	−3.8	−5.9	−2.5	−0.3	−6.2	−6.8	1.7
0.3	−2.3	0.4	−5.3	0.2	−2.2	−5.1			

(a) The researchers are willing to consider these 47 women as an SRS from the population of all nursing mothers. Suppose that the percent change in this population has standard deviation $\sigma = 2.5\%$.

Make a stemplot of the data to verify that the data follow a Normal distribution quite closely. (Don't forget that you need both a 0 and a −0 stem because there are both positive and negative values.)

(b) Use a 99% confidence interval to estimate the mean percent change in the population. 🔲 BONELOSS

14.22 This wine stinks. Sulfur compounds cause "off-odors" in wine, so winemakers want to know the odor threshold, the lowest concentration of a compound that the human nose can detect. The odor threshold for dimethyl sulfide (DMS) in trained wine tasters is about 25 micrograms per liter of wine (μg/l). The untrained noses of consumers may be less sensitive, however. Here are the DMS odor thresholds for 10 untrained students:

$$30 \quad 30 \quad 42 \quad 35 \quad 22 \quad 33 \quad 31 \quad 29 \quad 19 \quad 23$$

(a) Assume that the standard deviation of the odor threshold for untrained noses is known to be $\sigma = 7 \mu$g/l. Briefly discuss the other two "simple conditions," using a stemplot to verify that the distribution is roughly symmetric with no outliers.

(b) Give a 95% confidence interval for the mean DMS odor threshold among all students. 🔲 WINE2

14.23 Why are larger samples better? Statisticians prefer large samples. Describe briefly the effect of increasing the size of a sample on the margin of error of a 95% confidence interval.

 EXPLORING THE WEB

14.24 A statistics glossary. An editorial was published in the *Journal of the National Cancer Institute*, Vol. 101, No. 23 (December 2, 2009), that announced some online resources for journalists, including a statistics glossary. The glossary can be found at www.oxfordjournals.org/our_journals/jnc/resource/statistics%20glossary.pdf. Read the definition of a confidence interval. Is this an accurate definition? Explain your answer.

14.25 Getting around No Child Left Behind. The PBS Web site has an interesting article from 2007 discussing how school districts were getting around certain requirements of the No Child Left Behind law. You can find the article at www.pbs.org/newshour/bb/education/july-dec07/nclb_08-14.html. What does the article have to say about the use of confidence intervals in reporting results about the percent of students passing proficiency tests?

Corbis/Superstack

Tests of Significance: The Basics

Confidence intervals are one of the two most common types of statistical inference. Use a confidence interval when your goal is to estimate a population parameter. The second common type of inference, called *tests of significance*, has a *different goal:* to assess the evidence provided by data about some claim concerning a population. Here is the reasoning of statistical tests in a nutshell.

EXAMPLE 15.1 I'm a good free-throw shooter

I claim that I make 75% of my basketball free throws. To test my claim, you ask me to shoot 20 free throws. I make only 8 of the 20. "Aha!" you say. "Someone who makes 75% of his free throws would almost never make only 8 out of 20. So I don't believe your claim."

Your reasoning is based on asking what would happen if my claim were true and we repeated the sample of 20 free throws many times—I would almost never make as few as 8. This outcome is so unlikely that it gives strong evidence that my claim is not true.

You can say how strong the evidence against my claim is by giving the probability that I would make as few as 8 out of 20 free throws if I really make 75% in the long run. This probability is 0.0009. I would make as few as 8 of 20 only 9 times in 10,000 tries in the long run if my claim to make 75% were true. The small probability convinces you that my claim is false. ■

THE REASONING OF TESTS OF SIGNIFICANCE

Statistical tests use an elaborate vocabulary, but the basic idea is simple: *an outcome that would rarely happen if a claim were true is good evidence that the claim is not true.* The reasoning of statistical tests, like that of confidence intervals, is based on asking what would happen if we repeated the sample or experiment many times. We will act as if the "simple conditions" listed on page 286 are true: we have a perfect SRS from an exactly Normal population with standard deviation σ known to us. Here is an example we will explore.

Bloomberg via Getty Images

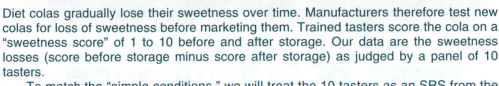

EXAMPLE 15.2 Sweetness loss in colas

Diet colas gradually lose their sweetness over time. Manufacturers therefore test new colas for loss of sweetness before marketing them. Trained tasters score the cola on a "sweetness score" of 1 to 10 before and after storage. Our data are the sweetness losses (score before storage minus score after storage) as judged by a panel of 10 tasters.

To match the "simple conditions," we will treat the 10 tasters as an SRS from the population of all trained tasters and assume that in this population sweetness losses for any cola are Normal with unknown mean μ and standard deviation $\sigma = 1$. The population mean μ measures true loss of sweetness and is different for different colas.

For a cola already on the market, 10 tasters had mean loss $\bar{x} = 0.3$. The taste test for a new cola gives $\bar{x} = 1.02$. Is there good evidence that either of these colas loses sweetness in storage? ■

The reasoning is the same as in Example 15.1. We make a claim and ask if the data give evidence *against* it. Let's spell out the steps.

1. We seek evidence that there *is* a sweetness loss, so the claim we test is that there *is not* a loss. This claim says that the mean loss for the population of all trained testers is $\mu = 0$.

2. If the claim that $\mu = 0$ is true, the sampling distribution of $\bar{x}$ from 10 tasters is Normal with mean $\mu = 0$ and standard deviation

$$\frac{\sigma}{\sqrt{n}} = \frac{1}{\sqrt{10}} = 0.316$$

Figure 15.1 shows this sampling distribution.

3. An outcome $\bar{x}$ that would rarely happen if $\mu = 0$ were true is evidence that μ is not 0. To see if an observed value of $\bar{x}$ would rarely happen, locate it on the distribution in Figure 15.1.

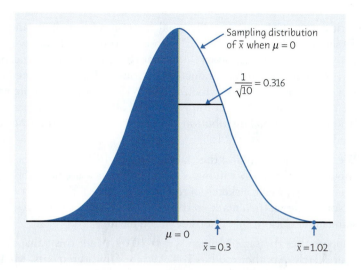

FIGURE 15.1

If the cola does not lose sweetness in storage, the mean score $\bar{x}$ for 10 tasters will have this sampling distribution. The actual result for one cola was $\bar{x} = 0.3$. That could easily happen just by chance. Another cola had $\bar{x} = 1.02$. That's so far out on the Normal curve that it is good evidence that this cola did lose sweetness.

EXAMPLE 15.3 Sweetness loss in colas

For a cola already on the market, 10 tasters had mean loss $\bar{x} = 0.3$. Look at Figure 15.1. It is clear that $\bar{x} = 0.3$ could easily occur just by chance when the population mean is $\mu = 0$. This outcome is not good evidence against the claim that $\mu = 0$.

The taste test for a new cola produced $\bar{x} = 1.02$. That's way out on the Normal curve in Figure 15.1—so far out that *an observed value this large would rarely occur just by chance if the true μ were 0*. This observed value is good evidence that the true μ is in fact greater than 0, that is, that the cola lost sweetness. The manufacturer must reformulate the cola and try again. ■

APPLY YOUR KNOWLEDGE

15.1 Student attitudes. The Survey of Study Habits and Attitudes (SSHA) is a psychological test that measures students' study habits and attitude toward school. Scores range from 0 to 200. The mean score for college students is about 115, and the standard deviation is about 30. A teacher suspects that the mean μ for older students is higher than 115. She gives the SSHA to an SRS of 25 students who are at least 30 years old. Suppose we know that scores in the population of older students are Normally distributed with standard deviation $\sigma = 30$.

(a) We seek evidence *against* the claim that $\mu = 115$. What is the sampling distribution of the mean score $\bar{x}$ of a sample of 25 students if the claim is true? Draw the density curve of this distribution. (Sketch a Normal curve, then mark on the axis the values of the mean and 1, 2, and 3 standard deviations on either side of the mean.)

(b) Suppose that the sample data give $\bar{x} = 118.6$. Mark this point on the axis of your sketch. In fact, the result was $\bar{x} = 125.8$. Mark this point on your sketch. Using your sketch, explain in simple language why one result is good evidence that the mean score of all older students is greater than 115 and why the other outcome is not.

15.2 **Measuring conductivity.** The National Institute of Standards and Technology (NIST) supplies a "standard iron rod" whose electrical conductivity is supposed to be exactly 10.1. Is there reason to think that the true conductivity is not 10.1? To find out, NIST measures the conductivity of one rod 6 times. Repeated measurements of the same thing vary, which is why NIST makes 6 measurements. These measurements are an SRS from the population of all possible measurements. This population has a Normal distribution with mean μ equal to the true conductivity and standard deviation $\sigma = 0.1$.

(a) We seek evidence *against* the claim that $\mu = 10.1$. What is the sampling distribution of the mean $\bar{x}$ in many samples of 6 measurements of one rod if the claim is true? Make a sketch of the Normal curve for this distribution. (Draw a Normal curve, then mark on the axis the values of the mean and 1, 2, and 3 standard deviations on either side of the mean.)

(b) Suppose that the sample mean is $\bar{x} = 10.09$. Mark this value on the axis of your sketch. Another rod has $\bar{x} = 9.95$ for 6 measurements. Mark this value on the axis as well. Explain in simple language why one result is good evidence that the true conductivity differs from 10.1 and why the other result gives no reason to doubt that 10.1 is correct.

STATING HYPOTHESES

A statistical test starts with a careful statement of the claims we want to compare. In Example 15.3, we saw that the taste test data are not plausible if the new cola loses no sweetness. Because the reasoning of tests looks for evidence *against* a claim, we start with the claim we seek evidence against, such as "no loss of sweetness."

NULL AND ALTERNATIVE HYPOTHESES

The claim tested by a statistical test is called the **null hypothesis.** The test is designed to assess the strength of the evidence *against* the null hypothesis. Usually the null hypothesis is a statement of "no effect" or "no difference."

The claim about the population that we are trying to find evidence *for* is the **alternative hypothesis.** The alternative hypothesis is **one-sided** if it states that a parameter is *larger than* or *smaller than* the null hypothesis value. It is **two-sided** if it states that the parameter is *different from* the null value (it could be either smaller or larger).

We abbreviate the null hypothesis as H_0 and the alternative hypothesis as H_a. *Hypotheses always refer to a population, not to a particular outcome. Be sure to state H_0 and H_a in terms of population parameters.*

In Examples 15.2 and 15.3, we are seeking evidence *for* loss in sweetness. The null hypothesis says "no loss" on the average in a large population of tasters. The alternative hypothesis says "there is a loss." So the hypotheses are

$$H_0: \mu = 0$$
$$H_a: \mu > 0$$

The alternative hypothesis is *one-sided* because we are interested only in whether the cola *lost* sweetness.

EXAMPLE 15.4 Studying job satisfaction

Does the job satisfaction of assembly workers differ when their work is machine-paced rather than self-paced? Assign workers either to an assembly line moving at a fixed pace or to a self-paced setting. All subjects work in both settings, in random order. This is a matched pairs design. After two weeks in each work setting, the workers take a test of job satisfaction. The response variable is the difference in satisfaction scores, self-paced minus machine-paced.

The parameter of interest is the mean μ of the differences in scores in the population of all assembly workers. The null hypothesis says that there is no difference between self-paced and machine-paced work, that is,

$$H_0: \mu = 0$$

The authors of the study wanted to know if the two work conditions have different levels of job satisfaction. They did not specify the direction of the difference. The alternative hypothesis is therefore *two-sided*:

$$H_a: \mu \neq 0 \ ■$$

The hypotheses should express the hopes or suspicions you have *before* you see the data. If you do not have a specific direction firmly in mind in advance, use a two-sided alternative.

APPLY YOUR KNOWLEDGE

15.3 Student attitudes. State the null and alternative hypotheses for the study of older students' attitudes described in Exercise 15.1. (Is the alternative hypothesis one-sided or two-sided?)

15.4 Measuring conductivity. State the null and alternative hypotheses for the study of electrical conductivity described in Exercise 15.2. (Is the alternative hypothesis one-sided or two-sided?)

15.5 Grading a teaching assistant. The examinations in a large statistics class are scaled after grading so that the mean score is 75. The professor thinks that one teaching assistant is a poor teacher and suspects that his students have a lower mean score than the class as a whole. The TA's students this semester can be considered a sample from the population of all students in the course, so the professor compares their mean score with 75. State the hypotheses H_0 and H_a.

P-VALUES

The reasoning of a statistical test is that *an outcome that would rarely happen if a claim were true is good evidence that the claim is not true*. The claim we seek evidence against is the null hypothesis H_0. We assess the strength of the evidence by giving a probability that says how rarely an outcome like this would happen if H_0 were true. This probability is called a *P-value*. Statistical tests generally work like this:

> ### TEST STATISTIC AND *P*-VALUE
>
> A **test statistic** calculated from the sample data measures how far the data diverge from what we would expect if the null hypothesis H_0 were true. Large values of the statistic show that the data are not consistent with H_0.
>
> The probability, computed assuming that H_0 is true, that the test statistic would take a value as extreme or more extreme than that actually observed is called the **P-value** of the test. The smaller the P-value, the stronger the evidence against H_0 provided by the data.

Small P-values are evidence against H_0 because they say that the observed result would be unlikely to occur if H_0 were true. Large P-values fail to give evidence against H_0. Statistical software will give you the P-value of a test when you enter your null and alternative hypotheses and your data. So your most important task is to understand what a P-value says.

EXAMPLE 15.5   Sweetening colas: one-sided *P*-value

The study of sweetness loss in Examples 15.2 and 15.3 tests the hypotheses

$$H_0: \mu = 0$$
$$H_a: \mu > 0$$

Because the alternative hypothesis says that $\mu > 0$, values of $\bar{x}$ greater than 0 favor H_a over H_0. The test statistic compares the observed $\bar{x}$ with the hypothesized value $\mu = 0$. For now, let's concentrate on the P-value.

For a cola already on the market, 10 tasters found mean sweetness loss $\bar{x} = 0.3$. For a new cola, the tasters reported $\bar{x} = 1.02$. *The P-value for each test is the probability of getting an $\bar{x}$ this large when the mean sweetness loss is really $\mu = 0$.*

The shaded area in Figure 15.2 shows the P-value when $\bar{x} = 0.3$. The Normal curve is the sampling distribution of $\bar{x}$ when the null hypothesis $H_0: \mu = 0$ is true. A Normal probability calculation (Exercise 15.6) shows that the P-value is $P(\bar{x} \geq 0.3) = 0.1711$.

FIGURE 15.2

The one-sided P-value for the cola with mean sweetness loss $\bar{x} = 0.3$ in Example 15.5.

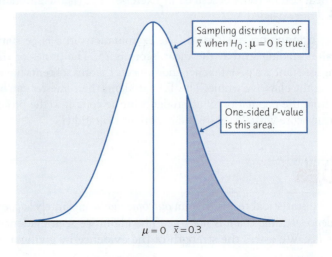

Sampling distribution of $\bar{x}$ when $H_0 : \mu = 0$ is true.

One-sided P-value is this area.

$\mu = 0 \quad \bar{x} = 0.3$

A value as large as $\bar{x} = 0.3$ would appear just by chance in 17% of all samples when $H_0: \mu = 0$ is true. So observing $\bar{x} = 0.3$ is not strong evidence against H_0.

On the other hand, you can calculate that the probability that $\bar{x}$ is 1.02 or larger when in fact $\mu = 0$ is only 0.0006. We would very rarely observe a mean sweetness loss of 1.02 or larger if H_0 were true. This small *P*-value provides strong evidence against H_0 and in favor of the alternative $H_a: \mu > 0$. ■

The alternative hypothesis sets the direction that counts as evidence against H_0. In Example 15.5, only large positive values count because the alternative is one-sided on the high side. If the alternative is two-sided, both directions count.

EXAMPLE 15.6 Job satisfaction: two-sided *P*-value

The study of job satisfaction in Example 15.4 requires that we test

$$H_0: \mu = 0$$
$$H_a: \mu \neq 0$$

Suppose we know that differences in job satisfaction scores (self-paced minus machine-paced) in the population of all workers follow a Normal distribution with standard deviation $\sigma = 60$.

Data from 18 workers give $\bar{x} = 17$. That is, these workers prefer the self-paced environment on the average. Because the alternative is two-sided, the *P*-value is the probability of getting an $\bar{x}$ at least as far from $\mu = 0$ *in either direction* as the observed $\bar{x} = 17$. The shaded areas in Figure 15.3 show this *P*-value. A Normal probability calculation (Exercise 15.7) finds that $P = 0.2302$. ■

The conclusion of Example 15.6 is *not* that H_0 is true. The study looked for evidence against $H_0: \mu = 0$ and failed to find strong evidence. That is all we can say. Tests of significance assess the evidence against H_0. If the evidence is strong, we can confidently reject H_0 in favor of the alternative. *Failing to find evidence against H_0 means only that the data are consistent with H_0, not that we have clear evidence that H_0 is true.*

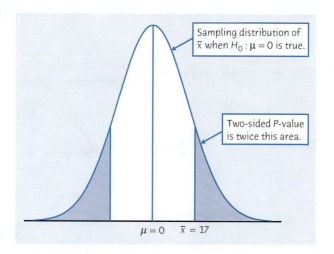

μ = 0   x̄ = 17

Sampling distribution of x̄ when $H_0 : \mu = 0$ is true.

Two-sided *P*-value is twice this area.

FIGURE 15.3

The two-sided *P*-value for sample mean $\bar{x} = 17$ in Example 15.6.

APPLY YOUR KNOWLEDGE

15.6 Sweetening colas: find the *P*-value. The *P*-value for the first cola in Example 15.5 is the probability (taking the null hypothesis $\mu = 0$ to be true) that $\bar{x}$ takes a value at least as large as 0.3.

(a) What is the sampling distribution of $\bar{x}$ when $\mu = 0$? This distribution appears in Figure 15.2.

(b) Do a Normal probability calculation to find the *P*-value. Your result should agree with Example 15.5 up to roundoff error.

15.7 Job satisfaction: find the *P*-value. The *P*-value in Example 15.6 is the probability (taking the null hypothesis $\mu = 0$ to be true) that $\bar{x}$ takes a value at least as far from 0 as 17.

(a) What is the sampling distribution of $\bar{x}$ when $\mu = 0$? This distribution is shown in Figure 15.3.

(b) Do a Normal probability calculation to find the *P*-value. Your result should agree with Example 15.6 up to roundoff error.

TESTS FOR A POPULATION MEAN

We have used tests for hypotheses about the mean μ of a population, under the "simple conditions," to introduce statistical tests. The test compares the sample mean $\bar{x}$ with the claimed population mean stated by the null hypothesis H_0. The *P*-value says how unlikely an $\bar{x}$ this extreme is if H_0 is true. Now we can reduce this test to a rule.

---

z TEST FOR A POPULATION MEAN

Draw an SRS of size n from a Normal population that has unknown mean μ and known standard deviation σ. To **test the null hypothesis that μ has a specified value,**

$$H_0: \mu = \mu_0$$

calculate the **one-sample z test statistic**

$$z = \frac{\bar{x} - \mu_0}{\sigma/\sqrt{n}}$$

In terms of a variable Z having the standard Normal distribution, the *P*-value for a test of H_0 against

$H_a: \mu > \mu_0$ is $P(Z \geq z)$

$H_a: \mu < \mu_0$ is $P(Z \leq z)$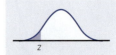

$H_a: \mu \neq \mu_0$ is $2P(Z \geq |z|)$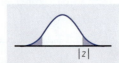

The test statistic z measures how far the observed sample mean $\bar{x}$ deviates from the hypothesized population value μ_0. The measurement is in the standard scale obtained by dividing by the standard deviation of $\bar{x}$. When H_0 is true, z has the standard Normal distribution. The pictures that illustrate the P-value look just like Figures 15.2 and 15.3 except that they are in the standard scale.

In practice, the steps in carrying out a test of significance mirror the overall four-step process for organizing realistic statistical problems.

TESTS OF SIGNIFICANCE: THE FOUR-STEP PROCESS

STATE: What is the practical question that requires a statistical test?

PLAN: Identify the parameter, state null and alternative hypotheses, and choose the type of test that fits your situation.

SOLVE: Carry out the test in three phases:

1. **Check the conditions** for the test you plan to use.

2. Calculate the **test statistic.**

3. Find the **P-value.**

CONCLUDE: Return to the practical question to describe your results in this setting.

EXAMPLE 15.7 Executives' blood pressures

STATE: The National Center for Health Statistics reports that the systolic blood pressure for males 35 to 44 years of age has mean 128 and standard deviation 15. The medical director of a large company looks at the medical records of 72 executives in this age group and finds that the mean systolic blood pressure in this sample is $\bar{x} = 126.07$. Is this evidence that the company's executives have a different mean systolic blood pressure from the general population?

PLAN: The null hypothesis is "no difference" from the national mean $\mu_0 = 128$. The alternative is two-sided because the medical director did not have a particular direction in mind before examining the data. So the hypotheses about the unknown mean μ of the executive population are

$$H_0: \mu = 128$$
$$H_a: \mu \neq 128$$

We know that the one-sample z test is appropriate for these hypotheses under the "simple conditions."

SOLVE: As part of the "simple conditions," suppose we know that executives' systolic blood pressures follow a Normal distribution with standard deviation $\sigma = 15$. Software can now calculate z and P for you. Going ahead by hand, the **test statistic** is

$$z = \frac{\bar{x} - \mu_0}{\sigma/\sqrt{n}} = \frac{126.07 - 128}{15/\sqrt{72}}$$
$$= -1.09$$

To help find the **P-value,** sketch the standard Normal curve and mark on it the observed value of z. Figure 15.4 shows that the P-value is the probability that a standard Normal variable Z takes a value at least 1.09 away from zero. From Table A or software, this probability is

$$P = 2P(Z < -1.09) = (2)(0.1379) = 0.2758$$

CONCLUDE: More than 27% of the time, an SRS of size 72 from the general male population would have a mean systolic blood pressure at least as far from 128 as that of the executive sample. The observed $\bar{x} = 126.07$ is therefore not good evidence that executives differ from other men. ▪

FIGURE 15.4

The P-value for the two-sided test in Example 15.7. The observed value of the test statistic is $z = -1.09$.

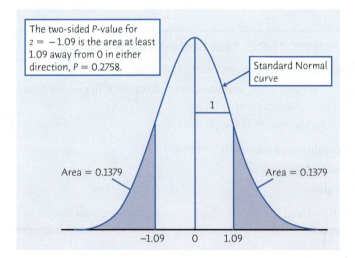

The two-sided P-value for $z = -1.09$ is the area at least 1.09 away from 0 in either direction, $P = 0.2758$.

Standard Normal curve

Area = 0.1379   Area = 0.1379

−1.09   0   1.09

  In this chapter we are acting as if the "simple conditions" stated on page 286 are true. In practice, you must verify these conditions.

1. **SRS:** The most important condition is that the 72 executives in the sample are an SRS from the population of all middle-aged male executives in the company. We should check this requirement by asking how the data were produced. If medical records are available only for executives with recent medical problems, for example, the data are of little value for our purpose because of the obvious health bias. It turns out that all executives are given a free annual medical exam, and that the medical director selected 72 exam results at random.

2. **Normal distribution:** We should also examine the distribution of the 72 observations to look for signs that the population distribution is not Normal.

3. **Known σ:** It really is unrealistic to suppose that we know that $\sigma = 15$. We will see in Chapter 18 that it is easy to do away with the need to know σ.

APPLY YOUR KNOWLEDGE

15.8 The z statistic. Published reports of research work are terse. They often report just a test statistic and P-value. For example, the conclusion of Example 15.7 might be stated as "($z = -1.09, P = 0.2758$)." Find the values of the one-sample z statistic needed to complete these conclusions:

(a) For the first cola in Example 15.5, $z = ?, P = 0.1714$.

(b) For the second cola in Example 15.5, $z = ?, P = 0.0006$.

(c) For Example 15.6, $z = ?, P = 0.2293$.

15.9   Measuring conductivity. Here are 6 measurements of the electrical conductivity of an iron rod:

$$10.08 \quad 9.89 \quad 10.05 \quad 10.16 \quad 10.21 \quad 10.11$$

The iron rod is supposed to have conductivity 10.1. Do the measurements give good evidence that the true conductivity is not 10.1?

The 6 measurements are an SRS from the population of all results we would get if we kept measuring conductivity forever. This population has a Normal distribution with mean equal to the true conductivity of the rod and standard deviation 0.1. Use this information to carry out a test, following the four-step process as illustrated in Example 15.7. CONDUCTIVITY

15.10   Bad weather, bad tip? People tend to be more generous after receiving good news. Are they less generous after receiving bad news? The average tip left by adult Americans is 20%. Give 20 patrons of a restaurant a message on their bill warning them that tomorrow's weather will be bad and record the tip percent they leave. Here are the tips as a percent of the total bill:[1]

18.0	19.1	19.2	18.8	18.4	19.0	18.5	16.1	16.8	18.2
14.0	17.0	13.6	17.5	20.0	20.2	18.8	18.0	23.2	19.4

Suppose that tip percents are Normal with $\sigma = 2$. Is there good evidence that the mean tip percent is less than 20? Follow the four-step process as illustrated in Example 15.7. TIPPING3

STATISTICAL SIGNIFICANCE

In Examples 15.5 and 15.6, we decided that P-value $P = 0.0006$ was strong evidence against the null hypothesis and that P-values $P = 0.1711$ and $P = 0.2302$ did not give convincing evidence. There is no rule for how small a P-value we should require to reject H_0—it's a matter of judgment and depends on the specific circumstances.

Nonetheless, we can compare a P-value with some fixed values that are in common use as standards for evidence against H_0. The most common fixed values are 0.05 and 0.01. If $P \leq 0.05$, there is no more than 1 chance in 20 that a sample would give evidence this strong just by chance when H_0 is actually true. If $P \leq 0.01$, we have a result that in the long run would happen no more than once per 100 samples if H_0 were true. These fixed standards for P-values are called **significance levels.** We use α, the Greek letter alpha, to stand for a significance level.

significance level

STATISTICAL SIGNIFICANCE

If the P-value is as small or smaller than α, we say that the data are **statistically significant at level α.**

"Significant" in the statistical sense does not mean "important." It means simply "not likely to happen just by chance." The significance level α makes "not likely" more exact. Significance at level 0.01 is often expressed by writing "The results were significant ($P < 0.01$)." Here P stands for the P-value. The actual P-value is more informative than a statement of significance because it allows us to assess significance at any level we choose. For example, a result with $P = 0.03$ is significant at the $\alpha = 0.05$ level but is not significant at the $\alpha = 0.01$ level.

In practice, you should decide in advance how strong the evidence must be for you to reject the null hypothesis. This means that the significance level α should be specified prior to collecting data and any analysis. To reinforce this, scientific journals require researchers to demonstrate statistical significance at the $\alpha = 0.05$ level or the $\alpha = 0.01$ level.

Before technology that gives P-values quickly and accurately became common, *tables of critical values* were used to assess significance. Critical values for the z statistic appear in the z^* row at the bottom of Table C, the same table we used for confidence intervals. At the top of the table, you see the confidence level C for each z^*. At the bottom of the table, you see both the one-sided and two-sided P-values for each z^*. Values of a test statistic z that are farther out than a z^* (in the direction given by the alternative hypothesis) are significant at the level that matches z^*. To assess significance at the $\alpha = 0.05$ level, for example, just compare your z with the z^* for $P = 0.05$. Because P-values are more informative than just "significant or not," it is better to use the table to get an approximate P-value.

SIGNIFICANCE FROM A TABLE OF CRITICAL VALUES

To find the approximate P-value for any z statistic, compare z (ignoring its sign) with the critical values in the z^* row of Table C. If z falls between two values of z^*, the P-value falls between the two corresponding values of P in the "One-sided P" or the "Two-sided P" row of Table C.

EXAMPLE 15.8   Is it significant?

z^*	2.054	2.326
One-sided P	.02	.01

The z statistic for a one-sided test is $z = 2.13$. How significant is this result? Compare $z = 2.13$ with the z^* row in Table C. It lies between $z^* = 2.054$ and $z^* = 2.326$. So the P-value lies between the corresponding entries in the "One-sided P" row, which are $P = 0.02$ and $P = 0.01$. This z *is* significant at the $\alpha = 0.02$ level and *is not* significant at the $\alpha = 0.01$ level.

Figure 15.5 illustrates the situation. The shaded area under the Normal curve is the P-value for $z = 2.13$. You can see that P falls between the areas to the right of the two critical values, for $P = 0.02$ and $P = 0.01$.

The z statistic in Example 15.7 is $z = -1.09$. The alternative hypothesis is two-sided. Compare $z = -1.09$ (ignoring the minus sign) with the z^* row in Table C. It lies between $z^* = 1.036$ and $z^* = 1.282$. So the P-value lies between the matching entries in the "Two-sided P" row, $P = 0.30$ and $P = 0.20$. This is enough to conclude that the data do not provide good evidence against the null hypothesis. ■

z^*	1.036	1.282
Two-sided P	.30	.20

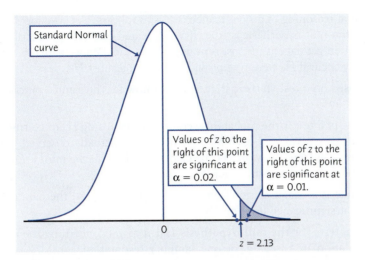

FIGURE 15.5

Is it significant? The test statistic value $z = 2.13$ falls between the critical values required for significance at the $\alpha = 0.02$ and $\alpha = 0.01$ levels. So the test is significant at $\alpha = 0.02$ and *is not* significant at $\alpha = 0.01$.

APPLY YOUR KNOWLEDGE

15.11 Significance from a table. A test of H_0: $\mu = 0$ against H_a: $\mu > 0$ has test statistic $z = 1.876$. Is this test significant at the 5% level ($\alpha = 0.05$)? Is it significant at the 1% level ($\alpha = 0.01$)?

15.12 Significance from a table. A test of H_0: $\mu = 0$ against H_a: $\mu \neq 0$ has test statistic $z = 1.876$. Is this test significant at the 5% level ($\alpha = 0.05$)? Is it significant at the 1% level ($\alpha = 0.01$)?

15.13 Testing software. You have computer software that claims to generate observations from a standard Normal distribution. If this is true, the numbers generated come from a population with $\mu = 0$ and $\sigma = 1$. A command to generate 100 observations gives outcomes with mean $\bar{x} = -0.2213$. Assume that the population σ remains fixed. We want to test

$$H_0: \mu = 0$$
$$H_a: \mu \neq 0$$

(a) Calculate the value of the z test statistic.

(b) Use Table C: is z significant at the 5% level ($\alpha = 0.05$)?

(c) Use Table C: is z significant at the 1% level ($\alpha = 0.01$)?

(d) Between which two Normal critical values z^* in the bottom row of Table C does z lie? Between what two numbers does the P-value lie? Does the test give good evidence against the null hypothesis?

▌ CHAPTER 15 SUMMARY

CHAPTER SPECIFICS

■ A **test of significance** assesses the evidence provided by data against a **null hypothesis** H_0 in favor of an **alternative hypothesis** H_a.

■ Hypotheses are always stated in terms of population parameters. Usually H_0 is a statement that no effect is present, and H_a says that a parameter differs from its null value in a specific direction (**one-sided alternative**) or in either direction (**two-sided alternative**).

- The essential reasoning of a significance test is as follows. Suppose for the sake of argument that the null hypothesis is true. If we repeated our data production many times, would we often get data as inconsistent with H_0 as the data we actually have? Data that would rarely occur if H_0 were true provide evidence against H_0.

- A test is based on a **test statistic** that measures how far the sample outcome is from the value stated by H_0.

- The **P-value** of a test is the probability, computed supposing H_0 to be true, that the test statistic will take a value at least as extreme as that actually observed. Small P-values indicate strong evidence against H_0. To calculate a P-value we must know the sampling distribution of the test statistic when H_0 is true.

- If the P-value is as small or smaller than a specified value α, the data are **statistically significant** at **significance level** α.

- **Significance tests for the null hypothesis H_0: $\mu = \mu_0$** concerning the unknown mean μ of a population are based on the **one-sample z test statistic**

$$z = \frac{\bar{x} - \mu_0}{\sigma/\sqrt{n}}$$

- The z test assumes an SRS of size n from a Normal population with known population standard deviation σ. P-values can be obtained either with computations from the standard Normal distribution or by using technology (software).

LINK IT

In this chapter we discuss tests of significance, the second type of statistical inference. The mathematics of probability, in particular the sampling distributions discussed in Chapter 11, provides the formal basis for a test of significance. The sampling distribution allows us to assess "probabilistically" the strength of evidence against a null hypothesis, either through a level of significance or a P-value. The goal of hypothesis testing, which is used to assess the evidence provided by data about some claim concerning a population, is different from the goal of confidence interval estimation, which is used to estimate a population parameter.

Although we apply the reasoning of tests of significance for the mean of a population that has a Normal distribution in a simple and artificial setting (we assume that we know the population standard deviation), we will use the same logic in future chapters to construct tests of significance for population parameters in more realistic settings.

CHECK YOUR SKILLS

15.14 A laboratory scale is known to have a standard deviation of $\sigma = 0.001$ gram in repeated weighings. Scale readings in repeated weighings are Normally distributed, with mean equal to the true weight of the specimen. Three weighings of a specimen on this scale give 3.414, 3.418, and 3.416 grams. The z statistic for testing H_0: $\mu = 3.410$ based on these 3 measurements is

    (a) $z = 0.006$.   (b) $z = 6$.   (c) $z = 10.392$.

15.15 Experiments on learning in animals sometimes measure how long it takes mice to find their way through a maze. The mean time is 19 seconds for one particular maze. A researcher thinks that a loud noise will cause the mice to complete the maze faster. She measures how long each of 10 mice takes with a noise as stimulus. The sample mean is $\bar{x} = 16.5$ seconds. The null hypothesis for the significance test is

    (a) H_0: $\mu = 19$.   (b) H_0: $\mu = 16.5$.   (c) H_0: $\mu < 19$.

15.16 The alternative hypothesis for the test in Exercise 15.15 is

(a) $H_a: \mu \neq 19$. (b) $H_a: \mu < 19$. (c) $H_a: \mu = 16.5$.

15.17 You read an article about an experiment in which the researcher conducted a test of significance. The article tells you that the P-value is $P = 0.19$. This means that

(a) the probability that the null hypothesis is true is 0.19.

(b) the value of the test statistic is not particularly large.

(c) neither of the above.

15.18 You use software to carry out a test of significance. The program tells you that the P-value is $P = 0.031$. This result is

(a) not significant at either $\alpha = 0.05$ or $\alpha = 0.01$.

(b) significant at $\alpha = 0.05$ but not at $\alpha = 0.01$.

(c) significant at both $\alpha = 0.05$ and $\alpha = 0.01$.

15.19 The gas mileage for a particular model car is known to have a standard deviation of $\sigma = 1.0$ miles per gallon in repeated tests in a controlled laboratory environment at a fixed speed. For a fixed speed, gas mileages in repeated tests are Normally distributed. Tests on three cars of this model at 35 miles per hour give gas mileages of 29.3, 29.9, and 29.8 miles per gallon. The z statistic for testing $H_0: \mu = 30$ miles per gallon based on these three measurements is

(a) $z = 0.286$. (b) $z = -0.5773$. (c) $z = -0.286$.

CHAPTER 15 EXERCISES

15.20 Women's heights. The average height of 18-year-old American women is 64.2 inches. Your high school won the women's state basketball championship this year, and you wonder whether the mean height of this year's female graduates from your high school is greater than the national average. You measure an SRS of 78 female graduates and find that $\bar{x} = 64.1$ inches. What are your null and alternative hypotheses?

15.21 Stating hypotheses. In planning a study of the birth weights of babies whose mothers did not see a doctor before delivery, a researcher states the hypotheses as

$$H_0: \bar{x} = 1000 \text{ grams}$$
$$H_a: \bar{x} < 1000 \text{ grams}$$

What's wrong with this?

In all exercises that call for P-values, give the actual value if you use software; otherwise, use Table C to give values between which P must fall.

15.22 Student study times. Exercise 14.16 (page 297) describes a class survey in which students claimed to study an average of $\bar{x} = 118$ minutes on a typical weeknight. Regard these students as an SRS from the population of all first-year students at this university. Does the survey give good evidence that students claim to study less than 2 hours per night on the average?

(a) State null and alternative hypotheses in terms of the mean study time in minutes for the population.

(b) What is the value of the test statistic z?

(c) What is the P-value of the test? Can you conclude that students do claim to study more than 2 hours per weeknight on the average?

15.23 I want more muscle. If young men thought that their own level of muscle was about what women prefer, the mean "muscle gap" in the study described in Exercise 14.17 (page 297) would be 0. We suspect (before seeing the data) that young men think women prefer more muscle than the young men themselves have.

(a) State null and alternative hypotheses for testing this suspicion.

(b) What is the value of the test statistic z?

(c) You can tell just from the value of z that the evidence in favor of the alternative is very strong (that is, the P-value is very small). Explain why this is true.

15.24 Hotel managers' personalities. Successful hotel managers must have personality characteristics often thought of as feminine (such as "compassionate") as well as those often thought of as masculine (such as "forceful"). The Bem Sex-Role Inventory (BSRI) is a personality test that gives separate ratings for female and male stereotypes, both on a scale of 1 to 7. A sample of 148 male general managers of three-star and four-star hotels had mean BSRI femininity score $\bar{y} = 5.29$.[2] The mean score for the general male population is $\mu = 5.19$. Do hotel managers, on the average, differ significantly in femininity score from men in general? Assume that the standard deviation of scores in the population of all male hotel managers is the same as the $\sigma = 0.78$ for the adult male population.

(a) State null and alternative hypotheses in terms of the mean femininity score μ for male hotel managers.

(b) Find the z test statistic.

(c) What is the P-value for your z? What do you conclude about male hotel managers?

15.25 Is this what *P* means? When asked to explain the meaning of "the *P*-value was *P* = 0.03," a student says, "This means there is only probability 0.03 that the null hypothesis is true." Explain what *P* = 0.03 really means in a way that makes it clear that the student's explanation is wrong.

15.26 Pig skulls show that you were rich. Every society has its own marks of wealth and prestige. In ancient China, it appears that owning pigs was such a mark. Evidence comes from examining burial sites. The skulls of sacrificed pigs tend to appear along with expensive ornaments, which suggests that the pigs, like the ornaments, signal the wealth and prestige of the person buried. A study of burials from around 3500 B.C. concluded that "there are striking differences in grave goods between burials with pig skulls and burials without them. . . . A test indicates that the two samples of total artifacts are significantly different at the 0.01 level."[3] Explain clearly why "significantly different at the 0.01 level" gives good reason to think that there really is a systematic difference between burials that contain pig skulls and those that lack them.

15.27 Alleviating test anxiety. Research suggests that pressure to perform well can reduce performance on exams. Are there effective strategies to deal with pressure? In an experiment, researchers had students take a test on mathematical skills. The same students were asked to take a second test on the same skills, but now each student was paired with a partner and only if both improved their scores would they receive a monetary reward for participating in the experiment. They were also told that their performance would be videotaped and watched by teachers and students. To help them cope with the pressure, ten minutes before the second exam they were asked to write as candidly as possible about their thoughts and feelings regarding the exam. "Students who expressed their thoughts before the high-pressure test showed a significant 5% math accuracy improvement from the pretest to posttest" (*P* < 0.03).[4] A colleague who knows no statistics says that an increase of 5% isn't a lot—maybe it's just an accident due to natural variation among the students. Explain in simple language how "*P* < 0.03" answers this objection.

15.28 Treating Parkinson's disease. A randomized comparative experiment compared the effects of two types of deep-brain stimulation (pallidal stimulation and subthalamic stimulation) on change in motor function, as blindly assessed on the Unified Parkinson's Disease Rating Scale, part III (UPDRS-III). The abstract of the study said: "Mean changes in the primary outcome did not differ significantly between the two study groups (*P* = 0.50)."[5] The *P*-value refers to a null hypothesis of "no change" in measurements between pallidal stimulation and subthalamic stimulation. Explain clearly why this value provides no evidence of change.

15.29 5% versus 1%. Sketch the standard Normal curve for the *z* test statistic and mark off areas under the curve to show why a value of *z* that is significant at the 1% level in a one-sided test is always significant at the 5% level. If *z* is significant at the 5% level, what can you say about its significance at the 1% level?

15.30 The wrong alternative. A graduate student is comparing final-exam test scores of male and female students in an introductory physics class. She starts with no expectations as to which sex will score more highly. After seeing that men did better than women on the first quiz, she tests a one-sided alternative about the mean final-exam scores,

$$H_0: \mu_M = \mu_F$$
$$H_a: \mu_M > \mu_F$$

She finds *z* = 1.9 with one-sided *P*-value *P* = 0.0287.

(a) Explain why she should have used the two-sided alternative hypothesis.

(b) What is the correct *P*-value for *z* = 1.9?

15.31 The wrong *P*. The report of a study of seat belt use by drivers says, "Hispanic drivers were not significantly more likely than White/non-Hispanic drivers to overreport safety belt use (27.4 vs. 21.1%, respectively; *z* = 1.33, *P* > 1.0)."[6] How do you know that the *P*-value given is incorrect? What is the correct one-sided *P*-value for test statistic *z* = 1.33?

*Exercises 15.32 to 15.35 ask you to answer questions from data. Assume that the "simple conditions" hold in each case. The exercise statements give you the **State** step of the four-step process. In your work, follow the **Plan, Solve,** and **Conclude** steps, illustrated in Example 15.7 for a test of significance.*

15.32 Pulling wood apart. How heavy a load (pounds) is needed to pull apart pieces of Douglas fir 4 inches long and 1.5 inches square? Here are data from students doing a laboratory exercise:

33,190	31,860	32,590	26,520	33,280
32,320	33,020	32,030	30,460	32,700
23,040	30,930	32,720	33,650	32,340
24,050	30,170	31,300	28,730	31,920

We are willing to regard the wood pieces prepared for the lab session as an SRS of all similar pieces of Douglas fir. Engineers also commonly assume that characteristics of materials vary Normally. Suppose that the strength of pieces of wood like these follows a Normal distribution with standard deviation 3000 pounds.

(a) Is there significant evidence at the $\alpha = 0.10$ level against the hypothesis that the mean is 32,500 pounds for the two-sided alternative?

(b) Is there significant evidence at the $\alpha = 0.10$ level against the hypothesis that the mean is 31,500 pounds for the two-sided alternative? WOOD

15.33 Bone loss by nursing mothers. As discussed in Exercise 14.21 (page 298), breast-feeding mothers secrete calcium into their milk. Some of the calcium may come from their bones, so mothers may lose bone mineral. Researchers measured the percent change in mineral content of the spines of 47 mothers during three months of breast-feeding.[7] Here are the data:

−4.7	−2.5	−4.9	−2.7	−0.8	−5.3	−8.3	−2.1	−6.8	−4.3
2.2	−7.8	−3.1	−1.0	−6.5	−1.8	−5.2	−5.7	−7.0	−2.2
−6.5	−1.0	−3.0	−3.6	−5.2	−2.0	−2.1	−5.6	−4.4	−3.3
−4.0	−4.9	−4.7	−3.8	−5.9	−2.5	−0.3	−6.2	−6.8	1.7
0.3	−2.3	0.4	−5.3	0.2	−2.2	−5.1			

The researchers are willing to consider these 47 women as an SRS from the population of all nursing mothers. Suppose that the percent change in this population has a Normal distribution with standard deviation $\sigma = 2.5\%$. Do these data give good evidence that, on the average, nursing mothers lose bone mineral? BONELOSS

15.34 This wine stinks. Sulfur compounds cause "off-odors" in wine, so winemakers want to know the odor threshold, the lowest concentration of a compound that the human nose can detect. The odor threshold for dimethyl sulfide (DMS) in trained wine tasters is about 25 micrograms per liter of wine (μg/l). The untrained noses of consumers may be less sensitive, however. Here are the DMS odor thresholds for 10 untrained students:

$$30 \quad 30 \quad 42 \quad 35 \quad 22 \quad 33 \quad 31 \quad 29 \quad 19 \quad 23$$

Assume that the odor threshold for untrained noses is Normally distributed with $\sigma = 7$ μg/l. Is there evidence that the mean threshold for untrained tasters is greater than 25 μg/l? WINE

15.35 Eye grease. Athletes performing in bright sunlight often smear black eye grease under their eyes to reduce glare. Does eye grease work? In one study, 16 student subjects took a test of sensitivity to contrast after 3 hours facing into bright sun, both with and without eye grease. This is a matched pairs design. Here are the differences in sensitivity, with eye grease minus without eye grease:[8]

0.07	0.64	−0.12	−0.05	−0.18	0.14	−0.16	0.03
0.05	0.02	0.43	0.24	−0.11	0.28	0.05	0.29

We want to know whether eye grease increases sensitivity on the average.

(a) What are the null and alternative hypotheses? Say in words what mean μ your hypotheses concern.

(b) Suppose that the subjects are an SRS of all young people with normal vision, that contrast differences follow a Normal distribution in this population, and that the standard deviation of differences is $\sigma = 0.22$. Carry out a test of significance. EYEGREASE

15.36 Tests from confidence intervals. A confidence interval for the population mean μ tells us which values of μ are plausible (those inside the interval) and which values are not plausible (those outside the interval) at the chosen level of confidence. You can use this idea to carry out a test of any null hypothesis $H_0: \mu = \mu_0$ starting with a confidence interval: *reject H_0 if μ_0 is outside the interval and fail to reject if μ_0 is inside the interval.*

The alternative hypothesis is always two-sided, $H_a: \mu \neq \mu_0$, because the confidence interval extends in both directions from $\bar{x}$. A 95% confidence interval leads to a test at the 5% significance level because the interval is wrong 5% of the time. In general, confidence level C leads to a test at significance level $\alpha = 1 - C$.

(a) In Example 15.7, a medical director found mean blood pressure $\bar{x} = 126.07$ for an SRS of 72 executives. The standard deviation of the blood pressures of all executives is $\sigma = 15$. Give a 90% confidence interval for the mean blood pressure μ of all executives.

(b) The hypothesized value $\mu_0 = 128$ falls *inside* this confidence interval. Carry out the z test for $H_0: \mu = 128$ against the two-sided alternative. Show that the test is *not significant* at the 10% level.

(c) The hypothesized value $\mu_0 = 129$ falls *outside* this confidence interval. Carry out the z test for $H_0: \mu = 129$ against the two-sided alternative. Show that the test *is significant* at the 10% level.

15.37 Tests from confidence intervals. A 95% confidence interval for a population mean is 30.7 ± 3.2. Use the method described in the previous exercise to answer these questions.

(a) With a two-sided alternative, can you reject the null hypothesis that $\mu = 33$ at the 5% ($\alpha = 0.05$) significance level? Why?

(b) With a two-sided alternative, can you reject the null hypothesis that $\mu = 34$ at the 5% significance level? Why?

EXPLORING THE WEB

15.38 Significance in journals. Choose a major journal in your field of study. Use a Web search engine to find its Web site—just search on the journal's name. Find a paper that uses a phrase like "significant ($P = 0.01$)" and summarize the findings in the paper.

15.39 A statistics glossary. An editorial was published in the *Journal of the National Cancer Institute*, Vol. 101, No. 23 (December 2, 2009), that announced some online resources for journalists, including a statistics glossary. The glossary can be found at www.oxfordjournals. org/our_journals/jnc/resource/statistics%20glossary.pdf. Read the definition of a *P*-value. Is this an accurate definition? Explain your answer.

Alex Segre/Alamy

Inference in Practice

To this point, we have met just two procedures for statistical inference. Both concern inference about the mean μ of a population when the "simple conditions" (page 286) are true: the data are an SRS, the population has a Normal distribution, and we know the standard deviation σ of the population. Under these conditions, a confidence interval for the mean μ is

$$\bar{x} \pm z^* \frac{\sigma}{\sqrt{n}}$$

To test a hypothesis $H_0: \mu = \mu_0$ we use the one-sample z statistic:

$$z = \frac{\bar{x} - \mu_0}{\sigma/\sqrt{n}}$$

We call these **z procedures** because they both start with the one-sample z statistic and use the standard Normal distribution.

This chapter expands our discussion of confidence intervals and tests, still using the z procedures as examples. In later chapters we will modify these procedures for inference about a population mean to make them useful in practice. We will also introduce procedures for confidence intervals and tests

z procedures

317

in most of the settings we met in learning to explore data. The understanding needed to use statistical inference effectively is the same, no matter how elaborate the details of the procedure are.

CONDITIONS FOR INFERENCE IN PRACTICE

 Any confidence interval or significance test can be trusted only under specific conditions. It's up to you to understand these conditions and judge whether they fit your problem. With that in mind, let's look back at the "simple conditions" for the z procedures.

The final "simple condition," that we know the standard deviation σ of the population, is rarely satisfied in practice. The z procedures are therefore of little practical use. Fortunately, it's easy to remove the "known σ" condition. Chapter 18 shows how. The first two "simple conditions" (SRS, Normal population) are harder to escape. In fact, they represent the kinds of conditions needed if we are to trust almost any statistical inference. As you plan inference, you should always ask, "Where did the data come from?" and you must often also ask, "What is the shape of the population distribution?"

Where did the data come from? *The most important requirement for any inference procedure is that the data come from a process to which the laws of probability apply.* Inference is most reliable when the data come from a random sample or a randomized comparative experiment. Random samples use chance to choose respondents. Randomized comparative experiments use chance to assign subjects to treatments. The deliberate use of chance ensures that the laws of probability apply to the outcomes, and this in turn ensures that statistical inference makes sense.

> **WHERE THE DATA COME FROM MATTERS**
>
> When you use statistical inference, you are acting as if your data are a random sample or come from a randomized comparative experiment.

If your data don't come from a random sample or a randomized comparative experiment, your conclusions may be challenged. To answer the challenge, you must usually rely on subject-matter knowledge, not on statistics. It is common to apply statistical inference to data that are not produced by random selection. When you see such a study, ask whether the data can be trusted as a basis for the conclusions of the study.

EXAMPLE 16.1 The psychologist and the sociologist

A psychologist is interested in how our visual perception can be fooled by optical illusions. Her subjects are students in Psychology 101 at her university. Most psychologists would agree that it's safe to treat the students as an SRS of all people with normal vision. There is nothing special about being a student that changes visual perception.

A sociologist at the same university uses students in Sociology 101 to examine attitudes toward poor people and antipoverty programs. Students as a group are younger than the adult population as a whole. Even among young people, students as a group come from more prosperous and better-educated homes. Even among students, this university isn't typical of all campuses. Even on this campus, students in a sociology course may have opinions that are quite different from those of engineering students. The sociologist can't reasonably act as if these students are a random sample from any interesting population. ■

Our first examples of inference, using the z procedures, act as if the data are an SRS from the population of interest. Let's look back at the examples in Chapters 14 and 15.

EXAMPLE 16.2 Is it really an SRS?

The NHANES survey that produced the BMI data for Example 14.1 used a complex multistage sample design, so it's a bit oversimplified to treat the BMI data as coming from an SRS from the population of young women.[1] Although the overall effect of the NHANES sample is close to an SRS, professional statisticians would use more complex inference procedures to match the more complex design of the sample.

The 20 patrons in the tipping study in Example 14.3 were chosen from those eating at a particular restaurant to receive one of several treatments being compared in a randomized comparative experiment. Recall that each treatment group in a completely randomized experiment is an SRS of the available subjects. Researchers sometimes act as if the available subjects are an SRS from some population if there is nothing special about where the subjects came from. In some cases, researchers collect demographic data on subjects to help justify the assumption that the subjects are a representative sample from some population. We are willing to regard the subjects as an SRS from the population of patrons of this particular restaurant, but perhaps this needs to be explored further.

The cola taste test in Example 15.2 uses scores from 10 tasters. All were examined to be sure that they have no medical condition that interferes with normal taste and then carefully trained to score sweetness using a set of standard drinks. We are willing to take their scores as an SRS from the population of trained tasters.

The medical director who examined executives' blood pressures in Example 15.7 actually chose an SRS from the medical records of all executives in this company. ■

These examples are typical. One is an actual SRS, two are situations in which common practice is to act as if the sample were an SRS, and in the remaining example procedures that assume an SRS are used for a quick analysis of data from a more complex random sample. *There is no simple rule for deciding when you can act as if a sample is an SRS. Pay attention to these cautions:*

■ *Practical problems such as nonresponse in samples or dropouts from an experiment can hinder inference even from a well-designed study.* The NHANES survey has about an 80% response rate. This is much higher than opinion polls and most other national surveys, so by realistic standards NHANES data are quite trustworthy. (NHANES uses advanced methods to try to correct for nonresponse, but these methods work best when response is high to start with.)

■ *Different methods are needed for different designs.* The z procedures aren't correct for random sampling designs more complex than an SRS. Later chapters give methods for some other designs, but we won't discuss inference for really complex designs like that used by NHANES. Always be sure that you (or your statistical consultant) know how to carry out the inference your design calls for.

■ *There is no cure for fundamental flaws like voluntary response surveys or uncontrolled experiments.* Look back at the bad examples in Chapters 8 and 9 and steel yourself to just ignore data from such studies.

What is the shape of the population distribution? Most statistical inference procedures require some conditions on the shape of the population distribution. Many of the most basic methods of inference are designed for Normal populations. That's the case for the z procedures and also for the more practical procedures for inference about means that we will meet in Chapters 18 and 19. Fortunately, this condition is less essential than where the data come from.

This is true because the z procedures and many other procedures designed for Normal distributions are based on Normality of the sample mean $\bar{x}$, not Normality of individual observations. The central limit theorem tells us that $\bar{x}$ is more Normal than the individual observations and that $\bar{x}$ becomes more Normal as the size of the sample increases. In practice, the z procedures are reasonably accurate for any roughly symmetric distribution for samples of even moderate size. If the sample is large, $\bar{x}$ will be close to Normal even if individual measurements are strongly skewed, as Figures 11.3 (page 244) and 11.4 (page 245) illustrate. Later chapters give practical guidelines for specific inference procedures.

There is one important exception to the principle that the shape of the population is less critical than how the data were produced. Outliers can distort the results of inference. *Any inference procedure based on sample statistics like the sample mean $\bar{x}$ that are not resistant to outliers can be strongly influenced by a few extreme observations.*

How can we decide if the population distribution is roughly Normal? Sometimes *experience with similar data* suggests that our data are likely to come from a roughly Normal distribution, or not. For example, heights of people of the same sex and similar ages are close to Normal, but weights are not. Always explore your data before doing inference. When the data are chosen at random from a population, the shape of the data distribution mirrors the shape of the population distribution. Make a stemplot or histogram of your data and look to see whether the shape is roughly Normal. Remember that small samples have a lot of chance variation, so that Normality is hard to judge from just a few observations. Always look for outliers and try to correct them or justify their removal before performing the z procedures or other inference based on statistics like $\bar{x}$ that are not resistant.

When outliers are present or the data suggest that the population is strongly non-Normal, consider alternative methods that don't require Normality and are not sensitive to outliers. Some of these methods appear in Chapter 26 (available online and on the text CD).

APPLY YOUR KNOWLEDGE

16.1 Rate the lecture. A professor is interested in how the 500 students in his class will rate today's lecture. He selects the first 20 students on his class list, reads the names at the beginning of the lecture, and asks them to go online to the course Web site and rate the lecture on a scale of 0 to 5. Which of the following is the most important reason why a confidence interval for the mean rating by all his students based on these data is of little use? Comment briefly on each reason to explain your answer.

(a) The number of students selected is small, so the margin of error will be large.

(b) Most of the students selected will not respond.

(c) The students selected can't be considered a random sample from the population of all students in the course.

16.2 Running red lights. A survey of licensed drivers inquired about running red lights. One question asked, "Of every ten motorists who run a red light, about how many do you think will be caught?" The mean result for 880 respondents was $\bar{x} = 1.92$ and the standard deviation was $s = 1.83$.[2] For this large sample, s will be close to the population standard deviation σ, so suppose we know that $\sigma = 1.83$.

(a) Give a 95% confidence interval for the mean opinion in the population of all licensed drivers.

(b) The distribution of responses is skewed to the right rather than Normal. This will not strongly affect the z confidence interval for this sample. Why not?

(c) The 880 respondents are an SRS from completed calls among 45,956 calls to randomly chosen residential telephone numbers listed in telephone directories. Only 5029 of the calls were completed. This information gives two reasons to suspect that the sample may not represent all licensed drivers. What are these reasons?

Ilene MacDonald/Alamy

16.3 Sampling shoppers. A marketing consultant observes 50 consecutive shoppers at a department store the Friday after Thanksgiving, recording how much each shopper spends in the store. Suggest some reasons why it may be risky to act as if 50 consecutive shoppers at this particular time are an SRS of all shoppers at this store.

CAUTIONS ABOUT CONFIDENCE INTERVALS

The most important caution about confidence intervals in general is a consequence of the use of a sampling distribution. A sampling distribution shows how a statistic such as $\bar{x}$ varies in repeated random sampling. This variation causes *random sampling error* because the statistic misses the true parameter by a random amount. No other source of variation or bias in the sample data influences the sampling distribution. So *the margin of error in a confidence interval ignores everything except the sample-to-sample variation due to choosing the sample randomly*.

THE MARGIN OF ERROR DOESN'T COVER ALL ERRORS

The margin of error in a confidence interval covers only random sampling errors.

Practical difficulties such as undercoverage and nonresponse are often more serious than random sampling error. The margin of error does not take such difficulties into account.

Recall from Chapter 8 that national opinion polls often have response rates less than 50% and that even small changes in the wording of questions can strongly influence results. In such cases, the announced margin of error is probably unrealistically small. And of course there is no way to assign a meaningful margin of error to results from voluntary response or convenience samples, because there is no random selection. Look carefully at the details of a study before you trust a confidence interval.

APPLY YOUR KNOWLEDGE

16.4   What's your weight. A Gallup Poll asked a national random sample of 501 adult women to state their current weight. The mean weight in the sample was $\bar{x} = 159$. We will treat these data as an SRS from a Normally distributed population with standard deviation $\sigma = 35$.

  (a) Give a 95% confidence interval for the mean weight of adult women based on these data.

  (b) Do you trust the interval you computed in part (a) as a 95% confidence interval for the mean weight of all U.S. adult women? Why or why not?

16.5   Good weather, good tips? Example 14.3 (page 291) described an experiment exploring the size of the tip in a particular restaurant when a message indicating that the next day's weather would be good was written on the bill. You work part-time as a server in a restaurant. You read a newspaper article about the study that reports that with 95% confidence the mean tip percent from restaurant patrons will be between 21.33 and 23.09 when the server writes a message on the bill stating that the next day's weather will be good. Can you conclude that if you begin writing a message on patron's bills that the next day's weather will be good, approximately 95% of the days you work your mean tip percent will be between 21.33 and 23.09? Why or why not?

16.6   Is your food safe? "Do you feel confident or not confident that the food available at most grocery stores is safe to eat?" When a Gallup Poll asked this question, 82% of the sample said they were confident.[3] Gallup announced the poll's margin of error for 95% confidence as ±3 percentage points. Which of the following sources of error are included in this margin of error?

  (a) Gallup dialed landline telephone numbers at random and so missed all people without landline phones, including people whose only phone is a cell phone.

  (b) Some people whose numbers were chosen never answered the phone in several calls or answered but refused to participate in the poll.

  (c) There is chance variation in the random selection of telephone numbers.

Creatas/Thinkstock

CAUTIONS ABOUT SIGNIFICANCE TESTS

Significance tests are widely used in most areas of statistical work. New pharmaceutical products require significant evidence of effectiveness and safety. Courts inquire about statistical significance in hearing class action discrimination cases. Marketers want to know whether a new package design will significantly increase sales. Medical researchers want to know whether a new therapy performs significantly better. In all these uses, statistical significance is valued because it points to an effect that is unlikely to occur simply by chance. Here are some points to keep in mind when you use or interpret significance tests.

How small a *P* is convincing? The purpose of a test of significance is to describe the degree of evidence provided by the sample against the null hypothesis. The *P*-value does this. But how small a *P*-value is convincing evidence against the null hypothesis? This depends mainly on two circumstances:

■ *How plausible is* H_0? If H_0 represents an assumption that the people you must convince have believed for years, strong evidence (small *P*) will be needed to persuade them.

■ *What are the consequences of rejecting* H_0? If rejecting H_0 in favor of H_a means making an expensive changeover from one type of product packaging to another, you need strong evidence that the new packaging will boost sales.

These criteria are a bit subjective. Different people will often insist on different levels of significance. Giving the *P*-value allows each of us to decide individually if the evidence is sufficiently strong.

Users of statistics have often emphasized standard levels of significance such as 10%, 5%, and 1%. For example, courts have tended to accept 5% as a standard in discrimination cases.[4] This emphasis reflects the time when tables of critical values rather than software dominated statistical practice. The 5% level ($\alpha = 0.05$) is particularly common. *There is no sharp border between "significant" and "not significant," only increasingly strong evidence as the P-value decreases. There is no practical distinction between the P-values 0.049 and 0.051. It makes no sense to treat $P \leq 0.05$ as a universal rule for what is significant.*

Significance depends on the alternative hypothesis You may have noticed that the *P*-value for a one-sided test is one-half the *P*-value for the two-sided test of the same null hypothesis based on the same data. The two-sided *P*-value combines two equal areas, one in each tail of a Normal curve. The one-sided *P*-value is just one of these areas, in the direction specified by the alternative hypothesis. It makes sense that the evidence against H_0 is stronger when the alternative is one-sided, because it is based on the data *plus* information about the direction of possible deviations from H_0. If you lack this added information, always use a two-sided alternative hypothesis.

Significance depends on sample size Significance depends both on the size of the effect you observe *and* on the size of the sample. Understanding this fact is essential to understanding significance tests.

EXAMPLE 16.3 Coaching and SAT scores

On the average, high school juniors who retake the SAT exam as seniors improve their Mathematics score by 13 points. Professor Gamma has designed a rigorous coaching program that she thinks will produce a larger increase. A group of juniors goes through this program and retakes the SAT as seniors. Their scores improve by an average of $\bar{x} = 15$ points. Is this significant evidence that the coaching program raises scores by more than 13 points on the average?

We'll assume the simple conditions: the students in the program are an SRS of the population of all juniors who take the SAT, and the distribution of Math score gains in the entire population is Normal with unknown mean μ and known standard deviation $\sigma = 30$. For testing

$$H_0: \mu = 13$$

$$H_a: \mu > 13$$

the z test statistic is

$$z = \frac{\bar{x} - \mu_0}{\sigma/\sqrt{n}} = \frac{15 - 13}{30/\sqrt{n}}$$

The gain of 2 points is not very impressive. But how significant it is depends on the sample size n:

Sample size	z statistic	P-value
50	0.4714	0.3187
100	0.6667	0.2525
500	1.4907	0.0680
1000	2.1082	0.0175
5000	4.7140	0.000001

There you have it: a very small effect can be highly significant if the sample size is very large. To see why, think of the z test statistic as follows:

$$z = \frac{\bar{x} - \mu_0}{\sigma/\sqrt{n}} = \frac{\text{size of the observed effect}}{\text{size of chance variation}}$$

The numerator $\bar{x} - \mu_0$ shows how far the data diverge from the null hypothesis. How significant this effect is depends on the size of the chance variation from sample to sample, measured by the standard deviation of $\bar{x}$ that is the denominator of z.

SAMPLE SIZE AFFECTS STATISTICAL SIGNIFICANCE

Because large random samples have small chance variation, very small population effects can be highly significant if the sample is large.

Because small random samples have a lot of chance variation, even large population effects can fail to be significant if the sample is small.

Statistical significance does not tell us whether an effect is large enough to be important. That is, **statistical significance is not the same thing as practical significance.**

Keep in mind that "statistical significance" means "the sample showed an effect larger than would often occur just by chance." Significance says nothing about how large the effect actually is. *Always look at the actual size of an effect as well as at its statistical significance.* A confidence interval is often helpful. For example, the 95% confidence interval for the mean score gain in Example 16.3 with a sample of size 1000 is

$$\bar{x} \pm z^* \frac{\sigma}{\sqrt{n}} = 2 \pm 1.960 \frac{30}{\sqrt{1000}}$$

$$= 2 \pm 1.86$$

$$= 0.14 \text{ to } 3.86 \text{ points}$$

An improvement this small, even if it is statistically significant, doesn't justify an intensive coaching program.

Beware of multiple analyses Statistical significance ought to mean that you have found an effect that you were looking for. The reasoning behind statistical significance works well if you decide what effect you are seeking, design a study to search for it, and use a test of significance to weigh the evidence you get. In other settings, significance may have little meaning.

EXAMPLE 16.4 Cell phones and brain cancer

Might the radiation from cell phones be harmful to users? Many studies have found little or no connection between using cell phones and various illnesses. Here is part of a news account of one study:

> A hospital study that compared brain cancer patients and a similar group without brain cancer found no statistically significant association between cell phone use and a group of brain cancers known as gliomas. But when 20 types of glioma were considered separately an association was found between phone use and one rare form. Puzzlingly, however, this risk appeared to decrease rather than increase with greater mobile phone use.[5]

Think for a moment. Suppose that the 20 null hypotheses (no association) for these 20 significance tests are all true. Then each test has a 5% chance of being significant at the 5% level. That's what $\alpha = 0.05$ means: results this extreme occur 5% of the time just by chance when the null hypothesis is true. Because 5% is 1/20, we expect about 1 of 20 tests to give a significant result just by chance. That's what the study observed. ■

Running one test and reaching the 5% level of significance is reasonably good evidence that you have found something. Running 20 tests and reaching that level only once is not. The caution about multiple analyses applies to confidence intervals as well. A single 95% confidence interval has probability 0.95 of capturing the true parameter each time you use it. The probability that all of 20 confidence intervals will capture their parameters is much less than 95%. If you think that multiple tests or intervals may have discovered an important effect, you need to gather new data to do inference about that specific effect.

iStockphoto

APPLY YOUR KNOWLEDGE

16.7 Is it significant? In the absence of special preparation, SAT Mathematics (SATM) scores in 2009 varied Normally with mean $\mu = 515$ and $\sigma = 116$. Fifty students go through a rigorous training program designed to raise their SATM scores by improving their mathematics skills. Either by hand or by using software, carry out a test of

$$H_0: \mu = 515$$
$$H_a: \mu > 515$$

(with $\sigma = 116$) in each of the following situations:

(a)   The students' average score is $\bar{x} = 541$. Is this result significant at the 5% level?

(b)   The average score is $\bar{x} = 542$. Is this result significant at the 5% level?

The difference between the two outcomes in (a) and (b) is of no importance. Beware attempts to treat $\alpha = 0.05$ as sacred.

16.8 **Detecting acid rain.** Emissions of sulfur dioxide by industry set off chemical changes in the atmosphere that result in "acid rain." The acidity of liquids is measured by pH on a scale of 0 to 14. Distilled water has pH 7.0, and lower pH values indicate acidity. Normal rain is somewhat acidic, so acid rain is sometimes defined as rainfall with a pH below 5.0. Suppose that pH measurements of rainfall on different days in a Canadian forest follow a Normal distribution with standard deviation $\sigma = 0.5$. A sample of n days finds that the mean pH is $\bar{x} = 4.8$. Is this good evidence that the mean pH μ for all rainy days is less than 5.0? The answer depends on the size of the sample.

Either by hand or using software, carry out three tests of

$$H_0: \mu = 5.0$$
$$H_a: \mu < 5.0$$

Use $\sigma = 0.5$ and $\bar{x} = 4.8$ in all three tests. But use three different sample sizes, $n = 5, n = 15$, and $n = 40$.

(a)   What are the P-values for the three tests? *The P-value of the same result $\bar{x} = 4.8$ gets smaller (more significant) as the sample size increases.*

(b)   For each test, sketch the Normal curve for the sampling distribution of $\bar{x}$ when H_0 is true. This curve has mean 5.0 and standard deviation $0.5/\sqrt{n}$. Mark the observed $\bar{x} = 4.8$ on each curve. *The same result $\bar{x} = 4.8$ gets more extreme on the sampling distribution as the sample size increases.*

16.9 **Confidence intervals help.** Give a 95% confidence interval for the mean pH μ for each sample size in the previous exercise. The intervals, unlike the P-values, give a clear picture of what mean pH values are plausible for each sample.

16.10 **Searching for ESP.** A researcher looking for evidence of extrasensory perception (ESP) tests 500 subjects. Four of these subjects do significantly better ($P < 0.01$) than random guessing.

(a)   You can't conclude that these 4 people have ESP. Why not?

(b)   What should the researcher now do to test whether any of these 4 subjects have ESP?

PLANNING STUDIES: Sample size for confidence intervals

A wise user of statistics never plans a sample or an experiment without at the same time planning the inference. The number of observations is a critical part of planning a study. Larger samples give smaller margins of error in confidence intervals and make significance tests better able to detect effects in the population. But taking observations costs both time and money. How many observations are enough? We will look at this question first for confidence intervals and then for tests. Planning a confidence interval is much simpler than planning a test. It is also more useful, because estimation is generally more informative than testing.

You can arrange to have both high confidence and a small margin of error by taking enough observations. The margin of error of the z confidence interval for the mean of a Normally distributed population is $m = z^*\sigma/\sqrt{n}$. To obtain a desired margin of error m, put in the value of z^* for your desired confidence level, and solve for the sample size n. Here is the result.

SAMPLE SIZE FOR DESIRED MARGIN OF ERROR

The z confidence interval for the mean of a Normal population will have a specified margin of error m when the sample size is

$$n = \left(\frac{z^*\sigma}{m}\right)^2$$

Notice that it is the size of the sample that determines the margin of error. The *size of the population does not influence the sample size we need.* (This is true as long as the population is much larger than the sample.)

EXAMPLE 16.5 How many observations?

In Example 14.3 (page 291), psychologists recorded the size of the tip left by 20 patrons in a restaurant when a message indicating that the next day's weather would be good was written on their bill. We know that the population standard deviation is $\sigma = 2$. We want to estimate the mean tip percent μ for patrons of this restaurant who receive this message on their bill within ± 0.5 with 90% confidence. How many patrons must we observe?

The desired margin of error is $m = 0.5$. For 90% confidence, Table C gives $z^* = 1.645$. Therefore,

$$n = \left(\frac{z^*\sigma}{m}\right)^2 = \left(\frac{1.645 \times 2}{0.5}\right)^2 = 43.3$$

Because 43 patrons will give a slightly larger margin of error than desired, and 44 patrons a slightly smaller margin of error, we must observe 44 patrons. *Always round up to the next higher whole number when finding n.* ■

APPLY YOUR KNOWLEDGE

16.11 Body mass index of young women. Example 14.1 (page 287) assumed that the body mass index (BMI) of all American young women follows a Normal distribution with standard deviation $\sigma = 7.5$. How large a sample would be needed to estimate the mean BMI μ in this population to within ± 1 with 95% confidence?

16.12 Number skills of young men. Suppose that scores on the mathematics part of the National Assessment of Educational Progress (NAEP) test for high school seniors follow a Normal distribution with standard deviation $\sigma = 30$. You want to estimate the mean score within ± 10 with 90% confidence. How large an SRS of scores must you choose?

CHAPTER 16 SUMMARY

CHAPTER SPECIFICS

- A specific confidence interval or test is correct only under specific conditions. The most important conditions concern the method used to produce the data. Other factors such as the shape of the population distribution may also be important.

- Whenever you use statistical inference, you are acting as if your data are a random sample or come from a randomized comparative experiment.

- Always do data analysis before inference to detect outliers or other problems that would make inference untrustworthy.

- The margin of error in a confidence interval accounts for only the chance variation due to random sampling. In practice, errors due to nonresponse or undercoverage are often more serious.

- There is no universal rule for how small a P-value in a test of significance is convincing evidence against the null hypothesis. Beware of placing too much weight on traditional significance levels such as $\alpha = 0.05$.

- Very small effects can be highly significant (small P) when a test is based on a large sample. A statistically significant effect need not be practically important. Plot the data to display the effect you are seeking, and use confidence intervals to estimate the actual values of parameters.

- On the other hand, lack of significance does not imply that H_0 is true. Even a large effect can fail to be significant when a test is based on a small sample.

- Many tests run at once will probably produce some significant results by chance alone, even if all the null hypotheses are true.

- When you plan a statistical study, plan the inference as well. In particular, ask what sample size you need for successful inference.

- The z confidence interval for a Normal mean has specified margin of error m when the sample size is

$$n = \left(\frac{z^* \sigma}{m} \right)^2$$

Here z^* is the critical value for the desired level of confidence. Always round n up when you use this formula.

LINK IT

In Chapters 14 and 15 we introduced the basic reasoning behind statistical estimation and tests of significance. We applied this reasoning to the problem of making inferences about a mean of a Normally distributed population in a simple and artificial setting (the population standard deviation is known). In this chapter we begin to move away from our simple and artificial conditions toward the reality of statistical practice. Later chapters deal with inference in fully realistic settings. Here we discuss more carefully conditions under which our procedures for inference do and do not hold. Where the data come from is crucial. Even if the population distribution is not Normal, our procedures are approximately correct if we have a moderate sample size and the shape of the population distribution is roughly symmetric. If the sample size is large, our procedures are approximately correct even if the population distribution is strongly skewed. However, any procedure based on sample statistics like the sample mean that are not resistant to outliers can be influenced by a few extreme observations. This is a caution that we first encountered in Chapter 2.

In this chapter we also provide some cautions about confidence intervals and tests of significance. Some of these echo statements made in Chapters 8 and 9. Some are based on the behavior of confidence intervals and significance tests. These cautions will help you evaluate studies that report confidence intervals or the results of a test of significance.

We conclude this chapter with material about planning a study that will use a confidence interval. The fundamental question is "What sample size do I need for successful inference?"

CHECK YOUR SKILLS

16.13 The most important condition for sound conclusions from statistical inference is usually

    (a) that the data can be thought of as a random sample from the population of interest.

    (b) that the population distribution is exactly Normal.

    (c) that the data contain no outliers.

16.14 The coach of a college men's soccer team records the resting heart rates of the 27 team members. You should not trust a confidence interval for the mean resting heart rate of all male students at this college based on these data because

    (a) with only 27 observations, the margin of error will be large.

    (b) heart rates may not have a Normal distribution.

    (c) the members of the soccer team can't be considered a random sample of all students.

16.15 You turn your Web browser to the online Harris Interactive Poll. Based on 2163 responses, the poll reports that 43% of U.S. adults said they would like to be richer, 21% said thinner, 14% said smarter, and 12% said younger. Nearly 1 in 10 (9%) said they would not want to choose any of the given options.[6] You should refuse to calculate a 95% confidence interval for the proportion of all U.S. adults who would like to be richer based on this sample because

    (a) the poll was taken a week ago.

    (b) inference from a voluntary response sample can't be trusted.

    (c) the sample is too large.

16.16 Many sample surveys use well-designed random samples but half or more of the original sample can't be contacted or refuse to take part. Any errors due to this nonresponse

    (a) have no effect on the accuracy of confidence intervals.

    (b) are included in the announced margin of error.

    (c) are in addition to the random variation accounted for by the announced margin of error.

16.17 A writer in a medical journal says: "An uncontrolled experiment in 37 women found a significantly improved mean clinical symptom score after treatment. Methodologic flaws make it difficult to interpret the results of this study." The writer is skeptical about the significant improvement because

    (a) there is no control group, so the improvement might be due to the placebo effect or to the fact that many medical conditions improve over time.

    (b) the P-value given was $P = 0.048$, which is too large to be convincing.

    (c) the response variable might not have an exactly Normal distribution in the population.

16.18 Vigorous exercise helps people live several years longer (on the average). Whether mild activities like slow walking extend life is not clear. Suppose that the added life expectancy from regular slow walking is just 2 months. A statistical test is more likely to find a significant increase in mean life if

    (a) it is based on a very large random sample.

    (b) it is based on a very small random sample.

    (c) The size of the sample doesn't have any effect on the significance of the test.

16.19 A medical experiment compared the herb echinacea with a placebo for preventing colds. One response variable was "volume of nasal secretions" (if you have a cold, you blow your nose a lot). Take the average volume of nasal secretions in people without colds to be $\mu = 1$. An increase to $\mu = 3$

indicates a cold. The significance level of a test of H_0: $\mu = 1$ versus H_a: $\mu > 1$ is defined as

(a) the probability that the test rejects H_0 when $\mu = 1$ is true.

(b) the probability that the test rejects H_0 when $\mu = 3$ is true.

(c) the probability that the test fails to reject H_0 when $\mu = 3$ is true.

CHAPTER 16 EXERCISES

16.20 Hotel managers. In Exercise 15.24 (page 313) you carried out a test of significance based on data from 148 general managers of three-star and four-star hotels. Before you trust your results, you would like more information about the data. What facts would you most like to know?

16.21 Color blindness in Africa. An anthropologist claims that color blindness is less common in societies that live by hunting and gathering than in settled agricultural societies. He tests a number of adults in two populations in Africa, one of each type. The proportion of color-blind people is significantly lower ($P < 0.05$) in the hunter-gatherer population. What additional information would you want to help you decide whether you believe the anthropologist's claim?

16.22 Sampling at the mall. A market researcher chooses at random from women entering a large suburban shopping mall. One outcome of the study is a 95% confidence interval for the mean of "the highest price you would pay for a pair of jeans."

(a) Explain why this confidence interval does not give useful information about the population of all women.

(b) Explain why it may give useful information about the population of women who shop at large suburban malls.

16.23 Sensitive questions. The National AIDS Behavioral Surveys found that 320 individuals in its random sample of 1334 urban heterosexuals aged 18 to 25 years said that they had multiple sexual partners in the past year. That's 24% of the sample. Why is this estimate likely to be biased? Do you think it is biased high or low? Does the margin of error of a 95% confidence interval for the proportion of all urban heterosexuals aged 18 to 25 with multiple partners allow for this bias?

16.24 College degrees. At the Statistics Canada Web site, www.statcan.gc.ca, you can find the percent of adults in each province or territory who have at least a university certificate, diploma, or degree at bachelor's level or above. It makes no sense to find $\bar{x}$ for these data and use it to get a confidence interval for the mean percent μ in all 13 provinces or territories. Why not?

16.25 An outlier strikes. You have data on an SRS of recent graduates from your college that shows how long each student took to complete a bachelor's degree. The data contain one high outlier. Will this outlier have a greater effect on a confidence interval for mean completion time if your sample is small or if it is large? Why?

16.26 Can we trust this interval? Here are data on the percent change in the total mass (in tons) of wildlife in several West African game preserves in the years 1971 to 1999:[7]

1971	1972	1973	1974	1975	1976	1977	1978
2.9	3.1	−1.2	−1.1	−3.3	3.7	1.9	−0.3

1979	1980	1981	1982	1983	1984	1985	1986
−5.9	−7.9	−5.5	−7.2	−4.1	−8.6	−5.5	−0.7

1987	1988	1989	1990	1991	1992	1993	1994
−5.1	−7.1	−4.2	0.9	−6.1	−4.1	−4.8	−11.3

1995	1996	1997	1998	1999
−9.3	−10.7	−1.8	−7.4	−22.9

Software gives the 95% confidence interval for the mean annual percent change as −6.66% to −2.55%. There are several reasons why we might not trust this interval.

(a) Examine the distribution of the data. What feature of the distribution throws doubt on the validity of statistical inference?

(b) Plot the percents against year. What trend do you see in this time series? Explain why a trend over time casts doubt on the condition that years 1971 to 1999 can be treated as an SRS from a larger population of years. **WILDLIFEMASS**

16.27 When to use pacemakers. A medical panel prepared guidelines for when cardiac pacemakers should be implanted in patients with heart problems. The panel reviewed a large number of medical studies to judge the strength of the evidence supporting each recommendation. For each recommendation, they ranked the evidence as level A (strongest), B, or C (weakest). Here, in scrambled order, are the panel's descriptions of the three levels of evidence.[8] Which is A, which B, and which C? Explain your ranking.

Evidence was ranked as level———when data were derived from a limited number of trials involving comparatively small numbers of patients or from well-designed data analysis of nonrandomized studies or observational data registries.

Evidence was ranked as level———if the data were derived from multiple randomized clinical trials involving a large number of individuals.

Evidence was ranked as level———when consensus of expert opinion was the primary source of recommendation.

16.28 What is significance good for? Which of the following questions does a test of significance answer? Briefly explain your replies.

(a) Is the sample or experiment properly designed?

(b) Is the observed effect due to chance?

(c) Is the observed effect important?

16.29 Why are larger samples better? Statisticians prefer large samples. Describe briefly the effect of increasing the size of a sample (or the number of subjects in an experiment) on each of the following:

(a) The margin of error of a 95% confidence interval.

(b) The P-value of a test, when H_0 is false and all facts about the population remain unchanged as n increases.

16.30 Divorce rates. Divorce rates vary from city to city in the United States. We have lots of data on many U.S. cities. Statistical software makes it easy to perform dozens of significance tests on dozens of variables to see which ones best predict divorce rate. One interesting finding is that those cities with major league ballparks tend to have significantly lower divorce rates than other cities. To improve your chances of a successful marriage, should you use this "significant" variable to decide where to live? Explain your answer.

16.31 A test goes wrong. Software can generate samples from (almost) exactly Normal distributions. Here is a random sample of size 5 from the Normal distribution with mean 8 and standard deviation 2:

$$4.47 \quad 5.51 \quad 8.10 \quad 11.63 \quad 7.91$$

These data match the conditions for a z test better than real data will: the population is very close to Normal and has known standard deviation $\sigma = 2$, and the population mean is $\mu = 8$. Although we know the true value of μ, we pretend that we do not and test the hypotheses

$$H_0: \mu = 6$$
$$H_a: \mu \neq 6$$

(a) What are the z statistic and its P-value? Is the test significant at the 5% level?

(b) We know that the null hypothesis does not hold, but the test failed to give strong evidence against H_0. Explain why this is not surprising. **RANDOMSAMPLE**

16.32 Reducing the gender gap. In many science disciplines women are outperformed by men on test scores. Will "values affirmation training" improve self-confidence and hence performance of women relative to men in science courses? A study conducted at a large university compares the scores of men and women at the end of a large introductory physics course on a nationally normed standardized test of conceptual physics, the Force and Motion Conceptual Evaluation (FMCE). Half the women in the course were given values affirmation training during the course; the other half received no training. The study reports that there was a significant difference ($P < 0.01$) in the gap between men's and women's scores, although the gap for women who received the values affirmation training was much smaller than that for women who did not receive training. The study also reports that a 95% confidence interval for the mean difference in scores on the FMCE exam between women who received the training and those who didn't is 13 ± 8 points. You are a faculty member in the physics department, and the provost, who is interested in women in science, asks you about the study.

(a) Explain in simple language what "a significant difference ($P < 0.01$)" means.

(b) Explain clearly and briefly what "95% confidence" means.

(c) Is this study good evidence that requiring values affirmation training of all female students would greatly reduce the gender gap in scores on science tests in college courses?

16.33 How far do rich parents take us? How much education children get is strongly associated with the wealth and social status of their parents. In social science jargon, this is "socioeconomic status," or SES. But the SES of parents has little influence on whether children who have graduated from college go on to yet more education. One study looked at whether college graduates took the graduate admissions tests for business, law, and other graduate programs. The effects of the parents' SES on taking the LSAT for law school were "both statistically insignificant and small."

(a) What does "statistically insignificant" mean?

(b) Why is it important that the effects were small in size as well as insignificant?

16.34 This wine stinks. How sensitive are the untrained noses of students? Exercise 14.22 (page 298) gives the lowest levels of dimethyl sulfide (DMS) that 10 students could detect. You want to estimate the mean DMS odor threshold among all students and you would be satisfied to estimate the mean to within ± 0.1 with 99% confidence. The standard deviation of the odor threshold for untrained noses is known to be $\sigma = 7$ micrograms per liter of wine. How large an SRS of untrained students do you need?

16.35 Pulling wood apart. You want to estimate the mean load needed to pull apart the pieces of wood in Exercise 14.20 (page 297) to within ±600 pounds with 95% confidence. How large a sample is needed?

 ## EXPLORING THE WEB

16.36 Statistically significant but not practically important. Find an example of a study in which a statistically significant result may not be practically important. Summarize the study and its conclusions in your own words. The CHANCE Web site at www.causeweb.org/wiki/chance/index.php/Main_Page is a good place to look for examples.

16.37 The American Psychological Association and tests. The report of the American Psychological Association's Task Force on Statistical Inference is an excellent brief introduction to wise use of inference. The report appeared in the journal *American Psychologist* in 1999. You can find a copy of the report on the Web in the list of *TFSI Publications/Links* from this journal at www.apa.org/science/leadership/bsa/statistical/index.aspx. Read the report. Are the authors opposed to the use of hypothesis testing? Describe one abuse of hypothesis testing that is cited in this report.

blickwinkel/Alamy

From Exploration to Inference: Part II Review

PART II SUMMARY

In Part I of this book, you mastered **data analysis,** the use of graphs and numerical summaries to organize and explore any set of data. Part II has introduced designs for data production, probability, and the reasoning of statistical inference. Parts III and IV will deal with inference in practice.

Designs for producing data are essential if the data are intended to represent some wider population or process. Figures 17.1 and 17.2 display the big ideas visually. You should now understand good designs for producing data and also why bad designs often produce data that are worthless for inference. The deliberate use of chance in producing data is a central idea in statistics. It not only reduces bias but allows us to use **probability,** the mathematics of chance, as the basis for inference. Fortunately, we need only some basic facts about probability in order to understand statistical inference.

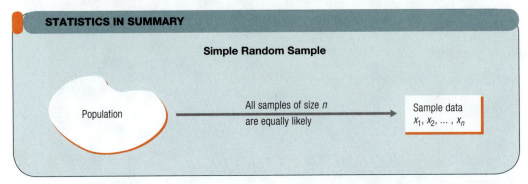

STATISTICS IN SUMMARY

Simple Random Sample

Population

All samples of size n
are equally likely

Sample data
$x_1, x_2, \ldots, x_n$

FIGURE 17.1

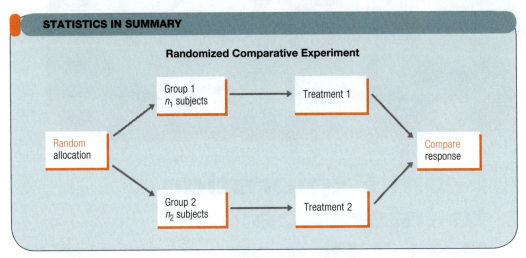

STATISTICS IN SUMMARY

Randomized Comparative Experiment

Random
allocation

Group 1
n_1 subjects

Treatment 1

Group 2
n_2 subjects

Treatment 2

Compare
response

FIGURE 17.2

Statistical inference draws conclusions about a population on the basis of sample data and uses probability to indicate how reliable the conclusions are. A confidence interval estimates an unknown parameter. A significance test shows how strong the evidence is for some claim about a parameter.

The probabilities in both confidence intervals and tests tell us what would happen if we used the method for the interval or test very many times.

■ A confidence level is the success rate of the method for a confidence interval. This is the probability that the method actually produces an interval that captures the unknown parameter. A 95% confidence interval gives a correct result 95% of the time when we use it repeatedly.

■ A P-value tells us how surprising the observed outcome would be if the null hypothesis were true. That is, P is the probability that the test would produce a result at least as extreme as the observed result if the null hypothesis really were true. Very surprising outcomes (small P-values) are good evidence that the null hypothesis is not true.

Figures 17.3 and 17.4 use the z procedures introduced in Chapters 14 and 15 to present in picture form the big ideas of confidence intervals and significance tests. These ideas are the foundation for the rest of this book. We will have much to say about many statistical methods and their use in practice. In every case, the basic reasoning of confidence intervals and significance tests remains the same.

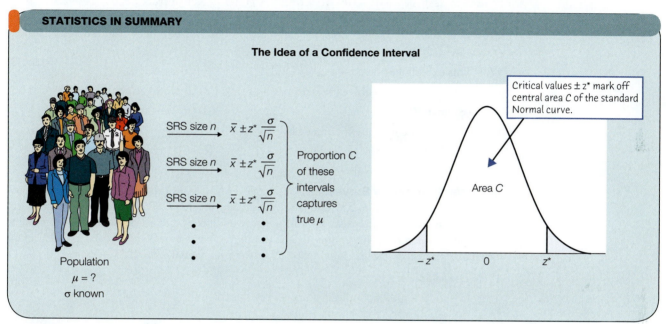

FIGURE 17.3

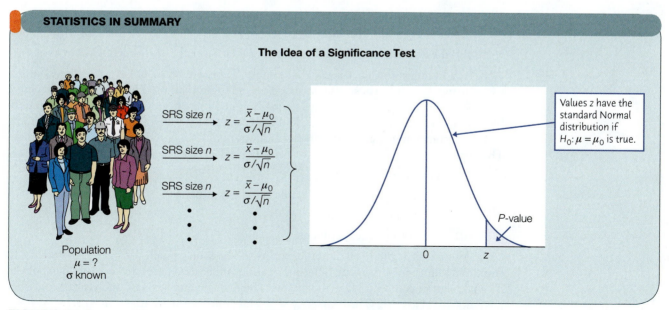

FIGURE 17.4

The questions below include both multiple-choice and short-answer questions and calculations. They will help you review the basic ideas and skills presented in Chapters 8 to 16.

Elephants and bees. *Elephants sometimes damage crops in Africa. It turns out that elephants dislike bees. They recognize beehives in areas where they are common and avoid them. Can this be used to keep elephants away from trees? A group in Kenya placed active beehives in some trees, empty beehives in others, and none in others.[1] Will elephant damage be less in trees with hives? Will even empty hives keep elephants away? Use this information to answer Questions 17.1 and 17.2.*

17.1 This experiment has

  (a) two factors, beehives present or absent.   (c) three treatments.

  (b) matched pairs.   (d) stratification by beehive.

17.2 The response in this experiment is

  (a) the type of crop.   (c) the presence or absence of hives.

  (b) the presence or absence of bees.   (d) elephant damage.

American Community Survey. *Each month the U.S. Census Bureau's American Community Survey mails survey forms to 250,000 households asking questions about demographic, social, economic, and housing characteristics such as mortgage and utility costs. Telephone calls are made to households that don't return the form. In one month, responses were obtained from 240,000 of the households contacted. Use this information to answer Questions 17.3 and 17.4.*

17.3 The sample is

  (a) the 250,000 households initially contacted.

  (b) the 240,000 households that responded.

  (c) the 10,000 households that did not respond.

  (d) all U.S. households.

17.4 The population of interest is

  (a) all households with mortgages.   (c) only U.S. households with phones.

  (b) the 250,000 households contacted.   (d) all U.S. households.

17.5 At a local health club, a researcher samples 75 people whose primary exercise is cardiovascular and 75 people whose primary exercise is strength training. The researcher's objective is to assess the effect of type of exercise on cholesterol. Each subject reported to a clinic to have his or her cholesterol measured. The subjects were unaware of the purpose of the study, and the technician measuring the cholesterol was not aware of the subjects' type of exercise. This is

  (a) an observational study.

  (b) an experiment, but not a double-blind experiment.

  (c) a double-blind experiment.

  (d) a matched pairs experiment.

17.6 A university's financial aid office wants to know how much it can expect students to earn from summer employment. This information will be used to set the level of financial aid. The population contains 3478 students who have completed at least one year of study but have not yet graduated. The university will send a questionnaire to an SRS of 100 of these students, drawn from an alphabetized list.

(a) Describe how you will label the students in order to select the sample.

(b) Use Table B, beginning at line 105, to select the first 5 students in the sample.

(c) What is the response variable in this study?

17.7 A common definition of "binge drinking" is 5 or more drinks at one setting for men, and 4 or more for women. An observational study finds that students who binge have lower average GPA than those who don't. Suggest two lurking variables that may be confounded with binge drinking, and be sure to give a reason why you have chosen each of these variables. The possibility of confounding means that we can't conclude that binge drinking *causes* lower GPA.

17.8 The evidence linking chocolate to chronic headaches is inconsistent. In one study, 64 women with chronic headaches ate a restricted diet for two weeks. They then ate candy bars containing either chocolate or carob, prepared to taste the same, and reported whether they had a headache in the next 12 hours.[2]

(a) Outline the design of this experiment.

(b) Use Table B, beginning at line 110, to choose the first 5 members of the chocolate group.

17.9 In 2000, when the federal budget showed a large surplus, the Pew Research Center asked random samples of adults two questions about using the remaining surplus. Both questions stated that Social Security would be "fixed."

Question A: *Should the money be used for a tax cut, or should it be used to fund new government programs?*

Question B: *Should the money be used for a tax cut, or should it be spent on programs for education, the environment, health care, crime-fighting and military defense?*

One of these questions drew 60% favoring a tax cut. The other drew only 22%. Which wording pulls respondents toward a tax cut? Why?

Snacking and movies. *In a study of human development, investigators showed two movies that were different types to a group of children. Crackers were available in a bowl at each movie, and the investigators compared the number of crackers eaten by children watching each movie. One movie was shown at 8 A.M. (right after the children had breakfast) and the other at 11 A.M. (right before the children had lunch). It was found that during the movie shown at 11 A.M., more crackers were eaten than during the movie shown at 8 A.M. The investigators concluded that the different types of movies had different effects on appetite. Use this information to answer Questions 17.10 and 17.11.*

17.10 The results cannot be trusted because

(a) the study was not double-blind. Neither the investigators nor the children should have been aware of which movie was being shown.

(b) the investigators were biased. They knew beforehand what the study would show.

(c) the investigators should have used several bowls of crackers randomly placed in the room.

(d) the time each movie was shown is a confounding variable.

17.11 The treatment in this experiment is

(a) the number of crackers eaten.   (c) the time each movie was shown.

(b) the different types of movies.   (d) the type of cracker.

17.12 The Web site of the PBS television program *NOVA Science Now* invites viewers to vote on issues such as re-creating the virus responsible for the deadly flu epidemic of 1918. This online poll is unusual in offering detailed arguments for both sides. Of the 790 viewers who read the arguments and voted, 64% said that re-creating the virus was justified.[3]

Explain to someone who knows no statistics why these 790 responses probably don't represent the opinions of all American adults.

17.13 A study attempts to determine whether a football filled with helium travels farther when kicked than one filled with air. Each subject kicks twice, once with a football filled with helium and once with a football filled with air. The order of the type of football kicked is randomized. This is an example of

    (a) a matched pairs experiment.

    (b) a randomized controlled experiment.

    (c) a stratified experiment.

    (d) the placebo effect.

A student survey. *To assess the opinion of students about campus safety at the Ohio State University, a reporter for the student newspaper interviews 15 students she meets walking on the campus late at night and who are willing to give their opinion. Use this information to answer Questions 17.14 and 17.15.*

17.14 The sample is

    (a) all students walking on campus late at night.

    (b) all students at universities with safety issues.

    (c) the 15 students interviewed.

    (d) all students approached by the reporter.

17.15 The sample obtained is

    (a) a simple random sample of students who feel safe.

    (b) a stratified random sample of students who feel safe.

    (c) a probability sample of students with night classes.

    (d) probably biased.

17.16 A randomly chosen subject arrives for a study of exercise and fitness. Describe a sample space for each of the following. (In some cases, you may have some freedom in your choice of S.)

    (a) The subject is either female or male.

    (b) After 10 minutes on an exercise bicycle, you ask the subject to rate his or her effort on the Rate of Perceived Exertion (RPE) scale. RPE ranges in whole-number steps from 6 (no exertion at all) to 20 (maximal exertion).

    (c) You measure VO2, the maximum volume of oxygen consumed per minute during exercise. VO2 is generally between 2.5 and 6.1 liters per minute.

    (d) You measure the maximum heart rate (beats per minute).

Internet search engines. *Internet search sites compete for users because they sell advertising space on their sites and can charge more if they are heavily used. Choose an Internet search attempt at random. Here is the probability distribution for the site the search uses:*[4]

Site	Google	Yahoo	MSN	Ask.com	Others
Probability	0.66	0.21	0.07	0.04	?

Use this information to answer Questions 17.17 and 17.18

17.17 What is the probability that a search attempt is made at a site other than the leading four?

(a) 0.02   (b) 0.34   (c) 0.98

(d) Cannot be determined from the information given.

17.18 What is the probability that a search attempt is directed to a site other than Google?

(a) 0.02   (b) 0.34   (c) 0.98

(d) Cannot be determined from the information given.

How many in the house? *In government data, a household consists of all occupants of a dwelling unit. Here is the distribution of household size in the United States:*

Number of persons	1	2	3	4	5	6	7
Probability	0.26	0.33	0.16	0.15	0.07	0.02	0.01

Choose an American household at random and let the random variable Y be the number of persons living in the household. Use this information to answer Questions 17.19 to 17.21.

17.19 Express "more than one person lives in this household" in terms of Y. What is the probability of this event?

17.20 What is $P(2 < Y \leq 4)$?

17.21 What is $P(Y \neq 2)$?

(a) 0.26   (b) 0.33   (c) 0.41   (d) 0.67

How many children? *How many children do women give birth to during their childbearing years? Choose at random an American woman who is past childbearing:*[5]

Number of children	0	1	2	3	4	5
Probability	0.193	0.174	0.344	0.181	0.074	0.034

(The few women with 6 or more children are included in the "5 children" group.) Use this information to answer Questions 17.22 to 17.25.

17.22 Check that this distribution satisfies the two requirements for a legitimate finite probability model.

17.23 Describe in words the event $P(X \leq 2)$. What is the probability of this event?

17.24 What is $P(X < 2)$?

(a) 0.289   (b) 0.344   (c) 0.367   (d) 0.711

17.25 Write the event "a woman gives birth to 3 or more children" in terms of values of X. What is the probability of this event?

Random number generators. *Many random number generators allow users to specify the range of the random numbers to be produced. Suppose that you specify that the random number Y can take any value between 0 and 5. The density curve of the outcome has a constant height between 0 and 5, and height 0 elsewhere. Use this information to answer Questions 17.26 to 17.28.*

17.26 The random variable Y is

(a) discrete.   (c) continuous and Normal.

(b) continuous, but not Normal.   (d) none of the above.

17.27 The height of the density curve between 0 and 5 is

(a) 0.2.   (b) 1.   (c) 5.   (d) none of the above.

17.28 Draw a graph of the density curve and find $P(1 \leq Y \leq 3)$.

An IQ test. *The Wechsler Adult Intelligence Scale (WAIS) is a common "IQ test" for adults. The distribution of WAIS scores for persons over 16 years of age is approximately Normal with mean 100 and standard deviation 15. Use this information to answer Questions 17.29 to 17.32.*

17.29 What is the probability that a randomly chosen individual has a WAIS score of 105 or higher?

(a) 0.0005   (b) 0.3707   (c) 0.4400   (d) 0.6293

17.30 What are the mean and standard deviation of the average WAIS score $\bar{x}$ for an SRS of 60 people?

(a) mean = 13.56, standard deviation = 15.

(b) mean = 105, standard deviation = 15.

(c) mean = 105, standard deviation = 1.94.

(d) mean = 105, standard deviation = 0.25.

17.31 What is the probability that the average WAIS score of an SRS of 60 people is 105 or higher?

(a) 0.0049   (b) 0.3607   (c) 0.9738   (d) none of the above.

17.32 Would your answers to any of Questions 17.29, 17.30, or 17.31 be affected if the distribution of WAIS scores in the adult population was distinctly non-Normal? Explain.

Reaction times. *The time that people require to react to a stimulus usually has a right-skewed distribution, as lack of attention or tiredness causes some lengthy reaction times. Reaction times for children with attention-deficit/hyperactivity disorder (ADHD) are more skewed, as their condition causes more frequent lack of attention. In one study, children with ADHD were asked to press the spacebar on a computer keyboard when any letter other than X appeared on the screen. With 2 seconds between letters, the mean reaction time was 445 milliseconds (ms) and the standard deviation was 82 ms.*[6] *Take these values to be the population μ and σ for ADHD children. Use this information to answer Questions 17.33 to 17.35.*

17.33 What are the mean and standard deviation of the mean reaction time $\bar{x}$ for a randomly chosen group of 15 ADHD children? For a group of 150 such children?

17.34 The distribution of reaction time is strongly skewed. Explain briefly why we hesitate to regard $\bar{x}$ as Normally distributed for 15 children but are willing to use a Normal distribution for the mean reaction time of 150 children.

17.35 What is the approximate probability that the mean reaction time in a group of 150 ADHD children is greater than 450 ms?

17.36 (Optional). Accidents, suicide, and murder are the leading causes of death for young adults. Here are the counts of violent deaths in a recent year among people 20 to 24 years of age:

	Female	Male
Accidents	1818	6457
Homicide	457	2870
Suicide	345	2152

(a) Choose a violent death in this age group at random. What is the probability that the victim was male?

(b) Find the conditional probability that the victim was male, given that the death was accidental.

Parallel systems (optional). *A system has two components that operate in parallel, as shown in Figure 17.5. Because the components operate in parallel, at least one of the components must function properly if the system is to function properly. The probabilities of failure for Components 1 and 2 during one period of operation are 0.20 and 0.03, respectively. Let F denote the event that Component 1 fails during one period of operation, and let G denote the event that Component 2 fails during one period of operation. The component failures are independent. Use this information to answer Questions 17.37 and 17.38.*

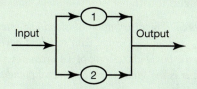

FIGURE 17.5

Parallel systems for Exercises 17.37 and 17.38.

17.37 The event corresponding to the system failing during one period of operation is

(a) F and G.   (b) F or G.   (c) not F or not G.   (d) not F and not G.

17.38 The probability that the system functions properly during one period of operation is closest to

(a) 0.994.   (b) 0.970.   (c) 0.940.   (d) 0.776.

17.39 (Optional). A survey of college students finds that 35% like country music, 25% like gospel music, and 15% like both. The proportion of students who like country music but not gospel music is

(a) 15%.   (b) 20%.   (c) 25%.   (d) 40%.

17.40 (Optional). Opinion polls find that 63% of American teens say that their parents put at least some pressure on them to get into a good college.[7] If you take an SRS of 1000 teens, the approximate distribution of the number in your sample who say that they feel at least some pressure from their parents to get into a good college is

(a) $N(0.63, 15.27)$.   (c) $N(630, 15.27)$.

(b) $N(0.63, 233.1)$.   (d) $N(630, 233.1)$.

17.41 (Optional). What kinds of Web sites do males aged 18 to 34 visit? About 50% of male Internet users in this age group visit an auction site such as eBay at least once a month.[8]

(a) If we interview a random sample of 12 male Internet users aged 18 to 34, what is the probability that exactly 8 of the 12 have visited an auction site in the past month?

(b) Suppose that we had interviewed a random sample of 500 men aged 18 to 34. What is the probability that at least 235 of the men in the sample visit an online auction site at least once a month? (Check that the Normal approximation is permissible and use it to find this probability.)

Pesticides in whale blubber: estimation. *The level of pesticides found in the blubber of whales is a measure of pollution of the oceans by runoff from land and can also be used to identify different populations of whales. A sample of 8 male minke whales in the West Greenland area of the North Atlantic found the mean concentration of the insecticide dieldrin to be $\bar{x} = 357$ nanograms per gram of blubber (ng/g).[9] Suppose that the concentration in all such whales varies Normally with standard deviation $\sigma = 50$ ng/g. Use this information to answer Questions 17.42 to 17.45.*

17.42 A 95% confidence interval to estimate the mean level of dieldrin is

(a) 344.75 to 369.25.   (c) 322.35 to 391.65.

(b) 339.32 to 374.68.   (d) 259.00 to 455.00.

17.43 A 90% confidence interval to estimate the mean level of dieldrin is

(a) 346.72 to 367.28.   (c) 311.36 to 402.54.

(b) 327.92 to 386.08.   (d) 274.75 to 439.25.

17.44 Find an 80% confidence interval for the mean concentration of dieldrin in the whale population.

17.45 What general fact about confidence intervals do the margins of error of your three intervals in the previous problems illustrate?

Estimating blood cholesterol. *The distribution of blood cholesterol level in the population of young men aged 20 to 34 years is close to Normal with standard deviation $\sigma = 41$ milligrams per deciliter (mg/dl). You measure the blood cholesterol of 14 cross-country runners. The mean level is $\bar{x} = 172$ mg/dl. Assume that σ is the same as in the general population. Use this information to answer Questions 17.46 to 17.48.*

17.46 A 90% confidence interval for the mean level μ among cross-country runners is

(a) 172 ± 4.82 mg/dl.   (c) 172 ± 21.48 mg/dl.

(b) 172 ± 18.03 mg/dl.   (d) none of the above.

17.47 How large a sample is needed to cut the margin of error in the previous exercise in half?

(a) 2   (b) 4   (c) 28   (d) 56

17.48 How large a sample is needed to cut the margin of error to ± 5 mg/dl?

(a) 14   (b) 68   (c) 182   (d) 259

17.49 The Environmental Protection Agency (EPA) fuel economy ratings say that the Toyota Prius hybrid car gets 48 miles per gallon (mpg) on the highway. Deborah wonders whether the actual long-term average highway mileage μ of her new Prius is less than 48 mpg. She keeps careful records of gas mileage for 3000 miles of highway driving. Her result is $\bar{x} = 47.2$ mpg. What are her null and alternative hypotheses?

(a) $H_0: \mu = 48$, $H_a: \mu < 48$.   (c) $H_0: \bar{x} = 48$, $H_a: \bar{x} < 48$.

(b) $H_0: \mu = 48$, $H_a: \mu > 48$.   (d) $H_0: \bar{x} = 48$, $H_a: \bar{x} > 48$.

17.50 The average amount of time that high school students spend on homework is about 5 hours per week. Only 25% of college freshmen say they spent at least 6 hours per week on homework in high school. Your college wonders if the average μ for its freshmen differs from the national average. A random sample of 500 freshmen claims to have spent an average of $\bar{x} = 6.2$ hours per week on homework in high school. What are the null and alternative hypotheses for a comparison of freshmen at your college with national freshmen?

(a) $H_0: \bar{x} = 5$, $H_a: \bar{x} \neq 5$.   (c) $H_0: \mu = 5$, $H_a: \mu \neq 5$.

(b) $H_0: \bar{x} = 6$, $H_a: \bar{x} > 6$.   (d) $H_0: \mu = 6$, $H_a: \mu > 6$.

Testing blood cholesterol. *The distribution of blood cholesterol level in the population of young men aged 20 to 34 years is close to Normal with mean 188 milligrams per deciliter (mg/dl) and standard deviation 41 mg/dl. You measure the blood cholesterol of 14 cross-country runners. The mean level is $\bar{x} = 172$ mg/dl. Assume that σ is the same as in the general population. Use this information to answer Questions 17.51 to 17.53.*

17.51 We suspect that the mean μ for all cross-country runners is lower than that for the population of young men aged 20 to 34 years. Thus, we decide to test the hypotheses $H_0: \mu = 188$, $H_a: \mu < 188$. The z test statistic for testing these hypotheses is

(a) 5.46.   (b) -5.46.   (c) 1.46.   (d) -1.46.

17.52 The result is significant at

  (a) $\alpha = 0.01$.

  (b) $\alpha = 0.05$ but not at $\alpha = 0.01$.

  (c) $\alpha = 0.10$ but not at $\alpha = 0.05$.

  (d) $\alpha = 0.25$ but not at $\alpha = 0.10$.

17.53 You increase the sample of cross-country runners from 14 to 56. Suppose that this larger sample gives the same mean level, $\bar{x} = 172$ mg/dl. Redo the test in the previous exercises. The result is significant at

  (a) $\alpha = 0.01$.

  (b) $\alpha = 0.05$ but not at $\alpha = 0.01$.

  (c) $\alpha = 0.10$ but not at $\alpha = 0.05$.

  (d) $\alpha = 0.25$ but not at $\alpha = 0.10$.

17.54 The Food and Drug Administration regulates the amount of dieldrin in raw food. For some foods, no more than 100 nanograms per gram (ng/g) is allowed. Using the information in Questions 17.42 to 17.45, is there good evidence that the mean concentration μ in whale blubber is above 100 ng/g? Carry out a test of the hypotheses $H_0\colon \mu = 100$, $H_a\colon \mu > 100$ assuming that the "simple conditions" (page 286) hold. The P-value of your test is

  (a) above 0.10.

  (b) less than or equal to 0.10 but greater than 0.05.

  (c) less than or equal to 0.05 but greater than 0.01.

  (d) no more than 0.01.

17.55 Infants weighing less than 1500 grams at birth are classed as "very low birth weight." Low birth weight carries many risks. One study followed 113 male infants with very low birth weight to adulthood. At age 20, the mean IQ score for these men was $\bar{x} = 87.6$.[10] IQ scores vary Normally with standard deviation $\sigma = 15$. Give a 95% confidence interval for the mean IQ score at age 20 for all very-low-birth-weight males.

17.56 IQ tests are scaled so that the mean score in a large population should be $\mu = 100$. We suspect that the very-low-birth-weight population has mean score less than 100. Does the study described in the previous exercise give good evidence that this is true? State hypotheses, carry out a test assuming that the "simple conditions" (page 286) hold, compute the P-value, and give your conclusion in plain language.

17.57 Very-low-birth-weight babies are more likely to be born to unmarried mothers and to mothers who did not complete high school. Is the study of the previous examples an experiment? Explain. Also explain clearly why confounding prevents us from concluding that very low birth weight in itself reduces adult IQ.

17.58 When our brains store information, complicated chemical changes take place. In trying to understand these changes, researchers blocked some processes in brain cells taken from rats and compared these cells with a control group of normal cells. They say that "no differences were seen" between the two groups in four response variables. They give P-values of 0.45, 0.83, 0.26, and 0.84 for these four comparisons.[11] Which of the following statements is correct?

  (a) It is literally true that "no differences were seen." That is, the mean responses were exactly alike in the two groups.

  (b) The mean responses were exactly alike in the two groups for at least one of the four response variables measured, but not for all of them.

(c) The statement "no differences were seen" means that the observed differences were not statistically significant at the significance level used by the researchers.

(d) The statement "no differences were seen" means that the observed differences were all less than 1 (and were actually 0.45, 0.83, 0.26, and 0.84 for these four comparisons).

17.59 Here are some of the results of the experiment described in Question 17.8 (page 337). There was no significant difference in headaches between the chocolate and carob groups ($P = 0.68$). But subjects who said they had a mild headache before eating the candy bar were more likely to report a headache afterward ($P < 0.001$). Explain carefully why $P = 0.68$ means that there is no evidence that chocolate and carob differ in their effects and why $P < 0.001$ is evidence that having a headache before eating the candy bar does increase reports of a headache after eating.

17.60 We often see televised reports of brushfires threatening homes in California. Some people argue that the modern practice of quickly putting out small fires allows fuel to accumulate and so increases the damage done by large fires. A detailed study of historical data suggests that this is wrong—the damage has risen simply because there are more houses in risky areas. As usual, the study report gives statistical information tersely. Here is the summary of a regression of number of fires on decade (9 data points, for the 1910s to the 1990s): "Collectively, since 1910, there has been a highly significant increase ($r^2 = 0.61$, $P < 0.01$) in the number of fires per decade."[12] How would you explain this statement to someone who knows no statistics? Include an explanation of both the description given by r^2 and its statistical significance.

SUPPLEMENTARY EXERCISES

Supplementary exercises apply the skills you have learned in ways that require more thought or more elaborate use of technology.

17.61 Sampling students. You want to investigate the attitudes of students at your school toward the school's policy on sexual harassment. You have a grant that will pay the costs of contacting about 500 students.

(a) Specify the exact population for your study. For example, will you include part-time students?

(b) Describe your sample design. Will you use a stratified sample?

(c) Briefly discuss the practical difficulties that you anticipate. For example, how will you contact the students in your sample?

17.62 The placebo effect. A survey of physicians found that some doctors give a placebo to a patient who complains of pain for which the physician can find no cause. If the patient's pain improves, these doctors conclude that it had no physical basis. The medical school researchers who conducted the survey claimed that these doctors do not understand the placebo effect. Why?

17.63 Informed consent. The requirement that human subjects give their informed consent to participate in an experiment can greatly reduce the number of available subjects. For example, a study of new teaching methods asks the consent of parents for their children to be taught by either a new method or the standard method. Many parents do not return the forms, so their children must continue to follow the standard curriculum. Why is it not correct to consider these children as part of the control group along with children who are randomly assigned to the standard method?

17.64 Fixing health care. The cost of health care and health insurance is the biggest health concern among Americans, even ahead of cancer and other diseases. Changing to a national government health insurance system is controversial. An opinion poll will give different results depending on the wording of the question asked. For each of the following claims, say whether including it in the question would *increase* or *decrease* the percent of a poll sample who support a government health insurance system.

(a) A national system would mean that everybody has health insurance.

(b) A national system would probably require an increase in taxes.

(c) Eliminating private insurance companies and their profits would reduce insurance costs.

(d) A national system would limit the medical treatments available in order to contain costs.

17.65 Market research. Stores advertise price reductions to attract customers. What type of price cut is most attractive? Market researchers prepared ads for athletic shoes announcing different levels of discounts (20%, 40%, or 60%). The student subjects who read the ads were also given "inside information" about the fraction of shoes on sale (50% or 100%). Each subject then rated the attractiveness of the sale on a scale of 1 to 7.[13]

(a) There are two factors. Make a sketch like Figure 9.2 (page 191) that displays the treatments formed by all combinations of levels of the factors.

(b) Outline a completely randomized design using 60 student subjects. Use software or Table B at line 111 to choose the subjects for the first treatment.

17.66 Making french fries. Few people want to eat discolored french fries. Potatoes are kept refrigerated before being cut for french fries to prevent spoiling and preserve flavor. But immediate processing of cold potatoes causes discoloring due to complex chemical reactions. The potatoes must therefore be brought to room temperature before processing. Design an experiment in which tasters will rate the color and flavor of french fries prepared from several groups of potatoes. The potatoes will be freshly picked or stored for a month at room temperature or stored for a month refrigerated. They will then be sliced and cooked either immediately or after an hour at room temperature.

(a) What are the factors and their levels, the treatments, and the response variables?

(b) Describe and outline the design of this experiment.

(c) It is efficient to have each taster rate fries from all treatments. How will you use randomization in presenting fries to the tasters?

17.67 The addition rule. The addition rule for probabilities, $P(A \text{ or } B) = P(A) + P(B)$, is not always true. Give (in words) an example of real-world events A and B for which this rule is not true.

17.68 Comparing wine tasters. Two wine tasters rate each wine they taste on a scale of 1 to 5. From data on their ratings of a large number of wines, we obtain the following probabilities for both tasters' ratings of a randomly chosen wine:

Taster 1	Taster 2				
	1	2	3	4	5
1	0.03	0.02	0.01	0.00	0.00
2	0.02	0.08	0.05	0.02	0.01
3	0.01	0.05	0.25	0.05	0.01
4	0.00	0.02	0.05	0.20	0.02
5	0.00	0.01	0.01	0.02	0.06

(a) Why is this a legitimate finite probability model?

(b) What is the probability that the tasters agree when rating a wine?

(c) What is the probability that Taster 1 rates a wine higher than Taster 2? What is the probability that Taster 2 rates a wine higher than Taster 1?

17.69 Distributions: means versus individuals. The z confidence interval and test are based on the sampling distribution of the sample mean $\bar{x}$. Suppose that the distribution of body mass index (BMI) among young women is Normal with mean $\mu = 27$ and standard deviation $\sigma = 7.5$.

(a) You take an SRS of 100 young women. According to the 99.7 part of the 68–95–99.7 rule, about what range of BMI values do you expect to see in your sample?

(b) You look at many SRSs of size 100. About what range of sample mean BMIs $\bar{x}$ do you expect to see?

17.70 Distributions: larger samples. In the setting of the previous exercise, how many women must you sample to cut the range of values of $\bar{x}$ in half? This will also cut the margin of error of a confidence interval for μ in half. Do you expect the range of individual scores in the new sample to also be much less than in a sample of size 100? Why?

17.71 Alcohol and mortality. It appears that people who drink alcohol in moderation have lower death rates than either people who drink heavily or people who do not drink at all. The protection offered by moderate drinking is concentrated among people over 50 and on deaths from heart disease. The Nurses' Health Study played an essential role in establishing these facts for women. This part of the study followed 85,709 female nurses for 12 years, during which time 2658 of the subjects died. The nurses completed a questionnaire that described their diet, including their use of alcohol. They were reexamined every two years. Conclusion: "As compared with nondrinkers and heavy drinkers, light-to-moderate drinkers had a significantly lower risk of death."[14]

(a) Was this study an experiment? Explain your answer.

(b) What does "significantly lower risk of death" mean in simple language?

(c) Suggest some lurking variables that might be confounded with how much a person drinks. The investigators used advanced statistical methods to adjust for many such variables before concluding that moderate drinkers really do have a lower risk of death.

17.72 Time in a restaurant. The owner of a pizza restaurant in France knows that the time customers spend in the restaurant on Saturday evening has mean 90 minutes and standard deviation 15 minutes. He has read that pleasant odors can influence customers, so he spreads a lavender odor throughout the restaurant. Here are the times (minutes) for customers on the next Saturday evening:[15] **RESTAURANT**

```
 92 126 114 106  89 137  93  76  98 108
124 105 129 103 107 109  94 105 102 108
 95 121 109 104 116  88 109  97 101 106
```

(a) Make a stemplot of the times. The distribution is roughly symmetric and single-peaked, so the distribution of $\bar{x}$ should be close to Normal.

(b) Suppose that the standard deviation $\sigma = 15$ minutes is not changed by the odor. Is there reason to think that the lavender odor has changed the mean time customers spend in the restaurant?

Follow the four-step process for significance tests (page 307).

17.73 Normal body temperature? Here are the daily average body temperatures (degrees Fahrenheit) for 20 healthy adults:[16] **BODYTEMP**

```
 98.74  98.83  96.80  98.12  97.89  98.09  97.87  97.42  97.30  97.84
100.27  97.90  99.64  97.88  98.54  98.33  97.87  97.48  98.92  98.33
```

(a) Make a stemplot of the data. The distribution is roughly symmetric and single-peaked. There is one mild outlier. We expect the distribution of the sample mean $\bar{x}$ to be close to Normal.

(b) Do these data give evidence that the mean body temperature for all healthy adults is not equal to the traditional 98.6 degrees? Follow the four-step process for significance tests (page 307). (Suppose that body temperature varies Normally with standard deviation 0.7 degree.)

17.74 Time in a restaurant. Use the data in Exercise 17.72 to estimate the mean time customers spend in this restaurant on Saturday evenings with 95% confidence. Follow the four-step process for confidence intervals (page 291). **RESTAURANT**

17.75 Normal body temperature? Use the data in Exercise 17.73 to estimate mean body temperature with 90% confidence. Follow the four-step process for confidence intervals (page 291). **BODYTEMP**

Inference about Variables

With the principles in hand, we proceed to practice, that is, to inference in fully realistic settings. In the remaining chapters of this book, you will meet many of the most commonly used statistical procedures. We have grouped these procedures into two classes, corresponding to our division of data analysis into exploring variables and distributions and exploring relationships. The five chapters of Part III concern inference about the distribution of a single variable and inference for comparing the distributions of two variables. Part IV deals with inference for relationships among variables. In Chapters 18 and 19, we analyze data on quantitative variables. We begin with the familiar Normal distribution for a quantitative variable. Chapters 20 and 21 concern categorical variables, so that inference begins with counts and proportions of outcomes. Chapter 22 reviews this part of the text.

The four-step process for approaching a statistical problem can guide much of your work in these chapters. You should review the outlines of the four-step process for a confidence interval (page 291) and for a test of significance (page 307). The statement of an exercise usually does the "*State*" step for you, leaving the "Plan," "Solve," and "Conclude" steps for you to complete. It is helpful to first summarize the "State" step in your own words to organize your thinking. Many examples and exercises in these chapters involve both carrying out inference and thinking about inference in practice. Remember that any inference method is useful only under certain conditions, and that you must judge these conditions before rushing to inference.

Regis Domergue/Photolibrary

Inference about a Population Mean

This chapter describes confidence intervals and significance tests for the mean μ of a population. We used the z procedures in this same setting to introduce the ideas of confidence intervals and tests. Now we discard the unrealistic condition that we know the population standard deviation σ and present procedures for practical use. We also pay more attention to the real-data setting of our work. The details of confidence intervals and tests change only slightly when you don't know σ. More important, you can interpret your results exactly as before. To illustrate this, Example 18.2 repeats an example from Chapter 14.

CONDITIONS FOR INFERENCE ABOUT A MEAN

Confidence intervals and tests of significance for the mean μ of a Normal population are based on the sample mean $\bar{x}$. Confidence intervals and P-values involve probabilities calculated from the sampling distribution of $\bar{x}$. Here are the conditions needed for realistic inference about a population mean.

349

> ## CONDITIONS FOR INFERENCE ABOUT A MEAN
> ■ We can regard our data as a **simple random sample** (SRS) from the population. This condition is very important.
>
> ■ Observations from the population have a **Normal distribution** with mean μ and standard deviation σ. In practice, it is enough that the distribution be symmetric and single-peaked unless the sample is very small. Both μ and σ are unknown parameters.

There is another condition that applies to all the inference methods in this book: *the population must be much larger than the sample, say at least 20 times as large.*[1] All our examples and exercises satisfy this condition. Practical settings in which the sample is a large part of the population are rather special, and we will not discuss them.

When the conditions for inference are satisfied, the sample mean $\bar{x}$ has the Normal distribution with mean μ and standard deviation $\sigma/\sqrt{n}$. Because we don't know σ, we estimate it by the sample standard deviation s. We then estimate the standard deviation of $\bar{x}$ by $s/\sqrt{n}$. This quantity is called the *standard error* of the sample mean $\bar{x}$.

> ## STANDARD ERROR
> When the standard deviation of a statistic is estimated from data, the result is called the **standard error** of the statistic. The standard error of the sample mean $\bar{x}$ is $s/\sqrt{n}$.

APPLY YOUR KNOWLEDGE

18.1   Travel time to work. A study of commuting times reports the travel times to work of a random sample of 1000 employed adults. The mean is $\bar{x} = 49.2$ minutes and the standard deviation is $s = 63.9$ minutes. What is the standard error of the mean?

18.2   Comparing breathing frequencies in swimming. Researchers from the United Kingdom studied the effect of two breathing frequencies on performance times and on several physiological parameters in front crawl swimming. The breathing frequencies were one breath every second stroke (B2) and one breath every fourth stroke (B4). Subjects were 10 male collegiate swimmers. Each subject swam 200 meters using each breathing frequency: once with breathing frequency B2 and once on a different day with breathing frequency B4. A paper states that the results are expressed as mean plus or minus the standard deviation.[2] One result reported in the paper states that the immediate postexercise heart rate for subjects when using breathing frequency B2 was 163 ± 15 beats per minute. What are $\bar{x}$ and the standard error of the mean for these subjects? (This exercise is also a warning to read carefully: that 163 ± 15 is *not* a confidence interval, yet summaries in this form are common in scientific reports.)

Oote Boe Photography/Alamy

THE *t* DISTRIBUTIONS

If we knew the value of σ, we would base confidence intervals and tests for μ on the one-sample z statistic

$$z = \frac{\bar{x} - \mu}{\sigma/\sqrt{n}}$$

This z statistic has the standard Normal distribution $N(0, 1)$. In practice, we don't know σ, so we substitute the standard error $s/\sqrt{n}$ of $\bar{x}$ for its standard deviation $\sigma/\sqrt{n}$. The statistic that results does not have a Normal distribution. It has a distribution that is new to us, called a *t distribution*.

THE ONE-SAMPLE *t* STATISTIC AND THE *t* DISTRIBUTIONS

Draw an SRS of size n from a large population that has the Normal distribution with mean μ and standard deviation σ. The **one-sample *t* statistic**

$$t = \frac{\bar{x} - \mu}{s/\sqrt{n}}$$

has the **t distribution** with $n - 1$ degrees of freedom.

The t statistic has the same interpretation as any standardized statistic: it says how far $\bar{x}$ is from its mean μ in standard deviation units. There is a different t distribution for each sample size. We specify a particular t distribution by giving its **degrees of freedom.** The degrees of freedom for the one-sample t statistic come from the sample standard deviation s in the denominator of t. We saw in Chapter 2 (page 41) that s has $n - 1$ degrees of freedom. There are other t statistics with different degrees of freedom, some of which we will meet later. We will write the t distribution with $n - 1$ degrees of freedom as $t(n - 1)$ for short.

degrees of freedom

Figure 18.1 on the next page compares the density curves of the standard Normal distribution and the t distributions with 2 and 9 degrees of freedom. The figure illustrates these facts about the t distributions:

■ The density curves of the t distributions are similar in shape to the standard Normal curve. They are symmetric about 0, single-peaked, and bell-shaped.

■ The spread of the t distributions is a bit greater than that of the standard Normal distribution. The t distributions in Figure 18.1 have more probability in the tails and less in the center than does the standard Normal. This is true because substituting the estimate s for the fixed parameter σ introduces more variation into the statistic.

■ As the degrees of freedom increase, the t density curve approaches the $N(0, 1)$ curve ever more closely. This happens because s estimates σ more accurately as the sample size increases. So using s in place of σ causes little extra variation when the sample is large.

Table C in the back of the book gives critical values for the t distributions. Each row in the table contains critical values for the t distribution whose degrees of freedom appear at the left of the row. For convenience, we label the table entries both by the

FIGURE 18.1

Density curves for the *t* distributions with 2 and 9 degrees of freedom and for the standard Normal distribution. All are symmetric with center 0. The *t* distributions are somewhat more spread out.

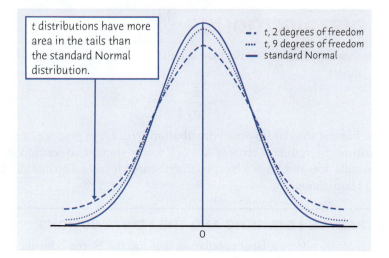

t distributions have more area in the tails than the standard Normal distribution.

- -• *t*, 2 degrees of freedom
- •••• *t*, 9 degrees of freedom
- —— standard Normal

0

confidence level C (in percent) required for confidence intervals and by the one-sided and two-sided *P*-values for each critical value. You have already used the standard Normal critical values in the *z** row at the bottom of Table C. By looking down any column, you can check that the *t* critical values approach the Normal values as the degrees of freedom increase. If you use statistical software, you don't need Table C.

EXAMPLE 18.1 *t* critical values

Figure 18.1 shows the density curve for the *t* distribution with 9 degrees of freedom. What point on this distribution has probability 0.05 to its right? In Table C, look in the df = 9 row above one-sided *P*-value .05 and you will find that this critical value is *t** = 1.833. To use software, enter the degrees of freedom and the probability you want to the *left,* 0.95 in this case. Here is Minitab's output:

```
Student's t distribution with 9 DF
P( X <= x )        x
   0.95 1.83311 ■
```

APPLY YOUR KNOWLEDGE

18.3 Critical values. Use Table C or software to find

(a) the critical value for a one-sided test with level $\alpha = 0.05$ based on the $t(4)$ distribution.

(b) the critical value for a 98% confidence interval based on the $t(26)$ distribution.

18.4 More critical values. You have an SRS of size 30 and calculate the one-sample *t* statistic. What is the critical value *t** such that

(a) *t* has probability 0.025 to the right of *t**?

(b) *t* has probability 0.75 to the left of *t**?

THE ONE-SAMPLE *t* CONFIDENCE INTERVAL

To analyze samples from Normal populations with unknown σ, just replace the standard deviation $\sigma/\sqrt{n}$ of $\bar{x}$ by its standard error $s/\sqrt{n}$ in the z procedures of Chapters 14, 15, and 16. The confidence interval and test that result are *one-sample t procedures*. Critical values and *P*-values come from the *t* distribution with $n - 1$ degrees of freedom. The one-sample *t* procedures are similar in both reasoning and computational detail to the z procedures.

THE ONE-SAMPLE *t* CONFIDENCE INTERVAL

Draw an SRS of size n from a large population having unknown mean μ. A level C **confidence interval for μ** is

$$\bar{x} \pm t^* \frac{s}{\sqrt{n}}$$

where t^* is the critical value for the $t(n - 1)$ density curve with area C between $-t^*$ and t^*. This interval is exact when the population distribution is Normal and is approximately correct for large n in other cases.

EXAMPLE 18.2 Good weather, good tips?

TIPPING2

Let's look again at the study of tipping in a restaurant that we met in Example 14.3. We follow the four-step process for a confidence interval, outlined on page 291.

STATE: Does the expectation of good weather lead to more generous behavior? Psychologists studied the size of the tip in a restaurant when a message indicating that the next day's weather would be good was written on the bill. Here are tips from 20 patrons, measured in percent of the total bill:[3]

20.8	18.7	19.9	20.6	21.9	23.4	22.8	24.9	22.2	20.3
24.9	22.3	27.0	20.4	22.2	24.0	21.1	22.1	22.0	22.7

This is one of three sets of measurements made, the others being tips received when the message on the bill said that the next day's weather would not be good or there was no message on the bill. We want to estimate the mean tip for comparison with tips under the other conditions.

PLAN: We will give a 95% confidence interval to estimate the mean tip percent μ for all patrons of this restaurant when they receive a message on their bill indicating that the next day's weather will be good.

SOLVE: We must first check the conditions for inference.

■ As in Chapter 14 (page 285), we are willing to regard these patrons as an SRS from all patrons of this restaurant.

```
18 | 7
19 | 9
20 | 3 4 6 8
21 | 1 9
22 | 0 1 2 2 3 7 8
23 | 4
24 | 0 9 9
25 |
26 |
27 | 0
```

FIGURE 18.2

Stemplot of the tip percents, for Example 18.2.

■ The stemplot in Figure 18.2 does not suggest any strong departures from Normality. We can proceed to calculation. For these data,

$$\bar{x} = 22.21 \quad \text{and} \quad s = 1.963$$

The degrees of freedom are $n - 1 = 19$. From Table C we find that for 95% confidence $t^* = 2.093$. The confidence interval is

$$\bar{x} \pm t^* \frac{s}{\sqrt{n}} = 22.21 \pm 2.093 \frac{1.963}{\sqrt{20}}$$
$$= 22.21 \pm 0.92$$
$$= 21.29 \text{ to } 23.13 \text{ percent}$$

CONCLUDE: We are 95% confident that the mean tip percent for all patrons of this restaurant when their bill contains a message that the next day's weather will be good is between 21.29 and 23.13. ■

Our work in Example 18.2 is very similar to what we did in Example 14.3 (page 291). To make the inference realistic we replaced the assumed $\sigma = 2$ by $s = 1.963$ calculated from the data and replaced the standard Normal critical value $z^* = 1.960$ by the t critical value $t^* = 2.093$.

The one-sample t confidence interval has the form

$$\text{estimate} \pm t^* \text{SE}_{\text{estimate}}$$

where "SE" stands for "standard error." We will meet a number of confidence intervals that have this common form. In Example 18.2, the estimate is the sample mean $\bar{x}$, and its standard error is

$$\text{SE}_{\bar{x}} = \frac{s}{\sqrt{n}}$$
$$= \frac{1.963}{\sqrt{20}} = 0.439$$

Software will find $\bar{x}$, s, $\text{SE}_{\bar{x}}$, and the confidence interval from the data. Figure 18.5 (page 359) displays typical software output for Example 18.2.

APPLY YOUR KNOWLEDGE

18.5 Critical values. What critical value t^* from Table C would you use for a confidence interval for the mean of the population in each of the following situations?

(a) A 95% confidence interval based on $n = 12$ observations.

(b) A 99% confidence interval from an SRS of 18 observations.

(c) A 90% confidence interval from a sample of size 6.

18.6 How much will I bet? Our decisions depend on how the options are presented to us. Here's an experiment that illustrates this phenomenon. Tell 20 subjects that they have been given $50 but can't keep it all. Then present them with a long series of choices between bets they can make with the $50. Scattered among these choices in random order are 64 choices that ask the subject to choose between betting a fixed amount and an all-or-nothing gamble. The odds for all the bets are the same, but in 32 of the choices, the fixed option reads "Keep $20," and in the other 32 choices, the fixed option reads "Lose $30." These two fixed options lead to exactly the same outcome, but people are more likely to choose the fixed option that says they lose money. Here are the percent differences ("Number of times chose 'Lose $30' " minus "Number of times chose 'Keep $20' " divided by the number of trials on which the 20 subjects chose the fixed-option gamble rather than the all-or-nothing bet).[4] **GAMBLING1**

| 37.5 | 30.8 | 6.2 | 17.6 | 14.3 | 8.3 | 16.7 | 20.0 | 10.5 | 21.7 |
| 30.8 | 27.3 | 22.7 | 38.5 | 8.3 | 10.5 | 8.3 | 10.5 | 25.0 | 7.7 |

(a) Make a stemplot. Is there any sign of a major deviation from Normality?

(b) All 20 subjects gambled a fixed amount more often when faced with a sure loss than when faced with a sure win. Give a 95% confidence interval for the mean percent increase in gambling a fixed amount when faced with a sure loss.

18.7 Ancient air. The composition of the earth's atmosphere may have changed over time. To try to discover the nature of the atmosphere long ago, we can examine the gas in bubbles inside ancient amber. Amber is tree resin that has hardened and been trapped in rocks. The gas in bubbles within amber should be a sample of the atmosphere at the time the amber was formed. Measurements on specimens of amber from the late Cretaceous era (75 to 95 million years ago) give these percents of nitrogen:[5] **ANCIENTAIR**

| 63.4 | 65.0 | 64.4 | 63.3 | 54.8 | 64.5 | 60.8 | 49.1 | 51.0 |

Assume (this is not yet agreed on by experts) that these observations are an SRS from the late Cretaceous atmosphere. Use a 90% confidence interval to estimate the mean percent of nitrogen in ancient air. Follow the four-step process as illustrated in Example 18.2. (Our present-day atmosphere is about 78.1% nitrogen).

David Sanger Photography/Alamy

THE ONE-SAMPLE *t* TEST

The *t* test for a population mean is very similar to the *z* test we met on page 306. The only difference is that the *P*-values come from a *t* distribution rather than from the standard Normal distribution.

THE ONE-SAMPLE *t* TEST

Draw an SRS of size n from a large population having unknown mean μ. To **test the hypothesis H_0: $\mu = \mu_0$**, compute the **one-sample t statistic**

$$t = \frac{\bar{x} - \mu_0}{s/\sqrt{n}}$$

In terms of a variable T having the $t(n-1)$ distribution, the P-value for a test of H_0 against

H_a: $\mu > \mu_0$ is $P(T \geq t)$

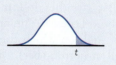

H_a: $\mu < \mu_0$ is $P(T \leq t)$

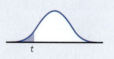

H_a: $\mu \neq \mu_0$ is $2P(T \geq |t|)$

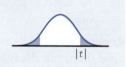

These P-values are exact if the population distribution is Normal and are approximately correct for large n in other cases.

DATA FILE

WATERQUAL

4-STEP

EXAMPLE 18.3   Water quality

We follow the four-step process for a significance test, outlined on page 307.

STATE: To investigate water quality, on August 8, 2010, the *Columbus Dispatch* took water samples at 20 Ohio State Park swimming areas. Those samples were taken to laboratories and tested for fecal coliform, which are bacteria found in human and animal feces. An unsafe level of fecal coliform means there's a higher chance that disease-causing bacteria are present and more risk that a swimmer will become ill. Ohio considers it unsafe if a 100-milliliter sample (about 3.3 ounces) of water contains more than 400 coliform bacteria. Here are the fecal coliform levels found by the laboratories:[6]

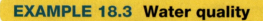

| 160 | 40 | 2800 | 80 | 2000 | 2000 | 1500 | 400 | 150 | 500 |
| 3000 | 2200 | 15 | 80 | 2000 | 2000 | 2600 | 600 | 1000 | 1500 |

Are these data good evidence that, on average, the fecal coliform levels in these swimming areas were unsafe?

PLAN: Experts caution that the tests are a snapshot of the quality of the water at the time they were taken. Fecal coliform levels can change as weather and other conditions change. So we ask the question in terms of the mean fecal coliform level μ for all these swimming areas. The null hypothesis is "level is not unsafe," and the alternative hypothesis is "level is unsafe."

$$H_0: \mu = 400$$
$$H_a: \mu > 400$$

SOLVE: First check the conditions for inference. We are willing to regard these particular 20 samples as an SRS from a large population of possible samples. Figure 18.3 is a histogram of the data. We can't accurately judge Normality from 20 observations; there are no outliers but the data are somewhat skewed. *P*-values for the *t* test may be only approximately accurate.

The basic statistics are

$$\bar{x} = 1231 \quad \text{and} \quad s = 1038$$

The one-sample *t* statistic is

$$t = \frac{\bar{x} - \mu_0}{s/\sqrt{n}} = \frac{1231 - 400}{1038/\sqrt{20}}$$
$$= 3.580$$

The *P*-value for $t = 3.580$ is the area to the right of 3.580 under the *t* distribution curve with degrees of freedom $n - 1 = 19$. Figure 18.4 shows this area. Software (see Figure 18.6) tells us that $P = 0.001$.

Without software, we can pin *P* between two values by using Table C. Search the df = 19 row of Table C for entries that bracket $t = 3.580$. The observed *t* lies between the critical values for one-sided *P* -values 0.001 and 0.0005.

CONCLUDE: There is quite strong evidence ($P < 0.001$) that, on average, fecal coliform levels in these Ohio State Park swimming areas are unsafe. ■

df = 19		
*t**	3.579	3.883
One-sided *P*	.001	.0005

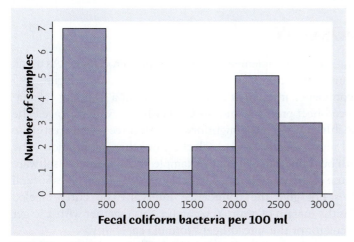

FIGURE 18.3

Histogram of the fecal coliform levels for Example 18.3.

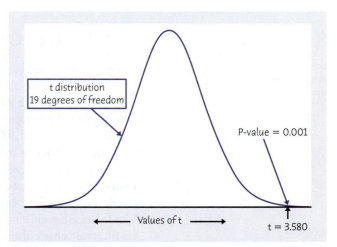

FIGURE 18.4

The *P*-value for the one-sided *t* test in Example 18.3.

APPLY YOUR KNOWLEDGE

18.8 Is it significant? The one-sample t statistic for testing

$$H_0: \mu = 0$$
$$H_a: \mu > 0$$

from a sample of $n = 20$ observations has the value $t = 1.84$.

(a)   What are the degrees of freedom for this statistic?

(b)   Give the two critical values t^* from Table C that bracket t. What are the one-sided P-values for these two entries?

(c)   Is the value $t = 1.84$ significant at the 5% level? Is it significant at the 1% level?

(d)   (Optional) If you have access to suitable technology, give the exact one-sided P-value for $t = 1.84$.

18.9 Is it significant? The one-sample t statistic from a sample of $n = 15$ observations for the two-sided test of

$$H_0: \mu = 64$$
$$H_a: \mu \neq 64$$

has the value $t = 2.12$.

(a)   What are the degrees of freedom for t?

(b)   Locate the two critical values t^* from Table C that bracket t. What are the two-sided P-values for these two entries?

(c)   Is the value $t = 2.12$ statistically significant at the 10% level? At the 5% level?

(d)   (Optional) If you have access to suitable technology, give the exact two-sided P-value for $t = 2.12$.

18.10 Ancient air, continued. Do the data of Exercise 18.7 give good reason to think that the percent of nitrogen in the air during the Cretaceous era was different from the present 78.1%? Carry out a test of significance, following the four-step process as illustrated in Example 18.3. ANCIENTAIR

● USING TECHNOLOGY

Any technology suitable for statistics will implement the one-sample t procedures. As usual, you can read and use almost any output now that you know what to look for. Figure 18.5 displays output for the 95% confidence interval of Example 18.2 from a graphing calculator, a statistical program, a spreadsheet program, and the CrunchIt! software package. The calculator, Minitab, and CrunchIt! outputs are straightforward. All three give the estimate $\bar{x}$ and the confidence interval plus a clearly labeled selection of other information. The confidence interval agrees with our hand calculation in Example 18.2. In general, software results are more accurate because of the rounding in hand calculations. Excel gives several descriptive measures but does not give the confidence interval. The entry labeled "Confidence Level (95.0%)" is the margin of error. You can use this together with $\bar{x}$ to get the interval using either a calculator or the spreadsheet's formula capability.

Figure 18.6 displays output for the t test in Example 18.3. The graphing calculator, Minitab, and CrunchIt! give the sample mean $\bar{x}$, the t statistic, and its P-value. Accurate

Texas Instruments Graphing Calculator

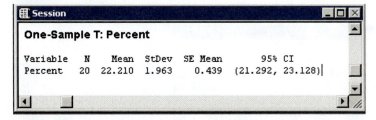

```
TInterval
 (21.292,23.128)
x̄=22.2100
Sx=1.9625
n=20.0000
```

FIGURE 18.5

The *t* confidence interval for Example 18.2: output from a graphing calculator, a statistical program, and a spreadsheet program, and a software package.

Minitab

Session □□⊠

One-Sample T: Percent

Variable	N	Mean	StDev	SE Mean	95% CI
Percent	20	22.210	1.963	0.439	(21.292, 23.128)

Excel

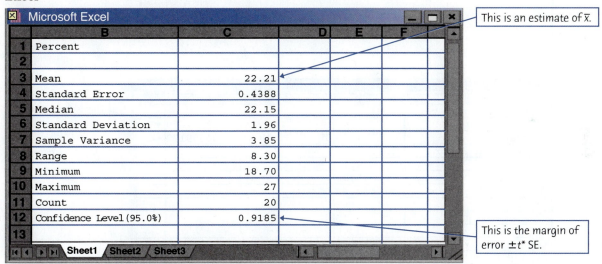

Microsoft Excel _ □ ⊠

	B	C	D	E	F
1	Percent				
2					
3	Mean	22.21			
4	Standard Error	0.4388			
5	Median	22.15			
6	Standard Deviation	1.96			
7	Sample Variance	3.85			
8	Range	8.30			
9	Minimum	18.70			
10	Maximum	27			
11	Count	20			
12	Confidence Level(95.0%)	0.9185			
13					

Sheet1 / Sheet2 / Sheet3

This is an estimate of x̄.

This is the margin of error ±*t** SE.

CrunchIt!

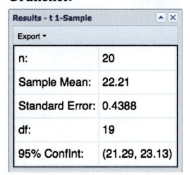

Results - t 1-Sample ▲ ⊠

Export ▾

n:	20
Sample Mean:	22.21
Standard Error:	0.4388
df:	19
95% ConfInt:	(21.29, 23.13)

Texas Instruments Graphing Calculator

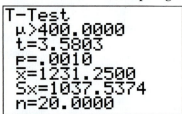

```
T-Test
 μ>400.0000
 t=3.5803
 P=.0010
 x̄=1231.2500
 Sx=1037.5374
 n=20.0000
```

FIGURE 18.6

The *t* test for Example 18.3: output from a graphing calculator, a statistical program, and a spreadsheet program, and a software package.

Minitab

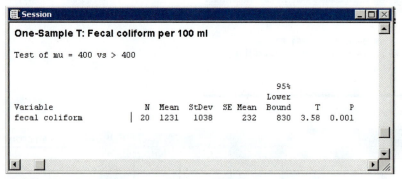

Session

One-Sample T: Fecal coliform per 100 ml

Test of mu = 400 vs > 400

					95% Lower		
Variable	N	Mean	StDev	SE Mean	Bound	T	P
fecal coliform	20	1231	1038	232	830	3.58	0.001

Excel

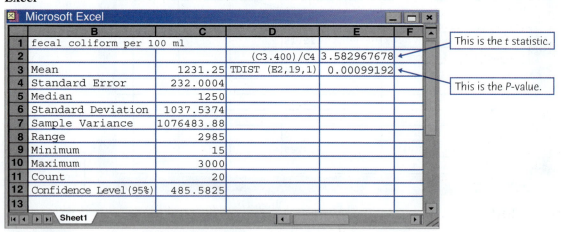

Microsoft Excel

	B	C	D	E	F
1	fecal coliform per 100 ml				
2			(C3.400)/C4	3.582967678	
3	Mean	1231.25	TDIST (E2,19,1)	0.00099192	
4	Standard Error	232.0004			
5	Median	1250			
6	Standard Deviation	1037.5374			
7	Sample Variance	1076483.88			
8	Range	2985			
9	Minimum	15			
10	Maximum	3000			
11	Count	20			
12	Confidence Level(95%)	485.5825			
13					

Sheet1

This is the *t* statistic.

This is the *P*-value.

CrunchIt!

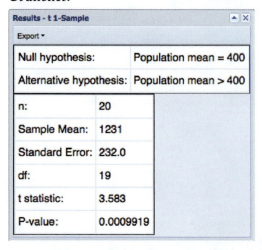

Results - t 1-Sample

Export ▾

Null hypothesis:	Population mean = 400
Alternative hypothesis:	Population mean > 400

n:	20
Sample Mean:	1231
Standard Error:	232.0
df:	19
t statistic:	3.583
P-value:	0.0009919

P-values are the biggest advantage of software for the *t* procedures. Excel is, as usual, more awkward than software designed for statistics. It lacks a one-sample *t* test menu selection but does have a function named TDIST for tail areas under *t* density curves. The Excel output shows functions for the *t* statistic and its *P*-value to the right of the main display, along with their values $t = 3.582967678$ and $P = 0.00099192$.

MATCHED PAIRS *t* PROCEDURES

Often the goal of an investigation is to demonstrate that a treatment causes an observed effect. In Chapter 9 we learned that randomized comparative studies are more convincing than single-sample investigations for demonstrating causation. For that reason, one-sample inference is less common than comparative inference. One common design to compare two treatments makes use of one-sample procedures. Matched pairs designs were discussed in Chapter 9. In a **matched pairs design,** subjects are matched in pairs and each treatment is given to one subject in each pair. Another situation calling for matched pairs is before-and-after observations on the same subjects.

matched pairs design

MATCHED PAIRS *t* PROCEDURES

To compare the responses to the two treatments in a matched pairs design, find the difference between the responses within each pair. Then apply the one-sample *t* procedures to these differences.

The parameter μ in a matched pairs *t* procedure is the mean difference in the responses to the two treatments within matched pairs of subjects in the entire population.

EXAMPLE 18.4 Do chimpanzees collaborate?

CHIMPS

STATE: Humans often collaborate to solve problems. Will chimpanzees recruit another chimp when solving a problem requires collaboration? Researchers presented chimpanzee subjects with food outside their cage that they could bring within reach by pulling two ropes, one attached to each end of the food tray. If a chimp pulled only one rope, the rope came loose and the food was lost. Another chimp was available as a partner, but only if the subject unlocked a door joining two cages. (Chimpanzees learn these things quickly.) The same 8 chimpanzee subjects faced this problem in two versions: the two ropes were close enough together that one chimp could pull both (no collaboration needed) or the two ropes were too far apart for one chimp to pull both (collaboration needed). Each subject faced each version of the problem in 24 trials. Table 18.1 shows how many times each subject opened the door to recruit a partner.[7] Is there evidence that chimpanzees recruit partners more often when a problem requires collaboration?

Manoj Shah/Getty

PLAN: Take μ to be the mean difference (collaboration required minus not) in the number of times a subject recruited a partner. The null hypothesis says that the need for collaboration has no effect, and H_a says that partners are recruited more often when the problem requires collaboration. So we test the hypotheses

$$H_0: \mu = 0$$
$$H_a: \mu > 0$$

TABLE 18.1 Trials (out of 24) on which chimpanzees recruited a partner

| CHIMPANZEE | COLLABORATION NEEDED | | DIFFERENCE |
	YES	NO	
Namuiska	16	0	16
Kalema	16	1	15
Okech	23	5	18
Baluku	19	3	16
Umugenzi	15	4	11
Indi	20	9	11
Bili	24	16	8
Asega	24	20	4

SOLVE: The subjects are "semi-free-ranging chimpanzees at Ngamba Island Chimpanzee Sanctuary in Uganda." We are willing to regard them as an SRS from their species. To analyze the data, we examine the difference in the number of times a chimp recruited a partner, so subtract the "no collaboration needed" count from the "collaboration needed" count for each subject. The 8 differences form a single sample from a population with unknown mean μ. They appear in the "Difference" column in Table 18.1. All the chimpanzees recruited a partner more often when the ropes were too far apart to be pulled by one chimp.

The stemplot in Figure 18.7 creates the impression of a left-skew. This is a bit misleading, as the *dotplot* in the bottom part of Figure 18.7 shows. A dotplot simply places the observations on an axis, stacking observations that have the same value. It gives a good picture of distributions with only whole-number values. We know that observations that can take only whole-number values cannot come from a Normal population. In practice, researchers are willing to treat such observations as coming from a Normal population if there are more than just a few possible values and the distribution appears approximately Normal. Of course, we can't assess approximate Normality from just 8 observations, but there are no signs of major departures from Normality. The researchers used the matched pairs *t* test.

The 8 differences have

$$\bar{x} = 12.375 \quad \text{and} \quad s = 4.749$$

The one-sample *t* statistic is therefore

$$t = \frac{\bar{x} - 0}{s/\sqrt{n}} = \frac{12.375 - 0}{4.749/\sqrt{8}}$$

$$= 7.37$$

Find the *P*-value from the $t(7)$ distribution. (Remember that the degrees of freedom are 1 less than the sample size.) Table C shows that 7.37 is greater than the critical value for one-sided $P = 0.0005$. The *P*-value is therefore less than 0.0005. Software says that $P = 0.000077$.

CONCLUDE: The data give very strong evidence ($P < 0.0005$) that chimpanzees recruit a collaborator more often when faced with a problem that requires a collaborator to solve. That is, chimpanzees recognize when collaboration is necessary, a skill that they share with humans. ■

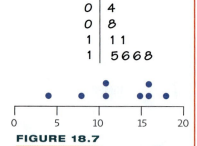

```
0 | 4
0 | 8
1 | 1 1
1 | 5 6 6 8
```

FIGURE 18.7

Stemplot and dotplot of the differences, for Example 18.4.

df = 7		
t^*	4.785	5.408
One-sided P	.001	.0005

Example 18.4 illustrates how to turn matched pairs data into single-sample data by taking differences within each pair. We are making inferences about a single population, the population of all differences within matched pairs. *It is incorrect to ignore the matching and analyze the data as if we had two samples of chimpanzees, one facing ropes close together and the other facing ropes far apart.* Inference procedures for comparing two samples assume that the samples are selected independently of each other. This condition does not hold when the same subjects are measured twice.

APPLY YOUR KNOWLEDGE

Many exercises from this point on ask you to give the P-value of a t test. If you have suitable technology, give the exact P-value. Otherwise, use Table C to give two values between which P lies.

18.11 The brain responds to sound. The usual way to study the brain's response to sounds is to have subjects listen to "pure tones." The response to recognizable sounds may differ. To compare responses, researchers anesthetized macaque monkeys. They fed pure tones and also monkey calls directly to their brains by inserting electrodes. Response to the stimulus was measured by the firing rate (electrical spikes per second) of neurons in various areas of the brain. Table 18.2 contains the responses for 37 neurons.[8] Researchers suspected that the response to monkey calls would be stronger than the response to a pure tone. Do the data support this idea? Complete the "Plan," "Solve," and "Conclude" steps of the four-step process, following the model of Example 18.4. BRAINRESPONSE

18.12 The brain responds, continued. How much more strongly do monkey brains respond to monkey calls than to pure tones? Give a 99% confidence interval to answer this question. BRAINRESPONSE

TABLE 18.2 Neuron response to tones and monkey calls

TONE	CALL	TONE	CALL	TONE	CALL	TONE	CALL
474	500	145	42	71	134	35	103
256	138	141	241	68	65	31	70
241	485	129	194	59	182	28	192
226	338	113	123	59	97	26	203
185	194	112	182	57	318	26	135
174	159	102	141	56	201	21	129
176	341	100	118	47	279	20	193
168	85	74	62	46	62	20	54
161	303	72	112	41	84	19	66
150	208						

ROBUSTNESS OF *t* PROCEDURES

The *t* confidence interval and test are exactly correct when the distribution of the population is exactly Normal. No real data are exactly Normal. The usefulness of the *t* procedures in practice therefore depends on how strongly they are affected by lack of Normality.

> ### ROBUST PROCEDURES
>
> A confidence interval or significance test is called **robust** if the confidence level or *P*-value does not change very much when the conditions for use of the procedure are violated.

The condition that the population is Normal rules out outliers, so the presence of outliers shows that this condition is not fulfilled. The *t* procedures are not robust against outliers unless the sample is large, because $\bar{x}$ and s are not resistant to outliers.

Fortunately, the *t* procedures are quite robust against non-Normality of the population except when outliers or strong skewness are present. (Skewness is more serious than other kinds of non-Normality.) As the size of the sample increases, the central limit theorem ensures that the distribution of the sample mean $\bar{x}$ becomes more nearly Normal and that the *t* distribution becomes more accurate for critical values and *P*-values of the *t* procedures.

Always make a plot to check for skewness and outliers before you use the *t* procedures for small samples. For most purposes, you can safely use the one-sample *t* procedures when $n \geq 15$ unless an outlier or quite strong skewness is present. Here are practical guidelines for inference on a single mean.[9]

> ### USING THE *t* PROCEDURES
>
> - Except in the case of small samples, the condition that the data are an SRS from the population of interest is more important than the condition that the population distribution is Normal.
> - *Sample size less than 15:* Use *t* procedures if the data appear close to Normal (roughly symmetric, single peak, no outliers). If the data are clearly skewed or if outliers are present, do not use *t*.
> - *Sample size at least 15:* The *t* procedures can be used except in the presence of outliers or strong skewness.
> - *Large samples:* The *t* procedures can be used even for clearly skewed distributions when the sample is large, roughly $n \geq 40$.

EXAMPLE 18.5 Can we use *t*?

Figure 18.8 shows plots of several data sets. For which of these can we safely use the *t* procedures?[10]

- Figure 18.8(a) is a histogram of the percent of each state's adult residents who are college graduates. *We have data on the entire population of 50 states, so inference is not needed.* We can calculate the exact mean for the population. There is no uncertainty due to having only a sample from the population, and no need for a confidence interval or test. *If these data were an SRS from a larger population, t inference would be safe despite the mild skewness because n = 50.*

■ Figure 18.8(b) is a stemplot of the force required to pull apart 20 pieces of Douglas fir. *The data are strongly skewed to the left with possible low outliers, so we cannot trust the t procedures for n = 20.*

■ Figure 18.8(c) is a stemplot of the lengths of 23 specimens of the red variety of the tropical flower *Heliconia*. *The data are mildly skewed to the right and there are no outliers. We can use the t distributions for such data.*

■ Figure 18.8(d) is a histogram of the heights of the students in a college class. *This distribution is quite symmetric and appears close to Normal. We can use the t procedures for any sample size.* ■

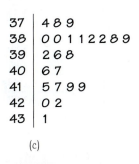

```
23 | 0
24 | 0
25 |
26 | 5
27 |
28 | 7
29 |
30 | 2 5 9
31 | 3 9 9
32 | 0 3 3 6 7 7
33 | 0 2 3 6
```
(b)

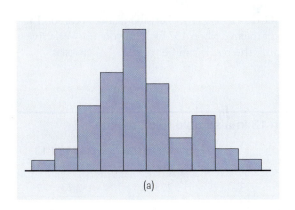

```
37 | 4 8 9
38 | 0 0 1 1 2 2 8 9
39 | 2 6 8
40 | 6 7
41 | 5 7 9 9
42 | 0 2
43 | 1
```
(c)

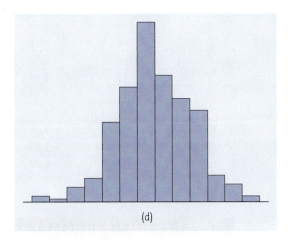

(d)

FIGURE 18.8

Can we use *t* procedures for these data? (a) Percent of adult college graduates in the 50 states. *No,* this is an entire population, not a sample. (b) Force required to pull apart 20 pieces of Douglas fir. *No,* there are just 20 observations and strong skewness. (c) Lengths of 23 tropical flowers of the same variety. *Yes,* the sample is large enough to overcome the mild skewness. (d) Heights of college students. *Yes, for any size sample,* because the distribution is close to Normal.

Eric Nathan /Alamy

APPLY YOUR KNOWLEDGE

18.13 Diamonds. A group of earth scientists studied the small diamonds found in a nodule of rock carried up to the earth's surface in surrounding rock. This is an opportunity to examine a sample from a single population of diamonds formed in a single event deep in the earth.[11] Table 18.3 presents data on the nitrogen content (parts per million) and the abundance of carbon 13 in these diamonds. (Carbon has several isotopes, forms with different numbers of neutrons in the nuclei of their atoms. Carbon 12 makes up almost 99% of natural carbon. The abundance of carbon 13 is measured by the ratio of carbon 13 to carbon 12, in parts per thousand more or less than a standard. The minus signs in the data mean that the ratio is smaller in these diamonds than in standard carbon.)

We would like to estimate the mean abundance of both nitrogen and carbon 13 in the population of diamonds represented by this sample. Examine the data for nitrogen. Can we use a *t* confidence interval for mean nitrogen? Explain your answer. Give a 90% confidence interval if you think the result can be trusted. **DIAMONDS**

18.14 Diamonds, continued. Examine the data in Table 18.3 on abundance of carbon 13. Can we use a *t* confidence interval for mean carbon 13? Explain your answer. Give a 90% confidence interval if you think the result can be trusted. **DIAMONDS**

TABLE 18.3 Nitrogen and carbon 13 in a sample of diamonds

DIAMOND	NITROGEN (PPM)	CARBON 13 RATIO	DIAMOND	NITROGEN (PPM)	CARBON 13 RATIO
1	487	−2.78	13	273	−2.73
2	1430	−1.39	14	94	−2.33
3	60	−4.26	15	69	−3.83
4	244	−1.19	16	262	−2.04
5	196	−2.12	17	120	−2.82
6	274	−2.87	18	302	−0.84
7	41	−3.68	19	75	−3.57
8	54	−3.29	20	242	−2.42
9	473	−3.79	21	115	−3.89
10	30	−4.06	22	65	−3.87
11	98	−1.83	23	311	−1.58
12	41	−4.03	24	61	−3.97

CHAPTER 18 SUMMARY

CHAPTER SPECIFICS

■ Tests and confidence intervals for the mean μ of a Normal population are based on the sample mean $\bar{x}$ of an SRS. Because of the central limit theorem, the resulting procedures are approximately correct for other population distributions when the sample is large.

- The standardized sample mean is the **one-sample z statistic**

$$z = \frac{\bar{x} - \mu}{\sigma/\sqrt{n}}$$

  If we knew σ, we would use the z statistic and the standard Normal distribution.

- In practice, we do not know σ. Replace the standard deviation $\sigma/\sqrt{n}$ of $\bar{x}$ by the **standard error** $s/\sqrt{n}$ to get the **one-sample t statistic**

$$t = \frac{\bar{x} - \mu}{s/\sqrt{n}}$$

- The t statistic has the **t distribution** with $n - 1$ degrees of freedom.

- There is a t distribution for every positive **degrees of freedom.** All are symmetric distributions similar in shape to the standard Normal distribution. The t distribution approaches the $N(0, 1)$ distribution as the degrees of freedom increase.

- A level C **confidence interval for the mean μ** of a Normal population is

$$\bar{x} \pm t^* \frac{s}{\sqrt{n}}$$

- The **critical value** t^* is chosen so that the t curve with $n - 1$ degrees of freedom has area C between $-t^*$ and t^*.

- **Significance tests** for H_0: $\mu = \mu_0$ are based on the t statistic. Use P-values or fixed significance levels from the $t(n - 1)$ distribution.

- Use these one-sample procedures to analyze **matched pairs** data by first taking the difference within each matched pair to produce a single sample.

- The t procedures are quite **robust** when the population is non-Normal, especially for larger sample sizes. The t procedures are useful for non-Normal data when $n \geq 15$ unless the data show outliers or strong skewness. When $n \geq 40$, the t procedures can be used even for clearly skewed distributions.

LINK IT

In Chapters 14 to 16 we began our study of inference. We focused on inference for a population mean based on a sample from a Normal population. We included the unrealistic assumption that we knew the population standard deviation σ. The reason was to make the underlying mathematics simpler. We were able to use what we learned about the Normal distribution in Chapters 3 and 10 and what we learned about the sampling distribution of the sample mean in Chapter 11 to construct confidence intervals for and conduct hypothesis tests about the population mean. Computing P-values and sample sizes was possible using what we had learned about Normal probability calculations.

In this chapter we continue our study of inference about a population mean based on a sample from a Normal population in the more realistic setting that we do not know σ. The basic ideas of Chapters 14 to 16 still apply, but now we use the t distribution rather than the Normal distribution. Unfortunately, the mathematics associated with the t distribution is more complicated than that associated with the Normal distribution. We must rely on approximations from tables or on statistical software to calculate P-values (and determining sample sizes is also more complicated when we use the t distribution). As we continue our study of statistical inference in realistic settings, statistical software will be invaluable.

As we saw in Chapter 9, statistical studies comparing two or more groups are preferable to one-sample procedures if we want to demonstrate that a treatment causes an observed response. As a first step toward developing methods for comparing means from two populations, we considered matched pairs studies (also discussed in Chapter 9) and saw that by looking at differences, we could use our one-sample t procedures to compare two means. In the next chapter, we consider inference for comparing the means of two populations when we have independent samples from the two populations. This will expand our tools for doing statistical inference in settings that we encounter in practice.

CHECK YOUR SKILLS

18.15 We prefer the t procedures to the z procedures for inference about a population mean because

  (a) z can be used only for large samples.

  (b) z requires that you know the population standard deviation σ.

  (c) z requires that you can regard your data as an SRS from the population.

18.16 You are testing H_0: $\mu = 10$ against H_a: $\mu < 10$ based on an SRS of 16 observations from a Normal population. The data give $\bar{x} = 8$ and $s = 4$. The value of the t statistic is

  (a) -0.5.

  (b) -2.

  (c) -8.

18.17 You are testing H_0: $\mu = 100$ against H_a: $\mu < 100$ based on an SRS of 25 observations from a Normal population. The t statistic is $t = -2.5$. The degrees of freedom for the t statistic are

  (a) 26.   (b) 25.   (c) 24.

18.18 You have an SRS of 12 observations from a Normally distributed population. What critical value would you use to obtain a 98% confidence interval for the mean μ of the population?

  (a) 2.718

  (b) 2.681

  (c) 2.650

18.19 Data on the blood cholesterol levels of 10 rats (milligrams per deciliter of blood) give $\bar{x} = 85$ and $s = 12$. A 99% confidence interval for the mean blood cholesterol of rats is

  (a) 76.4 to 93.6.

  (b) 73.0 to 97.0.

  (c) 72.7 to 97.3.

18.20 Which of the following would cause the most worry about the validity of the confidence interval you calculated in the previous exercise?

  (a) There is a clear outlier in the data.

  (b) A stemplot of the data shows a mild right-skew.

  (c) You do not know the population standard deviation σ.

18.21 Which of these settings does *not* allow use of a matched pairs t procedure?

  (a) You interview both the husband and the wife in 64 married couples and ask each about their ideal number of children.

  (b) You interview a sample of 64 unmarried male students and another sample of 64 unmarried female students and ask each about their ideal number of children.

  (c) You interview 64 female students in their freshman year and again in their senior year and ask each about their ideal number of children.

CHAPTER 18 EXERCISES

18.22 Body mass index of young women. In Example 14.1 (page 287) we developed a 95% z confidence interval for the mean body mass index (BMI) of women aged 20 to 29 years, based on a national random sample of 654 such women. We assumed there that the population standard deviation was known to be $\sigma = 7.5$. In fact, the sample data had mean BMI $\bar{x} = 26.8$ and standard deviation $s = 7.42$. What is the 95% t confidence interval for the mean BMI of all young women?

18.23 Read carefully. You read in the report of a psychology experiment: "Separate analyses for our two groups of 12 participants revealed no overall placebo effect for our student group (mean = 0.08, SD = 0.37, $t(11) = 0.49$) and a significant effect for our non-student group (mean = 0.35, SD = 0.37, $t(11) = 3.25$, $p < 0.01$)."[12] The null hypothesis is that the mean effect is zero. What are the correct values of the two t statistics based on the means and standard deviations? Compare each correct t-value with the critical values in Table C. What can you say about the two-sided P-value in each case?

18.24 Reading scores in Atlanta. The Trial Urban District Assessment (TUDA) is a government-sponsored study of student achievement in large urban school districts. TUDA gives a reading test scored from 0 to 500. A score of 243 is a "basic" reading level and a score of 281 is "proficient." Scores for a random sample of 3000 eighth-graders in Atlanta had $\bar{x} = 250$ with standard error 1.0.[13]

(a) We don't have the 3000 individual scores, but use of the t procedures is surely safe. Why?

(b) Give a 99% confidence interval for the mean score of all Atlanta eighth-graders. (Be careful: the report gives the standard error of $\bar{x}$, not the standard deviation s.)

(c) Urban children often perform below the basic level. Is there good evidence that the mean for all Atlanta eighth-graders is less than the basic level?

18.25 Color and cognition. In a randomized comparative experiment on the effect of color on the performance of a cognitive task, researchers randomly divided 69 subjects (27 males and 42 females ranging in age from 17 to 25 years) into three groups. Participants were asked to solve a series of 6 anagrams. One group was presented with the anagrams on a blue screen, one group saw them on a red screen, and one group had a neutral screen. The time, in seconds, taken to solve the anagrams was recorded. The paper reporting the study gives

$\bar{x} = 11.58$ and $s = 4.37$ for the times of the 23 members of the neutral group.[14]

(a) Give a 95% confidence interval for the mean time in the population from which the subjects were recruited.

(b) What conditions for the population and the study design are required by the procedure you used in (a)? Which of these conditions are important for the validity of the procedure in this case?

18.26 The placebo effect. The placebo effect is particularly strong in patients with Parkinson's disease. To understand the workings of the placebo effect, scientists measure activity at a key point in the brain when patients receive a placebo that they think is an active drug and also when no treatment is given.[15] The same 6 patients are measured both with and without the placebo, at different times.

(a) Explain why the proper procedure to compare the mean response to placebo with control (no treatment) is a matched pairs t test.

(b) The 6 differences (treatment minus control) had $\bar{x} = -0.326$ and $s = 0.181$. Is there significant evidence of a difference between treatment and control?

18.27 The conductivity of fibrous-glass board. How well materials conduct heat matters when designing houses, for example. Conductivity is measured in terms of watts of heat power transmitted per square meter of surface per degree Celsius of temperature difference on the two sides of the material. The National Institute of Standards and Technology (NIST) provides data on properties of materials. Here are 9 NIST measurements of the heat conductivity of a particular type of fibrous-glass board:[16] **HEATCONDUCT**

0.0339 0.0337 0.0334 0.0334 0.0333
0.0333 0.0333 0.0332 0.0330

(a) We can consider this an SRS of all specimens of fibrous-glass board of this type. Make a stemplot. Is there any sign of major deviation from Normality?

(b) Give a 95% confidence interval for the mean conductivity.

(c) Is there significant evidence at the 5% level that the mean conductivity of this type of fibrous-glass board is not 0.0330?

18.28 Exhaust from school buses. In a study of exhaust emissions from school buses, the pollution intake by passengers was determined for a sample of 9 school buses used in the Southern California Air Basin. The pollution intake is the amount of exhaust emissions, in grams per person, that would be breathed in while traveling on the bus during its usual 18-mile trip on congested freeways from South Central LA to a magnet school in West LA. (As a reference, the average intake of motor emissions of carbon monoxide in the LA area is estimated to be about 0.000046 grams per person.) Here are the amounts for the 9 buses when driven with the windows open:[17] ▧ EMISSIONS

1.15   0.33   0.40   0.33   1.35   0.38   0.25   0.40   0.35

(a) Make a stemplot. Are there outliers or strong skewness that would forbid use of the t procedures?

(b) A good way to judge the effect of outliers is to do your analysis twice, once with the outliers and a second time without them. Give two 90% confidence intervals, one with all the data and one with the outliers removed, for the mean pollution intake among all school buses used in the Southern California Air Basin that travel the route investigated in the study.

(c) Compare the two intervals in part (b). What is the most important effect of removing the outliers?

18.29 A big-toe problem. Hallux abducto valgus (call it HAV) is a deformation of the big toe that often requires surgery. Doctors used X-rays to measure the angle (in degrees) of deformity in 38 consecutive patients under the age of 21 who came to a medical center for surgery to correct HAV. The angle is a measure of the seriousness of the deformity. Here are the data:[18] ▧ DEFORMITY2

28 32 25 34 38 26 25 18 30 26 28 13 20
21 17 16 21 23 14 32 25 21 22 20 18 26
16 30 30 20 50 25 26 28 31 38 32 21

It is reasonable to regard these patients as a random sample of young patients who require HAV surgery. Carry out the "Solve" and "Conclude" steps for a 95% confidence interval for the mean HAV angle in the population of all such patients.

18.30 An outlier's effect. Our bodies have a natural electrical field that is known to help wounds heal. Does changing the field strength slow healing? A series of experiments with newts investigated this question. In one experiment, the two

hind limbs of 12 newts were assigned at random to either experimental or control groups. This is a matched pairs design. The electrical field in the experimental limbs was reduced to zero by applying a voltage. The control limbs were left alone. Here are the rates at which new cells closed a razor cut in each limb, in micrometers per hour:[19] ▧ NEWTS

Newt	1	2	3	4	5	6	7	8	9	10	11	12
Control limb	36	41	39	42	44	39	39	56	33	20	49	30
Experimental limb	28	31	27	33	33	38	45	25	28	33	47	23

(a) Make a stemplot of the differences between limbs of the same newt (control limb minus experimental limb). There is a high outlier.

(b) A good way to judge the effect of an outlier is to do your analysis twice, once with the outlier and a second time without it. Carry out two t tests to see if the mean healing rate is significantly lower in the experimental limbs, one test including all 12 newts and another that omits the outlier. What are the test statistics and their P-values? Does the outlier have a strong influence on your conclusion?

18.31 An outlier's effect. A good way to judge the effect of an outlier is to do your analysis twice, once with the outlier and a second time without it. The data in Exercise 18.29 follow a Normal distribution quite closely except for one patient with HAV angle 50 degrees, a high outlier. ▧ DEFORMITY3

(a) Find the 95% confidence interval for the population mean based on the 37 patients who remain after you drop the outlier.

(b) Compare your interval in (a) with your interval from Exercise 18.32. What is the most important effect of removing the outlier?

18.32 Men of few words? Researchers claim that women speak significantly more words per day than men. One estimate is that a woman uses about 20,000 words per day while a man uses about 7,000. To investigate such claims, one study used a special device to record the conversations of male and female university students over a four-day period. From these recordings, the daily word count of the 20 men in the study was determined. Here are their daily word counts:[20] ▧ TALKING

28,408	10,084	15,931	21,688	37,786
10,575	12,880	11,071	17,799	13,182
8,918	6,495	8,153	7,015	4,429
10,054	3,998	12,639	10,974	5,255

(a) Examine the data. Is it reasonable to use the t procedures (assume these men are an SRS of all male students at this university)?

(b) If your conclusion in part (a) is "Yes," do the data give convincing evidence that the mean number of words per day of men at this university differs from 7,000?

18.33 Genetic engineering for cancer treatment. Here's a new idea for treating advanced melanoma, the most serious kind of skin cancer. Genetically engineer white blood cells to better recognize and destroy cancer cells, then infuse these cells into patients. The subjects in a small initial study were 11 patients whose melanoma had not responded to existing treatments. One question was how rapidly the new cells would multiply after infusion, as measured by the doubling time in days. Here are the doubling times:[21] 🔴 CANCERTREAT

1.4   1.0   1.3   1.0   1.3   2.0   0.6   0.8   0.7   0.9   1.9

(a) Examine the data. Is it reasonable to use the t procedures?

(b) Give a 90% confidence interval for the mean doubling time. Are you willing to use this interval to make an inference about the mean doubling time in a population of similar patients?

18.34 Genetic engineering for cancer treatment, continued. Another outcome in the cancer experiment described in Exercise 18.33 is measured by a test for the presence of cells that trigger an immune response in the body and so may help fight cancer. Here are data for the 11 subjects: counts of active cells per 100,000 cells before and after infusion of the modified cells. The difference (after minus before) is the response variable. 🔴 MORECANCER

Before	14	0	1	0	0	0	0	20	1	6	0
After	41	7	1	215	20	700	13	530	35	92	108
Difference	27	7	0	215	20	700	13	510	34	86	108

(a) Examine the data. Is it reasonable to use the t procedures?

(b) If your conclusion in part (a) is "Yes," do the data give convincing evidence that the count of active cells is higher after treatment?

18.35 Kicking a helium-filled football. Does a football filled with helium travel farther than one filled with ordinary air? To test this, the *Columbus Dispatch* conducted a study. Two identical footballs, one filled with helium and one filled with ordinary air, were used. A casual observer

was unable to detect a difference in the two footballs. A novice kicker was used to punt the footballs. A trial consisted of kicking both footballs in a random order. The kicker did not know which football (the helium-filled or the air-filled football) he was kicking. The distance of each punt was recorded. Then another trial was conducted. A total of 39 trials were run. Here are the data for the 39 trials, in yards that the footballs traveled. The difference (helium minus air) is the response variable.[22] 🔴 FOOTBALL

Helium	25	16	25	14	23	29	25	26	22	26
Air	25	23	18	16	35	15	26	24	24	28
Difference	0	−7	7	−2	−12	14	−1	2	−2	−2
Helium	12	28	28	31	22	29	23	26	35	24
Air	25	19	27	25	34	26	20	22	33	29
Difference	−13	9	1	6	−12	3	3	4	2	−5
Helium	31	34	39	32	14	28	30	27	33	11
Air	31	27	22	29	28	29	22	31	25	20
Difference	0	7	17	3	−14	−1	8	−4	8	−9
Helium	26	32	30	29	30	29	29	30	26	
Air	27	26	28	32	28	25	31	28	28	
Difference	−1	6	2	−3	2	4	−2	2	−2	

(a) Examine the data. Is it reasonable to use the t procedures?

(b) If your conclusion in part (a) is "Yes," do the data give convincing evidence that the helium-filled football travels farther than the air-filled football?

18.36 Growing trees faster. The concentration of carbon dioxide (CO_2) in the atmosphere is increasing rapidly due to our use of fossil fuels. Because plants use CO_2 to fuel photosynthesis, more CO_2 may cause trees and other plants to grow faster. An elaborate apparatus allows researchers to pipe extra CO_2 to a 30-meter circle of forest. They selected two nearby circles in each of three parts of a pine forest and randomly chose one of each pair to receive extra CO_2. The response variable is the mean increase in base area for 30 to 40 trees in a circle during a growing season. We measure this in percent increase per year. Here are one year's data:[23] 🔴 TREES

Pair	Control plot	Treated plot
1	9.752	10.587
2	7.263	9.244
3	5.742	8.675

(a) State the null and alternative hypotheses. Explain clearly why the investigators used a one-sided alternative.

(b) Carry out a test and report your conclusion in simple language.

(c) The investigators used the test you just carried out. Any use of the t procedures with samples this size is risky. Why?

18.37 Fungus in the air. The air in poultry-processing plants often contains fungus spores. Inadequate ventilation can affect the health of the workers. The problem is most serious during the summer. To measure the presence of spores, air samples are pumped to an agar plate and "colony-forming units (CFUs)" are counted after an incubation period. Here are data from two locations in a plant that processes 37,000 turkeys per day, taken on four days in the summer. The units are CFUs per cubic meter of air.[24] 🔴 FUNGUS

	Day 1	Day 2	Day 3	Day 4
Kill room	3175	2526	1763	1090
Processing	529	141	362	224

(a) Explain carefully why these are matched pairs data.

(b) The spore count is clearly higher in the kill room. Give sample means and a 90% confidence interval to estimate how much higher. Be sure to state your conclusion in plain English.

(c) You will often see the t procedures used for data like these. You should regard the results as only rough approximations. Why?

18.38 Weeds among the corn. Velvetleaf is a particularly annoying weed in corn fields. It produces lots of seeds, and the seeds wait in the soil for years until conditions are right. How many seeds do velvetleaf plants produce? Here are counts from 28 plants that came up in a corn field when no herbicide was used:[25] 🔴 WEEDS

2450 2504 2114 1110 2137 8015 1623 1531 2008 1716
 721 863 1136 2819 1911 2101 1051 218 1711 164
2228 363 5973 1050 1961 1809 130 880

We would like to give a confidence interval for the mean number of seeds produced by velvetleaf plants. Alas, the t interval can't be safely used for these data. Why not?

18.39 Sweetening colas. Cola makers test new recipes for loss of sweetness during storage. Trained tasters rate the sweet-

ness before and after storage. Here are the sweetness losses (sweetness before storage minus sweetness after storage) found by 10 tasters for one new cola recipe: 🔴 COLA

2.0 0.4 0.7 2.0 −0.4 2.2 −1.3 1.2 1.1 2.3

Take the data from these 10 carefully trained tasters as an SRS from a large population of all trained tasters.

(a) Use these data to see if there is good evidence that the cola lost sweetness.

(b) It is not uncommon to see the t procedures used for data like these. However, you should regard the results as only rough approximations. Why?

18.40 How much oil? How much oil wells in a given field will ultimately produce is key information in deciding whether to drill more wells. Here are the estimated total amounts of oil recovered from 64 wells in the Devonian Richmond Dolomite area of the Michigan basin, in thousands of barrels:[26] 🔴 OIL

21.71	53.2	46.4	42.7	50.4	97.7	103.1	51.9
43.4	69.5	156.5	34.6	37.9	12.9	2.5	31.4
79.5	26.9	18.5	14.7	32.9	196	24.9	118.2
82.2	35.1	47.6	54.2	63.1	69.8	57.4	65.6
56.4	49.4	44.9	34.6	92.2	37.0	58.8	21.3
36.6	64.9	14.8	17.6	29.1	61.4	38.6	32.5
12.0	28.3	204.9	44.5	10.3	37.7	33.7	81.1
12.1	20.1	30.5	7.1	10.1	18.0	3.0	2.0

Take these wells to be an SRS of wells in this area.

(a) Give a 95% t confidence interval for the mean amount of oil recovered from all wells in this area.

(b) Make a graph of the data. The distribution is very skewed, with several high outliers. A computer-intensive method that gives accurate confidence intervals without assuming any specific shape for the distribution gives a 95% confidence interval of 40.28 to 60.32. How does the t interval compare with this? Should the t procedures be used with these data?

18.41 *E. coli* in swimming areas. To investigate water quality, the *Columbus Dispatch* took water samples at 16 Ohio State Park swimming areas in central Ohio. Those samples were taken to laboratories and tested for *E. coli*, which are bacteria that can cause serious gastrointestinal problems. If a 100-milliliter sample (about 3.3 ounces) of water contains more than 130 *E. coli* bacteria, it is considered unsafe. Here are the *E. coli* levels found by the laboratories:[27] 🔴 ECOLI

291.0	190.4	47.0	86.0	44.0	18.9	1.0	50.0
10.9	45.7	28.5	8.6	9.6	16.0	34.0	18.9

Take these water samples to be an SRS of the water in all swimming areas in central Ohio.

(a) Are these data good evidence that, on average, the *E. coli* levels in these swimming areas were unsafe?

(b) Make a graph of the data. The distribution is very skewed. Another method that gives *P*-values without assuming any specific shape for the distribution gives a *P*-value of 0.9997 for the question in part (a). How does the one-sample *t* test compare with this? Should the *t* procedures be used with these data?

*The following exercises ask you to answer questions from data without having the details outlined for you. The four-step process is illustrated in Examples 18.2, 18.3, and 18.4. The exercise statements give you the **State** step. Follow the **Plan, Solve,** and **Conclude** steps in your work.*

18.42 Natural weed control? Fortunately, we aren't really interested in the number of seeds velvetleaf plants produce (see Exercise 18.38). The velvetleaf seed beetle feeds on the seeds and might be a natural weed control. Here are the total seeds, seeds infected by the beetle, and percent of seeds infected for 28 velvetleaf plants: **WEEDCONTROL**

Seeds	2450	2504	2114	1110	2137	8015	1623	1531
	2008	1716						
Infected	135	101	76	24	121	189	31	44
	73	12						
Percent	5.5	4.0	3.6	2.2	5.7	2.4	1.9	2.9
	3.6	0.7						
Seeds	721	863	1136	2819	1911	2101	1051	218
	1711	164						
Infected	27	40	41	79	82	85	42	0
	64	7						
Percent	3.7	4.6	3.6	2.8	4.3	4.0	4.0	0.0
	3.7	4.3						
Seeds	2228	363	5973	1050	1961	1809	130	880
Infected	156	31	240	91	137	92	5	23
Percent	7.0	8.5	4.0	8.7	7.0	5.1	3.8	2.6

Do a complete analysis of the percent of seeds infected by the beetle. Include a 90% confidence interval for the mean percent infected in the population of all velvetleaf plants. Do you think that the beetle is very helpful in controlling the weed?

18.43 Recruiting T cells. There is evidence that cytotoxic T lymphocytes (T cells) participate in controlling tumor growth and that they can be harnessed to use the body's immune system to treat cancer. One study

investigated the use of a T cell–engaging antibody, blinatumomab, to recruit T cells to control tumor growth. The data below are T cell counts (1000 per microliter) at baseline (beginning of the study) and after 20 days on blinatumomab for 6 subjects in the study.[28] The difference (after 20 days minus baseline) is the response variable. **TCELLS**

Baseline	0.04	0.02	0.00	0.02	0.38	0.33
After 20 days	0.28	0.47	1.30	0.25	1.22	0.44
Difference	0.24	0.45	1.30	0.23	0.84	0.11

Do the data give convincing evidence that the mean count of T cells is higher after 20 days on blinatumomab?

18.44 Recruiting T cells, continued. Give a 95% confidence interval for the mean difference in T cell counts (after 20 days minus baseline) in the previous exercise. **TCELLS**

18.45 Mutual funds performance. Mutual funds often compare their performance with a benchmark provided by an "index" that describes the performance of the class of assets in which the fund invests. For example, the Vanguard International Growth Fund benchmarks its performance against the EAFE (Europe, Australasia, Far East) index. Table 18.4 gives annual returns (percent) for the fund and

TABLE 18.4 A mutual fund versus its benchmark index

YEAR	FUND RETURN (%)	INDEX RETURN (%)	YEAR	FUND RETURN (%)	INDEX RETURN (%)
1984	−1.02	7.38	1998	16.93	20.00
1985	56.94	56.16	1999	26.34	26.96
1986	56.71	69.44	2000	−8.60	−14.17
1987	12.48	24.63	2001	−18.92	−21.44
1988	11.61	28.27	2002	−17.79	−15.94
1989	24.76	10.54	2003	34.45	38.59
1990	−12.05	−23.45	2004	18.95	20.25
1991	4.74	12.13	2005	15.00	13.54
1992	−5.79	−12.17	2006	25.92	26.34
1993	44.74	32.56	2007	15.98	11.17
1994	0.76	7.78	2008	−44.94	−43.38
1995	14.89	11.21	2009	41.63	31.78
1996	14.65	6.05	2010	15.66	8.13
1997	4.12	1.78			

the index. Does the fund's performance differ significantly from that of its benchmark? 🌀 MUTUALFUND

(a) Explain clearly why the matched pairs t test is the proper choice to answer this question.

(b) Do a complete analysis that answers the question posed.

18.46 Right versus left. The design of controls and instruments affects how easily people can use them. Timothy Sturm investigated this effect in a course project, asking 25 right-handed students to turn a knob (with their right hands) that moved an indicator by screw action. There were two identical instruments, one with a right-hand thread (the knob turns clockwise) and the other with a left-hand thread (the knob turns counterclockwise). Table 18.5 gives the times in seconds each subject took to move the indicator a fixed distance.[29] 🌀 RIGHTLEFT

(a) Each of the 25 students used both instruments. Explain briefly how you would use randomization in arranging the experiment.

(b) The project hoped to show that right-handed people find right-hand threads easier to use. Do an analysis that leads to a conclusion about this issue.

18.47 Comparing two drugs. Makers of generic drugs must show that they do not differ significantly from the "reference" drugs that they imitate. One aspect in which drugs might differ is their extent of absorption in the blood. Table 18.6 gives data taken from 20 healthy nonsmoking male subjects for one pair of drugs.[30] This is a matched pairs design. Numbers 1 to 20 were assigned at random to the subjects. Subjects 1 to 10 received the generic drug first, followed by the reference drug. Subjects 11 to 20 received the reference drug first, followed by the generic drug. In all cases, a washout period separated the two drugs so that the first had disappeared from the blood before the subject took the second. By randomizing the order, we prevent the order in which the drugs were administered from being confounded with the difference in the absorption in the blood. Do the drugs differ significantly in the amount absorbed in the blood? 🌀 DRUGS

TABLE 18.5 Performance times (seconds) using right-hand and left-hand threads

SUBJECT	RIGHT THREAD	LEFT THREAD	SUBJECT	RIGHT THREAD	LEFT THREAD
1	113	137	14	107	87
2	105	105	15	118	166
3	130	133	16	103	146
4	101	108	17	111	123
5	138	115	18	104	135
6	118	170	19	111	112
7	87	103	20	89	93
8	116	145	21	78	76
9	75	78	22	100	116
10	96	107	23	89	78
11	122	84	24	85	101
12	103	148	25	88	123
13	116	147			

TABLE 18.6 Absorption extent for two versions of a drug

SUBJECT	REFERENCE DRUG	GENERIC DRUG
15	4108	1755
3	2526	1138
9	2779	1613
13	3852	2254
12	1833	1310
8	2463	2120
18	2059	1851
20	1709	1878
17	1829	1682
2	2594	2613
4	2344	2738
16	1864	2302
6	1022	1284
10	2256	3052
5	938	1287
7	1339	1930
14	1262	1964
11	1438	2549
1	1735	3340
19	1020	3050

18.48 Practical significance? Give a 90% confidence interval for the mean time advantage of right-hand over left-hand threads in the setting of Exercise 18.46. Do you think that the time saved would be of practical importance if the task were performed many times—for example, by an assembly-line worker? To help answer this question, find the mean time for right-hand threads as a percent of the mean time for left-hand threads. ⬤ **RIGHTLEFT**

18.49 Bad weather, bad tips? As part of the study of tipping in a restaurant that we met in Example 14.3 (page 291) the psychologists also studied the size of the tip in a restaurant when a message indicating that the next day's weather would be bad was written on the bill. Here are tips from 20 patrons, measured in percent of the total bill:[31] ⬤ **TIPPING3**

18.0 19.1 19.2 18.8 18.4 19.0 18.5 16.1 16.8 14.0
17.0 13.6 17.5 20.0 20.2 18.8 18.0 23.2 18.2 19.4

Do the data give convincing evidence that the mean tip percent for all patrons of this restaurant when their bill contains a message that the next day's weather will be bad is less than 20%? (20% is an often-recommended size for restaurant tips.)

EXPLORING THE WEB

18.50 A matched pairs study. Find an example of a matched pairs study on the Web. The *Journal of the American Medical Association* (jama.ama-assn.org), *Science Magazine* (www.sciencemag.org), the *Canadian Medical Association Journal* (www.cmaj.ca), the *Journal of Statistics Education* (www.amstat.org/publications/jse), or perhaps the *Journal of Quantitative Analysis in Sports* (www.bepress.com/jqas) are possible sources. To help locate an article, look through the abstracts of articles. Once you find a suitable article, read it, and then briefly describe the study (including why it is a matched pairs study) and its conclusions. If *P*-values, means, standard deviations, etc. are reported, be sure to include them in your summary. Also, be sure to give the reference (either the Web link or the journal, issue, year, title of the paper, authors, and page numbers).

18.51 An improper use of a t procedure. Search the Web for an example of an improper use of a *t* procedure. You might try using Google to do a search on "improper use of a *t*-test." Summarize the study in which the *t* procedure was used and discuss how it was used improperly. Be sure to provide a link to your example or an appropriate reference.

18.52 How big a sample size do you need? If you examine Table C, you will notice that critical values of the *t* distribution get closer and closer to the corresponding critical values of the Normal distribution as the number of degrees of freedom increase. You can see this by comparing the *z* critical values at the bottom of Table C with the *t* critical values in the corresponding column. This suggests that for very large sample sizes, inference based on the Normal probability calculations in Chapters 14 and 15 (pretending σ is known) and inference based on the *t* distribution as discussed in this chapter (σ is not known) may give essentially the same answer if sample sizes are large and we pretend that our estimate of σ is the true value of σ. Professor R. Webster West, Department of Statistics, Texas A&M University, has created an applet that allows one to compute t probabilities. The link to the applet is www.stat.tamu.edu/~west/applets/tdemo.html.

(a) Use this applet to determine how large a sample size (or how many degrees of freedom) is needed for the critical value of the t distribution to be within 0.01 of the corresponding critical value of the Normal distribution for a 90%, 95%, and 99% confidence interval for a population mean.

(b) Based on your findings, how large a sample size do you think is needed for inference using the Normal distribution and inference using the t distribution to give very similar results if σ (both the true value and its estimate) is 1? If σ (both the true value and its estimate) is 100?

Chapter 19

Two-Sample Problems

Comparing two populations or two treatments is one of the most common situations encountered in statistical practice. We call such situations *two-sample problems*.

TWO-SAMPLE PROBLEMS

■ The goal of inference is to compare the responses to two treatments or to compare the characteristics of two populations.

■ We have a separate sample from each treatment or each population.

Unlike the matched pairs designs studied earlier, there is no matching of the individuals in the two samples, and the two samples can be of different sizes. Inference procedures for two-sample data differ from those for matched pairs. Here are some typical two-sample problems.

EXAMPLE 19.1 Physical therapy

Does regular physical therapy help lower-back pain? A randomized experiment assigned patients with lower-back pain to two groups: 142 received an examination and advice from a physical therapist; another 144 received regular physical therapy for up to five weeks. After a year, the change in their level of disability (0% to 100%) was assessed by a doctor who did not know which treatment the patients had received. ■

IN THIS CHAPTER WE COVER...

■ Comparing two population means

■ Two-sample *t* procedures

■ Using technology

■ Robustness again

EXAMPLE 19.2 Social insight

A psychologist develops a test that measures social insight. He compares the social insight of female college students with that of male college students by giving the test to a sample of female students and a separate sample of male students. ■

APPLY YOUR KNOWLEDGE

Which data design? *Each situation described in Exercises 19.1 to 19.4 requires inference about a mean or means. Identify each as involving (1) a single sample, (2) matched pairs, or (3) two independent samples. The procedures of Chapter 18 apply to designs (1) and (2). We are about to learn procedures for (3).*

19.1 Managing the finances. Choose 50 engaged couples who have not been previously married. Interview the man and woman separately about how their joint finances will be handled after marriage. Compare the views of men and women.

19.2 Does peer discussion promote learning? Undergraduate students in a biology class were randomly divided into two groups. In the first group, students worked alone on a multiple-choice exam on material recently covered in the class. In the second group, students worked in teams of four on the same multiple-choice exam. The teams were encouraged to discuss the questions among themselves before answering the questions. All exams were graded and returned to the students. Then all students worked alone on another multiple-choice exam on the same material as the first exam. Compare the mean scores of the two groups on the second exam.

19.3 Chemical analysis. To check a new analytical method, a chemist obtains a reference specimen of known concentration from the National Institute of Standards and Technology. She then makes 20 measurements of the concentration of this specimen with the new method and checks for bias by comparing the mean result with the known concentration.

19.4 Chemical analysis, continued. Another chemist is checking the same new method. He has no reference specimen, but a familiar analytic method is available. He wants to know if the new and old methods agree. He takes a specimen of unknown concentration and measures the concentration 10 times with the new method and 10 times with the old method.

COMPARING TWO POPULATION MEANS

Comparing two populations or the responses to two treatments starts with data analysis: make boxplots, stemplots (for small samples), or histograms (for larger samples) and compare the shapes, centers, and spreads of the two samples. The most common goal of inference is to compare the average or typical responses in the two populations. When data analysis suggests that both population distributions are symmetric, and especially when they are at least approximately Normal, we want to compare the population means. Here are the conditions for inference about means.

> **CONDITIONS FOR INFERENCE COMPARING TWO MEANS**
>
> ■ We have **two SRSs,** from two distinct populations. The samples are **independent.** That is, one sample has no influence on the other. Matching violates independence, for example. We measure the same response variable for both samples.
>
> ■ Both populations are **Normally distributed.** The means and standard deviations of the populations are unknown. In practice, it is enough that the distributions have similar shapes and that the data have no strong outliers.

Call the variable we measure x_1 in the first population and x_2 in the second because the variable may have different distributions in the two populations. Here is how we describe the two populations:

Population	Variable	Mean	Standard deviation
1	x_1	μ_1	σ_1
2	x_2	μ_2	σ_2

There are four unknown parameters, the two means and the two standard deviations. The subscripts remind us which population a parameter describes. We want to compare the two population means, either by giving a confidence interval for their difference $\mu_1 - \mu_2$ or by testing the hypothesis of no difference, $H_0: \mu_1 = \mu_2$.

We use the sample means and standard deviations to estimate the unknown parameters. Again, subscripts remind us which sample a statistic comes from. Here is how we describe the samples:

Population	Sample size	Sample mean	Sample standard deviation
1	n_1	$\bar{x}_1$	s_1
2	n_2	$\bar{x}_2$	s_2

To do inference about the difference $\mu_1 - \mu_2$ between the means of the two populations, we start from the difference $\bar{x}_1 - \bar{x}_2$ between the means of the two samples.

To illustrate how we formulate the null and alternative hypotheses, consider the situation described in Example 19.2. A psychologist compares the social insight of female college students with that of male college students by giving the test to a sample of female students and a separate sample of male students. If we let μ_1 be the mean social insight of female college students and μ_2 be the mean social insight of male college students, then the null hypothesis of "no difference" between male and female students would be $H_0: \mu_1 = \mu_2$ or $H_0: \mu_1 - \mu_2 = 0$. If the psychologist makes no assumption about the difference between female and male social insight, then the alternative hypothesis is $H_a: \mu_1 \neq \mu_2$ or $H_a: \mu_1 - \mu_2 \neq 0$.

ACTIVITY

AP Photo/Toby Talbot

EXAMPLE 19.3 Daily activity and obesity

STATE: People gain weight when they take in more energy from food than they expend. James Levine and his collaborators at the Mayo Clinic investigated the link between obesity and energy spent on daily activity.[1]

Choose 20 healthy volunteers who don't exercise. Deliberately choose 10 who are lean and 10 who are mildly obese but still healthy. Attach sensors that monitor the subjects' every move for 10 days. Table 19.1 presents data on the time (in minutes per day) that the subjects spent standing or walking, sitting, and lying down. Do lean and obese people differ in the average time they spend standing and walking?

PLAN: Examine the data and carry out a test of hypotheses. We suspect in advance that lean subjects (Group 1) are more active than obese subjects (Group 2), so we test the hypotheses

$$H_0: \mu_1 = \mu_2$$
$$H_a: \mu_1 > \mu_2$$

SOLVE (first steps): Are the conditions for inference met? The subjects are volunteers, so they are not SRSs from all lean and mildly obese adults. The study tried to recruit comparable groups: all worked in sedentary jobs, none smoked or were taking medication,

TABLE 19.1 Time (minutes per day) spent in three different postures by lean and obese subjects

GROUP	SUBJECT	STAND/WALK	SIT	LIE
Lean	1	511.100	370.300	555.500
Lean	2	607.925	374.512	450.650
Lean	3	319.212	582.138	537.362
Lean	4	584.644	357.144	489.269
Lean	5	578.869	348.994	514.081
Lean	6	543.388	385.312	506.500
Lean	7	677.188	268.188	467.700
Lean	8	555.656	322.219	567.006
Lean	9	374.831	537.031	531.431
Lean	10	504.700	528.838	396.962
Obese	11	260.244	646.281	521.044
Obese	12	464.756	456.644	514.931
Obese	13	367.138	578.662	563.300
Obese	14	413.667	463.333	532.208
Obese	15	347.375	567.556	504.931
Obese	16	416.531	567.556	448.856
Obese	17	358.650	621.262	460.550
Obese	18	267.344	646.181	509.981
Obese	19	410.631	572.769	448.706
Obese	20	426.356	591.369	412.919

and so on. Setting clear standards like these helps make up for the fact that we can't reasonably get SRSs for so invasive a study. The subjects were not told that they were chosen from a larger group of volunteers because they did not exercise and were either lean or mildly obese. Because their willingness to volunteer isn't related to the purpose of the experiment, we will treat them as two independent SRSs.

A back-to-back stemplot (Figure 19.1) displays the data in detail. To make the plot, we rounded the data to the nearest 10 minutes and used 100s as stems and 10s as leaves. The distributions are a bit irregular, as we expect with just 10 observations. There are no clear departures from Normality such as extreme outliers or skewness. The lean subjects as a group spend much more time standing and walking than do the obese subjects. Calculating the group means confirms this:

Lean		Obese
	2	6 7
7 2	3	5 6 7
	4	1 1 2 3 6
8 8 6 4 1 0	5	
8 1	6	

FIGURE 19.1

Back-to-back stemplot of the times spent walking or standing, for Example 19.3.

Group	n	Mean $\bar{x}$	Std. dev. s
Group 1 (lean)	10	525.751	107.121
Group 2 (obese)	10	373.269	67.498

The observed difference in mean time per day spent standing or walking is

$$\bar{x}_1 - \bar{x}_2 = 525.751 - 373.269 = 152.482 \text{ minutes}$$

To complete the "Solve" step, we must learn the details of inference for comparing two means. After discussing these details, we complete the "Solve" and "Conclude" steps in Example 19.4. ■

TWO-SAMPLE *t* PROCEDURES

Whether an observed difference is surprising depends on the spread of the observations as well as on the two means. Widely different means can arise just by chance if the individual observations vary a great deal. To take variation into account, we standardize the observed difference $\bar{x}_1 - \bar{x}_2$ by dividing by its standard deviation. This standard deviation of the difference in sample means is

$$\sqrt{\frac{\sigma_1^2}{n_1} + \frac{\sigma_2^2}{n_2}}$$

Because we don't know the population standard deviations, we estimate them by the sample standard deviations from our two samples. The result is the **standard error,** or estimated standard deviation, of the difference in sample means:

standard error

$$\sqrt{\frac{s_1^2}{n_1} + \frac{s_2^2}{n_2}}$$

When we standardize the estimate by dividing it by its standard error, the result is the **two-sample *t* statistic:**

two-sample t statistic

$$t = \frac{\bar{x}_1 - \bar{x}_2}{\sqrt{\frac{s_1^2}{n_1} + \frac{s_2^2}{n_2}}}$$

The statistic t has the same interpretation as any z or t statistic: it says how far $\bar{x}_1 - \bar{x}_2$ is from 0 in standard deviation units.

The two-sample t statistic has approximately a t distribution. It does not have exactly a t distribution even if the populations are both exactly Normal. In practice, however, the approximation is very accurate. There are two practical options for using the two-sample t procedures:

Option 1. With software, use the statistic t with accurate critical values from the approximating t distribution. The degrees of freedom are calculated from the data by a somewhat messy formula. Moreover, the degrees of freedom may not be a whole number.

Option 2. Without software, use the statistic t with critical values from the t distribution with *degrees of freedom equal to the smaller of $n_1 - 1$ and $n_2 - 1$*. These procedures are always conservative for any two Normal populations. The confidence interval has a margin of error *as large as or larger than* is needed for the desired confidence level. The significance test gives a P-value *equal to or greater than* the true P-value.

The two options are exactly the same except for the degrees of freedom used for t critical values and P-values. As the sample sizes increase, confidence levels and P-values from Option 2 become more accurate. The gap between what Option 2 reports and the truth is quite small unless the sample sizes are both small and unequal.[2]

THE TWO-SAMPLE t PROCEDURES

Draw an SRS of size n_1 from a large Normal population with unknown mean μ_1, and draw an independent SRS of size n_2 from another large Normal population with unknown mean μ_2. A level C **confidence interval for $\mu_1 - \mu_2$** is given by

$$(x_1 - x_2) \pm t^* \sqrt{\frac{s_1^2}{n_1} + \frac{s_2^2}{n_2}}$$

Here t^* is the critical value for confidence level C for the t distribution with degrees of freedom from either Option 1 (software) or Option 2 (the smaller of $n_1 - 1$ and $n_2 - 1$).

To **test the hypothesis H_0: $\mu_1 = \mu_2$**, calculate the **two-sample t statistic**

$$t = \frac{\bar{x}_1 - \bar{x}_2}{\sqrt{\dfrac{s_1^2}{n_1} + \dfrac{s_2^2}{n_2}}}$$

Find P-values from the t distribution with degrees of freedom from either Option 1 (software) or Option 2 (the smaller of $n_1 - 1$ and $n_2 - 1$).

EXAMPLE 19.4 Daily activity and obesity

We can now complete Example 19.3.

SOLVE (inference): The two-sample t statistic comparing the average minutes spent standing and walking in Group 1 (lean) and Group 2 (obese) is

$$t = \frac{\bar{x}_1 - \bar{x}_2}{\sqrt{\dfrac{s_1^2}{n_1} + \dfrac{s_2^2}{n_2}}}$$

$$= \frac{525.751 - 373.269}{\sqrt{\dfrac{107.121^2}{10} + \dfrac{67.498^2}{10}}}$$

$$= \frac{152.482}{40.039} = 3.808$$

Software (Option 1) gives one-sided *P*-value *P* = 0.0008 based on df = 15.174.

   Without software, use the conservative Option 2. Because $n_1 - 1 = 9$ and $n_2 - 1 = 9$, there are 9 degrees of freedom. Because H_a is one-sided, the *P*-value is the area to the right of *t* = 3.808 under the *t*(9) curve. Figure 19.2 illustrates this *P*-value. Table C shows that *t* = 3.808 lies between the critical values *t** for 0.0025 and 0.001. So $0.001 < P < 0.0025$. Option 2 gives a larger (more conservative) *P*-value than Option 1. As usual, the practical conclusion is the same for both versions of the test.

df = 9

t*	3.690	4.297
One-sided *P*	.0025	.001

CONCLUDE: There is very strong evidence (*P* = 0.0008) that, on average, lean people spend more time walking and standing than do moderately obese people. ■

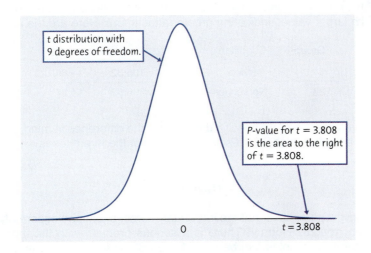

FIGURE 19.2

Using the conservative Option 2, the *P*-value in Example 19.4 comes from the *t* distribution with 9 degrees of freedom.

In figure: "t distribution with 9 degrees of freedom." — "P-value for t = 3.808 is the area to the right of t = 3.808." — 0 — t = 3.808

   The analysis in Example 19.4 doesn't tell us whether less activity *causes* obesity. It may be that some people are naturally more active and are therefore less likely to gain weight. Or it may be that people who gain weight reduce their activity level.

EXAMPLE 19.5 How much more active are lean people?

PLAN: Give a 90% confidence interval for $\mu_1 - \mu_2$, the difference in average daily minutes spent standing and walking between lean and mildly obese adults.

SOLVE and CONCLUDE: As in Example 19.4, the conservative Option 2 uses 9 degrees of freedom. Table C shows that the *t*(9) critical value is *t** = 1.833. We are 90% confident that $\mu_1 - \mu_2$ lies in the interval

$$(\bar{x}_1 - \bar{x}_2) \pm t^* \sqrt{\frac{s_1^2}{n_1} + \frac{s_2^2}{n_2}}$$

$$= (525.751 - 373.269) \pm 1.833 \sqrt{\frac{107.121^2}{10} + \frac{67.498^2}{10}}$$

$$= 152.482 \pm 73.390$$

$$= 79.09 \text{ to } 225.87 \text{ minutes}$$

Software using Option 1 gives the 90% interval as 82.35 to 222.62 minutes, based on t with 15.174 degrees of freedom. The Option 2 interval is wider because this method is conservative. ■

 **ACTIVITY**

EXAMPLE 19.6 Community service and attachment to friends

STATE: Do college students who have volunteered for community service work differ from those who have not? A study obtained data from 57 students who had done service work and 17 who had not. One of the response variables was a measure of "attachment to friends," with larger values indicating greater attachment. Here are the results:[3]

Group	Condition	n	$\bar{x}$	s
1	Service	57	105.32	14.68
2	No service	17	96.82	14.26

PLAN: The investigator had no specific direction for the difference in mind before looking at the data, so the alternative is two-sided. We will test the hypotheses

$$H_0: \mu_1 = \mu_2$$
$$H_a: \mu_1 \neq \mu_2$$

SOLVE: The investigator says that the individual scores, examined separately in the two samples, appear roughly Normal. There is a serious problem with the more important condition that the two samples can be regarded as SRSs from two student populations. We will discuss that after we illustrate the calculations.

The two-sample t statistic is

$$t = \frac{\bar{x}_1 - \bar{x}_2}{\sqrt{\dfrac{s_1^2}{n_1} + \dfrac{s_2^2}{n_2}}}$$

$$= \frac{105.32 - 96.82}{\sqrt{\dfrac{14.68^2}{57} + \dfrac{14.26^2}{17}}}$$

$$= \frac{8.5}{3.9677} = 2.142$$

Software (Option 1) says that the two-sided P-value is $P = 0.0414$.

Without software, use Option 2 to find a conservative P-value. There are 16 degrees of freedom, the smaller of

$$n_1 - 1 = 57 - 1 = 56 \quad \text{and} \quad n_2 - 1 = 17 - 1 = 16$$

Figure 19.3 illustrates the P-value. Find it by comparing $t = 2.142$ with the two-sided critical values for the $t(16)$ distribution. Table C shows that the P-value is between 0.05 and 0.04.

df = 16		
t^*	2.120	2.235
Two-sided P	.05	.04

CONCLUDE: The data give moderately strong evidence ($P < 0.05$) that students who have engaged in community service are, on the average, more attached to their friends. ■

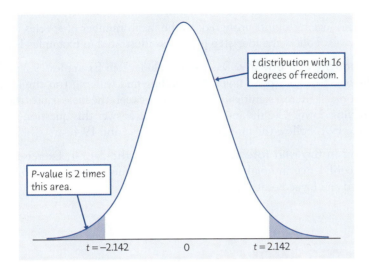

FIGURE 19.3
The *P*-value in Example 19.6. Because the alternative is two-sided, the *P*-value is double the area to the left of $t = -2.142$.

Is the *t* test in Example 19.6 justified? The student subjects were "enrolled in a course on U.S. Diversity at a large mid-western university." Unless this course is required of all students, the subjects cannot be considered a random sample even from this campus. Students were placed in the two groups on the basis of a questionnaire, 39 in the "no service" group and 71 in the "service" group. The data were gathered from a follow-up survey two years later; 17 of the 39 "no service" students responded (44%), compared with 80% response (57 of 71) in the "service" group. Nonresponse is confounded with group: students who had done community service were much more likely to respond. Finally, 75% of the "service" respondents were women, compared with 47% of the "no service" respondents. Sex, which can strongly affect attachment, is badly confounded with the presence or absence of community service. The data are so far from meeting the SRS condition for inference that the *t* test is meaningless.

APPLY YOUR KNOWLEDGE

In exercises that call for two-sample t procedures, use Option 1 if you have technology that implements that method. Otherwise, use Option 2 (degrees of freedom the smaller of $n_1 - 1$ and $n_2 - 1$).

19.5 Logging in the rain forest. "Conservationists have despaired over destruction of tropical rain forest by logging, clearing, and burning." These words begin a report on a statistical study of the effects of logging in Borneo.[4] Here are data on the number of tree species in 12 unlogged forest plots and 9 similar plots logged 8 years earlier: LOGGING2

Unlogged	22	18	22	20	15	21	13	13	19	13	19	15
Logged	17	4	18	14	18	15	15	10	12			

(a) The study report says, "Loggers were unaware that the effects of logging would be assessed." Why is this important? The study report also explains why the plots can be considered to be randomly assigned.

Digital Vision/Getty Images

(b) Does logging significantly reduce the mean number of species in a plot after 8 years? Follow the four-step process as illustrated in Examples 19.3 and 19.4.

19.6 Daily activity and obesity. We can conclude from Examples 19.3 and 19.4 that mildly obese people spend less time standing and walking (on the average) than lean people. Is there a significant difference between the mean times the two groups spend lying down? Use the four-step process to answer this question from the data in Table 19.1. Follow the model of Examples 19.3 and 19.4.

19.7 Logging in the rain forest, continued. Use the data in Exercise 19.5 to give a 99% confidence interval for the difference in mean number of species between unlogged and logged plots. LOGGING2

● USING TECHNOLOGY

Software should use Option 1 for the degrees of freedom to give accurate confidence intervals and P-values. Unfortunately, there is variation in how well software implements Option 1. Figure 19.4 displays output from a graphing calculator, two statistical programs, and a spreadsheet program for the test of Examples 19.3 and 19.4. All four claim to use Option 1. The two-sample t statistic is exactly as in Example 19.4, $t = 3.808$. You can find this in all four outputs (Minitab rounds to 3.81; Excel and the graphing calculator give additional decimal places). The different technologies use different methods to find the P-value for $t = 3.808$.

■ CrunchIt! and the calculator get Option 1 completely right. The accurate approximation uses the t distribution with approximately 15.174 (CrunchIt! rounds this to 15.17) degrees of freedom. The P-value is $P = 0.0008$.

■ Minitab uses Option 1, but it *truncates* the exact degrees of freedom to the next smaller whole number to get critical values and P-values. In this example, the exact df = 15.174 is truncated to df = 15, so that Minitab's results are slightly conservative. That is, Minitab's P-value (rounded to $P = 0.001$ in the output) is slightly larger than the full Option 1 P-value.

■ Excel *rounds* the exact degrees of freedom to the nearest whole number, so that df = 15.174 becomes df = 15. Excel's method agrees with Minitab's in this example. But when rounding moves the degrees of freedom up to the next higher whole number, Excel's P-values are slightly smaller than is correct. *This is misleading, another illustration of the fact that Excel is substandard as statistical software.*

Excel's label for the test, "Two-Sample Assuming Unequal Variances," is seriously misleading. *The two-sample t procedures we have described work whether or not the two populations have the same variance.* There is an old-fashioned special procedure that works only when the two variances are equal. We won't discuss this method because you should never use it.

Although different calculators and software give slightly different P-values, in practice you can just accept what your technology says. The small differences in P don't affect the conclusion. Even "between 0.001 and 0.0025" from Option 2 (Example 19.4) is close enough for practical purposes.

Texas Instruments Graphing Calculator

FIGURE 19.4

The two-sample t procedures applied to the data on activity and obesity: output from a graphing calculator, two statistical programs, and a spreadsheet program.

```
2-SampTTest
  µ1 >µ2
  t=3.808375604
  P=8.4101904ᴇ-4
  df=15.17355038
  x̄1=525.7513
↓x̄2=373.2692
```

Minitab

Session

Two-sample T for stand

group	N	Mean	StDev	SE Mean
1	10	526	107	34
2	10	373.3	67.5	21

Difference = mu (1) − mu (2)
Estimate for difference: 152.5
T-Test of difference = 0 (vs >): T-Value = 3.81 P-Value = 0.001 DF = 15

Microsoft Excel

Excel

	A	B	C
1	t-Test: Two-Sample Assuming Unequal Variances		
2			
3		*Lean*	*Obese*
4	Mean	525.7513	373.2692
5	Variance	11474.8903	4556.019849
6	Observations	10	10
7	Hypothesized Mean	0	
8	df	15	
9	t Stat	3.808375604	
10	P(T<=t) one-tail	0.000856818	
11	t Critical one-tail	1.753051038	
12	P(T<=t) two-tail	0.001713635	
13	P(T<t) two-tail	2.131450856	
14			

Sheet4

Results - t 2-Sample

Export ▾

Null hypothesis:	Difference of means = 0
Alternative hypothesis:	Difference of means > 0

Group	Std Dev	Sample Mean	n
1	107.1	525.8	10
2	67.50	373.3	10

df:	15.17
Difference of means:	152.5
t statistic:	3.808
P-value:	0.0008410

19.8 Perception of life expectancy. Do women and men differ in how they perceive their life expectancy? A researcher asked a sample of men and women to indicate their life expectancy. This was compared with values from actuarial tables, and the relative percent difference was computed (perceived life expectancy minus life expectancy from actuarial tables was divided by life expectancy from actuarial tables and converted to a percent). Here are the relative percent differences for all men and women over the age of 70 in the sample:[5] 🔥 LIFEEXPECTANCY

Men	−28	−23	−20	−19	−14	−13	
Women	−20	−19	−15	−12	−10	−8	−5

Figure 19.5 shows output for the two-sample t test using Option 1. (This output is from CrunchIt! software, which does Option 1 without rounding or truncating the degrees of freedom.) Do men and women over 70 years old differ in their perceptions of life expectancy? Using the output in Figure 19.5, write a summary in a sentence or two, including t, df, P, and a conclusion.

FIGURE 19.5

Two-sample t output from CrunchIt! for Exercise 19.8.

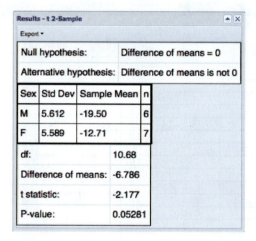

ROBUSTNESS AGAIN

The two-sample t procedures are more robust than the one-sample t methods, particularly when the distributions are not symmetric. When the sizes of the two samples are equal and the two populations being compared have distributions with similar shapes, probability values from the t table are quite accurate for a broad range of distributions when the sample sizes are as small as $n_1 = n_2 = 5$.[6] When the two population distributions have different shapes, larger samples are needed.

As a guide to practice, adapt the guidelines given on page 364 for the use of one-sample t procedures to two-sample procedures by replacing "sample size" with the "sum of the sample sizes," $n_1 + n_2$. These guidelines err on the side of safety, especially when the two samples are of equal size. *In planning a two-sample study, choose equal sample sizes whenever possible. The two-sample t procedures are most robust against non-Normality in this case, and the conservative Option 2 probability values are most accurate.*

APPLY YOUR KNOWLEDGE

19.9 Do good smells bring good business? Businesses know that customers often respond to background music. Do they also respond to odors? One study of this question took place in a small pizza restaurant in France on two Saturday evenings in May. On one of these evenings, a relaxing lavender odor was spread through the restaurant. On the other evening, no scent was used. Table 19.2 gives the time (minutes) that two samples of 30 customers spent in the restaurant and the amount they spent (in euros).[7] The two evenings were comparable in many ways (weather, customer count, and so on), so we are willing to regard the data as independent SRSs from spring Saturday evenings at this restaurant. The authors say,

TABLE 19.2 Time (minutes) and spending (euros) by restaurant customers

NO ODOR		LAVENDER	
MINUTES	EUROS SPENT	MINUTES	EUROS SPENT
103	15.9	92	21.9
68	18.5	126	18.5
79	15.9	114	22.3
106	18.5	106	21.9
72	18.5	89	18.5
121	21.9	137	24.9
92	15.9	93	18.5
84	15.9	76	22.5
72	15.9	98	21.5
92	15.9	108	21.9
85	15.9	124	21.5
69	18.5	105	18.5
73	18.5	129	25.5
87	18.5	103	18.5
109	20.5	107	18.5
115	18.5	109	21.9
91	18.5	94	18.5
84	15.9	105	18.5
76	15.9	102	24.9
96	15.9	108	21.9
107	18.5	95	25.9
98	18.5	121	21.9
92	15.9	109	18.5
107	18.5	104	18.5
93	15.9	116	22.8
118	18.5	88	18.5
87	15.9	109	21.9
101	25.5	97	20.7
75	12.9	101	21.9
86	15.9	106	22.5

"Therefore at this stage it would be impossible to generalize the results to other restaurants." ODORS2

(a) Does a lavender odor encourage customers to stay longer in the restaurant? Examine the time data and explain why they are suitable for two-sample t procedures. Use the two-sample t test to answer the question posed.

(b) Does a lavender odor encourage customers to spend more while in the restaurant? Examine the spending data. In what ways do these data deviate from Normality? With 30 observations, the t procedures are nonetheless reasonably accurate. Use the two-sample t test to answer the question posed.

19.10 **Compressing soil.** Farmers know that driving heavy equipment on wet soil compresses the soil and injures future crops. Here are data on the "penetrability" of the same type of soil at two levels of compression.[8] Penetrability is a measure of how much resistance plant roots will meet when they try to grow through the soil. SOILCOMPRESS

Compressed Soil									
2.86	2.68	2.92	2.82	2.76	2.81	2.78	3.08	2.94	2.86
3.08	2.82	2.78	2.98	3.00	2.78	2.96	2.90	3.18	3.16

Intermediate Soil									
3.14	3.38	3.10	3.40	3.38	3.14	3.18	3.26	2.96	3.02
3.54	3.36	.18	3.12	3.86	2.92	3.46	3.44	3.62	4.26

(a) Make stemplots to investigate the shape of the distributions. The penetrabilities for intermediate soil are skewed to the right and have a high outlier. Returning to the source of the data shows that the outlying sample had unusually low soil density, so that it belongs in the "loose soil" class. We are justified in removing the outlier.

(b) We suspect that the penetrability of compressed soil is less than that of intermediate soil. Do the data (with the outlier removed) support this suspicion?

19.11 **Weeds among the corn.** Lamb's-quarter is a common weed that interferes with the growth of corn. An agriculture researcher planted corn at the same rate in 16 small plots of ground, then weeded the plots by hand to allow a fixed number of lamb's-quarter plants to grow in each meter of corn row. No other weeds were allowed to grow. Here are the yields of corn (bushels per acre) for only the experimental plots controlled to have 1 weed per meter of row and 9 weeds per meter of row:[9] WEEDSANDCORN

1 weed/meter	166.2	157.3	166.7	161.1
9 weeds/meter	162.8	142.4	162.8	162.4

Explain carefully why a two-sample t confidence interval for the difference in mean yields may not be accurate.

19.12 **Compressing soil, continued.** Use the data in Exercise 19.10, omitting the outlier, to give a 90% confidence interval for the decrease in penetrability of compressed soil relative to intermediate soil. SOILCOMPRESS2

CHAPTER 19   SUMMARY

CHAPTER SPECIFICS

- The data in a **two-sample problem** come from two independent SRSs, each drawn from a separate population.

- Tests and confidence intervals for the difference between the means μ_1 and μ_2 of two Normal populations start from the difference $\bar{x}_1 - \bar{x}_2$ between the two sample means. Because of the central limit theorem, the resulting procedures are approximately correct for other population distributions when the sample sizes are large.

- Draw independent SRSs of sizes n_1 and n_2 from two Normal populations with parameters μ_1, σ_1 and μ_2, σ_2. The **two-sample t statistic** is

$$t = \frac{(\bar{x}_1 - \bar{x}_2) - (\mu_1 - \mu_2)}{\sqrt{\dfrac{s_1^2}{n_1} + \dfrac{s_2^2}{n_2}}}$$

  The statistic t has approximately a t distribution.

- There are two choices for the **degrees of freedom** of the two-sample t statistic. Option 1: software produces accurate probability values using degrees of freedom calculated from the data. Option 2: for conservative inference procedures, use degrees of freedom equal to the smaller of $n_1 - 1$ and $n_2 - 1$.

- The **confidence interval for $\mu_1 - \mu_2$** is

$$(\bar{x}_1 - \bar{x}_2) \pm t^* \sqrt{\dfrac{s_1^2}{n_1} + \dfrac{s_2^2}{n_2}}$$

  The critical value t^* from Option 1 gives a confidence level very close to the desired level C. Option 2 produces a margin of error at least as wide as is needed for the desired level C.

- **Significance tests for H_0: $\mu_1 = \mu_2$** are based on

$$t = \frac{\bar{x}_1 - \bar{x}_2}{\sqrt{\dfrac{s_1^2}{n_1} + \dfrac{s_2^2}{n_2}}}$$

  P-values calculated from Option 1 are very accurate. Option 2 P-values are always at least as large as the true P.

- The two-sample t procedures are quite **robust** against departures from Normality. Guidelines for practical use are similar to those for one-sample t procedures. Equal sample sizes are recommended.

LINK IT

In Chapter 18 we studied inference for the mean of a Normal population using procedures based on the t distribution. These procedures are more realistic than those studied in Chapters 14 to 16 because t procedures do not require that we know the population variance. In practice, the most common use of t procedures for a single population mean is with matched pairs data because most research studies make comparisons between two or more populations.

In this chapter, we discuss t procedures for comparing the means of two Normal populations when we have independent samples from these two populations. These t procedures are quite common in practice, and one encounters them in many research papers. Researchers typically report the means and standard deviations for the two samples and, in the case of tests of hypotheses, the value of the t statistic and the corresponding P-value.

In the next two chapters we extend our procedures for inference to additional settings that occur frequently in practice—in particular, to inference for population proportions. And we will see that the basic ideas about confidence intervals and tests of hypotheses that we learned in Chapters 14 to 16 still apply.

CHECK YOUR SKILLS

19.13 The 2009 National Assessment of Educational Progress (NAEP) gave a mathematics test to a random sample of eighth-graders in Texas. The mean score was 287 out of 500. To give a confidence interval for the mean score of all Texas eighth-graders, you would use

(a) the two-sample t interval.

(b) the matched pairs t interval.

(c) the one-sample t interval.

19.14 In the 2009 NAEP sample of Texas eighth-graders, the mean mathematics scores were 286 for female students and 287 for male students. To see if this difference is statistically significant, you would use

(a) the two-sample t test.

(b) the matched pairs t test.

(c) the one-sample t test.

19.15 A study of the effect of exposure to color (red or blue) on the ability to solve puzzles used 42 subjects. Half the subjects (21) were asked to solve a series of puzzles while in a red-colored environment. The other half were asked to solve the same series of puzzles while in a blue-colored environment. The time taken to solve the puzzles was recorded for each subject. To compare the mean times for the two groups of subjects using the two-sample t procedures with the conservative Option 2, the correct degrees of freedom is

(a) 41.   (b) 40.   (c) 20.

19.16 The 21 subjects in the red-colored environment had a mean time for solving the puzzles of 9.64 seconds with standard deviation 3.43; the 21 subjects in the blue-colored environment had a mean time of 15.84 seconds with standard deviation 8.65. The two-sample t statistic for comparing the population means has value

(a) 1.50.   (b) 3.05.   (c) 6.2.

19.17 A study of the use of social media asked a sample of 488 American adults under the age of 40 and a sample of 421 American adults aged 40 or over about their use of social media. Based on their answers, each subject was assigned a social media usage score on a scale of 0 to 25. Higher scores indicate greater usage. The subjects were chosen by random digit dialing of telephone numbers. Are the conditions for two-sample t inference satisfied?

(a) Maybe: the SRS condition is OK but we need to look at the data to check Normality.

(b) No: scores in a range between 0 and 25 can't be Normal.

(c) Yes: the SRS condition is OK and large sample sizes make the Normality condition unnecessary.

19.18 We suspect that younger adults use social media more than adults aged 40 or over. To see if this is true, test these hypotheses for the mean social media usage scores of all adults under 40 and all adults 40 and over:

(a) $H_0: \mu_{<40} = \mu_{\geq 40}$ versus $H_a: \mu_{<40} > \mu_{\geq 40}$

(b) $H_0: \mu_{<40} = \mu_{\geq 40}$ versus $H_a: \mu_{<40} \neq \mu_{\geq 40}$

(c) $H_0: \mu_{<40} = \mu_{\geq 40}$ versus $H_a: \mu_{<40} < \mu_{\geq 40}$

19.19 The two-sample t statistic for the social media use study ("under 40" mean minus "40 and over" mean) is $t = 3.18$. The P-value for testing the hypotheses from the previous exercise satisfies

(a) $0.001 < P < 0.005$.

(b) $0.0005 < P < 0.001$.

(c) $0.001 < P < 0.002$.

CHAPTER 19 EXERCISES

Exercises 19.20 to 19.27 are based on summary statistics rather than raw data. This information is typically all that is presented in published reports. You can perform inference procedures by hand from the summaries. Use the conservative Option 2 (degrees of freedom the smaller of $n_1 - 1$ and $n_2 - 1$) for two-sample t confidence intervals and P-values. You must trust that the authors understood the conditions for inference and verified that they apply. This isn't always true.

19.20 Do women talk more than men? Equip male and female students with a small device that secretly records sound for a random 30 seconds during each 12.5-minute period over two days. Count the words each subject speaks during each recording period, and from this, estimate how many words per day each subject speaks. The published report includes a table summarizing six such studies.[10] Here are two of the six:

Study	Sample Size Women	Sample Size Men	Estimated Average Number (SD) of Words Spoken per Day Women	Estimated Average Number (SD) of Words Spoken per Day Men
1	56	56	16,177 (7520)	16,569 (9108)
2	27	20	16,496 (7914)	12,867 (8343)

Readers are supposed to understand that, for example, the 56 women in the first study had $\bar{x} = 16,177$ and $s = 7520$. It is commonly thought that women talk more than men. Does either of the two samples support this idea? For each study:

(a) State hypotheses in terms of the population means for men (μ_M) and women (μ_F).

(b) Find the two-sample t statistic.

(c) What degrees of freedom does Option 2 use to get a conservative P-value?

(d) Compare your value of t with the critical values in Table C. What can you say about the P-value of the test?

(e) What do you conclude from the results of these two studies?

19.21 Alcohol and zoning out. Healthy men aged 21 to 35 were randomly assigned to one of two groups: half received 0.82 grams of alcohol per kilogram of body weight; half received a placebo. Participants were then given 30 minutes to read up to 34 pages of Tolstoy's *War and Peace* (beginning at chapter 1, with each page containing approximately 22 lines of text). Every two to four minutes participants were prompted to indicate whether they were "zoning out." The proportion of time participants indicated they were zoning out was recorded for each subject. The table below summarizes data on the proportion of episodes of zoning out.[11] (The study report gave the standard error of the mean $s/\sqrt{n}$, abbreviated as SEM, rather than the standard deviation s.)

Group	n	$\bar{x}$	SEM
Alcohol	25	0.25	0.05
Placebo	25	0.12	0.03

(a) What are the two sample standard deviations?

(b) What degrees of freedom does the conservative Option 2 use for two-sample t procedures for these samples?

(c) Using Option 2, give a 90% confidence interval for the mean difference between the two groups.

19.22 Stress and weight in rats. In a study of the effects of stress on behavior in rats, 71 rats were randomly assigned to either a stressful environment or a control (nonstressful) environment. After 21 days, the change in weight (in grams) was determined for each rat. The table below summarizes data on weight gain.[12] (The study report gave the standard error of the mean $s/\sqrt{n}$, abbreviated as SEM, rather than the standard deviation s.)

Group	n	$\bar{x}$	SEM
Stress	20	26	3
No stress	51	32	2

(a) What are the standard deviations for the two groups?

(b) What degrees of freedom does the conservative Option 2 use for two-sample t procedures for these data?

(c) Test the null hypothesis of no difference between the two group means against the two-sided alternative. Use the degrees of freedom from part (b).

19.23 Illusory pattern perceptions. When one experiences a lack of control in one's life, does one compensate by seeking structure elsewhere? Assign 36 undergraduate students to one of two conditions. All are asked to identify a concept associated with a series of "grainy" pictures that contain an embedded image and are presented to them sequentially. During the task they can ask questions to help them determine the associated concept. Half of the subjects (the lack-of-control group) receive feedback that is random and noncontingent on their questions. The other half receive useful feedback (the in-control group). After attempting to complete the task, all subjects are presented with 12 grainy pictures that are similar to those used in the task but lack an embedded image. All are asked whether they perceive an image in the pictures, and the number of pictures identified as containing an image is counted for each subject. Here are the summary statistics:[13]

Group	Group size	Mean	Std. dev.
Lack-of-control	18	5.16	3.5
In-control	18	3.47	2.0

(a) What degrees of freedom would you use in the conservative two-sample t procedures to compare the lack-of-control and in-control groups?

(b) What is the two-sample t test statistic for comparing the mean number of pictures identified as having an image for the two groups?

(c) Test the null hypothesis of no difference between the two population means against the two-sided alternative. Use your statistic from part (b) with degrees of freedom from part (a).

19.24 Cholesterol in Canadian young adults. A random sample of 2053 Canadian women aged 18 to 34 found mean blood cholesterol level $\bar{x} = 4.5$ millimoles per liter (mmol/l), with standard deviation $s = 0.8$ mmol/l. A sample of 1990 Canadian young men in the same study had $\bar{x} = 4.6$ mmol/l and $s = 0.9$ mmol/l.[14]

(a) We know that even small differences can be statistically significant if the samples are large. Is there a significant difference between the mean blood cholesterol levels of Canadian young women and young men?

(b) We also know that estimating the size of a difference helps us decide whether it is large enough to be important. Give a 95% confidence interval for the difference between female and male mean cholesterol levels.

19.25 Coaching and SAT scores. Coaching companies claim that their courses can raise the SAT scores of high school students. Of course, students who retake the SAT without paying for coaching generally raise their scores, too. A random sample of students who took the SAT twice found 427 who were coached and 2733 who were uncoached.[15] Starting with their Verbal scores on the first and second tries, we have these summary statistics:

		Try 1		Try 2		Gain	
	n	$\bar{x}$	s	$\bar{x}$	s	$\bar{x}$	s
Coached	427	500	92	529	97	29	59
Uncoached	2733	506	101	527	101	21	52

Let's first ask if the students who were coached increased their scores significantly.

(a) You could use the information on the Coached line to carry out either a two-sample t test comparing Try 1 with Try 2 for coached students or a matched pairs t test using Gain. Which is the correct test? Why?

(b) Carry out the proper test. What do you conclude?

(c) Give a 99% confidence interval for the mean gain of all students who are coached.

19.26 Coaching and SAT scores, continued. What we really want to know is whether coached students improve more than uncoached students, and whether any advantage is large enough to be worth paying for. Use the information in the previous exercise to answer these questions:

(a) Is there good evidence that coached students gained more, on the average, than uncoached students?

(b) How much more do coached students gain, on the average? Give a 99% confidence interval.

(c) Based on your work, what is your opinion: do you think coaching courses are worth paying for?

19.27 Coaching and SAT scores: critique. The data you used in the previous two problems came from a random sample of students who took the SAT twice. The response rate was 63%, which is pretty good for nongovernment surveys, so let's accept that the respondents do represent all students who took the exam twice. Nonetheless, we can't be sure that coaching actually *caused* the coached students to gain more than the uncoached students. Explain briefly but clearly why this is so.

Exercises 19.28 to 19.34 include the actual data. To apply the two-sample t procedures, use Option 1 if you have technology that implements that method. Otherwise, use Option 2.

19.28 Improving your tips. Researchers gave 40 index cards to a waitress at an Italian restaurant in New Jersey. Before delivering the bill to each customer, the waitress randomly selected a card and wrote on the bill the same message that was printed on the index card. Twenty of the cards had the message "The weather is supposed to be really good tomorrow. I hope you enjoy the day!" Another 20 cards contained the message "The weather is supposed to be not so good tomorrow. I hope you enjoy the day anyway!" After the customers left, the waitress recorded the amount of the tip (as a percent of the bill) before taxes. Here are the tip percents for those receiving the good-weather message:[16] 🔴 **TIPPING4**

20.8 18.7 19.9 20.6 21.9 23.4 22.8 24.9 22.2 20.3
24.9 22.3 27.0 20.5 22.2 24.0 21.2 22.1 22.0 22.7

The tip percents for the 20 customers who received the bad-weather message are

18.0 19.1 19.2 18.8 18.4 19.0 18.5 16.1 16.8 14.0
17.0 13.6 17.5 20.0 20.2 18.8 18.0 23.2 18.2 19.4

(a) Make stemplots or histograms of both sets of data. Because the distributions are reasonably symmetric with no extreme outliers, the t procedures will work well.

(b) Is there good evidence that the two different messages produce different percent tip percents? State hypotheses, carry out a two-sample t test, and report your conclusions.

19.29 Do good smells bring good business? In Exercise 19.9 (page 392) you examined the effects of a lavender odor on customer behavior in a small restaurant. Lavender is a relaxing odor. The researchers also looked at the effects of lemon, a stimulating odor. The design of the study is described in Exercise 19.9. Here are the times in minutes that customers spent in the restaurant when no odor was present: 🔴 **ODORS3**

103 68 79 106 72 121 92 84 72 92
85 69 73 87 109 115 91 84 76 96
107 98 92 107 93 118 87 101 75 86

When a lemon odor was present, customers lingered for these times:

78 104 74 75 112 88 105 97 101 89
88 73 94 63 83 108 91 88 83 106
108 60 96 94 56 90 113 97

(a) Examine both samples. Does it appear that use of two-sample t procedures is justified? Do the sample means suggest that a lemon odor changes the average length of stay?

(b) Does a lemon odor influence the length of time customers stay in the restaurant? State hypotheses, carry out a t test, and report your conclusions.

19.30 Improving your tips, continued. Use the data in Exercise 19.28 to give a 95% confidence interval for the difference between the mean tip percents for the two different messages. 🔴 **TIPPING4**

19.31 How strong are durable press fabrics? "Durable press" cotton fabrics are treated to improve their recovery from wrinkles after washing. Unfortunately, the treatment also reduces the strength of the fabric. A study compared the breaking strength of fabrics treated by two commercial durable press processes. Five swatches of the same fabric were assigned at random to each process. Here are the data, in pounds of pull needed to tear the fabric:[17] 🔴 **FABRICS**

| Permafresh | 29.9 | 30.7 | 30.0 | 29.5 | 27.6 |
| Hylite | 28.8 | 23.9 | 27.0 | 22.1 | 24.2 |

Is there good evidence that the two processes result in different mean breaking strengths?

(a) Do the sample means suggest that one of the processes is superior in breaking strength?

(b) Make stemplots for both samples. The Permafresh sample contains a mild outlier. With just 5 observations per group, we worry that this outlier will affect our conclusions.

(c) Test the hypothesis $H_0: \mu_1 = \mu_2$ against the two-sided alternative twice: once using all the data and again without the outlier in the Permafresh sample. Do the two tests lead to similar conclusions? Can we safely conclude that one treatment has significantly higher mean breaking strength than the other?

19.32 Reducing wrinkles. Of course, the reason for durable press treatment is to reduce wrinkling. "Wrinkle recovery angle" measures how well a fabric recovers from wrinkles. Higher is better. Here are data on the wrinkle recovery angle (in degrees) for the same fabric swatches discussed in the previous exercise: 🔴 **WRINKLES**

| Permafresh | 136 | 135 | 132 | 137 | 134 |
| Hylite | 143 | 141 | 146 | 141 | 145 |

Is there a significant difference in wrinkle resistance?

(a) Do the sample means suggest that one process has better wrinkle resistance?

(b) Make stemplots for both samples. There are no obvious deviations from Normality.

(c) Test the hypothesis $H_0: \mu_1 = \mu_2$ against the two-sided alternative. What do you conclude from part (a) and from the result of your test?

19.33 How much stronger? Continue your work from Exercise 19.31. A fabric manufacturer wants to know how large an advantage in strength fabrics treated by the Permafresh method have over fabrics treated by the Hylite process. Give a 90% confidence interval for the difference in mean breaking strengths. (Use all 5 fabric swatches.) 🔴 FABRICS

19.34 How much less wrinkling? In Exercise 19.32, you found that the Hylite process results in significantly greater wrinkle resistance than the Permafresh process. How large is the difference in mean wrinkle recovery angle? Give a 90% confidence interval. 🔴 WRINKLES

Do birds learn to time their breeding? *Blue titmice eat caterpillars. The birds would like lots of caterpillars around when they have young to feed, but they breed earlier than peak caterpillar season. Do the birds time when they breed based on the previous year's caterpillar supply? Researchers randomly assigned 7 pairs of birds to have the natural caterpillar supply supplemented while feeding their young and another 6 pairs to serve as a control group relying on natural food supply. The next year, they measured how many days after the caterpillar peak the birds produced their nestlings.[18] Exercises 19.35 to 19.37 are based on this experiment.*

19.35 Did the randomization produce similar groups? The first thing to do is to compare the two groups in the first year. The only difference should be the chance effect of the random assignment. The study report says: "In the experimental year, the degree of synchronization did not differ between food-supplemented and control females." For this comparison, the report gives $t = -1.05$. What type of t statistic (paired or two-sample) is this? What are the degrees of freedom for this statistic? Show that this t leads to the quoted conclusion.

19.36 Did the treatment have an effect? The investigators expected the control group to adjust their breeding date the next year, whereas the well-fed supplemented group had no reason to change. The report continues: "but in the following year food-supplemented females were more out of synchrony with the caterpillar peak than the controls." Here are the data (days behind the caterpillar peak): 🔴 BREEDING

Control	4.6	2.3	7.7	6.0	4.6	−1.2	
Supplemented	15.5	11.3	5.4	16.5	11.3	11.4	7.7

Carry out a t test and show that it leads to the quoted conclusion.

19.37 Year-to-year comparison. Rather than comparing the two groups in each year, we could compare the behavior of each group in the first and second years. The study report says: "Our main prediction was that females receiving additional food in the nestling period should not change laying date the next year, whereas controls, which (in our area) breed too late in their first year, were expected to advance their laying date in the second year."

Comparing days behind the caterpillar peak in Years 1 and 2 gave $t = 0.63$ for the control group and $t = -2.63$ for the supplemented group. Are these paired or two-sample t

statistics? What are the degrees of freedom for each t? Show that these t-values do *not* agree with the prediction.

*The remaining exercises ask you to answer questions from data without having the details outlined for you. The exercise statements give you the **State** step of the four-step process. Follow the **Plan, Solve,** and **Conclude** steps as illustrated in Examples 19.3 and 19.4 for tests and Example 19.5 for confidence intervals. Remember that examining the data and discussing the conditions for inference are part of the **Solve** step.*

19.38 Thinking about money changes behavior. Kathleen Vohs of the University of Minnesota and her coworkers carried out several randomized comparative experiments on the effects of thinking about money. Here's part of one such experiment.[19] Ask student subjects to unscramble 30 sets of five words to make a meaningful phrase from four of the five words. The control group unscrambled phrases like "cold it desk outside is" into "it is cold outside." The treatment group unscrambled phrases that lead to thinking about money, turning "high a salary desk paying" into "a high-paying salary." Then each subject worked a hard puzzle, knowing that he or she could ask for help. Here are the times in seconds until subjects asked for help. For the treatment group: 🔴 MONEYTHINK

609	444	242	199	174	55	251	466	443
531	135	241	476	482	362	69	160	

For the control group:

118	272	413	291	140	104	55	189	126
400	92	64	88	142	141	373	156	

The researchers suspected that money is connected with self-sufficiency, so that the treatment group will ask for help less quickly on the average. Do the data support this idea?

19.39 Active versus traditional learning. Can active learning improve knowledge retention? Two undergraduate calculus-based engineering statistics courses were taught in different academic quarters, with one employing active-learning methods and another using traditional learning methods. The traditional class was taught lecture-style with relatively little in-class interaction between peers and with the instructor. The active-learning course integrated four group projects into the curriculum, with in-class time devoted to group work on the projects and fewer homework assignments. To assess knowledge retention, two five-question versions of a test were created. They had similar but not identical questions covering core statistics topics, worth a total of 18 possible points. All students in both sections were randomly given one version of the test as part of their final exam. Then, eight months later, a volunteer subset of the original students were given the version that they had not taken previously. To encourage students to take the second version of the exam, a ten-dollar gift card to the university bookstore was given to each participant. The change in the score from the first version to the second is used to measure a student's long-term ability to retain the course material. 🔴 ACTIVELEARN

Here are the changes in exam scores for the 15 students in the Active group:[20]

        0 5 7 8 0 3 6 2 5 1
        3 2 4 3 5

The changes in exam scores for the 23 students in the Traditional group are

        7 0 8   2 4 3 1 2 5 8
        5 6 3 12 1 6 3 6 7 7
        5 6 2

Is there good evidence that active learning is superior to traditional learning?

19.40 Each day I am getting better in math. A "subliminal" message is below our threshold of awareness but may nonetheless influence us. Can subliminal messages help students learn math? A group of students who had failed the mathematics part of the City University of New York Skills Assessment Test agreed to participate in a study to find out.

All received a daily subliminal message, flashed on a screen too rapidly to be consciously read. The treatment group of 10 students (chosen at random) was exposed to "Each day I am getting better in math." The control group of 8 students was exposed to a neutral message, "People are walking on the street." All students participated in a summer program designed to raise their math skills, and all took the assessment test again at the end of the program. Table 19.3

TABLE 19.3 Mathematics skills scores before and after a subliminal message

TREATMENT GROUP		CONTROL GROUP	
BEFORE	AFTER	BEFORE	AFTER
18	24	18	29
18	25	24	29
21	33	20	24
18	29	18	26
18	33	24	38
20	36	22	27
23	34	15	22
23	36	19	31
21	34		
17	27		

gives data on the subjects' scores before and after the program.[21] Is there good evidence that the treatment brought about a greater improvement in math scores than the neutral message? How large is the mean difference in gains between treatment and control? (Use 90% confidence.) 🔴 SUBLIMINAL

19.41 Active versus traditional learning, continued.

(a) Use the data in Exercise 19.39 to give a 90% confidence interval for the difference in the mean change in score for students in the active and traditional classes. 🔴 ACTIVELEARN

(b) Give a 90% confidence interval for the mean change in score of students in the active-learning class.

19.42 Tropical flowers. Different varieties of the tropical flower *Heliconia* are fertilized by different species of hummingbirds. Over time, the lengths of the flowers and the forms of the hummingbirds' beaks have evolved to match each other. Here are data on the lengths in millimeters of two color varieties of the same species of flower on the island of Dominica:[22] 🔴 FLOWERS

H. caribaea red							
41.90	42.01	41.93	43.09	41.47	41.69	39.78	40.57
39.63	42.18	40.66	37.87	39.16	37.40	38.20	38.07
38.10	37.97	38.79	38.23	38.87	37.78	38.01	

H. caribaea yellow						
36.78	37.02	36.52	36.11	36.03	35.45	38.13	37.1
35.17	36.82	36.66	35.68	36.03	34.57	34.63	

Is there good evidence that the mean lengths of the two varieties differ? Estimate the difference between the population means. (Use 95% confidence.)

19.43 Student drinking. A professor asked her sophomore students, "How many drinks do you typically have per session? (A drink is defined as one 12 oz beer, one 4 oz glass of wine, or one 1 oz shot of liquor.)" Some of the students didn't drink. Table 19.4 gives the responses of the female and male students who did drink.[23] It is likely that some of the students exaggerated a bit. The sample is all students in one large sophomore-level class. The class is popular, so we are tentatively willing to regard its members as an SRS of sophomore students at this college. Do a complete analysis that reports on 🔴 DRINKS

(a) the drinking behavior claimed by sophomore women.

(b) the drinking behavior claimed by sophomore men.

(c) a comparison of the behavior of women and men.

TABLE 19.4 Drinks per session claimed by female and male students

FEMALE STUDENTS												
2.5	9	1	3.5	2.5	3	1	3	3	3	3	2.5	2.5
5	3.5	5	1	2	1	7	3	7	4	4	6.5	4
3	6	5	3	8	6	6	3	6	8	3	4	7
4	5	3.5	4	2	1	5	5	3	3	6	4	2
7	7	7	3.5	3	2.5	10	5	4	9	8	1	6
2	5	2.5	3	4.5	9	5	4	4	3	4	6	7
4	5	1	5	3	4	10	7	3	4	4	4	4
2	1	2.5	2.5									

MALE STUDENTS												
7	7.5	8	15	3	4	1	5	11	4.5	6	4	10
16	4	8	5	9	7	7	3	5	6.5	1	12	4
6	8	8	4.5	10.5	8	6	10	1	9	8	7	8
15	3	10	7	4	6	5	2	10	7	9	5	8
7	3	7	6	4	5	2	5	5.5	9	10	10	4
8	4	2	4	12.5	3	15	2	6	3	4	3	10
6	4.5	5										

EXPLORING THE WEB

19.44 A two-sample t test example. Find an example of a two-sample *t* test on the Web. The *Journal of the American Medical Association* (jama.ama-assn.org), *Science Magazine* (www.sciencemag.org), the *Canadian Medical Association Journal* (www.cmaj.ca), the *Journal of Statistics Education* (www.amstat.org/publications/jse), or perhaps the *Journal of Quantitative Analysis in Sports* (www.bepress.com/jqas) are possible sources. To help locate an article, look through the abstracts of articles. Once you find a suitable article, read it and then briefly describe the study (including why it is a two-sample study) and its conclusions. If *P*-values, means, standard deviations, *t* statistics, etc. are reported, be sure to include them in your summary. Also, be sure to give the reference (either the Web link or the journal, issue, year, title of the paper, authors, and page numbers).

19.45 Antibiotics after surgery. If your college has online access to the *Archives of Otolaryngology—Head and Neck Surgery*, read the article "Duration-Related Efficacy of Postoperative Antibiotics Following Pediatric Tonsillectomy: A Prospective, Randomized, Placebo-Controlled Trial" (available online at archotol.ama-assn.org/cgi/content/full/135/10/984). The authors appear to use two-sample *t* procedures in the paper. After reading the article, read the (brief) discussion on the *Chance* Web site, www.causeweb.org/wiki/chance/index.php/Chance_News_57.What are some criticisms or concerns expressed about the study in the *Chance* article?

iStockphoto

Inference about a Population Proportion

Our discussion of statistical inference to this point has concerned making inferences about population *means.* Now we turn to questions about the *proportion* of some outcome in a population. Here are some examples that call for inference about population proportions.

EXAMPLE 20.1 Risky behavior in the age of AIDS

How common is behavior that puts people at risk of AIDS? In the early 1990s, the landmark National AIDS Behavioral Surveys interviewed a random sample of 2673 adult heterosexuals. Of these, 170 had more than one sexual partner in the past year. That's 6.36% of the sample.[1] Based on these data, what can we say about the percent of all adult heterosexuals who have multiple partners? We want to *estimate a single population proportion*. This chapter concerns inference about one proportion. ■

> ### EXAMPLE 20.2 Young adults living with their parents
>
> A surprising number of young adults (ages 19 to 25) still live with their parents. A random sample of 2253 men and 2629 women in this age group found that 44% of the men but only 35% of the women lived at home. Is this significant evidence that the proportions living at home differ in the populations of all young men and all young women? We want to *compare two population proportions*. This is the topic of Chapter 21. ■

To do inference about a population mean μ, we use the mean $\bar{x}$ of a random sample from the population. The reasoning of inference starts with the sampling distribution of $\bar{x}$. Now we follow the same pattern, replacing means by proportions.

THE SAMPLE PROPORTION $\hat{p}$

We are interested in the unknown proportion p of a population that has some outcome. For convenience, call the outcome we are looking for a "success." In Example 20.1, the population is adult heterosexuals, and the parameter p is the proportion who have had more than one sexual partner in the past year. To estimate p, the National AIDS Behavioral Surveys used random dialing of telephone numbers to contact a sample of 2673 people. Of these, 170 said they had multiple sexual partners. The statistic that *sample proportion* estimates the parameter p is the **sample proportion**

$$\hat{p} = \frac{\text{number of successes in the sample}}{\text{total number of individuals in the sample}}$$

$$= \frac{170}{2673} = 0.0636$$

Read the sample proportion $\hat{p}$ as "p-hat."

How good is the statistic $\hat{p}$ as an estimate of the parameter p? To find out, we ask, "What would happen if we took many samples?" The sampling distribution of $\hat{p}$ answers this question. Here are the facts.[2]

SAMPLING DISTRIBUTION OF A SAMPLE PROPORTION

Draw an SRS of size n from a large population that contains proportion p of successes. Let $\hat{p}$ be the **sample proportion** of successes,

$$\hat{p} = \frac{\text{number of successes in the sample}}{n}$$

Then:

■ The **mean** of the sampling distribution of $\hat{p}$ is p.

■ The **standard deviation** of the sampling distribution is

$$\sqrt{\frac{p(1-p)}{n}}$$

■ As the sample size increases, the sampling distribution of $\hat{p}$ becomes **approximately Normal**. That is, for large n, $\hat{p}$ has approximately the $N(p, \sqrt{p(1-p)/n})$ distribution.

Figure 20.1 summarizes these facts in a form that helps you recall the big idea of a sampling distribution. The mean of the sampling distribution of $\hat{p}$ is the true value of the population proportion p. That is, $\hat{p}$ is an unbiased estimator of p. The standard deviation of $\hat{p}$ gets smaller as the sample size n gets larger, so that estimation is likely to be more accurate when the sample is larger. As is the case for $\bar{x}$, the standard deviation gets smaller only at the rate $\sqrt{n}$. We need four times as many observations to cut the standard deviation in half.

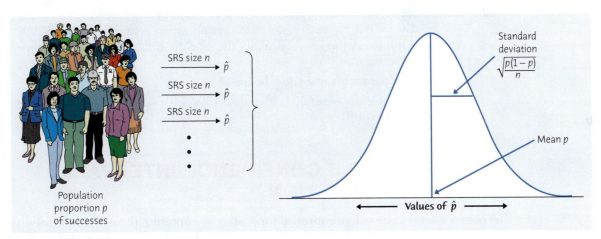

FIGURE 20.1

Select a large SRS from a population in which the proportion p are successes. The sampling distribution of the proportion $\hat{p}$ of successes in the sample is approximately Normal. The mean is p and the standard deviation is $\sqrt{p(1-p)/n}$.

EXAMPLE 20.3 Asking about risky behavior

Suppose that in fact 6% of all adult heterosexuals had more than one sexual partner in the past year (and would admit it when asked). The National AIDS Behavioral Surveys interviewed a random sample of 2673 people from this population. In many such samples, the proportion $\hat{p}$ of the 2673 people in the sample who had more than one partner would vary according to (approximately) the Normal distribution with mean 0.06 and standard deviation

$$\sqrt{\frac{p(1-p)}{n}} = \sqrt{\frac{(0.06)(0.94)}{2673}}$$

$$= \sqrt{0.0000211} = 0.00459 \quad ■$$

APPLY YOUR KNOWLEDGE

20.1 Prayer among the Millennials. The Millennial generation (so called because they were born after 1980 and began to come of age around the year 2000) are less religiously active than older Americans. One of the questions in the General Social Survey in 2010 was "How often does the respondent pray?" Among the 411 respondents in the survey between 18 and 30 years of age, 277 prayed at least once a week.[3]

(a) Describe the population and explain in words what the parameter p is.

(b) Give the numerical value of the statistic $\hat{p}$ that estimates p.

20.2 Texting. Consumers turned to their mobile devices in growing numbers and increasing frequency throughout 2010. Text messaging led as the top mobile activity, with 68% of American mobile subscribers texting in 2010.[4] A polling firm contacts an SRS of 1200 people chosen from the population of American mobile subscribers. If the sample were repeated many times, what would be the range of the sample proportions of mobile subscribers who have texted, according to the 95 part of the 68–95–99.7 rule?

20.3 Social-networking sites. About 70% of young adult Internet users (ages 18 to 29) use social-networking sites. Suppose that a sample survey contacts an SRS of 1500 young adult Internet users and calculates the proportion $\hat{p}$ in this sample who use social-networking sites.

(a) What is the approximate distribution of $\hat{p}$?

(b) If the sample size were 6000 rather than 1500, what would be the approximate distribution of $\hat{p}$?

LARGE-SAMPLE CONFIDENCE INTERVALS FOR A PROPORTION

To obtain a level C confidence interval for p, start by capturing the central probability C in the distribution of $\hat{p}$. To do this, go out z^* standard deviations from the mean p, where z^* is the critical value that captures the central area C under the standard Normal curve. Figure 20.2 shows the result. The confidence interval is

$$\hat{p} \pm z^* \sqrt{\frac{p(1-p)}{n}}$$

This won't do, because we don't know the value of p. So we replace the standard

standard error of $\hat{p}$

deviation by the **standard error of $\hat{p}$**

$$\sqrt{\frac{\hat{p}(1-\hat{p})}{n}}$$

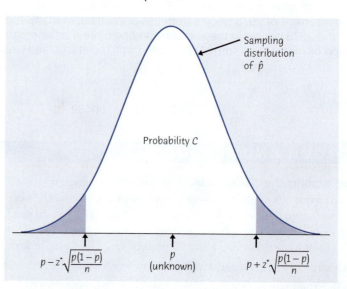

FIGURE 20.2

With probability C, $\hat{p}$ lies within $\pm z^* \sqrt{p(1-p)/n}$ of the unknown population proportion p. That is to say that in these samples p lies within $\pm z^* \sqrt{p(1-p)/n}$ of $\hat{p}$.

to get the confidence interval

$$\hat{p} \pm z^* \sqrt{\frac{\hat{p}(1 - \hat{p})}{n}}$$

Because the sampling distribution of $\hat{p}$ is only approximately Normal, we can trust this confidence interval only for large samples.

LARGE-SAMPLE CONFIDENCE INTERVAL FOR A POPULATION PROPORTION

Draw an SRS of size n from a large population that contains an unknown proportion p of successes. An approximate level C **confidence interval for p** is

$$\hat{p} \pm z^* \sqrt{\frac{\hat{p}(1 - \hat{p})}{n}}$$

where z^* is the critical value for the standard Normal density curve with area C between $-z^*$ and z^*.

Use this interval only when the numbers of successes and failures in the sample are both 15 or greater.

EXAMPLE 20.4 Estimating risky behavior

The four-step process for any confidence interval is outlined on page 291.

STATE: The National AIDS Behavioral Surveys found that 170 of a sample of 2673 adult heterosexuals had multiple partners. That is,

$$\hat{p} = \frac{170}{2673} = 0.0636$$

What can we say about the population of all adult heterosexuals?

PLAN: We will give a 99% confidence interval to estimate the proportion p of all adult heterosexuals who have multiple partners.

SOLVE: First verify the conditions for inference:

■ The sampling design was a complex random sample, and the survey used inference procedures for that design. The overall effect is close to an SRS, however.

■ The sample is large enough: the numbers of successes (170) and failures (2503) in the sample are both much larger than 15.

The sample size condition is easily satisfied. The condition that the sample be an SRS is only approximately met.

   A 99% confidence interval for the proportion p of all adult heterosexuals with multiple partners uses the standard Normal critical value $z^* = 2.576$. The confidence interval is

$$\hat{p} \pm z^* \sqrt{\frac{\hat{p}(1 - \hat{p})}{n}} = 0.0636 \pm 2.576 \sqrt{\frac{(0.0636)(0.9364)}{2673}}$$

$$= 0.0636 \pm 0.0122$$

$$= 0.0514 \text{ to } 0.0758$$

CONCLUDE: We are 99% confident that the percent of adult heterosexuals who have had more than one sexual partner in the past year lies between about 5.1% and 7.6%. ■

As usual, the practical problems of a large sample survey weaken our confidence in the AIDS survey's conclusions. Only households with landline telephones were contacted. About 30% of the people reached refused to cooperate. Some respondents may not have told the truth when asked about their sexual behavior. The survey report says that some response bias is probably present:

> It is more likely that the present figures are underestimates; some respondents may underreport their numbers of sexual partners and intravenous drug use because of embarrassment and fear of reprisal, or they may forget or not know details of their own or of their partner's HIV risk and their antibody testing history.[5]

Reading the report of a large study like the National AIDS Behavioral Surveys reminds us that statistics in practice involves much more than formulas for inference.

APPLY YOUR KNOWLEDGE

20.4   **Weight-lifting injuries.** Resistance training is a popular form of conditioning aimed at enhancing sports performance and is widely used among high school, college, and professional athletes, although its use for younger athletes is controversial. Researchers obtained a random sample of 4111 patients between the ages of 8 and 30 who were admitted to U.S. emergency rooms with injuries classified by the Consumer Product Safety Commission code "weightlifting." These injuries were further classified as "accidental" if caused by dropped weight or improper equipment use. Of the 4111 weight-lifting injuries, 1552 were classified as accidental.[6] Give a 90% confidence interval for the proportion of weight-lifting injuries in this age group that were accidental. Follow the four-step process as illustrated in Example 20.4.

20.5   **Computer/Internet-based crime.** With over 50% of adults spending more than an hour a day on the Internet, the number experiencing computer- or Internet-based crime continues to rise. A survey in 2010 of a random sample of 1025 adults, aged 18 and older, reached by random digit dialing found 113 adults in the sample who said that they or a household member had been the victim of a computer or Internet crime on their home computer in the past year.[7] Give the 99% confidence interval for the proportion p of all households that have experienced computer or Internet crime during the year before the survey was conducted. Follow the four-step process as illustrated in Example 20.4.

20.6   **Canadian attitudes toward guns.** Canadians support gun control more strongly than do Americans. A sample survey asked a random sample of 1505 adult Canadians, "Do you agree or disagree that all firearms should be registered?" Of the 1505 people in the sample, 1288 answered either "Agree strongly" or "Agree somewhat."[8]

(a)   The survey dialed residential telephone numbers at random in all 10 Canadian provinces (omitting the sparsely populated northern territories). Based on what you know about sample surveys, what is likely to be the biggest weakness of this survey?

(b) Nonetheless, act as if we have an SRS from adults in Canada. Give a 95% confidence interval for the proportion who support registration of all firearms.

20.7 No confidence interval. In the National AIDS Behavioral Surveys sample of 2673 adult heterosexuals, 0.2% (that's 0.002 as a decimal fraction) had both received a blood transfusion and had a sexual partner from a group at high risk of AIDS. Explain why we can't use the large-sample confidence interval to estimate the proportion p in the population who share these two risk factors.

CHOOSING THE SAMPLE SIZE

In planning a study, we may want to choose a sample size that will allow us to estimate the parameter within a given margin of error. The margin of error in the large-sample confidence interval for p is

$$m = z^* \sqrt{\frac{\hat{p}(1 - \hat{p})}{n}}$$

Here z^* is the standard Normal critical value for the level of confidence we want. Because the margin of error involves the sample proportion of successes $\hat{p}$, we need to guess this value when choosing n. Call our guess p^*. There are two ways to get p^*:

1. Use a guess p^* based on a pilot study or on past experience with similar studies. You can do several calculations to cover the range of values of $\hat{p}$ you might get.

2. Use $p^* = 0.5$ as the guess. The margin of error m is largest when $\hat{p} = 0.5$, so this guess is conservative in the sense that, if we get any other $\hat{p}$ when we do our study, we will get a margin of error smaller than planned.

Once you have a guess p^*, the recipe for the margin of error can be solved to give the sample size n needed. Here is the result.

SAMPLE SIZE FOR DESIRED MARGIN OF ERROR

The level C confidence interval for a population proportion p will have margin of error approximately equal to a specified value m when the sample size is

$$n = \left(\frac{z^*}{m}\right)^2 p^*(1 - p^*)$$

where p^* is a guessed value for the sample proportion. The margin of error will always be less than or equal to m if you take the guess p^* to be 0.5.

You can use the conservative guess $p^* = 0.5$ if you expect the true $\hat{p}$ to be roughly between 0.3 and 0.7. If the true $\hat{p}$ is close to 0 or 1, using $p^* = 0.5$ as your guess will give a sample much larger than you need. Try to use a better guess from a pilot study when you suspect that $\hat{p}$ will be less than 0.3 or greater than 0.7.

EXAMPLE 20.5 Planning a poll

Colin Anderson/BrandX/Age fotostock

STATE: Gloria Chavez and Ronald Flynn are the candidates for mayor in a large city. You are planning a sample survey to determine what percent of the voters intend to vote for Chavez. You will contact an SRS of registered voters in the city. You want to estimate the proportion p of Chavez voters with 95% confidence and a margin of error no greater than 3%, or 0.03. How large a sample do you need?

PLAN: Find the sample size n needed for margin of error $m = 0.03$ and 95% confidence. The winner's share in all but the most lopsided elections is between 30% and 70% of the vote. You can use the guess $p^* = 0.5$.

SOLVE: The sample size you need is

$$n = \left(\frac{1.96}{0.03}\right)^2 (0.5)(1 - 0.5) = 1067.1$$

Round the result up to $n = 1068$. (Rounding down would give a margin of error slightly greater than 0.03.)

CONCLUDE: An SRS of 1068 registered voters is adequate for margin of error ±3%. ■

As usual, a smaller margin of error calls for a larger sample. If you want a 2.5% margin of error rather than 3%, then (after rounding up)

$$n = \left(\frac{1.96}{0.025}\right)^2 (0.5)(1 - 0.5) = 1537$$

APPLY YOUR KNOWLEDGE

20.8 Canadians and doctor-assisted suicide. A Gallup Poll asked a sample of Canadian adults if they thought the law should allow doctors to end the life of a patient who is in great pain and near death if the patient makes a request in writing. The poll included 270 people in Québec, 221 of whom agreed that doctor-assisted suicide should be allowed.[9]

(a) What is the margin of error of the large-sample 95% confidence interval for the proportion of all Québec adults who would allow doctor-assisted suicide?

(b) How large a sample is needed to get the common ±3 percentage point margin of error? Use the previous sample as a pilot study to get p^*.

20.9 Can you taste PTC? PTC is a substance that has a strong bitter taste for some people and is tasteless for others. The ability to taste PTC is inherited. About 75% of Italians can taste PTC, for example. You want to estimate the proportion of Americans with at least one Italian grandparent who can taste PTC. Starting with the 75% estimate for Italians, how large a sample must you collect in order to estimate the proportion of PTC tasters within ±0.04 with 90% confidence?

SIGNIFICANCE TESTS FOR A PROPORTION

The test statistic for the null hypothesis $H_0: p = p_0$ is the sample proportion $\hat{p}$ standardized using the value p_0 specified by H_0,

$$z = \frac{\hat{p} - p_0}{\sqrt{\dfrac{p_0(1 - p_0)}{n}}}$$

This z statistic has approximately the standard Normal distribution when H_0 is true. P-values therefore come from the standard Normal distribution. Here is the procedure for tests.

SIGNIFICANCE TESTS FOR A PROPORTION

Draw an SRS of size n from a large population that contains an unknown proportion p of successes. To **test the hypothesis $H_0: p = p_0$**, compute the z statistic

$$z = \frac{\hat{p} - p_0}{\sqrt{\dfrac{p_0(1 - p_0)}{n}}}$$

Find P-values from the standard Normal distribution.

Use this test when the sample size n is so large that both np_0 and $n(1 - p_0)$ are 10 or more.[10]

EXAMPLE 20.6   Are boys more likely?

The four-step process for any significance test is outlined on page 307.

STATE: We hear that newborn babies are more likely to be boys than girls. Is this true? A random sample found 13,173 boys among 25,468 children.[11] The sample proportion of boys was

$$\hat{p} = \frac{13,173}{25,468} = 0.5172$$

Boys do make up more than half of the sample, but of course we don't expect a perfect 50-50 split in a random sample. Is this sample evidence that boys are more common than girls in the entire population?

Blaine Harrington III/CORBIS

PLAN: Take p to be the proportion of boys among all children of American mothers. We want to test the hypotheses

$$H_0: p = 0.5$$
$$H_a: p > 0.5$$

SOLVE: The conditions for inference are met, so we can go on to find the z test statistic:

$$z = \frac{\hat{p} - p_0}{\sqrt{\dfrac{p_0(1 - p_0)}{n}}}$$

$$= \frac{0.5172 - 0.5}{\sqrt{\dfrac{(0.5)(0.5)}{25,468}}} = 5.49$$

The *P*-value is the area under the standard Normal curve to the right of $z = 5.49$. Figure 20.3 reminds us that this area is very small. Table C shows that $P < 0.0005$, and software says that P is about 0.00000002.

CONCLUDE: There is very strong evidence that more than half of newborns are boys ($P < 0.0005$). ■

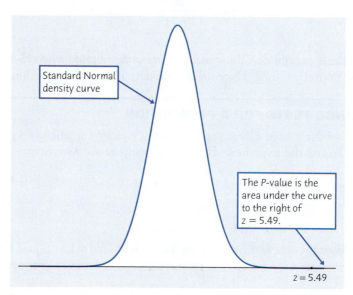

Standard Normal density curve

The *P*-value is the area under the curve to the right of $z = 5.49$.

$z = 5.49$

FIGURE 20.3

The one-sided *P*-value for Example 20.6 is the area under the standard Normal curve to the right of $z = 5.49$.

EXAMPLE 20.7 Estimating the chance of a boy

A 99% confidence interval for the proportion p of boys in the population of all newborns is

$$\hat{p} \pm z^* \sqrt{\frac{\hat{p}(1 - \hat{p})}{n}} = 0.5172 \pm 2.576 \sqrt{\frac{(0.5172)(0.4828)}{25{,}468}}$$

$$= 0.5172 \pm 0.0081$$

$$= 0.5091 \text{ to } 0.5253$$

We are 99% confident that between about 51% and 52.5% of children are boys. The confidence interval is more informative than the test in Example 20.6, which tells us only that more than half are boys. ■

APPLY YOUR KNOWLEDGE

© Ivan Vdovin/Alamy

20.10 Spinning euros. All euros have a national image on the "heads" side and a common design on the "tails" side. Spinning a coin, unlike tossing it, may not give heads and tails equal probabilities. Polish students spun the Belgium euro 250 times, with its portly king, Albert, displayed on the heads side. The result was 140 heads.[12] How significant is this evidence against equal probabilities? Follow the four-step process as illustrated in Example 20.6.

20.11 Vote for the best face? We often judge other people by their faces. It appears that some people judge candidates for elected office by their faces. Psychologists showed head-and-shoulders photos of the two main candidates in 32 races for the U.S. Senate to many subjects (dropping subjects who recognized one of the candidates) to see which candidate was rated "more competent" based on nothing but the photos. On election day, the candidates whose faces looked more competent won 22 of the 32 contests.[13] If faces don't influence voting, half of all races in the long run should be won by the candidate with the better face. Is there evidence that the candidate with the better face wins more than half the time? Follow the four-step process as illustrated in Example 20.6.

20.12 No test. Explain why we can't use the z test for a proportion in these situations:

(a) You toss a coin 10 times to test the hypothesis $H_0: p = 0.5$ that the coin is balanced.

(b) A college president says, "99% of the alumni support my firing of Coach Boggs." You contact an SRS of 200 of the college's 15,000 living alumni to test the hypothesis $H_0: p = 0.99$.

CHAPTER 20 SUMMARY

CHAPTER SPECIFICS

■ Tests and confidence intervals for a population proportion p when the data are an SRS of size n are based on the **sample proportion $\hat{p}$.**

■ When n is large, $\hat{p}$ has approximately the Normal distribution with mean p and standard deviation $\sqrt{p(1-p)/n}$.

■ The level C **confidence interval for p** is

$$\hat{p} \pm z^* \sqrt{\frac{\hat{p}(1-\hat{p})}{n}}$$

where z^* is the critical value for the standard Normal curve with area C between $-z^*$ and z^*. Use this interval only when the sample is so large that the counts of successes and failures are both 15 or greater.

■ The **sample size** needed to obtain a confidence interval with approximate margin of error m for a population proportion is

$$n = \left(\frac{z^*}{m}\right)^2 p^*(1-p^*)$$

where p^* is a guessed value for the sample proportion $\hat{p}$, and z^* is the standard Normal critical point for the level of confidence you want. If you use $p^* = 0.5$ in this formula, the margin of error of the interval will be less than or equal to m no matter what the value of $\hat{p}$ is.

■ **Significance tests for $H_0: p = p_0$** are based on the z statistic

$$z = \frac{\hat{p} - p_0}{\sqrt{\dfrac{p_0(1-p_0)}{n}}}$$

with P-values calculated from the standard Normal distribution. Use this test in practice when $np_0 \geq 10$ and $n(1-p_0) \geq 10$.

▌ LINK IT

The methods of this chapter can be used to compute confidence intervals and to test hypotheses about a population proportion. This may be the proportion in a population with some attribute of interest such as the population proportion of young adults who use social-networking sites. The proportion could also correspond to the probability of an outcome in an experiment such as the probability that a spinning coin will land on heads. Since the methods of this chapter are approximations, it is important to always check the conditions required for the approximations to work well, whether you are using the large-sample confidence interval or the z test.

When making inferences about a proportion in a population, an important assumption for the methods of this chapter is that the data are an SRS from the population. This is the most difficult assumption to guarantee because of the many difficulties associated with obtaining an SRS. These difficulties were described in Chapter 8. With nonresponse rates in many surveys that are over 80%, the final sample may not be representative of the population even when researchers initially selected an SRS. Because of this, most surveys of large populations need to use more complicated sampling schemes as well as modify the estimates to adjust for problems such as nonresponse.

In Chapters 18 and 19, we first considered inference about a single mean and then turned our attention to situations that required the comparison of two population means. In many instances, we want to compare two population proportions rather than making inferences about a single proportion. Methods to compare two population proportions will be described in the next chapter.

▌ CHECK YOUR SKILLS

20.13 A 2010 study finds that in a random sample of 3000 American adults aged 18 and over, 1410 owned an MP3 player such as an iPod. The sample proportion $\hat{p}$ who own an MP3 player is

(a) 47.   (b) 53.   (c) 0.47.

20.14 Based on the sample in the previous exercise, the 95% large-sample confidence interval for the proportion of all American adults aged 18 and over who own an MP3 player is

(a) 0.47 ± 0.009.

(b) 0.47 ± 0.015.

(c) 0.47 ± 0.018.

20.15 The sample survey in Exercise 20.13 actually called 4600 American adults aged 18 and over, but 1600 of those contacted refused to answer. This nonresponse could cause the survey result to be in error. The error due to nonresponse

(a) is in addition to the margin of error found in Exercise 20.14.

(b) is included in the margin of error found in Exercise 20.14.

(c) can be ignored because it isn't random.

20.16 How many American adults aged 18 and over must be interviewed to estimate the proportion who own MP3 players within ± 0.02 with 99% confidence? Use 0.5 as the conservative guess for p.

(a) $n = 1692$

(b) $n = 2401$

(c) $n = 4148$

20.17 An opinion poll asks an SRS of 100 college seniors how they view their job prospects. In all, 53 say "Good." Does this poll give reason to conclude that more than half of all seniors think their job prospects are good? The hypotheses for a test to answer this question are

(a) $H_0: p = 0.5, H_a: p > 0.5$.

(b) $H_0: p > 0.5, H_a: p = 0.5$.

(c) $H_0: p = 0.5, H_a: p \neq 0.5$.

20.18 The value of the z statistic for the test of the previous exercise is about

(a) $z = 12$.

(b) $z = 6$.

(c) $z = 0.6$.

20.19 A Gallup Poll found that 28% of American adults expect to inherit money or valuable possessions from a relative. The poll's margin of error was 3%. This means that

(a) the poll used a method that gets an answer within 3% of the truth about the population 95% of the time.

(b) we can be sure that the percent of all adults who expect an inheritance is between 25% and 31%.

(c) if Gallup takes another poll using the same method, the results of the second poll will lie between 25% and 31%.

CHAPTER 20 EXERCISES

20.20 Reporting cheating. Students are reluctant to report cheating by other students. A student project put this question to an SRS of 172 undergraduates at a large university: "You witness two students cheating on a quiz. Do you go to the professor?" Only 19 answered "Yes."[14] Give a 95% confidence interval for the proportion of all undergraduates at this university who would report cheating.

20.21 Do smokers know that smoking is bad for them? The Harris Poll asked a sample of smokers, "Do you believe that smoking will probably shorten your life, or not?" Of the 1010 people in the sample, 848 said "Yes."

(a) Harris called residential telephone numbers at random in an attempt to contact an SRS of smokers. Based on what you know about national sample surveys, what is likely to be the biggest weakness in the survey?

(b) We will nonetheless act as if the people interviewed are an SRS of smokers. Give a 95% confidence interval for the percent of smokers who agree that smoking will probably shorten their lives.

20.22 Prayer among the Millennials, continued. The Millennial generation (so called because they were born after 1980 and began to come of age around the year 2000) are less religiously active than older Americans. One of the questions in the General Social Survey in 2010 was "How often does the respondent pray?" Among the 411 respondents in the survey between 18 and 30 years of age, 277 prayed at least once a week.[15]

(a) Does the sample size meet the conditions for using the large-sample confidence interval?

(b) What is the large-sample 99% confidence interval for the proportion p of all adults between 18 and 30 years of age who pray at least once a week?

20.23 Harris announces a margin of error. Exercise 20.21 describes a Harris Poll survey of 1010 smokers. Harris announces a margin of error of ±3 percentage points for all samples of about this size. Opinion polls announce the margin of error for 95% confidence.

(a) What is the actual margin of error (in percent) for the confidence interval from this sample?

(b) The margin of error is largest when $\hat{p} = 0.5$. What would the margin of error (in percent) be if the sample had resulted in $\hat{p} = 0.5$?

(c) Why do you think that Harris announces a ±3% margin of error for all samples of about this size?

20.24 Internet searches and cell phones. The Pew Internet and American Life Project asked a random sample of 2485 cell phone users whether they had used their cell phone to look up health or medical information. Of these, 422 said "Yes."[16]

(a) Pew dialed cell phone numbers at random in the continental United States in an attempt to contact a random sample of adults. Based on what you know about national sample surveys, what is likely to be the biggest weakness in the survey?

(b) Act as if the sample is an SRS. Give a large-sample 90% confidence interval for the proportion p of all cell phone users who have used their cell phone to look up health or medical information.

(c) Three out of the five most popular health-related searches on cell phones have to do with sex: "pregnancy," "herpes," and "STD" (sexually transmitted diseases). Sex-related queries don't even show up on Google's and Yahoo's lists of the top five health searches on computers. What do you think explains the difference in the topics of health-related searches on cell phones versus computers? When drawing conclusions from a sample, you must always be careful to consider the relevant population.

20.25 Detecting genetically modified soybeans. Most soybeans grown in the United States and Canada are genetically modified (GM). Because some nations do not accept GM foods, grain-handling facilities routinely test soybean shipments for the presence of GM beans. In a study of the accuracy of these tests, researchers submitted shipments of soybeans containing 1% of GM beans to 23 randomly selected facilities. Eighteen detected the GM beans.[17] Explain why we can't use the large-sample confidence interval to estimate the percent of all grain-handling facilities that will correctly detect 1% of GM beans in a shipment.

20.26 Testing the waters. In August 2010, the Columbus Dispatch took water samples at 20 Ohio State Park swimming areas and tested for fecal coliform, which are bacteria found in human and animal feces. An unsafe level of fecal coliform means that there's a higher chance that disease-causing bacteria are present and more risk that a swimmer will become ill. Of the 20 swimming areas tested, 13 were found to have unsafe levels of fecal coliform according to state standards. Assume that the swimming areas tested represent a random sample of swimming areas throughout the state.[18] Explain why we can't use the large-sample confidence interval to estimate the proportion of all Ohio swimming areas with unsafe levels of fecal coliform.

20.27 Running red lights. A random digit dialing telephone survey of 880 drivers asked, "Recalling the last ten traffic lights you drove through, how many of them were red when you entered the intersections?" Of the 880 respondents, 171 admitted that at least one light had been red.[19]

(a) Give a 95% confidence interval for the proportion of all drivers who ran one or more of the last ten red lights they met.

(b) Nonresponse is a practical problem for this survey—only 21.6% of calls that reached a live person were completed. Another practical problem is that people may not give truthful answers. What is the likely direction of the bias: do you think more or fewer than 171 of the 880 respondents really ran a red light? Why?

20.28 The IRS plans an SRS. The Internal Revenue Service plans to examine an SRS of individual federal income tax returns from each state. One variable of interest is the proportion of returns claiming itemized deductions. The total number of tax returns in a state varies from more than 15 million in California to fewer than 250,000 in Wyoming.

(a) Will the margin of error for estimating the population proportion change from state to state if an SRS of 2000 tax returns is selected in each state? Explain your answer.

(b) Will the margin of error change from state to state if an SRS of 1% of all tax returns is selected in each state? Explain your answer.

20.29 Customer satisfaction. An automobile manufacturer would like to know what proportion of its customers are not satisfied with the service provided by the local dealer. The customer relations department will survey a random sample of customers and compute a 99% confidence interval for the proportion who are not satisfied.

(a) Past studies suggest that this proportion will be about 0.2. Find the sample size needed if the margin of error of the confidence interval is to be about 0.015.

(b) When the sample is actually contacted, 10% of the sample say they are not satisfied. What is the margin of error of the 99% confidence interval?

20.30 Surveying students. You are planning a survey of students at a large university to determine what proportion favor an increase in student fees to support an expansion of the student newspaper. Using records provided by the registrar, you can select a random sample of students. You will ask each student in the sample whether he or she is in favor of the proposed increase. Your budget will allow a sample of 100 students.

(a) For a sample of size 100, construct a table of the margins of error for 95% confidence intervals when $\hat{p}$ takes the values 0.1, 0.3, 0.5, 0.7, and 0.9.

(b) A former editor of the student newspaper offers to provide funds for a sample of size 500. Repeat the margin of error calculations in (a) for the larger sample size. Then write a short thank-you note to the former editor describing how the larger sample size will improve the results of the survey.

*In responding to Exercises 20.31 to 20.37, follow the **Plan, Solve,** and **Conclude** steps of the four-step process.*

20.31 College-educated parents. The National Assessment of Educational Progress (NAEP) includes a "long-term trend" study that tracks reading and mathematics skills over time and obtains demographic information. In the 2008 study, a random sample of 9600 17-year-old students was selected.[20] The NAEP sample used a multistage design, but the overall effect is quite similar to an SRS of 17-year-olds who are still in school.

(a) In the sample, 46% of students had at least one parent who was a college graduate. Estimate with 99% confidence the proportion of all 17-year-old students in 2008 who had at least one parent who was a college graduate.

(b) The sample does not include 17-year-olds who dropped out of school, so your estimate is valid only for students. Do you think the proportion of all 17-year-olds with at least one parent who was a college graduate would be higher or lower than 46%? Explain.

20.32 Downloading music. A husband and wife, Ted and Suzanne, share a digital music player that has a feature that randomly selects which song to play. A total of 3476 songs have been loaded into the player, some by Ted and the rest by Suzanne. They are interested in determining whether they have each loaded a different proportion of songs into the player. Suppose that when the player was in the random-selection mode, 22 of the first 30 songs selected were songs loaded by Suzanne. Let p denote the proportion of songs that were loaded by Suzanne. State the null and alternative hypotheses to be tested. How strong is the evidence that Ted and Suzanne have each loaded a different proportion of songs into the player?

20.33 Opinions about evolution. A sample survey funded by the National Science Foundation asked a random sample of American adults about biological evolution.[21] One question asked subjects to answer "True," "False," or "Not sure" to the statement "Human beings, as we know them today, developed from earlier species of animals." Of the 1484 respondents, 594 said "True." What can you say with 95% confidence about the percent of all American adults who think that humans developed from earlier species of animals?

20.34 Order in choice. Does the order in which wine is presented make a difference? Subjects were asked to taste two wine samples in sequence, and to then indicate which wine they preferred. Both samples given to the subjects were the *same* wine, although the subjects were expecting to taste two different samples of a particular variety. Of the 32 subjects in the study, 22 selected the wine presented first when presented with the two identical wine samples.[22]

(a) Do the data give good reason to conclude that the subjects are not equally likely to choose either of the two wines when presented with two identical wine samples in sequence?

(b) The subjects were recruited in Ontario, Canada, via advertisements to participate in a study of "attitudes and values towards wine." Can we generalize our conclusions to all wine drinkers? Explain.

20.35 Opinions about evolution, continued. Does the sample in Exercise 20.33 give good evidence to support the claim that "fewer than half of American adults think that humans developed from earlier species of animals"?

20.36 Order in choice: planning a study. How large a sample is needed to obtain margin of error ±0.05 in the study of choice order for tasting wine? Use the $\hat{p}$ from Exercise 20.34 as your guess for the unknown p.

20.37 Chick-fil-A gets it right. Which fast-food chain fills orders most accurately at the drive-thru window? The *Quick Service Restaurant (QSR)* magazine drive-thru study involved a total of 7594 visits to restaurants in the 25 largest fast-food chains in all 50 states. All visits occurred during the lunch hours of 11:00 A.M. to 2:30 P.M. or during the dinner hours of 4:00 to 7:00 P.M. During each visit, the researcher ordered a main item, a side item, and a drink. One item was left off of each order; for example, a field researcher could order a burger with no pickles. After receiving the order, all food and drink items were checked for complete accuracy. Any food or drink item received that was not exactly as ordered resulted in the order being classified as inaccurate. Also included in the measurement of accuracy were condiments requested, napkins, straws, and correct change. Any errors in these resulted in the order being classified as inaccurate. Chick-fil-A had the fewest inaccuracies, with only 14 of 196 orders classified as inaccurate.[23]

(a) What proportion of orders are filled *accurately* by Chick-fil-A? Use 95% confidence.

(b) Do you have any reservations about using the large-sample confidence interval in (a)? Explain.

EXPLORING THE WEB

20.38 Health care access/coverage. The Behavioral Risk Factor Surveillance System (BRFSS) is an ongoing data collection program designed to measure behavioral risk factors for the adult population (18 years of age or older) living in households. Data are collected from a random sample of adults (one per household) through a telephone survey. Go to the Web site apps.nccd.cdc.gov/BRFSS/ and under *Category* go to *Health Care Access/Coverage*. Under the topic *Adults aged 18–64 who have any kind of health care coverage*, you will find the percent with coverage in each state.

(a) Which state has the highest percent of coverage, and what is the reported value? Which state has the lowest percent, and what is its value? Are the reported percents statistics or parameters?

(b) Choose a state of interest to you and click on the link. In the table that opens, there is a line for n, and the entries are the numbers who answered "Yes" and "No." Find the percent in the sample who answered "Yes." Notice that it is different from the percent reported in the table. The table estimates are weighted to try to reduce bias. If it is determined that certain portions of the population are underrepresented in the sample, then that portion of the sample receives more weight when computing the estimate of the percent. The assumptions for an SRS are rarely met in practice, and more complicated methods are often necessary to estimate proportions and compute confidence intervals.

20.39 Find a poll. Search the Web for a recent poll in which the sample statistic is a proportion, for example, the proportion in the sample responding "Yes" to a question. Calculate a 95% confidence interval for the population proportion (assume that the sample is a random sample). State the question asked, how the sample was collected, the sample size, and the population of interest. Possible Web sites are www.gallup.com and www.cbsnews.com/sections/opinion/polls/main500160.shtml:

Chapter 21

Comparing Two Proportions

I n a two-sample problem, we want to compare two populations or the responses to two treatments based on two independent samples. When the comparison involves the *means* of two populations, we use the two-sample *t* methods of Chapter 19. Now we turn to methods to compare the *proportions* of successes in two populations.

TWO-SAMPLE PROBLEMS: Proportions

We will use notation similar to that used in our study of two-sample *t* statistics. The groups we want to compare are Population 1 and Population 2. We have a separate SRS from each population or responses from two treatments in a randomized comparative experiment. A subscript shows which group a parameter or statistic describes. Here is our notation:

Gillian Laub/Getty Images

415

Population	Population proportion	Sample size	Sample proportion
1	p_1	n_1	$\hat{p}_1$
2	p_2	n_2	$\hat{p}_2$

We compare the populations by doing inference about the difference $p_1 - p_2$ between the population proportions. The statistic that estimates this difference is the difference between the two sample proportions, $\hat{p}_1 - \hat{p}_2$.

EXAMPLE 21.1 Young adults living with their parents

STATE: A surprising number of young adults (ages 19 to 25) still live in their parents' home. A random sample by the National Institutes of Health included 2253 men and 2629 women in this age group.[1] The survey found that 986 of the men and 923 of the women lived with their parents. How large is the difference between the proportions of young men and young women who live with their parents?

PLAN: Take young men to be Population 1 and young women to be Population 2. The population proportions who live in their parents' home are p_1 for men and p_2 for women. We will use a confidence interval to estimate the difference $p_1 - p_2$.

SOLVE: Inference about population proportions is based on the sample proportions

$$\hat{p}_1 = \frac{986}{2253} = 0.4376 \text{ (men)}$$

$$\hat{p}_2 = \frac{923}{2629} = 0.3511 \text{ (women)}$$

We see that about 44% of the men but only about 35% of the women lived with their parents. To estimate $p_1 - p_2$, start from the difference between sample proportions

$$\hat{p}_1 - \hat{p}_2 = 0.4376 - 0.3511 = 0.0865$$

To complete the *Solve* step, we must know how this difference behaves. ■

THE SAMPLING DISTRIBUTION OF A DIFFERENCE BETWEEN PROPORTIONS

To use $\hat{p}_1 - \hat{p}_2$ for inference, we must know its sampling distribution. Here are the facts we need.

> ## SAMPLING DISTRIBUTION OF A DIFFERENCE BETWEEN PROPORTIONS
>
> Draw an SRS of size n_1 from a large population having proportion p_1 of successes, and draw an independent SRS of size n_2 from another large population having proportion p_2 of successes. For the difference $\hat{p}_1 - \hat{p}_2$ between the proportions of successes in the two samples,
>
> ■ The **mean** of the sampling distribution is $p_1 - p_2$.
>
> ■ The **standard deviation** of the sampling distribution is
>
> $$\sqrt{\frac{p_1(1 - p_1)}{n_1} + \frac{p_2(1 - p_2)}{n_2}}$$
>
> ■ When the samples are large, the distribution of $\hat{p}_1 - \hat{p}_2$ is **approximately Normal.**

Figure 21.1 displays the distribution of $\hat{p}_1 - \hat{p}_2$. The difference between sample proportions is an unbiased estimator of the difference between population proportions. The standard deviation of $\hat{p}_1 - \hat{p}_2$ involves the unknown parameters p_1 and p_2. Just as in the previous chapter, we must replace these by estimates in order to do inference.

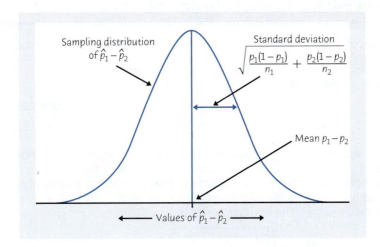

FIGURE 21.1

Select independent SRSs from two populations having proportions of successes p_1 and p_2. The proportions of successes in the two samples are $\hat{p}_1$ and $\hat{p}_2$. When the samples are large, the sampling distribution of the difference $\hat{p}_1 - \hat{p}_2$ is approximately Normal.

LARGE-SAMPLE CONFIDENCE INTERVALS FOR COMPARING PROPORTIONS

To obtain a confidence interval, replace the population proportions p_1 and p_2 in the standard deviation by the sample proportions. The result is the **standard error** of the statistic $\hat{p}_1 - \hat{p}_2$:

standard error

$$SE = \sqrt{\frac{\hat{p}_1(1 - \hat{p}_1)}{n_1} + \frac{\hat{p}_2(1 - \hat{p}_2)}{n_2}}$$

The confidence interval has the same form we met in the previous chapter:

$$\text{estimate} \pm z^* SE_{\text{estimate}}$$

LARGE-SAMPLE CONFIDENCE INTERVAL FOR COMPARING TWO PROPORTIONS

Draw an SRS of size n_1 from a large population having proportion p_1 of successes and draw an independent SRS of size n_2 from another large population having proportion p_2 of successes. When n_1 and n_2 are large, an approximate level C **confidence interval for $p_1 - p_2$** is

$$(\hat{p}_1 - \hat{p}_2) \pm z^*\text{SE}$$

In this formula the standard error SE of $\hat{p}_1 - \hat{p}_2$ is

$$\text{SE} = \sqrt{\frac{\hat{p}_1(1 - \hat{p}_1)}{n_1} + \frac{\hat{p}_2(1 - \hat{p}_2)}{n_2}}$$

and z^* is the critical value for the standard Normal density curve with area C between $-z^*$ and z^*.

Use this interval only when the numbers of successes and failures are each 10 or more in both samples.

EXAMPLE 21.2 Living with parents: men versus women

We can now complete Example 21.1. Here is a summary of the basic information:

Population	Population description	Sample size	Number of successes	Sample proportion
1	men	$n_1 = 2253$	986	$\hat{p}_1 = 986/2253 = 0.4376$
2	women	$n_2 = 2629$	923	$\hat{p}_2 = 923/2629 = 0.3511$

SOLVE: We will give a 95% confidence interval for $p_1 - p_2$, the difference between the proportions of young men and young women who live with their parents. To check that the large-sample confidence interval is safe to use, look at the counts of successes and failures in the two samples. All four counts are much larger than 10, so the large-sample method will be accurate. The standard error is

$$\begin{aligned}
\text{SE} &= \sqrt{\frac{\hat{p}_1(1 - \hat{p}_1)}{n_1} + \frac{\hat{p}_2(1 - \hat{p}_2)}{n_2}} \\
&= \sqrt{\frac{(0.4376)(0.5624)}{2253} + \frac{(0.3511)(0.6489)}{2629}} \\
&= \sqrt{0.0001959} = 0.01400
\end{aligned}$$

The 95% confidence interval is

$$\begin{aligned}
(\hat{p}_1 - \hat{p}_2) \pm z^*\text{SE} &= (0.4376 - 0.3511) \pm (1.960)(0.01400) \\
&= 0.0865 \pm 0.0274 \\
&= 0.059 \text{ to } 0.114
\end{aligned}$$

CONCLUDE: We are 95% confident that the percent of young men living with their parents is between 5.9 and 11.4 percentage points higher than the percent of young women who live with their parents. ■

The sample survey in this example selected a single random sample of young adults, not two separate random samples of young men and young women. To get two samples, we divided the single sample by sex. This means that we did not know the two sample sizes n_1 and n_2 until after the data were in hand. The two-sample z procedures for comparing proportions are valid in such situations. This is an important fact about these methods.

● USING TECHNOLOGY

Figure 21.2 (on page 420) displays software output for Example 21.2 from a graphing calculator and two statistical software programs. As usual, you can understand the output even without knowledge of the program that produced it. Minitab gives the test as well as the confidence interval, confirming that the difference between men and women is highly significant. In CrunchIt!, the test and the confidence interval must be requested using separate commands, resulting in the two outputs in the figure. Excel spreadsheet output is not shown because Excel lacks menu items for inference about proportions. You must use the spreadsheet's formula capability to program the confidence interval or test statistic and then to find the *P*-value of a test.

APPLY YOUR KNOWLEDGE

21.1 **Who texts?** Younger people use their cell phones to text more often than older people do. A random sample of 625 teens aged 12 to 17 who use their cell phones to text found that 475 sent more than 10 text messages in a typical day. In a random sample of 1917 adults aged 18 and over who use their cell phones to text, 786 sent more than 10 text messages in a typical day.[2] Give a 95% confidence interval for the difference between the proportions of cell phone users who send more than 10 texts a day for these two age groups. Follow the four-step process as illustrated in Examples 21.1 and 21.2.

21.2 **An issue of free speech.** In 2010, respondents to the General Social Survey were asked: "There are always some people whose ideas are considered bad or dangerous by other people. For instance, somebody who is against churches and religion. If such a person wanted to make a speech in your (city/town/community) against churches and religion, should he be allowed to speak, or not?"[3] Among the 407 respondents who considered themselves Democrats, 288 said, "Allow," while among the 293 respondents who considered themselves Republicans, 227 said, "Allow." Give a 95% confidence interval for the difference between the proportions of respondents from the two political parties who would allow such a person to speak. Follow the four-step process as illustrated in Examples 21.1 and 21.2.

21.3 **High school students in action.** A government survey randomly selected 8164 female high school students and 7881 male high school students.[4] Of these students, 2261 females and 3594 males met recommended levels of physical activity. (These levels are quite high: at least 60 minutes of activity that makes you breathe hard on at least 5 of the past 7 days.) Give a 99% confidence interval for the difference between the proportions of all female and male high school students who meet the recommended levels of activity.

FIGURE 21.2

Output from a graphing calculator, Minitab, and CrunchIt! for the 95% confidence interval of Example 21.2.

Texas Instruments Graphing Calculator

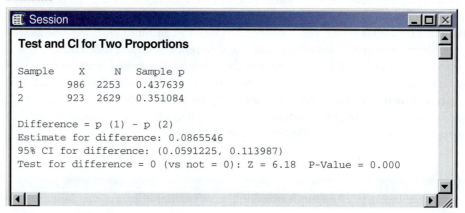

Minitab

Test and CI for Two Proportions

Sample	X	N	Sample p
1	986	2253	0.437639
2	923	2629	0.351084

Difference = p (1) – p (2)
Estimate for difference: 0.0865546
95% CI for difference: (0.0591225, 0.113987)
Test for difference = 0 (vs not = 0): Z = 6.18   P-Value = 0.000

CrunchIt!

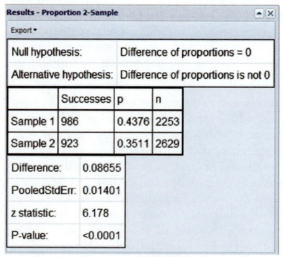

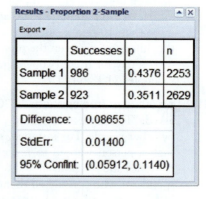

SIGNIFICANCE TESTS FOR COMPARING PROPORTIONS

An observed difference between two sample proportions can reflect an actual difference between the populations, or it may just be due to chance variation in random sampling. Significance tests help us decide if the effect we see in the samples is really there in the populations. The null hypothesis says that there is no difference between the two populations:

$$H_0: p_1 = p_2$$

The alternative hypothesis says what kind of difference we expect.

EXAMPLE 21.3 Interracial dating

STATE: "Would you date a person of a different race?" Researchers answered this question for black males and females by collecting data from the Internet dating site Match.com. When people post profiles on the site, they indicate which races they are willing to date. A random sample of 100 black males and a random sample of 100 black females were selected from the dating site, with 75 of the black males indicating their willingness to date white females and 56 of the black females indicating their willingness to date white males.[5] Is there reason to think that different proportions of black males and females on this Internet dating site would be willing to date whites?

PLAN: Call the population proportions p_1 for men and p_2 for women. We had no direction for the difference in mind before looking at the data, so we have a two-sided alternative:

$$H_0: p_1 = p_2$$
$$H_a: p_1 \neq p_2$$

SOLVE: The men and women can be considered separate SRSs of black men and women from the Internet dating site Match.com. The sample proportions who would be willing to date whites are

© *Radius Images/Alamy*

$$\hat{p}_1 = \frac{75}{100} = 0.75 \ (\text{men})$$

$$\hat{p}_2 = \frac{56}{100} = 0.56 \ (\text{women})$$

That is, 75% of the men but only 56% of the women would be willing to date whites. Is this apparent difference statistically significant? To continue the solution, we must learn the proper test. ■

    To do a test, standardize the difference between the sample proportions $\hat{p}_1 - \hat{p}_2$ to get a z statistic. If H_0 is true, both samples come from populations in which the same unknown proportion p would be willing to date whites. We therefore combine the two samples to estimate this single p, rather than estimating p_1 and p_2 separately. Call this the **pooled sample proportion.** It is

pooled sample proportion

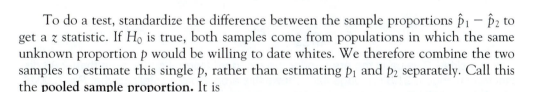

$$\hat{p} = \frac{\text{number of successes in both samples combined}}{\text{number of individuals in both samples combined}}$$

Use $\hat{p}$ in place of both $\hat{p}_1$ and $\hat{p}_2$ in the expression for the standard error SE of $\hat{p}_1 - \hat{p}_2$ to get a z statistic that has the standard Normal distribution when H_0 is true. Here is the test.

SIGNIFICANCE TEST FOR COMPARING TWO PROPORTIONS

Draw an SRS of size n_1 from a large population having proportion p_1 of successes, and draw an independent SRS of size n_2 from another large population having proportion p_2 of successes. To **test the hypothesis H_0: $p_1 = p_2$**, first find the pooled proportion $\hat{p}$ of successes in both samples combined. Then compute the z statistic

$$z = \frac{\hat{p}_1 - \hat{p}_2}{\sqrt{\hat{p}(1 - \hat{p})\left(\dfrac{1}{n_1} + \dfrac{1}{n_2}\right)}}$$

Find P-values from the standard Normal distribution.

Use this test when the counts of successes and failures are each 5 or more in both samples.[6]

EXAMPLE 21.4 Interracial dating, continued

SOLVE: The data come from an SRS and the counts of successes and failures are all much larger than 5. The pooled proportion of blacks who would date whites is

$$\hat{p} = \frac{\text{number "willing to date whites" among men and women combined}}{\text{number of men and women combined}}$$

$$= \frac{75 + 56}{100 + 100}$$

$$= \frac{131}{200} = 0.655$$

The z test statistic is

$$z = \frac{\hat{p}_1 - \hat{p}_2}{\sqrt{\hat{p}(1 - \hat{p})\left(\dfrac{1}{n_1} + \dfrac{1}{n_2}\right)}}$$

$$= \frac{0.75 - 0.56}{\sqrt{(0.655)(0.345)\left(\dfrac{1}{100} + \dfrac{1}{100}\right)}}$$

$$= \frac{0.19}{0.06723} = 2.83$$

The two-sided P-value is the area under the standard Normal curve more than 2.83 distant from 0. Figure 21.3 (on page 423) shows this area. Software tells us that $P = 0.0046$.

Without software, you can compare $z = 2.83$ with the bottom row of Table C (standard Normal critical values) to approximate P. It lies between the critical values 2.807 and 3.091 for two-sided P-values 0.005 and 0.002.

z^*	2.807	3.091
Two-sided P	.005	.002

CONCLUDE: There is strong evidence ($P < 0.005$) that black men are more likely than black women to be willing to date whites on comparable Internet dating sites. In a similar study by the authors, it was found that white men were more willing than white women to date blacks. ▪

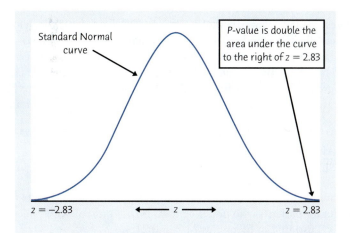

FIGURE 21.3
The *P*-value for the two-sided test of Example 21.4.

Standard Normal curve

P-value is double the area under the curve to the right of z = 2.83

z = −2.83   ⟵ z ⟶   z = 2.83

APPLY YOUR KNOWLEDGE

21.4 Seat belt use. The proportion of drivers who use seat belts depends on things like age (young people are more likely to go unbelted) and gender (women are more likely to use belts). It also depends on local law. In New York City, police can stop a driver who is not belted. In Boston at the time of the survey, police could cite a driver for not wearing a seat belt only if the driver had been stopped for some other violation. Here are data from observing random samples of female Hispanic drivers in these two cities in 2002:[7]

City	Drivers	Belted
New York	220	183
Boston	117	68

(a) Is this an experiment or an observational study? Why?

(b) Comparing local laws suggests the hypothesis that a smaller proportion of drivers wear seat belts in Boston than in New York. Do the data give good evidence that this is true for female Hispanic drivers? Follow the four-step process as illustrated in Examples 21.3 and 21.4.

21.5 Protecting skiers and snowboarders. Most alpine skiers and snowboarders do not use helmets. Do helmets reduce the risk of head injuries? A study in Norway compared skiers and snowboarders who suffered head injuries with a control group who were not injured. Of 578 injured subjects, 96 had worn a helmet. Of the 2992 in the control group, 656 wore helmets.[8] Is helmet use less common among skiers and snowboarders who have had head injuries? Follow the four-step process as illustrated in Examples 21.3 and 21.4. (Note that this is an observational study that compares injured and uninjured subjects. An experiment that assigned subjects to helmet and no-helmet groups would be more convincing.)

21.6 Breast cancer treatment. In sentinel lymph node dissection (SLND), surgeons remove two or three lymph nodes close to the breast that are most likely to contain cancer cells. If these "sentinel" lymph nodes are free of tumors, SLND alone is the accepted management for patients. When the sentinel lymph nodes contain

Jupiterimages/Age fotostock

metastases, axillary lymph node dissection (ALND; that is, the removal of further nodes) remains the standard of care, although its contribution to survival is controversial. ALND carries the additional risk of complications such as seroma, infection, and lymphedema. In one study, patients with sentinel metastases identified by SLND were randomized to undergo ALND or no further treatment (SLND alone). Here are the five-year disease-free survival numbers for the two groups:[9]

Group	Sample size	Disease-free after five years
ALND	420	345
SLND alone	436	366

How strong is the evidence that the proportions of disease-free patients after five years differ for patients who underwent ALND or only SLND? Follow the four-step process as illustrated in Examples 21.3 and 21.4.

CHAPTER 21 SUMMARY

CHAPTER SPECIFICS

■ The data in a **two-sample problem** are two independent SRSs, each drawn from a separate population.

■ Tests and confidence intervals to compare the proportions p_1 and p_2 of successes in the two populations are based on the difference $\hat{p}_1 - \hat{p}_2$ between the sample proportions of successes in the two SRSs.

■ When the sample sizes n_1 and n_2 are large, the sampling distribution of $\hat{p}_1 - \hat{p}_2$ is close to Normal with mean $p_1 - p_2$.

■ The level C **large-sample confidence interval for $p_1 - p_2$** is

$$(\hat{p}_1 - \hat{p}_2) \pm z^*\mathrm{SE}$$

where the **standard error** of $\hat{p}_1 - \hat{p}_2$ is

$$\mathrm{SE} = \sqrt{\frac{\hat{p}_1(1 - \hat{p}_1)}{n_1} + \frac{\hat{p}_2(1 - \hat{p}_2)}{n_2}}$$

and z^* is a standard Normal critical value. Use this interval only if the counts of successes and failures in both samples are 10 or greater.

■ **Significance tests for H_0: $p_1 = p_2$** use the **pooled sample proportion**

$$\hat{p} = \frac{\text{number of successes in both samples combined}}{\text{number of individuals in both samples combined}}$$

and the z statistic

$$z = \frac{\hat{p}_1 - \hat{p}_2}{\sqrt{\hat{p}(1 - \hat{p})\left(\dfrac{1}{n_1} + \dfrac{1}{n_2}\right)}}$$

P-values come from the standard Normal distribution. Use this test when there are 5 or more successes and 5 or more failures in both samples.

LINK IT

Most studies compare two or more treatments rather than investigating a single treatment. These can be observational studies or comparative experiments, and the differences in the type of conclusions that can be reached were described in Chapter 9. When there are two treatments and the response is a continuous measurement, the comparison between the treatments is often based on a comparison of the treatment means using the methods of Chapter 19.

This chapter considers the case where the response classifies individuals into two categories such as whether or not young adults live with their parents. The resulting proportions are then compared between two groups, such as the proportion of males living with their parents versus the proportion of females living with their parents. Since the methods of this chapter are approximate, it is important to always check the conditions required for the approximations to work well, whether you are using the large-sample confidence interval or the z test.

After the appropriate statistical method has been applied, care must be taken when stating the conclusion. The issues described in Chapter 9 are still important. For example, a lack of blinding can result in the expectations of the researcher influencing the results, while confounding can mix up the comparison of the two groups with other factors.

CHECK YOUR SKILLS

In the past decade there have been intensive antismoking campaigns sponsored by both federal and private agencies. The Behavioral Risk Factor Surveillance System (BRFSS) is an ongoing data collection program that monitors behaviors such as smoking on a statewide level using data collected from a random sample of adults through a telephone survey.[10] The first sample, taken in 1999 in Alaska, involved 2045 adults, of which 592 were current smokers. The second sample, taken in 2009 in Alaska, involved 2411 adults, of which 511 were smokers. The samples are to be compared to determine whether the proportion of U.S. adults in Alaska who smoke declined during the 10-year period between the samples. Exercises 21.7 to 21.11 are based on these surveys.

21.7 Take p_{1999} and p_{2009} to be the proportions of all adults in Alaska over 18 who were current smokers in these years. The hypotheses to be tested are

(a) $H_0: p_{1999} = p_{2009}$ versus $H_a: p_{1999} \neq p_{2009}$.

(b) $H_0: p_{1999} = p_{2009}$ versus $H_a: p_{1999} > p_{2009}$.

(c) $H_0: p_{1999} = p_{2009}$ versus $H_a: p_{1999} < p_{2009}$.

21.8 The sample proportions of adults who were current smokers in 1999 and 2009 are about

(a) $\hat{p}_{1999} = 0.21$ and $\hat{p}_{2009} = 0.29$.

(b) $\hat{p}_{1999} = 0.29$ and $\hat{p}_{2009} = 0.21$.

(c) $\hat{p}_{1999} = 0.21$ and $\hat{p}_{2009} = 0.25$.

21.9 The pooled sample proportion of adult smokers in Alaska is about

(a) $\hat{p} = 0.23$.   (b) $\hat{p} = 0.25$.   (c) $\hat{p} = 0.28$.

21.10 The z test for comparing the proportions of smokers in Alaska in 1999 and 2009 has

(a) $P < 0.01$.   (b) $0.01 < P < 0.05$.   (c) $P > 0.05$.

21.11 The 95% large-sample confidence interval for the difference $p_{1999} - p_{2009}$ between the proportions of smokers in Alaska in 1999 and 2009 is about

(a) 0.08 ± 0.013.

(b) 0.08 ± 0.021.

(c) 0.08 ± 0.026.

21.12 In an experiment to learn if substance M can help restore memory, the brains of 20 rats were treated to damage their memories. The rats were trained to run a maze. After a day, 10 rats were given M and 7 of them succeeded in the maze; only 2 of the 10 control rats were successful. The z test for "no difference" against "a higher proportion of the M group succeeds" has

(a) $z = 2.25, P < 0.02$.

(b) $z = 2.60, P < 0.005$.

(c) $z = 2.25, P < 0.04$ but not < 0.02.

21.13 The z test in the previous exercise

(a) may be inaccurate because the populations are too small.

(b) may be inaccurate because some counts of successes and failures are too small.

(c) is reasonably accurate because the conditions for inference are met.

CHAPTER 21 EXERCISES

21.14 Truthfulness in online profiles. Many teens have posted profiles on sites such as MySpace. A sample survey asked random samples of teens with online profiles if they included false information in their profiles. Of 170 younger teens (ages 12 to 14), 117 said "Yes." Of 317 older teens (ages 15 to 17), 152 said "Yes."[11]

(a) Do these samples satisfy the guidelines for the large-sample confidence interval?

(b) Give a 95% confidence interval for the difference between the proportions of younger and older teens who include false information in their online profiles.

21.15 Effects of an appetite suppressant. Subjects with preexisting cardiovascular symptoms who were receiving sibutramine, an appetite suppressant, were found to be at increased risk of cardiovascular events while taking the drug. The study included 9804 overweight or obese subjects with preexisting cardiovascular disease and/or type 2 diabetes. The subjects were randomly assigned to sibutramine (4906 subjects) or a placebo (4898 subjects) in a double-blind fashion. The primary outcome measured was the occurrence of any of the following events: nonfatal myocardial infarction or stroke, resuscitation after cardiac arrest, or cardiovascular death. The primary outcome was observed in 561 subjects in the sibutramine group and 490 subjects in the placebo group.[12]

(a) Find the proportion of subjects experiencing the primary outcome for both the sibutramine and the placebo group.

(b) Can we safely use the large-sample confidence interval for comparing the proportions of sibutramine and placebo subjects who experienced the primary outcome? Explain.

(c) Give a 95% confidence interval for the difference between the proportions of sibutramine and placebo subjects who experienced the primary outcome.

Adolescence, music, and algebra. *Research has suggested that musicians process music in the same cortical regions in which adolescents process algebra. When taking introductory algebra, will students who were enrolled in formal instrumental or choral music instruction during middle school outperform those who experienced neither of these modes of musical instruction? The sample consisted of 6026 ninth-grade students in Maryland who had completed introductory algebra. Of these, 3239 students had received formal instrumental or choral instruction during all three years of middle school, while the remaining students had not. Of those receiving formal musical instruction, 2818 received a passing grade on the Maryland Algebra/Data Analysis High School Assessment (HSA). In contrast, 2091 of the 2787 students not receiving musical instruction received a passing grade.[13] Exercises 21.16 to 21.18 are based on this study.*

21.16 Does music make a difference?

(a) Is there a significant difference between the proportions of students with and without musical instruction who receive a passing grade on the Maryland HSA? State hypotheses, find the test statistic, and use software or the bottom row of Table C to get a *P*-value.

(b) Is this an observational study or an experiment? Why?

(c) In view of your answer in (b), carefully state your conclusions about the relationship between music instruction and success in algebra.

21.17 How many students pass? Give a 95% confidence interval for the proportion of ninth-grade students who receive a passing grade on the HSA.

21.18 How big a difference? Give a 95% confidence interval for the difference between the proportions of students passing the HSA who received or did not receive formal musical instruction in middle school.

21.19 Effects of an appetite suppressant, continued. Exercise 21.15 describes a study to determine if subjects with preexisting cardiovascular symptoms were at an increased risk of cardiovascular events while taking sibutramine. Do the data give good reason to think that there is a difference between the proportions of treatment and placebo subjects who experienced the primary outcome? (Note that sibutramine is no longer available in the United States due to the manufacturer's concerns over increased risk of heart attack or stroke.)

(a) State hypotheses, find the test statistic, and use either software or the bottom row of Table C for the *P*-value. Be sure to state your conclusion.

(b) Explain simply why it was important to have a placebo group in this study.

21.20 Significant does not mean important. Never forget that even small effects can be statistically significant if the samples are large. To illustrate this fact, consider a sample of 148 small businesses. During a three-year period, 15 of the 106 headed by men and 7 of the 42 headed by women failed.[14]

(a) Find the proportions of failures for businesses headed by women and businesses headed by men. These sample proportions are quite close to each other. Give the *P*-value for the *z* test of the hypothesis that the same proportion of women's and men's businesses fail. (Use the two-sided alternative.) The test is very far from being significant.

(b) Now suppose that the same sample proportions came from a sample 30 times as large. That is, 210 out of 1260 businesses headed by women and 450 out of 3180 businesses headed by men fail. Verify that the proportions of failures are exactly the same as in (a). Repeat the z test for the new data, and show that it is now significant at the $\alpha = 0.05$ level.

(c) It is wise to use a confidence interval to estimate the size of an effect rather than just giving a P-value. Give 95% confidence intervals for the difference between the proportions of women's and men's businesses that fail for the settings of both (a) and (b). What is the effect of larger samples on the confidence interval? (In practice, we can't trust the large-sample confidence interval in setting (a).)

21.21 No inference: sample size. One of the processes that turn genes on or off (so to speak) is called "DNA methylation." Do low levels of this process help cause tumors? Compare mice altered to have low levels with normal mice. Of 33 mice with lowered levels of DNA methylation, 23 developed tumors. None of the control group of 18 normal mice developed tumors in the same time period.[15] Explain why we cannot safely use either the large-sample confidence interval or the test for comparing the proportions of normal and altered mice that develop tumors.

21.22 No inference: study design. Grain-handling facilities test for the presence of genetically modified (GM) soybeans in shipments to countries that do not allow GM beans. Batches of soybeans containing some GM beans were submitted to 23 grain-handling facilities. When batches contained 1% of GM beans, 18 of the facilities detected their presence. Only 7 of the 23 facilities detected GM beans when they made up one-tenth of 1% of the beans in the batches.[16] Explain why the study design does not allow us to use the methods of this chapter to compare the proportions of facilities that will detect the two levels of GM soybeans, even for large sample sizes.

In responding to Exercises 21.23 to 21.31, follow the **Plan,** **Solve,** *and* **Conclude** *steps of the four-step process.*

21.23 Are urban students more successful? North Carolina State University looked at the factors that affect whether students get a C or better in a required chemical engineering course. There were 65 students from urban or suburban backgrounds, and 52 of these students succeeded. Another 55 students were from rural or small-town backgrounds; 30 of these students succeeded in the course.[17] Is there good evidence that the proportion of students who succeed is different for urban/suburban versus rural/small-town backgrounds?

21.24 Female and male students. The North Carolina State University study in the previous exercise also compared the proportions of female and male students who succeeded in the course. They found that 23 of the 34 women and 60 of the 89 men succeeded. Is there evidence of a difference between the proportions of women and men who succeed?

21.25 More on urban and rural students. Continue your work from Exercise 21.23. Estimate the difference between the success rates for all urban/suburban and rural/small-town students who plan to study chemical engineering at North Carolina State. (Use 90% confidence.)

21.26 Smoking cessation. Chantix is different from most other quit-smoking products in that it targets nicotine receptors in the brain, attaches to them, and blocks nicotine from reaching them. As part of a larger randomized controlled trial, generally healthy smokers who smoked at least 10 cigarettes per day were assigned at random to take Chantix or a placebo. The study was double-blind, with the response measure being continuous absence from smoking for Weeks 9 through 12 of the study. Of the 352 subjects taking Chantix, 155 abstained from smoking during Weeks 9 through 12, while 61 of the 344 subjects taking the placebo abstained during this same time period.[18] Give a 99% confidence interval for the difference (treatment minus placebo) between the proportions of smokers who abstained from smoking during Weeks 9 through 12.

21.27 The Gold Coast. A historian examining British colonial records for the Gold Coast in Africa suspects that the death rate was higher among African miners than among European miners. In the year 1936, there were 223 deaths among 33,809 African miners and 7 deaths among 1541 European miners on the Gold Coast.[19] (The Gold Coast became the independent nation of Ghana in 1957.)

Consider this year as a random sample from the colonial era in West Africa. Is there good evidence that the proportion of African miners who died was higher than the proportion of European miners who died?

21.28 The ultimatum game. In the "ultimatum game," your partner gets $10, on the condition that it be shared with you. The partner makes you an offer. If you refuse, neither of you gets anything. So it's to your advantage to accept even the unfair offer of $2 out of the $10. But many people refuse unfair offers anyway. This is evidence that our emotions can influence our economic decisions. Here are data on the responses of 76 subjects randomly assigned to receive an offer of $2 from either a person they were introduced to or a computer:[20]

	Accept	Reject
Human offers	20	18
Computer offers	32	6

We suspect that emotion will lead to offers from another person being rejected more often than offers from an impersonal computer. Do a test to assess the evidence for this conjecture.

21.29 Acorns and mice. The mouse population in wooded areas rises and falls with the abundance of acorns, their favored food. Experimenters studied two similar forest areas in a year when the acorn crop failed. They added hundreds of thousands of acorns to one area to imitate an abundant acorn crop, while leaving the other area untouched. The next spring, 54 of the 72 mice trapped in the first area were in breeding condition, versus 10 of the 17 mice trapped in the second area.[21] Is there a significant difference between the proportions of mice ready to breed in good acorn years and bad acorn years?

21.30 Does preschool help? What are the long-term effects of preschool programs for poor children? To find out, investigators followed two groups of Michigan children from early childhood.[22] One group of 62 attended preschool as three- and four-year-olds. A control group of 61 children from the same area and similar backgrounds did not attend preschool. Over a 10-year period as adults, 38 of the preschool sample and 49 of the control sample needed social services (mainly welfare). Does the study provide significant evidence that children who attend preschool have less need for social services as adults? How large is the difference between the proportions of the preschool and no-preschool populations that require social services? Do inference to answer both questions. Be sure to explain exactly what inference you choose to do.

21.31 Hand sanitizers. Hand disinfection is frequently recommended to prevent transmission of the rhinovirus (RV) that causes the common cold. In particular, hand lotion containing 2% citric acid and 2% malic acid in 70% ethanol (HL+) has been found to have both immediate and persistent ability to inactivate RV on the hands in an experimental setting. Is hand disinfection effective in reducing the risk of infection in a natural setting? A total of 212 volunteers were assigned at random to either the HL+ group, which used the hand lotion every three hours or after hand washing, and a control group, which was asked to use routine hand washing but to avoid the use of alcohol-based hand sanitizers. Here are the data on the numbers of subjects with and without RV infection in the two groups over the 10-week study period:[23]

	RV Infection	
	Yes	No
HL+	49	67
Control group	49	47

(a) Is this an experiment or an observational study? Why?

(b) Do the data give good evidence that hand sanitizers reduce the chance of an RV infection?

21.32 Study design. The study in Exercise 21.30 randomly assigned 123 children to the two groups. The same data could have come from a study that followed children whose parents did or did not enroll them in preschool. Explain carefully how the conclusions we can draw depend on which design was used.

EXPLORING THE WEB

21.33 Hearing loss in adolescents. Go to the *Journal of the American Medical Association* Web site, http://jama.ama-assn.org/content/by/year, and find the article "Change in Prevalence of Hearing Loss in US Adolescents" by Shargorodsky et al. in the August 18, 2010, issue. If you cannot get the full text of the article, use the information in the abstract plus the information given below to answer the questions. NHANES III is the earlier sample and NHANES 2005–2006 is the more recent sample.

(a) Is this an observational study or an experiment?

(b) How many people were in the earlier sample and how many were in the later sample?

(c) If you do not have access to Table 2 of the full article, here are the facts that you will need: in the earlier study 480 people experienced some hearing loss, while in the later study 333 people experienced some hearing loss. Is there evidence of an increase in hearing loss for children aged 12 to 19 in the later study? State hypotheses, find the test statistic, and use either software or Table A to compute the *P*-value. Although the article used a more sophisticated analysis, your *P*-value should be quite close to the *P*-value of 0.02 reported in the abstract.

21.34 Compare two surveys. Go to the Web site www.pollingreport.com, which contains the results of surveys conducted by several survey organizations. Choose a topic of interest to you, and then, to see if attitudes have changed over time, find two surveys that were conducted at two different times but that ask the same question. For example, you might choose the topic of abortion and compare the percents of people who feel abortion should always be legal at points in time separated by several years. State hypotheses to check for a difference over time, find the test statistic, and use either software or Table A to compute the *P*-value. What is your conclusion in context?

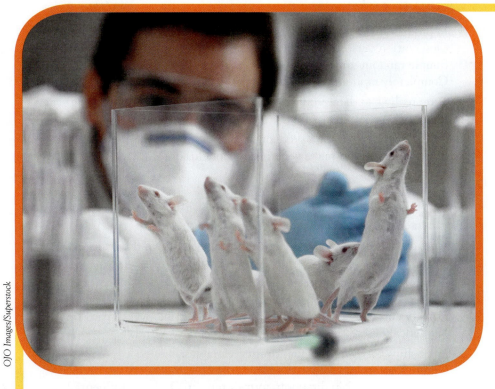

OJO Images/Superstock

Inference about Variables: Part III Review

PART III SUMMARY

The procedures of Chapters 18 to 21 are among the most common of all statistical inference methods. Now that you have mastered important ideas and practical methods for inference, it's time to review the big ideas of statistics in outline form. Here is a summary of Parts I and II of this book, leading up to Part III. The outline contains some important warnings: look for the Caution icon.

1. Data Production

■ Data basics:

    Individuals (subjects).

    Variables: categorical versus quantitative, units of measurement, explanatory versus response.

    Purpose of study.

■ Data production basics:
    Observation versus experiment.
    Simple random samples.
    Completely randomized experiments.

■ Beware: really bad data production (voluntary response, confounding) can make interpretation impossible.

■ Beware: weaknesses in data production (for example, sampling students at only one campus) can make generalizing conclusions difficult.

2. Data Analysis

■ Plot your data. Look for an overall pattern and striking deviations.

■ Add numerical descriptions based on what you see.

■ Beware: averages and other simple descriptions can miss the real story.

■ One quantitative variable:
    Graphs: stemplot, histogram, boxplot.
    Pattern: distribution shape, center, spread. Outliers?
    Density curves (such as Normal curves) to describe overall pattern.
    Numerical descriptions: five-number summary or $\bar{x}$ and s.

■ Relationships between two quantitative variables:
    Graph: scatterplot.
    Pattern: relationship direction, form, strength. Outliers? Influential
       observations?
    Numerical description for linear relationships: correlation, regression line.
    Beware the lurking variable: correlation does not imply causation.

■ Beware the effects of outliers and influential observations.

3. The Reasoning of Inference

■ Inference uses data to infer conclusions about a wider population.

■ When you do inference, you are acting as if your data come from random samples or randomized comparative experiments. Beware: if they don't, you may have "garbage in, garbage out."

■ Always examine your data before doing inference. Inference often requires a regular pattern, such as roughly Normal with no strong outliers.

■ Key idea: "What would happen if we did this many times?"

■ Confidence intervals: estimate a population parameter.
    95% confidence: I used a method that captures the true parameter 95% of
       the time in repeated use.
    Beware: the margin of error of a confidence interval does not include the
       effects of practical errors such as undercoverage and nonresponse.

■ Significance tests: assess evidence against H_0 in favor of H_a.
    P-value: If H_0 were true, how often would I get an outcome favoring the
       alternative this strongly? Smaller P = stronger evidence against H_0.
    Statistical significance at the 5% level, $P < 0.05$, means that an outcome
       this extreme would occur less than 5% of the time if H_0 were true.
    Beware: $P < 0.05$ is not sacred.

Beware: statistical significance is not the same as practical significance. Large samples can make small effects significant. Small samples can fail to declare large effects significant.

Always try to estimate the size of an effect (for example, with a confidence interval), not just its significance.

4. Methods of Inference

■ Choose the right inference procedure.

■ Carry out the details.

■ State your conclusion.

Part III of this book introduces the fourth and last part of this outline. To actually do inference, you must choose the right procedure and carry out the details. The Statistics in Summary flowchart on the next page offers a brief guide. It is important to do some of the review exercises because now, for the first time, you must decide which of several inference procedures to use. Learning to recognize problem settings in order to choose the right type of inference is a key step in advancing your mastery of statistics. This is the "Plan" step in the four-step process, in which you translate the real-world problem from the "State" step into a specific inference procedure.

The flowchart organizes one way of planning inference problems. Let's go through it from left to right.

1. *Do you want to test a claim or estimate an unknown quantity?* That is, will you need a test of significance or a confidence interval?

2. *Are your data a single sample representing one population or two samples chosen to compare two populations or responses to two treatments in an experiment?* Remember that to work with *matched pairs* data you form one sample from the differences within pairs.

3. *Is the response variable quantitative or categorical?* Quantitative variables take numerical values with some unit of measurement such as inches or grams. The most common inference questions about quantitative variables concern *mean* responses. If the response variable is categorical, inference most often concerns the *proportion* of some category (call it a "success") among the responses.

The flowchart leads you to a specific test or confidence interval, indicated by a formula at the end of each path. The formula is just an aid to guide you toward the "Solve" and "Conclude" steps. You (or your technology) will use the formula as part of the "Solve" step, but don't forget that you must do more.

■ *Are the conditions for this procedure met?* Can you act as if the data come from a random sample or randomized comparative experiment? Does data analysis show extreme outliers or strong skewness that forbid use of inference based on Normality? Do you have enough observations for your intended procedure?

■ *Do your data come from an experiment or from an observational study?* The details of inference methods are the same for both. But the design of the study determines what conclusions you can reach, because experiments give much better evidence that an effect uncovered by inference can be explained by direct causation.

You may ask, as you study the Statistics in Summary flowchart, "What if I have an experiment comparing four treatments, or samples from three populations?" The flowchart allows only one or two, not three or four or more. Be patient: methods for comparing more than two means or proportions, as well as some other settings for inference, appear in Part IV.

STATISTICS IN SUMMARY

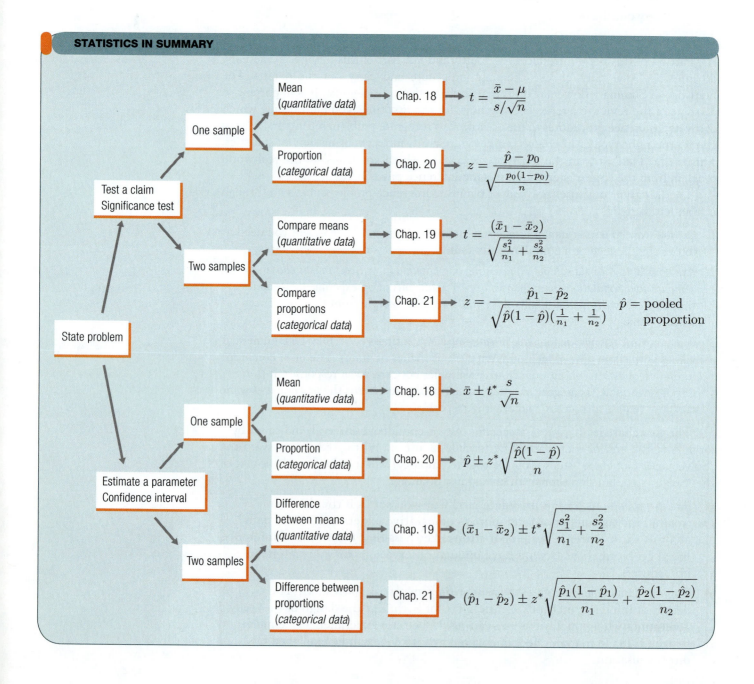

TEST YOURSELF

The questions below include both multiple-choice and short-answer questions and calculations. They will help you review the basic ideas and skills presented in Chapters 18 to 21.

Calcium and blood pressure. *In a randomized comparative experiment on the effect of dietary calcium on blood pressure, researchers divided 54 healthy white males at random into two groups. One group received calcium; the other, a placebo. At the beginning of the study, the researchers measured many variables on the subjects. The paper reporting the study gives $\bar{x} = 114.9$ and $s = 9.3$ for the seated systolic blood pressure of the 27 members of the placebo group. Use this information to answer Questions 22.1 and 22.2.*

22.1 A 95% confidence interval for the mean blood pressure in the population from which the subjects were recruited is

    (a) 113.1 to 116.7.   (b) 111.8 to 118.0.   (c) 111.2 to 118.6.   (d) 109.9 to 119.9.

22.2 What conditions for the population and the study design are required by the procedure you used to construct your confidence interval? Which of these conditions are important for the validity of the procedure in this case?

Does nature heal better? *Our bodies have a natural electrical field that is known to help wounds heal. Does changing the field strength slow healing? A series of experiments with newts investigated this question. The data below are the healing rates of cuts (micrometers per hour) in a matched pairs experiment. The pairs are the two hind limbs of the same newt, with the body's natural field in one limb (control) and half the natural value in the other limb (experimental).* [1]

Newt	1	2	3	4	5	6	7	8	9	10	11	12	13	14
Control	25	13	44	45	57	42	50	36	35	38	43	31	26	48
Experimental	24	23	47	42	26	46	38	33	28	28	21	27	25	45
Difference (control − experimental)	1	−10	−3	3	31	−4	12	3	7	10	22	4	1	3

The mean and standard deviation of the differences are 5.71 and 10.56 micrometers per hour, respectively. Use this information to answer Questions 22.3 and 22.4.

22.3 Is there good evidence that changing the electrical field from its natural level slows healing? The *P*-value for your test is

    (a) less than 0.01.   (c) between 0.05 and 0.10.

    (b) between 0.01 and 0.05.   (d) greater than 0.10.

22.4 Give a 99% confidence interval for the difference in healing rates (control minus experimental).

Game players. *A government survey randomly selected 6889 female high school students and 7028 male high school students.* [2] *Of these students, 1020 females and 1926 males played video or computer games for three or more hours a day. Use this information to answer Questions 22.5 to 22.8.*

22.5 The estimate of the proportion of males who play video or computer games for three or more hours a day is

(a) 0.148.   (b) 0.212.   (c) 0.231.   (d) 0.274.

22.6 The estimate of the proportion of females who play video or computer games for three or more hours a day is

(a) 0.148.   (b) 0.212.   (c) 0.231.   (d) 0.274.

22.7 The sampling distribution for the difference in the sample proportions has standard error

(a) 0.0026.   (b) 0.0043.   (c) 0.0053.   (d) 0.0068.

22.8 A 99% confidence interval for the difference between the proportions of male and female high school students who play video or computer games for at least three hours a day is

(a) 0.115 to 0.137.   (c) 0.108 to 0.144.

(b) 0.113 to 0.139.   (d) 0.106 to 0.146.

22.9 Wikipedia. A sample survey of 1497 adult Internet users found that 36% consult the online collaborative encyclopedia Wikipedia.[3]

(a) Give the standard error SE of $\hat{p}$, the proportion of all adult Internet users who refer to Wikipedia.

(b) Give a 95% confidence interval for the proportion of all adult Internet users who refer to Wikipedia.

Men and muscle. *Ask young men to estimate their own degree of body muscle by choosing from a set of 100 photos. Then ask them to choose what they think women prefer. The researchers know the actual degree of muscle, measured as kilograms per square meter of fat-free mass, for each of the photos. They can therefore measure the difference between what a subject thinks women prefer and the subject's own self-image. Call this difference the "muscle gap." Here are summary statistics for the muscle gap from two samples, one of American and European young men and the other of Chinese young men from Taiwan:[4]*

Group	n	$\bar{x}$	s
American/European	200	2.35	2.5
Chinese	55	1.20	3.2

Use this information to answer Questions 22.10 to 22.13.

22.10 A 95% confidence interval for the mean size of the muscle gap for all American and European young men is

(a) 2.35 ± 0.18.   (b) 2.35 ± 0.35.   (c) 2.35 ± 4.95.   (d) 1.15 ± 0.93.

22.11 A 95% confidence interval for the mean size of the muscle gap for all Chinese young men is

(a) 1.20 ± 0.43.   (b) 1.20 ± 0.86.   (c) 1.20 ± 6.40.   (d) 1.15 ± 0.93.

22.12 Is there a significant difference between the mean sizes of the muscle gap for American/European men and Chinese men? The value of the t statistic for testing the null hypothesis of no difference in the mean sizes of the muscle gap is

(a) 0.47.   (b) 1.15.   (c) 2.13.   (d) 2.47.

22.13 Is there a significant difference between the mean sizes of the muscle gap for American/European men and Chinese men? The degrees of freedom using the conservative Option 2 for the t statistic for testing the null hypothesis of no difference in the mean sizes of the muscle gap is

(a) 54.   (b) 126.5.   (c) 199.   (d) 253.

22.14 Butterflies mating. Here's how butterflies mate: a male passes to a female a packet of sperm called a spermatophore. Females may mate several times. Will they remate sooner if the first spermatophore they receive is small? Among 20 females who received a large spermatophore (greater than 25 milligrams), the mean time to the next mating was 5.15 days, with standard deviation 0.18 day. For 21 females who received a small spermatophore (about 7 milligrams), the mean was 4.33 days and the standard deviation was 0.31 day.[5] Is the observed difference in means statistically significant? Test using the conservative Option 2 for the degrees of freedom. The P-value is

(a) less than 0.01.   (c) between 0.05 and 0.10.

(b) between 0.01 and 0.05.   (d) greater than 0.10.

Mouse endurance. *A study of the inheritance of speed and endurance in mice found a trade-off between these two characteristics, both of which help mice survive. To test endurance, mice were made to swim in a bucket with a weight attached to their tails. (The mice were rescued when exhausted.) Here are data on endurance in minutes for female and male mice:*[6]

Group	n	Mean	Standard deviation
Female	162	11.4	26.09
Male	135	6.7	6.69

Use this information to answer Questions 22.15 to 22.18.

22.15 Both sets of endurance data are skewed to the right. Why are t procedures nonetheless reasonably accurate for these data?

22.16 A 90% confidence interval for the mean endurance of female mice swimming is

(a) 9.35 to 13.45.   (b) 8.00 to 14.80.   (c) 7.34 to 15.46.   (d) 7.14 to 15.66.

22.17 A 90% confidence interval for the mean difference (female minus male) in endurance times is

(a) 8.00 to 14.80.   (b) 1.20 to 8.20.   (c) 5.75 to 7.65.   (d) 2.25 to 7.15.

22.18 Do the data show that female mice have significantly higher endurance on the average than male mice?

22.19 Pre-readers in kindergarten. A school has two kindergarten classes. There are 31 children in Ms. Toodle's kindergarten class. Of these, 17 are "pre-readers"—children on the verge of reading. There are 29 children in Mr. Grimace's kindergarten class. Of these, 13 are pre-readers. The 90% confidence interval for the difference in proportions of children in these classes who are pre-readers is -0.152 to 0.352. Which of the following statements is correct?

(a) This confidence interval is not reliable because the samples are so small.

(b) This confidence interval is of no use because it contains 0, the value of no difference between classes.

(c) This confidence interval is reasonable because the sample sizes are both at least 10.

(d) This confidence interval is not reliable because these samples cannot be viewed as simple random samples taken from a larger population.

22.20 State of the economy. If we want to estimate p, the population proportion of likely voters who believe the state of the economy is the most urgent national concern, with 99% confidence and a margin of error no greater than 2%, how many likely voters need to be surveyed? Assume that you have no idea of the value of p.

(a) 2401   (b) 3484   (c) 4148   (d) 8256

Favoritism for college athletes? Sports Illustrated *surveyed a random sample of 757 Division I college athletes in 36 sports. One question asked was "Have you ever received preferential treatment from a professor because of your status as an athlete?" Of the athletes polled, 225 said "Yes." Use this information to answer Questions 22.21 to 22.23.*

22.21 The sample proportion of athletes who have received preferential treatment from a professor is

(a) 0.160.   (b) 0.297.   (c) 0.703.   (d) 0.840.

22.22 The standard error SE of $\hat{p}$, the proportion of athletes who have received preferential treatment from a professor, is

(a) 0.003.   (b) 0.017.   (c) 0.209.   (d) 0.457.

22.23 A 90% confidence interval for the proportion of athletes who have received preferential treatment from a professor is

(a) 0.276 to 0.320.   (c) 0.265 to 0.331.
(b) 0.270 to 0.326.   (d) 0.255 to 0.342.

Very-low-birth-weight babies. *Starting in the 1970s, medical technology allowed babies with very low birth weight (VLBW, less than 1500 grams, about 3.3 pounds) to survive without major handicaps. It was noticed that these children nonetheless had difficulties in school and as adults. A long-term study has followed 242 VLBW babies to age 20 years, along with a control group of 233 babies from the same population who had normal birth weight.[7] At age 20, 179 of the VLBW group and 193 of the control group had graduated from high school. Use this information to answer Questions 22.24 to 22.29.*

22.24 This is an example of

(a) an observational study.
(b) a nonrandomized experiment.
(c) a randomized controlled study.
(d) a matched pairs experiment.

22.25 Take p_{VLBW} and $p_{control}$ to be the proportions of all VLBW and normal-birth-weight (control) babies who would graduate from high school. The hypotheses to be tested are

(a) $H_0: p_{VLBW} = p_{control}$ versus $H_a: p_{VLBW} \neq p_{control}$.
(b) $H_0: p_{VLBW} = p_{control}$ versus $H_a: p_{VLBW} > p_{control}$.
(c) $H_0: p_{VLBW} = p_{control}$ versus $H_a: p_{VLBW} < p_{control}$.
(d) $H_0: p_{VLBW} > p_{control}$ versus $H_a: p_{VLBW} = p_{control}$.

22.26 The pooled sample proportion of babies who would graduate from high school is

(a) $\hat{p} = 0.74$.
(b) $\hat{p} = 0.78$.
(c) $\hat{p} = 0.81$.
(d) $\hat{p} = 0.83$.

22.27 The numerical value of the z test for comparing the proportions of all VLBW and normal-birth-weight (control) babies who would graduate from high school is

(a) $z = -1.65$.   (b) $z = -2.34$.   (c) $z = -2.77$.   (d) $z = -3.14$.

22.28 IQ scores were available for 113 men in the VLBW group and for 106 men in the control group. The mean IQ for the 113 men in the VLBW group was 87.6, and the standard deviation was 15.1. The 106 men in the control group had mean IQ 94.7, with standard deviation 14.9. Is there good evidence that mean IQ is lower among VLBW men than among controls from similar backgrounds? To test this with a two-sample t test, the test statistic would be

(a) $t = -1.72$.   (b) $t = -3.50$.   (c) $t = -5.00$.   (d) $t = -7.10$.

22.29 Of the 126 women in the VLBW group, 38 said they had used illegal drugs; 54 of the 124 control group women had done so. The IQ scores for the VLBW women who had used illegal drugs had mean 86.2 (standard deviation 13.4), and the normal-birth-weight controls who had used illegal drugs had mean IQ 89.8 (standard deviation 14.0). Is there a statistically significant difference between the two groups in mean IQ? The P-value for this test is

(a) less than 0.01.   (c) between 0.05 and 0.10.

(b) between 0.01 and 0.05.   (d) greater than 0.10.

Binge drinking. *According to the National Institute on Alcohol Abuse and Alcoholism (NIAAA) and the National Institutes of Health (NIH), 41% of college students nationwide engage in "binge-drinking" behavior: having 5 or more drinks on one occasion during the past two weeks. A college president wonders if the proportion of students enrolled at her college who binge drink is actually lower than the national proportion. In a commissioned study, 348 students are selected randomly from a list of all students enrolled at the college. Of these, 132 admit to having engaged in binge drinking. Use this information to answer Questions 22.30 to 22.32.*

22.30 Based on the results of the commissioned study, a 95% confidence interval for the proportion of all students at this college who engage in binge drinking is

(a) 0.328 to 0.430.   (c) 0.341 to 0.420.

(b) 0.338 to 0.423.   (d) 0.343 to 0.418.

22.31 The college president is more interested in testing her belief that the proportion of students at her college who engage in binge drinking is lower than the national proportion of 0.41. Her staff tests the hypotheses H_0: $p = 0.41$ versus H_a: $p < 0.41$. The P-value is

(a) between 0.15 and 0.20.   (c) between 0.05 and 0.10.

(b) between 0.10 and 0.15.   (d) below 0.05.

22.32 Which of the following conclusions is reasonable, based on the P-value computed in the previous exercise?

(a) There is little evidence to support a conclusion that the proportion of students at this particular college who binge drink is lower than the national proportion of 0.41.

(b) There is moderate but not strong evidence that the proportion of binge-drinking students at this college is lower than the national proportion of 0.41.

(c) There is strong evidence that the proportion of students at this college who binge drink is lower than the national proportion of 0.41.

(d) We can't reach any reasonable conclusion, because the assumptions necessary for a significance test for a proportion are not met in this case.

Listening to rap. *The Black Youth Project of the University of Chicago interviewed random samples of black, Hispanic, and white young people aged 15 to 25. We can consider this a stratified sample or three separate random samples of 634 blacks, 314 Hispanics, and 567 whites. The survey found that 58% of black youth listen to rap music every day, compared with 45% of Hispanics and 23% of whites. But attitudes were quite similar in the three groups. For example, 72% of blacks, 72% of Hispanics, and 68% of whites agreed that "rap music videos contain too many references to sex."[8] Questions 22.33 to 22.35 are based on this study.*

22.33 Give a 90% confidence interval for the proportion of all black young people who listen to rap every day.

22.34 Give a 90% confidence interval for the difference between the proportions of all Hispanic and all white young people who listen to rap every day.

22.35 Is there a significant difference between the proportions of black and white young people who think that rap videos contain too much sex? State hypotheses, find the test statistic, and use either software or the bottom row of Table C for the *P*-value. Be sure to state your conclusion.

Cholesterol in dogs. *High levels of cholesterol in the blood are not healthy in either humans or dogs. Because a diet rich in saturated fats raises the cholesterol level, it is plausible that dogs owned as pets have higher cholesterol levels than dogs owned by a veterinary research clinic. "Normal" levels of cholesterol based on the clinic's dogs would then be misleading. A clinic compared healthy dogs it owned with healthy pets brought to the clinic to be neutered. The summary statistics for blood cholesterol levels (milligrams per deciliter of blood) appear below.[9]*

Group	n	$\bar{x}$	s
Pets	26	193	68
Clinic	23	174	44

Questions 22.36 to 22.40 are based on this study.

22.36 A 95% confidence interval for the mean cholesterol level in pets is

(a) 179.7 to 206.3.   (c) 165.5 to 220.5.

(b) 176.8 to 209.2.   (d) 159.6 to 226.48.

22.37 Is there strong evidence that pets have a higher mean cholesterol level than clinic dogs? To test this with a two-sample *t* test, the values of the *t* statistic and its degrees of freedom using conservative Option 2 are

(a) $t = 1.17$, df $= 22$.   (c) $t = 8.92$, df $= 22$.

(b) $t = 1.17$, df $= 47$.   (d) $t = 8.92$, df $= 47$.

22.38 A 95% confidence interval for the difference in mean cholesterol levels between pets and clinic dogs is (use conservative Option 2 for the degrees of freedom)

(a) -26.1 to 64.1.   (b) -14.4 to 52.6.   (c) -8.7 to 46.7.   (d) 2.8 to 35.2.

22.39 What conditions must be satisfied to justify the procedures you used in Question 22.36? In Question 22.37? In Question 22.38?

22.40 Assuming that the cholesterol measurements have no outliers and are not strongly skewed, what is the chief threat to the validity of the results of this study?

Choosing an inference procedure. *In each of Questions 22.41 to 22.46, say which type of inference procedure from the Statistics in Summary flowchart (page 432) you would use, or explain why none of these procedures fits the problem. You do not need to carry out any procedures.*

22.41 Driving too fast. How seriously do people view speeding in comparison with other annoying behaviors? A large random sample of adults was asked to rate a number of behaviors on a scale of 1 (no problem at all) to 5 (very severe problem). Do speeding drivers get a higher average rating than noisy neighbors?

22.42 Preventing drowning. Drowning in bathtubs is a major cause of death in children less than 5 years old. A random sample of parents was asked many questions related to bathtub safety. Overall, 85% of the sample said they used baby bathtubs for infants. Estimate the percent of all parents of young children who use baby bathtubs.

22.43 Acid rain? You have data on rainwater collected at 16 locations in the Adirondack Mountains of New York State. One measurement is the acidity of the water, measured by pH on a scale of 0 to 14 (the pH of distilled water is 7.0). Estimate the average acidity of rainwater in the Adirondacks.

22.44 Athletes' salaries. Looking online, you find the salaries of the 27 players on the roster of the Chicago Cubs as of opening day of the 2008 baseball season. The team total was $118.6 million, seventh highest in the major leagues. Estimate the average salary of the Cubs players.

22.45 Looking back on love. How do young adults look back on adolescent romance? Investigators interviewed 40 couples in their midtwenties. The female and male partners were interviewed separately. Each was asked about his or her current relationship and also about a romantic relationship that lasted at least two months when they were aged 15 or 16. One response variable was a measure on a numerical scale of how much the attractiveness of the adolescent partner mattered. You want to compare the men and women on this measure.

22.46 Preventing AIDS through education. The Multisite HIV Prevention Trial was a randomized comparative experiment to compare the effects of twice-weekly small-group AIDS discussion sessions (the treatment) with a single one-hour session (the control). Compare the effects of treatment and control on each of the following response variables:

(a) A subject does or does not use condoms six months after the education sessions.

(b) The number of unprotected intercourse acts by a subject between four and eight months after the sessions.

(c) A subject is or is not infected with a sexually transmitted disease six months after the sessions.

■ SUPPLEMENTARY EXERCISES

*Supplementary exercises apply the skills you have learned in ways that require more thought or more use of technology. Some of these exercises start from actual data rather than from data summaries. Many of these exercises ask you to follow the **Plan, Solve,** and **Conclude** steps of the four-step process. Remember that the **Solve** step includes checking the conditions for the inference you plan.*

22.47 Do you have confidence? A report of a survey distributed to randomly selected emailaddresses at a large university says: "We have collected 427 responses from our sample of 2,100 as of April 30, 2004. This number of responses is large enough to achieve a 95% confidence interval with ±5% margin of sampling error in generalizing the results to our study population."[10] Why would you be reluctant to trust a confidence interval based on these data?

22.48 Monkeys and music. Humans generally prefer music to silence. What about monkeys? Allow a tamarin monkey to enter a V-shaped cage with food in both arms of the V. After the monkey eats the food, which arm will it prefer? The monkey's location determines what it hears, a lullaby played by a flute in one arm and silence in the other. Each of 4 monkeys was tested 6 times, on different days and with the music arm alternating between left and right (in case a monkey prefers one direction). The monkeys chose silence for about 65% of their time in the cage. The researchers reported a one-sample t test for the mean percent of time spent in the music arm, H_0: $\mu = 50\%$ against the two-sided alternative, $t = -5.26$, df $= 23$, $P < 0.0001$.[11]

Although the result is interesting, the statistical analysis is not correct. The degrees of freedom df $= 23$ show that the researchers assumed that they had 24 independent observations. Explain why the results of the 24 trials are not independent.

22.49 Starting to talk. At what age do infants speak their first word of English? Here are data on 20 children (ages in months):[12] FIRSTWORD

15	26	10	9	15	20	18	11	8	20
7	9	10	11	11	10	12	17	11	10

Is there good evidence that the mean age at first word among all normal children is greater than one year?

22.50 Fertilizing a tropical plant. Bromeliads are tropical flowering plants. Many are epiphytes that attach to trees and obtain moisture and nutrients from air and rain. Their leaf bases form cups that collect water and are home to the larvae of many insects. In an experiment in Costa Rica, Jacqueline Ngai and Diane Srivastava studied whether added nitrogen increases the productivity of bromeliad plants. Bromeliads were randomly assigned to nitrogen or control groups. Here are data on the number of new leaves produced over a seven-month period:[13] FERTILIZING

Control	11	13	16	15	15	11	12	
Nitrogen	15	14	15	16	17	18	17	13

Is there evidence that adding nitrogen increases the mean number of new leaves formed?

22.51 Starting to talk, continued. Use the data in Exercise 22.49 to give a 90% confidence interval for the mean age at which children speak their first word. FIRSTWORD

22.52 Dyeing fabrics. Different fabrics respond differently when dyed. This matters to clothing manufacturers, who want the color of the fabric to be just right. A researcher dyed fabrics made of cotton and of ramie with the same "procion blue" dye applied in the same way. Then she used a colorimeter to measure the lightness of the color on a scale in which black is 0 and white is 100. Here are the data for 8 pieces of each fabric:[14] FABRICDYE

Cotton	48.82	48.88	48.98	49.04	48.68	49.34	48.75	49.12
Ramie	41.72	41.83	42.05	41.44	41.27	42.27	41.12	41.49

Is there a significant difference between the fabrics? Which fabric is darker when dyed in this way?

22.53 More on dyeing fabrics. The color of a fabric depends on the dye used and also on how the dye is applied. This matters to clothing manufacturers, who want the color of the fabric to be just right. The study discussed in the previous exercise went on to dye fabric made of ramie with the same procion blue dye applied in two different ways. Here are the lightness scores for 8 pieces of identical fabric dyed in each way: FABRICDYE2

Method B	40.98	40.88	41.30	41.28	41.66	41.50	41.39	41.27
Method C	42.30	42.20	42.65	42.43	42.50	42.28	43.13	42.45

(a) This is a randomized comparative experiment. Outline the design.

(b) A clothing manufacturer wants to know which method gives the darker color (lower lightness score). Use sample means to answer this question. Is the difference between the two sample means statistically significant? Can you tell from just the P-value whether the difference is large enough to be important in practice?

22.54 Do parents matter? A professor asked her sophomore students, "Does either of your parents allow you to drink alcohol around him or her?" and "How many drinks do you typically have per session? (A drink is defined as one 12 oz beer, one 4 oz glass of wine, or one 1 oz shot of liquor)." Table 22.1 contains the responses of the female students who are not abstainers.[15] The sample is all students in one large sophomore-level class. The class is popular, so we are tentatively willing to regard its members as an SRS of sophomore students at this college. Does the behavior of parents make a significant difference in how many drinks students have on the average? FEMALESDRINK

TABLE 22.1 Drinks per session by female students

PARENT ALLOWS STUDENT TO DRINK

2.5	1	2.5	3	1	3	3	3	2.5	2.5	3.5	5	2
7	7	6.5	4	8	6	6	3	6	3	4	7	5
3.5	2	1	5	3	3	6	4	2	7	5	8	1
6	5	2.5	3	4.5	9	5	4	4	3	4	6	4
5	1	5	3	10	7	4	4	4	4	2	2.5	2.5

PARENT DOES NOT ALLOW STUDENT TO DRINK

9	3.5	3	5	1	1	3	4	4	3	6	5	3
8	4	4	5	7	7	3.5	3	10	4	9	2	7
4	3	1										

22.55 Parents' behavior. We wonder what proportion of female students have at least one parent who allows them to drink around him or her. Table 22.1 contains information about a sample of 94 students. Use this sample to give a 95% confidence interval for this proportion. FEMALESDRINK

22.56 Diabetic mice. The body's natural electrical field helps wounds heal. If diabetes changes this field, that might explain why people with diabetes heal slowly. A study of this idea compared normal mice and mice bred to spontaneously develop diabetes. The investigators attached sensors to the right hip and front feet of the mice and measured the difference in electrical potential (millivolts) between these locations. Here are the data:[16] MICE

Diabetic Mice						Normal Mice				
14.70	13.60	7.40	1.05	10.55	16.40	13.80	9.10	4.95	7.70	9.40
10.00	22.60	15.20	19.60	17.25	18.40	7.20	10.00	14.55	13.30	6.65
9.80	11.70	14.85	14.45	18.25	10.15	9.50	10.40	7.75	8.70	8.85
10.85	10.30	10.45	8.55	8.85	19.20	8.40	8.55	12.60		

(a) Make a stemplot of each sample of potentials. There is a low outlier in the diabetic group. Does it appear that potentials in the two groups differ in a systematic way?

(b) Is there significant evidence of a difference in mean potentials between the two groups?

(c) Repeat your inference without the outlier. Does the outlier affect your conclusion?

22.57 Keeping crackers from breaking. We don't like to find broken crackers when we open the package. How can makers reduce breaking? One idea is to microwave the crackers for 30 seconds right after baking them. Analyze the following results from two experiments intended to examine this idea.[17] Does microwaving significantly improve indicators of future breaking? How large is the improvement? What do you conclude about the idea of microwaving crackers?

(a) The experimenter randomly assigned 65 newly baked crackers to be microwaved and another 65 to a control group that is not microwaved. Fourteen days after baking, 3 of the 65 microwaved crackers and 57 of the 65 crackers in the control group showed visible checking, which is the starting point for breaks.

(b) The experimenter randomly assigned 20 crackers to be microwaved and another 20 to a control group. After 14 days, he broke the crackers. Here are summaries of the pressure needed to break them, in pounds per square inch:

	Microwave	Control
Mean	139.6	77.0
Standard deviation	33.6	22.6

22.58 Falling through the ice. Table 7.3 (page 163) gives the dates on which a wooden tripod fell through the ice of the Tanana River in Alaska, thus deciding the winner of the Nenana Ice Classic contest, for the years 1917 to 2010. Give a 95% confidence interval for the mean date on which the tripod falls through the ice. After calculating the interval in the scale used in the table (days from April 20, which is Day 1), translate your result into calendar dates and hours within the dates. (Each hour is 1/24, or 0.042, of a day.) 🔶 TANANA

22.59 A case for the Supreme Court. In 1986, a Texas jury found a black man guilty of murder. The prosecutors had used "peremptory challenges" to remove 10 of the 11 blacks and 4 of the 31 whites in the pool from which the jury was chosen.[18] The law says that there must be a plausible reason (that is, a reason other than race) for different treatment of blacks and whites in the jury pool. When the case reached the Supreme Court 17 years later, the Court said that "happenstance is unlikely to produce this disparity." Explain why the methods we know can't be safely used to do the inference that lies behind the Court's finding that chance is unlikely to produce so large a black-white difference.

Inference about Relationships

Statistical inference offers more methods than anyone can know well, as a glance at the offerings of any large statistical software package demonstrates. In an introductory text, we must be selective. Parts I to III have laid a foundation for understanding statistics:

- The nature and purpose of data analysis.
- The central ideas of designs for data production.
- The reasoning behind confidence intervals and significance tests.
- Experience applying these ideas in practice.

Each of the three chapters of Part IV offers an introduction to a more advanced topic in statistical inference. You may choose to read any or all of them, in any order.

What makes a statistical method "more advanced"? More complex data, for one thing. In Part III, we looked only at methods for inference about a single population parameter and for comparing two parameters. All the chapters in Part IV present methods for studying relationships between two variables. In Chapter 23, both variables are categorical, with data given as a two-way table of counts of outcomes. Chapter 24 considers inference in the setting of regressing a response variable on an explanatory variable. This is an important type of relationship between two quantitative variables. In Chapter 25 we meet methods for comparing the mean response in more than two groups. Here, the explanatory variable (group) is categorical and the response variable is quantitative.

443

With greater complexity comes greater reliance on technology. In these final three chapters you will more often be interpreting the output of statistical software or using software yourself. With effort, you can do the calculations needed in Chapter 23 with a basic calculator. In Chapters 24 and 25, the pain is too great and the contribution to learning too small. Fortunately, you can grasp the ideas without step-by-step arithmetic.

Another aspect of "more advanced" methods is new concepts and ideas. This is where we draw the line in deciding what statistical topics we can master in a first course. Part IV builds elaborate methods on the foundation we have laid without introducing fundamentally new concepts. Statistical practice does need additional big ideas, but the ideas you already know place you among the world's statistical sophisticates.

Axel/Dupeux/Corbis

Two Categorical Variables: The Chi-Square Test

In the first example in Chapter 21 (page 416), we compared young men and young women by looking at whether or not they lived with their parents. That is, we looked at a relationship between two categorical variables, gender (female or male) and "Where do you live?" (with parents or not). In fact, the data include four more outcomes for "Where do you live?": in another person's home, in your own place, in group quarters such as a dormitory, or "other." When there are more than two outcomes, or when we want to compare more than two groups, we need a new statistical test. The new test addresses a general question: *is there a relationship between two categorical variables?*

TWO-WAY TABLES

We saw in Chapter 6 that we can present data on two categorical variables in a **two-way table** of counts. That's our starting point. Let's continue our exploration of where college-age young people live.

two-way table

445

WHERELIVE

cell

EXAMPLE 23.1 Where do young people live?

A sample survey asked a random sample of young adults, "Where do you live now? That is, where do you stay most often?" Table 23.1 is a two-way table of all 2984 people in the sample (both men and women) classified by their age and by where they lived.[1] Living arrangement is a categorical variable. Even though age is quantitative, the two-way table treats age as dividing young adults into four categories. Table 23.1 gives the counts for all 20 combinations of age and living arrangement. Each of the 20 counts occupies a **cell** of the table. ■

TABLE 23.1 Young adults by age and living arrangement

LIVING ARRANGEMENT	AGE 19	AGE 20	AGE 21	AGE 22	TOTAL
Parents' home	324	378	337	318	1357
Another person's home	37	47	40	38	162
Your own place	116	279	372	487	1254
Group quarters	58	60	49	25	192
Other	5	2	3	9	19
Total	540	766	801	877	2984

As usual, we prepare for inference by first doing data analysis. Because we think that age helps explain where young people live, find the percents of people in each age group who have each living arrangement. The percents appear in Table 23.2. Each column adds to 100% (up to roundoff error) because we are looking at each age group separately. In the language of Chapter 6 (page 139), Table 23.2 shows the four *conditional distributions* of living arrangements given a specific age.

TABLE 23.2 Percents of each age group who have each living arrangement (read down columns)

LIVING ARRANGEMENT	AGE 19	AGE 20	AGE 21	AGE 22
Parents' home	60.0	49.3	42.1	36.3
Another person's home	6.9	6.1	5.0	4.3
Your own place	21.5	36.4	46.4	55.5
Group quarters	10.7	7.8	6.1	2.9
Other	0.9	0.3	0.4	1.0
Total	100.0	99.9	100.0	100.0

Figure 23.1 is Minitab's bar graph comparing the four conditional distributions. The graph shows a strong relationship between age and living arrangement. As young adults age from 19 to 22, the percent living with their parents drops and the percent living in their own place rises. The percent living in group quarters also declines with age as college students move out of dormitories. Are these differences among the four age groups large enough to be statistically significant?

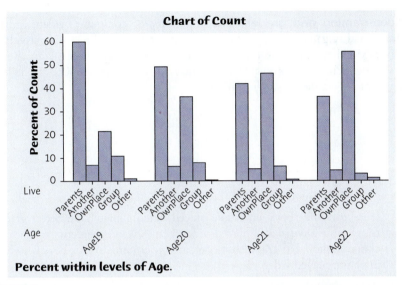

FIGURE 23.1

Minitab bar graph comparing the four conditional distributions of living arrangements given age, for Example 23.1.

APPLY YOUR KNOWLEDGE

23.1 Facebook at Penn State. The Pennsylvania State University has its main campus in University Park and more than 20 smaller "commonwealth campuses" around the state. The Penn State Division of Student Affairs polled a random sample of undergraduates about their use of online social networking. (The response rate was only about 20%, which casts some doubt on the usefulness of the data.) Facebook was the most popular site, with more than 80% of students having an account. Here is a comparison of Facebook use by undergraduates at the University Park and commonwealth campuses:[2] 🔴 FACEBOOKUSE

Use Facebook	University Park	Commonwealth
Do not use Facebook	68	248
Several times a month or less	55	76
At least once a week	215	157
At least once a day	640	394

Courtesy Pennsylvania State University

(a) What percent of University Park students fall in each Facebook category? What percent of commonwealth campus students fall in each category? Each column should add to 100% (up to roundoff error). These are the conditional distributions of Facebook use given campus setting.

(b) Make a bar graph that compares the two conditional distributions. What are the most important differences in Facebook use between the two campus settings?

23.2 Video-gaming and grades. The popularity of computer, video, online, and virtual reality games has raised concerns about their ability to negatively impact youth. The data in this exercise are based on a recent survey of 14- to 18-year-olds in Connecticut high schools. Here are the grade distributions of boys who have and have not played video games:[3] GAMING

	Grade Average		
	A's and B's	C's	D's and F's
Played games	736	450	193
Never played games	205	144	80

(a) It appears that boys who have played video games have better grades than those who have never played video games. Give percents to back up this claim. Make a bar graph that compares your percents for boys who have and have not played video games.

(b) Association does not prove causation. Explain why you can't conclude from this study that playing video games improves grades for boys.

IS THERE A RELATIONSHIP? EXPECTED CELL COUNTS

We want to test the null hypothesis that in the population of all American young adults there is *no difference* among the four distributions of living arrangements for people aged 19, 20, 21, and 22. If the null hypothesis is true, the differences in the sample are just accidents due to random selection of the sample. Put more generally, the null hypothesis is that there is *no relationship* between two categorical variables,

H_0: there is no relationship between age and where young people live

The alternative hypothesis says that there *is* a relationship but does not specify any particular kind of relationship,

H_a: there is some relationship between age and living arrangement

Any difference among the four distributions of living arrangements in the population of all young adults means that the null hypothesis is false and the alternative hypothesis is true. The alternative hypothesis is not one-sided or two-sided. We might call it "many-sided" because it allows any kind of difference.

To assess the significance of the relationship between two categorical variables in a two-way table:

▪ Use an *overall test* of the null hypothesis H_0 to see if there is good evidence of *any* relationship between the two variables.

▪ Do *data analysis* to describe the nature of the relationship in detail.

The overall test of the null hypothesis H_0 that the row and column variables are not related compares the observed counts in the table with the *expected counts*, the counts we would expect—except for random variation—if H_0 were true. If the observed counts are far from the expected counts, that is evidence against H_0. It is easy to find the expected counts.

EXPECTED COUNTS

The **expected count** in any cell of a two-way table when H_0 is true is

$$\text{expected count} = \frac{\text{row total} \times \text{column total}}{\text{table total}}$$

EXAMPLE 23.2 Where young people live: expected counts

Let's find the expected counts for the study of where young people live. Look back at the two-way table of counts, Table 23.1. That table includes the row and column totals. The expected count of 19-year-olds who live in their parents' home is

$$\frac{\text{row 1 total} \times \text{column 1 total}}{\text{table total}} = \frac{(1357)(540)}{2984} = 245.57$$

The expected count of 22-year-olds who live with their parents is

$$\frac{\text{row 1 total} \times \text{column 4 total}}{\text{table total}} = \frac{(1357)(877)}{2984} = 398.82$$

The actual counts are 324 and 318. More younger people and fewer older people live with their parents than we would expect if there were no relationship between age and living arrangement. Table 23.3 shows all 20 expected counts.

As this table shows, *the expected counts have exactly the same row and column totals (up to roundoff error) as the observed counts.* That's a good way to check your work. Comparing the actual counts (Table 23.1) and the expected counts (Table 23.3) shows in what ways the data diverge from the null hypothesis. ■

TABLE 23.3 Young adults by age and living arrangement: expected cell counts

LIVING ARRANGEMENT	AGE 19	AGE 20	AGE 21	AGE 22	TOTAL
Parents' home	245.57	348.35	364.26	398.82	1357
Another person's home	29.32	41.59	43.49	47.61	162
Your own place	226.93	321.90	336.61	368.55	1254
Group quarters	34.75	49.29	51.54	56.43	192
Other	3.44	4.88	5.10	5.58	19
Total	540	766	801	877	2984

APPLY YOUR KNOWLEDGE

23.3 Facebook at Penn State. The two-way table in Exercise 23.1 displays data on use of Facebook by two groups of Penn State students. It's clear that nonusers are much more frequent at the commonwealth campuses. Let's look just at students who have Facebook accounts: FACEBOOKUSE

Use Facebook	University Park	Commonwealth
Several times a month or less	55	76
At least once a week	215	157
At least once a day	640	394
Total Facebook users	910	627

The null hypothesis is that there is no relationship between campus and Facebook use, among students who have Facebook accounts.

(a) If this hypothesis is true, what are the expected counts for Facebook use among commonwealth campus students with Facebook accounts? This is one column of the two-way table of expected counts. Find the column total and verify that it agrees with the column total for the observed counts.

(b) Commonwealth campus students as a group are older and more likely to be married and employed than University Park students. What does comparing the observed and expected counts in this column show about Facebook use by these students with Facebook accounts?

23.4 Video-gaming and grades. Exercise 23.2 describes a comparison of the grade distribution of a sample of 14- to 18-year-old boys in Connecticut who do and don't play video games. The null hypothesis "no relationship" says that in the population of all 14- to 18-year-old boys in Connecticut, the proportions who have each grade average are the same for those who play and don't play video games. GAMING

(a) Find the expected counts if this hypothesis is true and display them in a two-way table. Add the row and column totals to your table and check that they agree with the totals for the observed counts.

(b) Are there any large deviations between the observed counts and the expected counts? What kind of relationship between the two variables do these deviations point to?

THE CHI-SQUARE TEST

To test whether the observed relationship between the row and column variables in a two-way table is statistically significant, we compare the observed and expected counts. The test statistic that makes the comparison is the *chi-square statistic*.

THE CHI-SQUARE TEST

Draw an SRS from a large population and make a two-way table of the sample counts for two categorical variables. To test the null hypothesis H_0 that there is no relationship between the row and column variables in the population, calculate the **chi-square statistic**

$$\chi^2 = \sum \frac{(\text{observed count} - \text{expected count})^2}{\text{expected count}}$$

The sum is over all cells in the table.

The **chi-square test** rejects H_0 when χ^2 is large. Software finds P-values from a **chi-square distribution.**

The symbol χ in the box is the Greek letter chi. Think of χ^2 as a measure of the distance of the observed counts from the expected counts. It is always zero or positive, and it is zero only when the observed counts are exactly equal to the expected counts. Large values of χ^2 are evidence against H_0 because they say that the observed counts are far from what we would expect if H_0 were true. *Although the alternative hypothesis H_a is many-sided, the chi-square test is one-sided* because any violation of H_0 tends to produce a large value of χ^2. Small values of χ^2 are not evidence against H_0.

EXAMPLE 23.3 Where young people live: the test statistic

In the study of where young people live, 324 19-year-olds lived with their parents. The expected count for this cell is 245.57. So the term of the chi-square statistic from this cell is

$$\frac{(\text{observed count} - \text{expected count})^2}{\text{expected count}} = \frac{(324 - 245.57)^2}{245.57}$$

$$= \frac{6151.26}{245.57} = 25.05$$

The chi-square statistic χ^2 is the sum of 20 terms like this one. Here they are, arranged to match the layout of the two-way table:

$$\chi^2 = 25.05 + 2.53 + 2.04 + 16.38$$
$$+ 2.01 + 0.71 + 0.28 + 1.94$$
$$+ 54.23 + 5.72 + 3.72 + 38.07$$
$$+ 15.56 + 2.33 + 0.13 + 17.51$$
$$+ 0.71 + 1.70 + 0.87 + 2.09$$
$$= 193.58$$

Software is very handy in finding χ^2. Figure 23.2 shows Minitab's chi-square output. We see that $\chi^2 = 193.548$ (more accurate than our rounded hand calculation). The P-value is 0 to three decimal places. The relationship between the age of young people and where they live is highly significant. ■

```
Session                                              —  □  X
```

> This key identifies the output for each cell in the table

```
Expected counts are printed below observed counts ◄
Chi-Square contributions are printed below expected counts

          Age 19   Age 29   Age 21   Age 22   Total
Parents      324      378      337      318    1357
          245.57   348.35   364.26   398.82
          25.049    2.525    2.040   16.379

Another       37       47       40       38     162
           29.32    41.59    43.49    47.61
           2.014    0.705    0.279    1.940

OwnPlace     116      279      372      437    1254
          226.93   321.90   336.61   368.55
          54.226    5.719    3.720   38.068

Group         58       60       49       25     192
           34.75    49.29    51.54    56.43
          15.564    2.329    0.125   17.505

Other          5        2        3        9      19
            3.44     4.88     5.10     5.58
           0.709    1.697    0.865    2.090

Total        540      766      801      877    2984

Chi-Sq = 193.548,   DF = 12,  P-Value = 0.000
2 cells with expected counts less than 5.
```

FIGURE 23.2

Minitab output showing observed and expected cell counts and contributions to chi-square for the study of where young people live, for Examples 23.3 and 23.4.

The chi-square test, like the z procedures for inference about proportions, is an approximate method that becomes more accurate as the counts in the cells of the table get larger. Approximate P-values come from a *chi-square distribution*, usually calculated by software. We must check that the counts are large enough to allow us to trust the P-value. Fortunately, the approximation is accurate for quite modest counts. Here is a practical guideline.[4]

CELL COUNTS REQUIRED FOR THE CHI-SQUARE TEST

You can safely use the chi-square test with P-values from the chi-square distribution when no more than 20% of the expected counts are less than 5 and all individual expected counts are 1 or greater. In particular, all four expected counts in a 2×2 table should be 5 or greater.

Note that the guideline uses *expected* cell counts. The expected counts for the living arrangements study of Example 23.1 appear in Table 23.3 and in the Minitab output in Figure 23.2. Only 2 of the 20 expected counts (that's 10%) are less than 5 and all are greater than 1, so the data meet the guideline for safe use of chi-square.

DATA ANALYSIS FOR CHI-SQUARE

The chi-square test is an overall test for detecting relationships between two categorical variables. If the test is significant, it is important to look at the data to learn the nature of the relationship. We have three ways to look at the living arrangements data:

■ **Compare selected percents:** which living arrangements occur in quite different percents of the four age groups? Table 23.2 illustrates this method.

■ **Compare observed and expected cell counts:** which cells have more or fewer observations than we would expect if H_0 were true?

■ **Look at the terms of the chi-square statistic:** which cells contribute the most to the value of χ^2?

Statistical software offers this information on request. Figure 23.1 shows Minitab output comparing the conditional distributions of living arrangements for different age groups. Figure 23.2 includes the observed counts and expected counts and also the term in the chi-square statistic for each cell, called the "contribution to chi-square." For example, the top-left cell has expected count 245.57 and contributes 25.049 to the chi-square statistic, as we calculated earlier. (Roundoff errors are smaller with software than in hand calculation.)

EXAMPLE 23.4 Where young people live: conclusion

There is very strong evidence ($\chi^2 = 193.548$, $P < 0.001$) that living arrangements of young people are not the same for ages 19, 20, 21, and 22. Comparing selected percents—specifically, the four conditional distributions of living arrangements for each age in Table 23.2 and Figure 23.1—shows how young people become more independent as they grow older.

A quick way to find the most important differences among the age groups is to look for the cells that contribute the most to the chi-square statistic, then compare observed and expected counts in these cells. Just 6 of the 20 cells in Figure 23.2 contribute 166.791 of the total chi-square $\chi^2 = 193.548$. These 6 cells occur in pairs:

■ 54.226 and 38.068: fewer 19-year-olds than expected and more 22-year-olds than expected live in their own place.

■ 25.049 and 16.379: more 19-year-olds than expected and fewer 22-year-olds than expected live in their parents' home.

■ 15.564 and 17.505: more 19-year-olds than expected and fewer 22-year-olds than expected live in group quarters.

These three trends display the increase in independent living between age 19 and age 22. ■

APPLY YOUR KNOWLEDGE

23.5 Facebook at Penn State. Figure 23.3 displays Minitab output for how frequently students at the University Park and Commonwealth campuses of Penn State University who have Facebook accounts make use of their accounts. The output includes the two-way table of observed counts, expected counts, and each cell's contribution to the chi-square statistic. FACEBOOKUSERS

(a) Verify from the output that the data meet the cell count requirement for use of chi-square.

FIGURE 23.3

Minitab output for the two-way table of Facebook use and Penn State campus category, for Exercise 23.5.

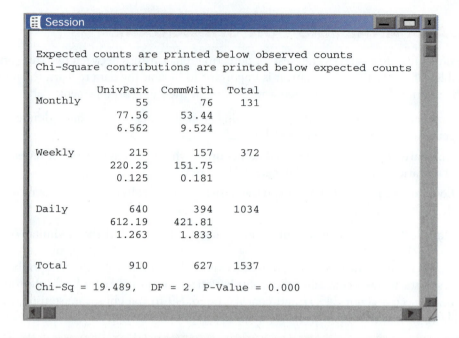

```
Session                                                    — ☐ X

Expected counts are printed below observed counts
Chi-Square contributions are printed below expected counts

            UnivPark  CommWith   Total
Monthly          55        76      131
              77.56     53.44
              6.562     9.524

Weekly          215       157      372
             220.25    151.75
              0.125     0.181

Daily           640       394     1034
             612.19    421.81
              1.263     1.833


Total           910       627     1537

Chi-Sq = 19.489,   DF = 2, P-Value = 0.000
```

(b) What hypotheses does chi-square test? What are the test statistic and its P-value?

(c) Which cells contribute the most to χ^2? Compare the observed and expected counts in these cells and comment on the most important differences in Facebook use between students at the two locations.

23.6 Video-gaming and grades. Your data analysis in Exercise 23.2 found that boys who have played video games tend to have higher grades than those who have not. Figure 23.4 (see page 455) gives Minitab output for the two-way table in Exercise 23.2. 🔴 **GAMING**

(a) Verify from the output that the data meet the cell count requirement for use of chi-square.

(b) What are the chi-square statistic and its P-value? Explain in simple language what it means to reject H_0 in this setting.

(c) Give an overall conclusion that refers to row percents to describe the nature of the relationship between playing video games and grades.

23.7 Is astrology scientific? The General Social Survey asked a random sample of adults about their education and about their view of astrology as scientific or not. Here are the data for people with three levels of higher education degrees:[5] 🔴 **ASTROLOGY**

	Degree Held		
Opinion	Associate's	Bachelor's	Graduate
Not at all scientific	11	70	32
Very or sort of scientific	17	15	9

Figure 23.5 (see page 455) gives Minitab chi-square output for these data. Follow the "Plan," "Solve," and "Conclude" steps of the four-step process in using the information in the output to describe how people with these levels of education differ in their opinions about astrology. Be sure that your "Solve" step includes data analysis and checking conditions for inference as well as a formal test.

FIGURE 23.4

Minitab output for the study of video-gaming and grades, for Exercise 23.6.

```
Session                                              _  □  X

                   A's and         D's and
                    B's      C's     F's      All

Played              736      450     193      1379
                    53.37    32.63   14.00    100.00
                    717.28   453.06  208.22   1379.00


Never played        205      144      80      429
                    47.79    33.57   18.65    100.00
                    223.28   140.94   64.78    429.00


All                 941      594     273      1808
                    52.05    32.85   15.10    100.00
                    941.00   594.00  273.00   1808.00


Cell Contents:     Count
                   % of Row
                   Expected count


Pearson Chi-Square = 6.739,   DF = 2, P-Value = 0.034
```

The key for cell entries in this table is at the bottom.

FIGURE 23.5

Minitab output for the two-way table of opinion about astrology and degree held, for Exercise 23.7.

```
Session                                              □  □  X

              Associate's  Bachelor's  Graduate    All

NotScience         11          70         32        113
                   39.29       82.35      78.05     73.38
                   20.55       62.37      30.08     113.00
                   4.435       0.933      0.122      *


Science            17          15          9         41
                   60.71       17.65      21.95     26.62
                   7.45        22.63      10.92     41.00
                   12.223      2.572      0.336      *


All                28          85         41        154
                   100.00      100.00     100.00    100.00
                   28.00       85.00      41.00     154.00
                    *           *          *         *


Cell Contents:     Count
                   % of Column
                   Expected count
                   Contribution to Chi-square


Pearson Chi-Square = 20.622, DF = 2, P-Value = 0.000
```

ANOTHER USE OF THE CHI-SQUARE TEST

One of the most useful properties of chi-square is that it tests the null hypothesis "the row and column variables are not related to each other" whenever this hypothesis makes sense for a two-way table. Some two-way tables classify a single sample by two categorical variables. Our earlier examples were of this kind. Other two-way tables compare the values of a categorical response variable in two separate samples. Here is an example of this setting.

AB/Getty Images

EXAMPLE 23.5 Are cell-only telephone users different?

STATE: Random digit dialing telephone surveys do not call cell phone numbers. If the opinions of people who have only cell phones differ from those of people who still have landline service, the poll results may not represent the entire adult population. The Pew Research Center interviewed separate random samples of cell-only and landline telephone users. We will compare the 96 cell-only users and the 104 landline users who were less than 30 years old. Here's what the Pew survey found about how these people describe their political party affiliation:[6]

Party affiliation	Cell-only sample	Landline sample
Democrat or lean Democratic	49	47
Refuse to lean either way	15	27
Republican or lean Republican	32	30
Total	96	104

PLAN: Carry out a chi-square test for

H_0: no relationship; that is, the distribution of party affiliation is the same in both populations

H_a: there is some relationship; that is, the party distribution in the cell-only population differs from that of landline users

Compare column percents or observed versus expected cell counts or terms of chi-square to see the nature of the relationship.

SOLVE: The Minitab output in Figure 23.6 (see page 457) includes the column percents. These give the conditional distributions of party given telephone use. Cell-only users are less likely to have no party affiliation (15.63% versus 25.96% of landline users). The party affiliations among the 158 people who prefer one party are nearly the same in both groups, 60% Democrat for cell-only, 61% Democrat for landline.

To see if the differences are significant, first check the guideline for use of chi-square. The samples are reasonably close to SRSs, though nonresponse was higher for the cell phone calls. The Minitab output shows that all expected counts are greater than 5. The chi-square test shows that there is no significant difference between the party affiliations of the two groups of young adults ($\chi^2 = 3.22$, $P = 0.200$). Comparing observed and expected counts again shows that cell-only young adults are less likely to have no party preference than would be expected if there were no relationship, and that landline users are more likely to have no preference. The two "refuse to lean" cells contribute 2.54 of the total chi-square $\chi^2 = 3.22$. But the overall comparison is not significant.

```
 ▦ Session                                        _  ▢  ▢  X

           Cell-only  Landline       All

Democrat           49        47        96
               51.04     45.19     48.00
               46.08     49.92     96.00
              0.1850    0.1708         *

RefuseToLean       15        27        42
               15.63     25.96     21.00
               20.16     21.84     42.00
              1.3207    1.2191         *

Republican         32        30        62
               33.33     28.85     31.00
               29.76     32.24     62.00
              0.1686    0.1556         *

All                96       104       200
              100.00    100.00    100.00
               96.00    104.00    200.00
                   *         *         *


Cell Contents:      Count
                    % of Column
                    Expected count
                    Contribution to Chi-square

Pearson Chi-Square = 3.220,  DF = 2, P-Value = 0.200
```

FIGURE 23.6

Minitab output for the two-way table of political party affiliation and telephone use, for Example 23.5.

CONCLUDE: There is no significant difference between the political party affiliations of young people who have a landline telephone and those who rely entirely on cell phones. The data do suggest that cell-only users are more likely to have some affiliation, so that a larger sample might find a significant difference. The Pew study found "little difference" to be true for all adults and for a variety of political questions. Traditional telephone sample surveys will live on, at least for a while. ■

APPLY YOUR KNOWLEDGE

23.8 Cell-only versus landline users. We suspect that people who rely entirely on cell phones will as a group be younger than those who have a landline telephone. Do data confirm this guess? Here is a two-way table that breaks down both of Pew's samples (see Example 23.5) by age group: ● CELLAGE

Age (years)	Landline sample	Cell-only sample
18–29	104	96
30–49	265	70
50–64	204	26
65 or older	179	8
Total	752	200

Do a complete analysis of these data, following the four-step process as illustrated in Example 23.5.

THE CHI-SQUARE DISTRIBUTIONS*

Software usually finds P-values for us. The P-value for a chi-square test comes from comparing the value of the chi-square statistic with critical values for a *chi-square distribution*.

> ### THE CHI-SQUARE DISTRIBUTIONS
>
> The **chi-square distributions** are a family of distributions that take only positive values and are skewed to the right. A specific chi-square distribution is specified by giving its **degrees of freedom.**
>
> The chi-square test for a two-way table with r rows and c columns uses critical values from the chi-square distribution with $(r-1)(c-1)$ degrees of freedom. The P-value is the area under the density curve of this chi-square distribution to the right of the value of the test statistic.

Figure 23.7 shows the density curves for three members of the chi-square family of distributions. As the degrees of freedom increase, the density curves become less skewed and larger values become more probable. Table D in the back of the book gives critical values for chi-square distributions. You can use Table D if you do not have software that gives you P-values for a chi-square test.

FIGURE 23.7

Density curves for the chi-square distributions with 1, 4, and 8 degrees of freedom. Chi-square distributions take only positive values and are right-skewed.

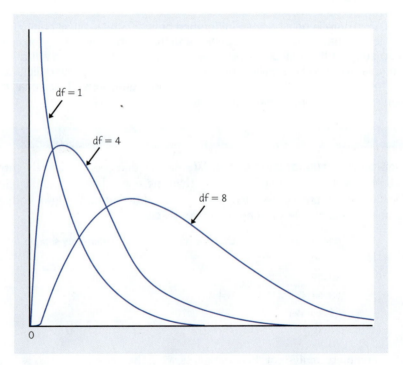

*This short section is optional if you will always use software for the chi-square test.

EXAMPLE 23.6 Using the chi-square table

The two-way table of 5 outcomes by 4 age groups for the living arrangements study (Table 23.1) has 5 rows and 4 columns. That is, $r = 5$ and $c = 4$. The chi-square statistic therefore has degrees of freedom

$$(r - 1)(c - 1) = (5 - 1)(4 - 1) = (4)(3) = 12$$

The output in Figure 23.2 gives 12 as the degrees of freedom.

The observed value of the chi-square statistic is $\chi^2 = 193.548$. Look in the df = 12 row of Table D. The value $\chi^2 = 193.548$ falls above the largest critical value in the table, for $P = 0.0005$. Remember that the chi-square test is always one-sided. So the P-value of $\chi^2 = 193.548$ is less than 0.0005. ■

df = 12		
p	.001	.0005
χ^*	32.91	34.82

We know that all z and t statistics measure the size of an effect in the standard scale centered at zero. We can roughly assess the size of any z or t statistic by the 68–95–99.7 rule, though this is exact only for z. The chi-square statistic does not have any such natural interpretation. But here is a helpful fact: *the mean of any chi-square distribution is equal to its degrees of freedom*. In Example 23.6, χ^2 would have mean 12 if the null hypothesis were true. The observed value $\chi^2 = 193.548$ is so much larger than 12 that we suspect it is significant even before we look at Table D.

APPLY YOUR KNOWLEDGE

23.9 Facebook at Penn State. The Minitab output in Figure 23.3 (page 454) gives the degrees of freedom for a table of Facebook use by students at two campus locations as DF = 2.

(a) Show that this is correct for a table with 3 rows and 2 columns.

(b) Minitab gives the chi-square statistic as Chi-Sq = 19.489. Where does this value fall when compared with critical values of the chi-square distribution with 2 degrees of freedom in Table D? How does Minitab's result P-Value = 0.000 compare with the P-value from the table?

(c) The two-way table included only students who have Facebook accounts. The original table in Exercise 23.1 had 4 rows and 2 columns. What is the proper degrees of freedom for that table?

23.10 Video-gaming and grades. The Minitab output in Figure 23.4 (page 455) gives 2 degrees of freedom for the table in Exercise 23.2.

(a) Verify that this is correct.

(b) The computer gives the value of the chi-square statistic as $\chi^2 = 6.739$. Between what two entries in Table D does this value lie? Verify that Minitab's P-value does fall between the tail probabilities p for these two entries.

(c) What is the mean value of the statistic χ^2 if the null hypothesis is true? How does the observed value of χ^2 compare with this mean?

THE CHI-SQUARE TEST FOR GOODNESS OF FIT*

The most common and most important use of the chi-square statistic is to test the hypothesis that there is *no relationship between two categorical variables*. A variation of the statistic can be used to test a different kind of null hypothesis: that *a categorical variable has a specified distribution*. Here is an example that illustrates this use of chi-square.

BIRTHDAY140

EXAMPLE 23.7 Never on Sunday?

Births are not evenly distributed across the days of the week. Fewer babies are born on Saturday and Sunday than on other days, probably because doctors find weekend births inconvenient.

A random sample of 140 births from local records shows this distribution across the days of the week:

Day	Sun.	Mon.	Tue.	Wed.	Thu.	Fri.	Sat.
Births	13	23	24	20	27	18	15

Sure enough, the two smallest counts of births are on Saturday and Sunday. Do these data give significant evidence that local births are not equally likely on all days of the week? ▪

The chi-square test answers the question of Example 23.7 by comparing observed counts with expected counts under the null hypothesis. The null hypothesis for births says that they *are* evenly distributed. To state the hypotheses carefully, write the discrete probability distribution for days of birth:

Day	Sun.	Mon.	Tue.	Wed.	Thu.	Fri.	Sat.
Probability	p_1	p_2	p_3	p_4	p_5	p_6	p_7

The null hypothesis says that the probabilities are the same on all days. In that case, all 7 probabilities must be 1/7. So the null hypothesis is

$$H_0: p_1 = p_2 = p_3 = p_4 = p_5 = p_6 = p_7 = \frac{1}{7}$$

The alternative hypothesis says that days are *not* all equally probable:

$$H_a: \text{not all } p_i = \frac{1}{7}$$

As usual in chi-square tests, H_a is a "many-sided" hypothesis that simply says that H_0 is not true. The chi-square statistic is also as usual:

$$\chi^2 = \sum \frac{(\text{observed count} - \text{expected count})^2}{\text{expected count}}$$

*This special topic is optional.

The expected count for an outcome with probability p is simply np. Under the null hypothesis, all the probabilities p_i are the same, so all 7 expected counts are equal to

$$np_i = 140 \times \frac{1}{7} = 20$$

These expected counts easily satisfy our guideline for using chi-square. The chi-square statistic is

$$\chi^2 = \sum \frac{(\text{observed count} - 20)^2}{20}$$
$$= \frac{(13-20)^2}{20} + \frac{(23-20)^2}{20} + \cdots + \frac{(15-20)^2}{20}$$
$$= 7.6$$

This new use of χ^2 requires a different degrees of freedom. To find the P-value, compare χ^2 with critical values from the chi-square distribution with degrees of freedom 1 less than the number of values the birth day can take. That's $7 - 1 = 6$ degrees of freedom. From Table D, we see that $\chi^2 = 7.6$ is smaller than the smallest entry in the df = 6 row, which is the critical value for tail area 0.25. The P-value is therefore greater than 0.25 (software gives the more exact value $P = 0.269$). These 140 births don't give convincing evidence that births are not equally likely on all days of the week.

The chi-square test applied to the hypothesis that a categorical variable has a specified distribution is called the test for *goodness of fit*. The idea is that the test assesses whether the observed counts "fit" the distribution. The chi-square statistic is the same as for the two-way table test, but the expected counts and degrees of freedom are different. Here are the details.

df = 6		
p	.25	.20
x^*	7.84	8.56

THE CHI-SQUARE TEST FOR GOODNESS OF FIT

A categorical variable has k possible outcomes, with probabilities $p_1, p_2, p_3, \ldots, p_k$. That is, p_i is the probability of the ith outcome. We have n independent observations from this categorical variable.

To test the null hypothesis that the probabilities have specified values

$$H_0: p_1 = p_{10}, p_2 = p_{20}, \ldots, p_k = p_{k0}$$

find the **expected count** for the ith possible outcome as np_{i0} and use the **chi-square statistic**

$$\chi^2 = \sum \frac{(\text{observed count} - \text{expected count})^2}{\text{expected count}}$$

The sum is over all the possible outcomes.

The P-value is the area to the right of χ^2 under the density curve of the chi-square distribution with $k - 1$ degrees of freedom.

In Example 23.7, the outcomes are days of the week, with $k = 7$. The null hypothesis says that the probability of a birth on the ith day is $p_{i0} = 1/7$ for all days. We observe $n = 140$ births and count how many fall on each day. These are the counts used in the chi-square statistic.

APPLY YOUR KNOWLEDGE

23.11 Saving birds from windows. Many birds are injured or killed by flying into windows. It appears that birds don't see windows. Can tilting windows down so that they reflect earth rather than sky reduce bird strikes? Place six windows at the edge of a woods: two vertical, two tilted 20 degrees, and two tilted 40 degrees. During the next four months, there were 53 bird strikes, 31 on the vertical windows, 14 on the 20-degree windows, and 8 on the 40-degree windows.[7] If the tilt has no effect, we expect strikes on windows with all three tilts to have equal probability. Test this null hypothesis. What do you conclude?

23.12 More on birth days. Births really are not evenly distributed across the days of the week. The data in Example 23.7 failed to reject this null hypothesis because of random variation in a quite small number of births. Here are data on 700 births in the same locale: **BIRTHDAYS700**

Day	Sun.	Mon.	Tue.	Wed.	Thu.	Fri.	Sat.
Births	84	110	124	104	94	112	72

(a) The null hypothesis is that all days are equally probable. What are the probabilities specified by this null hypothesis? What are the expected counts for each day in 700 births?

(b) Calculate the chi-square statistic for goodness of fit.

(c) What are the degrees of freedom for this statistic? Do these 700 births give significant evidence that births are not equally probable on all days of the week?

23.13 Police harassment? Police may use minor violations such as not wearing a seat belt to stop motorists for other reasons. A large study in Michigan first studied the population of drivers not wearing seat belts during daylight hours by observation at more than 400 locations around the state. Here is the population distribution of seat belt violators by age group:[8]

Age group	16 to 29	30 to 59	60 or older
Proportion	0.328	0.594	0.078

The researchers then looked at court records and called a random sample of 803 drivers who had actually been cited by police for not wearing a seat belt. Here are the counts:

Age group	16 to 29	30 to 59	60 or older
Count	401	382	20

Randy Duchaine/CORBIS

Does the age distribution of people cited differ significantly from the distribution of ages of all seat belt violators? Which age groups have the largest contributions to chi-square? Are these age groups cited more or less frequently than is justified? (The study found that males, blacks, and younger drivers were all overcited. This is an example in which the probabilities for the categories are not equal under the null hypothesis. You must use the given population probabilities and the sample size to compute the expected counts.)

23.14 Order in choice. Does the order in which wine is presented make a difference? Several choices of wine are presented one at a time, and subjects are asked to choose their preferred wine at the end of the sequence. In this study, subjects were asked to taste four wine samples in sequence. All four samples given to a subject were the *same* wine, although subjects were expecting to taste four different samples of a particular variety.[9] There were 33 subjects in the study, and the positions in the sequence they selected for their preferred wine were

Position	1	2	3	4
Count	15	5	2	11

(a) What percent of the subjects chose each position?

(b) If the subjects are equally likely to select each position, what are the expected counts for each position?

(c) Does the chi-square test for goodness of fit give good evidence that the subjects were not equally likely to choose each position? (State hypotheses, check the guideline for using chi-square, give the test statistic and its *P*-value, and state your conclusion.)

(d) The *primacy* effect is a tendency for subjects to choose the first wine tasted, while the *recency* effect is a tendency for subjects to choose the most recent wine tasted. Are either of these effects present in these data?

23.15 What's your sign? For reasons known only to social scientists, the General Social Survey (GSS) regularly asks its subjects about their astrological sign. Here are the counts of responses for the 2010 GSS: 🥧 SIGNS

Sign	Aries	Taurus	Gemini	Cancer	Leo	Virgo
Count	165	165	159	170	155	191
Sign	Libra	Scorpio	Sagittarius	Capricorn	Aquarius	Pisces
Count	183	152	147	175	165	168

If births are spread uniformly across the year, we expect all 12 signs to be equally likely. Are they? Follow the four-step process in your answer.

CHAPTER 23   SUMMARY

CHAPTER SPECIFICS

■ The **chi-square test** for a two-way table tests the null hypothesis H_0 that there is no relationship between the row variable and the column variable. The alternative hypothesis H_a says that there is some relationship but does not say what kind.

■ The test compares the observed counts of observations in the cells of the table with the counts that would be expected if H_0 were true. The **expected count** in any cell is

$$\text{expected count} = \frac{\text{row total} \times \text{column total}}{\text{table total}}$$

■ The **chi-square statistic** is

$$\chi^2 = \sum \frac{(\text{observed count} - \text{expected count})^2}{\text{expected count}}$$

■ The chi-square test compares the value of the statistic χ^2 with critical values from the **chi-square distribution** with $(r-1)(c-1)$ **degrees of freedom.** Large values of χ^2 are evidence against H_0, so the P-value is the area under the chi-square density curve to the right of χ^2.

■ The chi-square distribution is an approximation to the distribution of the statistic χ^2. You can safely use this approximation when all expected cell counts are at least 1 and no more than 20% are less than 5.

■ If the chi-square test finds a statistically significant relationship between the row and column variables in a two-way table, do data analysis to describe the nature of the relationship. You can do this by comparing well-chosen percents, comparing the observed counts with the expected counts, and looking for the largest **terms of the chi-square statistic.**

LINK IT

Part IV of the text studies relationships between variables. Chapters 4 and 5 introduced relationships between two quantitative variables, and these relationships will be described in greater detail in the next chapter. In this chapter, we considered the case of two categorical variables and developed a formal test for answering the question "Is there a relationship between the two categorical variables?" As with procedures described in earlier chapters, we must first consider how the data were produced, as this plays an important role in the conclusions we can reach. Were the data produced by an experiment or an observational study? If it is an observational study, are there lurking variables that can explain the observed relationship? In addition, we should begin with data analysis rather than a formal test. In the case of two-way tables, this typically involves looking at conditional distributions, both numerically and graphically, in order to first understand the nature of the relationship. When considering the relationship between the age of young adults and their living arrangements in Example 23.1, we saw from our data analysis that as young adults age from 19 to 22, the percent living with their parents drops as the percent living in their own place rises.

Even though there appears to be a clear relationship between age and living arrangement in Example 23.1, we must still determine whether the observed differences are large enough to be statistically significant. The chi-square test can be used for this, but it is an approximate procedure, and the conditions for cell sizes need to be checked before applying the test. If the differences are statistically significant, the chi-square test, unlike some of the simpler procedures in earlier chapters, tells us only that there is evidence of a relationship, not the nature of the relationship. Although there are formal statistical procedures to further investigate the nature of the relationship, at this point we need to be satisfied with describing the relationship between the two categorical variables using our data analysis tools.

CHECK YOUR SKILLS

Resistance training is a popular form of conditioning aimed at enhancing sports performance and is widely used among high school, college, and professional athletes, although its use for younger athletes is controversial. A random sample of 4111 patients between the ages of 8 and 30 admitted to U.S. emergency rooms with the injury code "weightlifting" was obtained. These injuries were classified as "accidental" if caused by dropped weight or improper equipment use. The patients were also classified into the four age categories "8–13," "14–18," "19–22," and "23–30." Here is a two-way table of the results:[10] 🔴 **WEIGHTLIFTING**

Age	Accidental	Not accidental
8–13	295	102
14–18	655	916
19–22	239	533
23–30	363	1008

23.16 The percent of the 14- to 18-year-olds in the sample whose injuries were classified as "accidental" is about

  (a) 42.2%.

  (b) 41.7%.

  (c) 74.3%.

23.17 The percent of the 14- to 18-year-olds in the sample whose injuries were classified as "accidental" is

  (a) higher than the percent for 23- to 30-year-olds.

  (b) about the same as the percent for 23- to 30-year-olds.

  (c) lower than the percent for 23- to 30-year-olds.

23.18 The expected count of 14- to 18-year-olds whose injuries were classified as "accidental" is about

  (a) 593.09.   (b) 655.   (c) 977.91.

23.19 The term in the chi-square statistic for the cell of 14- to 18-year-olds whose injuries were classified as "accidental" is about

  (a) 593.09.   (b) 3.919.   (c) 6.463.

23.20 (Optional) The degrees of freedom for the chi-square test for this two-way table are

  (a) 3.   (b) 4.   (c) 8.

23.21 The null hypothesis for the chi-square test for this two-way table is

  (a) The proportions of "Accidental" and "Not accidental" injuries are the same.

  (b) There is no difference in the probabilities of an "accidental" injury for each of the four age groups.

  (c) "Accidental" injuries are more likely for the younger age groups.

23.22 The alternative hypothesis for the chi-square test for this two-way table is

  (a) The proportions of "Accidental" and "Not accidental" injuries are different.

  (b) The probabilities of an "accidental" injury for each of the four age groups are not the same.

  (c) "Accidental" injuries are more likely for the younger age groups.

23.23 (Optional) Software gives chi-square statistic $\chi^2 = 325.459$ for this table. From the table of critical values, we can say that the *P*-value is

  (a) between 0.0025 and 0.001.

  (b) between 0.001 and 0.0005.

  (c) less than 0.0005.

CHAPTER 23 EXERCISES

If you have access to software or a graphing calculator, use it to speed your analysis of the data in these exercises. Exercises 23.24 to 23.35 don't require software.

23.24 Smoking cessation. A large randomized trial was conducted to assess the efficacy of Chantix for smoking cessation compared with bupropion (more commonly known as Wellbutrin or Zyban) and a placebo. Chantix is different from most other quit-smoking products in that it targets nicotine receptors in the brain, attaches to them, and blocks nicotine from reaching them, while bupropion is an antidepressant often used to help people stop smoking. Generally healthy smokers who smoked at least 10 cigarettes per day were assigned at random to take Chantix ($n = 352$), bupropion ($n = 329$), or a placebo ($n = 344$). The study was double-blind, with the response measure being continuous cessation from smoking for Weeks 9 through 12 of the study. Here is a two-way table of the results:[11] 🔴 **SMOKECESS**

	Treatment		
	Chantix	**Bupropion**	**Placebo**
No smoking in Weeks 9–12	155	97	61
Smoked in Weeks 9–12	197	232	283

(a) Give a 95% confidence interval for the difference between the proportions of smokers in the bupropion and placebo groups who did not smoke in Weeks 9 through 12 of the study.

(b) What proportion of each of the three groups in the sample did not smoke in Weeks 9 through 12 of the study? Are there statistically significant differences among these proportions? State hypotheses and give a test statistic and its P-value.

(c) Is this an observational study or an experiment? Why does this make a difference in the type of conclusion we can draw?

23.25 Attitudes toward recycled products. Some people think recycled products are lower in quality than other products, a fact that makes recycling less practical. Here are data on attitudes toward coffee filters made of recycled paper.[12]

RECYCLING

	Think the quality of the recycled product is		
	Higher	**Same**	**Lower**
Buyers	20	7	9
Nonbuyers	29	25	43

(a) Find the conditional distributions of opinions on the quality of recycled products for buyers and nonbuyers. Make a graph that compares the two conditional distributions. Use your work to describe the overall relationship between people who have and haven't bought recycled filters and their opinions on the quality of recycled products.

(b) Do buyers and nonbuyers of recycled filters differ significantly in their opinions on the quality of recycled products? State hypotheses, give the chi-square statistic and its P-value, and state your conclusion.

(c) Association does not prove causation. Explain how buying recycled filters might improve a person's opinion of their quality. Then explain how the opinion a person holds might influence his or her decision to buy or not. You see that the cause-and-effect relationship might go in either direction.

23.26 Do you use cocaine? Sample surveys on sensitive issues can give different results depending on how the question is asked. A University of Wisconsin study divided 2400 respondents into three groups at random. All were asked if they had ever used cocaine. One group of 800 was interviewed by phone; 21% said they had used cocaine. Another 800 people were asked the question in a one-on-one personal interview; 25% said "Yes." The remaining 800 were allowed to make an anonymous written response; 28% said "Yes."[13] Are there statistically significant differences among these proportions? State the hypotheses, convert the information given into a two-way table of counts, give the test statistic and its P-value, and state your conclusions.

23.27 Did the randomization work? After randomly assigning subjects to treatments in a randomized comparative experiment, we can compare the treatment groups to see how well the randomization worked. We hope to find no significant differences among the groups. A study of how to provide premature infants with a substance essential to their development assigned infants at random to receive one of four types of supplement, called PBM, NLCP, PL-LCP, and TG-LCP.[14]

(a) The subjects were 77 premature infants. Outline the design of the experiment if 20 are assigned to the PBM group and 19 to each of the other treatments.

(b) The random assignment resulted in 9 females in the TG-LCP group and 11 females in each of the other groups. Make a two-way table of group by gender and do a chi-square test to see if there are significant differences among the groups. What do you find?

23.28 More on video-gaming. The data for comparing two sample proportions can be presented in a two-way table containing the counts of successes and failures in both samples, with two rows and two columns. In Exercise 23.2, a survey of the consequences of video-gaming on 14- to 18-year-olds is described. Another question from the survey was about aggressive behavior as evidenced by getting into serious fights, and the comparison was between girls that have and have not played video games. Here are the data:

	Serious Fights	
	Yes	**No**
Played games	36	55
Never played games	578	1436

(a) Is there evidence that the proportions of all 14- to 18-year-old girls who played or have never played video games and have gotten into serious fights differ? Find the two sample proportions, the z statistic, and its P-value.

(b) Is there evidence that the proportions of 14- to 18-year-old girls who have or have not gotten into serious fights differ between those who have played or have never played video games? Find the chi-square statistic χ^2 and its P-value.

(c) Show that (up to roundoff error) your χ^2 is the same as z^2. The two P-values are also the same. These facts are always true, so you will often see chi-square for 2 × 2 tables used to compare two proportions.

(d) Suppose that we are interested in finding out if the data give good evidence that video-gaming is associated with *increased* aggression in girls as evidenced by getting into serious fights. Can we use the z test for this hypothesis? What about the χ^2 test? What is the important difference between these two procedures?

23.29 Unhappy rats and tumors. Some people think that the attitude of cancer patients can influence the progress of their disease. We can't experiment with humans, but here is a rat experiment on this theme. Inject 60 rats with tumor cells and then divide them at random into two groups of 30. All

the rats receive electric shocks, but rats in Group 1 can end the shock by pressing a lever. (Rats learn this sort of thing quickly.) The rats in Group 2 cannot control the shocks, which presumably makes them feel helpless and unhappy. We suspect that the rats in Group 1 will develop fewer tumors. The results: 11 of the Group 1 rats and 22 of the Group 2 rats developed tumors.[15]

(a) Make a two-way table of tumors by group. State the null and alternative hypotheses for this investigation.

(b) Although we have a two-way table, the chi-square test can't test a one-sided alternative. Carry out the z test and report your conclusion.

23.30 I think I'll be rich by age 30. A sample survey asked young adults (aged 19 to 25), "What do you think are the chances you will have much more than a middle-class income at age 30?" The Minitab output in Figure 23.8 shows the two-way table and related information, omitting a few subjects who refused to respond or who said they were already rich.[16] Use the output as the basis for a discussion of the differences between young men and young women in assessing their chances of being rich by age 30. **RICHBY30**

FIGURE 23.8

Minitab output for the sample survey responses, for Exercise 23.30.

```
 Session                                          _ □ X

                               Female      Male

A: Almost no chance               96        98
                                95.2      98.8
                              0.0076    0.0073

B: Some chance but probably not  426       286
                               349.2     362.8
                             16.8842   16.2525

C: A 50 50 chance                696       720
                               694.5     721.5
                              0.0032    0.0031

D: A good chance                 663       758
                               697.0     724.0
                              1.6543    1.5924

E: Almost certain                486       597
                               531.2     551.8
                              3.8424    3.6986


Cell Contents:      Count
                    Expected count
                    Contribution to Chi-square

Pearson Chi-Square = 43.946,  DF = 4, P-Value = 0.000
```

23.31 Sexy magazine ads? Look at full-page ads in magazines with a young adult readership. Classify ads that show a model as "not sexual" or "sexual" depending on how the model is dressed. Here are data on 1509 ads in magazines aimed at young men, at young women, or at young adults in general:[17] ⟨ SEXYADS

	Readers		
Ad type	Men	Women	General
Sexual	105	225	66
Not sexual	514	351	248

Figure 23.9 displays Minitab chi-square output. Use the information in the output to describe the relationship between the target audience and the sexual content of ads in magazines for young adults.

Mistakes in using the chi-square test are unusually common. Exercises 23.32 to 23.35 illustrate several kinds of mistake.

23.32 Sorry, no chi-square. An experimenter hid a toy from a dog behind either Screen A or Screen B. In the first phase the toy was always hidden behind Screen A, while in the second phase the toy was always hidden behind Screen B.

Will the dog continue to look behind Screen A in the second phase? This was tried under three conditions. In the Social-Communicative condition the experimenter communicated with the dog by establishing eye contact and addressing the dog while hiding the toy; in the Noncommunicative condition the toy was hidden without communication; and in the Nonsocial condition the toy was dragged by a string so that it could be hidden without any interaction from the experimenter. There were 12 dogs assigned at random to each condition, and each dog had up to three trials to find the toy hidden behind Screen B in Phase 2. An error occurred if the dog continued to search behind Screen A. The number of errors ranged from zero (the dog found the toy behind Screen B on the initial trial) up to 3 (the dog never correctly chose Screen B). Here are the data:[18] ⟨ HIDDENTOY

	Number of Errors			
Condition	0	1	2	3
Social-Communicative	0	3	3	6
Noncommunicative	5	3	1	3
Nonsocial	8	2	2	0

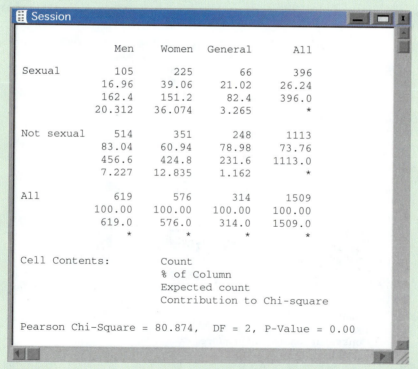

```
Session                                              _ □ X

              Men      Women    General      All

Sexual         105       225        66        396
             16.96     39.06     21.02      26.24
             162.4     151.2      82.4      396.0
            20.312    36.074     3.265          *

Not sexual     514       351       248       1113
             83.04     60.94     78.98      73.76
             456.6     424.8     231.6     1113.0
             7.227    12.835     1.162          *

All            619       576       314       1509
            100.00    100.00    100.00     100.00
             619.0     576.0     314.0     1509.0
                 *         *         *          *


Cell Contents:         Count
                       % of Column
                       Expected count
                       Contribution to Chi-square

Pearson Chi-Square = 80.874,   DF = 2, P-Value = 0.00
```

FIGURE 23.9
Minitab output for a study of ads in magazines, for Exercise 23.31.

(a) The data do show a difference in the number of errors for the different conditions. Show this by comparing suitable percents.

(b) The researchers used a more complicated but exact procedure rather than chi-square to assess significance for these data. Why can't the chi-square test be trusted in this case?

(c) If you use software, does the chi-square output for these data warn you against using the test?

23.33 Sorry, no chi-square. How do U.S. residents who travel overseas for leisure differ from those who travel for business? Here is the breakdown by occupation:[19]

Occupation	Leisure travelers	Business travelers
Professional/technical	36%	39%
Manager/executive	23%	48%
Retired	14%	3%
Student	7%	3%
Other	20%	7%
Total	100%	100%

Explain why we don't have enough information to use the chi-square test to learn whether these two distributions differ significantly.

23.34 Sorry, no chi-square. Here is more information about Internet use by students at Penn State, based on a random sample of 1852 undergraduates. Explain why it is not correct to use a chi-square test on this table to compare the University Park and commonwealth campuses. In order to use the chi-square test in a two-way table, each individual must fall into *one* cell of the table.

Internet use	University Park	Commonwealth
Viewed a video on YouTube or similar site	875	700
Legally purchased music or videos online	514	348
Downloaded a podcast	235	145
Participated in Internet gambling	114	93

23.35 Sorry, no chi-square. Does eating chocolate trigger headaches? To find out, women with chronic headaches followed the same diet except for eating chocolate bars and carob bars that looked and tasted the same. Each subject ate both chocolate and carob bars in random order

with at least three days between. Each woman then reported whether or not she had a headache within 12 hours of eating the bar. Here is a two-way table of the results for the 64 subjects:[20]

Bar	No headache	Headache
Chocolate	53	11
Carob (placebo)	38	26

The researchers carried out a chi-square test on this table to see if the two types of bar differ in triggering headaches. Explain why this test is incorrect. (*Hint:* There are 64 subjects. How many observations appear in the two-way table?)

The remaining exercises concern larger tables that require software for easy analysis. In many cases, you should follow the **Plan,** **Solve,** *and* **Conclude** *steps of the four-step process in your answers.*

23.36 Smokers rate their health. The University of Michigan Health and Retirement Study (HRS) surveys more than 22,000 Americans over the age of 50 every two years. A subsample of the HRS participated in the 2009 Internet-based survey that collected information on a number of topical areas, including health (physical and mental, health behaviors), psychosocial items, economics (income, assets, expectations, and consumption), and retirement.[21] Two of the questions asked on the Internet survey were "Would you say your health is excellent, very good, good, fair or poor?" and "Do you smoke cigarettes now?" The two-way table summarizes the answers to these two questions. ▶ SMOKERRATING

Health	Current Smoker	
	Yes	No
Excellent	25	484
Very good	115	1557
Good	145	1309
Fair	90	545
Poor	29	11

(a) Regard the HRS Internet sample as approximately an SRS of Americans over the age of 50, and give a 99% confidence interval for the proportion of Americans over the age of 50 who are current smokers.

(b) Compare the conditional distributions of self-evaluation of health for current smokers and non-smokers using both a table and a graph. What are the most important differences?

(c) Carry out the chi-square test for the hypothesis of no difference between the self-evaluation of health for current smokers and nonsmokers. What is the approximate P-value?

(d) Look at the terms of the chi-square statistic and compare observed and expected counts in the cells that contribute the most to chi-square. Based on this and your findings in part (b), write a short comparison of the differences in self-evaluation of health for current smokers and nonsmokers.

23.37 Who goes to religious services? The General Social Survey (GSS) asked this question: "Have you attended religious services in the last week?" Here are the responses for those whose highest degree was high school or above: **SERVICES**

	Highest Degree Held			
	High school	**Junior college**	**Bachelor's**	**Graduate**
Attended services	400	62	146	76
Did not attend services	880	101	232	105

(a) Carry out the chi-square test for the hypothesis of no relationship between the highest degree attained and attendance at religious services in the last week. What do you conclude?

(b) Make a 2 × 3 table by omitting the column corresponding to those whose highest degree was high school. Carry out the chi-square test for the hypothesis of no relationship between the type of advanced degree attained and attendance at religious services in the last week. What do you conclude?

(c) Make a 2 × 2 table by combining the counts in the three columns that have a highest degree beyond high school, so that you are comparing adults whose highest degree was high school with those whose highest degree was beyond high school. Carry out the chi-square test for the hypothesis of no relationship between attaining a degree beyond high school and attendance at religious services for this 2 × 2 table. What do you conclude?

(d) Using the results from these three chi-square tests, write a short report explaining the relationship between attendance at religious services in the last week and the highest degree attained. As part of your report, you should give the percents who attended religious services for each of the four degrees.

23.38 Condom usage among high school students. The Centers for Disease Control developed the Youth Risk Behavior Surveillance System (YRBSS) to monitor six categories of priority health risk behaviors among youth: behaviors that contribute to unintentional injuries and violence; tobacco use; alcohol and other drug use; sexual behaviors that contribute to unintended pregnancy and sexually transmitted diseases; unhealthy dietary behaviors; and physical inactivity. A multistage sample design is used to produce representative samples of students in grades 9 to 12, who then fill out a questionnaire on these behaviors. The data below are for the question "Did Not Use a Condom during Last Sexual Intercourse?" The two-way table of grade and condom usage includes only students who were currently sexually active. Here are the results:[22] **CONDOMUSE**

	Condom Used	
Grade	**Yes**	**No**
9th	300	532
10th	350	736
11th	601	956
12th	873	1068

Describe the most important differences between condom usage and grade. Is there a significant overall difference between the proportions who used condoms in the different grades?

23.39 How are schools doing? A nonprofit group conducted telephone interviews with random samples of 202 black parents of high school children, 202 Hispanic parents, and 201 white parents. One question asked was "Are the high schools in your state doing an excellent, good, fair or poor job, or don't you know enough to say?" Here are the survey results:[23] **HIGHSCHOOLS**

Opinion	**Black parents**	**Hispanic parents**	**White parents**
Excellent	12	34	22
Good	69	55	81
Fair	75	61	60
Poor	24	24	24
Don't know	22	28	14
Total	202	202	201

Are the differences in the distributions of responses for the three groups of parents statistically significant? What departures from the null hypothesis "no relationship between group and response" contribute most to the value of the chi-square statistic? Write a brief conclusion based on your analysis.

23.40 Complications of bariatric surgery. Bariatric surgery, or weight-loss surgery, includes a variety of procedures performed on people who are obese. Weight loss is achieved by reducing the size of the stomach with an implanted medical device (gastric banding), through removal of a portion of the stomach (sleeve gastrectomy), or by resecting and rerouting the small intestines to a small stomach pouch (gastric bypass surgery). Because there can be complications using any of these methods, the National Institutes of Health recommends bariatric surgery for obese people with a body mass index (BMI) of at least 40 and for people with a BMI of at least 35 and serious coexisting medical conditions such as diabetes. Serious complications include potentially life-threatening, permanently disabling, and fatal outcomes. Here is a two-way table for data collected in Michigan over several years giving counts of non-life-threatening complications, serious complications, and no complications for these three types of surgeries:[24] **BARIATRIC**

| | Type of Complication | | | |
Type of surgery	Non-life-threatening	Serious	None	Total
Gastric banding	81	46	5253	5380
Sleeve gastrectomy	31	19	804	854
Gastric bypass	606	325	8110	9041

(a) Is this study an experiment? Explain your answer.

(b) Is there a significant difference in the distributions of type of complication for the three types of surgery? Which surgeries have the greatest chance of complications? Can we conclude that it is the surgery that is more dangerous, or could there be other factors associated with the increased risk?

23.41 Market research. Before bringing a new product to market, firms carry out extensive studies to learn how consumers react to the product. Here are data from a study of a new laundry detergent.[25] The subjects are people who don't currently use the established brand that the new product will compete with. Give subjects free samples of both detergents. After they have tried both for a while, ask which they prefer. The answers may depend on other facts about how people do laundry. **LAUNDRY**

| | Laundry Practices | | | |
Preference	Soft water, warm wash	Soft water, hot wash	Hard water, warm wash	Hard water, hot wash
Prefer established brand	53	27	42	30
Prefer new product	63	29	68	42

How do water hardness and wash temperature influence the choice of detergent? In which settings does the new detergent do best? Are the differences between the detergents statistically significant?

EXPLORING THE WEB

23.42 Construct your own table. The Behavioral Risk Factor Surveillance System (BRFSS) is an ongoing data collection program designed to measure behavioral risk factors for the adult population (18 years of age or older) living in households. Data are collected from a random sample of adults (one per household) through a telephone survey. Go to the Web site apps.nccd.cdc.gov/BRFSS/ and under BRFSS Contents click on *Web Enabled Analysis Tool (WEAT)* and then click on *Cross Tabulation Analysis*. After selecting a year, a window will open that will allow you to produce two-way tables.

(a) Choose a state of interest to you and two variables for the two-way table. For example, you could choose Connecticut and look at the relationship between a demographic variable such as education level and a variable such as health care coverage. Once you have chosen your state and two variables, click on *run report* at the bottom of the page. A two-way table will appear in a new window.

(b) Is there a relationship between the two variables you selected? If the relationship is statistically significant, describe the relationship in a brief report using percents from the table and an appropriate graph.

23.43 What do the voters think? The American National Election Studies (ANES) is the leading academically run national survey of voters in the United States and is conducted before and after every presidential election. SDA (Survey Documentation and Analysis) is a set of programs that allows you to analyze survey data and includes the ANES survey as part of its archive. Go to the Web site sda.berkeley.edu/ and click on *Archive*. Go to the 2008 ANES survey.

(a) Open the pre-election survey data. Under Liberal/Conservative, choose the variable "liberal/conservative self-placement on a 7 point scale." Use this as your row variable. Under Issues, choose the variable "Iraq war increased or decreased the threat of terrorism." Use this as your column variable. In the details for the table, set Weight to No weight, and for N of Cases to Display, make sure the unweighted box is checked. For Percentaging, choose row percents. Now click on *Run the table*.

(b) To analyze the data, make a 3 × 3 table by combining the rows for extremely liberal and liberal; slightly liberal, middle of the road, and slightly conservative; and conservative and extremely conservative. Carry out a formal test to determine if there is a relationship between the two variables, and then describe the relationship in a brief report using percents from the table or an appropriate graph.

(c) Select two other variables of interest to you and analyze the relationship between them. If there is a more recent survey than 2008, you should use it.

Barbara Peacock/Getty Images

Inference for Regression

Whence a scatterplot shows a linear relationship between a quantitative explanatory variable x and a quantitative response variable y, we can use the least-squares line fitted to the data to predict y for a given value of x. When the data are a sample from a larger population, we need statistical inference to answer questions like these about the population:

■ Is there really a linear relationship between x and y in the population, or might the pattern we see in the scatterplot plausibly arise just by chance?

■ What is the slope (rate of change) that relates y to x in the population, including a margin of error for our estimate of the slope?

■ If we use the least-squares line to predict y for a given value of x, how accurate is our prediction (again, with a margin of error)?

This chapter shows you how to answer these questions. Here is an example we will explore.

473

CRYING

> ### EXAMPLE 24.1 Crying and IQ
>
> **STATE:** Infants who cry easily may be more easily stimulated than others. This may be a sign of higher IQ. Child development researchers explored the relationship between the crying of infants four to ten days old and their later IQ test scores. A snap of a rubber band on the sole of the foot caused the infants to cry. The researchers recorded the crying and measured its intensity by the number of peaks in the most active 20 seconds. They later measured the children's IQ at age three years using the Stanford-Binet IQ test. Table 24.1 contains data on 38 infants.[1] Do children with higher crying counts tend to have higher IQ?

TABLE 24.1 Infants' crying and IQ scores

CRYING	IQ	CRYING	IQ	CRYING	IQ	CRYING	IQ
10	87	20	90	17	94	12	94
12	97	16	100	19	103	12	103
9	103	23	103	13	104	14	106
16	106	27	108	18	109	10	109
18	109	15	112	18	112	23	113
15	114	21	114	16	118	9	119
12	119	12	120	19	120	16	124
20	132	15	133	22	135	31	135
16	136	17	141	30	155	22	157
33	159	13	162				

PLAN: Make a scatterplot. If the relationship appears linear, use correlation and regression to describe it. Finally, ask whether there is a *statistically significant* linear relationship between crying and IQ.

scatterplot

SOLVE (first steps): Figure 24.1 is a **scatterplot** of the crying data. Plot the explanatory variable (count of crying peaks) horizontally and the response variable (IQ) vertically. Look for the form, direction, and strength of the relationship as well as for outliers or other deviations. There is a moderately strong positive linear relationship, with no extreme outliers or potentially influential observations.

correlation

Because the scatterplot shows a roughly linear (straight-line) pattern, the **correlation** describes the direction and strength of the relationship. The correlation between crying and IQ is $r = 0.455$. We are interested in predicting the response from information about the explanatory variable. So we find the **least-squares regression line** for predicting IQ from crying. The equation of the regression line is

least-squares line

$$\hat{y} = a + bx$$
$$= 91.27 + 1.493x$$

CONCLUDE (first steps): Children who cry more vigorously do tend to have higher IQs. Because $r^2 = 0.207$, only about 21% of the variation in IQ scores is explained by crying intensity. Prediction of IQ will not be very accurate. It is nonetheless impressive that behavior soon after birth can even partly predict IQ three years later. Is this observed relationship statistically significant? We must now develop tools for inference in the regression setting. ■

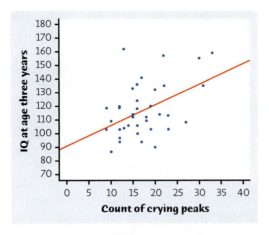

FIGURE 24.1

Scatterplot of the IQ scores of infants at age three years against the intensity of their crying soon after birth, with the least-squares regression line, for Example 24.1.

CONDITIONS FOR REGRESSION INFERENCE

We can fit a regression line to *any* data relating two quantitative variables, though the results are useful only if the scatterplot shows a linear pattern. Statistical inference requires more detailed conditions. Because the conclusions of inference always concern some *population*, the conditions describe the population and how the data are produced from it. The slope *b* and intercept *a* of the least-squares line are *statistics* calculated from the sample data. These statistics would take somewhat different values if we repeated the study with different infants. To do inference, think of *a* and *b* as estimates of unknown *parameters* that describe the population of all infants.

CONDITIONS FOR REGRESSION INFERENCE

We have n observations on an explanatory variable x and a response variable y. Our goal is to study or predict the behavior of y for given values of x.

■ For any fixed value of x, the response y varies according to a **Normal distribution.** Repeated responses y are **independent** of each other.

■ The mean response μ_y has a **straight-line relationship** with x given by a **population regression line**

$$\mu_y = \alpha + \beta x$$

The slope β and intercept α are unknown parameters.

■ The **standard deviation** of y (call it σ) is the same for all values of x. The value of σ is unknown.

There are thus three population parameters that we must estimate from the data: α, β, and σ.

These conditions say that in the population there is an "on the average" straight-line relationship between y and x. The population regression line $\mu_y = \alpha + \beta x$ says that the *mean* response μ_y moves along a straight line as the explanatory variable x changes. We can't observe the population regression line. The values of y that we do observe vary about their means according to a Normal distribution. In practice, we observe y for many different values of x, so that we see an overall linear pattern formed by points scattered about the population line. The standard deviation σ determines whether the points fall close to the population regression line (small σ) or are widely scattered (large σ).

Figure 24.2 shows the conditions for regression inference in picture form. The line in the figure is the population regression line. The mean response μ_y moves along this line as the explanatory variable x takes different values. The Normal curves show how y will vary when x is held fixed at different values. The mean depends on x, but the standard deviation is always the same. You must check the conditions for inference when you do inference about regression. We will see later how to do that.

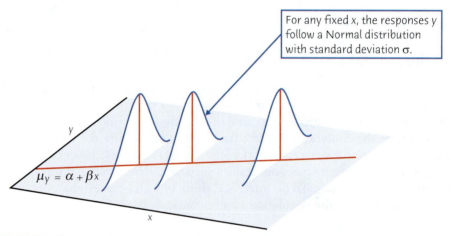

For any fixed x, the responses y follow a Normal distribution with standard deviation σ.

$\mu_y = \alpha + \beta x$

FIGURE 24.2

The conditions for regression inference in a picture. The line is the population regression line, which shows how the mean rxesponse μ_y changes as the explanatory variable x changes. For any fixed value of x, the observed response y varies according to a Normal distribution having mean μ_y and standard deviation σ.

ESTIMATING THE PARAMETERS

The first step in inference is to estimate the unknown parameters α, β, and σ.

ESTIMATING THE POPULATION REGRESSION LINE

When the conditions for regression are met and we calculate the least-squares line $\hat{y} = a + bx$, the slope b of the least-squares line is an unbiased estimator of the population slope β, and the intercept a of the least-squares line is an unbiased estimator of the population intercept α.

EXAMPLE 24.2 Crying and IQ: slope and intercept

The data in Figure 24.1 satisfy the condition of scatter about an invisible population regression line reasonably well. The least-squares line is $\hat{y} = 91.27 + 1.493x$. The slope is particularly important. *A slope is a rate of change.* The population slope β says how much higher average IQ is for children with one more peak in their crying measurement. Because $b = 1.493$ estimates the unknown β, we estimate that, on the average, IQ is about 1.5 points higher for each added crying peak.

We need the intercept $a = 91.27$ to draw the line, but it has no statistical meaning in this example. No child had fewer than 9 crying peaks, so we have no data near $x = 0$. We suspect that all normal children would cry when snapped with a rubber band, so that we will never observe $x = 0$. ■

The remaining parameter is the standard deviation σ, which describes the variability of the response y about the population regression line. The least-squares line estimates the population regression line. So the **residuals** estimate how much y varies about the population line. Recall that the residuals are the vertical deviations of the data points from the least-squares line:

residuals

$$\text{residual} = \text{observed } y - \text{predicted } y$$
$$= y - \hat{y}$$

There are n residuals, one for each data point. Because σ is the standard deviation of responses about the population regression line, we estimate it by a sample standard deviation of the residuals. We call this sample standard deviation the *regression standard error* to emphasize that it is estimated from data. The residuals from a least-squares line always have mean zero. That simplifies their standard error.

REGRESSION STANDARD ERROR

The **regression standard error** is

$$s = \sqrt{\frac{1}{n-2}\sum \text{residual}^2}$$
$$= \sqrt{\frac{1}{n-2}\sum (y - \hat{y})^2}$$

Use s to estimate the standard deviation σ of responses about the mean given by the population regression line.

Because we use the regression standard error so often, we just call it s. The quantity $\sum(y - \hat{y})^2$ is the sum of the squared deviations of the data points from the line. We average the squared deviations by dividing by $n - 2$, the number of data points less 2. It turns out that if we know $n - 2$ of the n residuals, the other two are determined. That is, $n - 2$ are the **degrees of freedom** of s. We first met the idea of degrees of freedom in the case of the ordinary sample standard deviation of n observations, which has $n - 1$ degrees of freedom. Now we observe two variables rather than one, and the proper degrees of freedom are $n - 2$ rather than $n - 1$.

degrees of freedom

Calculating s is unpleasant. You must find the predicted response for each x in your data set, then the residuals, and then s. In practice you will use software that does this arithmetic instantly. Nonetheless, here is an example to help you understand the standard error s.

CRYINGRES

EXAMPLE 24.3 Crying and IQ: residuals and standard error

Table 24.1 shows that the first infant studied had 10 crying peaks and a later IQ of 87. The predicted IQ for $x = 10$ is

$$\hat{y} = 91.27 + 1.493x$$
$$= 91.27 + 1.493(10) = 106.2$$

The residual for this observation is

$$\text{residual} = y - \hat{y}$$
$$= 87 - 106.2 = -19.2$$

That is, the observed IQ for this infant lies 19.2 points below the least-squares line on the scatterplot.

Repeat this calculation 37 more times, once for each subject. The 38 residuals are

−19.20	−31.13	−22.65	−15.18	−12.18	−15.15	−16.63	−6.18
−1.70	−22.60	−6.68	−6.17	−9.15	−23.58	−9.14	2.80
−9.14	−1.66	−6.14	−12.60	0.34	−8.62	2.85	14.30
9.82	10.82	0.37	8.85	10.87	19.34	10.89	2.55
20.85	24.35	18.94	32.89	18.47	51.32		

Check the calculations by verifying that the sum of the residuals is zero. It is 0.04, not quite zero, because of roundoff error. Another reason to use software in regression is that roundoff errors in hand calculation can accumulate to make the results inaccurate.

The variance about the line is

$$s^2 = \frac{1}{n-2} \sum \text{residual}^2$$
$$= \frac{1}{38-2}[(-19.20)^2 + (-31.13)^2 + \cdots + (51.32)^2]$$
$$= \frac{1}{36}(11{,}023.3) = 306.20$$

Finally, the regression standard error is

$$s = \sqrt{306.20} = 17.50 \ \blacksquare$$

We will study several kinds of inference in the regression setting. The regression standard error s is the key measure of the variability of the responses in regression. It is part of the standard error of all the statistics we will use for inference.

APPLY YOUR KNOWLEDGE

24.1 Wine and cancer in women. Some studies have suggested that a nightly glass of wine may not only take the edge off a day but also improve health. Is wine good for your health? A study of nearly 1.3 million middle-aged British women examined wine consumption and the relative risk of breast cancer. The relative risk is the proportion of those in the study who drank a given amount of wine and who developed breast cancer divided by the proportion of nondrinkers in the study who developed breast cancer. For example, if 10% of the women in the study who drank 10 grams of wine per day developed breast cancer and 9% of nondrinkers in the study developed breast cancer, the relative risk of breast cancer for women drinking 10 grams of wine per day would be 10%/9% = 1.11. A relative risk greater than 1 indicates a greater proportion of drinkers in the study developed breast cancer than nondrinkers. Wine intake is the mean wine intake, in grams per day, of all women in the study who drank some wine but less than or equal to 2 drinks per week; who drank between 3 and 6 drinks per week; who drank between 7 and 14 drinks per week; and who drank 15 or more drinks per week. Here are the data (for drinkers only):[2]  WINECANCER

Glowimages/AgeFotostock

Wine intake (grams per day) (x)	2.5	8.5	15.5	26.5
Relative risk (y)	1.00	1.08	1.15	1.22

(a) Examine the data. Make a scatterplot with wine intake as the explanatory variable and find the correlation. There is a strong linear relationship.

(b) Explain in words what the slope β of the population regression line would tell us if we knew it (note that these data represent averages over large numbers of women, and one must be careful not to interpret the data as applying to individuals). Based on the data, what are the estimates of β and the intercept α of the population regression line?

(c) Calculate by hand the residuals for the four data points. Check that their sum is 0 (up to roundoff error). Use the residuals to estimate the standard deviation σ that measures variation in the responses (relative risk) about the means given by the population regression line. You have now estimated all three parameters.

USING TECHNOLOGY

Inference about regression requires the regression standard error s and other calculations that are unpleasant with a basic calculator. Software or a graphing calculator that includes procedures for regression inference is almost essential for practical work.

Figure 24.3 shows regression output for the data of Table 24.1 from a graphing calculator, two statistical programs, and a spreadsheet program. When we entered the data into the programs, we called the explanatory variable "Crycount." The software outputs use that label. The graphing calculator just uses "x" and "y" to label the explanatory and response variables. You can locate the basic information in all the outputs. The regression slope is $b = 1.4929$, and the regression intercept is $a = 91.268$. The equation of the least-squares line is therefore (after rounding) just as given in Example 24.1. The regression standard error is $s = 17.4987$ and the squared correlation is $r^2 = 0.207$. Both of these results reflect the rather wide scatter of the points in Figure 24.1 about the least-squares line.

FIGURE 24.3

Regression of IQ on crying peaks: output from a graphing calculator, two statistical programs, and a spreadsheet program.

Texas Instruments Graphing Calculator

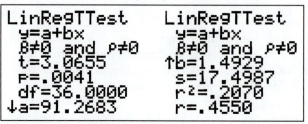

Minitab

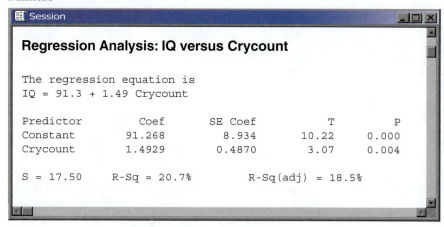

Crunchit

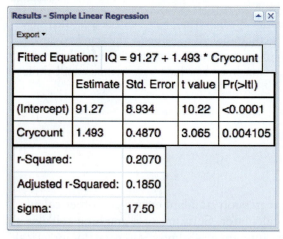

Excel

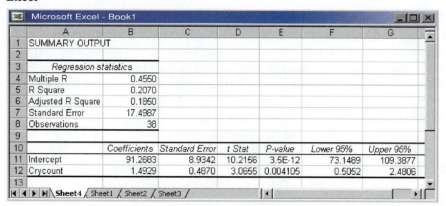

Each output contains other information, some of which we will need shortly and some of which we don't need. In fact, we left out some output to save space. Once you know what to look for, you can find what you want in almost any output and ignore what doesn't interest you.

24.2 Introspection and gray matter. The ability to introspect about self-performance is key to human subjective experience. Accurate introspection requires discriminating correct decisions from incorrect ones, a capacity that varies substantially across individuals. Are individual differences in introspective ability reflected in the anatomy of brain regions responsible for this function? The data below are a measure of introspective ability (labeled Aroc and based on the performance of subjects on a task) and a measure of gray-matter volume (Brodmann area) in the anterior prefrontal cortex of the brain of 29 subjects.[3] **GRAYMATTER**

Volume	0.55	0.58	0.59	0.59	0.59	0.61	0.62	0.63	0.63	0.63
Aroc	59	62	43	63	83	61	55	57	57	67
Volume	0.63	0.64	0.65	0.65	0.65	0.65	0.65	0.66	0.66	0.67
Aroc	72	62	58	62	65	70	75	60	63	71
Volume	0.67	0.67	0.68	0.69	0.70	0.70	0.71	0.72	0.75	
Aroc	71	80	68	72	66	73	61	80	75	

We want to predict Aroc from volume. Figure 24.4 shows Minitab regression output for these data.

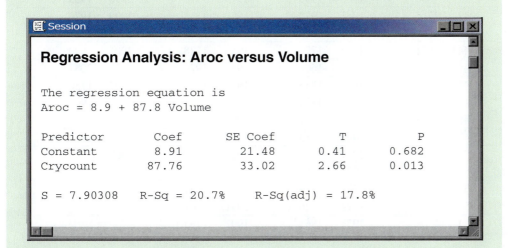

Regression Analysis: Aroc versus Volume

The regression equation is
Aroc = 8.9 + 87.8 Volume

Predictor	Coef	SE Coef	T	P
Constant	8.91	21.48	0.41	0.682
Crycount	87.76	33.02	2.66	0.013

S = 7.90308   R-Sq = 20.7%   R-Sq(adj) = 17.8%

FIGURE 24.4
Minitab output for the introspective ability data, for Exercise 24.2.

(a) Make a scatterplot suitable for predicting Aroc from volume. What is the squared correlation r^2?

(b) For regression inference, we must estimate the three parameters α, β, and σ. From the output, what are the estimates of these parameters?

(c) What is the equation of the least-squares regression line of Aroc on volume? Add this line to your plot. We will continue the analysis of these data in later exercises.

24.3 **Great Arctic rivers.** One effect of global warming is to increase the flow of water into the Arctic Ocean from rivers. Such an increase may have major effects on the world's climate. Six rivers (Yenisey, Lena, Ob, Pechora, Kolyma, and Severnaya Dvina) drain two-thirds of the Arctic in Europe and Asia. Several of these are among the largest rivers on earth. Table 24.2 presents the total discharge (amount of water flowing from these rivers) each year from 1936 to 2008.[4] Discharge is measured in cubic kilometers of water. Use software to analyze these data. ARCTIC

(a) Make a scatterplot of river discharge against time. Is there a clear increasing trend? Calculate r^2 and briefly interpret its value. There is considerable year-to-year variation, so we wonder if the trend is statistically significant.

(b) As a first step, find the least-squares line and draw it on your plot. Then find the regression standard error s, which measures scatter about this line. We will continue the analysis in later exercises.

TABLE 24.2 Arctic river discharge (cubic kilometers), 1936 to 2008

YEAR	DISCHARGE	YEAR	DISCHARGE	YEAR	DISCHARGE	YEAR	DISCHARGE
1936	1721	1955	1656	1974	2000	1993	1845
1937	1713	1956	1721	1975	1928	1994	1902
1938	1860	1957	1762	1976	1653	1995	1842
1939	1739	1958	1936	1977	1698	1996	1849
1940	1615	1959	1906	1978	2008	1997	2007
1941	1838	1960	1736	1979	1970	1998	1903
1942	1762	1961	1970	1980	1758	1999	1970
1943	1709	1962	1849	1981	1774	2000	1905
1944	1921	1963	1774	1982	1728	2001	1890
1945	1581	1964	1606	1983	1920	2002	2085
1946	1834	1965	1735	1984	1823	2003	1780
1947	1890	1966	1883	1985	1822	2004	1900
1948	1898	1967	1642	1986	1860	2005	1930
1949	1958	1968	1713	1987	1732	2006	1910
1950	1830	1969	1742	1988	1906	2007	2270
1951	1864	1970	1751	1989	1932	2008	2078
1952	1829	1971	1879	1990	1861		
1953	1652	1972	1736	1991	1801		
1954	1589	1973	1861	1992	1793		

TESTING THE HYPOTHESIS OF NO LINEAR RELATIONSHIP

Example 24.1 asked, "Do children with higher crying counts tend to have higher IQ?" Data analysis supports this conjecture. But is the positive association statistically significant? That is, is it too strong to often occur just by chance? To answer this question, test hypotheses about the slope β of the population regression line:

$$H_0: \beta = 0$$
$$H_a: \beta > 0$$

A regression line with slope 0 is horizontal. That is, the mean of y does not change at all when x changes. So H_0 says that there is *no linear relationship* between x and y in the population. Put another way, H_0 says that *linear regression of y on x is of no value for predicting y.*

The test statistic is just the standardized version of the least-squares slope b, using the hypothesized value $\beta = 0$ for the mean of b. It is another t statistic. Here are the details.

SIGNIFICANCE TEST FOR REGRESSION SLOPE

To **test the hypothesis $H_0: \beta = 0$,** compute the t statistic

$$t = \frac{b}{SE_b}$$

In this formula, the standard error of the least-squares slope b is

$$SE_b = \frac{s}{\sqrt{\Sigma(x - \bar{x})^2}}$$

The sum runs over all observations on the explanatory variable x.

Find P-values from the t distribution with $n - 2$ degrees of freedom.

The standard error of b is a multiple of the regression standard error s. The degrees of freedom $n = 2$ are the degrees of freedom of s. Although we give the formula for this standard error, you should not try to calculate it by hand. Regression software gives the standard error SE_b along with b itself.

EXAMPLE 24.4 Crying and IQ: is the relationship significant?

The hypothesis $H_0: \beta = 0$ says that crying has no straight-line relationship with IQ. We conjecture that there is a positive relationship, so we use the one-sided alternative $H_a: \beta > 0$.

Figure 24.1 shows that there is a positive relationship, and from Figure 24.3 we see $b = 1.4929$ and $SE_b = 0.4870$. Thus,

$$t = \frac{b}{SE_b} = \frac{1.4929}{0.4870} = 3.07$$

so it is not surprising that all the outputs in Figure 24.3 give $t = 3.07$ with two-sided P-value 0.004. The P-value for the one-sided test is half of this, $P = 0.002$. There is very strong evidence that IQ increases as the intensity of crying increases. ■

APPLY YOUR KNOWLEDGE

24.4   Wine and cancer in women. Exercise 24.1 gives data on daily wine consumption and the relative risk of breast cancer in women. Software tells us that the least-squares slope is $b = 0.009012$ with standard error $SE_b = 0.001112$.

(a)   What is the t statistic for testing $H_0: \beta = 0$?

(b)   How many degrees of freedom does t have? Use Table C to approximate the P-value of t against the one-sided alternative $H_a: \beta > 0$. What do you conclude?

24.5   Great Arctic rivers: testing. The most important question we ask of the data in Table 24.2 is this: is the increasing trend visible in your plot (Exercise 24.3) statistically significant? If so, changes in the Arctic may already be affecting the earth's climate. Use software to answer this question. Give a test statistic, its P-value, and the conclusion you draw from the test. ⬤ ARCTIC

TESTING LACK OF CORRELATION

The slope β of the population regression line is 0 exactly when the population correlation between x and y is 0. Testing the null hypothesis $H_0: \beta = 0$ is therefore exactly the same as testing that there is *no correlation* between x and y in the population from which we drew our data. You can use the test for zero slope to test the hypothesis of zero correlation between any two quantitative variables. That's a useful trick. It works even when there is no explanatory-response distinction, so that regression itself is not useful.

EXAMPLE 24.5   Testing lack of correlation

The scatterplot on the left in Figure 24.5 displays data from an experiment on the healing of cuts in the limbs of newts. The data are the healing rates (micrometers per hour) for the two front limbs of 18 newts. The right-hand scatterplot shows the first- and second-round scores for the 95 golfers in the 2010 Masters Tournament. (There are fewer than 95 points because of duplicate scores.)

We will test the hypotheses

$$H_0: \text{population correlation} = 0$$
$$H_a: \text{population correlation} \neq 0$$

for both sets of data. (The Masters scores are all whole numbers, but with $n = 95$ the robustness of the t procedures allows their use.) Software gives

```
newts      r=0.3581    t=1.5342    P=0.1445
masters    r=0.3465    t=3.56      P=0.001
```

The two-sided P-values for the t statistic for testing slope 0 are also the two-sided P-values for testing correlation 0. ■

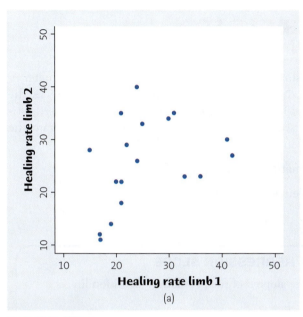

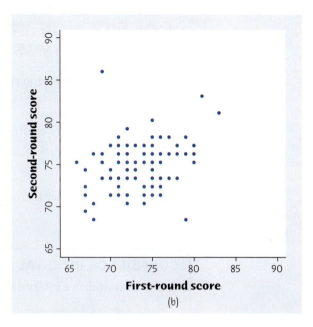

FIGURE 24.5

Two scatterplots for inference about the population correlation, for Example 24.5. (a) Healing rates for the two front limbs of 18 newts. (b) Scores on the first two rounds of the 2010 Masters Tournament.

The evidence for nonzero correlation is strong for the Masters scores ($t = 3.56$, $P = 0.001$) but not for the newts ($t = 1.5$, $P = 0.14$). Yet the correlation for the newts is slightly larger than that for the Masters, and the scatterplots suggest similar linear relationships for both. What happened? The larger sample size for the Masters data is largely responsible. The same r will have a smaller P-value for $n = 95$ than for $n = 18$. Our eyeball impression, even aided by calculating r, can't assess significance. We need the P-value from a formal test to guide us.

APPLY YOUR KNOWLEDGE

24.6 Wine and cancer in women: testing correlation. Exercise 24.1 gives data showing that the risk of breast cancer increases linearly with daily wine consumption. There are only 4 observations, so we worry that the apparent relationship may be just chance. Is the correlation significantly greater than 0? Return to your t statistic from Exercise 24.4. What is the one-sided P-value for this t? Apply your result to test the correlation. ⬛ WINECANCER

24.7 Does social rejection hurt? Exercise 4.37 (page 109) gives data from a study of whether social rejection causes activity in areas of the brain that are known to be activated by physical pain. The explanatory variable is a subject's score on a test of "social distress" after being excluded from an activity. The response variable is activity in an area of the brain that responds to physical pain. Your scatterplot (Exercise 4.37) shows a positive linear relationship. The research report gives the correlation r and the P-value for a test that r is greater than 0. Calculate r and the P-value. What do you conclude about the relationship? ⬛ REJECTION

CONFIDENCE INTERVALS FOR THE REGRESSION SLOPE

The slope β of the population regression line is usually the most important parameter in a regression problem. The slope is the rate of change of the mean response as the explanatory variable increases. The slope b of the least-squares line is an unbiased estimator of β. A confidence interval is more useful because it shows how accurate the estimate b is likely to be. The confidence interval for β has the familiar form

$$\text{estimate} \pm t^* \text{SE}_{\text{estimate}}$$

Because b is our estimate, the confidence interval is $b \pm t^* \text{SE}_b$.

CONFIDENCE INTERVAL FOR REGRESSION SLOPE

A level C **confidence interval for the slope** β of the population regression line is

$$b \pm t^* \text{SE}_b$$

Here t^* is the critical value for the $t(n-2)$ density curve with area C between $-t^*$ and t^*. The formula for SE_b appears in the box on page 483.

EXAMPLE 24.6 Crying and IQ: estimating the slope

All the software outputs in Figure 24.3 give the slope $b = 1.4929$ (or $b = 1.493$), and three also give the standard error $\text{SE}_b = 0.4870$. The outputs giving both use a similar arrangement, a table in which each regression coefficient is followed by its standard error. Excel also gives the lower and upper endpoints of the 95% confidence interval for the population slope β, 0.5052 and 2.4806.

Once we know b and SE_b, it is easy to find the confidence interval. There are 38 data points, so the degrees of freedom are $n - 2 = 36$. Because Table C does not have a row for df = 36, we must use either software or the next smaller degrees of freedom in the table, df = 30. To use software, enter 36 degrees of freedom. For 95% confidence, enter the cumulative proportion 0.975 that corresponds to upper-tail area 0.025. Minitab gives

```
Student's t distribution with 36 DF
P(X < = x)              x
   0.975     2.02809
```

The 95% confidence interval for the population slope β is

$$b \pm t^* \text{SE}_b = 1.4929 \pm (2.02809)(0.4870)$$
$$= 1.4929 \pm 0.9877$$
$$= 0.505 \text{ to } 2.481$$

This agrees with Excel's result. We are 95% confident that mean IQ increases by between about 0.5 and 2.5 points for each additional peak in crying. ▪

APPLY YOUR KNOWLEDGE

24.8 Wine and cancer in women: estimating slope. Exercise 24.1 gives data on wine consumption and the risk of breast cancer. Software tells us that the least-squares slope is $b = 0.009012$ with standard error $SE_b = 0.001112$. Because there are only 4 observations, the observed slope b may not be an accurate estimate of the population slope β. Give a 90% confidence interval for β.

24.9 Introspection and gray matter: estimating slope. Exercise 24.2 gives data on introspective ability and gray-matter volume of the brains of subjects. We want a 95% confidence interval for the slope of the population regression line. Starting from the information in the Minitab output in Figure 24.4, find this interval. Say in words what the slope of the population regression line tells us about the relationship between Aroc and gray-matter volume.

24.10 Great Arctic rivers: estimating slope. Use the data in Table 24.2 to give a 90% confidence interval for the slope of the population regression line of Arctic river discharge on year. Does this interval convince you that discharge is actually increasing over time? Explain your answer. ARCTIC

INFERENCE ABOUT PREDICTION

One of the most common reasons to fit a line to data is to predict the response to a particular value of the explanatory variable. We want a prediction with a margin of error that describes how accurate the prediction is likely to be.

EXAMPLE 24.7 Beer and blood alcohol

STATE: The EESEE story "Blood Alcohol Content" describes a study in which 16 student volunteers at the Ohio State University drank a randomly assigned number of cans of beer. Thirty minutes later, a police officer measured their blood alcohol content (BAC) in grams of alcohol per deciliter of blood. Here are the data:[5]

DATA FILE
BEERS

Student	1	2	3	4	5	6	7	8
Beers	5	2	9	8	3	7	3	5
BAC	0.10	0.03	0.19	0.12	0.04	0.095	0.07	0.06
Student	9	10	11	12	13	14	15	16
Beers	3	5	4	6	5	7	1	4
BAC	0.02	0.05	0.07	0.10	0.085	0.09	0.01	0.05

The students were equally divided between men and women and differed in weight and usual drinking habits. Because of this variation, many students don't believe that number of drinks predicts blood alcohol well. Steve thinks he can drive legally 30 minutes after he finishes drinking 5 beers. The legal limit for driving is BAC 0.08 in all states. We want to predict Steve's blood alcohol content, using no information except that he drinks 5 beers.

Jame Shaffer/The Image Works

PLAN: Regress BAC on number of beers. Use the regression line to predict Steve's BAC. Give a margin of error that allows us to have 95% confidence in our prediction.

SOLVE: The scatterplot in Figure 24.6 and the regression output in Figure 24.7 show that student opinion is wrong: number of beers predicts BAC quite well. In fact, $r^2 = 0.80$, so that number of beers explains 80% of the observed variation in BAC. To predict Steve's BAC after 5 beers, use the equation of the regression line:

$$\hat{y} = -0.0127 + 0.0180x$$
$$= -0.0127 + 0.0180(5) = 0.077$$

That's dangerously close to the legal limit of 0.08. What about 95% confidence? The "Predicted Values" part of the output in Figure 24.7 shows *two* 95% intervals. Which should we use? ▪

FIGURE 24.6

Scatterplot of students' blood alcohol content against the number of cans of beer consumed, with the least-squares regression line, for Example 24.7.

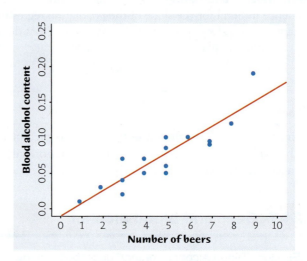

FIGURE 24.7

Minitab regression output for the blood alcohol content data, for Example 24.7.

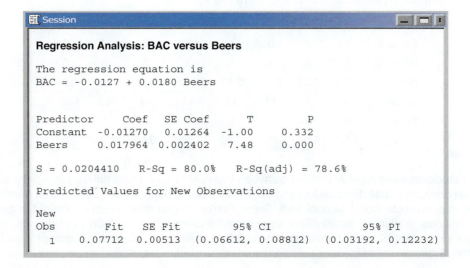

Session

Regression Analysis: BAC versus Beers

The regression equation is
BAC = -0.0127 + 0.0180 Beers

Predictor	Coef	SE Coef	T	P
Constant	-0.01270	0.01264	-1.00	0.332
Beers	0.017964	0.002402	7.48	0.000

S = 0.0204410   R-Sq = 80.0%   R-Sq(adj) = 78.6%

Predicted Values for New Observations

New Obs	Fit	SE Fit	95% CI	95% PI
1	0.07712	0.00513	(0.06612, 0.08812)	(0.03192, 0.12232)

The two intervals answer two different questions:

■ To predict the *mean BAC for all students* who drink 5 beers, use a *confidence interval* for the mean response when $x = 5$. This mean is a parameter, a fixed number whose value we don't know.

■ To predict *Steve's individual BAC* after 5 beers, use a **prediction interval.** A prediction interval estimates a single random response y rather than a parameter like the mean response.

prediction interval

The actual prediction is the same, $\hat{y} = 0.077$. But the margin of error is different for the two kinds of prediction. Individual students who drink 5 beers don't all have the same BAC. So we need a larger margin of error to pin down Steve's result than to estimate the mean BAC for all students who have 5 beers.

EXAMPLE 24.8 Beer and blood alcohol: conclusion

Steve is one individual, so we must use the prediction interval. The output in Figure 24.7 helpfully labels the confidence interval as "95% CI" and the prediction interval as "95% PI." We are 95% confident that Steve's BAC after 5 beers will lie between 0.032 and 0.122. The upper part of that range will get him arrested if he drives. The 95% confidence interval for the mean BAC of all students who drink 5 beers is much narrower, 0.066 to 0.088. ■

The confidence interval for a mean response and the prediction interval for an individual response have similar forms,

$$\hat{y} \pm t^*SE$$

The standard error SE for estimating an individual response is larger than the standard error SE needed to estimate a mean response. The formulas for both of these standard errors are a bit messy, so we rely on software for confidence and prediction intervals.

The interpretation of confidence intervals and prediction intervals is also similar: both give correct answers 95% of the time in repeated use. "Repeated use" for a prediction interval means that we measure BAC for 16 students who drink the same numbers of beers as in Example 24.7, calculate the prediction interval for 5 beers, then have one more student drink 5 beers. The interval covers the last student's BAC in 95% of all repetitions.

APPLY YOUR KNOWLEDGE

24.11 Wine and cancer in women: prediction. Exercise 24.1 gives data on wine consumption and the risk of breast cancer. For a new group of women who drink an average of 10 grams of wine per day, predict their relative risk of breast cancer.

(a) Figure 24.8 is part of the output from Minitab for prediction when $x = 10.0$. Which interval in the output is the proper 95% interval for predicting the relative risk?

(b) Minitab gives only one of the two standard errors used in prediction. It is $SE_{\hat{\mu}}$, the standard error for estimating the mean response. Use this fact along with the output to give a 90% confidence interval for the mean relative risk of breast cancer in all women who drink an average of 10 grams of wine per day.

FIGURE 24.8

Partial Minitab output for regressing relative risk of breast cancer on mean daily intake of wine, for Exercise 24.11.

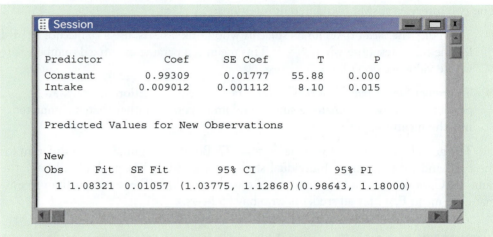

24.12 **Introspection and gray matter: prediction.** Analysis of the data in Exercise 24.2 shows that the relationship between gray-matter volume and introspective ability, as measured by Aroc, is roughly linear. We might want to predict the mean introspective ability of a person with a gray-matter volume of 0.60. Here is the Minitab output for prediction when $x = 0.60$:

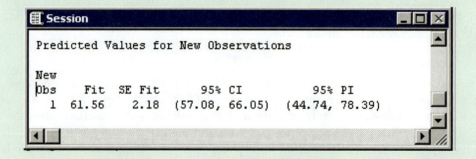

(a) Use the regression line from Figure 24.4 to verify that "Fit" is the predicted value for $x = 0.60$. (Start with the results in the "Coef" column of Figure 24.4 to reduce roundoff error.)

(b) What is the 95% interval we want?

CHECKING THE CONDITIONS FOR INFERENCE

You can fit a least-squares line to any set of explanatory-response data when both variables are quantitative, though the line is useful only when the scatterplot shows a roughly linear pattern. To use regression inference, however, the data must satisfy additional conditions. *Before you can trust the results of inference, you must check the conditions for inference one by one.*

The conditions involve the population regression line and the deviations of responses from this line. We can't observe the population line, but the least-squares line estimates it and the residuals estimate the deviations from the population line. *To check the conditions for regression inference, look at graphs of the residuals.* Regression software will calculate and save the residuals for you. Make a stemplot or histogram of the residuals and also a **residual plot,** a plot of the residuals against the explanatory variable x, with a horizontal line at the "residual = 0" position. The "residual = 0" line represents the position of the least-squares line in the scatterplot of y against x. Let's look at each condition in turn.

residual plot

■ **The relationship is linear in the population.** Look for curved patterns or other departures from a straight-line overall pattern in the residual plot. You can also use the original scatterplot, but the residual plot magnifies any effects.

■ **The response varies Normally about the population regression line.** Because different y-values usually come from different x-values, the responses themselves need not be Normal. It is the deviations from the population line—estimated by the residuals—that must be Normal. Check for clear skewness or other major departures from Normality in your stemplot or histogram of the residuals.

■ **Observations are independent.** In particular, repeated observations on the same individual are not allowed. You should not use ordinary regression to make inferences about the growth of a single child over time, for example. Signs of dependence in the residual plot are a bit subtle, so we usually rely on common sense.

■ **The standard deviation of the responses is the same for all values of x.** Look at the scatter of the residuals above and below the "residual = 0" line in the residual plot. The scatter should be roughly the same from one end to the other. You will sometimes find that, as the response y gets larger, so does the scatter of the residuals. Rather than remaining fixed, the standard deviation σ about the line changes with x as the mean response changes with x. There is no fixed σ for s to estimate. You cannot trust the results of inference when this happens.

You will always see some irregularity when you look for Normality and fixed standard deviation in the residuals, especially when you have few observations. Don't overreact to minor violations of the conditions. Like other t procedures, inference for regression is (with one exception) not very sensitive to lack of Normality, especially when we have many observations. Do beware of influential observations, which can greatly affect the results of inference.

The exception is the prediction interval for a single response y. This interval relies on Normality of individual observations, not just on the approximate Normality of statistics like the slope a and intercept b of the least-squares line. The statistics a and b become more Normal as we take more observations. This contributes to the robustness of regression inference, but it isn't enough for the prediction interval. We will not study methods that carefully check Normality of the residuals, so *you should regard prediction intervals as rough approximations.*

EXAMPLE 24.9 Climate change chases fish north

STATE: As the climate grows warmer, we expect many animal species to move toward the poles in an attempt to maintain their preferred temperature range. Do data on fish in the North Sea confirm this expectation? Table 24.3 gives data for 25 years on mean winter temperatures at the bottom of the North Sea (degrees Celsius) and the center of the distribution of anglerfish in degrees of north latitude.[6]

ANGLERFISH

TABLE 24.3 Winter temperature (degrees Celsius) and anglerfish latitude, 1977 to 2001

YEAR	TEMP.	LATITUDE	YEAR	TEMP.	LATITUDE	YEAR	TEMP.	LATITUDE
1977	6.26	57.20	1986	6.52	57.72	1994	7.02	58.71
1978	6.26	57.96	1987	6.68	57.83	1995	7.09	58.07
1979	6.27	57.65	1988	6.76	57.87	1996	7.13	58.49
1980	6.31	57.59	1989	6.78	57.48	1997	7.15	58.28
1981	6.34	58.01	1990	6.89	58.13	1998	7.29	58.49
1982	6.32	59.06	1991	6.90	58.52	1999	7.34	58.01
1983	6.37	56.85	1992	6.93	58.48	2000	7.57	58.57
1984	6.39	56.87	1993	6.98	57.89	2001	7.65	58.90
1985	6.42	57.43						

Dave Harasti

PLAN: Regress latitude on temperature. Look for a positive linear relationship and assess its significance. Be sure to check the conditions for regression inference.

SOLVE: The scatterplot in Figure 24.9 shows a clear positive linear relationship. The solid line in the plot is the least-squares regression line of the center of the fish distribution (north latitude) on winter ocean temperature. Software shows that the slope is $b = 0.818$. That is, each degree of ocean warming moves the fish about 0.8 degree of latitude farther north. The t statistic for testing $H_0: \beta = 0$ is $t = 3.6287$ with one-sided P-value $P = 0.0007$. There is very strong evidence that the population slope is positive, $\beta > 0$.

CONCLUDE: The data give highly significant evidence that anglerfish have moved north as the ocean has grown warmer. Before relying on this conclusion, we must check the conditions for inference. ■

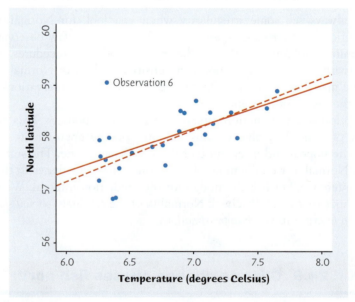

FIGURE 24.9
Scatterplot of the latitude of the center of the distribution of anglerfish in the North Sea against mean winter temperature at the bottom of the sea, for Example 24.9. The two regression lines are for the data with (solid) and without (dashed) Observation 6.

The software that did the regression calculations also finds the 25 residuals. In the same order as the observations in Example 24.9, they are

```
−0.3731    0.3869    0.0687   −0.0240    0.3714    1.4378   −0.8131
−0.8095   −0.2740   −0.0658   −0.0867   −0.1121   −0.5185    0.0415
 0.4234    0.3588   −0.2721    0.5152   −0.1821    0.2052   −0.0211
 0.0743   −0.4466   −0.0747    0.1899
```

Begin by making two graphs of the residuals. Figure 24.10 is a histogram of the residuals. Figure 24.11 is the residual plot, a plot of the residuals against the explanatory variable, sea-bottom temperature. The "residual = 0" line marks the position of the regression line.

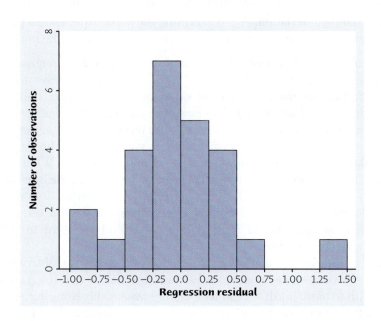

FIGURE 24.10

Histogram of the residuals from the regression of latitude on temperature in Example 24.9.

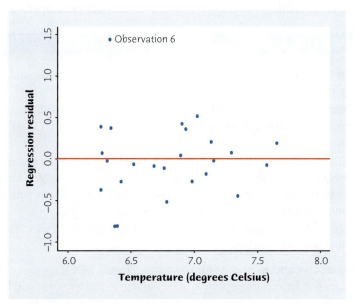

FIGURE 24.11

Residual plot for the regression of latitude on temperature in Example 24.9.

Patterns in residual plots are often easier to see if you use a wider vertical scale than your software's default plot and we suggest you do so if possible. Both graphs show that Observation 6 is a high outlier. Let's check the conditions for regression inference.

■ **Linear relationship.** The scatterplot in Figure 24.9 and the residual plot in Figure 24.11 both show a linear relationship except for the outlier.

■ **Normal residuals.** The histogram in Figure 24.10 is roughly symmetric and single-peaked. There are no important departures from Normality except for the outlier.

■ **Independent observations.** The observations were taken a year apart, so we are willing to regard them as close to independent. The residual plot shows no obvious pattern of dependence, such as runs of points all above or all below the line.

■ **Constant standard deviation.** Again excepting the outlier, the residual plot shows no unusual variation in the scatter of the residuals above and below the line as x varies.

The outlier is the only serious violation of the conditions for inference. How influential is the outlier? The dashed line in Figure 24.9 is the regression line without Observation 6. Because there are several other observations with similar values of temperature, dropping Observation 6 does not move the regression line very much. *Even though the outlier is not very influential for the regression line, it influences regression inference because of its effect on the regression standard error.* The standard error is $s = 0.4734$ with Observation 6 and $s = 0.3622$ without it. When we omit the outlier, the t statistic changes from $t = 3.6287$ to $t = 5.5599$, and the one-sided P-value changes from $P = 0.0007$ to $P < 0.00001$. Fortunately, the outlier does not affect the conclusion we drew from the data. Dropping Observation 6 makes the test for the population slope *more* significant and *increases* the percent of variation in fish location explained by ocean temperature.

One more caution about inference in this example: as usual in an observational study, the possibility of lurking variables makes us hesitant to conclude that rising temperature is *causing* anglerfish to move north. Ocean temperature was steadily rising during these years. The effect on fish latitude of any lurking variable that also increased over time—perhaps increased commercial fishing—is confounded with the effect of temperature.

APPLY YOUR KNOWLEDGE

24.13 Crying and IQ: residuals. The residuals for the study of crying and IQ appear in Example 24.3. **CRYINGRES**

(a) Make a stemplot to display the distribution of the residuals (round to the nearest whole number). Are there strong outliers or other signs of departures from Normality?

(b) Make a residual plot, residuals against crying peaks. Try a vertical scale of −60 to 60 to show patterns more clearly. Draw the "residual = 0" line. Does the residual plot show clear deviations from a linear pattern or clearly unequal spread about the line?

(c) Using the information given in Example 24.1, explain why the 38 observations are independent.

24.14 Introspection and gray matter: residuals. Figure 24.4 gives part of the Minitab output for the data on introspective ability and gray-matter volume in Exercise 24.2.

Figure 24.12 comes from another part of the output. It gives x, y, the predicted response $\hat{y}$, the residual $y - \hat{y}$, and related quantities for each of the 29 observations. Most statistical software provides similar output. Examine the conditions for regression inference one by one. This example illustrates mild violations of the conditions that did not prevent the researchers from doing inference. 🔴 GRAYMATTERRES

(a) **Linear relationship.** Your scatterplot and r^2 from Exercise 24.2 show that the relationship is roughly linear. Plot the residuals against volume. Are any deviations from a straight line apparent?

(b) **Normal variation about the line.** Make a stemplot of the residuals (round to the nearest integer, use split stems, and don't forget that -0 and 0 are separate stems). With only 29 observations, a small amount of skew is not disturbing. Minitab suggests that Observations 3 and 5 may be outliers. Does your plot confirm or refute this suggestion?

(c) **Independent observations.** The data come from 29 different subjects who were each measured separately.

(d) **Spread about the line stays the same.** Is there any evidence that the spread may be larger at one end?

```
 Session                                                    _ □ X

 Obs   Volume   Aroc    Fit   SE Fit   Residual   St Resid
  1    0.550   58.00   57.18   3.58        0.82       0.12
  2    0.580   62.00   59.81   2.71        2.19       0.30
  3    0.590   43.00   60.69   2.44      -17.69      -2.35R
  4    0.590   63.00   60.69   2.44        2.31       0.31
  5    0.590   83.00   60.69   2.44       22.31       2.97R
  6    0.610   61.00   62.44   1.95       -1.44      -0.19
  7    0.620   55.00   63.32   1.75       -8.32      -1.08
  8    0.630   57.00   64.20   1.60       -7.20      -0.93
  9    0.630   57.00   64.20   1.60       -7.20      -0.93
 10    0.630   67.00   64.20   1.60        2.80       0.36
 11    0.630   72.00   64.20   1.60        7.80       1.01
 12    0.640   62.00   65.08   1.50       -3.08      -0.40
 13    0.650   58.00   65.95   1.47       -7.95      -1.02
 14    0.650   62.00   65.95   1.47       -3.95      -0.51
 15    0.650   65.00   65.95   1.47       -0.95      -0.12
 16    0.650   70.00   65.95   1.47        4.05       0.52
 17    0.650   75.00   65.95   1.47        9.05       1.17
 18    0.660   60.00   66.83   1.51       -6.83      -0.88
 19    0.660   63.00   66.83   1.51       -3.83      -0.49
 20    0.670   71.00   67.71   1.62        3.29       0.43
 21    0.670   71.00   67.71   1.62        3.29       0.43
 22    0.670   80.00   67.71   1.62       12.29       1.59
 23    0.680   68.00   68.59   1.79       -0.59      -0.08
 24    0.690   72.00   69.46   2.00        2.54       0.33
 25    0.700   66.00   70.34   2.23       -4.34      -0.57
 26    0.700   73.00   70.34   2.23        2.66       0.35
 27    0.710   61.00   71.22   2.49      -10.22      -1.36
 28    0.720   80.00   72.10   2.77        7.90       1.07
 29    0.750   75.00   74.73   3.65        0.27       0.04

 R denotes an observation with a large standardized residual.
```

FIGURE 24.12

Residuals from Minitab for Exercise 24.14. The table gives the predicted value ("Fit") and the residual for each observation.

CHAPTER 24 SUMMARY

CHAPTER SPECIFICS

- **Least-squares regression** fits a straight line to data in order to predict a response variable y from an explanatory variable x. Inference about regression requires more conditions.

- The **conditions for regression inference** say that there is a **population regression line** $\mu_y = \alpha + \beta x$ that describes how the mean response varies as x changes. The observed response y for any x has a Normal distribution with mean given by the population regression line and with the same standard deviation σ for any value of x. Observations on y are independent.

- The **parameters to be estimated** are the intercept α and the slope β of the population regression line and also the standard deviation σ. The slope a and intercept b of the least-squares line estimate α and β. Use the **regression standard error s** to estimate σ.

- The regression standard error s has $n - 2$ **degrees of freedom.** All t procedures in regression inference have $n - 2$ degrees of freedom.

- To test **the hypothesis that the slope is zero in the population,** use the t statistic $t = b/SE_b$. This null hypothesis says that straight-line dependence on x has no value for predicting y. In practice, use software to find the slope b of the least-squares line, its standard error SE_b, and the t statistic.

- The t test for regression slope is also a test for **the hypothesis that the population correlation between x and y is zero.**

- **Confidence intervals for the slope** of the population regression line have the form $b \pm t^* SE_b$.

- **Confidence intervals for the mean response** and **prediction intervals for an individual response** when x has a given value both have the form $\hat{y} \pm t^* SE$. The standard error SE is larger for the prediction interval. Software often gives these intervals.

LINK IT

In Chapters 4 and 5 we studied scatterplots, correlation, and the least-squares regression line as methods for exploring data. In Chapter 5 we mentioned that we must exercise caution in how we interpret any relationships we observe through such exploratory analyses. We also mentioned that such interpretations rest on the assumption that the relationship is valid in some broader sense. And we promised to explore this more carefully later in this book. In this chapter we did so by considering inference for regression. Inference for regression allows us to determine whether the relationship we observe in a scatterplot is valid for some larger population. It also allows us to attach margins of error to our estimates of the slope and intercept, as well as to predictions based on the least-squares regression line.

In Chapters 4 and 5 we discussed several cautions about correlation and the least-squares regression line. These same cautions apply to inference for regression. We discussed a systematic approach using the residuals and what we know of the study design to determine if the assumptions behind inference for regression are reasonable.

This chapter considers inference for relationships between two quantitative variables. The previous chapter considered inference for relationships between two categorical variables.

In the next chapter, we consider inference for relationships between a quantitative and a categorical variable—in particular, for deciding whether the mean of a response is the same for more than two categories.

CHECK YOUR SKILLS

Florida reappraises real estate every year, so the county appraiser's Web site lists the current "fair market value" of each piece of property. Property usually sells for somewhat more than the appraised market value. Here are the appraised market values and actual selling prices (in thousands of dollars) of condominium units sold in a beachfront building in a 93-month period between 2003 and 2010:[7]

Selling price	Appraised value	Month	Selling price	Appraised value	Month
825	626	0	850	715	47
590	492	1	1100	997	54
1075	930	3	1164	953	59
890	790	9	1425	922	64
845	648	13	1865	1190	64
1100	942	14	1450	610	64
715	345	15	875	806	64
1325	1032	19	1510	1241	70
700	556	21	1375	813	70
1322	879	26	560	496	73
1900	1016	26	1050	774	79
1600	1040	28	605	470	86
980	442	34	675	545	88
940	771	37	693	690	93

Here is part of the Minitab output for regressing selling price on appraised value, along with prediction for a unit with appraised value $800,000:

```
Predictor       Coef     SE Coef        T       P
Constant        86.0       156.8     0.55   0.588
appraisal     1.2699      0.1938     6.55   0.000

S = 235.410 R-Sq = 62.3\% R-Sq(adj) = 60.8\%

Predicted Values for New Observations

New
Obs     Fit  SE Fit       95\% CI            95\% PI
  1  1101.9    44.7  (1010.0, 1193.9)  (609.4, 1594.5)
```

Exercises 24.15 to 24.21 are based on this information.

24.15 The equation of the least-squares regression line for predicting selling price from appraised value is

(a) price = 86.0 + 1.2699 × appraised value.

(b) price = 1.2699 + 86.0 × appraised value.

(c) price = 156.8 + 0.1938 × appraised value.

24.16 The slope β of the population regression line describes

(a) the average selling price in a population of units when a unit's appraised value is 0.

(b) the average increase in selling price in a population of units when appraised value increases by $1000.

(c) the exact increase in the selling price of an individual unit when its appraised value increases by $1000.

24.17 Is there significant evidence that selling price increases as appraised value increases? Minitab shows that the P-value for the test that answers this question is

(a) 0.588

(b) 0.1938

(c) less than 0.001.

24.18 The regression standard error for these data is

(a) 0.1938.

(b) 156.8

(c) 235.41.

24.19 Confidence intervals and tests for these data use the t distribution with degrees of freedom

(a) 28.

(b) 27.

(c) 26.

24.20 A 95% confidence interval for the population slope β is

(a) 1.2699 ± 0.3306.

(b) 1.2699 ± 322.3808.

(c) 1.2699 ± 0.3985.

24.21 Louisa owns a unit in this building appraised at $800,000. The Minitab output includes prediction for this appraised value. She can be 95% confident that her unit would sell for between

(a) $609,400 and $1,594,500.

(b) $1,010,000 and $1,193,900.

(c) $1,057,200 and $1,146,6900.

CHAPTER 24 EXERCISES

24.22 Genetically engineered cotton. A strain of genetically engineered cotton, know as Bt cotton, is resistant to certain insects, which results in larger yields of cotton. Farmers in northern China have increased the number of acres planted in Bt cotton. Because Bt cotton is resistant to certain pests, farmers have also reduced their use of insecticide. Scientists in China were interested in the long-term effects of Bt cotton cultivation and decreased insecticide use on insect populations that are not affected by Bt cotton. One such insect is the mirid bug. Scientists measured the number of mirid bugs per 100 plants and the proportion of Bt cotton planted at 38 locations in northern China for the 12-year period from 1997 to 2008. The scientists reported a regression analysis as follows:[8]

number of mirid bugs per 100 plants

$$= 0.54 + 6.81 \times \text{Bt cotton planting proportion}$$
$$r^2 = 0.90 \qquad P < 0.0001$$

(a) What does the slope $b = 6.81$ say about the relation between Bt cotton planting proportion and number of mirid bugs per 100 plants?

(b) What does $r^2 = 0.90$ add to the information given by the equation of the least-squares line?

(c) What null and alternative hypotheses do you think the P-value refers to? What does this P-value tell you?

(d) Does the large value of r^2 and the small P-value indicate that increasing the proportion of acres planted in Bt cotton causes an increase in mirid bugs?

Exercise 7.48 (page 165) gives data from a study of the "gate velocity" of molten metal that experienced foundry workers choose based on the thickness of the aluminum piston being cast. Gate velocity is measured in feet per second, and the piston wall thickness is in inches. A scatterplot (you need not make one) shows a moderately strong positive linear relationship. Figure 24.13 displays part of the Minitab regression output. Exercises 24.23 to 24.25 analyze these data.

FIGURE 24.13

Minitab output for the regression of gate velocity on piston thickness in casting aluminum parts, for Exercises 24.23 to 24.25.

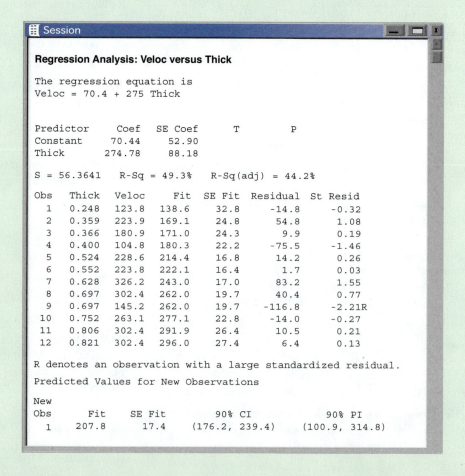

Regression Analysis: Veloc versus Thick

The regression equation is
Veloc = 70.4 + 275 Thick

Predictor	Coef	SE Coef	T	P
Constant	70.44	52.90		
Thick	274.78	88.18		

S = 56.3641   R-Sq = 49.3%   R-Sq(adj) = 44.2%

Obs	Thick	Veloc	Fit	SE Fit	Residual	St Resid
1	0.248	123.8	138.6	32.8	-14.8	-0.32
2	0.359	223.9	169.1	24.8	54.8	1.08
3	0.366	180.9	171.0	24.3	9.9	0.19
4	0.400	104.8	180.3	22.2	-75.5	-1.46
5	0.524	228.6	214.4	16.8	14.2	0.26
6	0.552	223.8	222.1	16.4	1.7	0.03
7	0.628	326.2	243.0	17.0	83.2	1.55
8	0.697	302.4	262.0	19.7	40.4	0.77
9	0.697	145.2	262.0	19.7	-116.8	-2.21R
10	0.752	263.1	277.1	22.8	-14.0	-0.27
11	0.806	302.4	291.9	26.4	10.5	0.21
12	0.821	302.4	296.0	27.4	6.4	0.13

R denotes an observation with a large standardized residual.

Predicted Values for New Observations

New Obs	Fit	SE Fit	90% CI	90% PI
1	207.8	17.4	(176.2, 239.4)	(100.9, 314.8)

24.23 Casting aluminum: is there a relationship? Figure 24.13 leaves out the t statistics and their P-values. Based on the information in the output, test the hypothesis that there is no straight-line relationship between thickness and gate velocity. State hypotheses, give a test statistic and its approximate P-value, and state your conclusion.

24.24 Casting aluminum: intervals. The output in Figure 24.13 includes prediction for piston wall thickness $x = 0.5$ inch. Use the output to give 90% intervals for

  (a) the slope of the population regression line of gate velocity on piston thickness.

  (b) the average gate velocity for a type of piston with thickness 0.5 inch.

24.25 Casting aluminum: residuals. The output in Figure 24.13 includes a table of the x and y variables, the fitted values $\hat{y}$ for each x, the residuals, and some related quantities. ALUMINUMRES

  (a) Plot the residuals against thickness (the explanatory variable). Use vertical scale -200 to 200 so that the pattern is clearer. Add the "residual $= 0$" line. Does your plot show a systematically nonlinear relationship? Does it show systematic change in the spread about the regression line?

  (b) Make a histogram of the residuals. Minitab identifies the residual for Observation 9 as a suspected outlier. Does your histogram agree?

  (c) Redoing the regression without Observation 9 gives regression standard error $s = 42.4725$ and predicted mean velocity 216 feet per second (90% confidence interval 191.4 to 240.6) for piston walls 0.5 inch thick. Compare these values with those in Figure 24.13. Is Observation 9 influential for inference?

Table 4.1 (page 96) gives 33 years' worth of data on boats registered in Florida and manatees killed by boats. Figure 4.2 (page 96) shows a strong linear relationship. The correlation is $r = 0.951$. Figure 24.14 (page 500) shows part of the Minitab regression output. Exercises 24.26 to 24.28 analyze the manatee data.

24.26 Manatees: conditions for inference. We know that there is a strong linear relationship. Let's check the other conditions for inference. Figure 24.14 includes a table of the two variables, the predicted values $\hat{y}$ for each x in the data, the residuals, and related quantities. MANATEESRES

  (a) Round the residuals to the nearest whole number and make a stemplot. The distribution is single-peaked and symmetric and appears close to Normal.

  (b) Make a residual plot, residuals against boats registered. Use a vertical scale from -25 to 25 to show the pattern more clearly. Add the "residual $= 0$" line. There is no clearly nonlinear pattern. The spread about the line may be a bit greater for larger values of the explanatory variable, but the effect is not large.

  (c) It is reasonable to regard the number of manatees killed by boats in successive years as independent. The number of boats grew over time. Someone says that pollution also grew over time and may explain the increase in manatee deaths. How would you respond to this idea?

24.27 Manatees: do more boats bring more kills? The output in Figure 24.14 omits the t statistics and their P-values. Based on the information in the output, is there good evidence that the number of manatees killed increases as the number of boats registered increases? State hypotheses and give a test statistic and its approximate P-value. What do you conclude?

24.28 Manatees: estimation. The output in Figure 24.14 includes prediction of the number of manatees killed when there are 1,050,000 boats registered in Florida. Give 95% intervals for

  (a) the increase in the number of manatees killed for each additional 1000 boats registered.

  (b) the number of manatees that will be killed next year if there are 1,050,000 boats registered next year.

24.29 Fidgeting keeps you slim: inference. Our first example of regression (Example 5.1, page 112) presented data showing that people who increased their nonexercise activity (NEA) when they were deliberately overfed gained less fat than other people. Use software to add formal inference to the data analysis for these data. FATGAIN

  (a) Based on 16 subjects, the correlation between NEA increase and fat gain was $r = -0.7786$. Is this significant evidence that people with higher NEA increase gain less fat? (Report a t statistic from regression output and give the one-sided P-value.)

  (b) The slope of the least-squares regression line was $b = -0.00344$, so that fat gain decreased by 0.00344 kilogram for each added calorie of NEA. Give a 90% confidence interval for the slope of the population regression line. This rate of change is the most important parameter to be estimated.

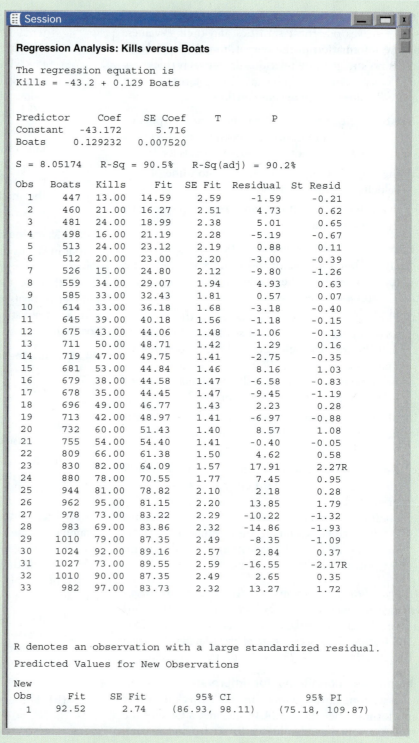

Minitab output for the regression of number of manatees killed by boats on the number of boats (in thousands) registered in Florida, for Exercises 24.26 to 24.28.

(c) Sam's NEA increases by 400 calories. His predicted fat gain is 2.13 kilograms. Give a 95% interval for predicting Sam's fat gain.

24.30 Predicting tropical storms. Exercise 5.44 (page 136) gives data on William Gray's predictions of the number of named tropical storms in Atlantic hurricane seasons from 1984 to 2010. Use these data for regression inference as follows. 🐌 STORMS2

(a) Does Professor Gray do better than random guessing? That is, is there a significantly positive correlation between his forecasts and the actual number of storms? (Report a t statistic from regression output and give the one-sided P-value.)

(b) Give a 95% confidence interval for the mean number of storms in years when Professor Gray forecasts 16 storms.

24.31 Coral growth. Sea surface temperatures across much of the tropics have been increasing since the mid-1970s. At the same time, the growth of coral has been decreasing. Scientists examined data on mean sea surface temperatures (SST) in degrees Celsius and mean coral growth in millimeters (mm) per year over a several-year period at locations in the Red Sea. Here are the data:[9] 🐌 CORAL

SST	29.68	29.87	30.16	30.22	30.48	30.65	30.90
Growth	2.63	2.58	2.60	2.48	2.26	2.38	2.26

(a) Do the data indicate that coral growth decreases linearly as SST increases? Is this change statistically significant?

(b) Use the data to predict with 95% confidence the mean coral growth (mm per year) when SST is 30.0 degrees Celsius.

24.32 Predicting tropical storms: residuals. Make a stemplot of the residuals (round to the nearest tenth) from your regression in Exercise 24.30. Explain why your plot suggests that we should not use these data to get a prediction interval for the number of storms in a single year. 🐌 STORMS2

24.33 Coral growth: residuals. Do the data in Exercise 24.31 on mean sea surface temperatures and coral growth in the Red Sea satisfy the conditions for regression inference? To examine this, here are the residuals: 🐌 CORALRES

SST	29.68	29.87	30.16	30.22	30.48	30.65	30.90
Residual	−0.067	−0.060	0.128	0.066	0.025	−0.024	−0.068

(a) **Linear relationship.** A plot of the residuals against the explanatory variable x magnifies the deviations from the least-squares line. Does the plot show any systematic deviation from a roughly linear pattern?

(b) **Normal variation about the line.** Make a histogram of the residuals. With only 7 observations, no clear shape emerges. Do strong skewness or outliers suggest lack of Normality?

(c) **Independent observations.** Why are the 7 observations independent?

(d) **Spread about the line stays the same.** Does your plot in (a) show any systematic change in spread as x changes?

24.34 Our brains don't like losses. Exercise 4.24 (page 105) describes an experiment that showed a linear relationship between how sensitive people are to monetary losses ("behavioral loss aversion") and activity in one part of their brains ("neural loss aversion"). 🐌 LOSSES

(a) Make a scatterplot with neural loss aversion as x and behavioral loss aversion as y. One point is a high outlier in both the x and y directions. In Exercise 5.32 (page 132) you found that this outlier is not influential for the least-squares line.

(b) The research report says that $r = 0.85$ and that the test for regression slope has $P < 0.001$. Verify these results, using all the observations.

(c) The report recognizes the outlier and says, "However, this regression also remained highly significant ($P = 0.004$) when the extreme data point (top right corner) was removed from the analysis." Repeat your analysis omitting the outlier. Show that the outlier influences regression inference by comparing the t statistic for testing slope with and without the outlier. Then verify the report's claim about the P-value of this test.

24.35 Time at the table. Does how long young children remain at the lunch table help predict how much they eat? Here are data on 20 toddlers observed over several months at a nursery school.[10] "Time" is the average number of minutes a child spent at the table when lunch was served. "Calories" is the average number of calories the child consumed during lunch, calculated from careful observation of what the child ate each day. 🐌 TIMEATTABLE

Time	21.4	30.8	37.7	33.5	32.8	39.5	22.8	34.1	33.9	43.8
Calories	472	498	465	456	423	437	508	431	479	454
Time	42.4	43.1	29.2	31.3	28.6	32.9	30.6	35.1	33.0	43.7
Calories	450	410	504	437	489	436	480	439	444	408

(a) Make a scatterplot. Find the correlation and the least-squares regression line. (Be sure to save the regression residuals.) Based on your work, describe the direction, form, and strength of the relationship.

(b) Check the conditions for regression inference. Parts (a) to (d) of Exercise 24.33 provide a handy outline. Use vertical limits −100 to 100 in your plot of the residuals against time to help you see the pattern. What do you conclude?

(c) Is there significant evidence that more time at the table is associated with more calories consumed? Give a 95% confidence interval to estimate how rapidly calories consumed changes as time at the table increases.

24.36 DNA on the ocean floor. We think of DNA as the stuff that stores the genetic code. It turns out that DNA occurs, mainly outside living cells, on the ocean floor. It is important in nourishing seafloor life. Scientists think that this DNA comes from organic matter that settles to the bottom from the top layers of the ocean. "Phytopigments," which come mainly from algae, are a measure of the amount of organic matter that has settled to the bottom. The data file on the text CD and Web site contains data on concentrations of DNA and phytopigments (both in grams per square meter) in 116 ocean locations around the world.[11] Look first at DNA alone. Describe the distribution of DNA concentration and give a confidence interval for the mean concentration. Be sure to explain why your confidence interval is trustworthy in the light of the shape of the distribution. The data show surprisingly high DNA concentration, and this by itself was an important finding. 🔴 **DNA**

24.37 Time at the table: prediction. Rachel attends the nursery school of Exercise 24.35. Over several months, Rachel averages 40 minutes at the lunch table. Give a 95% interval to predict Rachel's average calorie consumption at lunch. 🔴 **TIMEATTABLE**

*Exercises 24.38 to 24.42 ask practical questions involving regression inference without step-by-step instructions. Do complete regression analyses, using the **Plan, Solve,** and **Conclude** steps of the four-step process to organize your answers. Follow the model*

of Example 24.9 and the following discussion, and check the conditions as part of the **Solve** step.

24.38 DNA on the ocean floor. Another conclusion of the study introduced in Exercise 24.36 was that organic matter settling down from the top layers of the ocean is the main source of DNA on the seafloor. An important piece of evidence is the relationship between DNA and phytopigments. Do the data in the file on the text CD and Web site give good reason to think that phytopigment concentration helps explain DNA concentration? (Try vertical limits −1 to 1 to make the pattern of your residual plot clearer.)

24.39 Squirrels and their food supply. The introduction to Exercises 7.24 to 7.26 (page 158–159) gives data on the abundance of the pine cones that red squirrels feed on and the mean number of offspring per female squirrel over 16 years. The strength of the relationship is remarkable because females produce young before the food is available. How significant is the evidence that more cones lead to more offspring? (Use a vertical scale from −2 to 2 in your residual plot to show the pattern more clearly.) 🔴 **SQUIRRELS**

24.40 A big-toe problem. Table 7.4 (page 164) and Exercises 7.44 and 7.46 describe the relationship between two deformities of the feet in young patients. Metatarsus adductus (MA) may help predict the severity of hallux abducto valgus (HAV). The paper that reports this study says, "Linear regression analysis, using the hallux abducto angle as the response variable, demonstrated a significant correlation between the metatarsus adductus and hallux abducto angles."[12] Do a suitable analysis to verify this finding. The study authors note that the scatterplot suggests that the variation in y may change as x changes, so they offer a more elaborate analysis as well. 🔴 **DEFORMITY**

24.41 Beavers and beetles. Exercise 5.42 (page 135) describes a study that found that the number of stumps from trees felled by beavers predicts the abundance of beetle larvae. Is there good evidence that more beetle larvae clusters are present when beavers have left more tree stumps? Estimate how many more clusters accompany each additional stump, with 95% confidence. 🔴 **BEAVERS**

24.42 Sulfur, the ocean, and the sun. Sulfur in the atmosphere affects climate by influencing formation of clouds. The main natural source of sulfur is dimethyl sulfide (DMS) produced by small organisms in the upper layers of the oceans. DMS production is in turn influenced by the amount of energy the upper ocean receives from sunlight. Exercise 4.25 (page 106) gives monthly data on solar radiation dose (SRD, in watts per square meter) and surface DMS concentration (in nanomolars) for a region in the Mediterranean. Do the data provide convincing evidence that DMS increases as SRD increases? We also want to estimate the rate of increase, with 90% confidence. SULFUR

24.43 Tests for the intercept (optional).

Figure 24.7 (page 488) gives Minitab output for the regression of blood alcohol content (BAC) on number of beers consumed. The t test for the hypothesis that the population regression line has slope $\beta = 0$ has $P < 0.001$. The data show a positive linear relationship between BAC and beers. We might expect the intercept α of the population regression line to be 0, because no beers ($x = 0$) should produce no alcohol in the blood ($y = 0$). To test

$$H_0: \alpha = 0$$
$$H_a: \alpha \neq 0$$

we use a t statistic formed by dividing the least-squares intercept a by its standard error SE_a. Locate this statistic in the output of Figure 24.7 and verify that it is in fact a divided by its standard error. What is the P-value? Do the data suggest that the intercept is not 0?

24.44 Confidence intervals for the intercept (optional).

The output in Figure 24.7 (page 488) allows you to calculate confidence intervals for both the slope β and the intercept α of the population regression line of BAC on beers in the population of all students. Confidence intervals for the intercept α have the familiar form $a \pm t^* SE_a$ with degrees of freedom $n - 2$. What is the 95% confidence interval for the intercept? Does it contain 0, the value we might guess for α?

EXPLORING THE WEB

24.45 Predicting batting averages.

As you did in Exercise 5.48 (page 137), go to www.mlb.com/ and find the batting averages for a diverse set of 30 players for both the 2009 and 2010 seasons. You can click on the "Stats" tab to find the results for the current season as well as historical data. You should select only players who played in at least 50 games both seasons. Find the least-squares regression line for predicting batting average in 2010 from that in 2009 based on your sample of 30 players. In 2009, the major league leader in batting was Joe Mauer, who had a batting average of .365. Find a 95% prediction interval for the 2010 batting average of someone who hit .365 in 2009. How does this prediction compare with Joe Mauer's 2010 batting average?

24.46 Olympic medal counts.

In Exercise 4.39 (page 110) you made a scatterplot of the Winter Olympics medal counts for 2002 and 2006. We investigate these medal counts further. Go the *Chance News* Web site at www.causeweb.org/wiki/chance/index.php/Chance_News_61#Predicting_medal_counts and read the article "Predicting Medal Counts." Next, search the Web (as you did in Chapter 4) and locate the Winter Olympics medal counts for 2002 and 2006 (we found Winter Olympics medal counts on Wikipedia). Find the equation of the least-squares regression line for predicting the 2006 medal counts from the 2002 counts. Compute 95% confidence intervals for the slope and intercept of your regression line. Are your results consistent with the comment in the *Chance News* article that states "we would have done well simply predicting that the Vancouver totals would match the Torino totals"?

Roff Nussbaumer Photography/Alamy

One-Way Analysis of Variance: Comparing Several Means

The two-sample *t* procedures of Chapter 19 compare the means of two
populations or the mean responses to two treatments in an experiment.
Of course, studies don't always compare just two groups. We need a
method for comparing any number of means.

EXAMPLE 25.1 Comparing tropical flowers

STATE: Ethan Temeles and W. John Kress of Amherst College studied the
relationship between varieties of the tropical flower *Heliconia* and the hummingbirds that fertilize the flowers.[1] The researchers conjecture that flower
varieties fertilized by different hummingbird species should have distinct distributions of length.

Table 25.1 gives length measurements (in millimeters) for samples of
three varieties of *Heliconia,* each fertilized by a different species of hummingbird. Do the three varieties display distinct distributions of length? In particular, are the mean lengths of their flowers different?

FLOWERLENGTH

505

TABLE 25.1 Flower lengths (millimeters) for three *Heliconia* varieties

H. BIHAI

47.12	46.75	46.81	47.12	46.67	47.43	46.44	46.64
48.07	48.34	48.15	50.26	50.12	46.34	46.94	48.36

H. CARIBAEA RED

41.90	42.01	41.93	43.09	41.47	41.69	39.78	40.57
39.63	42.18	40.66	37.87	39.16	37.40	38.20	38.07
38.10	37.97	38.79	38.23	38.87	37.78	38.01	

H. CARIBAEA YELLOW

36.78	37.02	36.52	36.11	36.03	35.45	38.13	37.10
35.17	36.82	36.66	35.68	36.03	34.57	34.63	

PLAN: Use graphs and numerical descriptions to describe and compare the three distributions of flower length. Finally, ask whether the differences among the mean lengths of the three varieties are *statistically significant*.

SOLVE (first steps): We first met these data in Chapter 2 (page 56), where we compared the distributions. Figure 25.1 repeats side-by-side stemplots from Chapter 2. The lengths have been rounded to the nearest tenth of a millimeter. Here are the summary measures we will use in further analysis:

Sample	Variety	Sample size	Mean length	Standard deviation
1	*bihai*	16	47.60	1.213
2	red	23	39.71	1.799
3	yellow	15	36.18	0.975

FIGURE 25.1

Side-by-side stemplots comparing the lengths in millimeters of samples of flowers from three varieties of *Heliconia*, from Table 25.1.

```
        bihai              red               yellow
   34 |              34 |              34 | 6 6
   35 |              35 |              35 | 2 5 7
   36 |              36 |              36 | 0 0 1 5 7 8 8
   37 |              37 | 4 8 9        37 | 0 1
   38 |              38 | 0 0 1 1 2 2 8 9   38 | 1
   39 |              39 | 2 6 8        39 |
   40 |              40 | 6 7          40 |
   41 |              41 | 5 7 9 9      41 |
   42 |              42 | 0 2          42 |
   43 |              43 | 1            43 |
   44 |              44 |              44 |
   45 |              45 |              45 |
   46 | 3 4 6 7 8 8 9  46 |             46 |
   47 | 1 1 4         47 |             47 |
   48 | 1 2 3 4       48 |             48 |
   49 |              49 |              49 |
   50 | 1 3          50 |             50 |
```

CONCLUDE (first steps): The three varieties differ so much in flower length that there is little overlap among them. In particular, the flowers of *bihai* are longer than either red or yellow. The mean lengths are 47.6 mm for *H. bihai,* 39.7 mm for *H. caribaea* red, and 36.2 mm for *H. caribaea* yellow. Are these observed differences in sample means statistically significant? We must develop a test for comparing more than two population means. ■

THE ANALYSIS OF VARIANCE *F* TEST

Call the mean lengths for the three populations of flowers μ_1 for *bihai*, μ_2 for red, and μ_3 for yellow. The subscript reminds us which group a parameter or statistic describes. To compare these three population means, we might use the two-sample *t* test three times:

■ Test H_0: $\mu_1 = \mu_2$ to see if the mean length for *bihai* differs from the mean for red.

■ Test H_0: $\mu_1 = \mu_3$ to see if *bihai* differs from yellow.

■ Test H_0: $\mu_2 = \mu_3$ to see if red differs from yellow.

If we do three tests, we get three *P*-values, one for each test alone. That doesn't tell us how likely it is that *three* sample means are spread apart as far as these are. It may be that $\bar{x}_1 = 47.60$ and $\bar{x}_3 = 36.18$ are significantly different if we look at just two groups but not significantly different if we know that they are the largest and the smallest means in three groups. As we look at more groups, we expect the gap between the largest and smallest sample mean to get larger. (Think of comparing the tallest and shortest person in larger and larger groups of people.) *We can't safely compare many means by doing tests or confidence intervals for two means at a time.* Instead, we will use a single test to see if there is good evidence of *any* differences among the means that we want to compare.

The basic *conditions for inference* (more detail later) are that we have random samples from the three populations and that flower lengths are Normally distributed in each population and have the same standard deviation σ in each population. The three population means μ_1, μ_2, μ_3 and the common population standard deviation σ are all unknown.

We want to test the null hypothesis that there are *no differences* among the mean lengths for the three populations of flowers:

$$H_0: \mu_1 = \mu_2 = \mu_3$$

The alternative hypothesis is that there is *some difference*. That is, not all three population means are equal:

$$H_a: \text{not all of } \mu_1, \mu_2, \text{ and } \mu_3 \text{ are equal}$$

The alternative hypothesis is no longer one-sided or two-sided. It is "many-sided," because it allows any relationship other than "all three equal." For example, H_a includes the case in which $\mu_2 = \mu_3$ but μ_1 has a different value. The test of H_0 against H_a is called the **analysis of variance *F* test.** Analysis of variance is usually abbreviated as ANOVA. The ANOVA *F* test is almost always carried out by software that reports the test statistic and its *P*-value.

analysis of variance F test

EXAMPLE 25.2 Comparing tropical flowers: ANOVA

SOLVE (inference): Software tells us that for the flower length data in Table 25.1, the test statistic is $F = 259.12$ with P-value $P < 0.0001$ (see Figure 25.3 on page 510). There is very strong evidence that the three varieties of flowers do not all have the same mean length.

The F test does not say *which* of the three means are significantly different. It appears from our preliminary data analysis that *bihai* flowers are distinctly longer than either red or yellow. Red and yellow are closer together, but the red flowers tend to be longer.

CONCLUDE: There is strong evidence ($P < 0.0001$) that the population means are not all equal. The most important difference among the means is that the *bihai* variety has longer flowers than the red and yellow varieties. ■

Example 25.2 illustrates our approach to comparing means. The ANOVA F test (done by software) assesses the evidence for *some* difference among the population means. We rely on examination of the data to show what specific differences are present and whether they are large enough to be interesting.

APPLY YOUR KNOWLEDGE

25.1 Angry women, sad men. What are the relationships among the portrayal of anger or sadness, gender, and the degree of status conferred? Sixty-eight subjects were randomly assigned to view a videotaped interview in which either a male or a female professional described feeling either anger or sadness. The people being interviewed (we'll call them the "targets") wore professional attire and were ostensibly being interviewed for a job. The targets described an incident in which they and a colleague lost an account and, when asked by the interviewer how it made them feel, responded either that the incident made them feel angry or that it made them feel sad. The subjects were divided into four groups; each group evaluated one of the following four types of interviews:[2]

	Male target	Female target
Expressed anger	Group A	Group C
Expressed sadness	Group B	Group D

After watching the interview, subjects evaluated the target on a composite measure of status conferral that included items assessing how much status, power, and independence the target deserved in his or her future job. The measure of status ranged from 1 = none to 11 = a great deal.

(a) What are the null and alternative hypotheses for the ANOVA F test? Be sure to explain what means the test compares.

(b) Figure 25.2 is a graph displaying the means for the four groups. What is the approximate size of the mean difference in status conferred on angry men versus angry women? Which of these two groups has the higher mean status?

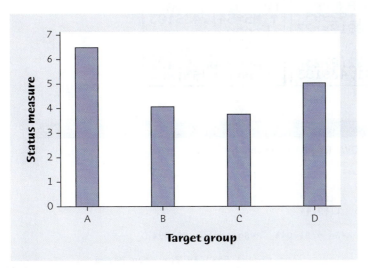

FIGURE 25.2

Bar graph comparing the mean status conferred for the four types of targets, for Exercise 25.1.

25.2 Road rage. "The phenomenon of road rage has been frequently discussed but infrequently examined." So begins a report based on interviews with 1382 randomly selected drivers.[3] The respondents' answers to interview questions produced scores on an "angry/threatening driving scale" with values between 0 and 19. What driver characteristics go with road rage? There were no significant differences among races or levels of education. What about the effect of the driver's age? Here are the mean responses for three age groups:

<30 yr	30–55 yr	>55 yr
2.22	1.33	0.66

The report says that $F = 34.96$, with $P < 0.01$.

(a) What are the null and alternative hypotheses for the ANOVA F test? Be sure to explain what means the test compares.

(b) Based on the sample means and the F test, what do you conclude?

USING TECHNOLOGY

Any technology used for statistics should perform analysis of variance. Figure 25.3 displays ANOVA output for the data of Table 25.1 from a graphing calculator, two statistical programs, and a spreadsheet program.

Minitab and Excel give the sizes of the three samples and their means. These agree with those in Example 25.1. Minitab also gives the standard deviations and Excel gives

FIGURE 25.3

ANOVA for the flower length data: output from a graphing calculator, two statistical programs, and a spreadsheet program.

Texas Instruments Graphing Calculator

```
One-way ANOVA        One-way ANOVA
 F=259.1192995        ↑ MS=541.436183
 p=1.918818ᴇ-27       Error
 Factor                 df=51
   df=2                 SS=106.565761
   SS=1082.87237        MS=2.08952472
↓ MS=541.436183         Sxp=1.44551884
```

Minitab

```
┌─ Session ───────────────────────────────── _ □ X ─┐
│                                                     │
│  One-way ANOVA: length versus variety               │
│                                                     │
│  Source   DF      SS      MS      F      P          │
│  Variety    2  1082.87  541.44  259.12  0.000       │
│  Error     51   106.57    2.09                      │
│  Total     53  1189.44                              │
│                                                     │
│  S = 1.446  R-Sq = 91.04%  R-Sq(adj) = 90.69%       │
│                                                     │
│                       Individual 95% CIs For Mean Based on │
│                                Pooled StDev         │
│  Level   N   Mean   StDev  --------+--------+--------+--------+  │
│  Bihai   16  47.598  1.213                          (-*-)     │
│  Red     23  39.711  1.799              (*-)          │
│  Yellow  15  36.180  0.975  (-*--)                   │
│                            --------+--------+--------+--------+  │
│                              38.5     42.0     45.5     49.0    │
│                                                     │
│  Pooled StDev = 1.446                               │
│                                                     │
└─────────────────────────────────────────────────────┘
```

Excel

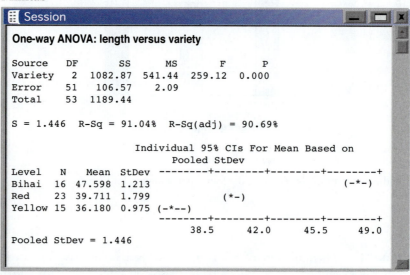

Microsoft Excel - ta25-01.dat

	A	B	C	D	E	F	G
1	Anova: Single Factor						
2							
3	SUMMARY						
4	*Groups*	*Count*	*Sum*	*Average*	*Variance*		
5	bihai	16	761.56	47.5975	1.471073		
6	red	23	913.36	39.7113	3.235548		
7	yellow	15	542.7	36.18	0.951257		
8							
9							
10	v						
11	*Source of variation*	*SS*	*df*	*MS*	*F*	*P-value*	*F crit*
12	Between Groups	1082.872	2	541.4362	259.1193	1.92E-27	3.178799
13	Within Groups	106.5658	51	2.089525			
14							
15	Total	1189.438	53				

Sheet4 / ta25-01 /

CrunchIt

Results - One-Way ANOVA

Export ▾

Source	Sum of Squares	df	Mean Square	F-value	P-value
Variety	1083	2	541.4	259.1	<0.0001
Error	106.6	51	2.090		
Total	1189	53			

the variances. All four outputs report the F test statistic, $F = 259.1$, and its P-value. Minitab sensibly reports the P-value as 0 to three decimal places, while CrunchIt! reports that $P < 0.0001$. This is all we need to know about the P-value in practice. Excel and the graphing calculator offer the specific value 1.92×10^{-27}. (This would be correct if the population distributions were exactly Normal. In practice, read such values simply as "P is very small.") There is very strong evidence that the three varieties of flowers do not all have the same mean length.

All four outputs report degrees of freedom (df), sums of squares (SS), and mean squares (MS). We don't need this information now. Minitab also gives confidence intervals for all three means that help us see which means differ and by how much. None of the intervals overlap, and *bihai* is much above the other two. These are 95% confidence intervals for each mean separately. We are *not* 95% confident that *all three* intervals cover the three means.

APPLY YOUR KNOWLEDGE

25.3 Logging in the rain forest. How does logging in a tropical rain forest affect the forest in later years? Researchers compared forest plots in Borneo that had never been logged (Group 1) with similar plots nearby that had been logged 1 year earlier (Group 2) and 8 years earlier (Group 3). The authors explain why we can consider the plots to be randomly selected. The data appear in Table 25.2. The variable

TABLE 25.2 Data from a study of logging in Borneo

GROUP	TREES	SPECIES	RICHNESS	GROUP	TREES	SPECIES	RICHNESS
1	27	22	0.81481	2	18	15	0.83333
1	22	18	0.81818	2	17	15	0.88235
1	29	22	0.75862	2	14	12	0.85714
1	21	20	0.95238	2	14	13	0.92857
1	19	15	0.78947	2	2	2	1.00000
1	33	21	0.63636	2	17	15	0.88235
1	16	13	0.81250	2	19	8	0.42105
1	20	13	0.65000	3	18	17	0.94444
1	24	19	0.79167	3	4	4	1.00000
1	27	13	0.48148	3	22	18	0.81818
1	28	19	0.67857	3	15	14	0.93333
1	19	15	0.78947	3	18	18	1.00000
2	12	11	0.91667	3	19	15	0.78947
2	12	11	0.91667	3	22	15	0.68182
2	15	14	0.93333	3	12	10	0.83333
2	9	7	0.77778	3	12	12	1.00000
2	20	18	0.90000				

Trees is the count of trees in a plot; Species is the count of tree species in a plot. The variable Richness is the number of species divided by the number of individual trees.[4]   **BORNEOLOGGING**

(a) Make side-by-side stemplots of Trees for the three groups. Use stems 0, 1, 2, and 3 and split the stems. What effects of logging are visible?

(b) Figure 25.4 shows Excel ANOVA output for Trees. What do the group means show about the effects of logging?

(c) What are the ANOVA F statistic and its P-value? What hypotheses does F test? What conclusions about the effects of logging on number of trees do the data lead to?

25.4 Political views and age. The University of Chicago's General Social Survey (GSS) is the nation's most important social science sample survey. The GSS asked a random sample of adults in 2008 both their age and where they placed themselves on the political spectrum from extremely liberal to extremely conservative. Is there a relationship between age and place on the political spectrum? The political spectrum categories in the original survey included slightly liberal, liberal, and extremely liberal, but these have been combined into the single category liberal, and similarly with conservative.[5]

(a) Figure 25.5 (on page 513) gives the Minitab ANOVA output for these data. What do the mean ages say about the relationship between age and political views?

(b) What are the ANOVA F statistic and its P-value? What hypotheses does F test? Briefly describe the conclusions you draw from these data.

Microsoft Excel Book 1

	A	B	C	D	E	F	G
1	Anova: Single Factor						
2							
3	SUMMARY						
4	*Groups*	*Count*	*Sum*	*Average*	*Variance*		
5	Group 1	12	285	23.75	25.6591		
6	Group 2	12	169	14.0833	24.8106		
7	Group 3	9	142	15.7778	33.1944		
8							
9							
10	ANOVA						
11	*Source of variation*	*SS*	*df*	*MS*	*F*	*P-value*	*F crit*
12	Between Groups	625.1566	2	312.57828	11.4257	0.000205	3.31583
13	Within Groups	820.7222	30	27.3574			
14							
15	Total	1445.879	32				

Sheet4 / Sheet1 / Sheet2 / Sheet3 /

FIGURE 25.4

Excel output for analysis of variance on the number of trees in forest plots, for Exercise 25.3.

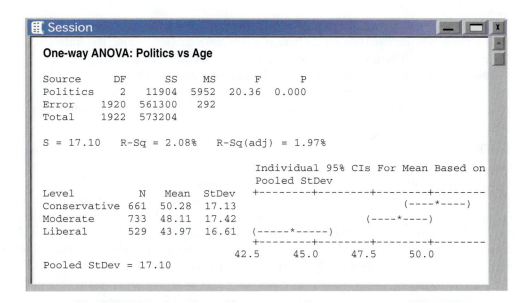

FIGURE 25.5

Minitab output for the data on respondents' ages for three different political viewpoints, for Exercise 25.4.

THE IDEA OF ANALYSIS OF VARIANCE

The details of calculating ANOVA are a bit daunting. The main idea of ANOVA is much more important. Here it is: when we ask if a set of sample means gives evidence for differences among the population means, what matters is not how far apart the sample means are but how far apart they are *relative to the variability of individual observations*.

Look at the two sets of boxplots in Figure 25.6. For simplicity, these distributions are all symmetric, so that the mean and median are the same. The center line in each boxplot is therefore the sample mean. Both sets of boxplots compare three samples with the same three means. Could differences this large easily arise just due to chance, or are they statistically significant?

■ The boxplots in Figure 25.6(a) have tall boxes, which indicates lots of variation among the individuals in each group. With this much variation among individuals, we would not be surprised if another set of samples gave quite different sample means. The observed differences among the sample means could easily happen just by chance.

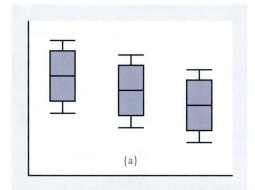

(a)

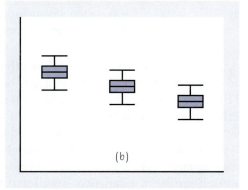

(b)

FIGURE 25.6

Boxplots for two sets of three samples each. The sample means are the same in (a) and (b). Analysis of variance will find a more significant difference among the means in (b) because there is less variation among the individuals within those samples.

■ The boxplots in Figure 25.6(b) have the same centers as those in Figure 25.6(a), but the boxes are much shorter. There is much less variation among the individuals in each group. It is unlikely that any sample from the first group would have a mean as small as the mean of the second group. Because means as far apart as those observed would rarely arise just by chance in repeated sampling, they are good evidence of real differences among the means of the three populations we are sampling from.

This comparison of the two parts of Figure 25.6 is too simple in one way. It ignores the effect of the sample sizes, an effect that boxplots do not show. *Small differences among sample means can be significant if the samples are large. Large differences among sample means can fail to be significant if the samples are small.* All we can be sure of is that for the same sample size, Figure 25.6(b) will give a much smaller *P*-value than Figure 25.6(a). Despite this qualification, the big idea remains: if sample means are far apart relative to the variation among individuals in the same groups, that's evidence that something other than chance is at work.

> ### THE ANALYSIS OF VARIANCE IDEA
>
> **Analysis of variance** compares the variation due to specific sources with the variation among individuals who should be similar. In particular, ANOVA tests whether several populations have the same mean by comparing how far apart the sample means are with how much variation there is within the samples.

It is one of the oddities of statistical language that methods for comparing means are named after the variance. The reason is that the test works by comparing two kinds of variation. Analysis of variance is a general method for studying sources of variation in responses. Comparing several means is the simplest form of ANOVA, called **one-way ANOVA.**

one-way ANOVA

> ### THE ANOVA *F* STATISTIC
>
> The **analysis of variance *F* statistic** for testing the equality of several means has this form:
>
> $$F = \frac{\text{variation among the sample means}}{\text{variation among individuals in the same sample}}$$

The *F* statistic can take only values that are zero or positive. It is zero only when all the sample means are identical and gets larger as they move farther apart. Large values of *F* are evidence against the null hypothesis H_0 that all population means are the same. Although the alternative hypothesis H_a is many-sided, the ANOVA *F* test is one-sided because any violation of H_0 tends to produce a large value of *F*.

The "variation" terms in the numerator and denominator of the *F* statistic are the **mean squares** that appear in the outputs in Figure 25.3. Roughly speaking, a mean square is similar to a variance. Recall that the variance of a set of data is an average of the squared deviations of the observations from their mean. Mean squares are average squared deviations that measure specific kinds of variation in the ANOVA setting.

mean squares

APPLY YOUR KNOWLEDGE

25.5 ANOVA calculation basics. Look at the Minitab output in Figure 25.3 (page 510).

(a) Verify that the F statistic is the "Variety" mean square (MS) divided by the "Error" mean square. Although we don't show the details of the algebra, the "Variety" mean square measures variation among the sample mean lengths for the three flower varieties. The "Error" mean square measures variation among individual flowers of the same variety.

(b) Verify that the quantity s is the square root of the "Error" mean square. In fact, s is the *pooled standard deviation*, which uses data from all three flower varieties to estimate the common population standard deviation σ.

25.6 The idea of ANOVA. Here is a simplified set of flower lengths similar to those in Table 25.1:

Bihai	red	yellow
48	39	37
52	40	34
50	41	38
49	38	36
46	37	40

(a) Using software, do ANOVA to compare the mean lengths. Report the sample mean and standard deviation for each variety, the mean squares for variety and error, the F statistic and its P-value, and the pooled standard deviation s. The differences among sample means are highly significant.

(b) Now modify the data by subtracting 10 from each *bihai* length and adding 1 to each yellow length (leave the red lengths unchanged). Do ANOVA and report the same statistics as in (a). The means of the new data are closer together, but the standard deviations are the same as in (a). Because ANOVA compares variation among the sample means with variation among individuals in the same sample, F is now much smaller and is not significant.

(c) The mean square for variety measures variation among the sample means. The mean square for error measures variation among flowers of the same variety. How are these mean squares affected by the change in the data from (a) to (b)?

CONDITIONS FOR ANOVA

Like all inference procedures, ANOVA is valid only in some circumstances. Here are the conditions under which we can use ANOVA to compare population means.

CONDITIONS FOR ANOVA INFERENCE

■ We have I **independent SRSs,** one from each of I populations. We measure the same response variable for each sample.

■ The ith population has a **Normal distribution** with unknown mean μ_i. One-way ANOVA tests the null hypothesis that all the population means are the same.

■ All the populations have the **same standard deviation** σ, whose value is unknown.

The first two conditions are familiar from our study of the two-sample t procedures for comparing two means. As usual, the design of the data production is the most important condition for inference. Biased sampling or confounding can make any inference meaningless. ANOVA, like other inference procedures, is often used when random samples are not available. You must judge each use on its merits, a judgment that usually requires some knowledge of the subject of the study in addition to some knowledge of statistics.

No real population has exactly a Normal distribution. Fortunately, procedures for comparing means are not very sensitive to lack of Normality. The ANOVA F test, like *robustness* the t procedures, is **robust.** What matters is Normality of the sample means, so ANOVA becomes safer as the sample sizes get larger, because of the central limit theorem effect. Remember to check for outliers that change the value of sample means and for extreme skewness. When there are no outliers and the distributions are roughly symmetric, you can safely use ANOVA for sample sizes as small as 4 or 5.

The third condition is annoying: unlike the t test for comparing two means (Chapter 19), ANOVA assumes that the variability of observations, measured by the standard deviation, is the same in all populations. It is not easy to check the condition that the populations have equal standard deviations. Statistical tests for equality of standard deviations are very sensitive to lack of Normality, so much so that they are of little practical value. You must either seek expert advice or rely on the robustness of ANOVA.

How serious are unequal standard deviations? ANOVA is not too sensitive to violations of the condition, especially when all samples have the same or similar sizes and no sample is very small. When designing a study, try to take samples of about the same size from all the groups you want to compare. The sample standard deviations estimate the population standard deviations, so check before doing ANOVA that the sample standard deviations are similar to each other. We expect some variation among them due to chance. Here is a rule of thumb that is safe in almost all situations.

CHECKING STANDARD DEVIATIONS IN ANOVA

The results of the ANOVA F test are approximately correct when the largest sample standard deviation is no more than twice as large as the smallest sample standard deviation.

EXAMPLE 25.3 Comparing tropical flowers: conditions for ANOVA

The study of *Heliconia* blossoms is based on three independent samples that the researchers consider to be random samples from all flowers of these varieties on the island of Dominica. The stemplots in Figure 25.1 show that the *bihai* and red varieties have slightly skewed distributions, but the sample means of samples of sizes 16 and 23 will have distributions that are close to Normal. The sample standard deviations for the three varieties are

$$s_1 = 1.213 \qquad s_2 = 1.799 \qquad s_3 = 0.975$$

These standard deviations satisfy our rule of thumb:

$$\frac{\text{largest } s}{\text{smallest } s} = \frac{1.799}{0.975} = 1.85 \quad (\text{less than 2})$$

We can safely use ANOVA to compare the mean lengths for the three populations. ■

EXAMPLE 25.4 Thinking about money changes behavior

THINKMONEY

STATE: Kathleen Vohs of the University of Minnesota and her coworkers carried out several randomized comparative experiments on the effects of thinking about money. Here's an outline of one of the experiments. Ask student subjects to unscramble 30 sets of five words to make a meaningful phrase from four of the five. The control group unscrambled phrases like "cold it desk outside is" into "it is cold outside." The "play money" group unscrambled similar sets of words, but a stack of Monopoly money was placed nearby. The "money prime" group unscrambled phrases that lead to thinking about money, turning "high a salary desk paying" into "a high-paying salary." Then each subject worked a hard puzzle, knowing that he or she could ask for help. Table 25.3 shows the time in seconds that each subject worked on the puzzle before asking for help.[6] Psychologists think that money tends to make people self-sufficient. If so, the two groups that were encouraged in different ways to think about money should take longer on the average to ask for help. Do the data support this idea?

TABLE 25.3 Time (seconds) until subjects ask for help with a puzzle

GROUP	TIME	GROUP	TIME	GROUP	TIME
Prime	609	Play	455	Control	118
Prime	444	Play	100	Control	272
Prime	242	Play	238	Control	413
Prime	199	Play	243	Control	291
Prime	174	Play	500	Control	140
Prime	55	Play	570	Control	104
Prime	251	Play	231	Control	55
Prime	466	Play	380	Control	189
Prime	443	Play	222	Control	126
Prime	531	Play	71	Control	400
Prime	135	Play	232	Control	92
Prime	241	Play	219	Control	64
Prime	476	Play	320	Control	88
Prime	482	Play	261	Control	142
Prime	362	Play	290	Control	141
Prime	69	Play	495	Control	373
Prime	160	Play	600	Control	156
		Play	67		

PLAN: Examine the data to compare the effect of the treatments and check that we can safely use ANOVA. If the data allow ANOVA, assess the significance of observed differences in mean times to ask for help.

SOLVE: Figure 25.7 shows side-by-side stemplots of the data in the three groups. We expect some irregularity in small samples, but there are no outliers or strong skewness that would hinder use of ANOVA. The Minitab ANOVA output in Figure 25.8 shows that the group standard deviations easily satisfy our rule of thumb. The control group subjects asked for help much sooner (mean 186.1 seconds) than did subjects in the two money groups (means 305.2 seconds and 314.1 seconds). The three means are significantly different ($F = 3.73$, $P = 0.031$).

CONCLUDE: The experiment gives good evidence that reminding people of money in either of two ways does make them less willing to ask others for help. This is consistent with the idea that money makes people feel more self-sufficient. ■

FIGURE 25.7

Side-by-side stemplots comparing the time until subjects asked for help with a puzzle, for Example 25.4.

Prime		Play		Control	
0	6 7	0	7 7	0	6 6 9 9
1	4 6 7	1	0	1	0 2 3 4 4 4 6 9
2	0 4 4 5	2	2 2 3 3 4 4 6 9	2	7 9
3	6	3	2 8	3	7
4	4 4 7 8 8	4	6	4	0 1
5	3	5	0 0 7	5	
6	1	6	0	6	

FIGURE 25.8

Minitab ANOVA output for comparing the three treatments in Example 25.4.

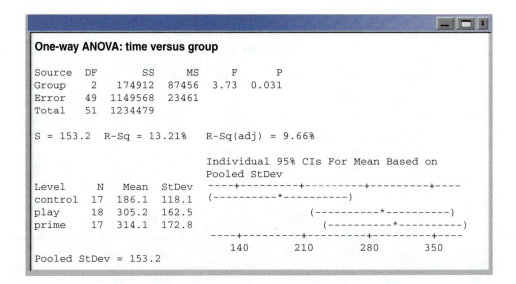

```
One-way ANOVA: time versus group

Source   DF        SS      MS      F      P
Group     2    174912   87456   3.73  0.031
Error    49   1149568   23461
Total    51   1234479

S = 153.2   R-Sq = 13.21%    R-Sq(adj) = 9.66%

                                Individual 95% CIs For Mean Based on
                                Pooled StDev
Level     N    Mean   StDev   ----+---------+---------+---------+----
control  17   186.1   118.1   (----------*----------)
play     18   305.2   162.5                     (----------*----------)
prime    17   314.1   172.8                       (----------*----------)
                              ----+---------+---------+---------+----
                               140       210       280       350

Pooled StDev = 153.2
```

APPLY YOUR KNOWLEDGE

25.7 Checking standard deviations. Verify that the sample standard deviations for these sets of data do allow use of ANOVA to compare the population means.

(a) The counts of trees in Exercise 25.3 and Figure 25.4.

(b) The ages of Exercise 25.4 and Figure 25.5.

25.8 Species richness after logging. Table 25.2 gives data on the species richness in rain forest plots, defined as the number of tree species in a plot divided by the number of trees in the plot. ANOVA may not be trustworthy for the richness data. Do data analysis: make side-by-side stemplots to examine the distributions of the response variable in the three groups, and also compare the standard deviations. What characteristic of the data makes ANOVA risky? 🔴 **BORNEOLOGGING**

25.9 Fertilizing bromeliads. Bromeliads are tropical flowering plants. Many are epiphytes that attach to trees and obtain moisture and nutrients from air and rain. Their leaf bases form cups that collect water and are home to the larvae of many insects. Jacqueline Ngai and Diane Srivastava examined the effects of adding nitrogen, phosphorus, or both to the cups. They randomly assigned 8 bromeliads to each of four treatment groups, including an unfertilized control group. A monkey destroyed one of the plants in the control group, leaving 7 bromeliads in that group. Here are the numbers of new leaves on each plant over the 7 months following fertilization:[7] 🔴 **BROMELIADS**

Nitrogen	Phosphorus	Both	Neither
15	14	14	11
14	14	16	13
15	14	15	16
16	11	14	15
17	13	14	15
18	12	13	11
17	15	17	12
13	15	14	

Analyze these data and discuss the results. Does nitrogen or phosphorus have a greater effect on the growth of bromeliads? Follow the four-step process as illustrated in Example 25.4.

F DISTRIBUTIONS AND DEGREES OF FREEDOM*

The ANOVA *F* statistic is

$$F = \frac{\text{variation among the sample means}}{\text{variation among individuals in the same sample}}$$

To find the *P*-value for this statistic, software uses the sampling distribution of *F* when the null hypothesis (all population means are equal) is true. This sampling distribution is an **F distribution.**

F distribution

The *F* distributions are a family of right-skewed distributions that take only values greater than 0. The density curves in Figure 25.9 illustrate their shapes. A specific *F* distribution is determined by the **degrees of freedom** of the numerator and denominator of the *F* statistic. When describing an *F* distribution, always give the numerator degrees

degrees of freedom

*This section is not required to do ANOVA with software.

FIGURE 25.9

Density curves for two *F* distributions. Both are right-skewed and take only positive values. The upper 5% critical values are marked under the curves.

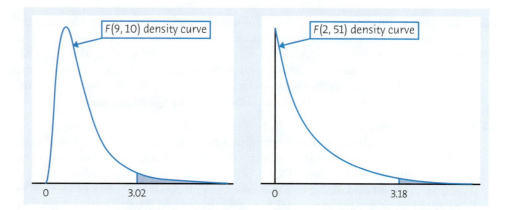

of freedom first. Our brief notation will be *F*(df1, df2) for the *F* distribution with df1 degrees of freedom in the numerator and df2 in the denominator. *Interchanging the degrees of freedom changes the distribution, so the order is important.* Tables of *F* critical points are awkward, because we need a separate table for every pair of degrees of freedom df1 and df2. Fortunately, software gives you *P*-values for the ANOVA *F* test without the need for a table.

EXAMPLE 25.5 Comparing flowers: the *F* distribution

Look again at the software output in Figure 25.3 for the flower length data. All four outputs give the degrees of freedom for the *F* test, labeled "df" or "DF." There are 2 degrees of freedom in the numerator and 51 in the denominator. *P*-values for the *F* test therefore come from the *F* distribution with 2 and 51 degrees of freedom: *F*(2, 51) with 2 and 51 degrees of freedom. The right-hand curve in Figure 25.9 is the density curve of this distribution. The 5% critical value marked on that curve is 3.18, and the 1% critical value is 5.05. The observed value *F* = 259.12 of the ANOVA *F* statistic lies far to the right of these values, so the *P*-value is extremely small. ■

Even without software, it is easy to find the proper degrees of freedom:

■ The numerator degrees of freedom are 1 fewer than the number of groups the *F* statistic compares.

■ The denominator degrees of freedom are the total number of observations in all groups, less the number of groups.

EXAMPLE 25.6 Degrees of freedom for *F*

In Examples 25.1 and 25.2, we compared the mean lengths for 3 varieties of flowers. The three sample sizes are $n_1 = 16$, $n_2 = 23$, $n_3 = 15$, so that the total number of observations is

$$n_1 + n_2 + n_3 = 16 + 23 + 15 = 54$$

> The ANOVA *F* test has numerator degrees of freedom 2 (1 less than the number of groups) and denominator degrees of freedom 51 (number of observations minus number of groups, $54 - 3$). These are the degrees of freedom given in the outputs in Figure 25.3. ■

APPLY YOUR KNOWLEDGE

25.10 Logging in the rain forest, continued. Exercise 25.3 compares the number of tree species in rain forest plots that had never been logged (Group 1) with similar plots nearby that had been logged 1 year earlier (Group 2) and 8 years earlier (Group 3). What are the sample sizes in the three groups? Find the degrees of freedom for the ANOVA *F* statistic. Check your work against the Excel output in Figure 25.4.

25.11 What music will you play? People often match their behavior to their social environment. One study of this idea first established that the type of music most preferred by black college students is R&B and that whites' most preferred music is rock. Will students hosting a small group of other students choose music that matches the makeup of the people attending? Two studies were done, using either black or white students as subjects. In the first study, 90 black business students were assigned at random to three equal-sized groups, and in the second study the same was done for 96 white students. In both studies, each subject sees a picture of the people he or she will host. Group 1 sees 6 blacks, Group 2 sees 3 whites and 3 blacks, and Group 3 sees 6 whites. Ask how likely the host is to play the type of music preferred by the other race. Use ANOVA to compare the three groups to see whether the racial mix of the gathering affects the choice of music.[8]

(a) For the white subjects, $F = 16.48$. What are the degrees of freedom?

(b) For the black subjects, $F = 2.47$. What are the degrees of freedom?

PhotoAlto/Alamy

CHAPTER 25 SUMMARY

CHAPTER SPECIFICS

■ **One-way analysis of variance (ANOVA)** compares the means of several populations. The **ANOVA F test** tests the null hypothesis that all the populations have the same mean. If the *F* test shows significant differences, examine the data to see where the differences lie and whether they are large enough to be important.

■ The **conditions for ANOVA** state that we have an **independent SRS** from each population; that each population has a **Normal distribution;** and that all populations have the **same standard deviation.**

■ In practice, ANOVA inference is relatively **robust** when the populations are non-Normal, especially when the samples are large. Before doing the *F* test, check the observations in each sample for outliers or strong skewness. Also verify that the largest sample standard deviation is no more than twice as large as the smallest standard deviation.

■ When the null hypothesis is true, the **ANOVA F statistic** for comparing I means from a total of N observations in all samples combined has the F **distribution** with $I - 1$ and $N - I$ degrees of freedom.

LINK IT

Analysis of variance is a general statistical method for studying sources of variation in a response. In this chapter, we have studied one-way ANOVA, which is a specific statistical technique designed to test the null hypothesis of the equality of the means of several populations. As such, it is an extension of the two-sample t test of Chapter 19, which tested the null hypothesis of the equality of *two* population means.

Rejection of the null hypothesis of equality of two means with the two-sample t test means that we have evidence that the two means are different. Rejection of the null hypothesis with a one-way ANOVA is a more ambiguous conclusion: it is evidence of a difference in the means of the populations, but the result does not tell us *which* differences between the means are statistically significant. This is similar to the chi-square test in Chapter 23, where rejection of the null hypothesis indicates that there is a relationship between the two categorical variables but says nothing about the nature of that relationship. Typically, after rejection of the null hypothesis in a one-way ANOVA, we perform a more detailed *follow-up analysis* to decide which of the means are different and to estimate how large these differences are. The details of this follow-up inference must be left to a more advanced course.

CHECK YOUR SKILLS

25.12 The purpose of analysis of variance is to compare

(a) the variances of several populations.

(b) the proportions of successes in several populations.

(c) the means of several populations.

An experiment to help determine if insects sleep gave caffeine to fruit flies to see if it affected their rest. The three treatments were a control, a low caffeine dose of 1 milligram of caffeine per milliliter of blood (mg/ml), and a higher dose of 5 mg/ml. Nine fruit flies were assigned at random to the three treatments, three to each treatment, and the minutes of rest were measured over a 12-hour period. Here are the minutes of rest for the three groups:

Control	Low dose	High dose
450	466	265
413	420	330
418	435	389

Here is partial Minitab output for ANOVA (several numbers have been omitted), along with the means and standard deviations of the rest times for the three groups:

Source	DF	SS	MS	F	P
Caffeine			11299		0.027
Error			1600		
Total					

Level	N	Mean	StDev
Control	3	427.00	20.07
Low	3	440.33	23.46
High	3	328.00	62.02

Exercises 25.13 to 25.18 are based on this study.

25.13 (Optional) The degrees of freedom for the ANOVA F statistic comparing mean minutes of rest are   CAFFEINE

(a) 2 and 7.

(b) 2 and 6.

(c) 3 and 7.

25.14 The null hypothesis for the ANOVA F test is

(a) that the population mean rest time is the same for all three levels of caffeine.

(b) that the population mean rest time decreases as the caffeine level increases.

(c) that the population mean rest time is lowest for the high level of caffeine.

25.15 The value of the ANOVA *F* statistic for testing equality of the population means of the three caffeine levels is

(a) 4.73.

(b) 4.82.

(c) 7.06.

25.16 The conclusion of the ANOVA test is that

(a) there is strong evidence ($P = 0.027$) that the mean rest time is not the same for all three groups.

(b) there is strong evidence ($P = 0.027$) that the mean rest time is lower in the high-caffeine group than in the other two.

(c) the data give no evidence ($P = 0.027$) to suggest that mean rest time differs among the three treatments.

25.17 For this study, we notice that

(a) ANOVA can be used on these data because ANOVA requires equal sample sizes.

(b) there is an extreme outlier in the data.

(c) the data show evidence of a violation of the assumption that the three populations have the same standard deviation.

25.18 To compare the treatments we might use three 90% two-sample *t* confidence intervals to compare each pair of treatments: the control versus low dose, the control versus high dose, and the low dose versus high dose. The weakness of doing this is that

(a) we don't know how confident we can be that all three intervals cover the true differences in means.

(b) 90% confidence is OK for one comparison, but it isn't high enough for three comparisons done at once.

(c) we can't compare two treatments that use different doses of caffeine.

25.19 A company runs a three-day workshop on strategies for working effectively in teams. On each day, a different strategy is presented. Forty-eight employees of the company attend the workshop. At the outset, all 48 are divided into 12 teams of 4. The teams remain the same for the entire workshop. Strategies are presented in the morning. In the afternoon, the teams are presented with a series of small tasks, and the number of these completed successfully using the strategy taught that morning is recorded for each team. The mean number of tasks completed successfully by all teams each day and the standard deviation follow:

Day	n	$\bar{x}$	s
1	12	17.25	7.10
2	12	17.64	14.14
3	12	17.21	14.03

In this study, we notice that

(a) the data show very strong evidence of a violation of the assumption that the three populations have the same standard deviation.

(b) ANOVA cannot be used on these data, because the sample sizes are less than 20.

(c) the assumption that the data are independent for the three days is unreasonable, because the same teams were observed each day.

CHAPTER 25 EXERCISES

Exercises 25.20 to 25.23 describe situations in which we want to compare the mean responses in several populations. For each setting, identify the populations and the response variable and give the null and alternative hypotheses for the ANOVA F statistic.

25.20 Morning or evening? Are you a morning person, an evening person, or neither? Does this personality trait affect how well you perform? A sample of 100 students took a psychological test that found 16 morning people, 30 evening

people, and 54 who were neither. All the students then took a test of their ability to memorize at 8 A.M. and again at 9 P.M. The response variable is the score at 8 A.M. minus the score at 9 P.M.

25.21 Does art sell products? How does visual art affect the perception and evaluation of consumer products? Subjects were asked to evaluate an advertisement for bathroom fittings that contained an art image, a nonart image, or no image. The art image was Vermeer's painting *Girl with a Pearl Earring*, while the nonart image was a photograph of the actress Scarlett Johansson, in the same pose and wearing the same garments as the girl in the painting, that was taken from the motion picture *Girl with a Pearl Earring*. Thus, the art and nonart image were a match on content. College students were divided at random into three groups of 39 each, with each group assigned to one of the three types of advertisements. Students evaluated the product in the advertisement on a scale of 1 to 7, with 1 being the most unfavorable rating and 7 being the most favorable. The paper reported that a one-way ANOVA on the product evaluation index had $F = 6.29$ with $P < 0.05$.[9]

25.22 Test accommodations. Many states require schoolchildren to take regular statewide tests to assess their progress. Children with learning disabilities who read poorly may not do well on mathematics tests because they can't read the problems. Most states allow "accommodations" for learning-disabled children. Randomly assign 100 learning-disabled children in equal numbers to three types of accommodation and a control group: math problems are read by a teacher, by a computer, or by a computer that also shows a video; and standard test conditions. Compare the mean scores on the state mathematics assessment.

25.23 Exercise and type 2 diabetes. It is generally accepted that regular exercise provides health benefits to individuals with type 2 diabetes, although it is unclear which exercise regimen (aerobic, resistance, or both) is the best. The subjects in this study were sedentary 30- to 75-year-old adults with type 2 diabetes and elevated hemoglobin A1c levels above 6.5%. The level of hemoglobin A1c correlates very well with a person's recent overall blood sugar levels. If the blood sugars have generally been running high during the previous few months, the level of hemoglobin A1c will be high. In a randomized controlled study, 41 subjects were assigned to a nonexercise control group, 73 to resistance training only, 72 to aerobic exercise only, and 76 to combined aerobic and resistance training. The weekly duration of exercise was similar for all three exercise groups, and subjects remained on the exercise regimens for 9 months. At the end of 9 months, the hemoglobin A1c levels of subjects were measured.[10]

25.24 Don't handle the merchandise? Although consumers often want to touch products before purchasing them, they generally prefer that others have not touched products they would like to buy. Can another person touching a product create a positive reaction? Subjects were given instructions to contact a sales associate at a university bookstore who would provide them with a shirt to try on. When meeting the sales associate, subjects were told that there was only one shirt left

and it was being tried on by another "customer." The other customer trying on the shirt was a confederate of the experimenter and was either an attractive, well-dressed professional female model or an average-looking female college student wearing jeans and a tee shirt. Subjects, who were either males or females, saw the confederate leaving the dressing room, where the shirt was left for them to try on. There was also a control group of subjects who were handed the shirt directly off the rack by the sales associate. Thus, there were five treatments: male subjects seeing a model, female subjects seeing a model, male subjects seeing a college student, female subjects seeing a college student, and the control group. Subjects evaluated the product on five dimensions, each dimension on a 7-point scale, with the five scores then averaged to give the subject's evaluation measure, with higher numbers indicating a more positive evaluation. Here are the sample sizes, means, and standard deviations for the five groups:[11]

Treatment group	n	$\bar{x}$	s
Males seeing a model	22	5.34	0.87
Males seeing a student	23	3.32	1.21
Females seeing a model	24	4.10	1.32
Females seeing a student	23	3.50	1.43
Controls	27	4.17	1.50

(a) Verify that the sample standard deviations allow the use of ANOVA to compare the population means. What do the means suggest about the effect of the subject's gender and the attractiveness of the confederate on the evaluation of the product?

(b) **(Optional)** The paper reports an ANOVA F statistic of 8.30. What are the degrees of freedom for the ANOVA F statistic and the P-value? State your conclusions.

25.25 Plants defend themselves. When some plants are attacked by leaf-eating insects, they release chemical compounds that attract other insects that prey on the leaf-eaters. A study carried out on plants growing naturally in the Utah desert demonstrated both the release of the compounds and that they not only repel the leaf-eaters but attract predators that act as the plants' bodyguards.[12] The investigators chose 8 plants attacked by each of three leaf-eaters and 8 more that were undamaged, 32 plants of the same species in all. They then measured emissions of several compounds during seven hours. Here are data (mean ± standard error of the mean for eight plants) for one compound. The emission rate is measured in nanograms (ng) per hour.

Group	Emission rate (ng/hr)
Control	9.22 ± 5.93
Hornworm	31.03 ± 8.75
Leaf bug	18.97 ± 6.64
Flea beetle	27.12 ± 8.62

(a) Make a graph that compares the mean emission rates for the four groups. Does it appear that emissions increase when the plant is attacked?

(b) What hypotheses does ANOVA test in this setting?

(c) We do not have all the data. What would you look for in deciding whether you can safely use ANOVA?

(d) What is the relationship between the standard error of the mean (SEM) and the standard deviation for a sample? What are the four sample standard deviations? Do they satisfy our rule of thumb for safe use of ANOVA?

25.26 Can you hear these words? To test whether a hearing aid is right for a patient, audiologists play a tape on which words are pronounced at low volume. The patient tries to repeat the words. There are several different lists of words that are supposed to be equally difficult. Are the lists equally difficult when there is background noise? To find out, an experimenter had subjects with normal hearing listen to four lists with a noisy background. The response variable was the percent of the 50 words in a list that the subject repeated correctly. The data set contains 96 responses.[13] Here are two study designs that could produce these data:

Design A. The experimenter assigns 96 subjects to 4 groups at random. Each group of 24 subjects listens to one of the lists. All individuals listen and respond separately.

Design B. The experimenter has 24 subjects. Each subject listens to all four lists in random order. All individuals listen and respond separately.

Does Design A allow use of one-way ANOVA to compare the lists? Does Design B allow use of one-way ANOVA to compare the lists? Briefly explain your answers.

25.27 More rain for California? The changing climate will probably bring more rain to California, but we don't know whether the additional rain will come during the winter wet season or extend into the long dry season in spring and summer. Kenwyn Suttle of the University of California at Berkeley and his coworkers randomly assigned plots of open grassland to three treatments: added water equal to 20% of annual rainfall either during January to March (winter) or during April to June (spring), and no added water (control). Here are some of the data, for plant biomass (in grams per square meter) produced by each plot in a single year:[14] ▓ BIOMASS2003

Winter	Spring	Control
264.1514	318.4182	129.0538
187.7312	281.6830	144.6578
291.1431	288.8433	172.7772
176.2879	382.6673	113.2813
141.7525	326.8877	142.1562
169.9737	293.8502	117.9808

Figure 25.10 shows Minitab ANOVA output for these data.

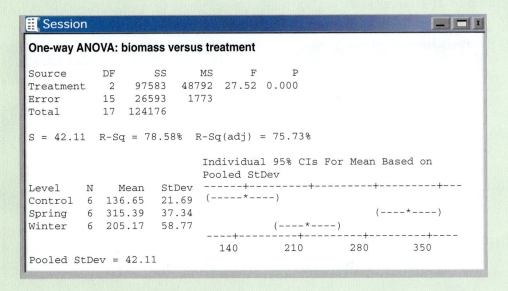

FIGURE 25.10

Minitab ANOVA output for comparing the total plant biomass of grassland plots under different water conditions, for Exercise 25.27.

(a) Make side-by-side stemplots of plant biomass for the three treatments, as well as a table of the sample means and standard deviations. What do the data appear to show about the effect of extra water in winter and in spring on biomass? Do these data satisfy the conditions for ANOVA?

(b) State H_0 and H_a for the ANOVA F test, and explain in words what ANOVA tests in this setting.

(c) Report your overall conclusions about the effect of added water on plant growth in California.

25.28 Can you hear these words? Figure 25.11 displays the Minitab output for one-way ANOVA applied to the hearing data described in Exercise 25.26. The response variable is "Percent," and "List" identifies the four lists of words. Based on this analysis, is there good reason to think that the four lists are not all equally difficult? Write a brief summary of the study findings.

25.29 Which blue is most blue? The color of a fabric depends on the dye used and also on how the dye is applied. This matters to clothing manufacturers, who want the color of the fabric to be just right. A manufacturer dyes fabric made of ramie with the same "procion blue" die applied in four different ways. She uses a colorimeter to measure the lightness of the color on a scale in which black is 0 and white is 100. Here are the data for 8 pieces of fabric dyed in each way:[15] 🔵 BLUEDYE

Method A	41.72	41.83	42.05	41.44	41.27	42.27	41.12	41.49
Method B	40.98	40.88	41.30	41.28	41.66	41.50	41.39	41.27
Method C	42.30	42.20	42.65	42.43	42.50	42.28	43.13	42.45
Method D	41.68	41.65	42.30	42.04	42.25	41.99	41.72	41.97

(a) This is a randomized comparative experiment. Outline the design.

(b) The clothing manufacturer wants to know which method gives the darkest color. Follow the four-step process in answering this question.

25.30 Do good smells bring good business? Businesses know that customers often respond to background music. Do they also respond to odors? Nicolas Gueguen and his colleagues studied this question in a small pizza restaurant in France on Saturday evenings in May. On one evening, a relaxing lavender odor was spread through the restaurant; on another evening, a stimulating lemon odor; a third evening served as a control, with no odor. The three evenings were comparable in many ways (weather, customer count, and so on), so we are willing to regard the data as independent SRSs from spring Saturday evenings at this restaurant. Table 25.4 (on page 527) contains data on how long (in minutes) customers stayed in the restaurant on each of the three evenings.[16] 🔴 GOODSMELLS

(a) Make stemplots of the customer times for each evening. Do any of the distributions show outliers, strong skewness, or other clear deviations from Normality?

(b) Do a complete analysis to see whether the groups differ in the average amount of time spent in the restaurant. Follow the four-step process in your work. Did you find anything surprising?

25.31 Good weather and tipping. Favorable weather has been shown to be associated with increased tipping. Will just the belief that future weather will be favorable lead to higher tips? The researchers gave 60 index cards to a waitress at an Italian restaurant in New Jersey. Before delivering the bill to each customer, the waitress randomly selected a

FIGURE 25.11

Minitab ANOVA output for comparing the percents heard correctly in four lists of words, for Exercise 25.28.

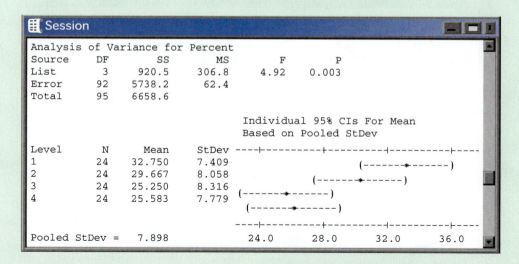

```
┌─────────────────────────────────────────────────────────────────────┐
│ ▦ Session                                                    ─ ☐ ↕    │
├─────────────────────────────────────────────────────────────────────┤
│ Analysis of Variance for Percent                                   ▲  │
│ Source     DF        SS        MS        F         P                  │
│ List        3     920.5     306.8      4.92     0.003                  │
│ Error      92    5738.2      62.4                                      │
│ Total      95    6658.6                                                │
│                                                                       │
│                                                                       │
│                              Individual 95% CIs For Mean              │
│                              Based on Pooled StDev                    │
│                                                                       │
│ Level       N      Mean     StDev  ----+---------+---------+---------+----  │
│ 1          24    32.750     7.409                        (------*------ )  │
│ 2          24    29.667     8.058                 (------*------)      │
│ 3          24    25.250     8.316   (------*------ )                   │
│ 4          24    25.583     7.779   (------*------ )                   │
│                                                                       │
│                                     ---+---------+---------+---------+----  │
│ Pooled StDev =     7.898             24.0      28.0      32.0      36.0 ▼  │
└─────────────────────────────────────────────────────────────────────┘
```

TABLE 25.4 Time (minutes) that customers remain in a restaurant when exposed to odors

LAVENDER ODOR									
92	126	114	106	89	137	93	76	98	108
124	105	129	103	107	109	94	105	102	108
95	121	109	104	116	88	109	97	101	106
LEMON ODOR									
78	104	74	75	112	88	105	97	101	89
88	73	94	63	83	108	91	88	83	106
108	60	96	94	56	90	113	97		
NO ODOR									
103	68	79	106	72	121	92	84	72	92
85	69	73	87	109	115	91	84	76	96
107	98	92	107	93	118	87	101	75	86

card and wrote on the bill the same message that was printed on the index card. Twenty of the cards had the message "The weather is supposed to be really good tomorrow. I hope you enjoy the day!" Another 20 cards contained the message "The weather is supposed to be not so good tomorrow. I hope you enjoy the day anyway!" The remaining 20 cards were blank, indicating that the waitress was not supposed to write any message. Choosing a card at random ensured that there was a random assignment of the diners to the three experimental conditions. Here are the tips as a percent of the total bill for the three messages:[17] 🍽 TIPPING

Good weather report	20.8	18.7	19.9	20.6	22.0	23.4	22.8	24.9	22.2	20.3
	24.9	22.3	27.0	20.4	22.2	24.0	21.2	22.1	22.0	22.7
Bad weather report	18.0	19.0	19.2	18.8	18.4	19.0	18.5	16.1	16.8	14.0
	17.0	13.6	17.5	19.9	20.2	18.8	18.0	23.2	18.2	19.4
No weather report	19.9	16.0	15.0	20.1	19.3	19.2	18.0	19.2	21.2	18.8
	18.5	19.3	19.3	19.4	10.8	19.1	19.7	19.8	21.3	20.6

Do the data support the hypothesis that there are differences among the tip percents for the three experimental conditions? Does a prediction of good weather seem to increase the tip percent? Follow the four-step process in data analysis and ANOVA. Be sure to check the conditions for ANOVA and to include an appropriate graph that compares the tip percents for the three conditions.

25.32 Durable press fabrics are weaker. "Durable press" cotton fabrics are treated to improve their recovery from wrinkles after washing. Unfortunately, the treatment also reduces the strength of the fabric. A study compared the breaking strength of untreated fabric with that of fabrics treated by three commercial durable press processes. Five specimens of the same fabric were assigned at random to each group. Here are the data, in pounds of pull needed to tear the fabric:[18] 🍽 WEAKFABRIC

Untreated	60.1	56.7	61.5	55.1	59.4
Permafresh 55	29.9	30.7	30.0	29.5	27.6
Permafresh 48	24.8	24.6	27.3	28.1	30.3
Hylite LF	28.8	23.9	27.0	22.1	24.2

The untreated fabric is clearly much stronger than any of the treated fabrics. We want to know if there is a significant difference in breaking strength among the three durable press treatments. Analyze the data for the three processes and write a clear summary of your findings. Which process do you recommend if breaking strength is a main concern? Use the four-step process to guide your discussion. (Although the standard deviations do not quite satisfy our rule of thumb, that rule is conservative, and many statisticians would use ANOVA for these data.)

25.33 Durable press fabrics wrinkle less. The data in Exercise 25.32 show that durable press treatment greatly reduces the breaking strength of cotton fabric. Of course, durable press treatment also reduces wrinkling. How much? "Wrinkle recovery angle" measures how well a fabric recovers from wrinkles. Higher is better. Here are data on the wrinkle recovery angle (in degrees) for the same fabric specimens discussed in the previous exercise: 🔺 **WRINKLEFABRIC**

Untreated	79	80	78	80	78
Permafresh 55	136	135	132	137	134
Permafresh 48	125	131	125	145	145
Hylite LF	143	141	146	141	145

The untreated fabric once again stands out, this time as inferior to the treated fabrics in wrinkle resistance. Examine the data for the three durable press processes and summarize your findings. How does the ranking of the three processes by wrinkle resistance compare with their ranking by breaking strength in Exercise 25.32? Explain why we can't trust the ANOVA F test.

25.34 Logging in the rain forest: species counts. Table 25.2 gives data on the number of trees per forest plot, the number of species per plot, and species richness. Exercise 25.3 analyzed the effect of logging on number of trees. Exercise 25.8 concludes that it would be risky to use ANOVA to analyze richness. Use software to analyze the effect of logging on the number of species. 🔺 **BORNEOLOGGING**

(a) Make a table of the group means and standard deviations. Do the standard deviations satisfy our rule of thumb for safe use of ANOVA? What do the means suggest about the effect of logging on the number of species?

(b) Carry out the ANOVA. Report the F statistic and its P-value and state your conclusion.

More rain for California? *Exercise 25.27 describes a randomized experiment carried out by Kenwyn Suttle and his coworkers to examine the effects of additional water on California grassland. The experimental units are 18 plots of grassland, assigned at random among three treatments: added water in the winter wet season, added water in the spring dry season, and no added water (control group). Field experiments, unlike laboratory experiments, are exposed to variations in the natural environment. The experiment therefore continued over five years, from 2001 to 2005. Table 25.5 gives data on the total plant biomass (grams per square meter) that grew on each plot during each year.[19] The "Plot" column shows how the random assignment of 18 of the 36 available plots worked. Exercises 25.35 to 25.37 are based on this information.*

TABLE 25.5 Plant biomass (g/m²) for three water conditions over five years

TREATMENT	PLOT	2001	2002	2003	2004	2005
Winter	3	136.8358	228.0717	264.1514	254.6453	344.3933
Winter	8	151.4154	189.9505	187.7312	233.8155	203.3908
Winter	14	136.1536	209.0485	291.1431	253.4506	331.9724
Winter	20	121.6323	189.6755	176.2879	228.5882	388.1056
Winter	27	124.1459	188.0090	141.7525	158.6675	382.8617
Winter	32	125.2986	215.2174	169.9737	212.3232	346.3042
Spring	4	338.1301	422.7411	318.4182	517.6650	344.0489
Spring	11	291.8597	339.8243	281.6830	342.2825	261.8016
Spring	18	244.8727	398.7296	288.8433	270.5785	262.7238
Spring	22	234.6599	400.6878	382.6673	212.5324	316.9683
Spring	25	197.5830	326.9497	326.8877	213.9879	224.1109
Spring	35	239.0122	444.1556	293.8502	240.1927	328.2783
Control	6	73.4288	148.8907	129.0538	178.9988	237.6596
Control	7	110.6306	182.6762	144.6578	205.5165	281.1442
Control	17	95.3405	196.8303	172.7772	242.6795	313.7242
Control	24	83.0584	186.1953	113.2813	231.7639	258.3631
Control	28	30.5886	154.0401	142.1562	134.9847	235.8320
Control	33	96.9709	213.2537	117.9808	212.4862	217.5060

25.35 Plot the means. Starting from the data in Table 25.5, you can calculate the mean plant biomass for each treatment in each year as follows: BIOMASSMEANS

Treatment	Year				
	2001	2002	2003	2004	2005
Winter	132.58	203.33	205.17	223.58	332.84
Spring	257.69	388.85	315.39	299.54	289.66
Control	81.67	180.31	136.65	201.07	257.37

Plot the means for each of the three treatments against year, connecting the yearly means for each treatment by lines to show the pattern over time. Use the same plot for all three treatments, with a different color for each treatment. From this plot, you can get an overall picture of the experiment's results.

(a) Across all five years, does more water in the wet season increase plant growth? What about more water in the dry season? Which seasonal addition of water has the larger effect?

(b) One-way ANOVAs comparing the mean plant biomass separately in each year find significant differences in three years and no significant difference in two years. Based on your plot, in which three years do you think the treatment means differ significantly?

(c) In 2005, there were unusually late rains during the spring. How does the effect of this natural rainfall show up in your plot? (You see that it would not be wise to do an experiment like this in just one year.)

25.36 The results for 2001. Your work in Exercise 25.27 shows that there were significant differences in mean plant biomass among the three treatments in 2003. Do a complete analysis of the data for 2001 and report your conclusions. BIOMASSALL

25.37 Conditions for ANOVA. Examine the data for the year 2004. The conditions for ANOVA inference are not met. In what way do these data fail to meet the conditions? (It is not very surprising that in five ANOVAs one will fail to satisfy our quite conservative conditions.) BIOMASSALL

25.38 Which test? Example 25.4 describes one of the experiments done by Kathleen Vohs and her coworkers to demonstrate that even being reminded of money makes people more self-sufficient and less involved with other people. Here are three more of these experiments. For each experiment, which statistical test from Chapters 18 to 25 would you use, and why?

(a) Randomly assign student subjects to money and control groups. The control group unscrambles neutral phrases, and the money group unscrambles money-oriented phrases, as described in Example 25.4. Then ask the subjects to volunteer to help the experimenter by coding data sheets, which takes about 5 minutes per sheet. Subjects said how many sheets they would volunteer to code. "Participants in the money condition volunteered to help code fewer data sheets than did participants in the control condition."

(b) Randomly assign student subjects to high-money, low-money, and control groups. After playing Monopoly for a short time, the high-money group is left with $4000 in Monopoly money, the low-money group with $200, and the control group with no money. Each subject is asked to imagine a future with lots of money (high-money group), a little money (low-money group), or just their future plans (control group). Another student walks in and spills a box of 27 pencils. How many pencils does the subject pick up? "Participants in the high-money condition gathered fewer pencils" than subjects in the other two groups.

(c) Randomly assign student subjects to three groups. All do paperwork while a computer on the desk shows a screensaver of currency floating underwater (Group 1), a screensaver of fish swimming underwater (Group 2), or a blank screen (Group 3). Each subject must now develop an advertisement and can choose whether to work alone or with a partner. Count how many in each group make each choice. "Choosing to perform the task with a coworker was reduced among money condition participants."

EXPLORING THE WEB

25.39 Confidence in the banking system. The General Social Survey (GSS) is a sociological survey used to collect data on demographic characteristics and attitudes of residents of the United States. The survey is conducted by the National Opinion Research Center of the University of Chicago, which interviews face-to-face a randomly selected sample of adults (18 and older). SDA (Survey Documentation and Analysis) is a set of programs that allows you to analyze survey data and includes the GSS survey as part of its archive. Go to the Web site sda.berkeley.edu/ and click on *Archive*. Unless there is a more recent file, open the 1972–2010 cumulative data file (without the quick tables option).

(a) In the "Analysis" tab on the top of the page, click on *Comparison of means*. Do an ANOVA that examines how the mean age of the respondents varies with their confidence in the banking and financial systems. To do this, type in the dependent variable as "Age" and the row (treatment) variable as "Confinan." For the selection filter, type in "Year(2010)" or the most recent year available. For weight, change it to "No Weight." Finally, in the table options, the *only* boxes that should be checked are "Std dev," "N," and "ANOVA stats." Make sure that the checks are removed from the other boxes. Now click on *Run the Table*.

(b) How many respondents are included in the analysis? What are the three means and standard deviations? Explain how the degrees of freedom were obtained. What are the F- and P-values? Write a brief report explaining the relationship between the average respondent age and confidence in the banking system.

25.40 Confidence in the banking system, continued. This exercise is a continuation of the previous Web exercise. You will download the data file and reproduce the analysis, as well as provide some additional plots. First, open the 1972–2010 cumulative data file following the instructions in the previous exercise.

(a) In the "Download" tab at the top of the page, click on *Customized Subset*. For the data file, if you highlight the CSV bubble, an Excel spreadsheet will be downloaded (unclick *Codebook*). For the selection filter, again type in "year(2010)" or the year used in the previous exercise. In the box for entering the names of individual variables, enter "Age" and "Confinan." Click *continue* at the bottom of the page. In the new window, click on *Create the Files* and in the next window click on *data files*. You can now either open or save the data file to your computer.

(b) Import the data into your statistical software package. You first need to "clean" the data a little because there are observations for which either the "Age" or the "Confinan" variable is missing. For the "Confinan" variable, any value other than a 1, 2, or 3 is a missing-value code. Delete these observations. For the "Age" variable, the missing value codes are 0, 98, and 99. Eliminate any observations with these values for "Age." You should now have the same number of observations as in the previous exercise.

(c) Draw comparative boxplots of the age distribution for the three values of "Confinan." Describe the shapes of the three distributions. What information can you obtain from the boxplots that was not included in the output for the previous exercise?

(d) Reproduce the one-way ANOVA table using your software. Your results should agree with those of the previous exercise.

Notes and Data Sources

Getting Started

1. Parts of this essay are shared with David S. Moore, "Introduction: learning from data," in Roxy Peck et al. (eds.), *Statistics: A Guide to the Unknown*, 4th ed., Thomson, 2006.
2. See, for example, Martin Enserink, "The vanishing promises of hormone replacement," *Science*, 297 (2002), pp. 325–326; and Brian Vastag, "Hormone replacement therapy falls out of favor with expert committee," *Journal of the American Medical Association*, 287 (2002), pp. 1923–1924. A National Institutes of Health panel's comprehensive report is *International Position Paper on Women's Health and Menopause*, NIH Publication 02-3284, 2002.
3. A. C. Nielsen, Jr., "Statistics in marketing," in *Making Statistics More Effective in Schools of Business*, Graduate School of Business, University of Chicago, 1986.
4. The data in Figure 2 are based on a component of the Consumer Price Index, from the Bureau of Labor Statistics Web site: www.bls.gov. We converted the index number into cents per gallon using retail price information from the Automobile Association of America, www.fuelgaugereport.com.
5. FUTURE II Study Group, "Quadrivalent vaccine against human papillomavirus to prevent high-grade cervical lesions," *New England Journal of Medicine*, 356 (2007), pp. 1915–1927.

Chapter 1

1. Data for 2008 from the *Statistical Abstract of the United States* at the Census Bureau Web site, www.census.gov.
2. *The Infinite Dial 2010: Digital Platforms and the Future of Radio*, at www.arbitron.com.
3. *Radio Today, 2011 Edition*, at www.arbitron.com.
4. Higher Education Research Institute 2010 Freshman Survey, at www.heri.ucla.edu.
5. Centers for Disease Control and Prevention, National Center for Health Statistics, *Births: Final Data for 2008*, National Vital Statistics Reports, 59, No. 1, December 2010, at www.cdc.gov/nchs. These are the most recent data available at the end of 2010, but the numbers change only slightly from year to year.
6. From the 2006 American Community Survey, at factfinder.census.gov.
7. Our eyes do respond to area, but not quite linearly. It appears that we perceive the ratio of two bars to be about the 0.7 power of the ratio of their actual areas. See W. S. Cleveland, *The Elements of Graphing Data*, Wadsworth, 1985, pp. 278–284.
8. 2011 *Statistical Abstract of the United States*, Table 16, at www.census.gov.
9. From the Gary Community School Corporation, courtesy of Celeste Foster, Purdue University.
10. From the College Board Web site, www.collegeboard.com.
11. The health care expenditures per capita in 2009 were obtained from the data repository at the World Health Organization at apps.who.int/ghodata/?vid=1901. All amounts are in international dollars at purchasing-power parity. That is, the exchange rate between each currency and the dollar is set not at the fluctuating market rate but at the rate that gives a dollar the same buying power in each country.
12. The U.S. Geological Survey maintains data for various water parameters at monitoring sites throughout the United States at waterdata.usgs.gov/nwis. The data can be graphed or downloaded. The data in Figure 1.12 are for USGS 254754080344300 SHARK RIVER SLOUGH NO.1.
13. College Entrance Examination Board, *Trends in College Pricing, 2010*, at www.trends.collegeboard.org. The averages are "enrollment weighted," so that they give average tuition over *students* rather than over *colleges*. The reported averages have been adjusted to constant 2010 dollars.
14. See Note 6.
15. *DuPont 2010 Color Popularity Report*, at www2.dupont.com.
16. Keith N. Hampton et al., "Social networking sites and our lives," June 2011, Pew Internet and American Life Project at www.pewinternet.org.

17. Centers for Disease Control and Prevention, National Center for Health Statistics, *Deaths: Preliminary Data for 2009*, 59, No. 4, March 2011, at www.cdc.gov/nchs.

18. "2010 Student surveys: complete results," *Macleans.ca*, February 15, 2010, at oncampus.macleans.ca.

19. Tom Lloyd et al., "Fruit consumption, fitness, and cardiovascular health in female adolescents: the Penn State Young Women's Health Study," *American Journal of Clinical Nutrition*, 67 (1998), pp. 624–630.

20. Data provided by Darlene Gordon from her PhD thesis, "Relationships among academic self-concept, academic achievement, and persistence with self-attribution, study habits, and perceived school environment," Purdue University, 1997.

21. National Institutes of Health, Essential Fatty Acids Education site, efaeducation.nih.gov.

22. 2011 *Statistical Abstract of the United States*, Table 161, at www.census.gov.

23. As of the end of 2010, yearly data were available through 2007 at the United Nations Web site unstats.un.org/unsd/mdg/SeriesDetail.aspx?srid=751&crid=.

24. National Oceanic and Atmospheric Administration, at www.beringclimate.noaa.gov/.

25. David M. Fergusson and L. John Horwood, "Cannabis use and traffic accidents in a birth cohort of young adults," *Accident Analysis and Prevention*, 33 (2001), pp. 703–711.

26. From a plot in K. Krishna Kumar et al., "Unraveling the mystery of Indian monsoon failure during El Niño," *Science*, 314 (2006), pp. 115–119.

27. See Note 13.

28. Census Bureau, New Residential Construction page, at www.census.gov/const/startsua.pdf. These are monthly data that are not seasonally adjusted.

29. Ozone Hole Watch, at ozonewatch.gsfc.nasa.gov/index.html.

Chapter 2

1. From the 2003 American Community Survey, at the Census Bureau Web site, www.census.gov. The data are a subsample of the 13,194 individuals in the ACS North Carolina sample who had travel times greater than zero.

2. This isn't a mathematical theorem. The mean can be less than the median in right-skewed distributions that take only a few values, many of which lie exactly at the median. The rule almost never fails for distributions taking many values, and most counterexamples don't appear clearly skewed in graphs even though they may be slightly skewed according to technical measures of skewness. See Paul T. von Hippel, "Mean, median, and skew: correcting a textbook rule," *Journal of Statistics Education*, 13, No. 2 (2005), www.amstat.org/publications/jse/.

3. National Association of College and University Business Officers, 2010 Endowment Study, at www.nacubo.org.

4. From the Census Bureau, www.census.gov/const/uspricemon.pdf.

5. U.S. Census Bureau, *Income, Poverty, and Health Insurance Coverage in the United States: 2009*, September 2010, at www.census.gov.

6. U.S. Department of Energy, www.fueleconomy.gov/feg/download.shtml.

7. We thank Patricia Humphrey for supplying the test scores for students at Georgia Southern University.

8. From the Environmental Protection Agency, www.epa.gov/radon/pubs/consguid.html.

9. Ethan J. Temeles and W. John Kress, "Adaptation in a plant-hummingbird association," *Science*, 300 (2003), pp. 630–633. We thank Ethan J. Temeles for providing the data.

10. C. H. Cannon, D. R. Peart, and M. Leighton, "Tree species diversity in commercially logged Bornean rainforest," *Science*, 281 (1998), pp. 1366–1367. We thank Charles Cannon for providing the data.

11. Raymond Fisman and Edward Miguel, "Cultures of corruption: evidence from diplomatic parking tickets," National Bureau of Economic Research Working Paper 12312, June 2006, at www.nber.org.

12. D. G. Jakovljevic and A. K. McConnell, "Influence of different breathing frequencies on the severity of inspiratory muscle fatigue induced by high-intensity front crawl swimming," *Journal of Strength and Conditioning Research*, 23, No. 4 (2009), pp. 1169–1174.

13. Patrick J. Purcell, *Retirement Savings and Household Wealth in 2007*, Congressional Research Service, April 2009.

14. T. Bjerkedal, "Acquisition of resistance in guinea pigs infected with different doses of virulent tubercle bacilli," *American Journal of Hygiene*, 72 (1960), pp. 130–148.

15. See Note 5 for Chapter 1.

16. Data for 1986 from David Brillinger, University of California, Berkeley. See David R. Brillinger, "Mapping aggregate birth data," in A. C. Singh and P. Whitridge (eds.), *Analysis of Data in Time*, Statistics Canada, 1990, pp. 77–83. A boxplot similar to Figure 2.5 appears in David R. Brillinger, "Some examples of random process environmental data analysis," in P. K. Sen and C. R. Rao (eds.), *Handbook of Statistics*, Vol. 18, *Bioenvironmental and Public Health Statistics*, North-Holland, 2000.

17. Paul E. O'Brien et al., "Laparascopic adjustable gastric banding in severely obese adolescents," *Journal of the American Medical Association*, 303 (2010), pp. 519–526. We thank the authors for providing the data.
18. The current roster as of January 2011 was obtained from `canadiens.nhl.com`, and their salaries were obtained from `forecaster.thehockeynews.com`.
19. Nicolas Guéguen and Christine Petr, "Odors and consumer behavior in a restaurant," *Journal of Hospitality Management*, 25 (2006), pp. 335–339. We thank Nicolas Guéguen for providing the data.
20. James A. Levine et al., "Inter-individual variation in posture allocation: possible role in human obesity," *Science*, 307 (2005), pp. 584–586. We thank James Levine for providing the data.
21. Bruce Rind and David Strohmetz, "Effects of beliefs about future weather conditions on restaurant tipping,"*Journal of Applied Social Psychology*, 31 (2001), pp. 2160–2164. We thank the authors for supplying the original data.
22. A sample of responses to the 1901 Census of Canada is available at the Canadian Families Project of the University of Victoria Web site, `www.uvic.ca/hrd/cfp/data`. The sample and the data are described in Canadian Families Project, *The National Sample of the 1901 Census of Canada*, 2002, on this Web site. Table 2.5 is a random sample of the 47,417 positive incomes in the census sample. The information on bread and beef prices (for 1900) comes from James Powell, *A History of the Canadian Dollar*, Bank of Canada, no date, at `www.bank-canada.ca/en/d`.

Chapter 3

1. See Note 9 for Chapter 1.
2. Monsoon rainfall from B. Parthasarathy, Indian Institute of Tropical Meteorology, at `www.iges.org`. The data cover the years 1871 to 2000.
3. Margaret A. McDowell et al., "Anthropometric reference data for children and adults: United States, 2003–2006," National Health Statistics Reports, No. 10 (October 2008), at `www.cdc.gov/nchs`. This report provides the means of various anthropometric measurements. Standard deviations were computed from the first and third quartiles assuming Normality.
4. All SAT facts are from the College Board Web site, `www.collegeboard.com`, and all ACT facts are from the ACT Web site, `www.act.org`.
5. See Note 3.
6. From the 2009–2010 "Guide for the College Bound Student Athlete" at `www.ncaastudent.org/NCAA_Guide.pdf`.
7. All MCAT facts are from the Medical College Admission Test Web site, `www.aamc.org/students/mcat/`.
8. Detailed data appear in P. S. Levy et al., *Total Serum Cholesterol Values for Youths 12–17 Years*, Vital and Health Statistics, Series 11, No. 155, National Center for Health Statistics, 1976.
9. See Note 20 for Chapter 2.
10. See Note 3.
11. See Note 20 for Chapter 1.
12. The data were provided by Nicolas Fisher.
13. See Note 7 for Chapter 2.
14. See Note 2.

Chapter 4

1. Neal E. Cantin et al., "Ocean warming slows coral growth in the central Red Sea," *Science*, 329 (2010), pp. 322–325.
2. Data for 2007 graduates from the College Board Web site, `www.collegeboard.com`.
3. Initial concerns were based on government data for 2005, presented in "An accident waiting to happen?" *Consumer Reports*, March 2007, pp. 16–19. Data for 2010 were found online at `web.mit.edu/airlinedata/www/default.html` (go to the *Employee Data and Analysis* link for each airline) and at the Department of Transportation Web site at `airconsumer.dot.gov/reports/2011/February/2011FebruaryATCR.PDF`.
4. The Florida Department of Highway Safety and Motor Vehicles (`www.flhsmv.gov/dmv/vslfacts.html`) gives the number of registered vessels. The Florida Wildlife Commission maintains a manatee death database at `research.myfwc.com/manatees`.
5. See Note 1.
6. Data for Figure 4.4(b) come from William Gray's Web site, `hurricane.atmos.colostate.edu`. Data for Figure 4.4(c) were provided by Drina Iglesia, Purdue University, from a study reported in D. D. S. Iglesia, E. J. Cragoe, Jr., and J. W. Vanable, "Electric field strength and epithelization in the newt (*Notophthalmus viridescens*)," *Journal of Experimental Zoology*, 274 (1996), pp. 56–62. Data for Figure 4.4(d) are for the Wilshire 5000 stock index. As a fine point, plots (b), (c), and (d) are square with the same scales on both axes because both variables measure similar quantities in the same units.

7. This exercise is motivated by Scott Berry, "Statistical fallacies in sports," *Chance*, 19, No. 4 (2006), pp. 50–56, where scores from the 2006 Masters are analyzed.

8. Andrew J. Oswald et al., "Objective confirmation of subjective measures of human well-being: evidence from the U.S.A.," *Science*, 327 (2010), pp. 576–579.

9. From a graph in Naomi E. Allen et al., "Moderate alcohol intake and cancer incidence in women," *Journal of the National Cancer Institute*, 101 (2009), pp. 296–305.

10. From a graph in Magdalena Bermejo et al., "Ebola outbreak killed 5000 gorillas," *Science*, 314 (2006), p. 1564.

11. From a graph in Bernt-Erik Saether, Steiner Engen, and Erik Mattysen, "Demographic characteristics and population dynamical patterns of solitary birds," *Science*, 295 (2002), pp. 2070–2073.

12. From a graph in Sabrina M. Tom et al., "The neural basis of loss aversion in decision-making under risk," *Science*, 315 (2007), pp. 515–518.

13. From a graph in Sergio M. Vallina and Rafel Simó, "Strong relationship between DMS and the solar radiation dose over the global surface ocean," *Science*, 315 (2007), pp. 506–508.

14. From a graph in Camilla A. Hinde et al., "Parent-offspring conflict and coadaptation," *Science*, 327 (2010), pp. 1373–1376.

15. See Note 21 in Chapter 2.

16. From a graph in Martin Wild et al., "From dimming to brightening: decadal changes in solar radiation at Earth's surface," *Science*, 308 (2005), pp. 847–850.

17. Brian J. Whipp and Susan A. Ward, "Will women soon outrun men?" *Nature*, 355 (1992), p. 25.

18. From a graph in Glenn J. Tattersall et al., "Heat exchange from the toucan bill reveals a controllable vascular thermal radiator," *Science*, 325 (2009), pp. 468–470.

19. From a graph in Naomi I. Eisenberger, Matthew D. Lieberman, and Kipling D. Williams, "Does rejection hurt? An fMRI study of social exclusion," *Science*, 302 (2003), pp. 290–292.

Chapter 5

1. From a graph in James A. Levine, Norman L. Eberhardt, and Michael D. Jensen, "Role of nonexercise activity thermogenesis in resistance to fat gain in humans," *Science*, 283 (1999), pp. 212–214.

2. See Note 1 for Chapter 4.

3. From a graph in Tania Singer et al., "Empathy for pain involves the affective but not sensory components of pain," *Science*, 303 (2004), pp. 1157–1162. Data for other brain regions showed a stronger correlation and no outliers.

4. Contributed by Marigene Arnold, Kalamazoo College.

5. Gannett News Service article appearing in the *Lafayette (Ind.) Journal and Courier*, April 23, 1994.

6. P. Goldblatt (ed.), *Longitudinal Study: Mortality and Social Organization*, Her Majesty's Stationery Office, 1990. At least, so claims Richard Conniff, *The Natural History of the Rich*, Norton, 2002, p. 45. The Goldblatt report is not available to us.

7. Laura L. Calderon et al., "Risk factors for obesity in Mexican-American girls: dietary factors, anthropometric factors, physical activity, and hours of television viewing," *Journal of the American Dietetic Association*, 96 (1996), pp. 1177–1179.

8. *The Health Consequences of Smoking: 1983*, Public Health Service, Washington, DC, 1983.

9. Data provided by Robert Dale, Purdue University.

10. G. L. Kooyman et al., "Diving behavior and energetics during foraging cycles in king penguins," *Ecological Monographs*, 62 (1992), pp. 143–163.

11. S. Chu, "Diamond ring pricing using simple linear regression," *Journal of Statistics Education*, 4 (1996), available online at www.amstat.org/publications/jse/v4n3/datasets.chu.html.

12. Karl Pearson and A. Lee, "On the laws of inheritance in man," *Biometrika*, 2 (1902), p. 357. These data also appear in D. J. Hand et al., *A Handbook of Small Data Sets*, Chapman & Hall, 1994. This book offers more than 500 data sets that can be used in statistical exercises.

13. See Note 11 for Chapter 4.

14. From a presentation by Charles Knauf, Monroe County (NY) Environmental Health Laboratory.

15. Frank J. Anscombe, "Graphs in statistical analysis," *The American Statistician*, 27 (1973), pp. 17–21.

16. Debora L. Arsenau, "Comparison of diet management instruction for patients with non–insulin dependent diabetes mellitus: learning activity package vs. group instruction," MS thesis, Purdue University, 1993.

17. From a graph in G. D. Martinsen, E. M. Driebe, and T. G. Whitham, "Indirect interactions mediated by changing plant chemistry: beaver browsing benefits beetles," *Ecology*, 79 (1998), pp. 192–200.

18. P. Velleman, *ActivStats 2.0*, Addison Wesley Interactive, 1997.

19. From William Gray's Web site, hurricane.atmos.colostate.edu. Forecasts are those made each June.

20. Data for 1936 to 1999 are from a graph in Bruce J. Peterson et al., "Increasing river discharge to the Arctic Ocean," *Science*, 298 (2002), pp. 2171–2173. Data for 2000 to 2008 are from a graph in I. Ashik et al.,

"Arctic report card: update for 2010," available online at `www.arctic.noaa.gov/reportcard/ArcticReportCard_full_report.pdf`. The graph is on page 41 of the report.

21. See Note 17 for Chapter 4.

Chapter 6

1. The National Longitudinal Study of Adolescent Health interviewed a stratified random sample of 27,000 adolescents, then reinterviewed many of the subjects six years later, when most were aged 19 to 25. These data are from the Wave III reinterviews in 2000 and 2001, found at the Web site of the Carolina Population Center, `www.cpc.unc.edu`.

2. Rani A. Desai et al., "Video-gaming among high school students: health correlates, gender differences, and problematic gaming," *Pediatrics*, 126 (2010), pp. 1416–1424.

3. From the October 2008 Current Population Survey, at `www.census.gov`.

4. These data are from an April 20, 2010, report, "Teens and mobile phones," by Amanda Lenhart, Rich Ling, Scott Campbell, and Kristen Purcell of the Pew Internet and American Life Project. Found online at `pewinternet.org/Reports/2010/Teens-and-Mobile-Phones.aspx`.

5. This General Social Survey exercise presents a table constructed using the search function at the GSS archive, `sda.berkeley.edu/archive.htm`. These data are from the 2008 GSS.

6. Gregory D. Myer et al., "Youth versus adult Weightlifting injuries presenting to United States emergency rooms: accidental versus nonaccidental injury mechanisms," *Journal of Strength and Conditioning Research*, 23 (2009), pp. 2054–2060.

7. Sanders Korenman and David Neumark, "Does marriage really make men more productive?" *Journal of Human Resources*, 26 (1991), pp. 282–307.

8. D. Gonzales et al., "*Journal of the American Medical Association* varenicline, an $\alpha 4\beta 2$ nicotinic acetylcholine receptor partial agonist, vs. sustained-release bupropion and placebo for smoking cessation," *New England Journal of Medicine*, 340 (1999), pp. 685–691.

9. Michael Gurian, "Where have the men gone? No place good," *Washington Post*, December 4, 2005, at `www.washingtonpost.com`. The data are from the 2009 *Digest of Education Statistics* at the Web site of the National Center for Education Statistics, `nces.ed.gov`.

10. Nancy J. O. Birkmeyer, "Hospital complication rates with bariatric surgery in Michigan," *Journal of the American Medical Association*, 304 (2010), pp. 435–442.

11. The data for the University of Michigan Health and Retirement Study can be downloaded from `ssl.isr.umich.edu/hrs/start.php`.

12. R. Shine, T. R. L. Madsen, M. J. Elphick, and P. S. Harlow, "The influence of nest temperatures and maternal brooding on hatchling phenotypes in water pythons," *Ecology*, 78 (1997), pp. 1713–1721.

Chapter 7

1. Data for Cohort 2 in Richard A. Morgan et al., "Cancer regression in patients after transfer of genetically engineered lymphocytes," *Science*, 314 (2006), pp. 126–129. The doubling time data are given in the paper, and the immune response data appear in the supplementary online material.

2. See Note 15 in Chapter 1.

3. Data provided by Brigitte Baldi, University of California at Irvine.

4. From a graph in Stan Boutin et al., "Anticipatory reproduction and population growth in seed predators," *Science*, 314 (2006), pp. 1928–1930.

5. J. T. Dwyer et al., "Memory of food intake in the distant past," *American Journal of Epidemiology*, 130 (1989), pp. 1033–1046.

6. Data from a plot in Josef P. Rauschecker, Biao Tian, and Marc Hauser, "Processing of complex sounds in the macaque nonprimary auditory cortex," *Science*, 268 (1995), pp. 111–114. The paper states that there are $n = 41$ observations, but only $n = 37$ can be read accurately from the plot.

7. Mei-Hui Chen, "An exploratory comparison of American and Asian consumers' catalog patronage behavior," MS thesis, Purdue University, 1994.

8. "Dancing in step," *Economist*, March 22, 2001.

9. Janice E. Williams et al., "Anger proneness predicts coronary heart disease risk," *Circulation*, 101 (2000), pp. 2034–2039.

10. From a graph in Peter A. Raymond and Jonathan J. Cole, "Increase in the export of alkalinity from North America's largest river," *Science*, 301 (2003), pp. 88–91.

11. From the Nenana Ice Classic Web site, `www.nenanaakiceclassic.com`. See Raphael Sagarin and Fiorenza Micheli, "Climate change in nontraditional data sets," *Science*, 294 (2001), p. 811, for a careful discussion.

12. Data for 2004 from Alan Heston, Robert Summers, and Bettina Aten, *Penn World Table Version 6.2*, Center for International Comparisons of Production, Income, and Prices at the University of Pennsylvania, September 2006, at `pwt.econ.upenn.edu`.

13. Louie H. Yang, "Periodical cicadas as resource pulses in North American forests," *Science*, 306 (2004), pp. 1565–1567. The data are simulated Normal values that match the means and standard deviations reported in this article.

14. Alan S. Banks et al., "Juvenile hallux abducto valgus association with metatarsus adductus," *Journal of the American Podiatric Medical Association*, 84 (1994), pp. 219–224.

15. Todd W. Anderson, "Predator responses, prey refuges, and density-dependent mortality of a marine fish," *Ecology*, 81 (2001), pp. 245–257.

16. From a graph in Craig Packer et al., "Ecological change, group territoriality, and population dynamics in Serengeti lions," *Science*, 307 (2005), pp. 390–393.

17. Peter H. Chen, Neftali Herrera, and Darren Christiansen, "Relationships between gate velocity and casting features among aluminum round castings," no date. Provided by Darren Christiansen.

18. Data compiled from a table of percents in "Americans view higher education as key to the American dream," press release by the National Center for Public Policy and Higher Education, at www.highereducation.org, May 3, 2000.

19. G. Adams et al., "A study of differences in Canadian university students' gambling and proximity to a casino," *Journal of Gambling Issues*, 19 (January 2007), pp. 9–17, at www.camh.net/egambling.

Chapter 8

1. From the *New York Times*/CBS News Poll at www.nytimes.com. The methodological statement is similar for most polls listed.

2. Gary S. Foster and Craig M. Eckert, "Up from the grave: a sociohistorical reconstruction of an African American community from cemetary data in the rural Midwest," *Journal of Black Studies*, 33 (2003), pp. 468–489.

3. Pew Forum on Religion and Public Life, *Spirit and Power: A 10-Country Survey of Pentecostals*, October 2006, at www.pewforum.org.

4. Information from various articles in the special issue on cell phone surveys, *Public Opinion Quarterly*, 71, No. 5 (2007). See also the Pew study cited in Note 6 for a comparison of a standard RDD survey with a rigorous survey that reduced nonresponse from 73% to 49%. The 2009 cell phone use numbers were obtained from the CDC Web site www.cdc.gov.

5. For information about the 2009 American Community Survey of households (there is a separate sample of group quarters), go to www.census.gov/acs.

6. The Pew press release and the full report "Polls face growing resistance, but still representative" (dated April 20, 2004) are at people-press.org/reports. Following the standards of the American Association for Public Opinion Research, the report gives a contact rate (75.5%), a cooperation rate (38.2%), and an overall response rate (26.6%).

7. For more detail on the limits of memory in surveys, see N. M. Bradburn, L. J. Rips, and S. K. Shevell, "Answering autobiographical questions: the impact of memory and inference on surveys," *Science*, 236 (1987), pp. 157–161.

8. The immigration questions are from the *New York Times/CBS News Poll* taken May 18 to 23, 2007, found at www.pollingreport.com. The responses on welfare are from a *New York Times*/CBS News Poll reported in the *New York Times*, July 5, 1992. Many other examples appear in T. W. Smith, "That which we call welfare by any other name would smell sweeter," *Public Opinion Quarterly*, 51 (1987), pp. 75–83. The survey on the effect of question order in Example 8.9 is cited in Daniel Kahnemann et al., "Would you be happier if you were richer? A focusing illusion," *Science*, 312 (2006), pp. 1908–1910.

9. Giuliana Coccia, "An overview of non-response in Italian telephone surveys," *Proceedings of the 99th Session of the International Statistical Institute*, 1993, Book 3, pp. 271–272.

10. You can go to www.pollingreport.com to see a compilation of the results from many polling agencies on a variety of issues.

11. From the Web site of the Gallup Organization, www.gallup.com. Individual poll reports remain on this site for only a limited time.

12. Information about areas codes can be found on the North American Numbering Plan Administration Web site, www.nanpa.com.

13. Robert C. Parker and Patrick A. Glass, "Preliminary results of double-sample forest inventory of pine and mixed stands with high- and low-density LiDAR," in Kristina F. Connoe (ed.), *Proceedings of the 12th Biennial Southern Silvicultural Research Conference*, U.S. Department of Agriculture, Forest Service, Southern Research Station, 2004. The researchers actually sampled every 10th plot. This is a systematic sample; see Exercise 8.36.

14. Bryan E. Porter and Thomas D. Berry, "A nationwide survey of self-reported red light running: measuring prevalence, predictors, and perceived consequences," *Accident Analysis and Prevention*, 33 (2001), pp. 735–741.

15. The article can be found at www2.macleans.ca/2010/07/16/sometimes-a-gaffe-is-more-than-a-gaffe/.

16. Information about the Ontario College of Pharmacists obtained from their Web site, www.ocpinfo.com.

17. Clyde O. McDaniel, Jr., "Dating roles and reasons for dating," *Journal of Marriage and the Family*, 31 (1969), pp. 97–107.

18. The Health Care in Canada Survey can be found by going to survey reports and presentations at www.hcic-sssc.ca.

19. Lydia Saad, "Gallup Poll: Many Americans say Gulf beaches, wildlife will never recover," at www.gallup.com/poll/140762/Americans-Say-Gulf-Beaches-Wildlife-Recover.aspx.

20. Mario A. Parada et al., "The validity of self-reported seatbelt use: Hispanic and non-Hispanic drivers in El Paso," *Accident Analysis and Prevention*, 33 (2001), pp. 139–143.

Chapter 9

1. I. J. Goldberg et al., "Wine and your heart: a science advisory for healthcare professionals from the Nutrition Committee, Council on Epidemiology and Prevention, and Council on Cardiovascular Nursing of the American Heart Association," *Circulation*, 103 (2001), pp. 472–475.

2. J. E. Muscat et al., "Handheld cellular telephone use and risk of brain cancer," *Journal of the American Medical Association*, 284 (2000), pp. 3001–3007.

3. Hyunjin Song and Norbert Schwarz, "If it's hard to read, it's hard to do: processing fluency affects effort prediction and motivation," *Psychological Science*, 19 (2008), pp. 986–988.

4. Hsin-Chieh Yeh et al., "Smoking, smoking cessation, and risk for type 2 diabetes mellitus: a cohort study," *Annals of Internal Medicine*, 152 (2010), pp. 10–17.

5. Charles A. Nelson III et al., "Cognitive recovery in socially deprived young children: the Bucharest Early Intervention Project," *Science*, 318 (2007), pp. 1937–1940.

6. The description of the factors and the response is based on a portion of the study by Alice Healy et al., "Terrorism after 9/11: reactions to simulated news reports," *American Journal of Psychology*, 122 (2009), pp. 153–165.

7. See Note 17 for Chapter 2.

8. K. B. Suttle, Meredith A. Thomsen, and Mary E. Power, "Species interactions reverse grassland responses to changing climate," *Science*, 315 (2007), pp. 640–642. See Chapter 25 for an analysis of some data from this experiment.

9. Julie Mares et al., "Healthy diets and the subsequent prevalence of nuclear cataract in women," *Archives of Opthalmology*, 128 (2010), pp. 738–749.

10. Marielle H. Emmelot-Vonk et al., "Effect of testosterone supplementation on functional mobility, cognition, and other parameters in older men," *Journal of the American Medical Association*, 299 (2008), pp. 39–52.

11. David L. Strayer, Frank A. Drews, and William A. Johnston, "Cell phone–induced failures of visual attention during simulated driving," *Journal of Experimental Psychology: Applied*, 9 (2003), pp. 23–32.

12. See Note 12 for Chapter 2.

13. Brad J. Bushman, "Violence and sex in television programs do not sell products in advertisements," *Psychological Science*, 16 (2005), pp. 702–707.

14. K. J. Mukamal et al., "Prior alcohol consumption and mortality following acute myocardial infarction," *Journal of the American Medical Association*, 285 (2001), pp. 1965–1970.

15. Rita F. Redburg, "Vitamin E and cardiovascular health," *Journal of the American Medical Association*, 294 (2005), pp. 107–109.

16. Jo Phelan et al., "The stigma of homelessness: the impact of the label 'homeless' on attitudes towards poor persons," *Social Psychology Quarterly*, 60 (1997), pp. 323–337.

17. Esther Duflo, Rema Hanna, and Stephan Ryan, "Monitoring works: getting teachers to come to school," report dated November 21, 2007, at econ-mit.edu/files/2066.

18. John H. Kagel, Raymond C. Battalio, and C. G. Miles, "Marijuana and work performance: results from an experiment," *Journal of Human Resources*, 15 (1980), pp. 373–395.

19. Shailja V. Nigdikar et al., "Consumption of red wine polyphenols reduces the susceptibility of low-density lipoproteins to oxidation in vivo," *American Journal of Clinical Nutrition*, 68 (1998), pp. 258–265. (There were in fact only 30 subjects, some of whom received more than one treatment, with a four-week period intervening.)

20. The description of the factors and the response is based on a portion of the study by Brian Wnasik and Perre Chandon, "Can 'low-fat' nutrition labels lead to obesity?" *Journal of Marketing Research*, 43 (2006), pp. 605–617.

21. Ian G. Williamson et al., "Antibiotics and topical nasal steroid for treatment of acute maxillary sinusitis," *Journal of the American Medical Association*, 298 (2007), pp. 2487–2496.

22. Based on Evan H. DeLucia et al., "Net primary production of a forest ecosystem with experimental CO_2 enhancement," *Science*, 284 (1999), pp. 1177–1179. The investigators used the block design.
23. The study is described in Gina Kolata, "New study finds vitamins are not cancer preventers," *New York Times*, July 21, 1994. Look in the *Journal of the American Medical Association* of the same date for the details.
24. R. C. Shelton et al., "Effectiveness of St. John's wort in major depression," *Journal of the American Medical Association*, 285 (2001), pp. 1978–1986.

Data Ethics Notes

1. John C. Bailar III, "The real threats to the integrity of science," *Chronicle of Higher Education*, April 21, 1995, pp. B1–B2.
2. See the details on the Web site of the Office for Human Research Protections of the Department of Health and Human Services, www.hhs.gov/ohrp.
3. The difficulties of interpreting guidelines for informed consent and for the work of institutional review boards in medical research are a main theme of Beverly Woodward, "Challenges to human subject protections in U.S. medical research," *Journal of the American Medical Association*, 282 (1999), pp. 1947–1952. The references in this paper point to other discussions. Updated regulations and guidelines appear on the OHRP Web site (see Note 2).
4. Quotation from the *Report of the Tuskegee Syphilis Study Legacy Committee*, May 20, 1996. A detailed history is James H. Jones, Bad Blood: *The Tuskegee Syphilis Experiment*, Free Press, 1993.
5. Dr. Hennekens's words are from an interview in the Annenberg/Corporation for Public Broadcasting video series *Against All Odds: Inside Statistics*. The lack of certainty that Dr. Hennekens refers to is now called "clinical equipoise" in discussions of ethics.
6. R. D. Middlemist, E. S. Knowles, and C. F. Matter, "Personal space invasions in the lavatory: suggestive evidence for arousal," *Journal of Personality and Social Psychology*, 33 (1976), pp. 541–546.
7. For a review of domestic violence experiments, see C. D. Maxwell et al., *The Effects of Arrest on Intimate Partner Violence: New Evidence from the Spouse Assault Replication Program*, U.S. Department of Justice, NCH188199, 2001. Available online at www.ojp.usdoj.gov/nij/pubs-sum/188199.htm.

Chapter 10

1. The Gallup Poll is based on telephone interviews. Each adult interviewed by Gallup had a known chance of being among those selected, but this chance depended on characteristics such as gender, age, type of phone (cell or landline), and geographic location. Gallup used special weights to adjust for differences in the probability of being selected to obtain an estimate of the proportion of all adults who bought a lottery ticket in the population of all U.S. adults. The actual estimate used by Gallup was close to 46%, and Gallup used this result to estimate what was true for the population.
2. Note that pennies have rims that make spinning more stable. The probability of a head in spinning a coin depends on the type of coin and also on the surface. See Exercise 20.10 for an account of 56% heads in spinning a Belgian one-euro coin. *Chance News 11.02* at www.dartmouth.edu/~chance reports about 45% heads in more than 20,000 spins of American pennies by Robin Lock's students at Saint Lawrence University.
3. The percents were found at the GMAT Web site, www.gmac.com/gmac/ResearchandTrends/GMATStats/ProfileofCandidates.htm.
4. Data for 2006 from the Web site of Statistics Canada, www.statcan.ca.
5. You can find a mathematical explanation of Benford's law in Ted Hill, "The first-digit phenomenon," *American Scientist*, 86 (1996), pp. 358–363; and Ted Hill, "The difficulty of faking data," *Chance*, 12, No. 3 (1999), pp. 27–31. Applications in fraud detection are discussed in the second paper by Hill and in Mark A. Nigrini, "I've got your number," *Journal of Accountancy*, May 1999, available online at www.aicpa.org/pubs/jofa/joaiss.htm.
6. Based on a November 2007 Gallup poll. Found at www.gallup.com/poll/1648/Personal-Health-Issues.aspx# 2.
7. Information from www.indiana.edu/r̃egistra/gradedist/.
8. Thomas K. Cureton et al., *Endurance of Young Men*, Monographs of the Society for Research in Child Development, Vol. 10, No. 1, 1945.
9. Based on a January 2007 Gallup poll. Found at www.gallup.com/poll/15370/Party-Affiliation.aspx.
10. See Note 15 for Chapter 1.
11. National population estimates for July 1, 2008, at the Census Bureau Web site www.census.gov. The table

omits people who consider themselves to belong to more than one race.

12. Based on data from the *2010 Statistical Abstract of the United States*, Table 58, at www.census.gov.

Chapter 11

1. U.S. Census Bureau, *Income, Poverty, and Health Insurance in the United States: 2009*, Current Population Reports P60-238. Available online at www.census.gov/prod/2010pubs/p60-238.pdf.

2. Strictly speaking, the formula for the standard deviation of assumes that we draw an SRS of size n from an *infinite* population. If the population has finite size N, this standard deviation is multiplied by . This "finite population correction" approaches 1 as N increases. When the population is at least 20 times as large as the sample, the correction factor is between about 0.97 and 1. It is reasonable to use the simpler form in these settings.

3. See Note 20 for Chapter 2.

4. Found online at pages.stern.nyu.edu/adamodar/New_Home_Page/datafile/histret.html. Sophisticates will note that for compounding over several years we want the geometric mean return, which was 9.38%.

Chapter 12

1. This is one of several tests discussed in Bernard M. Branson, "Rapid HIV testing: 2005 update," a presentation by the Centers for Disease Control and Prevention, at www.cdc.gov. The Malawi clinic result is reported by Bernard M. Branson, "Point-of-care rapid tests for HIV antibody," *Journal of Laboratory Medicine*, 27 (2003), pp. 288–295.

2. Robert P. Dellavalle et al., "Going, going, gone: lost Internet references," *Science*, 302 (2003), pp. 787–788.

3. From the U.S. Department of Commerce Bureau of Economic Analysis at www.bea.gov, March 2011. Motor vehicle sales information is included with the National Economic Accounts.

4. Information about Internet users comes from sample surveys carried out by the Pew Internet and American Life Project, at www.pewinternet.org.

5. S. H. Sicherer, "Prevalence of peanut and tree nut allergy in the US determined by random digit dial telephone survey," *Journal of Allergy and Clinical Immunology*, 103 (1999), pp. 559–562.

6. Probabilities from trials with 2897 people known to be free of HIV antibodies and 673 people known to be infected, reported in J. Richard George, "Alternative specimen sources: methods for confirming positives," 1998 Conference on the Laboratory Science of HIV, found online at the Centers for Disease Control and Prevention, www.cdc.gov.

7. From the statistics page of the National Science Foundation Web site, www.nsf.gov/statistics.

8. See Note 4 for Chapter 1.

9. From the Internal Revenue Service Web site, www.irs.gov/taxstats.

10. Sales in 2006 from the Web site of the Entertainment Software Association, at www.theesa.com.

11. Projections from U.S. Department of Education, *Projections of Education Statistics to 2016*, December 2007, at nces.ed.gov.

12. Data from Patricia Heithaus and the Department of Biology at Kenyon College. Provided by Brad Hartlaub.

13. F. J. G. M. Klaassen and J. R. Magnus, "How to reduce the service dominance in tennis? Empirical results from four years at Wimbledon," in S. J. Haake and A. O. Coe (eds.), *Tennis Science and Technology*, Blackwell, 2000, pp. 277–284.

14. Amanda Lenhart et al., "Teens and mobil phones," April 20, 2010, from the Pew Internet and American Life Project, www.pewinternet.org.

15. From the National Institutes of Health's National Digestive Diseases Information Clearinghouse, at www.wrongdiagnosis.com.

16. The probabilities given are realistic, according to the fundraising firm SCM Associates, at scmassoc.com.

17. B. Budowle et al., "Population data on the thirteen CODIS core short tandem repeat loci in African Americans, U.S. Caucasians, Hispanics, Bahamians, Jamaicans, and Trinidadians,"*Journal of Forensic Sciences*, 1999, pp. 1277–1286.

18. Marilyn vos Savant, Ask Marilyn column, *Parade Magazine*, p. 16, September 9, 1990, p. 16.

Chapter 13

1. From the Canadian Internet Use Survey at www.statcan.gc.ca/daily-quotidien/100510/dq100510a-eng.htm.

2. The survey question is reported in Trish Hall, "Shop? Many say 'Only if I must,'" *New York Times*, November 28, 1990. In fact, 66% (1650 of 2500) in the sample said "Agree."

3. Information obtained from the Planned Parenthood Web site, www.plannedparenthood.org.

4. Results for the full 2009 season at www.pgatour.com.

5. From the General Motors Web site www.gm.com/news-article.jsp?brand=gm&id=/content/Pages/news/us/en/2011/Jan/0117_chev_global.html

6. C. E. Finley et al., "Retention rates and weight loss in a commercial weight loss program," *International Journal of Obesity*, 31 (2006), pp. 292–298.
7. Associated Press news item dated December 9, 2007, found at www.msnbc.msn.com.

Chapter 14

1. Margaret A. McDowell et al., "Anthropometric reference data for children and adults: U.S. population, 1999–2002," National Center for Health Statistics, Advance Data from Vital and Health Statistics, No. 361, 2005, at www.cdc.gov/nchs.
2. Information about the NAEP test can be found online at nationsreportcard.gov/math_2009/.
3. See Note 21 for Chapter 2.
4. See Note 20 for Chapter 1.
5. Chi-Fu Jeffrey Yang, Peter Gray, and Harrison G. Pope, Jr., "Male body image in Taiwan versus the West," *American Journal of Psychiatry*, 162 (2005), pp. 263–269.
6. M. Ann Laskey et al., "Bone changes after 3 mo of lactation: influence of calcium intake, breast-milk output, and vitamin D–receptor genotype," *American Journal of Clinical Nutrition*, 67 (1998), pp. 685–692.

Chapter 15

1. See Note 21 for Chapter 2.
2. Ajay Ghei, "An empirical analysis of psychological androgeny in the personality profile of the successful hotel manager," MS thesis, Purdue University, 1992.
3. Seung-Ok Kim, "Burials, pigs, and political prestige in Neolithic China," *Current Anthropology*, 35 (1994), pp. 119–141.
4. Gerardo Ramirez and Sian L. Bellock, "Writing about testing worries boosts exam performance in the classroom," *Science*, 331 (2011), pp. 211–213.
5. Kenneth A. Follett et al., "Pallidal versus subthalamic deep-brain stimulation for Parkinson's disease," *New England Journal of Medicine*, 362, No. 22 (2010), pp. 2077–2091.
6. Mario A. Parada et al., "The validity of self-reported seatbelt use: Hispanic and non-Hispanic drivers in El Paso," *Accident Analysis and Prevention*, 33 (2001), pp. 139–143.
7. See Note 6 for Chapter 14.
8. Data simulated from a Normal distribution based on information in Brian M. DeBroff and Patricia J. Pahk, "The ability of periorbitally applied antiglare products to improve contrast sensitivity in conditions of sunlight exposure," *Archives of Ophthamology*, 121 (2003), pp. 997–1001.

Chapter 16

1. See www.cdc.gov/nchs/tutorials/NHANES/SurveyDesign/intro_iii.htm.
2. See Note 14 for Chapter 8.
3. From the Gallup Web site, www.gallup.com. The poll was taken in July 2008.
4. For a discussion of statistical significance in the legal setting, see D. H. Kaye, "Is proof of statistical significance relevant?" *Washington Law Review*, 61 (1986), pp. 1333–1365. Kaye argues: "Presenting the *P*-value without characterizing the evidence by a significance test is a step in the right direction. Interval estimation, in turn, is an improvement over *P*-values."
5. Warren E. Leary, "Cell phones: questions but no answers," *New York Times*, October 26, 1999.
6. Poll published August 26, 2010, at www.harrisinteractive.com/NewsRoom/HarrisPolls/tabid/447/mid/1508/ articleId/555/ctl/ReadCustom%20Default/Default.aspx. A note at the bottom of the page says: "Because the sample is based on those who agreed to participate in the Harris Interactive panel, no estimates of theoretical sampling error can be calculated."
7. Justin S. Brashares et al., "Bushmeat hunting, wildlife declines, and fish supply in West Africa," *Science*, 306 (2004), pp. 1180–1183. The data used here (and in Figure 1B of the article) are found in the online supplementary material.
8. Gabriel Gregoratos et al., "ACC/AHA guidelines for implantation of cardiac pacemakers and antiarrhythmia devices: executive summary," *Circulation*, 97 (1998), pp. 1325–1335.

Chapter 17

1. Based on a news item "Bee off with you," *Economist*, November 2, 2002, p. 78.
2. Simplified from D. A. Marcus et al., "A double-blind provocative study of chocolate as a trigger of headache," *Cephalalgia*, 17 (1997), pp. 855–862.
3. Votes as of June 27, 2007, at www.pbs.org/wgbh/nova/sciencenow.
4. Data for U.S. searches in February 2008 from Hitwise, at www.hitwise.com.
5. U.S. Census Bureau, *Fertility of American Women: June 2004*, at www.census.gov.
6. Aaron S. Hervey et al., "Reaction time distribution analysis of neuropsychological performance in an ADHD sample," *Child Neuropsychology*, 12 (2006), pp. 125–140.
7. From a Gallup Poll taken in 2003, www.gallup.com.

8. John Schwartz, "Leisure pursuits of today's young men," *New York Times*, March 29, 2004. The source cited is comScore Media Matrix.

9. K. E. Hobbs et al., "Levels and patterns of persistent organochlorines in minke whale (*Balaenoptera acutorostrata*) stocks from the North Atlantic and European Arctic," *Environmental Pollution*, 121 (2003), pp. 239–252.

10. Maureen Hack et al., "Outcomes in young adulthood for very-low-birth-weight infants," *New England Journal of Medicine*, 346 (2002), pp. 149–157.

11. Mikyoung Park et al., "Recycling endosomes supply AMPA receptors for LTP," *Science*, 305 (2004), pp. 1972–1975.

12. Jon E. Keeley, C. J. Fotheringham, and Marco Morais, "Reexamining fire suppression impacts on brushland fire regimes," *Science*, 284 (1999), pp. 1829–1831.

13. Simplified from Sanjay K. Dhar, Claudia González-Vallejo, and Dilip Soman, "Modeling the effects of advertised price claims: tensile versus precise pricing," *Marketing Science*, 18 (1999), pp. 154–177.

14. Charles S. Fuchs et al., "Alcohol consumption and mortality among women," *New England Journal of Medicine*, 332 (1995), pp. 1245–1250.

15. See Note 21 for Chapter 2.

16. Data simulated from a Normal distribution with $\mu = 98.2$ and $\sigma = 0.7$. These values are based on P. A. Mackowiak, S. S. Wasserman, and M. M. Levine, "A critical appraisal of 98.6 degrees F, the upper limit of the normal body temperature, and other legacies of Carl Reinhold August Wunderlich," *Journal of the American Medical Association*, 268 (1992), pp. 1578–1580.

Chapter 18 Notes

1. Note 2 for Chapter 11 explains the reason for this condition in the case of inference about a population mean.

2. See Note 12 for Chapter 2.

3. See Note 21 for Chapter 2.

4. From a graph in Benedetto De Martino et al., "Frames, biases, and rational decision-making in the human brain," *Science*, 313 (2006), pp. 684–687. We simplified the design a bit for easier comprehension: the starting amounts and gambles offered differed from trial to trial, though still matched in pairs; 32 very unbalanced "catch trials" were mixed with the 64 experimental trials to be sure subjects were paying attention; and all money amounts were in British pounds, not dollars.

5. R. A. Berner and G. P. Landis, "Gas bubbles in fossil amber as possible indicators of the major gas composition of ancient air," *Science*, 239 (1988), pp. 1406–1409. The 95% *t* confidence interval is 54.78 to 64.40. A bootstrap BCa interval is 55.03 to 62.63. So *t* is reasonably accurate despite the skew and the small sample.

6. This study is available online at www.dispatch.com/live/content/databases/index.html.

7. Alice P. Melis, Brian Hare, and Michael Tomasello, "Chimpanzees recruit the best collaborators," *Science*, 311 (2006), pp. 1297–1300. A Normal quantile plot does not show major lack of Normality, and a saddlepoint approximation that allows for skew gives $P = 0.0039$. So the *t* test is reasonably accurate despite the skew and small sample size.

8. Josef P. Rauschecker, Biao Tian, and Marc Hauser, "Processing of complex sounds in the macaque nonprimary auditory cortex," *Science*, 268 (1995), pp. 111–114.

9. For a qualitative discussion explaining why skewness is the most serious violation of the Normal shape condition, see Dennis D. Boos and Jacqueline M. Hughes-Oliver, "How large does n have to be for the Z and t intervals?" *American Statistician*, 54 (2000), pp. 121–128. Our recommendations are based on extensive computer work. See, for example, Harry O. Posten, "The robustness of the one-sample *t*-test over the Pearson system," *Journal of Statistical Computation and Simulation*, 9 (1979), pp. 133–149; and E. S. Pearson and N. W. Please, "Relation between the shape of population distribution and the robustness of four simple test statistics," *Biometrika*, 62 (1975), pp. 223–241.

10. For more advanced users, a good way to ascertain if the *t* procedures are safe is to compare the 95% confidence interval produced by *t* with the BCa interval from a bootstrap with at least 1000 resamples. For (b) the *t* interval is 29,428 to 32,254 and a BCa interval is 29,106 to 31,894. For (c), on the other hand, *t* gives 38.93 to 40.49 and BCa gives 38.97 to 40.44. These results confirm the judgment that *t* is safe for (c) but not for (b).

11. Table 1 of E. Thomassot et al., "Methane-related diamond crystallization in the earth's mantle: stable isotopes evidence from a single diamond-bearing xenolith," *Earth and Planetary Science Letters*, 257 (2007), pp. 362–371.

12. From the online supplement to Tor D. Wager et al., "Placebo-induced changes in fMRI in the anticipation and experience of pain," *Science*, 303 (2004), pp. 1162–1167.

13. TUDA results for 2009 from the National Center for Education Statistics, at nationsreportcard.gov/tuda.asp.

14. Ravi Mehta and Rui Zhu, "Blue or red? Exploring the effect of color on cognitive task performances," *Science*, 323 (2009), pp. 1226–1229.

15. Raul de la Fuente-Fernandez et al., "Expectation and dopamine release: mechanism of the placebo effect in Parkinson's disease," *Science*, 293 (2001), pp. 1164–1166.

16. Robert R. Zarr and Dennis D. Leber, "Evaluation and selection of candidate thermal insulation materials for NIST SRM 1450d, fibrous-glass board," available online from the National Institute of Standards and Technology Web site, `www.nist.gov/manuscript-publication-search.cfm?pub_id=902936`.

17. J. D. Marshall et al., "Vehicle self-pollution intake fraction: children's exposure to school bus emissions," *Environmental Science and Technology*, 39 (2005), pp. 2559–2563.

18. See Note 14 for Chapter 7.

19. See Note 6 for Chapter 4.

20. Matthias R. Mehl et al., "Are women really more talkative than men?" *Science*, 317 (2007), p. 82.

21. See Note 1 for Chapter 7.

22. M. B. Laferty, "OSU scientist gets a kick out of sports controversy," *Columbus Dispatch*, November 21, 1993.

23. We thank Jason Hamilton, University of Illinois, for providing the data. The study is reported in Evan H. DeLucia et al., "Net primary production of a forest ecosystem with experimental CO_2 enhancement," *Science*, 284 (1999), pp. 1177–1179. No method for inference can be trusted with $n = 3$. In this study, each observation is very costly, so the small n is inevitable.

24. Michael W. Peugh, "Field investigation of ventilation and air quality in duck and turkey slaughter plants," MS thesis, Purdue University, 1996.

25. Harry B. Meyers, "Investigations of the life history of the velvetleaf seed beetle, *Althaeus folkertsi* Kingsolver," MS thesis, Purdue University, 1996. The 95% t interval is 1227.9 to 2507.6. A 95% bootstrap BCa interval is 1444 to 2718, confirming that t inference is inaccurate for these data.

26. J. Marcus Jobe and Hutch Jobe, "A statistical approach for additional infill development," *Energy Exploration and Exploitation*, 18 (2000), pp. 89–103. The comparison interval is the BCa interval based on 1000 bootstrap resamples.

27. This study is available online at `www.dispatch.com/live/content/databases/index.html`.

28. Ralf Bargou et al., "Tumor regression in cancer patients by very low doses of a T cell engaging antibody," *Science*, 321 (2008), pp. 974–977.

29. Data provided by Timothy Sturm.

30. Liann Yuh, "A biopharmaceutical example for undergraduate students," manuscript, no date.

31. See Note 21 for Chapter 2.

Chapter 19 Notes

1. See Note 20 for Chapter 2.

2. Detailed information about the conservative t procedures can be found in Paul Leaverton and John J. Birch, "Small sample power curves for the two sample location problem," *Technometrics*, 11 (1969), pp. 299–307; Henry Scheffé, "Practical solutions of the Behrens-Fisher problem," *Journal of the American Statistical Association*, 65 (1970), pp. 1501–1508; and D. J. Best and J. C. W. Rayner, "Welch's approximate solution for the Behrens-Fisher problem," *Technometrics*, 29 (1987), pp. 205–210.

3. Kathleen G. McKinney, "Engagement in community service among college students: is it affected by significant attachment relationships?" *Journal of Adolescence*, 25 (2002), pp. 139–154. To see the questions in the Inventory of Parent and Peer Attachments, go to `chipts.cch.ucla.edu/assessment/IB/List_Scales/inventory%20parent%20and %20peer%20 attachment.htm`.

4. See Note 10 for Chapter 2.

5. P. A. Handcock, "The effect of age and sex on the perception of time in life," *American Journal of Psychology*, 123 (2010), pp. 1–13.

6. See the extensive simulation studies in Harry O. Posten, "The robustness of the two-sample t-test over the Pearson system," *Journal of Statistical Computation and Simulation*, 6 (1978), pp. 295–311; and Harry O. Posten, H. Yeh, and Donald B. Owen, "Robustness of the two-sample t-test under violations of the homogeneity assumption," *Communications in Statistics*, 11 (1982), pp. 109–126.

7. See Note 19 for Chapter 2. Although the spending data are quite discrete, a bootstrap BCa 95% confidence interval for the difference in means based on 1000 resamples is 2.394 to 4.826, close to the Option 1 95% interval 2.209 to 4.736. So the sample means are sufficiently Normal to allow use of t procedures.

8. Parmeshwar S. Gupta, "Reaction of plants to the density of soil," *Journal of Ecology*, 21 (1933), pp. 452–474.

9. Data provided by Samuel Phillips, Purdue University.

10. See Note 20 in Chapter 18.

11. Michael A. Sayette et al., "Lost in the sauce, the effects of alcohol on mind wandering," *Psychological Science*, 20 (2009), pp. 747–752.

12. Eduardo Dias-Ferreira et al., "Chronic stress causes frontostriatal reorganization and affects decision-making," *Science*, 325 (2009), pp. 621–625. Many of the details appear in the supporting online material.

13. Jennifer A. Whitson and Adam D. Galinsky, "Lacking control increases illusory pattern perception," *Science,* 322 (2008), pp. 115–117.
14. World Health Organization Global InfoBase: Canada, at www.who.int/infobase.
15. Wayne J. Camera and Donald Powers, "Coaching and the SAT I," *TIP* (online journal at www.siop.org/tip), July 1999.
16. See Note 21 in Chapter 2.
17. Sherri A. Buzinski, "The effect of position of methylation on the performance properties of durable press treated fabrics," CSR490 honors paper, Purdue University, 1985.
18. Fabrizio Grieco, Arie J. van Noordwijk, and Marcel E. Visser, "Evidence for the effect of learning on timing of reproduction in blue tits," *Science,* 296 (2002), pp. 136–138. The data in Exercise 19.36 are from a graph in this paper.
19. Kathleen D. Vohs, Nicole L. Mead, and Miranda R. Goode, "The psychological consequences of money," *Science,* 314 (2006), pp. 1154–1156. We thank Kathleen Vohs for supplying the data.
20. Paul Kvam, "The effect of active learning methods on student retention in engineering statistics," *The American Statistician,* 54 (2000), pp. 136–140.
21. Data provided by Warren Page, New York City Technical College, from a study done by John Hudesman.
22. See Note 9 for Chapter 2.
23. Data provided by Marigene Arnold, Kalamazoo College.

Chapter 20

1. Joseph H. Catania et al., "Prevalence of AIDS-related risk factors and condom use in the United States," *Science,* 258 (1992), pp. 1101–1106.
2. See Note 2 for Chapter 11. The same finite population correction applies here.
3. The data were obtained from the GSS Cumulative Datafile 1972–2010 at sda.berkeley.edu/archive.htm. No weights were used, and the data were filtered to include ages between 18 and 30 and year equal to 2010.
4. The 2010 U.S. Digital Year in Review, at www.comscore.com.
5. The quotation is from page 1104 of the article cited in Note 1.
6. See Note 6 for Chapter 6.
7. Lydia Saad, "In U.S., 11% of households report computer crimes, a new high," December 2010, at www.gallup.com. The sampling scheme was more complex than an SRS, so the computation in the sample reporting crimes and treating this as an SRS is oversimplified.
8. G. A. Mauser and H. Taylor Buckner, "Canadian attitudes toward gun control: the real story," Mackenzie Institute, 1997, at teapot.usask.ca/cdn-firearms/Mauser/gunstory.html.
9. Gary Edwards and Josephine Mazzuca, "Three quarters of Canadians support doctor-assisted suicide," Gallup Poll press release, March 24, 1999, at www.gallup.com.
10. In fact, *P*-values for two-sided tests are more accurate than those for one-sided tests. Our rule of thumb is a compromise to avoid the confusion of too many rules.
11. Matthew A. Carlton and William D. Stansfield, "Making babies by the flip of a coin?" *American Statistician,* 59 (2005), pp. 180–182.
12. Data found on the New Scientist Web site, www.newscientist.com/article/dn1748-euro-coin-accused-of-unfair-flipping.html.
13. Alexander Todorov et al., "Inferences of competence from faces predict election outcomes," *Science,* 308 (2005), pp. 1623–1626.
14. Michele L. Head, "Examining college students' ethical values," Consumer Science and Retailing honors project, Purdue University, 2003.
15. See Note 3.
16. Elizabeth Cohen, "Your top health searches, asked and answered," Pew Internet and American Life Project, 2010, at pewinternet.org. The cell phone sample used random digit dialing drawn through a systematic sampling from dedicated wireless 100-blocks and shared service 100-blocks with no directory-listed landline numbers, so acting as if we have an SRS is oversimplified.
17. John Fagan et al., "Performance assessment under field conditions of a rapid immunological test for transgenic soybeans," *International Journal of Food Science and Technology,* 36 (2001), pp. 357–367.
18. See Note 6 for Chapter 18.
19. See Note 14 for Chapter 8.
20. Bobby D. Rampey et al., *The Nation's Report Card: Trends in Academic Progress in Reading and Mathematics, 2008,* can be found on the Web site nces.ed.gov/nationsreportcard/ under *Long-term Trend Assessments.*
21. Jon D. Miller, Eugenie C. Scott, and Shinji Okamoto, "Public acceptance of evolution," *Science,* 313 (2006), pp. 765–766. The information in the exercise appears in the supplementary online material.

22. A. Mantonakis et al., "Order in choice: effects of serial position on preferences," *Psychological Science*, 20 (2009), pp. 1309–1312.
23. Laura Tutor, "The best drive through in America, 2002," on the Web site `http://www.qsrmagazine.com/reports`.

Chapter 21

1. See Note 1 for Chapter 6.
2. Based on data in Amanda Lenhart, "Cell phones and American adults," September 2010, at `pewinternet.org`.
3. The data were obtained from the GSS Cumulative Datafile 1972–2010 at `sda.berkeley.edu/archive.htm`.
4. From the 2009 Youth Risk Behavior Surveillance System at `apps.nccd.cdc.gov/youthonline/App/Default.aspx`. The data are from a complex multistage sample, so acting as if we have SRSs is oversimplified.
5. Shauna B. Wilson et al., "Dating across race: an examination of African American Internet personal advertisements," *Journal of Black Studies*, 37 (2007), pp. 964–982.
6. This rule of thumb is quite conservative. It is in fact safe to arrange the data as a 2 × 2 table and apply the rule of thumb from Chapter 23 that all four *expected* counts must be 5 or greater. We give the conservative rule here because expected counts are messy to explain in the present context.
7. JoAnn K. Wells, Allan F. Williams, and Charles M. Farmer, "Seat belt use among African Americans, Hispanics, and whites," *Accident Analysis and Prevention*, 34 (2002), pp. 523–529.
8. Steiner Sulheim et al., "Helmet use and risk of head injuries in alpine skiers and snowboarders," *Journal of the American Medical Association*, 295 (2006), pp. 919–924.
9. Armando E. Giuliano et al., "Axillary dissection vs. no axillary dissection in woman with invasive breast cancer and sentinel node metastasis," *Journal of the American Medical Association*, 305 (2011), pp. 569–575. The sample sizes for the two groups and the proportions of patients in each group that are disease-free after 5 years have been chosen to match those in the paper.
10. From the Prevalence and Trends Data of the Behavioral Risk Factor Surveillance System at `www.cdc.gov/BRFSS/`.
11. See Amanda Lenhart and Mary Madden, "Teens, privacy and online social networks," Pew Internet and American Life Project, 2007, at `www.pewinternet.org`.
12. W. P. T. James et al., "Effect of sibutramine on cardiovascular outcomes in overweight and obese subjects," *New England Journal of Medicine*, 363 (2010), pp. 905–917.
13. Barbara Helmrich, "Window of opportunity? Adolescence, music and algebra," *Journal of Adolescent Research*, 25 (2010), pp. 557–577.
14. Arne L. Kalleberg and Kevin T. Leicht, "Gender and organizational performance: determinants of small business survival and success," *Academy of Management Journal*, 34 (1991), pp. 136–161.
15. François Gaudet et al., "Induction of tumors in mice by genomic hypomethylation," *Science*, 300 (2003), pp. 489–492.
16. See Note 17 for Chapter 20.
17. Richard M. Felder et al., "Who gets it and who doesn't: a study of student performance in an introductory chemical engineering course," *1992 ASEE Annual Conference Proceedings*, American Society for Engineering Education, Washington, DC, 1992, pp. 1516–1519.
18. See Note 8 for Chapter 6.
19. Data courtesy of Raymond Dumett, Purdue University.
20. Based on Alan G. Sanfey et al., "The neural basis of economic decision-making in the ultimatum game," *Science*, 300 (2003), pp. 1755–1758. The paper reports a chi-square test (equivalent to a two-sided z test). This analysis is incorrect for the paper's data, as there were in fact only 19 participants, each appearing twice in each row of the table given in the exercise. Exercise 21.28 therefore amends the data, assuming 76 participants, so that the elementary analysis is correct.
21. Clive G. Jones et al., "Chain reactions linking acorns to gypsy moth outbreaks and Lyme disease risk," *Science*, 279 (1998), pp. 1023–1026.
22. The study is reported in William Celis III, "Study suggests Head Start helps beyond school," *New York Times*, April 20, 1993. See `www.highscope.org`.
23. R. B. Turner et al., "Hand disinfection for the prevention of viral respiratory illness," ICAAC abstract 101, 2010.

Chapter 22

1. See Note 6 for Chapter 4.
2. See Note 4 for Chapter 21.
3. Lee Rainie and Bill Tancer, "36% of online American adults consult Wikipedia," Pew Internet and American Life Project, 2007, at `www.pewinternet.org`.
4. See Note 5 for Chapter 14.
5. K. S. Oberhauser, "Fecundity, lifespan and egg mass in butterflies: effects of male-derived nutrients and female

size," *Functional Ecology,* 11 (1997), pp. 166–175.

6. Michael R. Dohm, Jack P. Hayes, and Theodore Garland, Jr., "Quantitative genetics of sprint running speed and swimming endurance in laboratory house mice (*Mus domesticus*)," *Evolution,* 50 (1996), pp. 1688–1701.

7. See Note 10 for Chapter 17. The exercises are simplified, in that the measures reported in this paper were statistically adjusted for "sociodemographic status."

8. From the Web site of the Black Youth Project, blackyouthproject.uchicago.edu.

9. V. D. Bass, W. E. Hoffmann, and J. L. Dorner, "Normal canine lipid profiles and effects of experimentally induced pancreatitis and hepatic necrosis on lipids," *American Journal of Veterinary Research,* 37 (1976), pp. 1355–1357.

10. Jin Ha Lee and J. Stephen Downie, "Survey of music information needs, uses, and seeking behaviors: preliminary findings," *Proceedings of the 5th International Conference on Music Information Retrieval,* 2004, at ismir2004.ismir.net.

11. Josh McDermott and Marc D. Hauser, "Nonhuman primates prefer slow tempos but dislike music overall," *Cognition,* 104 (2007), pp. 654–668. Failure to take account of repeated measures on the same subjects is one of the most common errors observed in statistical analysis.

12. These data were originally collected by L. M. Linde of UCLA but were first published by M. R. Mickey, O. J. Dunn, and V. Clark, "Note on the use of stepwise regression in detecting outliers," *Computers and Biomedical Research,* 1 (1967), pp. 105–111. The data have been used by several authors. We found them in N. R. Draper and J. A. John, "Influential observations and outliers in regression," *Technometrics,* 23 (1981), pp. 21–26.

13. Jacqueline T. Ngai and Diane S. Srivastava, "Predators accelerate nutrient cycling in a bromeliad ecosystem," *Science,* 314 (2006), p. 963. We thank Jacqueline Ngai for providing the data.

14. Yvan R. Germain, "The dyeing of ramie with fiber reactive dyes using the cold pad-batch method," MS thesis, Purdue University, 1988.

15. Data provided by Marigene Arnold, Kalamazoo College.

16. Data provided by Corinne Lim, Purdue University, from a student project supervised by Professor Joseph Vanable.

17. Saiyad S. Ahmed, "Effects of microwave drying on checking and mechanical strength of low-moisture baked products," MS thesis, Purdue University, 1994.

18. Michael O. Finkelstein and Bruce Levin, "Statistical proof of discrimination in peremptory challenges," *Chance,* 17, No. 1 (2004), pp. 35–38.

Chapter 23

1. See Note 1 for Chapter 6.

2. Pennsylvania State University Division of Student Affairs, "Net behaviors November 2006," *Penn State Pulse,* at www.sa.psu.edu.

3. See Note 2 for Chapter 6.

4. There are many computer studies of the accuracy of chi-square critical values for χ^2. Our guideline goes back to W. G. Cochran (1954). Later work has shown that it is often conservative in the sense that, if the expected cell counts are all similar and the degrees of freedom exceed 1, the chi-square approximation works well for an average expected count as small as 1 or 2. Our guideline protects against dissimilar expected counts. It has the added advantage that it is safe in the 2×2 case, where the chi-square approximation is least good. So our guideline is helpful for beginners—there is no single condition that is not conservative and applies to 2×2 and larger tables with similar and dissimilar expected cell counts. There are exact procedures that (with software) should be used for tables that do not satisfy our guideline. For a survey, see Alan Agresti, "A survey of exact inference for contingency tables," *Statistical Science,* 7 (1992), pp. 131–177.

5. All General Social Survey exercises in this chapter present tables constructed using the search function at the GSS archive, sda.berkeley.edu/archive.htm. Most concern data from the 2010 GSS.

6. Pew Research Center for the People and the Press, "The cell phone challenge to survey research," news release for May 15, 2006, at www.people-press.org.

7. Based on a news item in *Science,* 305 (2004), p. 1560. The study, by Daniel Klem, appeared in the *Wilson Journal.*

8. David W. Eby et al., "The effect of changing from secondary to primary safety belt enforcement on police harassment," *Accident Analysis and Prevention,* 36 (2000), pp. 819–828.

9. See Note 22 from Chapter 20.

10. See Note 6 for Chapter 6.

11. See Note 8 for Chapter 6.

12. Lien-Ti Bei, "Consumers' purchase behavior toward recycled products: an acquisition-transaction utility theory perspective," MS thesis, Purdue University, 1993.

13. Modified from Felicity Barringer, "Measuring sexuality through polls can be shaky," *New York Times,* April 25, 1993.

14. Virgilio P. Carnielli et al., "Intestinal absorption of long-chain polyunsaturated fatty acids in preterm infants fed breast milk or formula," *American Journal of Clinical Nutrition,* 67 (1998), pp. 97–103.

15. Adapted from M. A. Visintainer, J. R. Volpicelli, and M. E. P. Seligman, "Tumor rejection in rats after inescapable or escapable shock," *Science*, 216 (1982), pp. 437–439.

16. See Note 1 for Chapter 6.

17. Tom Reichert, "The prevalence of sexual imagery in ads targeted to young adults," *Journal of Consumer Affairs*, 37 (2003), pp. 403–412.

18. József Topál et al., "Differential sensitivity to human communication in dogs, wolves and human infants," *Science*, 325 (2009), pp. 1269–1272. Many statistical software packages offer "exact tests" that are valid even when there are small expected counts.

19. U.S. Department of Commerce, Office of Travel and Tourism Industries, in-flight survey, 2007, at `tinet.ita.doc.gov`.

20. See Note 2 for Chapter 17. We have simplified slightly: the table in the paper is exactly as in the exercise but contains data for 63 subjects plus data from one type of bar for 3 subjects who dropped out. Although the authors say that their chi-square refers to this table, they give a nonsignificant value that contradicts what the table shows.

21. See Note 11 for Chapter 6.

22. Two way tables from the Youth Risk Behavior Surveillance System can be constructed from the website `apps.nccd.cdc.gov/youthonline/App/Default.aspx`.

23. Data compiled from a table of percents in "Americans view higher education as key to the American dream," press release by the National Center for Public Policy and Higher Education, May 3, 2000, at `www.higheredu-cation.org`.

24. See Note 10 for Chapter 6.

25. Data produced by Ries and Smith, found in William D. Johnson and Gary G. Koch, "A note on the weighted least squares analysis of the Ries-Smith contingency table data," *Technometrics*, 13 (1971), pp. 438–447.

Chapter 24

1. Samuel Karelitz et al., "Relation of crying activity in early infancy to speech and intellectual development at age three years," *Child Development*, 35 (1964), pp. 769–777.

2. See Note 9 for Chapter 4.

3. From a graph in Stephen M. Fleming et al., "Relating introspective accuracy to individual differences in brain structure," *Science*, 329 (2010), pp. 1541–1543.

4. Data for 1936–1999 are from a graph in Bruce J. Peterson et al., "Increasing river discharge to the Arctic Ocean," *Science*, 298 (2002), pp. 2171–2173. Data for 2000–2008 are from a graph in I. Ashik et al., "Arctic report card: update for 2010," available online at `www.arctic.`

`noaa.gov/reportcard/ArcticReportCard_full_report.pdf`. The graph is on page 41 of the report.

5. Electronic Encyclopedia of Statistical Examples and Exercises (EESEE) at the text Web site, `www.whfreeman.com/essentialstats`.

6. From a graph in Allison L. Perry et al., "Climate change and distribution shifts in marine fishes," *Science*, 308 (2005), pp. 1912–1915. The explanatory variable is the five-year running mean of winter (December to March) sea-bottom temperature.

7. Data for the building at 1800 Ben Franklin Drive, Sarasota, Florida, starting in March 2003. From the Web site of the Sarasota County Property Appraiser, `www.sarasotaproperty.net`.

8. Yanhui Lu et al., "Mirid bug outbreaks in multiple crops correlated with wide-scale adoption of Bt cotton in China," *Science*, 328 (2010), pp. 1151–1154.

9. See Note 1 for Chapter 4.

10. Based on Marion E. Dunshee, "A study of factors affecting the amount and kind of food eaten by nursery school children," *Child Development*, 2 (1931), pp. 163–183. This article gives the means, standard deviations, and correlation for 37 children, from which the data in the exercise are simulated.

11. From Table S2 in the online supplement to Antonio Dell'Anno and Roberto Danovaro, "Extracellular DNA plays a key role in deep-sea ecosystem functioning," *Science*, 309 (2005), p. 2179.

12. See Note 14 for Chapter 7.

Chapter 25

1. See Note 9 for Chapter 2.

2. Victoria L. Brescoll and Eric L. Uhlmann, "Can an angry woman get ahead? Status conferral, gender and expression of emotion in the workplace," *Psychological Science*, 19 (2008), pp. 268–273. The description and data are based on study 1 in this article.

3. Elisabeth Wells-Parker et al., "An exploratory study of the relationship between road rage and crash experience in a representative sample of US drivers," *Accident Analysis and Prevention*, 34 (2002), pp. 271–278.

4. See Note 10 for Chapter 2.

5. The data from the General Social Survey for this exercise was constructed using the search function and download capabilities at the GSS archive, `sda.berkeley.edu/archive.htm`.

6. See Note 23 for Chapter 19.

7. See Note 13 for Chapter 22.

8. David B. Wooten, "One-of-a-kind in a full house: some consequences of ethnic and gender distinctiveness," *Journal of Consumer Psychology*, 4 (1995), 205–224.

9. Henrik Hagvedt and Vanessa M. Patrick, "Art infusion: the influence of visual art on the perception and evaluation of consumer products," *Journal of Marketing Research*, XLV (2008), pp. 379–389.

10. Timothy Church et al., "Effects of aerobic and resistance training on hemoglobin A1c levels in patients with type 2 diabetes: a randomized controlled trial,"*Journal of the American Medical Association*, 304 (2010), pp. 2253–2262.

11. Jennifer J. Argo et al., "Positive consumer contagion: responses to attractive others in a retail context,"*Journal of Marketing Research*, XLV (2008), pp. 690–701.

12. Data from the online supplement to Andre Kessler and Ian T. Baldwin, "Defensive function of herbivore-induced plant volatile emissions in nature," *Science*, 291 (2001), pp. 2141–2144.

13. The data and the full story can be found in the Data and Story Library at `lib.stat.cmu.edu`. The original study is by Faith Loven, "A study of interlist equivalency of the CID W-22 word list presented in quiet and in noise," MS thesis, University of Iowa, 1981.

14. See Note 8 for Chapter 9. We thank Kenwyn Suttle for providing these data, for the year 2003.

15. See Note 14 for Chapter 22.

16. See Note 19 for Chapter 2.

17. See Note 21 for Chapter 2.

18. Sherri A. Buzinski, The effect of position of methylation on the performance properties of durable press treated fabrics, CSR490 honors paper, Purdue University, 1985.

19. See Note 8 for Chapter 9.

Tables

Table entry for z is the area under the standard Normal curve to the left of z.

Table entry

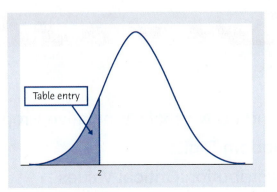

TABLE A Standard Normal cumulative proportions

z	.00	.01	.02	.03	.04	.05	.06	.07	.08	.09
−3.4	.0003	.0003	.0003	.0003	.0003	.0003	.0003	.0003	.0003	.0002
−3.3	.0005	.0005	.0005	.0004	.0004	.0004	.0004	.0004	.0004	.0003
−3.2	.0007	.0007	.0006	.0006	.0006	.0006	.0006	.0005	.0005	.0005
−3.1	.0010	.0009	.0009	.0009	.0008	.0008	.0008	.0008	.0007	.0007
−3.0	.0013	.0013	.0013	.0012	.0012	.0011	.0011	.0011	.0010	.0010
−2.9	.0019	.0018	.0018	.0017	.0016	.0016	.0015	.0015	.0014	.0014
−2.8	.0026	.0025	.0024	.0023	.0023	.0022	.0021	.0021	.0020	.0019
−2.7	.0035	.0034	.0033	.0032	.0031	.0030	.0029	.0028	.0027	.0026
−2.6	.0047	.0045	.0044	.0043	.0041	.0040	.0039	.0038	.0037	.0036
−2.5	.0062	.0060	.0059	.0057	.0055	.0054	.0052	.0051	.0049	.0048
−2.4	.0082	.0080	.0078	.0075	.0073	.0071	.0069	.0068	.0066	.0064
−2.3	.0107	.0104	.0102	.0099	.0096	.0094	.0091	.0089	.0087	.0084
−2.2	.0139	.0136	.0132	.0129	.0125	.0122	.0119	.0116	.0113	.0110
−2.1	.0179	.0174	.0170	.0166	.0162	.0158	.0154	.0150	.0146	.0143
−2.0	.0228	.0222	.0217	.0212	.0207	.0202	.0197	.0192	.0188	.0183
−1.9	.0287	.0281	.0274	.0268	.0262	.0256	.0250	.0244	.0239	.0233
−1.8	.0359	.0351	.0344	.0336	.0329	.0322	.0314	.0307	.0301	.0294
−1.7	.0446	.0436	.0427	.0418	.0409	.0401	.0392	.0384	.0375	.0367
−1.6	.0548	.0537	.0526	.0516	.0505	.0495	.0485	.0475	.0465	.0455
−1.5	.0668	.0655	.0643	.0630	.0618	.0606	.0594	.0582	.0571	.0559
−1.4	.0808	.0793	.0778	.0764	.0749	.0735	.0721	.0708	.0694	.0681
−1.3	.0968	.0951	.0934	.0918	.0901	.0885	.0869	.0853	.0838	.0823
−1.2	.1151	.1131	.1112	.1093	.1075	.1056	.1038	.1020	.1003	.0985
−1.1	.1357	.1335	.1314	.1292	.1271	.1251	.1230	.1210	.1190	.1170
−1.0	.1587	.1562	.1539	.1515	.1492	.1469	.1446	.1423	.1401	.1379
−0.9	.1841	.1814	.1788	.1762	.1736	.1711	.1685	.1660	.1635	.1611
−0.8	.2119	.2090	.2061	.2033	.2005	.1977	.1949	.1922	.1894	.1867
−0.7	.2420	.2389	.2358	.2327	.2296	.2266	.2236	.2206	.2177	.2148
−0.6	.2743	.2709	.2676	.2643	.2611	.2578	.2546	.2514	.2483	.2451
−0.5	.3085	.3050	.3015	.2981	.2946	.2912	.2877	.2843	.2810	.2776
−0.4	.3446	.3409	.3372	.3336	.3300	.3264	.3228	.3192	.3156	.3121
−0.3	.3821	.3783	.3745	.3707	.3669	.3632	.3594	.3557	.3520	.3483
−0.2	.4207	.4168	.4129	.4090	.4052	.4013	.3974	.3936	.3897	.3859
−0.1	.4602	.4562	.4522	.4483	.4443	.4404	.4364	.4325	.4286	.4247
−0.0	.5000	.4960	.4920	.4880	.4840	.4801	.4761	.4721	.4681	.4641

Table entry for z is the area under the standard Normal curve to the left of z.

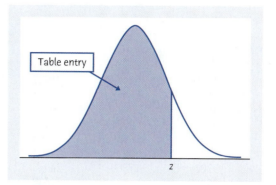

Table entry

TABLE A Standard Normal cumulative proportions (*continued*)

z	.00	.01	.02	.03	.04	.05	.06	.07	.08	.09
0.0	.5000	.5040	.5080	.5120	.5160	.5199	.5239	.5279	.5319	.5359
0.1	.5398	.5438	.5478	.5517	.5557	.5596	.5636	.5675	.5714	.5753
0.2	.5793	.5832	.5871	.5910	.5948	.5987	.6026	.6064	.6103	.6141
0.3	.6179	.6217	.6255	.6293	.6331	.6368	.6406	.6443	.6480	.6517
0.4	.6554	.6591	.6628	.6664	.6700	.6736	.6772	.6808	.6844	.6879
0.5	.6915	.6950	.6985	.7019	.7054	.7088	.7123	.7157	.7190	.7224
0.6	.7257	.7291	.7324	.7357	.7389	.7422	.7454	.7486	.7517	.7549
0.7	.7580	.7611	.7642	.7673	.7704	.7734	.7764	.7794	.7823	.7852
0.8	.7881	.7910	.7939	.7967	.7995	.8023	.8051	.8078	.8106	.8133
0.9	.8159	.8186	.8212	.8238	.8264	.8289	.8315	.8340	.8365	.8389
1.0	.8413	.8438	.8461	.8485	.8508	.8531	.8554	.8577	.8599	.8621
1.1	.8643	.8665	.8686	.8708	.8729	.8749	.8770	.8790	.8810	.8830
1.2	.8849	.8869	.8888	.8907	.8925	.8944	.8962	.8980	.8997	.9015
1.3	.9032	.9049	.9066	.9082	.9099	.9115	.9131	.9147	.9162	.9177
1.4	.9192	.9207	.9222	.9236	.9251	.9265	.9279	.9292	.9306	.9319
1.5	.9332	.9345	.9357	.9370	.9382	.9394	.9406	.9418	.9429	.9441
1.6	.9452	.9463	.9474	.9484	.9495	.9505	.9515	.9525	.9535	.9545
1.7	.9554	.9564	.9573	.9582	.9591	.9599	.9608	.9616	.9625	.9633
1.8	.9641	.9649	.9656	.9664	.9671	.9678	.9686	.9693	.9699	.9706
1.9	.9713	.9719	.9726	.9732	.9738	.9744	.9750	.9756	.9761	.9767
2.0	.9772	.9778	.9783	.9788	.9793	.9798	.9803	.9808	.9812	.9817
2.1	.9821	.9826	.9830	.9834	.9838	.9842	.9846	.9850	.9854	.9857
2.2	.9861	.9864	.9868	.9871	.9875	.9878	.9881	.9884	.9887	.9890
2.3	.9893	.9896	.9898	.9901	.9904	.9906	.9909	.9911	.9913	.9916
2.4	.9918	.9920	.9922	.9925	.9927	.9929	.9931	.9932	.9934	.9936
2.5	.9938	.9940	.9941	.9943	.9945	.9946	.9948	.9949	.9951	.9952
2.6	.9953	.9955	.9956	.9957	.9959	.9960	.9961	.9962	.9963	.9964
2.7	.9965	.9966	.9967	.9968	.9969	.9970	.9971	.9972	.9973	.9974
2.8	.9974	.9975	.9976	.9977	.9977	.9978	.9979	.9979	.9980	.9981
2.9	.9981	.9982	.9982	.9983	.9984	.9984	.9985	.9985	.9986	.9986
3.0	.9987	.9987	.9987	.9988	.9988	.9989	.9989	.9989	.9990	.9990
3.1	.9990	.9991	.9991	.9991	.9992	.9992	.9992	.9992	.9993	.9993
3.2	.9993	.9993	.9994	.9994	.9994	.9994	.9994	.9995	.9995	.9995
3.3	.9995	.9995	.9995	.9996	.9996	.9996	.9996	.9996	.9996	.9997
3.4	.9997	.9997	.9997	.9997	.9997	.9997	.9997	.9997	.9997	.9998

TABLE B Random digits

LINE								
101	19223	95034	05756	28713	96409	12531	42544	82853
102	73676	47150	99400	01927	27754	42648	82425	36290
103	45467	71709	77558	00095	32863	29485	82226	90056
104	52711	38889	93074	60227	40011	85848	48767	52573
105	95592	94007	69971	91481	60779	53791	17297	59335
106	68417	35013	15529	72765	85089	57067	50211	47487
107	82739	57890	20807	47511	81676	55300	94383	14893
108	60940	72024	17868	24943	61790	90656	87964	18883
109	36009	19365	15412	39638	85453	46816	83485	41979
110	38448	48789	18338	24697	39364	42006	76688	08708
111	81486	69487	60513	09297	00412	71238	27649	39950
112	59636	88804	04634	71197	19352	73089	84898	45785
113	62568	70206	40325	03699	71080	22553	11486	11776
114	45149	32992	75730	66280	03819	56202	02938	70915
115	61041	77684	94322	24709	73698	14526	31893	32592
116	14459	26056	31424	80371	65103	62253	50490	61181
117	38167	98532	62183	70632	23417	26185	41448	75532
118	73190	32533	04470	29669	84407	90785	65956	86382
119	95857	07118	87664	92099	58806	66979	98624	84826
120	35476	55972	39421	65850	04266	35435	43742	11937
121	71487	09984	29077	14863	61683	47052	62224	51025
122	13873	81598	95052	90908	73592	75186	87136	95761
123	54580	81507	27102	56027	55892	33063	41842	81868
124	71035	09001	43367	49497	72719	96758	27611	91596
125	96746	12149	37823	71868	18442	35119	62103	39244
126	96927	19931	36809	74192	77567	88741	48409	41903
127	43909	99477	25330	64359	40085	16925	85117	36071
128	15689	14227	06565	14374	13352	49367	81982	87209
129	36759	58984	68288	22913	18638	54303	00795	08727
130	69051	64817	87174	09517	84534	06489	87201	97245
131	05007	16632	81194	14873	04197	85576	45195	96565
132	68732	55259	84292	08796	43165	93739	31685	97150
133	45740	41807	65561	33302	07051	93623	18132	09547
134	27816	78416	18329	21337	35213	37741	04312	68508
135	66925	55658	39100	78458	11206	19876	87151	31260
136	08421	44753	77377	28744	75592	08563	79140	92454
137	53645	66812	61421	47836	12609	15373	98481	14592
138	66831	68908	40772	21558	47781	33586	79177	06928
139	55588	99404	70708	41098	43563	56934	48394	51719
140	12975	13258	13048	45144	72321	81940	00360	02428
141	96767	35964	23822	96012	94591	65194	50842	53372
142	72829	50232	97892	63408	77919	44575	24870	04178
143	88565	42628	17797	49376	61762	16953	88604	12724
144	62964	88145	83083	69453	46109	59505	69680	00900
145	19687	12633	57857	95806	09931	02150	43163	58636
146	37609	59057	66967	83401	60705	02384	90597	93600
147	54973	86278	88737	74351	47500	84552	19909	67181
148	00694	05977	19664	65441	20903	62371	22725	53340
149	71546	05233	53946	68743	72460	27601	45403	88692
150	07511	88915	41267	16853	84569	79367	32337	03316

Table entry for C is the critical value t* required for confidence level C. To approximate one- and two-sided P-values, compare the value of the t statistic with the critical values of t* that match the P-values given at the bottom of the table.

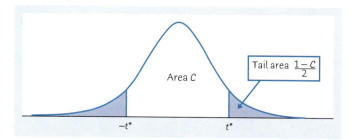

TABLE C t distribution critical values

DEGREES OF FREEDOM	CONFIDENCE LEVEL C											
	50%	60%	70%	80%	90%	95%	96%	98%	99%	99.5%	99.8%	99.9%
1	1.000	1.376	1.963	3.078	6.314	12.71	15.89	31.82	63.66	127.3	318.3	636.6
2	0.816	1.061	1.386	1.886	2.920	4.303	4.849	6.965	9.925	14.09	22.33	31.60
3	0.765	0.978	1.250	1.638	2.353	3.182	3.482	4.541	5.841	7.453	10.21	12.92
4	0.741	0.941	1.190	1.533	2.132	2.776	2.999	3.747	4.604	5.598	7.173	8.610
5	0.727	0.920	1.156	1.476	2.015	2.571	2.757	3.365	4.032	4.773	5.893	6.869
6	0.718	0.906	1.134	1.440	1.943	2.447	2.612	3.143	3.707	4.317	5.208	5.959
7	0.711	0.896	1.119	1.415	1.895	2.365	2.517	2.998	3.499	4.029	4.785	5.408
8	0.706	0.889	1.108	1.397	1.860	2.306	2.449	2.896	3.355	3.833	4.501	5.041
9	0.703	0.883	1.100	1.383	1.833	2.262	2.398	2.821	3.250	3.690	4.297	4.781
10	0.700	0.879	1.093	1.372	1.812	2.228	2.359	2.764	3.169	3.581	4.144	4.587
11	0.697	0.876	1.088	1.363	1.796	2.201	2.328	2.718	3.106	3.497	4.025	4.437
12	0.695	0.873	1.083	1.356	1.782	2.179	2.303	2.681	3.055	3.428	3.930	4.318
13	0.694	0.870	1.079	1.350	1.771	2.160	2.282	2.650	3.012	3.372	3.852	4.221
14	0.692	0.868	1.076	1.345	1.761	2.145	2.264	2.624	2.977	3.326	3.787	4.140
15	0.691	0.866	1.074	1.341	1.753	2.131	2.249	2.602	2.947	3.286	3.733	4.073
16	0.690	0.865	1.071	1.337	1.746	2.120	2.235	2.583	2.921	3.252	3.686	4.015
17	0.689	0.863	1.069	1.333	1.740	2.110	2.224	2.567	2.898	3.222	3.646	3.965
18	0.688	0.862	1.067	1.330	1.734	2.101	2.214	2.552	2.878	3.197	3.611	3.922
19	0.688	0.861	1.066	1.328	1.729	2.093	2.205	2.539	2.861	3.174	3.579	3.883
20	0.687	0.860	1.064	1.325	1.725	2.086	2.197	2.528	2.845	3.153	3.552	3.850
21	0.686	0.859	1.063	1.323	1.721	2.080	2.189	2.518	2.831	3.135	3.527	3.819
22	0.686	0.858	1.061	1.321	1.717	2.074	2.183	2.508	2.819	3.119	3.505	3.792
23	0.685	0.858	1.060	1.319	1.714	2.069	2.177	2.500	2.807	3.104	3.485	3.768
24	0.685	0.857	1.059	1.318	1.711	2.064	2.172	2.492	2.797	3.091	3.467	3.745
25	0.684	0.856	1.058	1.316	1.708	2.060	2.167	2.485	2.787	3.078	3.450	3.725
26	0.684	0.856	1.058	1.315	1.706	2.056	2.162	2.479	2.779	3.067	3.435	3.707
27	0.684	0.855	1.057	1.314	1.703	2.052	2.158	2.473	2.771	3.057	3.421	3.690
28	0.683	0.855	1.056	1.313	1.701	2.048	2.154	2.467	2.763	3.047	3.408	3.674
29	0.683	0.854	1.055	1.311	1.699	2.045	2.150	2.462	2.756	3.038	3.396	3.659
30	0.683	0.854	1.055	1.310	1.697	2.042	2.147	2.457	2.750	3.030	3.385	3.646
40	0.681	0.851	1.050	1.303	1.684	2.021	2.123	2.423	2.704	2.971	3.307	3.551
50	0.679	0.849	1.047	1.299	1.676	2.009	2.109	2.403	2.678	2.937	3.261	3.496
60	0.679	0.848	1.045	1.296	1.671	2.000	2.099	2.390	2.660	2.915	3.232	3.460
80	0.678	0.846	1.043	1.292	1.664	1.990	2.088	2.374	2.639	2.887	3.195	3.416
100	0.677	0.845	1.042	1.290	1.660	1.984	2.081	2.364	2.626	2.871	3.174	3.390
1000	0.675	0.842	1.037	1.282	1.646	1.962	2.056	2.330	2.581	2.813	3.098	3.300
z*	0.674	0.841	1.036	1.282	1.645	1.960	2.054	2.326	2.576	2.807	3.091	3.291
One-sided P	.25	.20	.15	.10	.05	.025	.02	.01	.005	.0025	.001	.0005
Two-sided P	.50	.40	.30	.20	.10	.05	.04	.02	.01	.005	.002	.001

Table entry for p is the critical value χ* with probability p lying to its right.

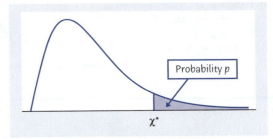

Probability p

χ*

TABLE D Chi-square distribution critical values

df	.25	.20	.15	.10	.05	.025	.02	.01	.005	.0025	.001	.0005
1	1.32	1.64	2.07	2.71	3.84	5.02	5.41	6.63	7.88	9.14	10.83	12.12
2	2.77	3.22	3.79	4.61	5.99	7.38	7.82	9.21	10.60	11.98	13.82	15.20
3	4.11	4.64	5.32	6.25	7.81	9.35	9.84	11.34	12.84	14.32	16.27	17.73
4	5.39	5.99	6.74	7.78	9.49	11.14	11.67	13.28	14.86	16.42	18.47	20.00
5	6.63	7.29	8.12	9.24	11.07	12.83	13.39	15.09	16.75	18.39	20.51	22.11
6	7.84	8.56	9.45	10.64	12.59	14.45	15.03	16.81	18.55	20.25	22.46	24.10
7	9.04	9.80	10.75	12.02	14.07	16.01	16.62	18.48	20.28	22.04	24.32	26.02
8	10.22	11.03	12.03	13.36	15.51	17.53	18.17	20.09	21.95	23.77	26.12	27.87
9	11.39	12.24	13.29	14.68	16.92	19.02	19.68	21.67	23.59	25.46	27.88	29.67
10	12.55	13.44	14.53	15.99	18.31	20.48	21.16	23.21	25.19	27.11	29.59	31.42
11	13.70	14.63	15.77	17.28	19.68	21.92	22.62	24.72	26.76	28.73	31.26	33.14
12	14.85	15.81	16.99	18.55	21.03	23.34	24.05	26.22	28.30	30.32	32.91	34.82
13	15.98	16.98	18.20	19.81	22.36	24.74	25.47	27.69	29.82	31.88	34.53	36.48
14	17.12	18.15	19.41	21.06	23.68	26.12	26.87	29.14	31.32	33.43	36.12	38.11
15	18.25	19.31	20.60	22.31	25.00	27.49	28.26	30.58	32.80	34.95	37.70	39.72
16	19.37	20.47	21.79	23.54	26.30	28.85	29.63	32.00	34.27	36.46	39.25	41.31
17	20.49	21.61	22.98	24.77	27.59	30.19	31.00	33.41	35.72	37.95	40.79	42.88
18	21.60	22.76	24.16	25.99	28.87	31.53	32.35	34.81	37.16	39.42	42.31	44.43
19	22.72	23.90	25.33	27.20	30.14	32.85	33.69	36.19	38.58	40.88	43.82	45.97
20	23.83	25.04	26.50	28.41	31.41	34.17	35.02	37.57	40.00	42.34	45.31	47.50
21	24.93	26.17	27.66	29.62	32.67	35.48	36.34	38.93	41.40	43.78	46.80	49.01
22	26.04	27.30	28.82	30.81	33.92	36.78	37.66	40.29	42.80	45.20	48.27	50.51
23	27.14	28.43	29.98	32.01	35.17	38.08	38.97	41.64	44.18	46.62	49.73	52.00
24	28.24	29.55	31.13	33.20	36.42	39.36	40.27	42.98	45.56	48.03	51.18	53.48
25	29.34	30.68	32.28	34.38	37.65	40.65	41.57	44.31	46.93	49.44	52.62	54.95
26	30.43	31.79	33.43	35.56	38.89	41.92	42.86	45.64	48.29	50.83	54.05	56.41
27	31.53	32.91	34.57	36.74	40.11	43.19	44.14	46.96	49.64	52.22	55.48	57.86
28	32.62	34.03	35.71	37.92	41.34	44.46	45.42	48.28	50.99	53.59	56.89	59.30
29	33.71	35.14	36.85	39.09	42.56	45.72	46.69	49.59	52.34	54.97	58.30	60.73
30	34.80	36.25	37.99	40.26	43.77	46.98	47.96	50.89	53.67	56.33	59.70	62.16
40	45.62	47.27	49.24	51.81	55.76	59.34	60.44	63.69	66.77	69.70	73.40	76.09
50	56.33	58.16	60.35	63.17	67.50	71.42	72.61	76.15	79.49	82.66	86.66	89.56
60	66.98	68.97	71.34	74.40	79.08	83.30	84.58	88.38	91.95	95.34	99.61	102.7
80	88.13	90.41	93.11	96.58	101.9	106.6	108.1	112.3	116.3	120.1	124.8	128.3
100	109.1	111.7	114.7	118.5	124.3	129.6	131.1	135.8	140.2	144.3	149.4	153.2

Answers to Selected Exercises

Chapter 1 Picturing Distributions with Graphs

1.1: (a) The individuals are the car makes and models. (b) For each individual, the variables recorded are vehicle type (categorical), transmission type (categorical), number of cylinders (usually treated as quantitative), city mpg (quantitative), highway mpg (quantitative), and carbon footprint (quantitative).

1.3: (a) 80.6%. Hence, 100% − 80.6% = 19.4% of the radio audience listens to stations with other formats. (b) See below. (c) Shares do not sum to 100%. If you include a wedge for "Other" that accounts for 19.4% of the total, a pie chart would be reasonable.

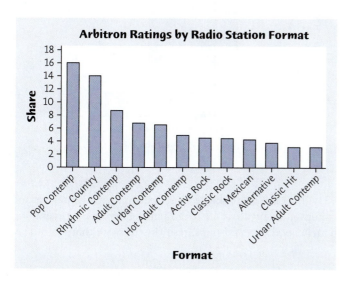

1.5: A pie chart would make it more difficult to distinguish between the weekend days and the weekdays. Some births are scheduled (induced labor, for example), and probably most of these are scheduled for weekdays.

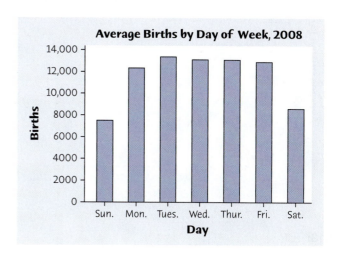

1.7: The distribution looks left-skewed and unimodal with center at about 13% and range from about 7% to about 18%. Alaska is unusually low at 7.6%, while Florida seems unusually high at 17.2%.

1.9:

```
 7 | 6
 8 |
 9 | 0
10 | 236
11 | 267
12 | 11223347789
13 | 0012444455555677899
14 | 333555678
15 | 468
16 |
17 | 2
```

The midpoint is 13.4%. The spread is 7.6% to 17.2%.

1.11: (a) See below. (b) Tuition has steadily climbed during the 30-year period. (c) There is a sharp increase from 2000 to 2010. (d) It would be better to use percent increases, rather than dollar increases.

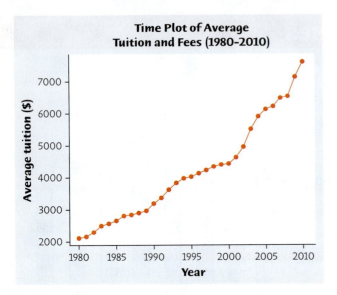

Time Plot of Average Tuition and Fees (1980-2010)

1.13: (c).

1.15: (a).

1.17: (b).

1.19: (a) Individuals are students who have finished medical school. (b) 6, including "Name." "Age" and "USMLE" are quantitative. The others are categorical.

1.21: "Other colors" should account for 4%.

1.23: (a) See below. (b) You would need to know the total number of deaths in this age group, or the number of deaths due to "other" causes.

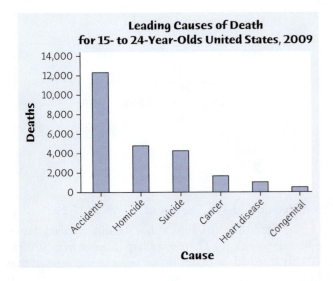

Leading Causes of Death for 15- to 24-Year-Olds United States, 2009

1.25: This distribution is right-skewed, with center around 2 servings, and spread from 0 to 8 servings. There are no outliers. About 12% (9 out of 74) consumed six or more servings, and about 35% (26 out of 74) ate fewer than two servings (which means zero or one serving).

1.27:

1. Are you female or male → Histogram (c).

2. Are you right-handed or left-handed → Histogram (b).

3. Heights → Histogram (d).

4. Time spent studying → Histogram (a).

1.29: (a) States vary in population, so you would expect more nurses in California than in New Hampshire, for example. Number of nurses per 100,000 people provides a better measure of how many nurses are available to serve a state's population. (b) A histogram is provided below. The District of Columbia, South Dakota, and Massachusetts are the three states that differ from the others. Perhaps they could be considered outliers. It's difficult to know why these states have more nurses than other states.

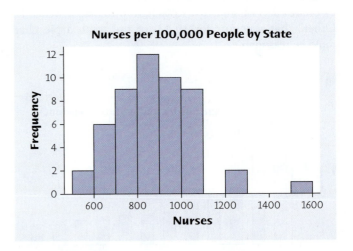

Nurses per 100,000 People by State

1.31: This is a right-skewed distribution, with center around 25 pups and spread of 17 to 56 pups. There were several extremely good years for pups, resulting in more than 45 births.

```
1 | 777789
2 | 0122344
2 | 555579
3 | 12333
3 | 899
4 | 3
4 | 77
5 | 4
5 | 6
```

1.33: The decline in population is not described by the stemplot made in Exercise 1.31.

Pups over Time

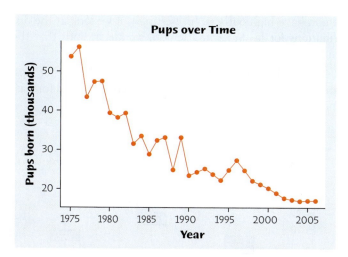

1.35: Coins with earlier (lower) dates are older and rarer. There are more coins with larger dates (newer coins) than with smaller dates (older coins).

1.37: (a) Graph (a). Vertical scaling can impact one's perception of the data. (b) In both graphs, tuition starts around $2000 and rises to $7700. Both plots describe the same data.

1.39: (a) See below. There is a trend, as well as year-to-year variability.

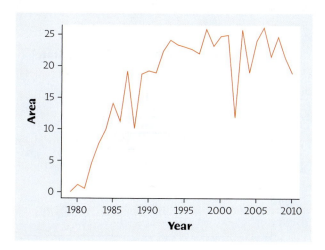

(b) See below. The midpoint is 19.3 millions of km^2. A stemplot fails to capture the relationship between size of hole and year.

```
0 | 0004
0 | 79
1 | 0114
1 | 899999
2 | 11222333444
2 | 5556
```

Chapter 2   Describing Distributions with Numbers

2.1: Mean breaking strength = 30,841 pounds. Only 6 pieces have strengths less than the mean. The mean is so small relative to the data because of the sharp left-skew.

2.3: Mean = 31.25 minutes. Median = 22.5 minutes. The mean is significantly larger than the median due to the right-skew.

2.5: The histogram shows a right-skew. Hence, the mean is larger than the median. Here, the mean is 4.61 and the median is 3.95 tons per person.

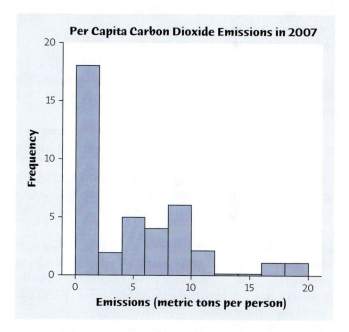

2.7: (a) Minimum = 9, Q_1 = 16, median = 18, Q_3 = 22, maximum = 51. (b) The boxplot shows right-skew in the distribution of mpg values.

2.9: IQR = 22 − 16 = 6, so Q_3 + 1.5 × IQR = 22 + 1.5 × 6 = 31. Five values are greater than 31 and would be identified as potential outliers (33, 35, 41, 41, 51). Since Q_1 − 1.5 × IQR = 16 − 1.5 × 6 = 7, there are no potential outliers below 7.

2.11: Both data sets have the same mean and standard deviation (about 7.5 and 2.0, respectively). However, simple stemplots reveal that Data set A has a very left-skewed distribution, while Data set B has a slightly right-skewed distribution.

2.13: Group 1: $\bar{x}$ = 23.7500, s = 5.06548. Group 2: $\bar{x}$ = 14.0833, s = 4.98102. Group 3: $\bar{x}$ = 15.7778, s = 5.76146.

2.15: (b).

2.17: (b).

2.19: (b).

2.21: (a).

2.23: In both cases (for the under-35 crowd and for all households), the distribution of account sizes is right-skewed. Lots of people have very small retirement savings accounts.

2.25: (a)

Variable	Minimum	Q_1	Median	Q_3	Maximum
Strength	23,040	30,315	31,975	32,710	33,650

(b) Notice that the minimum is much farther from Q_1 than the maximum is from Q_3. This suggests a long left tail, consistent with a left-skewed distribution.

2.27: (a) Median $= 2$, $Q_1 = 1$, $Q_3 = 4$. (b) $\bar{x} =$ $[(15)(0) + (11)(1) + (15)(2) + (11)(3) + (8)(4) + (5)(5) + (3)(6) + (3)(7) + (3)(8)]/74 = 194/74 = 2.62$ servings. The mean is larger than the median because the distribution is right-skewed.

2.29: (a) If countries or years have very different numbers of babies born, it would be unreasonable to compare across years or across countries by counts. (b) 4,243,333 babies. (c) The distribution is left-skewed. (d) The median is the 2,121,667th baby weight and falls in the interval 3000 to 3499 grams. Q_3 is in the interval 3500 to 3999 grams. Q_1 is in the interval 2500 to 2999 grams.

2.31: Both distributions are very similar. On weekdays more babies are born, and there is consistency from weekday to weekday, though Mondays appear to have slightly fewer births. On weekends, fewer births take place. Many more births take place in the United States.

2.33: More than half of all American households do not carry credit card debt.

2.35: The TI-89 calculator used by the authors reported $s = 1$ for the list

$$100,000,000,001 \quad 100,000,000,002 \quad 100,000,000,003$$

At some point, the calculator will fail. But for virtually any practical setting, a decent calculator will correctly compute.

2.37: Answers will vary. One solution is $(-100, 1, 2, 3, 4, 5, 6)$.

2.39: The distribution of salaries is very right-skewed. The median salary is $1,425,000 (mean is $2,520,646, consistent with a strong right-skew). The middle half of players earn between $756,250 and $4,416,500, although a handful earn more than $5,000,000.

2.41: Comparing side-by-side boxplots, lavender seems to produce the highest customer expenditures. Both no odor and

lemon have high outliers. Interestingly, if we look at the distributions for lavender and lemon, we see in both that the minimum is equal to Q_1.

2.43: Good weather forecasts generally yielded better tips, while there was little to no difference between a bad forecast and no forecast.

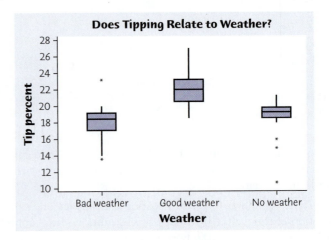

2.45: (a) 7.6, 12.3, 13.4, 14.3, 17.2. (b) The boxplot suggests rough symmetry. (c) There are two outliers (7.6% for Alaska and 9.0% for Utah) using the $1.5 \times IQR$ rule.

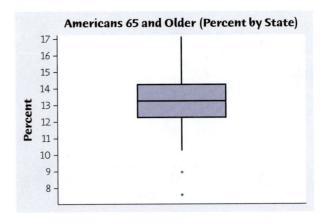

2.47: There are no salaries greater than $9,906,875. This is the salary that is $1.5 \times IQR$ greater than Q_3.

Chapter 3   The Normal Distributions

3.1: Sketches will vary.

3.3: $\mu = 2.5$. The median is also 2.5 because the distribution is symmetric.

3.5:

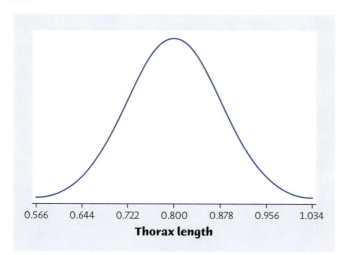

3.7: (a) In 95% of all years, monsoon rain levels are between 688 and 1016 mm—two standard deviations above and below the mean: $852 \pm 2(82) = 688$ to 1016 mm. (b) The driest 2.5% of monsoon rainfalls are less than 688 mm; this is more than two standard deviations below the mean.

3.9: A woman 6 feet tall has standardized score $z = \frac{72 - 64.3}{2.7} = 2.85$ (quite tall, relatively). A man 6 feet tall has standardized score $z = \frac{72 - 69.9}{3.1} = 0.68$.

3.11: Let x be the monsoon rainfall in a given year. (a) $x \le 697$ mm corresponds to $z \le \frac{697 - 852}{82} = -1.89$, for which Table A gives $0.0294 = 2.94\%$. (b) $683 < x < 1022$ corresponds to $\frac{683 - 852}{82} < z < \frac{1022 - 852}{82}$, or $-2.06 < z < 2.07$. This proportion is $0.9808 - 0.0197 = 0.9611 = 96.11\%$.

3.13: (a) Using Table A and looking for an area as close as possible to 0.1500, we find this value has $z = -1.04$ (software would give the more precise $z = -1.0364$). (b) Now we want the value such that the proportion above is 0.70. This means that we want a proportion of 0.30 below. Using Table A and looking for an area as close to 0.3000 as possible, we find this value has $z = -0.52$ (software gives $z = -0.5244$).

3.15: (a) Income distributions are typically skewed to the right. (b) Although the distribution of home prices in a very large metropolitan area tends to be right-skewed, perhaps the distribution is more symmetric in a suburb, where the houses tend to be similar. (c) In a forest, there are likely to be many more relatively short trees than relatively tall trees.

3.17: (b).

3.19: (c).

3.21: (c).

3.23: 70 is two standard deviations below the mean (that is, it has standard score $z = -2$), so about 2.5% (half of the outer 5%; there is 95% in the center of the distribution) of adults would have WAIS scores below 70.

3.25: (a) We want the proportion less than z to be 0.60, so $z = 0.25$. (Software gives $z = 0.2533$.) (b) If 15% are more than z, then 85% are less than or equal to z. Hence, $z = 1.04$. (Software gives $z = 1.0364$.)

3.27: About 0.2119: $x < 5.0$ corresponds to $z < \frac{5.0 - 5.4}{0.54} = -0.74$, for which Table A gives 0.2296.

3.29: $0.8720 < x < 0.8780$ corresponds to $\frac{0.8720 - 0.8750}{0.0012} < z < \frac{0.8780 - 0.8750}{0.0012}$, or $-2.50 < z < 2.50$, for which Table A gives $0.9938 - 0.0062 = 0.9876$.

3.31: Cars with better mileage than the Camaro correspond to $x > 19$, which corresponds to $z > \frac{19 - 20.3}{4.3} = -0.30$. $1 - 0.3821 = 0.6179$, or 61.79%.

3.33: The first and third quartiles have $z = -0.67$ and $z = 0.67$, respectively. The first quartile is $20.3 - (0.67)(4.3) = 17.42$ mpg, and the third quartile is $20.3 + (0.67)(4.3) = 23.18$ mpg.

3.35: Let x be the MCAT score for a randomly selected student. The event $x < 32$ corresponds to $z < \frac{32 - 25.0}{6.4} = 1.09$. Hence, 0.8621 is the corresponding proportion, or 86.21%. William's MCAT score is the 86.21st percentile.

3.37: If x is the height of a randomly selected woman in this age group, we want the proportion corresponding to $x > 69.9$ inches. This corresponds to $z > \frac{69.9 - 64.3}{2.7} = 2.07$, which has proportion $1 - 0.9808 = 0.0192$, or 1.92%.

3.39: If the distribution is Normal, it must be symmetric about its mean—and in particular, the 10th and 90th percentiles must be equal distances below and above the mean—so the mean is 250 points. If 225 points below (above) the mean is the 10th (90th) percentile, this is 1.28 standard deviations below (above) the mean, so the distribution's standard deviation is $225/1.28 = 175.8$ points.

3.41: (a) There are two somewhat low IQs: 72 qualifies as an outlier by the $1.5 \times IQR$ rule, while 74 is on the boundary. However, for a small sample, this stemplot looks reasonably Normal. (b) We compute $\bar{x} = 105.84$ and $s = 14.27$ and find $23/31 = 74.2\%$ of the scores in the range $\bar{x} \pm 1s$, or 91.6 to 120.1, and $29/31 = 93.5\%$ of the scores in the range $\bar{x} \pm 2s$, or 77.3 to 134.4. For an exactly Normal distribution, we would expect these proportions to be 68% and 95%. Given the small sample, this is reasonably close agreement.

```
 7 | 24
 7 |
 8 |
 8 | 69
 9 | 13
 9 | 68
10 | 023334
10 | 578
11 | 11222444
11 | 89
12 | 0
12 | 8
13 | 02
```

3.43: (a) The mean (5.43) is almost identical to the median (5.44), and the quartiles are similar distances from the median: $M - Q_1 = 0.39$ while $Q_3 - M = 0.35$. This suggests that the distribution is reasonably symmetric. (b) $x < 5.05$ corresponds to $z < \frac{5.05 - 5.43}{0.54} = -0.70$, and $x < 5.79$ corresponds to $z < \frac{5.79 - 5.43}{0.54} = 0.67$. Table A gives these proportions as 0.2420 and 0.7486. These are quite close to 0.25 and 0.75, which is what we would expect for the quartiles, so they are consistent with the idea that the distribution is close to Normal.

3.45: (a) Mean = 847.58 mm, and median = 860.8 mm. (b) The histogram shows a left-skew.

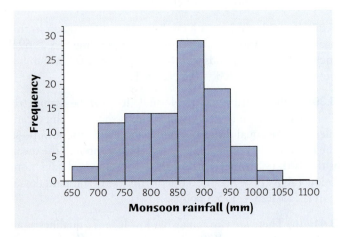

Chapter 4 Scatterplots and Correlation

4.1: (a) Explanatory: time spent studying; response: grade. (b) Explore the relationship. (c) Explanatory: time spent online using Facebook; Response: GPA. (d) Explore the relationship.

4.3: The researchers suspect that lean body mass is explanatory, so it should be on the horizontal axis.

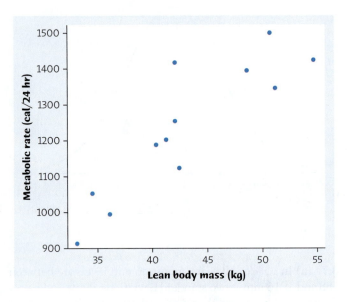

4.5: The scatterplot shows a positive direction, linear form, and moderately strong association.

4.7: (a) Women are marked with filled circles, men with open circles. (b) For both men and women, the association is linear and positive. The women's points show a stronger association. As a group, males typically have larger values for both variables (they tend to have more mass and tend to burn more calories per day).

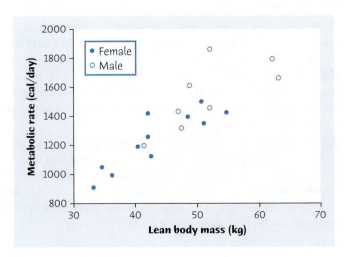

4.9: r would not change; units do not affect correlation.

4.11: $\bar{x} = 50$ mph, $s_x = 15.8114$ mph, $\bar{y} = 26.8$ mpg, and $s_y = 2.6833$ mpg. Refer to the table of standardized scores below, then note that $r = 0/4 = 0$. The correlation is zero because these variables do not have a straight-line relationship; the association is neither positive nor negative.

z_x	z_y	$z_x z_y$
−1.2649	−1.0435	1.3199
−0.6325	0.4472	−0.2828
0	1.1926	0
0.6325	0.4472	0.2828
1.2649	−1.0435	−1.3199
		0

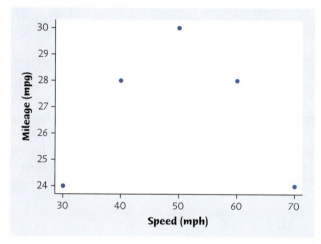

4.13: (b).

4.15: (c).

4.17: (b) Correlation is unaffected by units.

4.19: (a) The lowest first-round score was 66, scored by one golfer. This golfer scored 75 in the second round. (b) Lyle scored 86 in the second round, and 69 in the first round. (c) The correlation is very small but positive, so it is closest to 0.1. Knowing a golfer's first-round score would not be useful in predicting a second-round score.

4.21: (a) The scatterplot reveals a very strong and positive linear relationship between wine intake and relative risk for cancer. We expect correlation to be close to +1. (b) Using software, $r = 0.9851$. The data suggest that women who consume more wine tend to have higher risk of breast cancer. However, this is an observational study, and no causal relationship can be determined. The women who drink more wine may differ in many respects from women who drink less wine.

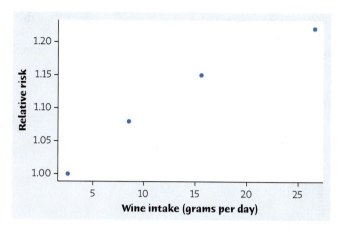

4.23: (a) The scatterplot shows a linear negative relationship. Correlation is an appropriate measure of strength: $r = -0.7485$. (b) The sparrowhawk is a long-lived territorial species.

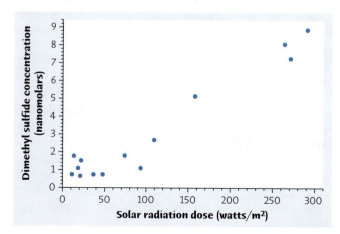

4.25: (a) SRD is the explanatory variable, so it should be on the horizontal axis. (b) The scatterplot shows a positive linear association. The correlation is $r = 0.9685$.

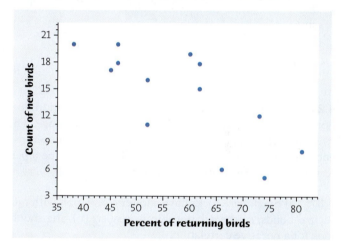

4.27: (a) See below. (b) The scatterplot suggests that there is not a linear relationship. Here, $r = -0.1749$. (c) Neither theory is strongly supported, but the latter is more strongly supported.

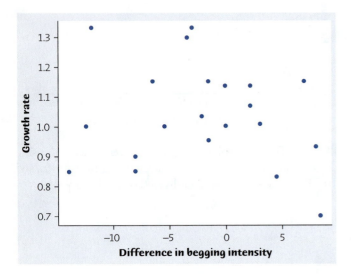

4.29: (a) Correlation would not change, as correlation does not depend on units. (b) Correlation would not change. The strength and direction of the linear relationship between risk and wine intake does not change. (c) There would be a perfect positive linear relationship with $r = +1$.

4.31: (a) Small-cap stocks have a lower correlation with municipal bonds, so the relationship is weaker. (b) She should look for a negative correlation.

4.33: (a) Because sex is a categorical variable, we cannot compute the correlation between sex and any other variable. Some writers and speakers use "correlation" as a synonym for "association," but this is not correct. (b) $r = 1.09$ is impossible, because r is restricted to be between -1 and 1. (c) Correlation has no units.

4.35: We will not use correlation, but we will examine the plot to see if women are beginning to outrun men. By inspection, one might guess that the "lines" that fit these data sets will meet around 1998. This is how the researchers made this leap. Men's and women's times have, indeed, grown closer over time. Both sexes have improved their record marathon times over the years, but women's times have improved at a faster rate. However, plots like this are designed to lure the reader into extrapolating—and extrapolation is never a good idea.

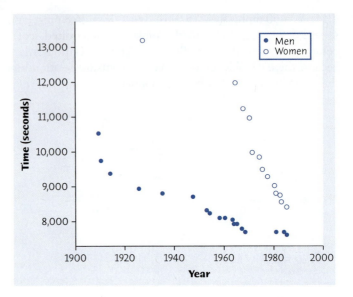

4.37: A scatterplot shows a fairly strong positive linear association. There are no outliers; each variable has low and high values, but those points do not deviate from the pattern of the rest. $r = 0.8782$. Social exclusion does appear to trigger a pain response: higher social distress measurements are associated with increased activity in the pain-sensing area of the brain. However, no cause-and-effect conclusion is possible since this was not a designed experiment.

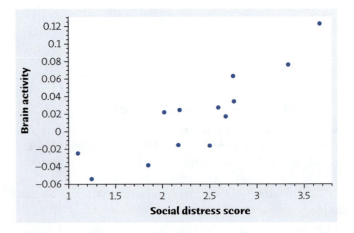

Chapter 5   Regression

5.1: (a) Slope $= 1.016$. On average, highway mileage increases by 1.016 mpg for each additional 1 mpg change in city mileage. (b) Intercept $= 6.554$ mpg. This is the highway mileage for a nonexistent car that gets 0 mpg in the city.

(c) For a car that gets 16 mpg in the city, we predict highway mileage to be $6.554 + (1.016)(16) = 22.81$ mpg. For a car that gets 28 mpg in the city, we predict highway mileage to be $6.554 + (1.016)(28) = 35.002$ mpg.

5.3: (a) $\bar{x} = 30.280$, $s_x = 0.4296$, $\bar{y} = 2.4557$, $s_y = 0.1579$, and $r = -0.8914$. Hence, $b = r\frac{s_y}{s_x} = (-0.8914)\frac{0.1579}{0.4296} = -0.3276$, and $a = \bar{y} - b\bar{x} = 2.4557 - (-0.3276)(30.280) = 12.3754$. (b) Software agrees with these values to 3 decimal places, since we rounded to the 4th decimal place.

5.5: The farther r is from 0 (in either direction), the stronger the linear relationship is between two variables.

5.7: (a) The residuals are computed in the table below using $\hat{y} = 12.3754 - 0.3276x$. (b) They sum to zero, except for rounding error. (c) From software, the correlation between x and $y - \hat{y}$ is 0.000025, which is zero except for rounding.

x	y	ŷ	y − ŷ
29.68	2.63	2.652	−0.022
29.87	2.58	2.590	−0.010
30.16	2.60	2.495	0.105
30.22	2.48	2.475	0.005
30.48	2.26	2.390	−0.130
30.65	2.38	2.335	0.045
30.90	2.26	2.253	0.007
			0

5.9: (a) In the plot, the outlier (Hawaiian Airlines) is the point identified with "H". Since this point is an outlier and falls outside the linear trend suggested by the other data points, it is influential and will affect the regression line by "pulling" it. (b) With the outlier, $r = -0.397$. If the outlier is deleted from the data, $r = -0.143$. Notice that with the outlier, the correlation suggests a somewhat stronger linear relationship. (c) The two regression lines (one including the outlier and the other without) are plotted. We see that the line based on the full data set (including the outlier) has been pulled down toward the outlier, indicating that the outlier is influential. The regression line based on the complete (original) data set, including the outlier, is $\hat{y} = 22.115 - 0.093x$. Using this, when $x = 74.7$, we predict 15.17% delays. The other regression line (fitted without the outlier) is $\hat{y} = 19.835 - 0.026x$, so our prediction is 17.89% delays. The outlier impacts predictions because it impacts the regression line.

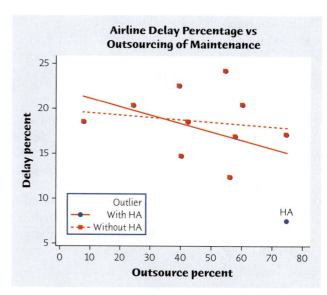

5.11: A student's intelligence may be a lurking variable: stronger students (who are more likely to succeed when they get to college) are more likely to choose to take these math courses, while weaker students may avoid them.

5.13: Socioeconomic status is a possible lurking variable: children from upper-class families can more easily afford higher education, and they would typically have had better preparation for college as well.

5.15: (b) 7.5. The regression line seems to pass through the point (110, 7.5).

5.17: (b) As the number of packs increases, average age at death decreases. Hence, correlation is negative and so is the slope of the regression line.

5.19: (a).

5.21: (c).

5.23: (a) The slope is 0.0138 minutes per meter. (b) 5.45 minutes. (c) See below.

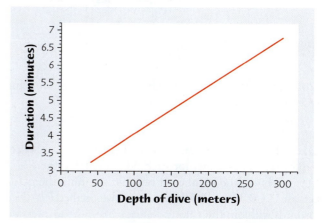

5.25: (a) The regression equation is $\hat{y} = -0.126 + 0.0608x$. For $x = 2.0$, this formula gives $\hat{y} = -0.0044$. (b) $r^2 = 77.1\%$. (c) $r = \sqrt{r^2} = 0.878$; the sign is positive because it has the same sign as the slope coefficient.

5.27: Since we wish to regress husbands' heights on wives' heights, the women's heights will be the x-values, and the men's heights will be the y-values. (a) $b = (0.5)(\frac{3.9}{3.1}) = 0.629$, and $a = 69.9 - (0.629)(64.3) = 29.46$ inches. The regression equation is $\hat{y} = 29.46 + 0.629x$. (b) $\hat{y} = 29.46 + (0.629)(67) = 71.603$ inches. The plot, with this pair identified, is provided below. (c) We don't expect this prediction to be very accurate because the heights of men having wives 67 inches tall varies a lot.

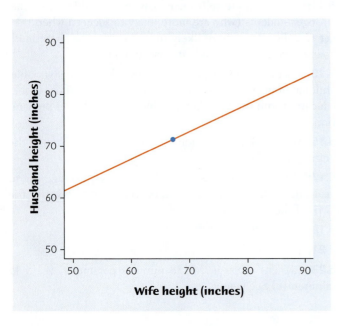

5.29: $r = \sqrt{0.16} = 0.40$ (high attendance goes with high grades, so the correlation must be positive).

5.31: (a) $\hat{y} = 31.9 - 0.304x$. (b) The slope (-0.304) tells us that, on the average, for each additional 1% increase in returning birds, the number of new birds joining the colony decreases by 0.304. (c) When $x = 60$, we predict $\hat{y} = 13.66$ new birds will join the colony.

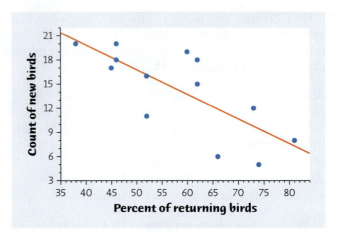

5.33: (a) A plot follows. The relationship between absorbence and nitrates is extremely linear. From software, $r = 0.99994 > 0.997$, so the calibration does not need to be repeated. From software, $\hat{y} = -14.522 + 8.825x$. For absorbence of 40: $-14.522 + (8.825)(40) = 338.478$ mg/liter. (c) We expect estimates of nitrate concentration from absorbence to be very accurate. $r^2 = (0.99994)^2 = 0.9999$, or 99.99% of the variation in nitrate concentration is explained by the regression on absorbence.

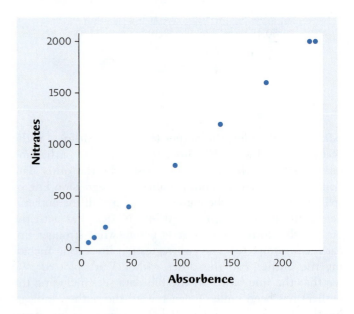

5.35: (a) The two unusual observations are indicated on the following scatterplot. (b)

$$r_1 = 0.4819 \text{ (all observations)}$$
$$r_2 = 0.5684 \text{ (without Subject 15)}$$
$$r_3 = 0.3837 \text{ (without Subject 18)}$$

Both outliers change the correlation. Removing Subject 15 increases *r* because its presence makes the scatterplot less linear. Removing Subject 18 decreases *r* because its presence decreases the relative scatter about the linear pattern.

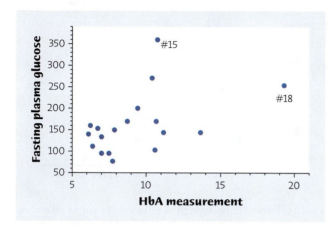

5.37: The equations are

$$\hat{y} = 66.4 + 10.4x \text{ (all observations)}$$
$$\hat{y} = 69.5 + 8.92x \text{ (without Subject 15)}$$
$$\hat{y} = 52.3 + 12.1x \text{ (without Subject 18)}$$

While the equation changes in response to removing either subject, one could argue that neither subject is particularly influential, because the line moves very little over the range of *x* (HbA) values.

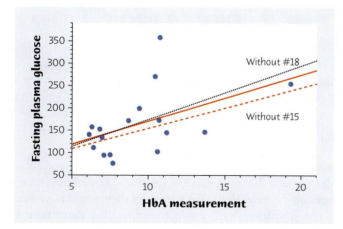

5.39: Responses will vary. For example, students who choose the online course might have more self-motivation or have better computer skills (which might be helpful in doing well in the class).

5.41: For a player who shot 80 in the first round, we predict a second-round score of $\hat{y} = 52.74 + (0.297)(80) = 76.5$. For a player who shot 70 in the first round, we predict a second-round score of $\hat{y} = 52.74 + (0.297)(70) = 73.53$. Notice that the player who shot 80 in the first round (worse than average) is predicted to have a worse-than-average score in the second round, but better than in the first round. Similarly, the player who shot 70 in the first round (better than average) is predicted to do better than average in the second round, but not as well (relatively) as in the first round. Both players are predicted to "regress" to the mean.

5.43: In the scatterplot, right-hand points are filled circles and left-hand points are open circles. In general, the right-hand points lie below the left-hand points, meaning that the right-hand times are shorter, so the subject is likely right-handed. There is no striking pattern for the left-hand points; the pattern for right-hand points is obscured because they are squeezed at the bottom of the plot. While neither plot looks particularly linear, we might nonetheless find the two regression lines: for the right hand, $\hat{y} = 99.4 + 0.0283x$ ($r = 0.305$, $r^2 = 9.3\%$), and for the left hand, $\hat{y} = 172 + 0.262x$ ($r = 0.318$, $r^2 = 10.1\%$). Neither regression is particularly useful for prediction; distance accounts for only 9.3% (right) and 10.1% (left) of the variation in time.

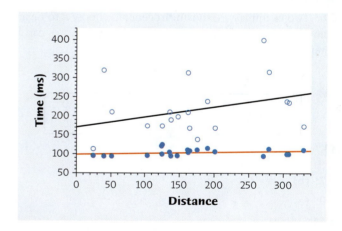

5.45: We see that during the most recent 10 to 15 years, the volume of discharge has increased more rapidly, but before then, the rate increased slowly, if at all. If there is a relationship between year and discharge, it isn't strongly linear, and use of a regression line would not be useful to predict discharge from year.

Chapter 6   Two-Way Tables

6.1: (a) This table describes $736 + 450 + 193 + 205 + 144 + 80 = 1808$ people. $736 + 450 + 193 = 1379$ played video games. (b) The percent of boys earning A's and B's is

$(736 + 205)/1808 = 0.5205 = 52.05\%$. We do this for all three grade levels. The complete marginal distribution for grades is

Grade	Percent
A's and B's	52.05
C's	32.85
D's and F's	15.10

Of all boys, $32.85\% + 15.10\% = 47.95\%$ received a grade of C or lower.

6.3: There are 1379 players. Of these, $736/1379 = 53.37\%$ earned A's or B's. Similarly, there are 429 nonplayers. Of these, $205/429 = 47.79\%$ earned A's or B's. Continuing in like manner, the conditional distribution of grades for players is

Grades	Players	Nonplayers
A's and B's	53.37%	47.79%
C's	32.63%	33.56%
D's and F's	14.00%	18.65%

It doesn't look like there's a big difference between these conditional distributions.

6.5: Two examples are shown. In general, choose a to be any number from 10 to 50, and then all the other entries can be determined.

30	20
30	20

50	0
10	40

6.7: (b).

6.9: (a).

6.11: (c).

6.13: (b).

6.15: The two distributions are given below. For example, among the people who feel that astrology is not at all scientific, the percent with junior college degrees is $87/(87 + 198 + 111) = 0.2197$, or 21.97%.

Opinion	Not at all scientific	Very or sort of scientific
Junior college	22.0%	33.6%
Bachelor's	50.0%	44.5%
Graduate	28.0%	21.9%

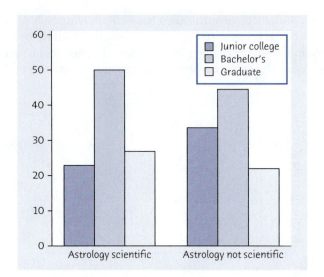

Loosely, adults who believe that astrology is not at all scientific tend to have relatively more college education than adults who believe that astrology is very or sort of scientific.

6.17: The table gives the two marginal distributions. The marginal distribution of marital status is found by taking, for example, $337/8235 = 0.041$, or 4.1%, for the "Single" group. The marginal distribution of job grade is found by taking, for example, $955/8235 = 0.116$, or 11.6%, for Grade 1. As rounded here, both sets of percents add to 100%.

Single	Married	Divorced	Widowed
4.1%	93.9%	1.5%	0.5%

Grade 1	Grade 2	Grade 3	Grade 4
11.6%	51.5%	30.2%	6.7%

6.19: Divide the entries in the first column by the first column total; for example, from Exercise 6.17, 17.2% is $0.172 = 58/337$. The percents should add to 100%, except for possible rounding error.

Job grade	1	2	3	4
% of single men	17.2%	65.9%	14.8%	2.1%

6.21: Age is the main lurking variable. Married men would generally be older than single men, so they would have been in the workforce longer and therefore had more time to advance in their careers.

6.23: The table represents the responses of 516 men and 636 women. To find the conditional distributions, divide each entry in the table by its column total. These percents are given in that table; for example, $76/516 = 0.1473$, or 14.73%. Men are more likely to view animal testing as justified if it might save human lives: over two-thirds of men agree or strongly agree with this statement, compared with slightly less than half of women. The percents who disagree or strongly disagree tell a similar story: 16% of men versus 30% of women.

Response	Male	Female
Strongly agree	14.7%	9.3%
Agree	52.3%	38.8%
Neither	16.9%	21.9%
Disagree	11.8%	19.3%
Strongly disagree	4.3%	10.7%

6.25: The table provides the percents of subjects with various complications for each treatment. For example, for subjects with gastric banding, 81/5380 = 0.0151, or 1.5%, had non-life-threatening complications. Gastric bypass surgery carries the greatest risk for both non-life-threatening and serious complications. Gastric banding seems to be the safest procedure, with the lowest rates for both types of complications.

	Non-life-threatening	Serious	None
Gastric banding	1.5%	0.9%	97.6%
Sleeve gastrectomy	3.6%	2.2%	94.1%
Gastric bypass	6.7%	3.6%	89.7%

6.27: (a) The two-way table is provided below. (b) In order of increasing temperature, the proportions hatching are 16/27 = 0.593, or 59.3%; 38/56 = 0.679, or 67.9%; and 75/104 = 0.721, or 72.1%. The percent hatching increases with temperature; the cold temperature did not prevent hatching, but it made it less likely. The difference between the percents hatching at hot and neutral temperatures is fairly small and may not be big enough to be called significant.

	Cold	Neutral	Hot
Hatched	16	38	75
Did not hatch	11	18	29

Chapter 7 Exploring Data: Part I Review

7.1: (c).
7.3: (c).
7.5: (b).
7.7: (a).
7.9: (d).
7.11: (b).
7.13: (b).
7.15: (a).

7.17: (a) $P(X > 90) = P(Z > 1.81) = 1 - 0.9649 = 0.0351$, or 3.51%. (b) The middle 50% of all observations lie between the first and third quartiles, so the IQR is the range in which these observations lie. In Chapter 3, we see that the first and third quartiles are 0.67 standard deviations above and below the mean. Hence, these values are $75 - 0.67(8.3) = 69.44$ and $75 + 0.67(8.3) = 80.56$ ksi. The range (IQR) in which the middle values lie is therefore $80.56 - 69.44 = 11.12$ ksi.

7.19: (a) Minimum = 7.2, Q_1 = 8.5, M = 9.3, Q_3 = 10.9, maximum = 12.8. (b) M = 27. (c) 25% of values exceed Q_3 = 30. (d) Yes. Virtually all Torrey pine needles are longer than virtually all Aleppo pine needles. There is no overlap in the distributions, as seen by comparing, say, the minimum for Torrey pine needles (21) with the maximum for Aleppo pine needles (12.8).

7.21: (b).
7.23: (c).
7.25: (c).
7.27: (d).
7.29: (d).
7.31: (c).
7.33: (a).
7.35: (a) No. (b) $r^2 = 0.64$, or 64%.

7.37: (a) A graph (either a stemplot or a histogram) shows that the distribution is slightly right-skewed; one observation is somewhat low but not really an outlier. (b) Because of the slight right-skew, we might expect the mean to be slightly larger, but the low observation will tend to counteract that. We find that $\bar{x} = 563.1$ and M = 560 km^3 of water. (c) Because the distribution is not too skewed, one could choose the mean and standard deviation. Here, s = 136.5 km^3 of water. Alternatively, use the five-number summary: Minimum = 290, Q_1 = 445, M = 560, Q_3 = 670, Maximum = 900 (all in km^3 of water).

```
2 | 9
3 |
3 | 6999
4 | 1222234
4 | 5678
5 | 00114
5 | 5566889
6 | 0001344
6 | 778889
7 | 011
7 | 7
8 | 0
8 | 8
9 | 0
```

7.39: A stemplot is shown; a histogram would also be a good choice. The distribution is roughly Normal, though with enough irregularity that students may not be willing to call it Normal. The two low numbers and one high number are not extreme enough to be called outliers. The mean, standard deviation, and five-number summary (all in days) are $\bar{x}$ = 15.287, s = 5.918, and Minimum = 1, Q_1 = 11, M = 16, Q_3 = 19, Maximum = 31. The median date is therefore May 5.

```
0 | 11
0 |
0 | 455
0 | 77
0 | 88999
1 | 00000000111111111
1 | 22222333
1 | 4445555
1 | 66666666777777
1 | 8899999999
2 | 0001111
2 | 2222333333
2 | 455
2 | 67
2 |
3 | 1
```

7.41: There is clearly no discernible pattern in the boxes, but the minimum values suggest a cyclical pattern (the minimum is 1 in every other group of years).

7.43: Back-to-back stemplots show little difference overall. Both shapes are somewhat irregular, but neither is clearly higher or lower. Means and medians are also similar.

```
  Cicada plants |   Control plants
              0 | 1 |
                | 1 | 3
              4 | 1 | 445
              7 | 1 | 77
             99 | 1 | 89999
         111100 | 2 | 0111
     3333332222 | 2 | 2
           5544 | 2 | 4444445555
        7777666 | 2 | 66666
            999 | 2 | 89
            110 | 3 |
                | 3 |
              5 | 3 |
```

	$\bar{x}$	M
Cicada group	0.2426 mg	0.2380 mg
Control group	0.2221 mg	0.2410 mg

The data give little reason to believe that cicadas make good fertilizer, at least on the basis of this response variable.

7.45: The scatterplot suggests a positive linear association, albeit with lots of scatter, so correlation and regression are reasonable tools to summarize the relationship. r = 0.6821, $\hat{y}$ = 0.1205 + 0.008569x. The regression line explains r^2 = 46.5% of the variation in the proportion killed. The analysis provides weak support for the idea that the proportion of perch killed rises with the number of perch present.

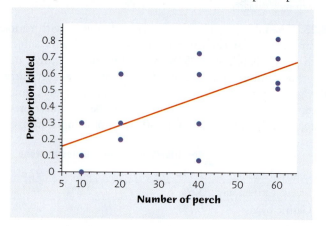

7.47: The scatterplot suggests a fairly strong negative linear association, so correlation and regression are reasonable tools to use here. r = −0.8035, $\hat{y}$ = 92.29 − 0.05762x; the equation explains r^2 = 64.6% of the variation in burned grassland. When wildebeest numbers are higher, the percent of grassland burned tends to be lower. Each additional 100 wildebeest decrease burned area by about 0.058%, on the average.

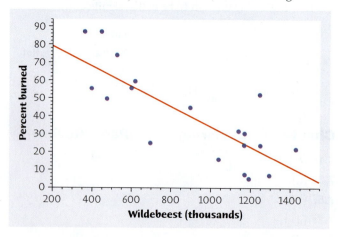

7.49: Some possible observations are the following. All three groups were basically identical in the percent rating schools as "poor." Hispanics appear to be more likely to rate their children's schools as "excellent" but less likely to call them "good."

7.51: (a) $\hat{y} = 93.92 + 0.7783x$. The third point (pure tone, 241; call, 485 spikes/second) is A (circled in plot). The first point (474 and 500 spikes/second) is B; it is marked with a square. (b) The correlation drops only slightly (from 0.6386 to 0.6101) when A is removed; it drops more drastically (to 0.4793) without B. (c) When either point is removed, the slope decreases. Without A, the line is $\hat{y} = 98.42 + 0.6792x$; without B, it is $\hat{y} = 101.1 + 0.6927x$.

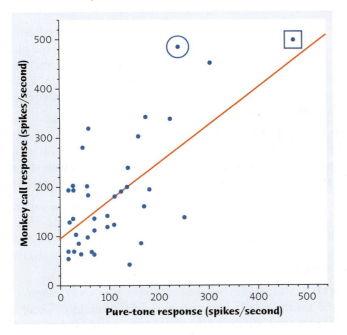

Chapter 8 Producing Data: Sampling

8.1: (a) The population is (all) college students. (b) The sample is the 104 students at the researcher's college who returned the questionnaire.

8.3: (a) The population is all 45,000 people who made credit card purchases. (b) The sample is the 137 people who returned the survey form.

8.5: Since all the students surveyed are enrolled in a special senior honors class, these students may be more likely to be interested in joining the club (and more willing to pay $35 to do so). The direction of bias is likely to overestimate the proportion of all psychology majors willing to pay to join this club. This is a convenience sample.

8.7: Number from 01 to 26 alphabetically (down the columns). With the applet: Population = 1 to <u>26</u>, select a sample of size <u>5</u>, then click <u>Reset</u> and <u>Sample</u>. With Table B, enter at line 134 and choose 16 = Ippolito, 18 = Jung, 13 = Gupta, 21 = Modur, and 04 = Bonds.

8.9: With the election close at hand, the polling organization wants to increase the accuracy of its results. Larger samples provide better information about the population.

8.11: The higher no-answer was probably the second period—more families are likely to be gone for vacations or to be outside enjoying the warmer weather, and so on.

8.13: (a).

8.15: (b).

8.17: (c) Notice that in (b) "07" appears in the sample twice.

8.19: (b).

8.21: The population is the 1000 envelopes stuffed during a given hour. The sample is the 40 envelopes selected.

8.23: With the applet: Population = 1 to <u>287</u>, select a sample of size <u>20</u>, then click <u>Reset</u> and <u>Sample</u>. Using Table B, number the area codes 001 to 287. Then enter at line 135, and pay attention to the instructions that if we use the table, we'll pick only 5 numbers. The selected area codes are 255, 100, 120, 126, and 008.

8.25: (a) Alphabetize the 6168 names (using middle initials or a student ID to distinguish between two people with the same name). Label these students with an ID 0001 to 6168. (b) Using Table B, entering at line 135, the sample is 5556, 5839, 1007, 1120, 1513, 1260, 0842, and 1447.

8.27: (a) False. Such regularity holds only in the long run. (b) True. All pairs of digits (there are 100, from 00 to 99) are equally likely. (c) False. Four random digits have chance 1/10,000 to be 0000, so this sequence will occasionally occur.

8.29: Answers will vary. One possible answer follows. (a) One might guess that the population of people who own only a cell phone and no landline phone is more likely to regularly text and would therefore be more likely to approve of texting while driving. (b) As explained, this group would be more supportive of texting while driving, so the sample percent that favors making texting while driving illegal would decrease.

8.31: (a) Assign labels 0001 through 5024, enter the table at line 104, and select 1388, 0746, 0227, 4001, and 1858. (b) More than 171 respondents have run red lights. We would not expect very many people to claim they *have* run red lights when they have not, but some people will deny running red lights when they have.

8.33: (a) Each person has a 10% chance: 4 of 40 men, and 3 of 30 women. (b) This is not an SRS, because not every group of 7 people can be chosen; the only possible samples are those with 4 men and 3 women.

8.35: Label the members of District 1 001, 002,..., 997. Label those of District 2 001, 002,..., 803. Continue in like manner for each district. Sampling 5 members from District 1 using Table B and entering at line 122, our sample is 138, 738, 159, 895, and 052. Sampling 5 members from District 2 using Table B and entering at line 131, our sample is 050, 071, 663, 281, and 194. We use different lines so that the samples will be independent.

8.37: (a) This design would omit households without telephones, those with only cell phones, and those with unlisted numbers. Such households would likely be made up of poor individuals (who cannot afford a phone), those who choose not to have landline phones, and those who do not wish to have their phone numbers published. (b) Those with unlisted numbers would be included in the sampling frame when a random digit dialer is used.

8.39: (a) The wording is clear but will almost certainly be slanted toward a high positive response. (b) The question makes the case for a national health care system and so will slant responses toward "Yes." (c) This survey question is most likely to produce a response similar to "Uhh … yes? I mean, no? I'm sorry, could you repeat the question?"

8.41: (a) Automated random digit dialing is a fast, economical way to randomly dial landline telephone numbers. (b) In some families, the adult who answers the phone regularly may be systematically different from an adult who does not. (c) There could be (and probably are) big differences between landline phone users and cellular phone users. The design in question is a stratified sample.

8.43: In general, online polls, call-in polls, and voluntary response polls tend to attract responses from those who have strong opinions on the subject, and therefore, such polls are often not representative of the population as a whole.

Chapter 9 Producing Data: Experiments

9.1: This is an observational study. No treatment was assigned to the subjects; we merely observed cell phone usage (and presence/absence of cancer). Explanatory variable: cell phone usage; response variable: whether or not a subject has brain cancer.

9.3: This is an observational study, so it is not reasonable to conclude any cause-and-effect relationship.

9.5: Individuals: pine seedlings. Factor: amount of light. Treatments: full light, 25% light, or 5% light. Response variable: dry weight at the end of the study.

9.7: Making a comparison between the treatment group and the percent finding work *last year* is not helpful. Over a year, many things can change. (To draw conclusions, we would need to make the $500 bonus offer to some people and not to others and then compare the two groups.)

9.9: (a) See the following diagram. (b) If using Table B, label 01 to 36 and take two digits at a time.

9.11: In a controlled scientific study, the effects of factors other than the nonphysical treatment (for example, the placebo effect, differences in the prior health of the subjects) can be eliminated or accounted for, so that the differences in improvement observed between the subjects can be attributed to the differences in treatments.

9.13: (a) The researchers simply observed the diets of subjects; they did not alter them. (That is, no treatments were assigned.) (b) Such language is reasonable because with observational studies, no cause-and-effect conclusion is reasonable.

9.15: In this case, "lack of blindness" means that the experimenter knows which subjects were taught to meditate. He or she may have some expectation about whether or not meditation will lower anxiety; this could unconsciously influence the diagnosis.

9.17: (a) *Completely randomized design:* Randomly assign 15 students to Group 1 (easy mazes) and the other 15 to Group 2 (hard mazes). Compare the time estimates of Group 1 with those of Group 2. (b) *Matched pairs design:* Each student does the activity twice, once with the easy mazes and once with the hard mazes. Randomly decide (for each student) which set of mazes will be used first. Compare each student's "easy" and "hard" time estimate (for example, by looking at each "hard" minus "easy" difference).

9.19: (c).

9.21: (a) Each of the 36 subjects needs a label.

9.23: (a) The choice should be made randomly.

9.25: (a) This is an observational study; the subjects chose their own "treatments" (how much to drink). Explanatory variable: alcohol consumption; response variable: whether or not a subject dies. (b) Many answers are possible. For example, some nondrinkers might avoid drinking because of other health concerns.

9.27: Answers will vary. (a) A survey might ask questions about opinions on tuition, fees, and book costs. (b) An experiment might involve randomly assigning different levels of sanctions for infringements of rules (say, underage drinking) and observing student behavior changes.

9.29:

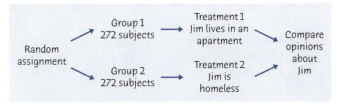

9.31: (a) See below. (b) Label the subjects from 01 through 30. From line 120, we choose subjects corresponding to the numbers 16, 04, 26, 21, 19, 07, 22, 10, 25, 13, 15, 05, 29, 09, and 08 for the first group, and the rest for the second group. Hence, the marijuana group consists of Mattos, Bower, Williams, Sawant, Reichert, Deis, Scannell, Giriunas, Stout, Kennedy, Mani, Burke, Zaccai, Fritz, and Fleming. All other subjects are assigned to the weak marijuana group. (c) This could be a double-blind experiment, assuming that subjects can't distinguish between the types of marijuana smoked. Also, the persons measuring the work output of subjects don't know what kind of marijuana a subject smoked.

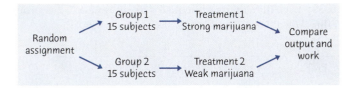

9.33: (a) Two factors: type of granola (two levels: regular and low-fat); serving size label (three levels: 2 servings, 1 serving, and no label). There are 6 treatment combinations. At 20 subjects per treatment, there were 120 subjects in the experiment. (b) The outline looks like the one in Exercise 9.9 except that there are 6 groups of 20 subjects each, with treatments as described in (a).

9.35: (a) See below. (b) Assign labels from 001 to 240. (c) Randomly select 53 subjects for Treatment 1, then 64 for Treatment 2, then 60 for Treatment 3. The remaining 63 subjects belong to Treatment 4. If Table B is used, subjects chosen will vary with starting line.

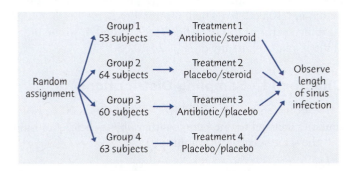

9.37: "No significant difference" does *not* mean the groups are identical. While there almost certainly were *some* differences in these variables between the four groups, those differences were no bigger than we might expect from true random allocation.

9.39: (a) Label the circles 1 to 6, then randomly select three (using Table B or simply by rolling a die) to receive the extra CO_2. Observe the growth in all six regions, and compare the mean growth within the three treated circles with the mean growth in the other three (control) circles. (b) Select pairs of circles in each of three different areas of the forest. For each pair, randomly select one circle to receive the extra CO_2 (using Table B or by flipping a coin). For each pair, compute the difference in growth (treated minus control).

9.41: (a) Explanatory variable: beta-carotene/vitamin(s) taken each day; response variable: whether or not colon cancer develops. (b) Diagram is shown below; equal group sizes are convenient but not necessary. (c) Neither the subjects nor the researchers who examined them knew who was getting which treatment. (d) The observed differences were no more than what might reasonably occur by chance even if there is no effect due to the treatments. (e) Fruits and vegetables contain fiber; this could account for the benefits of those foods.

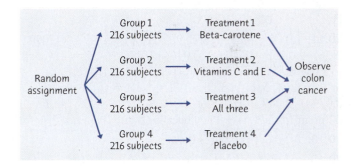

Chapter 10 Introducing Probability

10.1: In the long run, out of a large number of Texas hold'em games in which you hold a pair, the fraction in which you can make four of a kind will be about 2/245. It *does not* mean that exactly 2 out of 245 such hands would yield four of a kind.

10.3: (a) The counts and proportions for each row are shown in the table below.

Row	Count	Proportion
101	3	3/40 = 0.075
102	5	5/50 = 0.125
103	6	6/40 = 0.15
104	4	4/10 = 0.10
105	3	3/40 = 0.075

(b) There are 21 zeros among the first 200 digits of the table (rows 101 to 105), for a proportion of 0.105.

10.5: (a) See below. (b) Each of the 16 outcomes has probability 1/16.

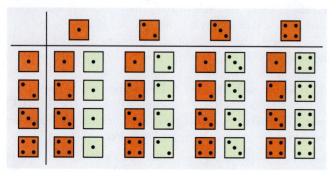

10.7: (a) 23% (17% + 6%) majored in engineering or science. This makes use of Rule 3, because (assuming there are no double majors) "undergraduate students in engineering" and "undergraduate students in science" have no students in common. (b) 47%. This makes use of Rule 4.

10.9: (a) The given probabilities have sum 0.90, so P(other language) = 0.10. (b) P(not English) = 1 − 0.08 = 0.92. (Or add the other three probabilities.) (c) P(neither English nor French) = 0.02 + 0.10 = 0.12.

10.11: (a) A = {4, 5, 6, 7, 8, 9}, so P(A) = 0.097 + 0.079 + 0.067 + 0.058 + 0.051 + 0.046 = 0.398. (b) B = {2, 4, 6, 8}, so P(B) = 0.176 + 0.097 + 0.067 + 0.051 = 0.391. (c) A or B = {2, 4, 5, 6, 7, 8, 9}, so P(A or B) = 0.176 + 0.097 + 0.079 + 0.067 + 0.058 + 0.051 + 0.046 = 0.574. This is different from P(A) + P(B) because A and B are not disjoint.

10.13: (a) 0.6. (b) 0.6. (c) 0.4.

10.15: (a) $P(X \geq 35)$. (b) $P(X \geq 35) = P(Z \geq \frac{35 - 25}{6.4}) = P(Z \geq 1.56) = 1 - 0.9406 = 0.0594$.

10.17: (a) The student runs the mile in 8 minutes or more. $P(Y \geq 8) = P(Z \geq \frac{8 - 7.11}{0.74}) = P(Z \geq 1.20) = 1 - 0.8849 = 0.1151$. (b) $Y < 6$. $P(Y < 6) = P(Z < \frac{6 - 7.11}{0.74}) = P(Z < -1.50) = 0.0668$.

10.19: (b) The set {0, 1, 2, 3, 4, 5} lists all possible counts.

10.21: (b) The other probabilities add to 0.98, so this must be 0.02.

10.23: (b) 24% (0.16 + 0.05 + 0.02 + 0.01 = 0.24, or 24%) have 3 or more cars.

10.25: (a) There are sixteen possible outcomes: {HHHH, HHHM, HHMH, HMHH, MHHH, HHMM, HMHM, HMMH, MHHM, MHMH, MMHH, HMMM, MHMM, MMHM, MMMH, MMMM}. (b) The sample space is {0, 1, 2, 3, 4}.

10.27: (a) 1 − 0.73 = 0.27. (b) P(at least a high school education) = 1 − P (has not finished high school) = 1 − 0.13 = 0.87.

10.29: (a) All probabilities are between 0 and 1, and they add to 1. (We must assume that no one takes more than one language.) (b) 0.43 = 1 − 0.57. (c) 0.40 = 0.30 + 0.08 + 0.02.

10.31: Of the seven cards, there are three 9s, two red 9s, and two 7s. (a) P(draw a 9) = 3/7. (b) P(draw a red 9) = 2/7. (c) P(don't draw a 7) = 1 − P(draw a 7) = 1 − 2/7 = 5/7.

10.33: Each of the 90 guests has probability 1/90 of winning the prize. Since there are 42 women, the probability is 42/90 = 0.467.

10.35: (a) It is legitimate because every person must fall into exactly one category, the probabilities are all between 0 and 1, and they add up to 1. (b) P(15- to 19-year-old who lives alone) = 0.001. (c) P(15- to 19-year-old) = 0.171—the sum of the numbers in the first column. (d) P(lives alone) = 0.073—the sum of the numbers in the third row.

10.37: (a) 1 − 0.171 = 0.829. (b) 1 − 0.073 = 0.927.

10.39: (a) All 9 digits are equally likely, so each has probability 1/9:

Value of W	1	2	3	4	5	6	7	8	9
Probability	1/9	1/9	1/9	1/9	1/9	1/9	1/9	1/9	1/9

(b) $P(W \geq 6) = 4/9 = 0.444$, or twice as big as the Benford's law probability.

10.41: (a) BBB, BBG, BGB, GBB, GGB, GBG, BGG, GGG. Each has probability 1/8. (b) $P(X = 2) = 3/8 = 0.375$. (c) See table.

Value of X	0	1	2	3
Probability	1/8	3/8	3/8	1/8

10.43: (a) $P(0.5 < Y < 1.3) = 0.4$. (b) $P(Y \geq 0.8) = 0.6$.

10.45: $P(8.9 \leq x \leq 9.1) = P(\frac{8.9 - 9}{0.075} \leq Z \leq \frac{9.1 - 9}{0.075}) = P(-1.33 \leq Z \leq 1.33) = 0.9082 - 0.0918 = 0.8164$.

10.47: (a) Because there are 10,000 equally likely four-digit numbers (0000 through 9999), the probability of an exact match is 1/10,000. (b) There is a total of 24 = 4 × 3 × 2 × 1 arrangements of the four digits 5, 9, 7, and 4, so the probability of a match in any order is 24/10,000.

Chapter 11 Sampling Distributions

11.1: Both 3.8 and 160.2 active cells per 100,000 cells are statistics (related to one sample—the subjects before infusion and the same subjects after infusion).

11.3: Although the probability of having to pay for a total loss for 1 or more of the 12 policies is very small, if this were to happen, it would be financially disastrous. On the other hand, for thousands of policies, the law of large numbers says that the average claim on many policies will be close to the mean, so the insurance company can be assured that the premiums they collect will (almost certainly) cover the claims.

11.5: (a) $\mu = 694/10 = 69.4$. (b) The table below shows the results for line 116. Note that we need to choose 5 digits because the digit 4 appears twice. (c) The results for the other lines are also in the table; the histogram is provided below.

Line	Digits	Scores	$\bar{x}$
116	14459	$63 + 72 + 72 + 59 = 266$	66.5
117	3816	$55 + 75 + 63 + 65 = 258$	64.5
118	7319	$66 + 55 + 63 + 59 = 243$	60.75
119	95857	$59 + 72 + 75 + 66 = 272$	68
120	3547	$55 + 72 + 72 + 66 = 265$	66.25
121	7148	$66 + 63 + 72 + 75 = 276$	69
122	1387	$63 + 55 + 75 + 66 = 259$	64.75
123	54580	$72 + 72 + 75 + 86 = 305$	76.25
124	7103	$66 + 63 + 86 + 55 = 270$	67.5
125	9674	$59 + 65 + 66 + 72 = 262$	65.5

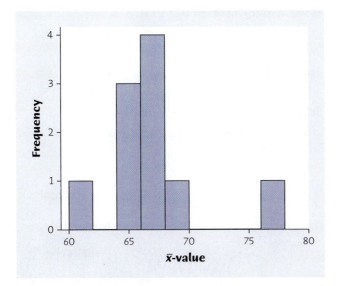

11.7: (a) Because the population is Normal, the sample mean will be Normal with mean $\mu = 188$ mg/dl and standard deviation $\sigma = 41/\sqrt{10} = 12.965$ mg/dl. (b) The overlaid distributions are shown in the following graph. We can clearly see that the distribution of the sample mean is narrower than the original distribution.

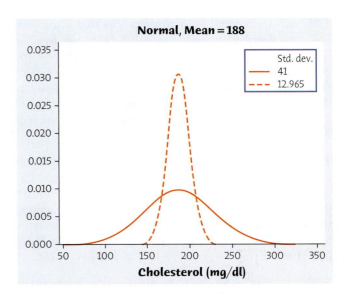

11.9: The central limit theorem says that despite the skewness of the population distribution, the average loss among 10,000 policies will be approximately $N(\$75, \$300/\sqrt{10,000}) = N(\$75, \$3)$. Now $P(\bar{x} > \$85) = P(Z > \frac{85 - 75}{3}) = P(Z > 3.33) = 1 - 0.9996 = 0.0004$.

11.11: (b) This was the true value for the election.

11.13: (a) The mean of the sample means ($\bar{x}$'s) is the same as the population mean (μ).

11.15: (c) The central limit theorem says that the mean from a large sample has (approximately) a Normal distribution.

11.17: 1 is a parameter; 1.07 is a statistic.

11.19: In the long run, the gambler earns an average of 94.7 cents per bet. In other words, the gambler loses (and the house gains) an average of 5.3 cents for each $1 bet.

11.21: (a) $P(20 < X < 30) = P(-0.78 < Z < 0.78) = 0.5646$. (b) If $n = 25$ students, the sampling distribution of $\bar{x}$ is $N(25, 6.4/\sqrt{25}) = N(25, 1.28)$. (c) $P(20 < \bar{x} < 30) = P(-3.91 < Z < 3.91) \approx 1$.

11.23: (a) Let $\bar{x}$ be the mean number of minutes per day that the 5 randomly selected mildly obese people spend walking. Then $\bar{x}$ has the $N(373, 67/\sqrt{5}) = N(373$ min., 29.96 min.) distribution. Now $P(\bar{x} > 420) = P(Z > \frac{420 - 373}{29.96}) = P(Z > 1.57) \approx 0.0582$. (b) Let $\bar{x}$ be the sample mean number of minutes per day for the 5 randomly selected lean people. $\bar{x}$ has the $N(526, 107/\sqrt{5}) = N(526$ min., 47.85 min.) distribution. $P(\bar{x} > 420) = P(Z > -2.22) = 0.9868$.

11.25: (a) The central limit theorem says that $\bar{x}$ will have a Normal distribution with mean 8.8 beats per five seconds and standard deviation $1/\sqrt{12} = 0.288675$ beats per five seconds. (b) $P(\bar{x} < 8) = P(Z < -2.77) = 0.0028$. (c) If the total number of beats in one minute is less than 100, then the average over 12 five-second intervals needs to be less than $100/12 = 8.333$ beats per five seconds. $P(\bar{x} < 8.333) = P(Z < -1.62) = 0.0526$.

11.27: If W is total weight, then the sample mean weight is $\bar{x} = W/22$. The event that the total weight exceeds 4500 pounds is equivalent to the event that $\bar{x}$ exceeds $4500/22 = 204.55$ lb. The central limit theorem says that $\bar{x}$ is approximately Normal with mean 190 lb and standard deviation $35/\sqrt{22} = 7.462$ lb. Therefore, $P(W > 4500) = P(\bar{x} > 204.55) = P(Z > \frac{204.55 - 190}{7.462}) = P(Z > 1.95) = 0.0256$.

11.29: (a) 99.7% of all observations fall within 3 standard deviations, so we want $3\sigma/\sqrt{n} = 1$. The standard deviation of x must therefore be $1/3 = 0.33$ point. (b) We need to choose n so that $6.4/\sqrt{n} = 0.33$. This means $\sqrt{n} = 19.2$, so $n = 368.64$. Because n must be a whole number, take $n = 369$.

11.31: (a) With $n = 14{,}000$, $\mu_{\bar{x}} = \$0.60$ and $\sigma_{\bar{x}} = \$18.96/\sqrt{14{,}000} = \$0.1602$. (b) $P(\$0.50 < \bar{x} < \$0.70) = P(-0.62 < Z < 0.62) = 0.4648$.

Chapter 12   General Rules of Probability

12.1: It is unlikely that these events are independent. In particular, it is reasonable to expect that younger adults are more likely than older adults to be college students.

12.3: If we assume that each site is independent of the others (and that they can be considered a random sample from the collection of sites referenced in scientific journals), then $P(\text{all seven are still good}) = (0.87)^7 = 0.3773$.

12.5: (a) A Venn diagram is provided. (b) The events are

{A and B}	= {student is at least 25 and local}
{A and not B}	= {student is at least 25 and not local}
{B and not A}	= {student is less than 25 and local}
{neither A nor B}	= {student is less than 25 and not local}

(c) $P(A \text{ and } B)$ is given. Subtracting this from the given probabilities for A and B gives $P(A \text{ and not } B)$ and $P(B \text{ and not } A)$. Those probabilities add to 0.90, so $P(\text{neither } B \text{ nor } W) = 0.10$.

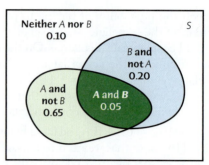

12.7 $P(B \mid \text{not } A) = \frac{P(B \text{ and not } A)}{P(\text{not } A)} = \frac{P(B) - P(B \text{ and } A)}{P(\text{not } A)} = \frac{0.2}{0.3} = 0.667$.

12.9: Let H be the event that an adult belongs to a club, and T be the event that he or she goes at least twice a week. We have been given $P(H) = 0.10$ and $P(T \mid H) = 0.40$. Note also that $P(T \text{ and } H) = P(T)$, since one has to be a member of the club in order to attend. So $P(T) = P(H)P(T \mid H) = (0.10)(0.40) = 0.04$. About 4% of all adults go to health clubs at least twice a week.

12.11: (a) and (b) These probabilities are provided below. (c) The product of these conditional probabilities gives the probability of a flush in spades by the general multiplication rule: we must draw a spade, and then another, and then a third, a fourth, and a fifth. The product of these probabilities is about 0.0004952. (d) Because there are four possible suits in which to have a flush, the probability of a flush is four times that found in (c), or about 0.001981.

$$P(\text{1st card } \spadesuit) = \tfrac{13}{52} = \tfrac{1}{4} = 0.25$$
$$P(\text{2nd card } \spadesuit \mid 1 \spadesuit \text{ picked}) = \tfrac{12}{51} = \tfrac{4}{17} \doteq 0.2353$$
$$P(\text{3rd card } \spadesuit \mid 2 \spadesuit\text{s picked}) = \tfrac{11}{50} = 0.22$$
$$P(\text{4th card } \spadesuit \mid 3 \spadesuit\text{s picked}) = \tfrac{10}{49} \doteq 0.2041$$
$$P(\text{5th card } \spadesuit \mid 4 \spadesuit\text{s picked}) = \tfrac{9}{48} = \tfrac{3}{16} = 0.1875$$

12.13: (a) See below. (b) $P(\text{positive}) = 0.009985 + 0.00594 = 0.015925$.

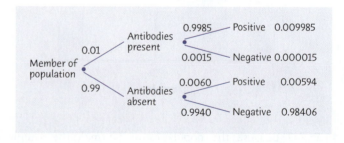

12.15: $P(\text{has antibody} \mid \text{positive}) = \frac{0.009985}{0.015925} = 0.627$.

12.17: (b) $P(W \text{ or } S) = P(W) + P(S) - P(W \text{ and } S) = 0.52 + 0.25 - 0.11 = 0.66$.

12.19: (c) $1{,}623/7{,}629 = 0.2127$.

12.21: (c) We want the fraction of engineering doctorates conferred on women. Hence, A (engineering degree) is what has been given. Hence, $P(B \mid A)$.

12.23: $(0.75)^8 = 0.1001$.

12.25: (a) $(\frac{1}{20})(\frac{9}{20})(\frac{1}{20}) = 0.001125$. (b) The other (non-cherry) symbol can show up on the middle wheel, with probability $(\frac{1}{20})(\frac{11}{20})(\frac{1}{20}) = 0.001375$, or on either of the outside wheels, with probability $(\frac{19}{20})(\frac{9}{20})(\frac{1}{20}) = 0.021375$ (each). (c) Combining all three cases from part (b), we have P(exactly 2 cherries) $= 0.001375 + 2 \cdot 0.021375 = 0.044125$.

12.27: Let I be the event "infection occurs" and let F be "the repair fails." We have been given $P(I) = 0.03$, $P(F) = 0.14$, and $P(I \text{ and } F) = 0.01$. We want to find $P(\text{not } I \text{ and not } F)$. First, use the general addition rule: $P(I \text{ or } F) = P(I) + P(F) - P(I \text{ and } F) = 0.03 + 0.14 - 0.01 = 0.16$. Now observe that the desired probability is the complement of "I or F": $P(\text{not } I \text{ and not } F) = 1 - P(I \text{ or } F) = 1 - 0.16 = 0.84$.

12.29: $P(D) = 0.4 = 0.1 + 0.1 + 0.2$.

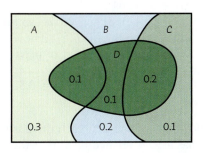

12.31: (a) $P(\text{income} \geq \$30{,}000) = 0.315 + 0.180 + 0.031 = 0.526$. (b) $P(\text{income} \geq \$75{,}000 \mid \text{income} \geq \$30{,}000) = \frac{P(\text{income} \geq \$75{,}000)}{P(\text{income} \geq \$30{,}000)} = \frac{0.211}{0.526} = 0.4011$.

12.33: (a) $P(\text{two boys} \mid \text{at least one boy}) = \frac{P(\text{two boys})}{P(\text{at least one boy})} = \frac{0.25}{0.75} = \frac{1}{3}$. (b) $P(\text{two boys} \mid \text{older child is a boy}) = \frac{P(\text{two boys})}{P(\text{older child is boy})} = \frac{0.25}{0.50} = \frac{1}{2}$.

12.35: Let W be the event "the person is a woman" and A be "the person earned an associate's degree." (a) $P(W) = 2139/3560 = 0.6008$. (b) $P(A \mid W) = 556/2139 = 0.2599$. (c) $P(W \text{ and } A) = P(W)P(A \mid W) = (0.6008)(0.2599) = 0.1561$. Except for rounding, this agrees with the directly computed probability: $P(W \text{ and } A) = 556/3560 = 0.1562$.

12.37: $P(\text{cover} > 2/3 \mid \text{not } D) = 176/662 = 0.2659$, or 26.59%.

12.39:

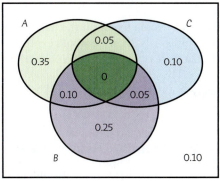

$P(\text{no offer}) = P(\text{not } A \text{ and not } B \text{ and not } C) = 0.10$.

12.41: $P(B \mid C) = 0.05/0.20 = 0.25$. $P(C \mid B) = 0.05/0.40 = 0.125$.

12.43: The probability of each outcome is the product of the individual branch probabilities leading to it. The total probability of the serving player winning a point is $0.4307 + 0.208034 = 0.6387$.

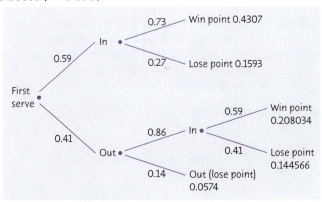

12.45: $P(\text{first serve in} \mid \text{server won point}) = \frac{P(\text{first serve in and server won point})}{P(\text{server won point})} = \frac{0.4307}{0.6387} = 0.6743$, or 67.43%.

12.47: (a) Let $C = \{\text{teen owns a cell phone}\}$ and $T = \{\text{texts}\}$. We are given $P(C) = 0.75$ and $P(T \mid C) = 0.87$. So $P(C \text{ and } T) = P(C) \cdot P(T \mid C) = (0.75)(0.87) = 0.6525$. (b) Let $M = \{\text{more than 6000 texts a month}\}$. We want $P(C \text{ and } T \text{ and } M) = P(C) \cdot P(T \mid C) \cdot P(M \mid C \text{ and } T) = (0.75)(0.87)(0.15) = 0.0979$.

12.49: Let $R = \{\text{recent donor}\}$, $P = \{\text{pledged}\}$, and $C = \{\text{contributed}\}$. (a) The percent of calls resulting in a contribution can be found by considering all the branches of the tree that end in a contribution, meaning that we compute, for example, $P(C \text{ and } R) = P(R) \cdot P(P \mid R) \cdot P(C \mid R \text{ and } P)$. This gives $P(C) = (0.5)(0.4)(0.8) + (0.3)(0.3)(0.6) + (0.2)(0.1)(0.5) = 0.224$, or 22.4%. (b) $P(R \mid C) = \frac{P(C \text{ and } R)}{P(C)} = \frac{(0.5)(0.4)(0.8)}{0.224} = 0.7143$, or 71.4%.

12.51: The proportion having combination (16, 17) is $2(0.232)(0.212) = 0.098368$.

12.53: If the DNA profile found on the hair is possessed by 1 in 1.6 million individuals, then we would expect about 3 individuals in the database of 4.5 million convicted felons to demonstrate a match. This comes from (4.5 million)/(1.6 million) = 2.8125, which was rounded up to 3.

Chapter 13   Binomial Distributions

13.1: Binomial. (1) We have a fixed number of observations ($n = 15$). (2) It is reasonable to believe that each call is independent of the others. (3) "Success" means reaching a live person; "failure" is any other outcome. (4) Each randomly dialed number has chance $p = 0.2$ of reaching a live person.

13.3: Not binomial. The trials aren't independent. If one tile in a box is cracked, there are likely more cracked tiles.

13.5: (a) C, the number caught, is binomial with $n = 10$ and $p = 0.7$. M, the number missed, is binomial with $n = 10$ and $p = 0.3$. (b) We find $P(M = 3) = \binom{10}{3}(0.3)^3(0.7)^7 = (120)(0.027)(0.08235) = 0.2668$. With software, we find $P(M \geq 3) = 0.6172$.

13.7: (a) X is binomial with $n = 10$ and $p = 0.3$; Y is binomial with $n = 10$ and $p = 0.7$. (b) The mean of Y is $(10)(0.7) = 7$ errors caught, and the mean of X is $(10)(0.3) = 3$ errors missed. (c) The standard deviation of Y (or X) is $\sigma = \sqrt{10(0.7)(0.3)} = 1.4491$ errors.

13.9: Let X be the number of 1s and 2s; then X has a binomial distribution with $n = 90$ and $p = 0.477$ (in the absence of fraud). This should have a mean of 42.93 and standard deviation $\sigma = \sqrt{22.4524} = 4.7384$. Therefore, $P(X \leq 29) = P(Z \leq \frac{29 - 42.93}{4.7384}) = P(Z \leq -2.94) = 0.0016$. This probability is quite small, so we have reason to be suspicious.

13.11: (a) $\mu = (1000)(0.24) = 240$ and $\sigma = \sqrt{1000(0.24)(1 - 0.24)} = 13.5056$ first-generation Canadians. (b) To check whether the Normal approximation can be applied, note that $np = 240$ and $n(1 - p) = 760$ are both more than 10. We compute $P(210 \leq X \leq 270) = P(\frac{210 - 240}{13.5056} \leq Z \leq \frac{270 - 240}{13.5056}) = P(-2.22 \leq Z \leq 2.22) = 0.9736$.

13.13: (c) The selections are not independent; once we choose one student, it changes the probability that the next student is a business major.

13.15: (a) 0.2304.

13.17: (a) Two lines of the table means that we have $2(40) = 80$ digits. This is the number of "successes" (8 or 9) in $n = 80$ independent trials with $p = 0.20$.

13.19: (a) No. There is no fixed number of observations. (b) A binomial distribution is reasonable here; a "large city" will have a population much larger than 100 (the sample size), and each randomly selected juror has the same (unknown) probability p of opposing the death penalty. (c) In a Pick 3 game, Joe's chance of winning the lottery is the same every week, so assuming that a year consists of 52 weeks (observations), this distribution would be binomial.

13.21: (a) $n = 20$ and $p = 0.25$. (b) $\mu = np = 5$ correct guesses. (c) $P(X = 5) = \binom{20}{5}(0.25)^5(0.75)^{15} = 0.2023$.

13.23: (a) $18/38 = 0.47368$. (b) X has the binomial ($n = 4$, $p = 0.47368$) distribution. (c) $P(\text{break even}) = P(X = 2) = \binom{4}{2}(0.47368)^2(1 - 0.47368)^2 = 0.37292$. (d) $P(\text{lose money}) = P(X < 2) = P(X = 0) + P(X = 1) = 0.07674 + 0.27625 = 0.35299$.

13.25: X, the number of wins betting on "red" 200 times, is binomial with $n = 200$ and $p = 0.47368$. $np = 94.736 > 10$ and $n(1 - p) = 105.264 > 10$. $\mu = np = 94.736$, $\sigma = \sqrt{200(0.47368)(1 - 0.47368)} = 7.06126$, so $P(X < 100) = P(X \leq 99) = P(Z \leq 0.60) = 0.7257$. The exact binomial probability is 0.7502. As the number of plays (n) increases, the probability of losing money will increase. For example, if $n = 400$, $P(X < 200) = P(Z \leq 0.95) = 0.8289$. The exact binomial probability is 0.8424.

13.27: (a) We must assume that each drive is independent, and that he has a 52% chance of hitting the fairway each time. Both of these assumptions are suspect. (b) The average number of fairways hit is $np = (14)(0.52) = 7.28$ fairways hit.

13.29: (a) X, the number of positive tests, has a binomial distribution with $n = 1000$ and $p = 0.004$. (b) $\mu = np = (1000)(0.004) = 4$ positive tests. (c) To use the Normal approximation, we need np and $n(1 - p)$ both bigger than 10, and as we saw in (b), $np = 4$.

13.31: Let D be the number of members who drop out in the first 4 weeks. Then D has the binomial distribution with $n = 300$ and $p = 0.25$, assuming customer results are independent. Let $S = 300 - D$ be the number still enrolled after 4 weeks. Then S has the binomial distribution with $n = 300$ and $p = 0.75$. (a) For D, $\mu = np = (300)(0.25) = 75$ and $\sigma = \sqrt{np(1 - p)} = \sqrt{300(0.25)(1 - 0.25)} = 7.5$ customers. (b) We use the Normal approximation to the distribution of S, since $np = 225$ and $n(1 - p) = 75$ are both larger than 10. Now, $P(S \geq 210) = P(Z \geq -2) = 0.9772$.

13.33: We have $\mu = 5000$ and $\sigma = 50$ heads, so using the Normal approximation, we compute $P(X \geq 5067$ or $X \leq 4933) = 2P(Z \geq 1.34) = 0.1802$. This is not unreasonable behavior for a fair coin.

13.35: The number N of infections among untreated BJU students is binomial with $n = 1400$ and $p = 0.80$, so the mean is 1120 and the standard deviation is 14.9666 students. 75% of that group is 1050, and the Normal approximation is safe: $P(N \geq 1050) = P(Z \geq \frac{1050 - 1120}{14.9666}) = P(Z \geq -4.68)$, which is very near 1.

13.37: Let V and U be (respectively) the number of new infections among the vaccinated and unvaccinated children. (a) $P(V = 1) = 0.3741$ and $P(U = 1) = 0.0960$. Because these events are independent, $P(V = 1$ and $U = 1) = P(V = 1)P(U = 1) = 0.0359$. (b) $P(2 \text{ infections}) = P(V = 0$ and $U = 2) + P(V = 1$ and $U = 1) + P(V = 2$ and $U = 0) = P(V = 0)P(U = 2) + P(V = 1)P(U = 1) + P(V = 2)P(U = 0) = 0.1977$.

Chapter 14 Confidence Intervals: The Basics

14.1: (a) The sampling distribution of $\bar{x}$ has mean μ (unknown) and standard deviation $\frac{\sigma}{\sqrt{n}} = \frac{34}{\sqrt{51,000}} = 0.1506$. (b) According to this rule, 95% of all values of $\bar{x}$ fall within 2 standard deviations of the sampling distribution of μ—that is, within $2(0.1506) = 0.3012$. (c) 153 ± 0.3012, or between 152.7 and 153.3.

14.3: For 85% confidence, there are three regions in the standard Normal curve: 7.5%, 85%, and 7.5%. The area to the left of z^* is 92.5%. Using Table A, we find that the z^* for 85% confidence is 1.44. See the graph below.

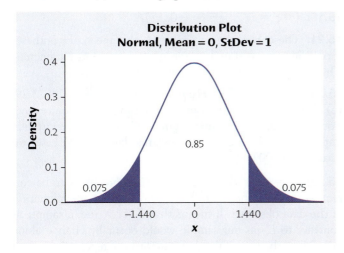

14.5: (a) A stemplot is provided. The two low scores (72 and 74) are both possible outliers, but there are no other apparent deviations from Normality.

```
 7 | 24
 7 |
 8 |
 8 | 69
 9 | 13
 9 | 68
10 | 023334
10 | 578
11 | 11222444
11 | 89
12 | 0
12 | 8
13 | 02
```

(b) The problem states that these girls are an SRS of the population, which is very large, so conditions for inference are met. In (a), we saw that the scores are consistent with having come from a Normal population. Our 99% confidence interval for μ is given by $105.84 \pm 2.576\frac{15}{\sqrt{31}} = 98.90$ to 112.78 IQ points. We are 99% confident that the mean IQ of seventh-grade girls in this district is between 98.90 and 112.78 points.

14.7: With $z^* = 1.96$ and $\sigma = 7.5$, the margin of error is $z^* \frac{\sigma}{\sqrt{n}} = \frac{14.7}{\sqrt{n}}$. (a) and (b) The margins of error are given in the table. (c) Margin of error decreases as n increases. (Specifically, every time the sample size n is quadrupled, the margin of error is halved.)

n	Margin of error
100	1.47
400	0.735
1600	0.3675

14.9: (a) The standard deviation of $\bar{x}$ is $\frac{\sigma}{\sqrt{n}} = \frac{0.001}{\sqrt{3}} = 0.000577$ gram, so the margin of error is $1.96 \frac{\sigma}{\sqrt{n}} = 1.96(0.000577) = 0.00113$ gram.

14.11: (c) The margin of error is now $\frac{(2.576)(0.001)}{\sqrt{8}} = 0.00091$.

14.13: (c) The margin of error is $1.960(1.167) = 2.29$, so the confidence interval is 150 ± 2.29.

14.15: (a) The larger the sample size, the smaller the margin of error, provided that the confidence level and population standard deviation remain the same.

14.17: The margin of error for 90% confidence is $1.645\frac{2.5}{\sqrt{200}} = 0.2908$ kg/m^2, so the interval is $2.35 \pm 0.2908 = 2.0592$ to 2.6408 kg/m^2.

14.19: The mistake is in saying that 95% of other polls would have results close to the results of this poll. Other surveys should be close to the truth—not necessarily close to the results of this survey.

14.21: (a) The stemplot (below) does look reasonably Normal.

```
-8 | 3
-7 | 80
-6 | 88552
-5 | 97633221
-4 | 9977430
-3 | 86310
-2 | 755322110
-1 | 800
-0 | 83
 0 | 234
 1 | 7
 2 | 2
```

(b) The problem states that we may consider these women to be an SRS of the population. In (a), we concluded that the data appear as though they may have come from a Normal distribution. The 99% confidence interval for μ is given by $-3.587\% \pm 2.576 \frac{2.5\%}{\sqrt{47}} = -4.526\%$ to -2.648%. We are 99% confident that the mean percent change in spinal mineral content of nursing mothers is between -4.526% and -2.648%. That is, the mean spinal mineral content in nursing mothers decreases by between 2.65% and 4.53% with 99% confidence.

14.23: Regardless of the level of confidence (the 95% confidence level has nothing to do with it), larger samples reduce margins of error, providing greater precision in estimating μ.

Chapter 15 Tests of Significance: The Basics

15.1: (a) If $\mu = 115$, the distribution is approximately Normal with mean $\mu = 115$ and standard deviation $\frac{\sigma}{\sqrt{n}} = 6$. (b) The actual result lies out toward the high tail of the curve, while 118.6 is fairly close to the middle. If $\mu = 115$, observing a value similar to 118.6 would not be too surprising, but 125.8 is less likely, and it therefore provides some evidence that $\mu > 115$.

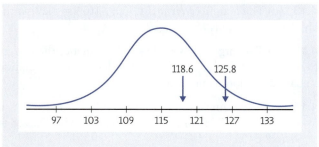

15.3: $H_0: \mu = 115$ vs. $H_a: \mu > 115$. Because the teacher suspects that older students have a higher mean, we have a one-sided alternative.

15.5: $H_0: \mu = 75$ vs. $H_a: \mu < 75$. The professor suspects that this TA's students perform worse than the population of all students in the class, on average.

15.7: With $\sigma = 60$ and $n = 18$, the standard deviation is $\frac{\sigma}{\sqrt{18}} = 14.1421$, so when $\mu = 0$, the distribution of $\bar{x}$ is $N(0, 14.1421)$. (b) The P-value is $P = 2P(\bar{x} \geq 17) = 2P(Z \geq \frac{17 - 0}{14.1421}) = 0.2302$.

15.9: Let μ be the rod's true conductivity (the mean of all measurements of its conductivity). $H_0: \mu = 10.1$ vs. $H_a: \mu \neq 10.1$. Assume we have a Normal distribution and an SRS. The standard deviation of $\bar{x}$ is $\frac{0.1}{\sqrt{6}} = 0.048$, so the test statistic is $z = \frac{10.0833 - 10.1}{0.048} = -0.35$ P-value $= 2P(Z \leq -0.35) = 0.728$. This sample gives little reason to doubt that the true conductivity is 10.1.

15.11: Using Table A, $z = 1.876$ is significant at the $\alpha = 0.05$ level because it is larger than 1.645. It is not significant at the $\alpha = 0.01$ level because it is smaller than 2.326.

15.13: (a) The test statistic is $z = \frac{-0.2213 - 0}{1/\sqrt{100}} = -2.213$. (b) Because $2.213 > 1.96$, the test is significant at the $\alpha = 0.05$ level. (c) The test is not significant at the $\alpha = 0.01$ level because $2.213 < 2.326$. (d) In Table C, 2.213 falls between 2.054 (0.04 two-sided P) and 2.326 (0.02). The test gives good evidence against the null hypothesis. We can believe that this software is not generating values from a standard Normal distribution.

15.15: (a) The null hypothesis states that μ takes on the "default" value, 19 seconds.

15.17: (c) The P-value refers to the probability of getting a sample as contrary to the null hypothesis as the sample observed, assuming H_0 is true.

15.19: (b) $z = \frac{29.667 - 30}{1/\sqrt{3}} = -0.5776$.

15.21: These hypotheses use $\bar{x}$ for the mean. Hypotheses should always be stated in terms of population parameters. The correct symbol for the population mean is μ.

15.23: (a) $H_0: \mu = 0$ vs. $H_a: \mu > 0$. (b) $z = \frac{2.35 - 0}{2.5/\sqrt{200}} = 13.29$. (c) This value of z is far outside the range we would expect from the $N(0, 1)$ distribution. Under H_0, it would be virtually impossible to observe a sample mean as large as 2.35 based on a sample of 200 men. Hence, we would easily reject H_0.

15.25: "$P = 0.03$" *does* mean that H_0 is not likely to be correct, but only in the sense that it provides a poor explanation of the data observed. It means that if H_0 is true, a sample as contrary to H_0 as our sample would occur by chance alone only 3% of the time if the experiment were repeated over and over. However, it does *not* mean that there is a 3% chance that H_0 is true.

15.27: The person making the objection is confusing practical significance with statistical significance. In fact, a 5% increase isn't a lot in a pragmatic sense. $P = 0.03$ means that random chance does not easily explain the difference observed. That is, there does seem to be an increase in mean improvement for those who expressed their anxieties, but the significance test does not address whether the difference is large enough to matter.

15.29: In the sketch, the "significant at 1%" region includes only the dark shading ($z > 2.326$). The "significant at 5%" region of the sketch includes both the light and the dark shading ($z > 1.645$). Significant at the 1% level implies significant at the 5% level (or at any level higher than 1%). The converse is false: something that occurs "fewer than 5 times in 100 repetitions" is not necessarily as rare as something that happens "less than once in 100 repetitions," so a test that is significant at the 5% level is not necessarily significant at the 1% level.

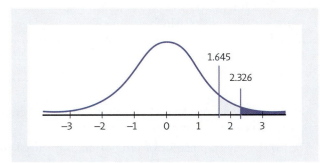

15.31: (a) Because a P-value is a probability, it can never be greater than 1. (b) The correct P-value is $P(Z \geq 1.33) = 0.0918$.

15.33: H_0: $\mu = 0\%$ vs. H_a: $\mu < 0\%$. $z = \frac{-3.587 - 0}{2.5/\sqrt{47}} = -9.84$; P-value $= P(Z \leq -9.84) \approx 0$. There is overwhelming evidence that, on average, nursing mothers lose bone mineral.

15.35: (a) H_0: $\mu = 0$ vs. H_a: $\mu > 0$, where μ is the mean sensitivity difference in the population. (b) $z = \frac{0.10125 - 0}{0.22/\sqrt{16}} = 1.84$. P-value $= 0.0329$. The sample gives significant evidence (at the $\alpha = 0.05$ level) that eye grease increases sensitivity.

15.37: (a) No, because 33 falls in the 95% confidence interval, which is (27.5, 33.9). (b) Yes, because 34 does not fall in the 95% confidence interval.

Chapter 16   Inference in Practice

16.1: The most important reason is (c). This is a convenience sample consisting of the first 20 students on a list. This is not an SRS. Anything we learn from this sample will not extend to the larger population.

16.3: Any number of things could go wrong with this convenience sample. The day after Thanksgiving is widely regarded (rightly or wrongly) as a day on which retailers offer great deals—and the kinds of shoppers found that day probably don't represent shoppers generally. Also, the sample isn't random.

16.5: No. The confidence interval does not describe the range of future values of $\bar{x}$.

16.7: Computing by hand, we get results almost identical to those obtained using the Applet. The standard deviation of $\bar{x}$ is $\frac{\sigma}{\sqrt{n}} = \frac{116}{\sqrt{50}} = 16.405$. The test statistic is $\frac{x - 515}{16.405}$. (a) If $\bar{x} = 541$, the test statistic is $z = 1.58$. The P-value is $P = P(Z \geq 1.58) = 0.057$. Hence, this is (barely) not significant at the 5% level. (b) If $\bar{x} = 542$, the test statistic is $z = 1.65$. The P-value is $P = P(Z \geq 1.65) = 0.049$. Hence, this is (barely) significant at the 5% level. Notice that there's no practical difference between $\bar{x} = 541$ and $\bar{x} = 542$, yet the decision we would make changes if we strictly apply the 5% significance level.

16.9: In each case, the interval is $4.8 \pm 1.96(\frac{0.5}{\sqrt{n}})$.

16.11: $n = (\frac{(1.96)(7.5)}{1})^2 = 216.09$. Take $n = 217$.

16.13: (a) All statistical methods are based on probability samples. We must have a random sample in order to apply them.

16.15: (b) Inference from a voluntary response sample is never reasonable. Online Web surveys are voluntary response surveys.

16.17: (a) There is no control group. Any observed improvement may be due to the treatment or to another cause.

16.19: (a) The significance level α is the probability of rejecting H_0 when H_0 is true.

16.21: We need to know that the samples taken from both populations (hunter-gatherers, agricultural) are random. Are the samples large? Recall that if the samples are very large, then even a small, practically insignificant difference in prevalence of color blindness in the two samples will be deemed statistically significant.

16.23: Many people might be reluctant to relate details of their sex lives, or perhaps some will be inclined to exaggerate. The margin of error does not allow for this bias.

16.25: The effect is greater if the sample is small. With a larger sample, the impact of any one value is small.

16.27: Opinion—even expert opinion—unsupported by data is the weakest type of evidence, so the third description is level C. The second description refers to experiments (clinical trials) and large samples; that is the strongest evidence (level A). The first description is level B: stronger than opinion but not as strong as experiments with large numbers of subjects.

16.29: (a) The margin of error decreases. (b) The P-value decreases (the evidence against H_0 becomes stronger).

16.31: (a) $z = \frac{7.524 - 6}{2/\sqrt{5}} = 1.704$. P-value $= 2P(Z \geq 1.704) = 0.0884$ (using software). This is not significant at the 5% level of significance. (b) We would not reject 6 as a plausible value of μ even though (unknown to the researcher) $\mu = 5$. This isn't surprising since $\bar{x} = 7.524$.

16.33: (a) "Statistically insignificant" means that the differences observed were no more than might have been expected to occur by chance even if SES had no effect on LSAT results. (b) If the results are based on a small sample, then even if the null hypothesis were not true, the test might not be sensitive enough to detect the effect. Knowing the effects were small tells us that the test was not insignificant merely because of a small sample size.

16.35: $n = \left(\frac{(1.96)(3000)}{600}\right)^2 = 96.04$. Take $n = 97$.

Chapter 17   From Exploration to Inference: Part II Review

17.1: (c) Hives with bees; hives with no bees; no hives.

17.3: (b).

17.5: (a) The subjects were not assigned to exercise type.

17.7: Many answers are possible. One possible lurking variable is "student attitude about purpose of college" (students with a view that college is about partying rather than studying may be more likely to binge drink and more likely to have lower grades).

17.9: Question A had 60% favoring a tax cut, while Question B had 22% favoring a tax cut.

17.11: (b).

17.13: (a).

17.15: (d) It's not a random sample, and those walking at night probably have a different view of campus safety than those in the campus community broadly defined.

17.17: (a) $1 - 0.66 - 0.21 - 0.07 - 0.04 = 0.02$.

17.19: $Y > 1$ or $Y \geq 2$. $P(Y \geq 2) = 1 - 0.26 = 0.74$.

17.21: (d) $1 - 0.33 = 0.67$.

17.23: $P(X \leq 2)$ is the probability of women giving birth to 2 or fewer children during their childbearing years. $P(X \leq 2) = 0.193 + 0.174 + 0.344 = 0.711$.

17.25: $P(X \geq 3) = 0.181 + 0.074 + 0.034 = 0.289$.

17.27: (a) The height of the density curve is $1/5 = 0.2$, since the area under the density function must be 1.

17.29: (b) 0.3707, since this is $P(Z \geq 1/3)$, or $P(Z \geq 0.33)$.

17.31: (a) 0.0049, since this is $P(Z \geq 2.58)$.

17.33: Whether $n = 15$ or $n = 150$, the mean of $\bar{x}$ is 445 ms. If $n = 15$, the standard deviation of $\bar{x}$ is $82/\sqrt{15} = 21.17$ ms. If $n = 150$, the standard deviation of $\bar{x}$ is $82/\sqrt{150} = 6.70$ ms.

17.35: $P(\bar{x} > 450) = P(Z > 0.75) = 0.2266$.

17.37: (a).

17.39: (b) $35\% - 15\% = 20\%$.

17.41: (a) This is a binomial distribution; $\binom{12}{8}(0.50)^8(1 - 0.50)^4 = 0.1208$. (b) If $n = 500$ and $p = 0.50$, then $np = 250$ and $n(1 - p) = 250$, both of which are more than 10. Hence, the Normal approximation is reasonable. With mean $np = 250$ and standard deviation $\sqrt{np(1 - p)} = 11.18$, $P(X \geq 235) = P(Z \geq \frac{235 - 250}{11.18}) = P(Z \geq -1.34) = 0.9099$.

17.43: (b).

17.45: As the confidence level decreases, the margin of error decreases, resulting in a narrower confidence interval.

17.47: (d) To cut the margin of error in half, we need to quadruple the sample size from 14 to 56.

17.49: (a).

17.51: (d) $z = \frac{172 - 188}{41/\sqrt{14}} = -1.46$.

17.53: (a) Now $z = \frac{172 - 188}{41/\sqrt{56}} = -2.92$, so P-value $= 0.0018$.

17.55: 84.83 to 90.37.

17.57: The study was an observational study, not an experiment, because nobody assigned birth weights (the treatment) to the babies. In an observational study, a lurking variable may be driving both variables in the study (birth weight and IQ in this case).

17.59: $P = 0.68$ means that the observed difference is easily explained by random chance. $P < 0.001$ means that the observed difference was exceedingly unlikely to have occurred by chance alone.

17.61: (a) One possible population: all full-time undergraduate students in the fall term on a list provided by the registrar. (b) A stratified sample with 125 students from each year is one possibility. (c) Mailed or emailed questionnaires might have high nonresponse rates. Telephone interviews exclude those without phones and may mean repeated calling for those who are not home. Face-to-face interviews might be more costly than your funding will allow. Some students might be sensitive about responding to questions about sexual harassment.

17.63: Parents who fail to return the consent form may be more likely to place less priority on education and therefore may give their children less help with homework, and so forth. Including those children in the control group is likely to lower that group's score.

17.65: (a) The table shows the six treatments—three levels of Factor A (discount level) and two levels of Factor B (fraction of shoes on sale). (b) See below. From line 111 of Table B, the first 10 subjects (Group 1) are 48, 60, 51, 30, 41, 27, 12, 38, 50, and 59.

Factor B
Fraction of shoes on sale

		50%	100%
Factor A	20%	1	2
Discount level	40%	2	4
	60%	5	6

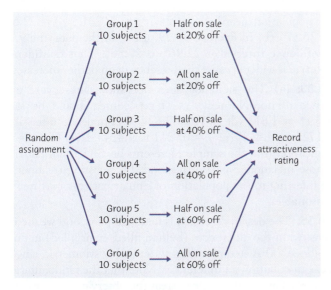

17.67: There are many possible answers; the key is that the events A and B must be able to occur together.

17.69: (a) Out of 100 BMIs, nearly all should be in the range $\mu \pm 3\sigma = 27 \pm 22.5 = 4.5$ to 49.5. (b) The sample mean $\bar{x}$ has a $N(\mu, \sigma/\sqrt{100}) = N(27, 0.75)$ distribution, so nearly all such means should be in the range $27 \pm 3(0.75) = 27 \pm 2.25$, or 24.75 to 29.25.

17.71: (a) This is an observational study: behavior is observed, but no treatment is imposed. (b) "Significant" means

unlikely to happen by chance. (c) Answers will vary. For example, some nondrinkers might avoid drinking because of other health concerns.

17.73: (a) The stemplot (see below) confirms the description given in the text. (b) Let μ be the mean body temperature. We test H_0: $\mu = 98.6°$ vs. H_a: $\mu \neq 98.6°$; the alternative is two-sided because we had no suspicion (before looking at the data) that μ might be higher or lower than 98.6°. Assume that we have a Normal distribution and an SRS. $z = \frac{98.203 - 98.6}{0.7/\sqrt{20}} = -2.54$. P-value $= 2P(Z < -2.54) = 0.0110$. We have fairly strong evidence—significant at $\alpha = 0.05$ but not at $\alpha = 0.01$—that mean body temperature is not equal to 98.6°.

```
 96 | 8
 97 | 344
 97 | 888889
 98 | 0133
 98 | 5789
 99 |
 99 | 6
100 | 2
```

17.75: Assume that we have a Normal distribution and an SRS. Our 90% confidence interval for μ is $98.203 \pm 1.645(\frac{0.7}{\sqrt{20}}) = 98.203 \pm 0.257$, or 97.95° to 98.46°. We are 90% confident that the mean body temperature for healthy adults is between 97.95° and 98.46°.

Chapter 18   Inference about a Population Mean

18.1: $s/\sqrt{n} = 63.9/\sqrt{1000} = 2.0207$ minutes.

18.3: (a) $t^* = 2.132$. (b) $t^* = 2.479$.

18.5: (a) df $= 12 - 1 = 11$, so $t^* = 2.201$. (b) df $= 18 - 1 = 17$, so $t^* = 2.898$. (c) df $= 6 - 1 = 5$, so $t^* = 2.015$.

18.7: We are told to view the observations as an SRS. A stemplot shows some left-skewness; however, for such a small sample, the data are not unreasonably skewed. There are no outliers. $t^* = 1.860$ (df $= 8$); $59.5889 \pm 1.860\frac{6.2553}{\sqrt{9}} = 55.71\%$ to 63.47%. We are 90% confident that the mean percent of nitrogen in ancient air is between 55.71% and 63.47%.

18.9: (a) df $= 15 - 1 = 14$. (b) $t = 2.12$ is bracketed by $t^* = 1.761$ (with two-tail probability 0.10) and $t^* = 2.145$ (with two-tail probability 0.05). Since this is a two-sided significance test, $0.05 < P < 0.10$. (c) This test is significant at the 10% level since $P < 0.10$. It is not significant at the 5% level since $P > 0.05$. (d) From software, $P = 0.0524$.

18.11: Let μ be the mean difference (monkey call minus pure tone) in firing rate. H_0: $\mu = 0$ vs. H_a: $\mu > 0$. We must assume that the monkeys can be regarded as an SRS. For each monkey, we compute the call minus pure-tone differences; a stemplot of these differences shows no outliers or deviations from Normality. $t = \frac{70.378 - 0}{88.447/\sqrt{37}} = 4.84$ with df $= 36$. This has a very small P-value: $P < 0.0001$. We have very strong evidence that macaque neural response to monkey calls is stronger than the response to pure tones.

18.13: A stemplot suggests that the distribution of nitrogen contents is heavily skewed. Although t procedures are robust, they should not be used if the population being sampled from is this heavily skewed. In this case, t procedures are not reliable.

18.15: (b) We virtually never know the value of σ.

18.17: (c) df $= 25 - 1 = 24$.

18.19: (c) $85 \pm 3.250\frac{12}{\sqrt{10}}$.

18.21: (b) If you sample 64 unmarried male students, and then sample 64 unmarried female students, no matching is present.

18.23: For the student group: $t = \frac{0.08 - 0}{0.37/\sqrt{12}} = 0.749$ (not 0.49, as stated). For the non-student group: $t = \frac{0.35 - 0}{0.37/\sqrt{12}} = 3.277$ (rather than 3.25, a difference that might be due to rounding error). From Table C, the first P-value is between 0.4 and 0.5 (software gives 0.47), and the second P-value is between 0.005 and 0.01 (software gives 0.007).

18.25: (a) We have df $= 23 - 1 = 22$, so $t^* = 2.074$. A 95% confidence interval for the mean solution time is $11.58 \pm 2.074(\frac{4.37}{\sqrt{23}}) = 9.69$ to 13.47 seconds. (b) We must assume that the 23 individuals in the neutral group can be regarded as an SRS from the population. Since the sample size is at least 15, we don't need to assume that the population is Normal. Indeed, t procedures can be used as long as the distribution of solution times for the neutral group is not heavily skewed and as long as there are no outliers in the sample.

18.27: (a) A stemplot is provided. A 0 in the row with stem 333 corresponds to a data value of 0.03330. Since the sample size is less than 15, we look to see if the data appear close to Normal. The stemplot is roughly symmetric with one peak and no outliers. (b) df $= 8$, and $t^* = 2.30600$ (using software to obtain t^* to 5 significant figures). $0.03339 \pm 2.30600(\frac{0.00027}{\sqrt{9}}) = 0.03318$ to 0.03360 watts. (c) Since 0.0330 is not contained in the 95% confidence interval computed in (b), we would reject H_0: $\mu = 0.0330$ at the 5% significance level in favor of the two-sided alternative. There is strong evidence that the mean conductivity is different from 0.0330 watts.

```
330 | 0
331 |
332 | 0
333 | 000
334 | 00
335 |
336 |
337 | 0
338 |
339 | 0
```

18.29: $t^* = 2.042$ (using df $= 30$ with Table C) or $t^* = 2.0262$ (using df $= 37$ with software). The confidence interval is nearly identical in both cases:

$$\bar{x} \pm t^*\left(\frac{s}{\sqrt{38}}\right) = 22.95° \text{ to } 27.89° \quad (t^* = 2.042) \quad \text{or}$$
$$= 22.96° \text{ to } 27.88° \quad (t^* = 2.0262)$$

We are 95% confident that the mean HAV angle among such patients is between 22.95° and 27.89°.

18.31: (a) Without the outlier, the mean is $\bar{x} = 24.76°$, and the standard deviation decreases to $s = 6.34°$. Using df $= 36$ with software, $t^* = 2.0281$, so a 95% confidence interval for the population mean becomes $24.76 \pm 2.0281(\frac{6.34}{\sqrt{37}}) = 22.64°$ to $26.87°$. (b) In Exercise 18.29, using all the data, the 95% confidence interval is 22.96° to 27.88°. That confidence interval is wider because the presence of an outlier increases s.

18.33: (a) The stemplot does not show any severe evidence of non-Normality, so t procedures should be safe. (b) $t^* = 1.812$ (df $= 10$). The 90% confidence interval is $1.1727 \pm 1.812(\frac{0.4606}{\sqrt{11}}) = 0.9211$ to 1.4243 days. There is no indication that the sample represents an SRS of all patients whose melanoma has not responded to existing treatments, so inferring to the population of similar patients may not be reasonable.

18.35: The design described is matched pairs, and we are interested in the differences (helium filled $-$ air filled) in punt distance. (a) A stemplot suggests a roughly symmetric, single-peak distribution for differences. Note that the randomization described means that we can treat the observations as an SRS from a population of all differences (for this kicker). Hence, t procedures seem to be appropriate here. (b) Let μ denote the mean difference (helium filled $-$ air filled). H_0: $\mu = 0$ vs. H_a: $\mu > 0$. $t = \frac{0.462 - 0}{6.867/\sqrt{39}} = 0.420$. With df $= 38$, $P = 0.3384$, using software. There is virtually no evidence that the mean distance for helium-filled footballs is greater than that for air-filled footballs.

18.37: (a) Weather conditions that change from day to day can affect spore counts. So the two measurements made on the same day form a matched pair. (b) Take the differences (kill room counts − processing counts). The 90% confidence interval for μ is $1824.5 \pm 2.353 \left(\frac{834.1}{\sqrt{4}}\right) = 843.2$ to 2805.8 CFU/m^3. The interval is so wide because the sample size is very small, but we are confident that the mean counts in the kill room are higher. (c) The data are counts, which are at best only approximately Normal, and we have only a small sample.

18.39: (a) H_0: $\mu = 0$ vs. H_a: $\mu > 0$, where μ is the mean loss in sweetness (sweetness before storage minus sweetness after storage). $t = \frac{1.02 - 0}{1.196/\sqrt{10}} = 2.697$ with df = 9. $P = 0.012$. There is strong evidence that storage reduces sweetness for this cola. (b) We have only 10 observations, and it isn't possible to assess Normality of the distribution of score differences. Indeed, a stemplot of these data reveals possible skew in this distribution.

```
-1 | 3
-0 | 4
 0 | 47
 1 | 12
 2 | 0023
```

18.41: (a) Let μ represent the mean *E. coli* counts for all possible 100 ml samples taken from all central Ohio swimming areas. H_0: $\mu = 130$ vs. H_a: $\mu > 130$. $t = \frac{56.28125 - 130}{77.28992/\sqrt{16}} = -3.815$ with df = 15, so $P = 0.9991$. There is no evidence that swimming areas in central Ohio have mean *E. coli* counts greater than 130 bacteria per 100 ml. (b) Note that the stems of the stemplot are in units of 100, and data were rounded to the nearest 10. For example, 2|9 represents 290, which corresponds to the original sample value of 291, while 0|0 represents 0, which corresponds to the original sample value of 1. Due to extreme skew and the presence of outliers, t procedures should not be used here. Both tests provide similar P-values, and both tests reach the obvious conclusion, but this is not validation of the t test.

```
0 | 01112223345559
1 | 9
2 | 9
```

18.43: H_0: $\mu = 0$ vs. H_a: $\mu > 0$, where μ represents the mean increase in T cell counts after 20 days on blinatumomab. A stemplot suggests that t procedures are reasonable, with no evidence of non-Normality and no outliers. df = 5 and $t = \frac{0.5283 - 0}{0.4574/\sqrt{6}} = 2.829$, $P = 0.0184$. We would reject H_0 at the 5% (or even 2%) significance level. The data give convincing evidence that the mean count of T cells is higher after 20 days on blinatumomab.

```
0 | 122
0 | 48
1 | 3
```

18.45: (a) Fund and index performances are certainly not independent; for example, a good year for one is likely to be a good year for the other. (b) Let μ be the mean difference (fund minus EAFE). H_0: $\mu = 0$ vs. H_a: $\mu \neq 0$. A stemplot shows no reason to doubt Normality. We must assume that the data we have can be viewed as an SRS. $t = \frac{-0.0754 - 0}{7.9979/\sqrt{24}} = -0.05$, for which $P > 0.5$ (software gives 0.96). We have very little reason to doubt that $\mu = 0$; VIG Fund performance is not significantly different from its benchmark.

18.47: H_0: $\mu = 0$ vs. H_a: $\mu \neq 0$, where μ denotes the mean difference in absorption (generic minus reference). We assume that the subjects can be considered an SRS. A stemplot of the differences looks reasonably Normal with no outliers, so the t procedures should be safe. $t = \frac{37 - 0}{1070.6/\sqrt{20}} = 0.15$. With df = 19 we see that $P > 0.5$ (software gives $P = 0.88$). We cannot conclude that the two drugs differ in mean absorption level.

18.49: Let μ denote the average tip percent for all patrons receiving a bad weather forecast. H_0: $\mu = 20\%$ vs. H_a: $\mu < 20\%$. We assume that we may consider the sample to be an SRS taken from the population of all patrons receiving such a weather report. A stemplot of these data reveals no reason to suspect that t procedures are not appropriate. There are no outliers, and the data are roughly symmetric with one peak. $t = \frac{18.19 - 20}{2.105/\sqrt{20}} = -3.845$. With df = 19, $P = 0.0005$ (using software). There is overwhelming evidence that the mean tip percent for patrons receiving a bad weather report is less than 20%.

Chapter 19   Two-Sample Problems

19.1: This is a matched pairs design. Each couple is a matched pair.

19.3: This involves a single sample.

19.5: (a) If the loggers had known that a study would be done, they might have (consciously or subconsciously) cut down fewer trees than they typically would, in order to reduce the impact of logging. (b) H_0: $\mu_1 = \mu_2$ vs. H_a: $\mu_1 > \mu_2$, where μ_1 is the mean number of species in unlogged plots and μ_2 is the mean number of species in plots logged 8 years earlier. We assume that the data come from SRSs of the two populations. Stemplots suggest some deviation from Normality and a possible low outlier for the logged-plot counts, but neither sample shows strong evidence of non-Normality. With $\bar{x}_1 = 17.50$, $\bar{x}_2 = 13.67$, $s_1 = 3.53$, $s_2 = 4.50$, $n_1 = 12$, and $n_2 = 9$: SE = $\sqrt{\frac{s_1^2}{n_1} + \frac{s_2^2}{n_2}} = 1.813$ and $t = \frac{\bar{x}_1 - \bar{x}_2}{SE} = 2.11$. Using df as the smaller of $9 - 1$ and $12 - 1$, we have df = 8, and $0.025 < P < 0.05$. Using software, we have df = 14.8 and $P = 0.026$. There is strong evidence that the mean number of species in unlogged plots is greater than that in logged plots 8 years after logging.

19.7: $\bar{x}_1 = 17.50$, $\bar{x}_2 = 13.67$, and SE $= 1.813$. Using df $= 8$, $t^* = 3.355$. A 99% confidence interval for the mean difference in number of species in unlogged and logged plots is $\bar{x}_1 - \bar{x}_2 \pm t^* $ SE $= -2.253$ to 9.913 species. Software gives a 99% confidence interval of -1.52 to 9.19 species, using df $= 14.796$.

19.9: (a) A back-to-back stemplot of the time data is provided. The distributions appear to be reasonably Normal, and the discussion in the exercise justifies our treating the data as independent SRSs, so we can use the t procedures. We wish to test H_0: $\mu_1 = \mu_2$ vs. H_a: $\mu_1 < \mu_2$, where μ_1 is the population mean time in the restaurant with no scent, and μ_2 is the mean time in the restaurant with a lavender odor. With $\bar{x}_1 = 91.27$, $\bar{x}_2 = 105.700$, $s_1 = 14.930$, $s_2 = 13.105$, $n_1 = 30$, and $n_2 = 30$: SE $= \sqrt{\frac{s_1^2}{n_1} + \frac{s_2^2}{n_2}} = 3.627$ and $t = \frac{\bar{x}_1 - \bar{x}_2}{\text{SE}} = -3.98$. Using software, df $= 57.041$ and $P = 0.0001$. Using the more conservative df $= 29$ (lesser of $30 - 1$ and $30 - 1$) and Table C, $P < 0.0005$. There is very strong evidence that customers spend more time, on average, in the restaurant when the lavender scent is present. (b) A back-to-back stemplot of the spending data is provided. The distributions are skewed and have many gaps. We wish to test H_0: $\mu_1 = \mu_2$ vs. H_a: $\mu_1 < \mu_2$, where μ_1 is the population mean amount spent in the restaurant with no scent, and μ_2 is the mean amount spent in the restaurant with lavender odor. With $\bar{x}_1 = \$17.5133$, $\bar{x}_2 = \$21.1233$, $s_1 = \$2.3588$, $s_2 = \$2.3450$, $n_1 = 30$, and $n_2 = 30$: SE $= \sqrt{\frac{s_1^2}{n_1} + \frac{s_2^2}{n_2}} = \$0.6073$ and $t = \frac{\bar{x}_1 - \bar{x}_2}{\text{SE}} = -5.95$. Using software, df $= 57.041$ and $P < 0.0001$. Using the more conservative df $= 29$ and Table C, $P < 0.0005$. There is very strong evidence that customers spend more money, on average, when the lavender scent is present.

No scent		Lavender
	6	
98	6	
322	7	
965	7	6
44	8	
7765	8	89
32221	9	234
86	9	578
31	10	1234
9776	10	5566788999
	11	4
85	11	6
1	12	14
	12	69
	13	
	13	7

No scent		Lavender
9	12	
	13	
	14	
99999999999999	15	
	16	
	17	
555555555555	18	55555555555
	19	
5	20	7
9	21	5599999999
	22	3558
	23	
	24	99
5	25	59

19.11: We have two small samples ($n_1 = n_2 = 4$), so the t procedures are not reliable unless both distributions are Normal.

19.13: (c) We have one sample and only one score from each member of the sample.

19.15: (c) Here, df is the lesser of $21 - 1$ and $21 - 1$.

19.17: (c) If random digit dialing produces an SRS, then our samples are SRSs from their respective populations. Also, the samples are large enough to overcome problems of potential non-Normality.

19.19: (b).

19.21: (a) Call the subjects who were given alcohol Group 1, and those who were given a placebo Group 2. Then, since SEM $= s/\sqrt{n}$, we have $s = \text{SEM}\sqrt{n}$. Hence, $s_1 = 0.05\sqrt{25} = 0.25$ and $s_2 = 0.03\sqrt{25} = 0.15$. (b) Using the conservative Option 2, df $= 24$ (the lesser of 25 and $25 - 1$). (c) With $n_1 = n_2 = 25$, SE $= \sqrt{\frac{s_1^2}{n_1} + \frac{s_2^2}{n_2}} = 0.0583$. With df $= 24$, we have $t^* = 1.711$. A 90% confidence interval for the mean difference in proportions is given by $0.25 - 0.12 \pm 1.711(0.0583) = 0.03$ to 0.23.

19.23: (a) Using the conservative two-sample t procedures, df $= 17$ (the lesser of 18 and $18 - 1$). (b) Using the data summary provided in the problem description, $t = \frac{5.16 - 3.47}{\sqrt{\frac{3.5^2}{18} + \frac{2.0^2}{18}}} = 1.779$.

(c) H_0: $\mu_1 = \mu_2$ vs. H_a: $\mu_1 \neq \mu_2$, where μ_1 is the mean for the lack-of-control group, and μ_2 is the mean for the in-control group. Using Table C, with df $= 17$, $0.05 < P < 0.10$. There is at best weak evidence of a difference in means between the in-control and lack-of-control groups.

19.25: (a) The appropriate test is the matched pairs test because a student's score on Try 1 is certainly correlated with his or her score on Try 2. Using the differences, we have $\bar{x} = 29$

and $s = 59$. (b) H_0: $\mu = 0$ vs. H_a: $\mu > 0$; $t = \frac{29 - 0}{59/\sqrt{427}} = 10.16$ with df $= 426$. $P < 0.0005$. Coached students do improve their scores, on average. (c) Table C gives $t^* = 2.626$ for df $= 100$, while software gives $t^* = 2.587$ for df $= 426$. The confidence interval is $\bar{x} \pm t^*s/\sqrt{n}$. Using the conservative value of t^*, this yields 21.50 to 36.50 points. Using software, the confidence interval is 21.61 to 36.39.

19.27: This was an observational study, not an experiment. The students (or their parents) chose whether or not to be coached; students who choose coaching might have other motivating factors that help them do better the second time.

19.29: (a) Based on the stemplots, the t procedures should be safe. Both the stemplots and the means suggest that customers stayed (very slightly) longer when there was no odor. (b) H_0: $\mu_1 = \mu_2$ vs. H_a: $\mu_1 \neq \mu_2$, where μ_1 is the mean time in restaurant with no odor, and μ_2 is the mean time in restaurant with lemon odor. $\bar{x}_1 = 91.2667$, $\bar{x}_2 = 89.7857$, $s_1 = 14.9296$, $s_2 = 15.4377$, $n_1 = 30$, and $n_2 = 28$. We find SE $= 3.9927$ and $t = 0.371$. This is not at all significant: $P > 0.5$ (df $= 27$, using Table C with Option 2 for conservative df) or $P = 0.7121$ (df $= 55.4$, using software). We cannot conclude that mean time in the restaurant is different when the lemon odor is present.

19.31: (a) We provide some summary statistics describing the two samples. The second line for Permafresh, denoted with *, has the low outlier of interest omitted.

	n	$\bar{x}$	s
Permafresh	5	29.54	1.1675
Permafresh*	4	30.025	0.4992
Hylite	5	25.20	2.6693

(b)

```
Permafresh  |    | Hylite
            | 22 | 1
            | 23 | 9
            | 24 | 2
            | 25 |
            | 26 |
          6 | 27 | 0
            | 28 | 8
         95 | 29 |
         70 | 30 |
```

(c) With summary statistics listed in the table, we find the following test statistics and P-values:

	t	df	Conservative P	Software df	P
All points	3.33	4	$0.02 < P < 0.04$	5.48	0.0184
Outlier removed	3.96	3	$0.02 < P < 0.04$	4.35	0.0147

The mild outlier in the Permafresh sample had almost no effect on our conclusion. Despite the small sample sizes, there is good evidence that the mean breaking strengths of the two processes differ.

19.33: The 90% confidence interval is $\bar{x}_1 - \bar{x}_2 \pm t^*SE$, where $t^* = 2.132$ (df $= 4$) or $t^* = 1.981$ (df $= 5.476$). This gives either

$4.34 \pm 2.778 = 1.562$ to 7.118 pounds (with df $= 4$) or

$4.34 \pm 2.581 = 1.759$ to 6.921 pounds (with df $= 5.476$)

19.35: This is a two-sample t statistic, comparing two independent groups (supplemented and control). Using the conservative df $= 5$, $t = -1.05$ would have a P-value between 0.30 and 0.40, which (as the report said) is not significant. The test statistic $t = -1.05$ would not be significant for any value of df.

19.37: These are paired t statistics: for each bird, the number of days behind the caterpillar peak was observed, and the t-values were computed based on the pairwise differences between the first and second years. For the control group, df $= 5$, and for the supplemented group, df $= 6$. The control t is not significant (so the birds in that group did *not* "advance their laying date in the second year"), while the supplemented group t is significant with one-sided $P = 0.0195$ (so those birds did change their laying date).

19.39: H_0: $\mu_1 = \mu_2$ vs. H_a: $\mu_1 > \mu_2$, where μ_1 is the mean score for the Active group, and μ_2 is the mean score for the Traditional group. We must assume that the data come from SRSs of the intended population. Stemplots for each sample show no heavy skew and no outliers. $\bar{x}_1 = 3.6$, $\bar{x}_2 = 4.74$, $s_1 = 2.41$, $s_2 = 2.85$, $n_1 = 15$, and $n_2 = 23$. Of course, since $\bar{x}_1 < \bar{x}_2$, we will not conclude that $\mu_1 > \mu_2$. SE $= \sqrt{\frac{s_1^2}{n_1} + \frac{s_2^2}{n_2}} = 0.86$ and $t = \frac{3.6 - 4.74}{SE} = -1.32$, for which $P > 0.50$, regardless of df. The software df $= 33.42$ and $P = 0.9026$. There is no support for a conclusion that active learning yields higher average scores than traditional learning.

19.41: (a) $t^* = 1.761$ (using df $= 14$) or $t^* = 1.692$ (using software). A 90% confidence interval for $\mu_1 - \mu_2$ is $3.6 - 4.74 \pm t^*(0.86)$, or -2.65 to 0.37 (using df $= 14$) or -2.60 to 0.32 (using df $= 33.42$). (b) Now we want a 90% confidence interval for the mean change in score for the Active class. That is, we construct a 90% confidence interval for μ_1. df $= 14$ and $t^* = 1.761$. $3.6 \pm 1.761\frac{2.41}{\sqrt{15}} = 2.50$ to 4.70.

19.43: Answers will vary. A back-to-back stemplot of responses for men and women reveals that the distribution of claimed drinks per day for women is slightly skewed but has no outliers. For men, the distribution is slightly skewed and contains four outliers. However, these outliers are not too extreme. In all problems, it seems that use of the t procedures is reasonable.

(a) We construct a 95% confidence interval for μ_w, the mean number of claimed drinks for women. $t^* = 1.990$ (df $= 80$ in Table C) or $t^* = 1.9855$ (df $= 94$, software) and SE $= 2.1472/\sqrt{95} = 0.2203$. A 95% confidence interval for μ_w is $4.2737 \pm 1.990(0.223) = 3.84$ to 4.71 drinks. With 95% confidence, the mean number of claimed drinks for women is between 3.84 and 4.71 drinks. (b) We construct a 95% confidence interval for μ_m, the mean number of claimed drinks for men. Here, $t^* = 1.990$ (df $= 80$ in Table C or software) and SE $= 3.3471/\sqrt{81} = 0.3719$. A 95% confidence interval for μ_m is $6.5185 \pm 1.990(0.3719) = 5.78$ to 7.26 drinks. With 95% confidence, the mean number of claimed drinks for men is between 5.78 and 7.26 drinks. (c) $H_0: \mu_m = \mu_w$ vs. $H_a: \mu_m \neq \mu_w$. SE $= \sqrt{\frac{2.1472^2}{95} + \frac{3.3471^2}{81}} = 0.4322$ and $t = \frac{4.2737 - 6.5185}{SE} = -5.193$. Regardless of the choice of df (80 or 132.15), this is highly significant ($P < 0.001$). We have very strong evidence that the claimed number of drinks is different for men and women. To construct a 95% confidence interval for $\mu_m - \mu_w$, we use $t^* = 1.990$ (df $= 80$) or $t^* = 1.9781$ (df $= 132.15$). $\bar{x}_1 - \bar{x}_2 \pm t^* \sqrt{\frac{s_1^2}{n_1} + \frac{s_2^2}{n_2}} = 2.2448 \pm 0.8601$ or 2.2448 ± 0.8549. After rounding either interval, we report that with 95% confidence, on average, sophomore men who drink claim an additional 1.4 to 3.1 drinks per day compared with sophomore women who drink.

Chapter 20 Inference for a Population Proportion

20.1: (a) The population consists of all persons between the ages of 18 and 30 living in the United States. The parameter p is the proportion of this population that prays at least once a week. (b) $\hat{p} = \frac{277}{411} = 0.674$, or 67.4%.

20.3: (a) Approximately Normal with mean $p = 0.70$ and standard deviation $\sqrt{\frac{0.70(1 - 0.70)}{1500}} = 0.0118$. (b) Approximately Normal with mean $p = 0.70$ and standard deviation $\sqrt{\frac{0.70(1 - 0.70)}{6000}} = 0.0059$. Notice that quadrupling the sample size (from 1500 to 6000) results in halving the standard deviation of $\hat{p}$ (0.0059 is one-half of 0.0118).

20.5: We are told that the sample is random and will assume that the sample is close to an SRS. Since both the number of successes (113) and the number of failures ($1025 - 113 = 912$)

are much greater than 15, we may assume that the sampling distribution of $\hat{p}$ is approximately Normal. $\hat{p} = \frac{113}{1025} = 0.1102$ and SE $= \sqrt{\frac{\hat{p}(1 - \hat{p})}{1025}} = 0.0098$. A 99% confidence interval for p is given by $0.1102 \pm 2.576(0.0098) = 0.0850$ to 0.1354, or 8.5% to 13.5%. Based on this sample, we are 99% confident that between 8.5% and 13.5% of Internet users were victims of computer or Internet crime during the year before this survey was taken.

20.7: There were only 5 or 6 "successes" in the sample (because 5/2673 and 6/2673 both round to 0.2%).

20.9: $n = (\frac{z^*}{m})^2 p^*(1 - p^*) = (\frac{1.645}{0.04})^2 (0.75)(1 - 0.75) = 317.1$, so use $n = 318$.

20.11: Let p be the proportion of times the "best face" wins. $H_0: p = 0.50$ vs. $H_a: p > 0.50$. Since the sample consists of 32 trials, we expect 16 successes (best face wins) and 16 failures (best face does not win). The sample is large enough to use the Normal approximation to describe the sampling distribution of $\hat{p}$. We assume that the sample is an SRS. Here, $\hat{p} = \frac{22}{32} = 0.6875$ and $SE_{\hat{p}} = \sqrt{\frac{0.50(1 - 0.50)}{32}} = 0.0884$. $z = \frac{\hat{p} - p_0}{SE} = \frac{0.6875 - 0.50}{0.0884} = 2.12$, and $P = 0.0170$. There is strong evidence that the proportion of times the "best face" wins is more than 0.50.

20.13: (c) $\hat{p} = \frac{1410}{3000} = 0.47$.

20.15: (a).

20.17: (a) The alternative hypothesis expresses the idea that "more than half think their job prospects are good."

20.19: (a) The definition of the confidence level, C, is that an interval constructed in this manner will contain the true value of the parameter C*100% of the time.

20.21: (a) The survey excludes those who have no phones or have only cell phone service. (b) Note that we have plenty of successes and plenty of failures, so conditions for the large-sample confidence interval are met. $\hat{p} = \frac{848}{1010} = 0.8396$, and the large-sample 95% confidence interval is $\hat{p} \pm z^* \sqrt{\frac{\hat{p}(1 - \hat{p})}{n}} = 0.8396 \pm 1.96 \sqrt{\frac{0.8396(1 - 0.8396)}{1010}} = 0.8170$ to 0.8622.

20.23: (a) $\hat{p} = \frac{848}{1010} = 0.8396$, $SE_{\hat{p}} = 0.01155$, so the margin of error is $1.96 SE_{\hat{p}} = 0.02263 = 2.26\%$. (b) If instead $\hat{p} = 0.50$, then $SE_{\hat{p}} = 0.01573$ and the margin of error for 95% confidence would be $1.96 SE_{\hat{p}} = 0.03084 = 3.08\%$. (c) For samples of about this size, the margin of error is no more than about $\pm 3\%$ no matter what $\hat{p}$ is.

20.25: 1% of 23 is 0.23; this is much less than 15, so we cannot use large-sample inference with this information.

20.27: (a) Large-sample methods are safe because we have 880 trials, with 171 successes and $880 - 171 = 709$ failures. For the large-sample interval: $\hat{p} = \frac{171}{880} = 0.1943$, $SE_{\hat{p}} = 0.01334$, the margin of error is $1.96 SE_{\hat{p}} = 0.02614$, and the 95% confidence interval is 0.1682 to 0.2204. (b) More than 171 respondents have run red lights. We would not expect very many people to claim that they have run red lights when they have not, but some people will deny running red lights when they have.

20.29: (a) $n = \left(\frac{z^*}{m}\right)^2 p^*(1 - p^*) = \left(\frac{2.576}{0.015}\right)^2 (0.2)(1 - 0.2) = 4718.8$, so use $n = 4719$. (b) $2.576 \sqrt{\frac{(0.1)(0.9)}{4719}} = 0.01125$.

20.31: (a) We are told to treat this sample as an SRS of 17-year-olds still in school. The sample size is very large, with $n = 9600$, so we have $9600(0.46) = 4416$ kids with a parent who graduated from college and 5184 kids who did not have a parent who graduated from college. The number of successes and failures is very large (more than the required 15), so the large-sample confidence interval is appropriate. We have $SE_{\hat{p}} = \sqrt{\frac{\hat{p}(1 - \hat{p})}{9600}} = 0.0051$, so a margin of error for 99% confidence is $2.576(0.0051) = 0.0131$, and a 99% confidence interval for the proportion is 0.4469 to 0.4731, or 44.69% to 47.31%. With 99% confidence, the proportion of 17-year-old students who are still in school and have at least one parent who graduated from college is between about 0.447 and 0.473. (b) Perhaps parents who are college graduates are more likely to have children who finish school. If so, then the proportion of the entire population is likely to be lower.

20.33: Let p be the proportion of American adults who think that humans developed from earlier species of animals. We have an SRS with a very large sample size (and more than 15 each successes and failures), so the large-sample method can be used. $\hat{p} = \frac{594}{1484} = 0.4003$, $SE_{\hat{p}} = 0.01272$, the margin of error is $1.96 SE_{\hat{p}} = 0.02493$, and the 95% confidence interval is 0.3754 to 0.4252. We are 95% confident that the percent of American adults thinking that humans developed from earlier species of animals is between about 37.5% and 42.5%.

20.35: Let p represent the proportion of American adults who think that humans developed from earlier species of animals. $H_0: p = 0.50$ vs. $H_a: p < 0.50$. We have an SRS with a very large sample size, so expected counts (successes and failures) are easily large enough to apply the large-sample z test. $\hat{p} = \frac{594}{1484} = 0.4003$, so $z = \dfrac{0.4003 - 0.50}{\sqrt{\dfrac{0.50(1 - 0.50)}{1484}}} = -7.68$, for

which $P < 0.0001$. We have very strong evidence that fewer than half of adults believe that humans developed from earlier species of animals.

20.37: We will give a 95% confidence interval for p, the proportion of Chick-fil-A orders correctly filled. We will assume that the 196 visits constitute a random sample of all possible visits. In our sample, we have 182 successes (correctly filled orders) and 14 failures (incorrectly filled orders). Because there are fewer than 15 failures (although not much fewer), our interval may be somewhat suspect. We have $\hat{p} = \frac{182}{196} = 0.9286$, $SE_{\hat{p}} = 0.0183$, the margin of error is $1.96 SE_{\hat{p}} = 0.0360$, and the 95% confidence interval is 0.8926 to 0.9646. We are 95% confident that the proportion of orders filled correctly by Chick-fil-A is between 0.893 and 0.965, or 89.3% to 96.5%. (b) Because we have only 14 incorrect orders, we have 1 fewer failure than is needed to have full faith in our method.

Chapter 21 Comparing Two Proportions

21.1: Let p_1 denote the proportion of younger people who text often and p_2 denote the proportion for older people. We have two large samples: 625 younger people and 1917 older people. The number of successes in each sample (475 and 786, respectively) and the number of failures in each sample (150 and 1131) are large enough to use large-sample methods. $\hat{p}_1 = \frac{475}{625} = 0.76$, and $\hat{p}_2 = \frac{786}{1917} = 0.41$. $SE = \sqrt{\frac{\hat{p}_1(1 - \hat{p}_1)}{625} + \frac{\hat{p}_2(1 - \hat{p}_2)}{1917}} = 0.0204$, so the margin of error for 95% confidence is $1.96(0.0204) = 0.0400$, and a 95% confidence interval for the difference in proportions is 0.3100 to 0.3900, or 31% to 39%. With 95% confidence, the proportion of teenagers who text a lot exceeds that of persons 18 and over by between 0.31 and 0.39.

21.3: Let p_1 denote the proportion of males who meet recommended levels, and let p_2 denote the proportion of females. We have many successes and failures in both samples, so large-sample methods are reasonable. $\hat{p}_1 = \frac{3594}{7881} = 0.4560$ and $\hat{p}_2 = \frac{2261}{8164} = 0.2769$. $SE = 0.0075$, and the margin of error is $2.576 SE = 0.0193$. A 99% confidence interval for the difference in proportions between males and females meeting recommended levels of physical activity is 0.1598 to 0.1984, or 16.0% to 19.8%.

21.5: Let p_1 and p_2 be (respectively) the proportions of injured skiers and injured snowboarders who wear helmets. $H_0: p_1 = p_2$ vs. $H_a: p_1 < p_2$. The smallest count is 96, so the significance testing procedure is safe. $\hat{p}_1 = \frac{96}{578} = 0.1661$ and $\hat{p}_2 = \frac{656}{2992} = 0.2193$. $\hat{p} = \frac{96 + 656}{578 + 2992} = 0.2106$. $SE = \sqrt{\hat{p}(1 - \hat{p})(\frac{1}{578} + \frac{1}{2992})} = 0.01853$. $z = \frac{0.1661 - 0.2193}{SE} = -2.87$ and $P = 0.0021$. We have strong evidence (significant at $\alpha = 0.01$) that skiers and snowboarders with head injuries are less likely to use helmets than skiers and snowboarders without head injuries.

21.7: (b) We look for evidence that the proportion for 2009 is lower than for 1999.

21.9: (b) $\hat{p} = \frac{511 + 592}{2411 + 2045} = 0.2475$, which rounds to 0.25.

21.11: (c) For a 95% confidence interval, the margin of error is $1.96 \sqrt{\frac{\hat{p}_{1999}(1 - \hat{p}_{1999})}{2411} + \frac{\hat{p}_{2009}(1 - \hat{p}_{2009})}{2045}} = 0.026$.

21.13: (b) We have only three failures in the treatment group and only two successes in the control group.

21.15: (a) For the sibutramine group, $\hat{p}_1 = \frac{561}{4906} = 0.114$. For the control (placebo) group, $\hat{p}_2 = \frac{490}{4898} = 0.100$. (b) The counts are 561, 4345, 490, and 4408—easily large enough for use of the large sample confidence interval procedure. (c) The 95% confidence interval is $\hat{p}_1 - \hat{p}_2 \pm 1.96 \sqrt{\frac{\hat{p}_1(1 - \hat{p}_1)}{4906} + \frac{\hat{p}_2(1 - \hat{p}_2)}{4898}} = 0.014 \pm 0.012 = 0.002$ to 0.026, or 0.2% to 2.6%.

21.17: We estimate the overall proportion of ninth-graders who passed the HSA test. As computed in Exercise 21.16, $\hat{p} = \frac{2818 + 2091}{3239 + 2787} = \frac{4909}{6026} = 0.815$. A 95% confidence interval for the proportion p is given by $\hat{p} \pm 1.96 \sqrt{\frac{\hat{p}(1 - \hat{p})}{6026}} = 0.815 \pm 0.010 = 0.805$ to 0.825, or 80.5% to 82.5%.

21.19: (a) Let p_1 and p_2 be (respectively) the proportions of subjects in the sibutramine and placebo groups that experienced a primary outcome. We test $H_0: p_1 = p_2$ vs. $H_a: p_1 \neq p_2$. The test statistic is $z = \dfrac{0.114 - 0.100}{\sqrt{0.107(1 - 0.107)(\frac{1}{4906} + \frac{1}{4898})}} = 2.24$. Software gives us $P = 0.025$. We reject H_0 and conclude that primary outcomes are different between the two groups; the group with sibutramine had significantly more such events. (b) If there were no placebo control group in this study, we could not say for sure that the observed events were due to pre-existing conditions or the drug.

21.21: None of the normal mice developed tumors; we cannot use our methods.

21.23: Let p_1 be the proportion of students from urban/suburban backgrounds who succeed, and let p_2 be that proportion for students from rural/small-town backgrounds. $H_0: p_1 = p_2$ vs. $H_a: p_1 \neq p_2$. All counts are greater than 5, so it should be safe to use the significance test. $\hat{p}_1 = \frac{52}{65} = 0.8$ and $\hat{p}_2 = \frac{30}{55} = 0.5455$. $\hat{p} = \frac{52 + 30}{65 + 55} = 0.6833$ and SE $= \sqrt{\hat{p}(1 - \hat{p})(\frac{1}{65} + \frac{1}{55})} = 0.08523$. $z = \frac{0.8 - 0.5455}{\text{SE}} = 2.99$, for which $P = 0.0028$. We have strong evidence that there is a difference in success rates between urban/suburban students and rural/small-town students.

21.25: The smallest count is 13, so the large-sample procedures are safe. $\hat{p}_1 = \frac{52}{65} = 0.8$, $\hat{p}_2 = \frac{30}{55} = 0.5455$, and the 90% confidence interval is $\hat{p}_1 - \hat{p}_2 \pm 1.645 \sqrt{\frac{\hat{p}_1(1 - \hat{p}_1)}{65} + \frac{\hat{p}_2(1 - \hat{p}_2)}{55}} = 0.1172$ to 0.3918. We are 90% confident that the success rate for urban/suburban students is between about 11.7 and 39.2 percentage points higher than for rural/small-town students.

21.27: Let p_1 be the proportion of deaths among African miners, and let p_2 be the proportion among European miners. $H_0: p_1 = p_2$ vs. $H_a: p_1 > p_2$. The smallest success/failure count is 7, so the conditions for a significance test are met. $\hat{p}_1 = \frac{223}{33,809} = 0.006596$ and $\hat{p}_2 = \frac{7}{1541} = 0.004543$. $\hat{p} = \frac{223 + 7}{33,809 + 1541} = 0.006506$ and SE $= \sqrt{\hat{p}(1 - \hat{p})(\frac{1}{33,809} + \frac{1}{1541})} = 0.002094$. $z = \frac{0.006596 - 0.004543}{\text{SE}} = 0.98$ and $P = 0.1635$. We do not have enough evidence to conclude that the death rates are higher for African miners than for European miners.

21.29: Let p_1 be the proportion of mice ready to breed in good acorn years and p_2 the proportion in bad acorn years. $H_0: p_1 = p_2$ vs. $H_a: p_1 \neq p_2$. All counts are greater than 5, so the conditions for a significance test are met (but not those for a confidence interval). The sample proportions are $\hat{p}_1 = \frac{54}{72} = 0.75$ and $\hat{p}_2 = \frac{10}{17} = 0.5882$. The pooled proportion is $\hat{p} = \frac{54 + 10}{72 + 17} = 0.7191$. The test statistic is $z = \dfrac{0.75 - 0.5882}{\sqrt{0.7191(1 - 0.7191)(\frac{1}{72} + \frac{1}{17})}} = 1.335$. With $P = 0.1819$, we have insufficient evidence to say there is a difference in the proportions of mice ready to breed in good and in bad acorn years.

21.31: (a) This is an experiment because the researchers assigned subjects to the groups being compared. (b) Let p_1 and p_2 be (respectively) the proportions that have an RV infection in the HL+ group and the control group. $H_0: p_1 = p_2$ vs. $H_a: p_1 < p_2$. We have large enough counts to safely use large-sample significance testing procedures. $\hat{p}_1 = \frac{49}{49 + 67} = 0.4224$, $\hat{p}_2 = \frac{49}{49 + 47} = 0.5104$, and $\hat{p} = \frac{49 + 49}{116 + 96} = 0.4623$. SE $= \sqrt{\hat{p}(1 - \hat{p})(\frac{1}{116} + \frac{1}{96})} = 0.0688$. $z = \frac{0.4224 - 0.5104}{\text{SE}} = -1.28$ and $P = 0.1003$. We do not have enough evidence to reject the null hypothesis; there is little evidence to conclude that the proportion of HL+ users with an RV infection is less than that of non-HL+ users.

Chapter 22　Inference about Variables: Part III Review

22.1: (c) The margin of error is $2.056(9.3)/\sqrt{27} = 3.7$.

22.3: (b) $t = 2.023$, df $= 13$.

22.5: (d) $\hat{p} = 1926/7028 = 0.274$.

22.7: (d) The standard error is 0.0068.

22.9: (a) The standard error is 0.0124. (b) A 95% confidence interval is 0.336 to 0.384.

22.11: (b) The margin of error is $2.005(3.2)/\sqrt{55} = 0.865$.

22.13: (a) df is the lesser of $(55 - 1)$ and $(200 - 1)$.

22.15: With such large samples, t procedures are reasonable.

22.17: (b) The margin of error is 3.52. The point estimate is $11.4 - 6.7 = 4.7$.

22.19: (d)

22.21: (b) $\hat{p} = 225/757 = 0.297$.

22.23: (b) $0.297 \pm 1.645(0.017)$.

22.25: (c) It seems reasonable that the researchers suspect that VLBW babies are less likely to graduate from high school.

22.27: (b) $z = \dfrac{0.7397 - 0.8283}{\sqrt{\hat{p}(1-\hat{p})\left(\frac{1}{242} + \frac{1}{233}\right)}} = -2.34$.

22.29: (d) $t = \dfrac{86.2 - 89.8}{\sqrt{\frac{13.4^2}{38} + \frac{14^2}{54}}} = -1.25$, and the test is two-sided.

22.31: (b) $z = \dfrac{0.379 - 0.41}{\sqrt{0.41(1 - 0.41)/348}} = -1.18$, so $P = 0.1190$.

22.33: $0.58 \pm 1.645\sqrt{\dfrac{0.58(1 - 0.58)}{634}} = 0.58 \pm 0.03 = 0.55$ to 0.61.

22.35: $H_0: p_b = p_w$ vs. $H_a: p_b \neq p_w$. With $\hat{p} = [0.72(634) + 0.68(567)]/(634 + 567) = 0.701$, $z = \dfrac{0.72 - 0.68}{\sqrt{0.701(1 - 0.701)\left(\frac{1}{634} + \frac{1}{567}\right)}} = 1.51$ and $P = 2P(Z > 1.51) = 0.131$. There is little evidence of a difference between black and white young people in the proportion believing that rap music videos contain too many references to sex.

22.37: (a) $t = \dfrac{193 - 174}{\sqrt{\frac{68^2}{26} + \frac{44^2}{23}}} = 1.174$, and df $= 22$, the lesser of $23 - 1 = 22$ and $26 - 1 = 25$.

22.39: We must assume that each sample is an SRS taken from its respective population (clinic dogs and pet dogs). We must also assume that the populations (cholesterol levels of pet dogs and cholesterol levels of clinic dogs) are Normal.

22.41: Matched pairs test for difference in means.

22.43: If the sample can be viewed as an SRS, a t confidence interval for a population mean.

22.45: Matched pairs t test or confidence interval.

22.47: The response rate for the survey was only about 20% $(427/2100 = 0.203)$, which might make the conclusions unreliable.

22.49: $H_0: \mu = 12$ vs. $H_a: \mu > 12$, where μ denotes the mean age at first word, measured in months. We regard the sample as an SRS; a stemplot shows that the data are right-skewed with a high outlier (26 months). If we proceed with the t procedures in spite of this, we find $\bar{x} = 13$ and $s = 4.9311$ months. $t = \dfrac{13 - 12}{4.9311/\sqrt{20}} = 0.907$, with df $= 19$, and $P = 0.1879$. (*Note:* If you delete the outlier, $\bar{x} = 12.3158$, $s = 3.9729$, and $t = 0.346$, yielding $P = 0.3665$.) We cannot conclude that the mean age at first word is greater than one year.

22.51: Let μ be the mean age at first word, measured in months. For df $= 19$, $t^* = 1.729$, and the 90% confidence interval is $13 \pm 1.729\frac{4.9311}{\sqrt{20}} = 11.09$ to 14.91 months. We are 90% confident that the mean age at first word for normal children is between 11 and 15 months.

22.53: (a) The design is shown below. (b) $H_0: \mu_B = \mu_C$ vs. $H_a: \mu_B \neq \mu_C$. $\bar{x}_B = 41.2825$, $s_B = 0.2550$, $\bar{x}_C = 42.4925$, and $s_C = 0.2939$; $n_B = n_C = 8$. SE $= 0.1376$ and $t = \dfrac{x_B - x_C}{SE} = -8.79$. With df $= 7$ (or 13.73 from software), $P < 0.001$. There is overwhelming evidence that Method B gives a darker color on average. However, the magnitude of this difference may be too small to be important in practice.

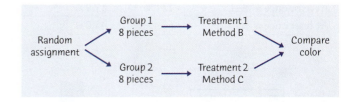

22.55: Let p be the proportion of female students with at least one parent who allows drinking. We are told that the sample represents an SRS. Large-sample methods may be used. $\hat{p} = 0.6915$ and SE $= 0.04764$, so the margin of error is 1.96SE $= 0.09337$, and the interval is 0.5981 to 0.7849. With 95% confidence, the proportion of female students who have at least one parent who allows drinking is 0.598 to 0.785.

22.57: (a) Only 3 of the microwaved crackers showed checking. There are fewer than 5 checked crackers, so we cannot use a large-sample confidence interval or hypothesis test. (b) We want to compare μ_1 and μ_2, the mean breaking pressures of microwaved and control crackers. We test $H_0: \mu_1 = \mu_2$ vs. $H_a: \mu_1 \neq \mu_2$ and construct a 95% confidence interval for $\mu_1 - \mu_2$. We assume that the data can be considered SRSs from the two populations, and that the population distributions are not far from Normal. SE $= 9.0546$ and $t = 6.914$, so the *P*-value is very small, regardless of whether we use df = 19 or df = 33.27. A 95% confidence interval for the difference in mean breaking pressures between these cracker types is 43.65 to 81.55 pounds per square inch (using df = 19 and $t^* = 2.093$) or 44.18 to 81.02 psi (using df = 33.27 and $t^* = 2.0339$). There is very strong evidence that microwaving crackers changes their mean breaking strength. We are 95% confident that microwaving crackers increases their mean breaking strength by between 43.65 and 81.55 psi.

22.59: Two of the counts are too small to allow us to perform a significance test safely.

Chapter 23   Two Categorical Variables: The Chi-Square Test

23.1: (a) The proportion of University Park campus students who do not use Facebook is 68/978 = 0.0695, which rounds to 0.070 and is represented as 7% in the table. (b) The bar graph reveals that students on the main campus are much more likely to use Facebook at least daily, while commonwealth campus students are more likely not to use it at all.

	Univ. Park	Commonwealth
Do not use Facebook	7.0%	28.3%
Several times a month or less	5.6%	8.7%
At least once a week	22.0%	17.9%
At least once a day	65.4%	45.0%

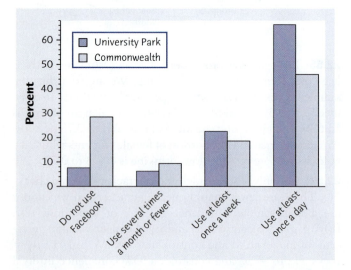

23.3: (a) Expected counts are shown in the table. For example, $\frac{(131)(627)}{1537} = 53.44$. (b) Commonwealth students

actually use Facebook less than once weekly more often than we would expect. Also, Commonwealth students use Facebook daily less often than we would expect.

	Expected counts	
	University Park	Commonwealth
Monthly	77.56	53.44
Weekly	220.25	151.75
Daily	612.19	421.81

23.5: (a) All expected counts are well above 5 (the smallest is 53.44). (b) H_0: There is no relationship between campus and Facebook use vs. H_a: There is a relationship between campus and Facebook use. Using software, we have $\chi^2 = 19.489$ and $P < 0.0005$. (c) The largest contributions come from the first row, reflecting the fact that monthly use is lower among University Park students and higher among commonwealth students.

23.7: H_0: There is no relationship between education level and astrology opinion vs. H_a: There is some relationship between education level and astrology opinion. Examining the output provided in Figure 23.5, we see that all expected cell counts are greater than 5 and all observed cell counts are at least 1, so conditions for use of the chi-square test are satisfied. $\chi^2 = 7.244$ and $P = 0.027$. There is strong evidence of an association between education level and opinion about astrology.

23.9: (a) df = $(r - 1)(c - 1) = (3 - 1)(2 - 1) = 2$. (b) The largest critical value shown for df = 2 is 15.20; since the computed value (19.489) is greater than this, we conclude that $P < 0.0005$. (c) With $r = 4$ and $c = 2$, the appropriate degrees of freedom would be df = 3.

23.11: H_0: $p_1 = p_2 = p_3 = \frac{1}{3}$ vs. H_a: Not all three are equally likely. The expected counts are each $53 \times \frac{1}{3} = 17.67$. The chi-square statistic is then $\chi^2 = \Sigma \frac{(\text{observed count} - 17.67)^2}{17.67} = \frac{(31 - 17.67)^2}{17.67} + \frac{(14 - 17.67)^2}{17.67} + \frac{(8 - 17.67)^2}{17.67} = 10.06 + 0.76 + 5.29 = 16.11$. df = 2. From Table D, $\chi^2 = 16.11$ falls beyond the 0.005 critical value, so $P < 0.005$. There is very strong evidence that the three tilts differ.

23.13: The details of the computation are shown below. The expected counts are found by multiplying the expected frequencies by 803 (the total number of observations).

	Expected frequency	Observed count	Expected count	$O - E$	$\frac{(O - E)^2}{E}$
16 to 29	0.328	401	263.384	137.616	71.9032
30 to 59	0.594	382	476.982	−94.982	18.9139
60 to older	0.078	20	62.634	−42.634	29.0203
		803			119.8374

The difference is significant: $\chi^2 = 119.84$, df $= 2$, and $P < 0.0005$ (using software, $P = 0.000$ to three decimal places).

23.15: $H_0: p_1 = p_2 = \cdots = p_{12} = \frac{1}{12}$ vs. H_a: The 12 astrological sign birth probabilities are not equally likely. Under H_0, we expect $1995/12 = 166.25$ subjects per sign. All cells have expected counts greater than 5, and all cells have at least one observation. A chi-square test is appropriate. Hence, $\chi^2 = \frac{(165 - 166.25)^2}{166.25} + \frac{(165 - 166.25)^2}{166.25} + \cdots + \frac{(168 - 166.25)^2}{166.25} = 10.49$. With df $= 12 - 1 = 11$, using Table D, $P > 0.25$. The technology P-value of $P = 0.4868$. There is little evidence that some astrological signs are more likely in birth than others.

23.17: (a) For 23- to 30-year-olds, the percent is 26.5%.

23.19: (c) $(655 - 593.09)^2/593.09 = 6.46$.

23.21: (b) This is the hypothesis of no association between "age" and "type of injury."

23.23: (c) The largest entry in the table corresponding to df $= 3$ is 17.73.

23.25: (a) The table below summarizes conditional distributions of opinion for each type of consumer. For example, there are $20 + 7 + 9 = 36$ buyers, so the proportion of buyers who think that the quality of the recycled product is higher is $20/36 = 0.556$, or 55.6%.

| | **Think the quality of recycled product is** | | |
	Higher	**Same**	**Lower**
Buyers	55.6%	19.4%	25.0%
Nonbuyers	29.9%	25.8%	44.3%

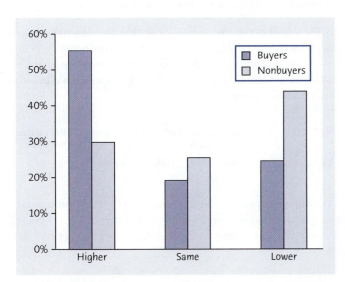

It seems that buyers of recycled products are more likely to feel that recycled products are of higher quality, while nonbuyers are more likely to feel that recycled products are of lower quality. (b) H_0: No association between "opinion of quality" and "buyer status" vs. H_a: There is some association between buyer status and opinion of quality. All expected cell counts are more than 5, so the guidelines for the chi-square test are satisfied. $\chi^2 = 7.64$, df $= 2$, and $0.01 < P < 0.025$. There is strong evidence of an association between buyer status and opinion of quality.

| | **Expected counts** | | |
	Better	**Same**	**Lower**
Buyers	13.26	8.66	14.08
Nonbuyers	35.74	23.34	37.92

(c) We see that there is a relationship between opinion of quality and whether someone buys the recycled product. However, it is impossible to determine whether (i) prior opinion on quality drives the decision to buy or not to buy; or (ii) perhaps the quality of both types of products is excellent, and whichever product you happen to buy drives your opinion of that product.

23.27: (a) See below. To perform the randomization, label the infants 01 to 77, and choose pairs of random digits. (b) See the table for expected counts. $\chi^2 = 0.568$, df $= 3$, and $P = 0.904$. There is no reason to doubt that the randomization "worked."

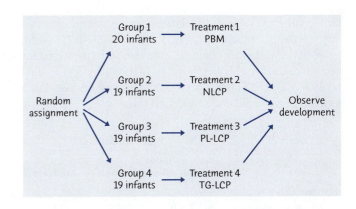

| | **Expected counts** | |
	Female	**Male**
PBM	10.91	9.09
NLCP	10.36	8.64
PL-LCP	10.36	8.64
TG-LCP	10.36	8.64

23.29: (a) H_0: $p_1 = p_2$ vs. H_a: $p_1 < p_2$. (b) The z test must be used because the chi-square procedure measures evidence in support of any association and is implicitly two-sided. $\hat{p}_1 = 0.3667$ and $\hat{p}_2 = 0.7333$. $\hat{p} = (11 + 22)/(30 + 30) = 0.55$ and SE $= 0.12845$, so $z = -2.85$ and $P = 0.0022$. We have strong evidence that rats that can stop the shock (and therefore presumably have better attitudes) develop tumors less often than rats that cannot (and therefore presumably are depressed).

23.31: H_0: There is no relationship between sexual content of ads and magazine audience vs. H_a: There is some relationship between sexual content of ads and magazine audience. Examining the Minitab output, we see that conditions for use of the chi-square test are satisfied since all expected cell counts exceed 5. $\chi^2 = 80.874$ with df $= 2$, leading to $P < 0.0005$. Magazines aimed at women are much more likely to have sexual depictions of models than the other two types of magazines.

23.33: We need cell counts, not just percents. If we had been given the number of travelers in each group—leisure and business—we could have estimated this.

23.35: To do a chi-square test, each subject can be counted only once.

23.37: (a) H_0: There is no relationship between degree held and service attendance vs. H_a: There is some relationship between degree held and service attendance. Expected counts are shown in the table below. $\chi^2 = 14.19$ with df $= 3$, yielding $P = 0.0027$. There is strong evidence of an association between degree held and service attendance.

| | Expected counts | | | |
	High school	Junior college	Bachelor's	Graduate
Attended services	437.3	55.7	129.2	61.8
Did not attend services	842.7	107.3	248.9	119.1

(b) Expected counts are shown. $\chi^2 = 0.73$ with df $= 2$, yielding $P > 25$ (0.694 with software). In this table, we find no evidence of association between religious service attendance and degree held.

| | Expected counts | | |
	Junior College	Bachelor's	Graduate
Attended services	64.1	148.7	71.2
Did not attend services	98.9	229.3	109.8

(c) Expected counts are shown. $\chi^2 = 13.40$ with df $= 1$, yielding $P < 0.0005$ (0.0002 with software). There is overwhelming evidence of association between level of education (High school vs. Beyond high school) and religious service attendance.

| | Expected counts | |
	High school	Beyond High school
Attended services	437.3	246.7
Did not attend services	842.7	475.3

(d) In general, we find that people with degrees beyond high school attend services more often than expected, while people with high school degrees attend services less often than expected. Of those with high school degrees, 31.3% attended services, while the percents are 38.0%, 38.6%, and 42.0%, respectively, for people with junior college, bachelor's, and graduate degrees.

23.39: H_0: There is no relationship between race and opinion about schools vs. H_a: There is some relationship between race and opinion about schools. All expected cell counts exceed 5, so use of a chi-square test is appropriate. $\chi^2 = 22.426$ with df $= 8$, yielding $P = 0.004$. We have strong evidence of a relationship between race and opinion about schools.

23.41: H_0: There is no relationship between laundry habits and preference vs. H_a: There is some relationship between laundry habits and preference. To compare people with different laundry habits, we compare the percent in each class who prefer the new product.

	Soft water, warm wash	Soft water, hot wash	Hard water, warm wash	Hard water, hot wash
Prefer new product	54.3%	51.8%	61.8%	58.3%

The differences are not large, but the "hard water, warm wash" group is most likely to prefer the new detergent. With expected cell counts exceeding 5, a chi-square test is appropriate.

$\chi^2 = 2.058$ with df = 3, yielding $P = 0.560$. The data provide no evidence to conclude that laundry habits and brand preference are related.

Chapter 24   Inference for Regression

24.1: (a) See below.

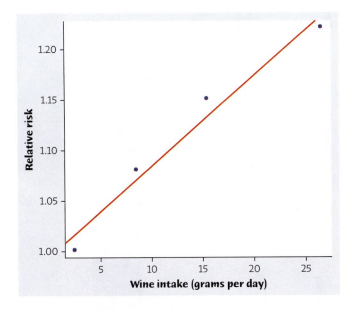

(b) We estimate that an increase in intake of 1 gram per day increases relative risk of breast cancer by 0.0009. According to our estimate, wine intake of 0 grams per day is associated with a relative risk of breast cancer of 0.9931 (about 1). (c) $\hat{y} = 0.9931 + 0.0009x$. See the table below. $s^2 = 0.00079/2 = 0.000395$. We estimate σ by $s = \sqrt{0.000395} = 0.01987$.

| | | | Residual | |
x	y	$\hat{y}$	$y - \hat{y}$	$(y - \hat{y})^2$
2.5	1.00	1.0156	−0.0156	0.00024
8.5	1.08	1.0697	0.0103	0.00011
15.5	1.15	1.1328	0.0172	0.00030
26.5	1.22	1.2319	−0.0119	0.00014
			0	0.00079

24.3: (a) See the following plot. Discharge seems to be increasing over time, but there is also a lot of variation in this

trend, and our impression is easily influenced by the most recent years' data. $r^2 = 0.225$. (b) $\hat{y} = -3690.08 + 2.80x$; $s = 111$.

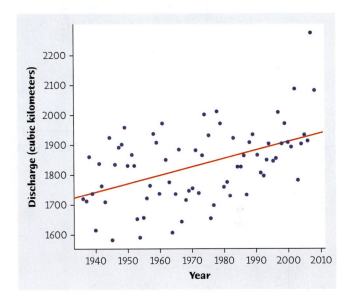

24.5: $H_0: \beta = 0$ vs. $H_a: \beta > 0$. Using Table C, we obtain $P < 0.0005$ ($P = 0.0002$ with software). There is strong evidence of an increase in Arctic discharge over time.

24.7: $r = 0.878$ and $n = 13$. H_0: Population correlation = 0 vs. H_a: Population correlation > 0. Using Table C, $P < 0.0005$. There is overwhelming evidence of a positive linear relationship between social distress score and activity in the part of the brain known to be activated by physical pain.

24.9: df = $29 - 2 = 27$. $t^* = 2.052$. $87.76 \pm 2.052(33.02) = 87.76 \pm 67.76 = 20.00$ to 155.52. With 95% confidence, each unit increase in gray-matter volume results in an increase of introspective ability (as measured by Aroc) of between 20.00 and 155.52 units.

24.11: (a) We should use a prediction interval. With 95% confidence, the relative risk of breast cancer for women drinking 10 g of red wine per day is 0.98643 to 1.18000. (b) $\hat{\mu} = 1.08321$, $SE_{\hat{\mu}} = 0.01057$, $t^* = 2.920$. Hence, a 90% confidence interval for the mean relative risk of breast cancer in all women drinking 10 g of red wine per day is $1.08321 \pm 2.920(0.01057) = 1.052$ to 1.114.

24.13: (a) A stemplot of the residuals is provided after rounding each residual to the nearest whole number. The distribution of residuals appears close to Normal, with perhaps one outlier in the right tail (a residual of 51).

```
-3 | 1
-2 | 433
-1 | 975532
-0 | 99997666322
 0 | 00339
 1 | 01114899
 2 | 14
 3 | 3
 4 |
 5 | 1
```

(b) See below. There appears to be roughly equal spread in the residuals about the line. Notice the outlier mentioned in (a).

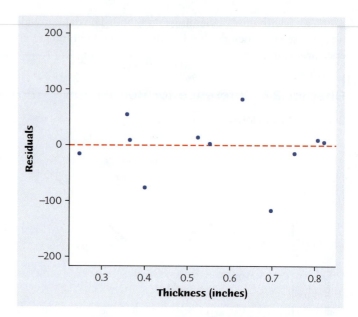

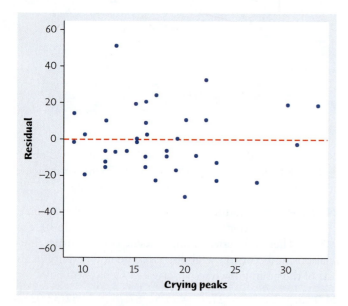

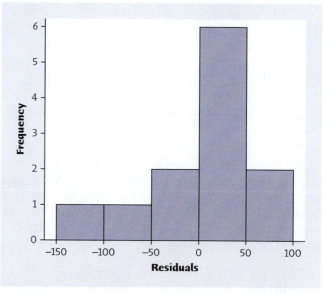

(c) The residuals sum to zero, so only $n - 1$ observations are independent.

24.15: (a) $a = 86.0$ and $b = 1.2699$.

24.17: (c)

24.19: (c) df $= 28 - 2 = 26$.

24.21: (a) The prediction interval is appropriate.

24.23: $H_0: \beta = 0$ vs. $H_a: \beta \neq 0$; $t = \frac{b}{SE_b} = \frac{274.78}{88.18} = 3.116$ with df $= 12 - 2 = 10$. The two-sided P-value is between 0.01 and 0.02. There is strong evidence of a linear relationship between thickness and gate velocity.

24.25: (a) The scatterplot shows no obvious nonlinearity or change in spread. (b) The histogram is quite spread out but not strikingly non-Normal. (c) There are some changes, but they might not be considered substantial: the regression standard error is about 25% smaller, the prediction for $x = 0.5$ inch is about 8 ft/s larger, and the confidence interval is narrower, due to the reduced standard error.

24.27: $H_0: \beta = 0$ vs. $H_a: \beta > 0$; df $= 33 - 2 = 31$, $t = \frac{b}{SE_b} = \frac{0.129232}{0.00752} = 17.185$, yielding $P < 0.0005$. There is overwhelming evidence that manatee kills increase with boats registered.

24.29: (a) The test for $H_0: \beta = 0$ is equivalent to the test for H_0: Population correlation is 0. For testing $H_0: \beta = 0$ vs. $H_a: \beta \neq 0$, we have $t = -4.64$ and $P < 0.0005$. For a one-sided test, P is half the size. For testing H_0: Population correlation is 0 vs. H_a: Population correlation is negative, we have $P < 0.00025$. There is overwhelming evidence of a negative population correlation. (b) $SE_b = 0.0007414$, df $= 14$, $t^* = 1.761$. A 90% confidence interval for β is $-0.0034415 \pm 1.761(0.0007414) = -0.0034415 \pm$

0.00131 = −0.00475 to −0.00213. (c) This question calls for a prediction interval. The interval is 0.488 to 3.769 kg.

24.31: (a) The scatterplot reveals a fairly strong negative linear relationship between SST and coral growth. $H_0: \beta = 0$ vs. $H_a: \beta < 0$; $t = 5.487$, df $= 7 - 2 = 5$; $P = 0.003$. There is strong evidence of a negative linear relationship between SST and coral growth. (b) $\hat{\mu} = 12.37587 - 0.32761(30) = 2.5476$ mm/year. $SE_{\mu} = 0.0362$, df $= 5$, $t^* = 2.571$. A 95% confidence interval for the mean coral growth per year when water temperature is 30 degrees is $2.5476 \pm 2.571(0.0362) = 2.4545$ to 2.6407 mm per year.

24.33: (a) There is a potential outlier, but there is no evidence of a systematic departure from nonlinearity in the relationship between SST and coral growth. (b) There is some evidence (albeit difficult to detect with only 7 observations) that residuals are non-Normal. (c) It is not clear that observations are independent. (d) There may be a trend in the residual plot—negative residuals are associated with low and high temperatures, while large positive residuals are associated with moderate temperatures.

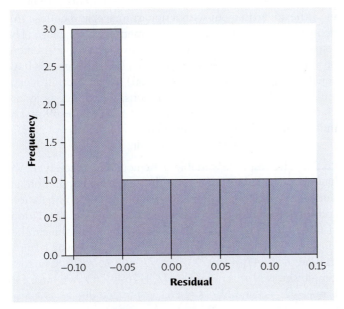

24.35: (a) $\hat{y} = 560.65 - 3.0771x$, $r = -0.6492$. Generally, the longer a child remains at the table, the fewer calories he or she will consume. This relationship is moderately strong and linear. (b) All the conditions for inference appear to be upheld. (c) The slope is significantly different from 0: $t = -3.62$, $P = 0.002$, $SE_b = 0.8498$, df $= 18$, $t^* = 2.101$. The 95% confidence interval for β is $-3.0771 \pm 2.101(0.8498) = -4.8625$ to -1.2917 calories per minute.

24.37: $\hat{y} = 560.65 - 3.0771(40) = 437.57$ calories. $SE_{\hat{y}} = s\sqrt{1 + \frac{1}{n} + \frac{(x^* - \bar{x})^2}{\sum(x - \bar{x})^2}} = 23.4\sqrt{1 + \frac{1}{20} + \frac{(40 - 34.01)^2}{758.07}} = 24.51$ calories. A 95%

prediction interval is given by $437.57 \pm 2.101(24.51) = 386$ to 489 calories.

24.39: $\hat{y} = 1.4146 + 0.4399x$. The slope is significantly different from zero ($t = 4.33$, $P = 0.001$). To assess the evidence that more cones leads to more offspring, we should use the one-sided alternative, $H_a: \beta > 0$, for which P is half as large (so $P < 0.001$). The conditions for inference seem to be satisfied: the relationship appears linear in the scatterplot; a histogram of the residuals looks fairly Normal; the observations should be independent; there may be a slight concern about more variation for moderate number of cones. One might also choose to find a confidence interval for β: df $= 14$, $t^* = 2.145$. A 95% confidence interval for β is $0.4399 \pm 2.145(0.1016) = 0.2220$ to 0.6578 offspring per cone.

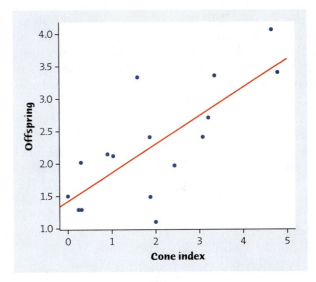

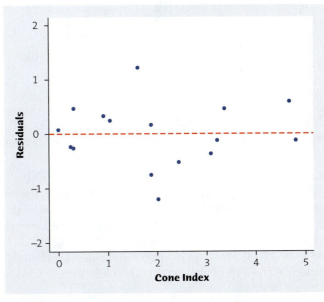

24.41: $\hat{y} = -1.286 + 11.894x$. An examination of the residuals does not suggest any severe violations of the conditions for regression inference. To test $H_0: \beta = 0$ vs. $H_a: \beta > 0$, the test statistic is $t = 10.47$ (df = 21), yielding $P < 0.0005$. For df = 21, $t^* = 2.080$ for 95% confidence, so with b and $SE_b = 1.136$. We are 95% confident that β is between 9.531 and 14.257 clusters.

24.43: $t = -1.00 = \frac{a}{SE_a} = \frac{-0.01270}{0.01264}$. $P = 0.332$, so we do not have enough evidence to conclude that the intercept α differs from 0.

Chapter 25 One-Way Analysis of Variance: Comparing Several Means

25.1: (a) $H_0: \mu_A = \mu_B = \mu_C = \mu_D$ vs. H_a: not all means agree. (b) Referring to Figure 25.2, comparing Groups A and C, we see that the mean status for men expressing anger is about 6.3, while the mean status for women expressing anger is about 4. The mean difference is about 2.3. Notice that comparing Groups B and D, we see that women expressing sadness receive higher status scores than men expressing sadness, but the difference is relatively small (about 1).

25.3: (a) The stemplots appear to suggest that logging reduces the number of trees per plot and that recovery is slow (the 1-year-after and 8-years-after stemplots are similar). (b) The means lead one to the same conclusion as in (a): the first mean is much larger than the other two. (c) For H_0: $\mu_1 = \mu_2 = \mu_3$ vs. H_a: not all means are the same, we find that $F = 11.43$ with df = 2 and 30, which has $P = 0.000205$, so we conclude that these differences are significant: the number of trees per plot really is lower in logged areas.

Never logged		1 year ago		8 years ago	
0		0	2	0	4
0		0	9	0	
1		1	2244	1	22
1	699	1	57789	1	5889
2	0124	2	0	2	22
2	7789	2		2	
3	3	3		3	

25.5: (a) MSE = 2.09 and MSVariety = 541.11. $F = 541.44/2.09 = 259.06$. These agree to within roundoff error. (b) $\sqrt{2.09} = 1.446$, which agrees with the value shown.

25.7: (a) $s_1^2 = 25.6591$, $s_2^2 = 24.8106$, and $s_3^2 = 33.1944$. $s_1 = 5.065$, $s_2 = 4.981$, and $s_3 = 5.761$. The largest standard deviation (5.761) is not more than twice the size of the smallest standard deviation (4.981). Conditions are satisfied. (b) The three standard deviations are $s_L = 16.61$, $s_M = 17.42$, and $s_C = 17.13$. The ratio of largest to smallest standard deviation is $17.42/16.61 = 1.05$, which is less than 2. Conditions are satisfied.

25.9: Side-by-side stemplots show some irregularity but no outliers or strong skewness. ANOVA output shows that the group standard deviations easily satisfy our rule of thumb $(2.059/1.302 = 1.58 < 2)$. The differences among the groups were significant at $\alpha = 0.05$: $F = 3.44$, df = 3, and 27, $P = 0.031$. Nitrogen had a positive effect, the phosphorus and control groups were similar, and the plants that got both nutrients fell between the others.

25.11: (a) $I = 3$ and $N = 96$, so df = 2 and 93. (b) $I = 3$ and $N = 90$, so df = 2 and 87.

25.13: (b) $I - 1 = 3 - 1 = 2$, and $N - I = 9 - 3 = 6$.

25.15: $F = $ MSCaffeine/MSError $= 11,299/1600 = 7.06$.

25.17: (c) The largest standard deviation is 62.02, and the smallest is 20.07. Hence, the largest standard deviation is more than twice the smallest.

25.19: (c) We do not have three independent samples from three populations.

25.21: The populations are college students who might view the advertisement with art image, college students who might view the advertisement with a nonart image, and college students who might view the advertisement with no image. The response variable is student evaluation of the advertisement on the 1 to 7 scale. $H_0: \mu_1 = \mu_2 = \mu_3$ (all three groups have equal mean advertisement evaluation) vs. H_a: not all means are equal. There are $I = 3$ populations; the samples sizes are $n_1 = n_2 = n_3 = 39$, so there are $N = 39 + 39 + 39 = 117$ individuals in the total sample. There are then $I - 1 = 3 - 1 = 2$ and $N - I = 117 - 3 = 114$ df.

25.23: The response variable is hemoglobin A1c level. We have $I = 4$ populations; a control (sedentary) population, an aerobic exercise population, a resistance training population, and a combined aerobic and resistance training population. $H_0: \mu_1 = \mu_2 = \mu_3 = \mu_4$ (all four groups have equal mean hemoglobin A1c levels) vs. H_a: not all means are equal. Sample sizes are $n_1 = 41$, $n_2 = 73$, $n_3 = 72$, and $n_4 = 76$. Our total sample size is $N = 41 + 73 + 72 + 76 = 262$. We have $I - 1 = 4 - 1 = 3$ and $N - I = 262 - 4 = 258$ df.

25.25: (a) The graph suggests that emissions rise when a plant is attacked because the mean control emission rate is half the smallest of the other rates. (b) The null hypothesis is "all groups have the same mean emission rate." The alternative is "at least one group has a different mean emission rate." (c) The most important piece of additional information would be whether the data are sufficiently close to Normally distributed. (From the description, it seems reasonably safe to assume that these are more or less random samples.) (d) The SEM equals $s/\sqrt{8}$, so we can find the standard deviations by multiplying by $\sqrt{8}$; they are 16.77, 24.75, 18.78, and 24.38.

However, this factor of $\sqrt{8}$ would cancel out in the process of finding the ratio of the largest and smallest standard deviations, so we can simply find this ratio directly from the SEMs: $\frac{8.75}{5.93} = \frac{24.75}{16.77} = 1.48$, which satisfies our rule of thumb.

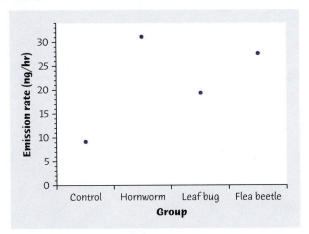

25.27: (a) The means suggest that extra water in the spring has the greatest effect on biomass, with a lesser effect from added water in the winter. ANOVA is risky with these data; the standard deviation ratio is nearly 3, and the winter and spring distributions may have skewness or outliers (although it is difficult to judge with such small samples). (b) H_0: $\mu_w = \mu_s = \mu_c$ vs. H_a: at least one mean is different. (c) ANOVA gives a statistically significant result ($F = 27.52$, df = 2 and 15, $P < 0.0005$), but as noted in (a), the conditions for ANOVA are not satisfied. Based on the stemplots and the means, however, we should still be safe in concluding that added water increases biomass.

25.29: (a) The design, with four treatments, is shown.

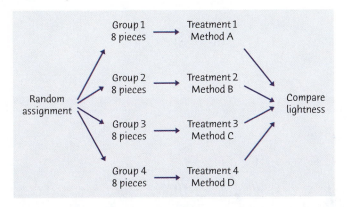

(b) ANOVA should be safe: it is reasonable to view the samples as SRSs from the four populations, the distributions do not show drastic deviations from Normality, and the standard deviations satisfy our rule of thumb (0.392/0.250 = 1.568). The means have rather small differences in lightness score; Method C is lightest and Method B is darkest. The differences in mean lightness are nonetheless highly significant ($F = 22.77$, $P < 0.001$). The manufacturer will prefer Method B. Whether these differences are large enough to be important in practice requires more information about the scale of lightness scores.

25.31: First, we see that the ratio of largest standard deviation to smallest standard deviation is 2.388/1.959 = 1.219, which is less than 2. There is some evidence of non-Normality, and perhaps one outlier in the "no weather report" group. We proceed, as the samples are reasonably large. $F = 20.679$ with $3 - 1 = 2$ and $60 - 3 = 57$ df. $P = 0.000$, to three decimal places. There is overwhelming evidence that the mean tip percents are not the same for all three groups.

25.33: First, we note that the mean angle for untreated fabric is 79 degrees, showing much less wrinkle resistance than any of the treated fabrics. ANOVA on four groups gives $F = 153.76$ and $P < 0.001$. A comparison of wrinkle recovery angle for the three durable press treatments is more interesting.

The ANOVA F test cannot be trusted because the standard deviations violate our rule of thumb: 10.16/1.92 = 5.29. This is much larger than 2. In particular, Permafresh 48 shows much more variability from piece to piece than either of the other treatments. Large variability in performance is a serious defect in a commercial product, so it appears that Permafresh 48 is unsuited for use on these grounds. The data are very helpful to a maker of durable press fabrics despite the fact that the formal test is not valid.

25.35: (a) There is a slight increase in growth when water is added in the wet season, but a much greater increase when it is added during the dry season. (b) The means differ significantly during the first three years. (c) The year 2005 is the only one for which the winter biomass was higher than the spring biomass.

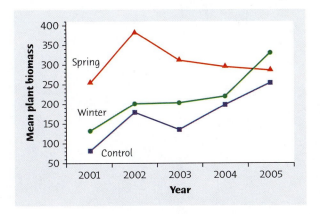

25.37: In addition to a high standard deviation ratio (117.18/35.57 = 3.29), the spring biomass distribution has a high outlier.

Data Table Index

Index

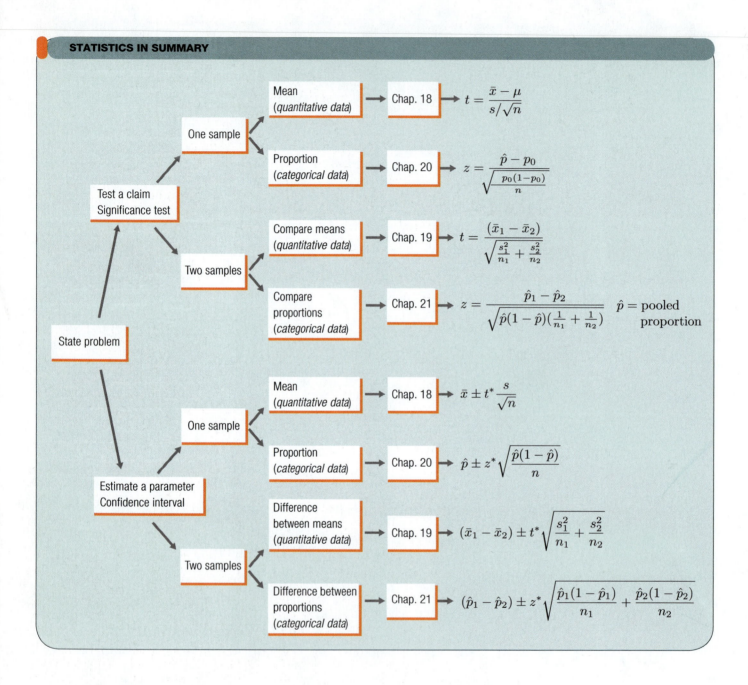

Mean
(*quantitative data*) → Chap. 18 → $t = \dfrac{\bar{x} - \mu}{s/\sqrt{n}}$

One sample

Proportion
(*categorical data*) → Chap. 20 → $z = \dfrac{\hat{p} - p_0}{\sqrt{\dfrac{p_0(1-p_0)}{n}}}$

Test a claim
Significance test

Compare means
(*quantitative data*) → Chap. 19 → $t = \dfrac{(\bar{x}_1 - \bar{x}_2)}{\sqrt{\dfrac{s_1^2}{n_1} + \dfrac{s_2^2}{n_2}}}$

Two samples

Compare proportions
(*categorical data*) → Chap. 21 → $z = \dfrac{\hat{p}_1 - \hat{p}_2}{\sqrt{\hat{p}(1-\hat{p})(\frac{1}{n_1} + \frac{1}{n_2})}}$ $\hat{p} = $ pooled proportion

State problem

Mean
(*quantitative data*) → Chap. 18 → $\bar{x} \pm t^* \dfrac{s}{\sqrt{n}}$

One sample

Proportion
(*categorical data*) → Chap. 20 → $\hat{p} \pm z^* \sqrt{\dfrac{\hat{p}(1-\hat{p})}{n}}$

Estimate a parameter
Confidence interval

Difference between means
(*quantitative data*) → Chap. 19 → $(\bar{x}_1 - \bar{x}_2) \pm t^* \sqrt{\dfrac{s_1^2}{n_1} + \dfrac{s_2^2}{n_2}}$

Two samples

Difference between proportions
(*categorical data*) → Chap. 21 → $(\hat{p}_1 - \hat{p}_2) \pm z^* \sqrt{\dfrac{\hat{p}_1(1-\hat{p}_1)}{n_1} + \dfrac{\hat{p}_2(1-\hat{p}_2)}{n_2}}$